THE GREEN GUIDE
Paris

Overview of Paris and Eiffel Tower / ©Peter Wrenn / Michelin

MICHELIN

The Green Guide PARIS

Editorial Director	Cynthia Clayton Ochterbeck
Editor	Gwen Cannon
Contributing Writers	Beebe Bahrami, Veronica Coquard, Paige Donner, Steven Durose, Françoise Klingen, Anne-Marie Scott, Heather Stimmler-Hall
Production Manager	Natasha George
Cartography	Peter Wrenn
Photo Researcher	Nicole D. Jordan
Interior Design	Chris Bell
Layout	Nicole D. Jordan
Cover Design	Chris Bell, Christelle Le Déan
Cover Layout	Michelin Travel Partner, Natasha George
Contact Us	Michelin Travel and Lifestyle North America One Parkway South Greenville, SC 29615 USA travel.lifestyle@us.michelin.com www.michelintravel.com
	Michelin Travel Partner Hannay House 39 Clarendon Road Watford, Herts WD17 1JA UK ✆01923 205240 travelpubsales@uk.michelin.com www.ViaMichelin.com
Special Sales	For information regarding bulk sales, customized editions and premium sales, please contact us at: travel.lifestyle@us.michelin.com www.michelintravel.com

HOW TO USE THIS GUIDE

PLANNING YOUR TRIP

The blue-tabbed PLANNING YOUR TRIP section at the front of the guide gives you **ideas for your trip** and **practical information** to help you organize it. You'll find tours, practical information, a host of outdoor activities, a calendar of events, information on shopping, sightseeing, kids' activities and more.

INTRODUCTION

The orange-tabbed INTRODUCTION section delves into the modern city in **Paris Today**. The **History** chapter spans the first Celtic settlers to present times. **Art and Culture** covers architecture, art, literature film and music.

DISCOVERING

The green-tabbed DISCOVERING section features Principal Sights by region, featuring the most interesting local **Sights**, **Walking Tours**, nearby **Excursions**, and detailed **Driving Tours**. Admission prices shown are normally for a single adult.

ADDRESSES

We've selected the best hotels, restaurants, cafés, shops, nightlife and entertainment to fit all budgets. See the Legend on the cover flap for an explanation of the price categories. See the back of the guide for an index of where to find hotels and restaurants.

Sidebars

Throughout the guide you will find blue, orange and green-coloured text boxes with lively anecdotes, detailed history and background information.

🍃 A Bit of Advice 🍃

Green advice boxes found in this guide contain practical tips and handy information relevant to your visit or to a sight in the Discovering section.

STAR RATINGS★★★

Michelin has given star ratings for more than 100 years. If you're pressed for time, we recommend you visit the ★★★, or ★★ sights first:

★★★ **Highly recommended**
★★ **Recommended**
★ **Interesting**

MAPS

🍃 Principal Sights map.
🍃 Arrondissements map
🍃 Metro map
🍃 Area maps
🍃 Walking Tour maps
🍃 Floor plans of major museums and churches

All maps in this guide are oriented north, unless otherwise indicated by a directional arrow. The term "Local Map" refers to a map within the chapter or Tourism Region. A complete list of the maps found in the guide appears at the back of this book.

PLANNING YOUR TRIP

INTRODUCTION TO PARIS

CONTENTS

© Vidler Steve / age fotostock

DISCOVERING PARIS

YOUR STAY IN PARIS

Welcome to Paris

To discover Paris is to discover a city of villages, each with its own distinct style and atmosphere. From the narrow, medieval streets winding through the Latin Quarter and the steep stairs of Montmartre to the chic Haussmannian buildings of the Grands Boulevards and the tree-lined avenue des Champs-Élysées, a stroll through the City of Light is the best way to enjoy the multifaceted personality of this world-class metropolis.

THE 1ST, 2ND, 3RD & 4TH
(pp86–171)

The centre of Paris includes the Île de la Cité with Ste-Chapelle and Notre-Dame Cathedral and the charming Île St-Louis with its boutiques and ice cream stands. The Louvre Museum, Tuileries Gardens and the Palais Royal make up the 1st *arrondissement*, while the small 2nd is home to the wholesale district and covered passages. The 3rd is known for its cutting-edge fashion and contemporary art galleries, while the medieval streets of the 4th are full of museums, clothing boutiques, the historic Jewish Quarter and some of the best little cafés in the city.

THE 5TH, 6TH & 7TH *(pp172–221)*

The Left Bank is home to the Latin Quarter, the student district around the Sorbonne and Panthéon. Further

Île de la Cité
©Peter Wrenn/Michelin

west are the chic Luxembourg Gardens and the famous cafés of the boulevard St-Germain. The high-end fashion boutiques and art galleries of the 6th merge into the diplomatic and residential district of the 7th, dominated by two iconic monuments, Les Invalides and the Eiffel Tower.

THE 8TH, 9TH, 10TH & 17TH
(pp222–262)

The 8th is known for the world famous avenue des Champs-Élysées and its nearby couture houses. The Arc de Triomphe marks the beginning of the discreetly elegant 17th, while the Opéra Garnier and the Grands Magasins of the boulevard Haussmann define the bustling 9th. The northeastern borders of the 9th and 17th have an edgier vibe as they become more gentrified, along with the 10th and its popular Canal St-Martin and busy train stations.

Canal St-Martin

© Y. Kanazawa/Michelin

Palais de Tokyo

© S. Quillon/MICHELIN

THE 11TH & 12TH (pp263–275)

The eastern districts of Paris are known for their laid-back atmosphere and lively nightlife, particularly around the rue Oberkampf and the place de la Bastille. Once known as the workers' district, the Faubourg St-Antoine is still home to many furniture makers, while two of the city's best open-air food markets can be found at the boulevard Richard Lenoir and the place d'Aligre. The revived Bercy district and its vast park are a welcome green space along the Seine, as well as the vast Bois de Vincennes and its château to the east.

THE 13TH, 14TH & 15TH (pp276–292)

The large southern *arrondissements* of Paris include Chinatown, Butte-aux-Cailles and the contemporary Bibliothèque district in the 13th, the peaceful Parc Montsouris and the Catacombes dominated by the Montparnasse Tower in the 14th, and the pleasant residential district with the Parc André-Citroën in the 15th. These districts, now connected by the new Tramway, offer many shopping opportunities in typically Parisian neighbourhoods.

THE 16TH (pp293–306)

The immense 16th *arrondissement* is considered one of the very chic places to live in Paris. Among the residential streets are several museums, including those in the Palais Chaillot and Palais de Tokyo. Its two prime shopping streets are avenue Victor Hugo and the rue de Passy with its Franck & Fils department store. To the west is the vast Bois de Boulogne, with its sports stadiums, gardens, lakes and children's park.

THE 18TH, 19TH & 20TH (pp307–325)

Home to the bucolic Butte de Montmartre, with its Sacré-Cœur Basilica and Moulin Rouge Cabaret, the 18th is one of the most popular districts in Paris. To the east visitors will find the up-and-coming 19th, with the contemporary Parc de la Villette of museums and concert halls, the Bassin de la Villette waterway, and the 19C Parc des Buttes Chaumont. The 20th's Belleville district is known for its artist ateliers and modern park, while Père-Lachaise Cemetery remains one of the largest green spaces within Paris.

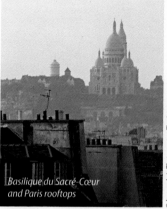

Basilique du Sacré-Cœur and Paris rooftops

© Jacques Loïc/Photononstop/Tips Images

Musée des Arts et métiers, Le Temple
SONNET Sylvain / hemis.fr

PLANNING YOUR TRIP

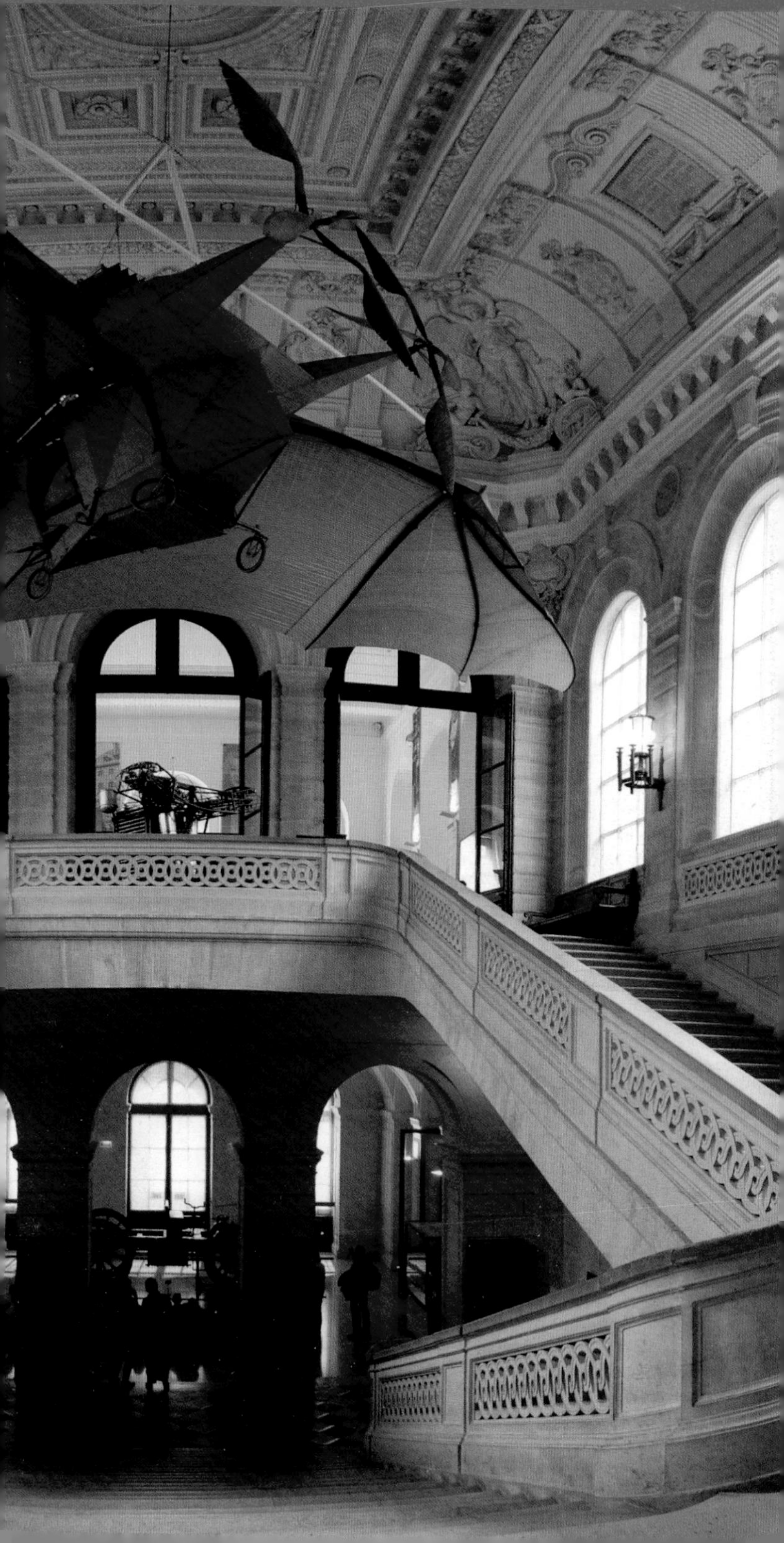

When and Where to Go

There is so much to see in Paris that it is a good idea to plan your visit carefully to maximize your time. An excellent starting point for any day out in the city is the absolute centre – the place du Parvis, in front of the Cathedral of Notre-Dame.

WHEN TO GO
SEASONS

Paris is a wonderful city to visit at any time of year. The city enjoys a typical temperate climate of cold winters and hot summers, while spring and autumn both have their unpredictable share of glorious sunny days and gloomy wet ones.

In **summer**, you can sit beneath the trees with a cold drink, idle away an evening on a café terrace, or take an open-boat tour on the Seine. The heat can be stifling at times: this is the period when Parisians converge on the seasonal beach of Paris Plage, the open-air cafés along the Seine, and outdoor swimming pools.

Autumn weather is generally crisp and sunny with intermittent grey skies; Parisians are back from their own holidays and there is an air of energy and bustle.

Winter can be severe, although there is rarely any snow and when the sun lights up the sky, Paris is most attractive. In December the streets and shop windows are bright with Christmas illuminations.

As for Paris in the **spring**, it tends to be cold and wet, but the buds on the trees and the blooming gardens mark a happy ending to the chilly winter.

WEATHER FORECAST

7-day national forecast: ☎3250 (followed by "1") updated 3 times daily (.034€/minute).

7-day local forecast: ☎3250 followed by the number of the *département* ((78 for Yvelines, for example) updated 3 times daily (.034€/minute).

36-hour city forecast: ☎3250 followed by the number of the *département* of the selected city (75 for Paris, for example) updated 3 times daily (.034€/minute). This information is also available at www.meteofrance.fr.

MUST SEES

Eiffel Tower – One of the most famous monuments in the world, affording superb views of the city.

Triumphal Way – Vista extending from the Arche de la Défense to the Arc de Triomphe then on to the

The Louvre and the pyramid

© Arnaud Chicurel/hemis.fr

Musée Rodin, Faubourg St-Germain

© Bruno Bernier/Fotolia.com

Concorde along the Champs-Élysées, right through to the Louvre.

Louvre Museum – One of the largest and most prestigious European art collections in the world, from Antiquity to 1850.

Orsay Museum and Faubourg St-Germain – 19C and 20C national art collections (including Impressionist painting) housed in a former 19C railway station surrounded by elegant 18C mansions.

Île de la Cité and banks of the Seine – Notre-Dame and Ste-Chapelle, two jewels of Gothic architecture in the historic centre of Paris.

Montmartre Hill – Crowned by the Sacré-Cœur Basilica, it symbolizes the 19C artistic world and bohemian life.

Latin Quarter – Lively student district.

Le Marais and its museums – One of the oldest districts of Paris, tastefully restored: Musée de la Chasse et de la Nature, Musée Carnavalet, Musée d'Art et d'Histoire du Judaïsme and others.

Invalides and Army Museum – Masterpiece of 17C architecture housing Napoléon's tomb.

Centre Georges Pompidou and Beaubourg district – The futuristic National Museum of Modern Art in the heart of one of the capital's oldest and liveliest districts.

Rue du Faubourg-St-Honoré, Madeleine, Opéra Garnier – Luxury boutiques and imposing buildings.

La Villette, Cité des Sciences et de l'Industrie – Fascinating interactive museum complex.

Trocadéro and Alma district – Wide avenues lined with elegant mansions and a wealth of museums (Musée des Arts Asiatiques-Guimet, Musée d'Art Moderne de la Ville de Paris, Musée de la Marine, Musée Baccarat).

Make up your own itinerary from the list above or follow one of the itineraries suggested below.

MEAN TEMPERATURES

	Jan	Feb	Mar	Apr	May	Jun
Min/max °F	21/59	23/59	30/70	34/75	41/81	46/88
Min/max °C	-6/15	-5/15	-1/21	1/24	5/27	8/31
	Jul	Aug	Sept	Oct	Nov	Dec
Min/max °F	52/91	50/88	45/84	34/75	28/63	25/55
Min/max °C	11/33	10/31	7/29	1/24	-2/17	-4/13

TWO-DAY TRIP

DAY 1 – Morning – Notre-Dame, Les Quais, Ste-Chapelle. **Afternoon – Louvre** or the **Orsay Museum** *(closed Mon)* walk through the **Tuileries Gardens** and on to **Place de la Concorde, Champs-Élysées, Eiffel Tower**.

DAY 2 – Morning – Le Marais, place des Vosges, Centre Pompidou *(closed Tue)*. **Afternoon –** Boat tour starting from **Pont Neuf, Latin Quarter, Luxembourg Gardens**. Take the metro at Notre-Dame-des-Champs (line 12) to **Montmartre** to finish the evening.

FOUR-DAY TRIP

DAY 1 – Morning – Notre-Dame, the banks of the **Seine, Ste-Chapelle**. **Afternoon – Louvre**, Tuileries *(lunch in the museum or in the gardens)*; a stroll around **place Vendôme, La Madeleine, Concorde** and to the **Opéra Garnier**.

DAY 2 – Morning – Quartier Latin/ St-Germain-des-Prés, Musée d'Orsay *(closed Mon)*. **Afternoon – Cité des Sciences et de l'Industrie** at **La Villette** *(closed Mon)*, lunch at the Café de la Musique, Montmartre in the evening.

DAY 3 – Morning – Versailles Château *(closed Mon)*, park and gardens *(bring a picnic or eat at the restaurant by the Grand Canal)*. Return to town in the **afternoon** via the RER, get off at Alma station, and enjoy a river tour aboard a *bateau-mouche*.

DAY 4 – Morning – Place des Vosges and the **Marais, Centre Pompidou** *(closed Tue – lunch in the museum or in the neighbourhood)*. **Afternoon – Invalides, Eiffel Tower, Trocadéro, Champs-Élysées**.

HISTORIC PARIS

Ancient Paris – The oldest part of Paris, historically speaking, includes the **Île de la Cité** (place Dauphine, Palais de Justice, Ste-Chapelle, Conciergerie) and the **Marais** (place des Vosges, rue des Francs-Bourgeois lined with fine mansions and a wealth of museums).

Monumental Paris – This itinerary includes two magnificent vistas: one encompasses the Trocadéro, the Eiffel Tower, the Champ de Mars and the École Militaire next to the Invalides, the other extends from Tuileries Gardens and place de la Concorde along the Champs-Élysées to the Arc de Triomphe; the River Seine provides an inspiring link between the two.

Jardin du Palais Royal

© Franck Boston/Fotolia.com

Quai de Bourbon at night

© Erick Nguyen/Dreamstime.com

Right-Bank Paris – The Right Bank is dominated by the extensive buildings of the Louvre. Just north across rue de Rivoli is the **Palais Royal** and its peaceful gardens. To the west is avenue de l'Opéra heading towards the Opéra Garnier, rue de la Paix and place Vendôme, home to prestigious jewellery shops, rue St-Honoré and rue Royale, lined with leading fashion houses, and the Madeleine. From there, metro line 12 will take you directly to Lamarck Caulaincourt station at the foot of Montmartre Hill. As a reward for climbing to the top, you will enjoy a superb view from the Sacré-Cœur Basilica.

Left-Bank Paris – Strolling through the Odéon, St-Germain-des-Prés and St-Sulpice districts then across Luxembourg Gardens to the south, you will get the feel of the Left-Bank atmosphere. Further east stand the Panthéon and the Sorbonne overlooking the Latin Quarter. At the heart of this lively university district, the Musée de Cluny takes visitors on a delightful journey back to medieval times. Heading west along the embankment, you will walk past the *bouquinistes'* stalls displaying second-hand books and old prints. Walk as far as the Musée d'Orsay for fine views of the Right-Bank monuments including the Louvre.

RIVERSIDE PARIS
Along the Seine – The river banks are the favourite haunt of Parisians in summer and winter alike. They like to stroll along past lovers oblivious to the world around them, musicians who practise their instruments, unperturbed by onlookers, and anglers convinced that the Seine abounds with fish. Many strollers browse through the old books and prints displayed on the *bouquinistes'* stalls, hoping to find a rare copy or manuscript, although they know it is most unlikely nowadays.

Around Île St-Louis – Quai de Bourbon and quai d'Anjou, running along the northern edge of the island, offer a peaceful stroll past elegant 17C mansions full of old-world charm. Anyone venturing along rue St-Louis-en-l'Île finds it hard to resist Berthillon's delicious ice cream! From quai de Béthune and quai d'Orléans, the east end of Notre-Dame looks breathtakingly lovely and Pont Louis-Philippe affords a beautiful view of the Panthéon.

Along the Canal St-Martin – Dainty metallic footbridges spanning the canal at regular intervals, barges negotiating the locks and anglers lost in their thoughts form the peaceful setting of the Canal St-Martin linking the Bassin de la Villette and the Paris-Arsenal marina.

FASHION AND LUXURY

Paris is generally acknowledged as the capital of fashion. Couture houses and luxury boutiques are located in well-defined areas.

On the Right Bank: South of the Champs-Élysées, along avenue Montaigne, avenue George V, avenue Marceau and rue François-I (fashion houses); along rue du Faubourg St-Honoré leading to place Vendôme and rue de la Paix (fashion, jewellery); place des Victoires, rue des Francs-Bourgeois and rue des Rosiers (fashion boutiques); department stores along boulevard Haussmann, around the Madeleine; rue de Rivoli (department stores and boutiques).

On the Left Bank: Le Bon Marché (department store) along rue de Sèvres and boutiques along rue du Bac, rue du Dragon, rue des Sts-Pères, rue du Vieux Colombier, rue du Cherche-Midi, rue du Four, rue de Rennes and rue Bonaparte leading to boulevard St-Germain.

OFF THE BEATEN PATH

Some districts have retained their Old-World charm and atmosphere: Montmartre hill with its vineyard and windmill, Canal St-Martin and its metallic footbridges, the Butte aux Cailles hilltop near Gobelins, the St-Séverin Quarter near place St-Michel.

Other districts, on the contrary, look so modern that they stand out against the traditional Parisian townscape: the Bibliothèque district along the Seine (13th *arr*), place de Catalogne (14th *arr*) and La Défense.

Some museums and monuments can also be termed unusual: Musée de la Curiosité et de la Magie (Marais district), Musée Cernuschi (Parc Monceau), Cathédrale St-Alexandre Nevski (Monceau), Musée du Vin (Passy), Les Catacombes (Denfert-Rochereau), the Paris sewers (Alma).

GREEN PARIS
PARKS AND GARDENS

Paris has evolved into a city of trees and flowers, boasting almost 400 parks, public and private gardens, little squares, and, of course, its two vast stretches of woodland (Bois de Boulogne and Bois de Vincennes – 846ha/2 090 acres and 995ha/2 458 acres respectively) where lakes and waterfalls complement fountains and ponds.

Thanks to its varied landscape of woods, parks and gardens, Paris allows a surprising diversity of flora and fauna to thrive in the very heart of this urban metropolis. Some of the gardens provide a setting for a range of temporary or year-round exhibitions: flower shows, classical and avant-garde artwork. Here is a list, with metro stations, of some of the nicest parks in town:

Bagatelle (Ⓜ Sablons) for its irises and rose garden; the botanical gardens and greenhouses of the **Jardin des Plantes** (Ⓜ Jussieu); **Parc Montsouris** (Ⓜ Cité Universitaire) with its English-style gardens; the most picturesque of the landscaped parks, the **Buttes-Chaumont** (Ⓜ Buttes-Chaumont); the calm, elegant **Palais Royal Gardens** (Ⓜ Palais Royal); the cherry trees in the gardens of the university residence (Ⓜ Cité Universitaire). The **Luxembourg Gardens** (Ⓜ Luxembourg, Port Royal, Rennes) where courting couples and students from the Latin Quarter come to relax in the sunshine; **Parc Monceau** whose wrought-iron gates open on to a collection of statues of Musset, Maupassant and Chopin (Ⓜ Monceau); the sophisticated **Parc André-Citroën** gardens complete with hi-tech glasshouses (Ⓜ Javel).

As if this wealth of greenery were not enough, several new parks have sprung up on the cityscape in recent years: the magnificent **Parc de Bercy** (12th *arr*); the **Jardin de l'Atlantique** (15th *arr*) laid out on a huge concrete slab over the Gare Montparnasse; the **Promenade plantée** from Bastille to

Luxembourg Gardens

© Peter Wrenn/MICHELIN

Vineyard of Montmartre

S. Sauvignier/MICHELIN

the Vincennes woods; meanwhile the **Tuileries Gardens** (1st *arr*) have been restored to their former glory.

VINEYARDS

The area occupied by vineyards in the Île de France region as a whole remained considerable until the 18C and even today, Paris surprisingly boasts nine vineyards producing red and white wines. The most interesting are **Montmartre** (rue des Saules, 75018, Ⓜ Lamarck Caulaincourt) with 1 762 vines; **Parc de Belleville** (rue des Couronnes, rue Piat, rue Julien-Lacroix or rue Jouye-Rouve, 75020, Ⓜ Couronnes), with 140 vines tucked away inside the Parc de Belleville; **Parc Georges-Brassens** (rue des Morillons, rue des Périchaux or rue Brancion, 75015, Ⓜ Porte de Vanves) with 700 vines; and **Parc de Bercy** (41 rue Paul Belmondo, 75012, Ⓜ Cour St-Émilion) with 350 vines.

The **Musée du Vin** is situated in a quiet street of the 16th *arrondissement* (⟨ *see PASSY*).

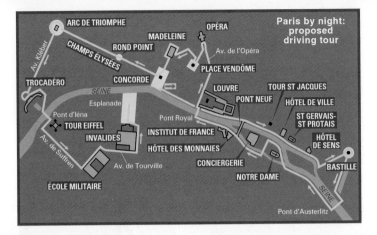

PARIS BY NIGHT

The city is floodlit throughout the year from nightfall (between 5.15pm and 10.20pm according to the season) to midnight (1am on Saturdays, the eve of bank holidays and during the summer months). The fountains are turned off during the cold weather from 1 January to 1 April.

At Christmas, many streets including the Champs-Élysées, avenue Montaigne, rue Royale or boulevard Haussmann take on a magical quality with trees and shop windows decked in seasonal lights.

On foot or by car, the main sights line the **banks of the Seine**: **place de la Concorde** with its two fountains; the **Champs-Élysées** climbing up to the **Arc de Triomphe**; **Cour Napoléon** and **Pei's Pyramid**, which, together with the majestic walls of the Louvre, are reflected in the rippling waters of the flat fountains; place André-Malraux and the arcades fronting the **Comédie-Française**; the area around the abbey of **St-Germain-des-Prés** although not as white as the limestone of the **Sacré-Cœur**, takes on a paler hue beneath the lights; the **Invalides** with its striking gilded dome; **Notre-Dame**, which is even more impressive when the floodlights of the river boats pick out the exquisite detail of its sculpted façade, and the **esplanade du Palais de Chaillot** from which there is a wonderful view of the Champ de Mars and the École Militaire, while fountains play below in the **Trocadéro** Gardens. On the other bank of the Seine, stop directly underneath the **Eiffel Tower** to gaze upwards at the latticed ironwork: monumental and yet delicate.

PARIS FOR PEDESTRIANS

Paris' neighbourhoods are perhaps best explored on foot. In addition to tours mapped in this book, you may want to try the three **signposted walks** in Paris: the west-east oriented one from Bois de Boulogne to Bois de Vincennes crosses parks such as the Champs de Mars, Jardin du Luxembourg, Jardin des Plantes and Bercy; the north-south oriented walk links two Hausmann parks: Buttes-Chaumont and Montsouris; the third (west-east) links porte Maillot to porte Dorée. Each route totals about 20km/12.4mi. Details about the walks are provided in *Paris à Pied*, a topoguide published by the **Fédération française de randonnée pédestre** (*64 rue du Dessous des Berges, 75013, Paris;* ℘*01 44 89 93 90; www.ffrandonnee.fr*).

Context Paris offers themed guided walks in English such as Art & Architecture of Gothic Paris, Marais Mansions, and Trends in Parisian Cuisine. *For more information:* ℘*09 75 18 04 15; www.contexttravel.com*.

PARIS BY BUS

The bus is another excellent means of exploring Paris. There are several different tourist buses and coaches (with or without commentary) and, alternatively, Parisian **RATP** buses. Riding the regular transport system is a good way to see historic Paris in the company of the locals, for only a modest sum of money.

Balabus – (Line 07) This bus crosses Paris from east to west, from Gare de Lyon to La Défense. (*Balabus* or *Bb* is indicated on bus stops.) The buses run only on Sundays and public holidays *(12.30pm–8.30pm)*, from the last Sunday in April to the last Sunday in September.

Montmartrobus – (Line 07) This bus tours Montmartre between the town hall of the 18th *arrondissement* and place Pigalle. Bus fare is standard.

Big Bus Paris – ℘01 53 95 39 53. http://eng.bigbustours.com/paris/home.html.

- ♦ **Key stops:** Eiffel Tower, Champ de Mars, Louvre -Pyramide, Notre-Dame, Musée d'Orsay, Opéra Garnier, Champs-Élysées-Étoile, Grand Palais, Trocadéro. Bus tour with running commentary.
- ♦ **Duration:** 2hr 20min for the complete circuit, although it is possible to get on or off at any stop on the route.
- ♦ **Prices:** 29€, 16€/child for 1-day tour. Tickets can be bought on the bus *(or online: 10 percent discount)*, and are valid 2 consecutive days.
- ♦ **Departure:** Every 15min from the Eiffel Tower, starting at 10am.

Cityrama – 2 rue des Pyramides, 75001, Ⓜ Pyramides. ℘01 44 55 60 00. www.cityrama.fr. Tour of the city aboard panoramic buses.

Paris L'OpenTour – 13 rue Auber, 75009, Ⓜ Opéra or Havre-Caumartin. ℘01 42 66 56 56. www.paris. opentour.com/fr. com. Double-decker, open-top, hop-on-hop-off bus tours. 50 stops, marked "L'OpenTour" (every 10–15min; 2 Nov–Mar every 20–30min). Four routes (Grand Tour, Montmartre–Grands Boulevards,

"Les cars rouges" - L'OpenTour bus

© S. Sauvignier/MICHELIN

Bastille–Bercy, Montparnasse–St-Germain), commentary on personal earphones. 1-day pass 32€, 2-day pass 36€; (4–11 years 16€ 1 or 2 days).

RATP BUSES

Like all forms of public transport, Parisian buses – depending to some extent on the line – can be slightly unpredictable in terms of punctuality and comfort: they can get extremely crowded, so it is best to avoid rush hours if possible. Nonetheless, the bus remains a great way to see Paris. All bus trips in Paris and the immediate suburbs require one ticket, called a "carnet" (no transfers). They are the same as the tickets used in the metro, but you can save money by buying a pass (ⓒ*see Best Fares)* or a book of 10 tickets ahead of time. On board the bus, you can buy tickets individually from the driver, at a higher price (2€ instead of 1,80€).

Line 21 (Gare St-Lazare–Stade Charlety Porte-de-Gentilly) – Opéra, Palais Royal, the Louvre, then along the Seine, before crossing the river towards the Latin Quarter and Luxembourg Gardens.

Line 72 (Parc-de-St-Cloud–Hôtel de Ville) – the Right Bank of the Seine:

Alma Marceau, the Grand Palais, place de la Concorde, Palais Royal, the Louvre, place du Châtelet and the Hôtel de Ville.

Line 73 (La Garenne Colombes–Musée d'Orsay) – place de l'Étoile, the Champs-Élysées, place de la Concorde and the Musée d'Orsay.

Line 96 (Gare Montparnasse–Porte des Lilas) – The St-Sulpice area, Odéon, the Latin Quarter, Île de la Cité, Châtelet–Hôtel de Ville, the Marais and finally Belleville.

PASSAGES OF PARIS

Here is one more suggestion for a thematic tour of the town: seek out the **Passages of Paris**. These covered alleyways, mostly built in the 19C, were once popular shopping and meeting places where Parisians could stroll peacefully and at a safe distance from the many horses in the streets. As times changed, streets became cleaner, and pavements more prevalent, these lovely arcades slowly fell out of favour. But fortunately, many have been restored and new shops have been opened in them, alongside the quaint older ones.

Galerie Véro-Dodat – 19 rue Jean-Jacques-Rousseau, 75001 MPalais Royal. Opened in 1826, this arcade undoubtedly boasts the finest interior decoration. High-quality shops with windows encased in brass surrounds have been rebuilt in the original style, their windows full of old-fashioned charm like the old toy shop (Robert Capia).

Galerie Vivienne – 4 rue des Petits-Champs, 75002 MBourse. Built in 1823, this is one of the most beautiful arcades in Paris. The Petit Siroux bookshop was established in 1826.

Passage Brady – 18 rue du Faubourg–Saint-Denis, 75010 MStrasbourg Saint-Denis. Scents and perfumes of India waft through this arcade, where you will find restaurants and food shops.

Passage Choiseul – 23 rue St-Augustin, 75002 MQuatre Septembre. One of the exits of the famous Bouffes-Parisiens Theatre

opens on this picturesque covered alleyway. Opened in 1827 this arcade, the longest in Paris, contains several restaurants and bookstores, a famous stationery store (Lavrut) and various jewellery and clothing shops.

Passage du Grand-Cerf – 145 rue St-Denis, 75002 MÉtienne Marcel. This arcade was built between 1825 and 1835. Paved in marble, it boasts an elegant and very high glass roof, wrought-iron walkways, and wood-framed shop windows.

Passage Jouffroy – 10 boulevard Montmartre, 75009 MGrands Boulevards. The Musée Grévin is in the middle of the passage, the first arcade in the city to be heated. There is an interesting second-hand bookshop which has some rare editions, a good, old-fashioned toy store, some clothing shops and gift boutiques.

Passage Jouffroy

© S. Sauvignier/MICHELIN

Passage des Panoramas – 11 boulevard Montmartre, 75002 MGrands Boulevards. Built in 1800, its name comes from the paintings created there by Fulton (destroyed in 1831). There are several shops which deal in collectors' items, an engraver's shop and a tearoom.

Passage Verdeau – 6 rue de la Grange-Batelière, 75009 MRichelieu-Drouot, Rue Montmartre. This arcade extends beyond passage Jouffroy, not far from the Hôtel Drouot and stocks antiques and old books (La France Ancienne).

What to See and Do

CYCLING

Paris has some 700km/435mi of cycle lanes and more are under construction. A north–south axis links the cycle path at Canal de l'Ourcq and place de la Bataille-de-Stalingrad to Porte de Vanves. Another, running from east to west, joins the Bois de Vincennes and the Bois de Boulogne, both of which have a network of cycle paths complete with signposts. There are also combination bike–bus lanes. Designated areas where cyclists can leave their bikes are dotted around the capital; the French railway SNCF facilitates the free entry of bikes on the RER lines B, C and D, although only at particular times and stations. On Sundays and holidays, certain roads are closed to traffic for the benefit of pedestrians and cyclists:

- Roads running parallel to the **Seine** from 9am to 5pm (quai des Tuileries, quai Henri IV, quai Anatole France and quai Branly).
- **Canal St-Martin** 10am to 8pm (Oct–Mar until 6pm) (quai de Jemmapes, quai de Valmy).
- In the **Mouffetard area** from 10am to 6pm (place Marcelin-Berthelot, rue de Cluny, rue de l'École Polytechnique, rue de Lanneau, rue Mouffetard, rue Descartes), the only drawback is that it is uphill!
- On the **Butte de Montmartre** from 11am to 6pm, a steep hill.

Ⓛ **Remember:** Parisian motorists do not always take much notice of cyclists even though, theoretically, the groups share the same status on the roads. It is therefore advisable to be extremely careful, especially of parked cars as unaware drivers may open car doors without prior warning. Remember that all road users, including cyclists, must adhere to the French Vehicle Code (www.americansinfrance.net/Driving). Always keep an eye on your bicycle – even if it is equipped with a padlock; detachable parts such as the saddle and the front wheel are easily stolen and resold.

Ⓛ **Road regulations** require:
- Bell and lights.
- Use of designated parking areas.
- Wearing of a cycle helmet (highly recommended, not mandatory).
- Use of cycle paths.

BICYCLE HIRE

Below are some useful addresses; for further information, consult the *Paris à Vélo* map, published by the **Mairie de Paris** and available from town

Vélib' bike station

©AlexO/Fotolia.com

halls and the **Office du Tourisme de Paris**. Always carry your passport with you, as it will be essential for hiring anything in Paris. A cycle helmet, basket and bike lock – and sometimes baby seats – are included in the price.

Paris à vélo, c'est sympa! – 22 rue Alphonse Baudin, 75011, Ⓜ Richard-Lenoir (line 5). ☎ 01 48 87 60 01. www.parisvelosympa.com/en. Standard bike (adult or child) 15€/day, 12€/half-day, 25€/2 days (250€ security deposit required). This company offers guided tours (French, English, Dutch, German, Italian and Spanish) year round (from 35€; under 26 years from 29€). Baby seats can be provided and you can hire a bike or a tandem. No reservations necessary.

Vélib' – This very popular self-hire bike service in Paris is available 24hr a day seven days a week. Simply go to the self-service machines and follow the instructions to choose from a range of bikes, using your credit card (note: American cards without a microchip will not work) or directly purchase a 1-day or a 7-day ticket online at www.velib.paris.fr.

ROLLERBLADING

Pari Roller – ☎ 01 43 36 89 81, www.pari-roller.com. Meeting point: place Raoul Dautry, 75014 (Ⓜ Montparnasse Bienvenue). Every Friday (weather permitting) a free 3hr rollerblading rally takes place in Paris at 10pm, following a different itinerary on each occasion. The event is overseen by policemen, themselves on rollerblades, who prevent the traffic accessing the roads used by the rollerbladers. Some 15 000 people gather every week in front of the Gare Montparnasse, the starting point. There is a relaxed, fun atmosphere, and it's a good way to meet people. *Not suitable for beginners as a good breaking technique is essential.*

Rollers & Coquillages – 75011, Ⓜ Bastille. www.rollers-coquillages.org. Meeting point: place de la Bastille on Sundays at 2.30pm. This free 3hr rally is suitable for beginners and experienced skaters; the itinerary is different on each occasion, check the website.

Rollers Squad Institut (RSI) – 7 rue Jean-Giono, 75013, Ⓜ Quai-de-la-Gare. ☎ 01 56 61 99 61. www.rsi.asso.fr. Open Mon, Thu–Fri 10am–6pm. This association organizes free, year-round roller-skating tours such as a child-friendly (8 years and older) skate Sundays 2.45pm–5pm and two tours for adults Saturdays 2.45pm–6pm and Sundays 2.45pm–5pm. Meeting point: esplanade des Invalides.

BOATING

Paris would not be Paris without its *bateaux-mouches*, an institution. No visit is complete without taking in Notre-Dame, the Eiffel Tower, and the rest of the riverside from on board one of these legendary boats.

ON THE SEINE

Bateaux-Mouches – Boarding point: Pont de l'Alma (Right Bank), 75008, Ⓜ Alma-Marceau. ☎ 01 42 25 96 10. www.bateaux-mouches.fr. Round trip from Pont de l'Alma to Notre-Dame. ⌖ 13€, under 12 years 5.50€ (lunch 55€ and dinner cruises from 99€).

Les Vedettes du Pont-Neuf – **Boarding point:** place du Vert-Galant, 75001, Ⓜ Pont-Neuf. ☎ 01 46 33 98 38. http://vedettesdupontneuf.com. Itinerary: from Pont-Neuf to Pont d'Iéna, including a circuit around Île de la Cité and Île St-Louis. Commentary in French and English. Duration: 1hr. ⌖ 14€, child 7€ (9-10€/5€ online).

Les Bateaux Parisiens – Boarding point: Port de la Bourdonnais, 75007, RER Champs de Mars Tour Eiffel or Ⓜ Bir-Hakeim. ☎ 01 44 11 33 44. www.bateauxparisiens.com. Boarding point: quai de Montebello, opposite Notre-Dame (end Mar–early Nov), Metro/RER C St-Michel. ☎ 01 43 26 92 55. Duration: 1hr. ⌖ 14€, under 12 years 6€. Departures every 30min 10am to 10.30pm (Jun–Aug until 11pm); Oct–Mar departures every hour

Batobus on the Seine

© Peter Wrenn/Michelin

10.30am to 9.30pm (Sat–Sun 10am to 10.30pm).

Batobus – **Port de la Bourdonnais**, 75007, RER C Champs de Mars Tour Eiffel or Ⓜ Bir-Hakeim. ☎08 25 05 01 01 (0.15€/min). www.batobus. com. Eight hop-on- hop-off stops, no commentary: Eiffel Tower (Port de la Bourdonnais), Musée d'Orsay (quai de Solférino), St-Germain-des-Prés (quai Malaquais), Notre-Dame (quai de Montebello), Jardin des Plantes (near Austerlitz bridge), Hôtel de Ville (near Arcole bridge), Louvre (quai du Louvre), Champs-Élysées (Port des Champs-Élysées, near Pont Alexandre-III). Times vary from 10am–7pm in winter, 10am–9.30pm in summer. Departures every 20min (winter every 25min). Closed 5 Jan–8 Feb. ☞16€, under 16 years 7€ for 1 day; 18€, under 16 years 9€ for 2 days.

CANAL SAINT-MARTIN

Canauxrama – Boarding point at Port de Plaisance-Paris-Arsenal, opposite 50 boulevard de la Bastille, 75012, Ⓜ Bastille. Departure times: 9.45am and 2.30pm. Another boarding point at Bassin-de-la-Villette, 13 quai de la Loire, 75019, Ⓜ Jaurès. Departure times: 9.45am and 2.45pm. Reservation recommended by calling

☎01 42 39 15 00 or online: www. canauxrama.com. This 2.5hr barge trip takes you from Port de Plaisance to Parc de la Villette or vice versa, crossing four locks and two swing bridges. Commentary. ☞17€, under 12 years 9€, under 4 years free.

Paris Canal – Reservation strongly advised. ☎01 42 40 96 97. www. pariscanal.com. Cruise along the Canal St-Martin negotiating locks and swing bridges and navigating through a 2km/1.2mi-long tunnel beneath the Bastille. Departures Tuesday–Sunday late March–mid-November at 9.45am and 2.25pm in front of the Musée d'Orsay (Ⓜ Solférino) and at 10.30am and 2.30pm from the Parc de la Villette (Ⓜ Porte de Pantin). Boarding point at 12 Port de Solférino, quai Anatole France. Duration: 2hr30min. ☞20€, 12–25 years 17€, under 12 years 13€. Family rate (2 adults, 2 children) 50€.

MARNE RIVER CRUISE

Canauxrama – By reservation only ☎01 42 39 15 00. www.canauxrama. com. Departure May–September Wednesday–Sunday at 9am from Paris-Arsenal marina, 75012, Ⓜ Bastille. All-day cruise to Bry-sur-Marne. ☞36€/person without lunch. ♿*Not recommended for children.*

VIEWS OF PARIS

The Eiffel Tower is, of course, the best place from which to view Paris, but by no means is it the only one. Here are some ideas of places that offer unexpectedly stunning views over the City of Light, by day or by night:

Montmartre: From in front of the Sacré-Cœur, place Émile Goudeau.

Belleville and Ménilmontant: From the summit of the Parc de Belleville, at the end of rue Piat.

Passy: Place du Trocadéro.

Parvis de la Défense: Looking towards Paris from the Grande Arche.

FAVOURITE TOURIST VIEWS

Montparnasse Tower – Ⓜ Montparnasse Bienvenüe (🔎 see MONTPARNASSE).

The Eiffel Tower – Ⓜ Bir-Hakeim (🔎 see EIFFEL TOWER).

The Arc de Triomphe – Ⓜ Charles de Gaulle Étoile (🔎 see Avenue des Champs Élysées).

Notre-Dame (towers) – Ⓜ Cité (🔎 see Notre-Dame Cathedral).

Panthéon (upper parts) – RER Luxembourg (🔎 see Le QUARTIER LATIN).

Pompidou Centre (5th floor terrace) – Ⓜ Rambuteau or Hôtel de Ville or RER Châtelet-Les Halles. 🕿 01 44 78 12 33. www.centrepompidou.fr. Museum and exhibitions: *Wed–Mon 11am–9pm (Thu 11pm); last admission 1hr before closing.* Access to the terrace requires a ticket to the museum or to an exhibition.

Sacré-Cœur (dome) – Ⓜ Anvers or Abesses (🔎 see MONTMARTRE).

Printemps Maison – Ⓜ Havre-Caumartin. Mon–Sat 9.35am–8pm (Thu 8.45pm). Free entry via the escalator.

Institut du Monde Arabe (9th-floor terrace) – Ⓜ Jussieu. No charge (🔎 see Jussieu).

Hôtel Concorde-Lafayette (bar with panoramic view) – Ⓜ Porte Maillot.

The Grande Arche at La Défense – Ⓜ and RER La Défense (🔎 see La DÉFENSE).

GUIDED TOURS

Guided tours of monuments, districts and exhibitions are organized by the following organizations:

Centre des monuments nationaux – Service visites-conférences Paris île-de-France, 62 Rue Saint-Antoine 75004, 🕿 01 44 54 19 30. Mon–Fri 9am–noon, 2pm–6pm (Fri until 5pm). www.monum.fr.

Association pour la Sauvegarde et la mise en valeur du Paris historique – 44–46 rue François-Miron, 75004, 🕿 01 48 87 74 31. Daily 2pm–6pm. www.paris-historique.org.

Association Fondation pour la Connaissance de Paris – 21 rue du Repos, 75020, 🕿 01 43 70 70 87.

Ecoute du Passé – 44 rue Maubeuge 75009, 🕿 01 42 65 30 47.

Communautés d'accueil dans les sites artistiques – 🕿 01 42 34 56 10. www.cathedraledeparis.com. Free guided tours of Notre-Dame.
🕭 These guided tours, in English Wed (2pm), Thu (2pm) and Sat (2.30pm), are publicized in weekly entertainment guides (such as *Pariscope*), at the Paris Tourism Office, and posted at the sight entrances.

ART

Antiquities: Louvre; Musée de Cluny; Musée de l'Homme; Arènes de Lutèce.

Painting: Louvre; Musée d'Orsay; Musée National d'Art Moderne; Centre Georges Pompidou; Château de Versailles; Musée d'Art Moderne de la Ville de Paris (Palais de Tokyo); Musée Carnavalet; Musée Picasso; Musée Marmottan-Monet; Musée Maillol; Musée du Petit Palais; Musée Gustave-Moreau; Musée Eugène-Delacroix; Musée de l'Orangerie; Musée de Montmartre; Musée d'Art naïf Max-Fourny.

Sculpture: Louvre; Notre-Dame de Paris; Musée d'Orsay; Basilique St-Denis; Musée des Monuments Français; Musée Rodin; Musée Maillol; Musée Bourdelle; Musée Bouchard; Musée Zadkine; Espace Dalí; Fontaine Stravinski; Jardin des Tuileries.

Eiffel Tower and Carrousel

© Patricia Grube/Michelin

Literature: Maison de Balzac; Maison de Victor Hugo; Musée de la Vie Romantique; Musée Adam-Mickiewicz.

Furniture: Louvre; Musée de Cluny; Musée des Arts Décoratifs; Musée Cognacq-Jay; Musée Jacquemart-André; Musée Nissim de Camondo; Hôtel de Soubise; Faubourg St-Antoine.

Tapestries: Louvre; Musée de Cluny; Musée Nissim de Camondo; Manufacture des Gobelins.

Silver, glass and china: Château de Vincennes; Musée Baccarat; Musée Bouilhet-Christofle.

Fashion: Musée des Arts Décoratifs; Musée de la Mode et du Costume; Faubourg St-Honoré; Musée de l'Éventail; Musée Fragonard; Musée de la Contrefaçon.

Music: Musée de l'Opéra Garnier; Cité de la Musique.

Ethnic: Musée des Arts asiatiques-Guimet; Musée de l'Homme; Musée Cernuschi; Institut du Monde Arabe; Musée Dapper; Musée Arménien; Centre Bouddhique du Bois de Vincennes; Musée d'Art et d'Histoire du Judaïsme, Quai Branly.

SCIENCE

Natural History: Musée d'Histoire Naturelle, Jardin des Plantes.

Astronomy: Palais de la Découverte; Musée des Arts et Métiers; l'Observatoire; La Villette Planetarium.

Medicine: Hôpital Militaire du Val-de-Grâce's Musée du Service de Santé des Armées; Institut Pasteur; Musée des Moulages de l'Hôpital St-Louis.

Mineralogy: École Supérieure des Mines; Musée de Minéralogie; Galerie de Minéralogie.

Technology: Cité des Sciences et de l'Industrie; Palais de la Découverte; Musée des Arts et Métiers.

The Cheat by George de la Tour, Louvre

©Scala, Florence/Musée du Louvre

BOOKS
GASTRONOMY
Paris on a Plate (2006)
by Stephen Downes.

A gastronomic diary set in Paris during the author's youth. He recounts his experiences eating in famous restaurants and makes some observations about Paris street life. Also examines how the restaurant business changed after the introduction of big money.

FICTION
The Lollipop Shoes (2007)
by Joanne Harris.

A sequel to her best-known novel, *Chocolat*. Five years on, Vianne has moved to Montmartre with Anouk and now has another daughter, Rosette. Vianne is no longer the free spirit she was, due to the demands of motherhood. Into their lives steps the bohemian Zozie de l'Alba, who helps Vianne regain her life. What is her motive?

HISTORY
Paris: The Secret History (2006)
by Andrew Hussey.

The author, head of the French Department at the University of London's Paris Campus, contends that Parisians have always prized secrecy and that the city has for years hosted secret societies of occultists, freemasons and other organizations.He views the City of Light as a city of darkness.

FILMS
Hotel du Nord (1938) directed by
Marcel Carné.

Starring Louis Jouvet and Arletty. The relative peace of a small hotel bar is disrupted when two lovers seek a room for the night. They are determined to take each other's lives but Pierre fails in his task.

An American in Paris (1951) directed
by Vincente Minelli.

Starring Gene Kelly and Leslie Caron. Jerry, an American expatriate living in Paris and hoping to be a successful painter, falls in love with Lise, a young Frenchwoman he meets in a restaurant. She is already in a relationship but after singing/dancing his way through Paris, Jerry and Lise finally get together.

Les Amants du Pont Neuf (1991)
directed by Leos Carax.

A tragic love story between an alcoholic street performer and an artist living on the streets of Paris who is losing her sight. They live under renovation scaffolding on the Pont Neuf among the homeless, but the movie takes place throughout the city.

Amélie (2001) directed
by Jean-Pierre Jeunet.

Starring Audrey Tautou. The imaginative Amélie has a strong sense of justice. When she takes a job in a Montmartre bar, she discovers that her main role in life is to help others and creates deceptions that allow her to intervene in others' lives.

Paris, Je t'Aime (2006).

An international production made up of 18 short films by 22 different directors (including Joel and Ethan Coen, Gerard Depardieu and Wes Craven) showing different Paris neighbourhoods.

Ratatouille (2007) directed
by Brad Bird and Jan Pinkava.

A Pixar animated film about a food-loving country rat named Rémy who comes to Paris and unexpectedly finds himself at the helm of one of the city's great haute cuisine restaurants.

Midnight in Paris (2011) directed
by Woody Allen.

Various scenes of this vibrant homage to the French capital were filmed in Paris palaces such as the Ritz, the Bristol and the Meurice.

ACTIVITIES FOR KIDS 👤👤
Paris is a great city for kids, with several large parks divided into multiple play areas to suit tots of all ages. There are also marionette

theatres, museums catering specifically to young children, and even a few that the most demanding teens would find fascinating.

THE 1ST, 2ND, 3RD AND 4TH
(pp86–171)

The Tuileries Gardens have the largest play areas for kids, but the Jardins des Enfants at Les Halles is worth a visit, and there is a small playground in the square Jean XXIII behind Notre-Dame. The Doll Museum and Magic Museum are great for rainy days.

THE 5TH, 6TH AND 7TH
(pp172–221)

Luxembourg Gardens is one of the best-loved parks in Paris, with pony rides, huge play areas for small and large kids, sailboats to push around the basin and a marionette theatre. The Jardin des Plantes, with its small zoo, merry-go-round and natural history museums, is also a favourite for kids of all ages. In the 7th there are small play areas and vast lawns on the Champ de Mars, at the foot of the Eiffel Tower.

THE 8TH, 9TH, 10TH AND 17TH
(pp222–262)

The Champs-Élysées is home to a popular marionette theatre, as well as the Palais de la Découverte, a planetarium and children's science museum in the Grand Palais. The Parc Monceau provides peaceful playground space. When the weather isn't cooperating, try a visit to the Grévin Wax Museum on the Grands Boulevards.

THE 11TH AND 12TH (pp263–275)

Bercy Parc is a great place to let kids run free. There's a grassy lawn for ball games, a skate park, two gardens connected by footbridges, a labyrinth hill and a large lake. One of Paris' Green Lungs, the Bois de Vincennes, is located on the outer edge of the 12th arrondissement, with several lakes, pony rides, bike rental, playgrounds

In This Guide

Sights and attractions geared to children are marked with a ♟♙ symbol. In Paris some museums propose supervised educational activities such as quizzes and treasure hunts, whereas workshops give youngsters the opportunity to try artistic techniques for themselves. These sessions are generally held on Wednesdays and during school holidays and last between one and three hours.

in the Parc Floral, and the imposing tower keep of the Château de Vincennes fortress.

THE 13TH, 14TH AND 15TH
(pp276–292)

Square René le Gall has a large playground in a leafy, tranquil setting. The vast Parc Montsouris in the 14th has play equipment, a waterfall and small lake. Two modern parks in the 15th, the Parc Georges Brassens and the Parc André-Citroën, have playgrounds, open lawns and fountains. The last has an anchored hot-air balloon for great Paris views.

THE 16TH (pp293–306)

The Bois de Boulogne has several parks, pony rides, bike rental, boat rides, and the popular Jardin d'Acclimatation amusement park. The Jardins du Ranelagh also have a playground and merry-go-round.

THE 18TH, 19TH AND 20TH
(pp307–325)

The carrousel at the foot of Sacré-Cœur is a popular place for children. The vast Parc de Belleville, with its Maison de l'Air, and the bucolic Buttes-Chaumont, with its hills and footbridges, make for a great day out.

Calendar of Events

The following events may change dates or venues from year to year. Check the tourist office online: www.parisinfo.com or http://75.agendaculturel.fr.

LAST SUNDAY IN JANUARY
Prix d'Amérique – Hippodrome de Vincennes. ☎01 49 77 17 17. www.hippodromes-parisiens.fr.

LATE JANUARY OR FEBRUARY
Chinese New Year – Grand parade, Chinatown (avenue de Choisy, avenue d'Ivry, 13th *arr*). ☎01 44 08 14 69. www.mairie13.paris.fr.
Festival mondial du Cirque de demain – Under the circus tent of the Cirque de Phenix (Pelouse de Reuilly, Bois de Vincennes). ☎01 40 55 50 56. www.cirquededemain.com.

FEBRUARY
Carnaval de Paris – Begins at the foot of rue Le Vau (20th *arr*) and arrives at the place de l'Hôtel-de-Ville (4th *arr*) the Sunday preceding Mardi gras. ☎06 26 67 76 39 or ☎09 53 72 16 61. www.carnaval-paris.org.

END FEBRUARY–EARLY MARCH
Salon international de l'Agriculture – Paris Expo Porte de Versailles. ☎01 49 09 60 00. www.salon-agriculture.com.

EARLY MARCH
Semi-Marathon de Paris – Starts and finishes at the esplanade du Château de Vincennes. 21.1km/13.1mi race. ☎01 41 3315 68. www.semideparis.com.

END MARCH
Salon du Livre de Paris (Book Fair) – Paris Expo Porte de Versailles. ☎01 47 56 64 31. www.salondulivreparis.com.
Art Paris – Avenue Winston-Churchill (8th *arr*). Modern and contemporary art from140 galleries from France and abroad under the nave of the Grand Palais. www.artparis.fr.

MARCH–APRIL
Festival Banlieues Bleues – Jazz festival of internationally renowned musicians with concerts in several towns in the suburbs of Seine-St-Denis. ☎01 49 22 10 10. www.banlieuesbleues.org.

Paris Plages, Mid-July–Mid-August

© S. Sauvignier/MICHELIN

EARLY APRIL
Marathon de Paris – 42km/26mi race from Champs-Élysées to the avenue Foch. ℘01 41 33 15 68. www.schneiderelectricparis marathon.com.

APRIL–OCTOBER
Horticultural Presentations – Monthly blooms. Parc floral de Paris, Château de Vincennes esplanade.
℘01 49 57 15 15.

END APRIL–EARLY MAY
Paris Fair – (Foire de Paris) Paris Expo Porte de Versailles.
℘01 49 09 60 00.
www.foiredeparis.fr.

MAY–OCTOBER
Musique côté jardins – Some 400 free concerts in the gardens of Paris. www.paris.fr.
Shakespeare Theatre Festival in the Gardens – At the Pré Catelan (Bois de Boulogne).
℘01 40 19 95 33.

END MAY–EARLY JUNE
Internationaux de France de tennis – Stade Roland-Garros.
℘01 47 43 48 00. www.fft.fr.
St-Germain Fair – Market stands, poetry readings, live music, bookselling, antiques and ceramics. St-Germain-des-Prés. www.foiresaintgermain.org.

1ST HALF OF JUNE
Festival Paris en toutes lettres – Author signings and books events throughout Paris. www.paris.fr.

MID-JUNE
Prix du président de la République– Hippodrome de Vincennes.℘ 01 49 77 17 17. www.cheval-francais.com.
Festival Jazz-Musette des Puces – A music festival at the St-Ouen flea markets. ℘ 01 40 11 77 36. www.festivaldespuces.com.

EARLY JUNE–JULY
Paris Jazz Festival – Open-air concerts weekend afternoons at the Parc Floral de Vincennes. www.parisjazzfestival.fr.

21 JUNE
Fête de la Musique – Citywide free music festival. www.fetedelamusique.culture.fr.

END JUNE
Marche des Fiertés lesbiennes, gays, bi et trans – Gay Pride Parade from Denfert-Rochereau to Bastille. ℘01 72 70 39 22. http://marche.inter-lgbt.org.

END JUNE–END AUGUST
Tuileries Fun Fair (Fête foraine des Tuileries) – Jardin des Tuileries.

EARLY JULY
Festival Paris-cinéma – Film festival in cinemas throughout the city. www.pariscinema.org.

JULY
Finish of the Tour de France cyclists – On the Champs-Élysées. www.letour.fr.

13–14 JULY
Bastille Day – Dance parties and fireworks; military parade on the 14th on the Champs-Élysées.

MID-JULY–MID-AUGUST
Paris Quartier d'été – Music, theatre and dance events in venues throughout Paris. ℘ 01 44 94 98 00. www.quartierdete.com.
Paris Plages – The route along the Seine is transformed into a beach with lounge chairs, ice cream stands. www.paris.fr/parisplages.

AUGUST
Festival Classique au Vert – Parc floral de Paris (Bois de Vincennes) Saturday and Sunday, free classical concerts. www.classiqueauvert.paris.fr

Fête de Ganesha – Parade for the Hindu god Ganesh (Sri Manicka Vinayakar Alayam temple) in 10th and 18th arr. 📞01 40 34 21 89.

EARLY–MID-SEPTEMBER
Jazz à la Villette – Jazz festival at the Parc de la Villette of concerts, many free, under the open sky. 📞01 44 84 44 84. www.jazzalavillette.com.

MID-SEPTEMBER–END DECEMBER
Festival d'automne – Autumn festival of theatre, contemporary dance and music throughout Paris. 📞01 53 45 17 00. www.festival-automne.com.

2ND HALF OF SEPTEMBER
Biennale internationale des Antiquaires et Salon du Collectionneur – At the Grand Palais, for antique dealers on even years, and antique collectors on odd years. 📞01 44 51 74 74. www.antiquaires-sna.com.

3RD WEEKEND OF SEPTEMBER
Journées européennes du patrimoine – During the National Heritage Days, visit any historic monument in Paris normally closed to the public. journeesdupatrimoine.culture.fr
Festival America, North American Literature and Culture – Vincennes – even years. 📞01 43 98 65 09. www.festival-america.og.

LATE SEPTEMBER–MID-OCTOBER
Fête de la Science – Science workshops and conferences in various venues (e.g. Cité des Sciences, Jardin des Plantes, Palais de la Découverte). www.fetedelascience.fr.

EARLY OCTOBER
La Nuit Blanche – An all-night contemporary art festival in venues throughout the city. www.paris.fr

Mondial de l'automobile – (Salon de l'Auto) Car show. Paris Expo Porte de Versailles – every two years. 📞01 56 88 22 40. www.mondial-automobile.com
Qatar Prix de l'Arc de Triomphe – Hippodrome de Longchamp. 📞0 821 213 213. www.france-galop.com.

2ND WEEK OF OCTOBER
Fête des Vendanges – Harvest festival at the Butte de Montmartre. 📞01 46 06 00 32. www.fetedes vendangesdemontmartre.com.

MID-OCTOBER
Les 20 km de Paris – A race from the Pont d'Iéna (at the foot of the Eiffel Tower) to the quai Branly. 📞01 46 19 83 66. www.20kmparis.com.

END OCTOBER
Foire Internationale d'Art Contemporain (Fiac) – Contemporary art, Grand Palais . Performances and conferences at the Louvre, Museum national d'Histoire naturelle and other venues. www.fiacparis.com.

NOVEMBER
Mois de la Photo – Every even year in museums and galleries around Paris. 📞01 44 78 75 00. www.mep-fr.org.

END NOVEMBER–EARLY DECEMBER
Salon du Cheval – Horse show at the Paris Expo (Porte de Versailles). www.salon-cheval.com. 📞01 30 80 80 87

EARLY DECEMBER
Salon Nautique – Boat show at the Paris Expo (Porte de Versailles). www.salonnautiqueparis.com.

DECEMBER–EARLY MARCH
Paris sur Glace – Open-air skating rink (patinoire en plein air) at Parvis de l'Hôtel de Ville. www.paris.fr.

Know Before You Go

USEFUL WEBSITES
CYBERSPACE

www.ambafrance-us.org
The French Embassy's website provides basic information (geography, demographics, history), a news digest and business-related information. It offers special pages for children, and pages devoted to culture, language study and travel, and you can reach other selected French sites (regions, cities, ministries) with a hypertext link.

www.ambafrance-ca.org
The Cultural Service of the French Embassy in Ottawa has a varied site with many links to other sites for French literature, news updates and E-texts in both French and English.

www.France.fr/en.html
This official website introduces readers to the country's history, geography, gastronomy, economy and other topics of interest.

www.visiteurope.com
The European Travel Commission provides useful information on travelling to and around 34 European countries, and includes links to commercial booking services (e.g. vehicle hire), rail schedules, weather reports and more.

www.parisbalades.com
This website covers a lot of ground, and has especially good information about architecture from all periods with links to the museums of Paris and other useful sites.

www.contexttravel.com
A selection of guided tours through different neighbourhoods and museums with well-qualified group leaders.

TOURIST OFFICES
FRENCH TOURIST OFFICES ABROAD

For information, brochures, maps and assistance in planning a trip to France, travellers should apply to the official French tourist office in their own country:

♦ **Australia – New Zealand**
Sydney – Level 13, 25 Bligh Street, Sydney, NSW 2000
℘61 + (02) 9 231 52 44.
http:/au.rendezvousenfrance.com

♦ **Canada**
Montreal
1800 avenue McGill College, Bureau 1010, Montreal PQ H3A 3J6
℘(514) 288 2026
ca.rendezvousenfrance.com

♦ **Ireland**
Dublin
Merrion St. Upper, Dublin 2, Ireland ℘1 662 9345
uk.rendezvousenfrance.com

♦ **United Kingdom**
London
London Maison de France
Lincoln House, 300 High Holborn, London WC1V 7JH
℘207 061 66 00
uk.franceguide.com

♦ **United States, East Coast**
New York
444 Madison Avenue, 16th Floor, NY 10022-6903
℘(212) 838 7830
us.rendezvousenfrance.com

United States, West Coast
Los Angeles
9454 Wilshire Boulevard, Suite 715, Beverly Hills, CA 90212-2967
℘(310) 271 6665
us.rendezvousenfrance.com

Request further information from the French public information hotline:
France-on-Call (410) 286 8310

TOURIST OFFICES IN PARIS
Office du Tourisme et des Congrès de Paris, 25 rue des Pyramides, 75001 Paris, Ⓜ Pyramides. ℰ08 92 68 30 00 (0.34€/min). www.parisinfo.com. Daily 9am–7pm; closed 1 May. **Gare de Lyon**, 12th *arr*, Mon–Sat 8am–6pm. **Gare du Nord**, 10th *arr* daily 8am–6pm; closed 1 Jan, 1 May, 25 Dec. **Gare de l'Est**, 10th *arr* Mon–Sat 8am–7pm. **Anvers**, 72 bd Rochechouart, 75018 daily 10am–6pm; closed 1 Jan, 1 May, 25 Dec; **Montmartre**, 21 place du Tertre, 18th *arr*, daily 10am–7pm.

INTERNATIONAL VISITORS
EMBASSIES AND CONSULATES
- **Australia Embassy**
  4 rue Jean-Rey, 75724 Paris Cedex 15. ℰ01 40 59 33 00
  www.france.embassy.gov.au
- **Canada Embassy**
  35 avenue Montaigne, 75008 Paris ℰ01 44 43 29 00
  www.canadainternational.gc.ca
- **Ireland Consulate**
  4 rue Rude, 75116 Paris
  ℰ01 44 17 67 00
  www.embassyofireland.fr
- **New Zealand Embassy**
  103 rue de Grenelle, 75007 Paris ℰ01 45 00 43 43
  www.nzembassy.com/fr/france
- **UK Embassy**
  35 rue du Faubourg-St-Honoré, 75008 Paris ℰ01 44 51 31 00; Fax 01 44 51 31 27
- **UK Consular Services**
  16 rue d'Anjou, 75008 Paris
  ℰ01 44 51 31 00
- **USA Embassy & Consulate**
  2 avenue Gabriel, 75008 Paris
  ℰ01 43 12 22 22
  http://france.usembassy.gov

ENTRY REQUIREMENTS
Passport – Nationals of countries within the Schengen Area of EU countries need only a national identity card. Nationals of all other countries, including other EU member states (such as the UK), must carry a valid passport. Loss or theft must be reported to your embassy, or consulate and the local police.
Visa – An **entry visa** is required for Canadian and US citizens who intend to stay more than 3 months and for Australian and New Zealand citizens. Apply to the French Consulate.

CUSTOMS REGULATIONS
The Customs Office (UK) website http://customs.hmrc.gov.uk has the latest travel advice for France, including entry requirements, safety and security, travel warnings and health. The website of the US Customs Service www.cbp.gov has information you need to know before you travel. Americans can bring home, tax-free, up to US$800 worth of goods; Canadians up to CND$300; Australians up to AUS$400 and New Zealanders up to NZ$700. Persons living in a Member State of the European Union are not restricted in regard to purchasing goods for private use, but the recommended allowances for alcoholic beverages and tobacco are set out in the table below.

HEALTH
No insurance is necessary to receive medical care in France; however, it is advisable to take out comprehensive insurance cover as the recipient of medical treatment in French hospitals or clinics must pay the bill. Nationals of non-EU countries should check

DUTY-FREE ALLOWANCE	
Spirits (whisky, gin, vodka, etc.)	10l/2.6gal
Fortified wines (vermouth, port, etc.)	20l/5.3gal
Wine (not more than 60 sparkling)	90l/23.7gal
Beer	110l/29gal
Cigarettes	3 200
Cigarillos	400
Cigars	200
Smoking tobacco	3kg/6.6lb

with their insurance companies about policy limitations. Reimbursement can then be negotiated with the insurance company according to the policy held. All prescription drugs should be clearly labelled; it is recommended that you carry a copy of the prescription and to always pack urgent medications in your carry-on baggage.

US citizens concerned about travel and health can contact the International Association for Medical Assistance to Travellers: ✆716 754 4883, www.iamat.org.

British and Irish citizens should apply to the Department of Health (www.dh.gov.uk) for the **European Health Insurance Card**, or EHIC, which entitles the holder to free or reduced-cost urgent treatment for accident or sudden illness in EU countries, as well as a refund of part of the cost of treatment on application in person or by post to the local Social Security Offices (*Caisse Primaire d'Assurance Maladie*).

ACCESSIBILITY

Paris remains a city of stairs, but many buildings have now been retro-fitted with ramps and lifts.

The sights described in this guide that are easily accessible to people of reduced mobility are indicated in the *Discovering Paris* section by the ♿ symbol.

For information on transport, holidaymaking and sports associations for the disabled, see the "Visiter Paris avec un handicap" section of the website of the **Office du Tourisme et des Congrès de Paris** (www.parisinfo.com). Web-surfers can find information for slow walkers, mature travellers and others with special needs at www.access-able.com.

For information on museum access for the disabled, contact the Direction des affaires culturelles – Bureau des Musées, 70 rue des Archives, 75003. ✆01 42 76 83 66.

The **Michelin Guide France** and **Michelin Camping and Caravanning in France** indicate hotels and campsites with facilities suitable for physically handicapped people. Call hotels directly before booking to find out the exact nature of their accessible rooms, lifts and bathroom facilities, as there are no standard measurements.

Getting There and Getting Around

BY PLANE

Paris is served by two international airports: **Roissy-Charles de Gaulle** 23km/14.3mi to the north of Paris on the A1, and **Orly** 11km/6.8mi to the south along the A6. Domestic flights are handled by Orly. Public services giving access to and from Paris include Air France coaches, public transport (RATP) buses, private minibuses, RER trains and taxis. Check if the train or bus is running before buying a ticket from a machine (it's nonrefundable).

ROISSY-CHARLES DE GAULLE

Les Cars Air France run every 30min from 5am to 11.40pm. **Line 2** stops at Paris-Porte Maillot (blvd Gouvion St-Cyr) and Paris-Place de Étoile (corner with avenue Carnot). 1st/last departure de Gaulle Airport and Place de Étoile 5.45am–11pm; 50–60min; 17€. **Line 4** stops at Gare de Montparnasse (rue du Commandant Mouchotte) and Gare de Lyon. 1st/last departure de Gaulle Airport 6am–10pm (Gare Montparnasse 10.30pm); 60-70min; 17.50€. www.lescarsairfrance.com. Purchase tickets online, at airport desks, automated machines or on-board.

Bus RATP runs the ROISSYBUS between Roissy-CDG and Paris-Opéra (rue Scribe, corner with rue Auber,

Ⓜ Opéra) from 6.30am to 12.30am, and from Paris-Opéra to Roissy-CDG from 5.45am to 12.30am. Departures every 15–30min. Approximate journey time: 60min. ℘08 36 68 77 14. 11€.

Underground trains RER line B runs every 10-20min from Roissy-CDG to Paris Châtelet-Les Halles from 5am to 11.30pm, and from Paris Châtelet-Les Halles to Roissy-CDG from 5.26am to 12.47am. Average journey time to Gare du Nord: 28min. 9.75€.

Taxis are subject to road traffic conditions; it is best to allow 1hr journey time into Paris. Expect to pay 35-65€, plus 1€ extra per item of baggage over 5kg/11lb.

Shuttle services offer a good alternative to expensive cabs and to lugging baggage on the RER: Paris Airports Service (34€ for 2 people from Roissy-CGD or Orly; reduced rates depend on the number of people in your party) ℘01 55 98 10 80, www.parisairportservice.com.

Useful numbers – Airport Information ℘01 48 62 22 80 or 08 92 68 15 15. www.taxi-paris.net or www.aeroportsdeparis.fr.

ORLY

Les Cars Air France Line 1 runs every 20min from 6am to 11.40pm from Orly Airport to Les Invalides (rue Esnault Pelterie), Place Charles de Gaulle-de l'Étoile (corner with avenue Carnot), and Gare de Montparnasse (rue du Commandant Mouchotte).1st and last departure from Paris-Place de l'Etoile to Orly Airport 5am to 10.40pm. Approximate journey time: 60min. 12.50€. www.lescarsairfrance.com. Purchase tickets online, at airport desks or on-board.

Bus RATP runs the OrlyBus between Orly Sud and Orly Ouest terminals and Paris-place Denfert-Rochereau (outside RER station) from 6am to 12.30m and from Paris-place Denfert-Rochereau to Orly Sud and Orly Ouest terminals from 5.35am to midnight. Departures every 8-15min. Average journey time: 25-35min. 7€. ℘08 36 68 77 14 (0.34€/min. www.ratp.fr.

Underground trains RER line C run from Paris-Gare d'Austerlitz to Pont de Rungis-Aéroport d'Orly (connection with the air terminals is then by shuttle) from 5.12am to 12.27pm, and from Pont de Rungis-Aéroport d'Orly to Paris between 4.53am and 11.38pm. Average journey time to Gare d'Austerlitz: 35min.Combined ticket (métro + RER + shuttle) 6.40€.

Underground trains RER line B run as far as Antony and connect with ORLYVAL (automated trains serving Orly Airport south and west terminals). Scheduled departures from Antony to Orly Sud or Orly Ouest every 7min, between 6am and 11pm. Average journey time between Paris-Châtelet-Les Halles and Orly: 35min. Combined ticket (Paris via Antony) 12.05€. ℘08 36 68 77 14.

Taxis are subject to traffic conditions. Average time between Orly and Downtown Paris 25min (except rush hours: 7am-9am and 4pm-7pm. Allow at least 45min into Paris. Around 45€, plus 1€ extra per item of baggage over 5kg/11lb.

Useful numbers – Airport information (24hr) ℘01 49 75 15 15. www.aeroportsdeparis.fr.

AIRLINE OFFICES

- **Air France:** 49 avenue Opéra, 75002. ℘08 20 820 820. www.airfrance.fr.
- **Air Canada** – 10 rue de la Paix, 75002. ℘08 25 88 08 81/01 44 50 20 02. www.aircanada.com.
- **Aer Lingus** – ℘01 70 20 00 72/ 08 21 23 02 67. www.flyaerlingus.com.
- **American Airlines** – ℘08 10 87 28 72. www.aa.com.
- **British Midland Airways** – ℘08 90 71 00 81. www.bmiregional.com.

BY SHIP

There are numerous **cross-Channel services** (passenger and car ferries, hovercraft) from the United Kingdom and Ireland and also the rail Shuttle through the Channel

Tunnel (**Eurostar**, ☎08705 18 61 86 from the UK; ☎08 10 63 03 04 from France; www.eurotunnel.com or www.eurostar.com). To choose the most suitable route between your port of arrival and your destination use *www.viamichelin.com*, the *Michelin Tourist and Motoring Atlas France*, Michelin map 911 (which gives travel times and mileages) or Michelin maps from the 1:200 000 series (these maps have yellow covers).

♦ **P & O Ferries**
Channel House, Channel View Road, Dover CT17 9TJ.
☎08716 64 64 64.
www.poferries.com.

♦ **DFDS Seaways**
Norfolk House
Eastern Docks, Dover CT16 1JA.
☎0870 870 10 20.
www.norfolkline.com.

♦ **Irish Ferries**
PO Box 19, Alexandra Road, Ferryport, Dublin 1. ☎0818 300 400 in Ireland, 08705 17 17 17 in the UK. www.irishferries.com.

BY TRAIN

Eurostar runs via the Channel Tunnel between **London** (St Pancras) and **Paris** (Gare du Nord) in 3hr (bookings and information ☎08705 186 186; ☎+44 1233 617 575 outside the UK); www.eurostar.com.
Eurail Global Pass, **Eurail Select Pass**, **Eurail Global Pass Youth**, **Saver** and **Flexi** travel passes for various lengths of time may be purchased in North America. Contact your travel agent or **Rail Europe**, ☎1 888 382 7245 in the US, 1 800 361 7245 in Canada. Information on schedules can be obtained on websites for these agencies and the **SNCF**, respectively: www.raileurope.com, www.sncf.fr. Tickets bought in France must be validated *(composter)* by using the orange automatic date-stamping machines at the platform entrance (⊚failure to do so will result in a fine). Paris has six mainline stations: **Gare du Nord** (northern France, Belgium, Denmark, Germany, Holland,

Scandinavia, the UK); **Gare de l'Est** (eastern France, Austria, Germany, Luxembourg); **Gare de Lyon** (eastern and southern France, the Alps, Greece, Italy, Switzerland); **Gare d'Austerlitz** (southwest France, Portugal, Spain); **Gare Montparnasse** (western France and TGV to southwest France); **Gare St-Lazare** (northwest France).
The French railway company SNCF operates a telephone information, reservation and prepayment service in English from 7am to 10pm (French time). In France call ☎08 36 35 35 39 (when calling from outside France, start with 00 and then drop the initial 0). Accessibility facilities for rail travel in Europe ☎212 888 7800.

BY COACH/BUS

♦ **Eurolines (National Express)**
For travel to all over Europe by coach (bus). ☎08705 808080 (in the UK), ☎08 92 89 90 91 (in France); www.eurolines.co.uk. Helplines for disabled visitors ☎01 21 423 8479 and for deaf or hard-of-hearing visitors ☎01 21 455 0086. For information on bus travel in Paris, see By Public Transport.

♦ **Eurolines (Paris)**
28 Avenue du Général de Gaulle, 93541, Bagnolet. ☎08 92 89 90 91. www.eurolines.fr.

♦ **www.eurolines.com** has information on travelling by coach in Europe.

BY PUBLIC TRANSPORT

See metro map on inside back cover.
Paris is justly renowned for its excellent and inexpensive public transport system.
The **RATP** – Independent Paris Transport Authority – was created in 1949 to manage the urban metro, bus, tram and RER (Regional Express Rail) networks. Today there are 16 metro lines and 302 metro stations, 5 RER lines and 257 RER stations, 351 bus lines and 12 000 bus stops in Paris and the suburbs.

Etienne Marcel metro station

© Yoshimi Kanazawa/MICHELIN

BEST FARES

A book of 10 t+ tickets (called **un carnet**) costs 14.10€, child 7.05€: use one for each metro or bus ride within Paris and keep it with you (inspectors may ask to see it). Children under age 4 ride for free on a lap; under-10s pay half-fare *(demi-tarif)*. Passes may be purchased for different travel zones (zones 1–2, Paris; 3, near suburbs including St-Denis, La Défense, Le Bourget; 5, the airports, Disneyland, Versailles; 8, Provins). **Paris Visite** is a 1-, 2-, 3- or 5-day pass on all modes of transport: métro, RER (RATP et SNCF), Transilien SNCF, bus and tramway (RATP et OPTILE), Orlyval (linking Orly Airport to RER B) and funiculaire de Montmartre. Advantages: access to first class on SNCF trains in the valid zones; half-fare for children under age 12; no photo required; discounts for tourist attractions. Cost from 11.15€/1 day, 3 zones; child 5.55€. The monthly and weekly **Navigo** passes are valid from the first of the month or from Monday to Sunday, at an advantageous rate (e.g. two zones for one week, 21.25€); photograph required; www.navigo.fr.

Mobilis is a one-day pass valid for unlimited travel in the zones selected (but does not include services to airports), costing from 7€ (1–2 zones) to 16.60€ (5 zones); www.ratp.fr.

Ticket windows in stations open at 6.30am (first train around 5.30am depending on the station) but tickets can also be purchased from machines in stations and in *tabacs* and other shops with the RATP sign outside. The last metro leaves the end of the line around 12.30am. Insert your metro ticket in the turnstile and recover it, keeping it with you until you exit the metro.
For information 24/7, ℰ 08 92 68 77 14. You can also plan online at: www.ratp.fr.

RER

The Regional Express Network includes five lines: **line A** runs from St-Germain-en-Laye, Cergy and Poissy

---

The Metro

Construction – Parisians first took the metro on 19 July 1900. The first Paris line was on the Right Bank, from Porte de Vincennes to Porte Maillot. The engineer responsible was Fulgence Bienvenüe and Guimard designed the emblematic Art Nouveau metro entrance, in the so-called noodle style.

Facts and figures – There are more than 219.9km/136.6mi of track for the 16 lines, not including the RER, and 302 stations of which 90 are interchanges. No point in the capital is more than 500m/547yd from a metro station.

to Boissy-St-Léger and Marne-la-Vallée; **line B** from Robinson and St-Rémy-lès-Chevreuse to Roissy-Charles de Gaulle, and Mitry Claye; **line C** links Versailles (Left Bank), St-Quentin-en-Yvelines, Argenteuil and Pontoise and Dourdan, Massy-Palaiseau and St-Martin d'Etampes; **line D** links Orry-la-Ville and Creil to Melun and Malesherbes; **line E** goes from St-Lazare (downtown Paris) to Chelles-Gournay and Tournan. Regular services run between approximately 5am and 1.20am. Metro tickets may be used for RER trains within the metro system – outside these, special fares and tickets apply (including to airports, Versailles and Disneyland-Paris).

BUSES

References in the main text will help you to find the stop to look for on the bus itineraries. Bus routes are displayed in bus shelters as well as inside the buses themselves. Buses normally operate between 6.30am and 8.30pm (Mon–Sat); designated lines operate until around 12.30am and on Sundays and holidays (service assuré les dimanches et fêtes); 47 night buses (noctilien) operate between 12.30am and 5.30am. On the bus, validate your ticket by passing it through the machine by the door. A single ticket can be purchased from the driver for 2€ but it is not valid for metro transfer.

BY CAR

Documents – Travellers from other European Union countries and North America can drive in France with a valid national or home-state **driving licence**. An **international driving licence** is useful because the information on it appears in nine languages (keep in mind that traffic officers are empowered to fine motorists). A permit is available (US$15) from the National Automobile Club, ✆800 622 2136, www.nationalautoclub.com; or contact your local branch of the American Automobile Association. It

is necessary to have the registration papers (logbook) of the vehicle and a nationality plate of the approved size.
Insurance – Certain motoring organisations (AAA, AA™, RAC™) offer accident insurance and breakdown service schemes for members.
Highway Code – The minimum driving age is 18. Traffic drives on the right. All passengers must wear **seat belts**. Children under the age of ten must travel in the back seat of the vehicle. Full or dipped headlights must be switched on in poor visibility and at night; use side-lights only when the vehicle is stationary.
In the case of a **breakdown**, a red warning triangle or hazard warning lights are obligatory. In the absence of stop signs at intersections, cars must **yield to the right**. Traffic on main roads outside built-up areas (priority indicated by a yellow diamond sign) and on roundabouts has right of way. The regulations on **drinking and driving** (limited to 0.5g/l) and **speeding** are strictly enforced – usually by an on-the-spot fine and/or confiscation of the vehicle.
Petrol (gas) – French service stations dispense: sans plomb 98 (super unleaded 98), sans plomb 95 (super unleaded 95), diesel/gazole (diesel) and some have GPL (LPG). Prices are listed on signboards on the motorways; it is usually cheaper to fill up after leaving the motorway.
Tolls – In France, most motorway sections are subject to a toll (péage). You can pay in cash or with a credit card (Visa, MasterCard).

DRIVING IN PARIS

Parking is restricted and while parking garages are well indicated on Michelin maps and on street signs, they are expensive. It's best to use the metro and the bus, which are usually faster than driving. Taxis are abundant. Parking on the street, when authorized, is subject to a fee; tickets should be obtained from the ticket machines (horodateurs – some machines take credit cards if there's a

"CB" sticker; otherwise you must pay with a prepaid *carte de stationnement*–(purchase at *tabacs*) and display the ticket inside the windscreen on the driver's side; failure to display may result in a fine, or towing and impoundment. It is easier to drive around in August, but the riverside motorways are closed to traffic.

Beware *axes rouges* or red routes, along main thoroughfares where parking is prohibited to maintain free flow of traffic (between Gare de Lyon and Gare de l'Est, via Bastille, République, quai des Célestins and quai de la Rapée). *NEVER use the lanes reserved for buses and taxis; severe fines are enforced.* Paris is served by a six-lane 35km/21.7mi outer ring-road, the **boulevard périphérique** (speed limit 70kmph/43mph). Traffic from the motorways into Paris all merges on to the *périphérique* before filtering into the city centre via the *Portes*. As traffic can move at considerable speed during off-peak periods, it is advisable to have pinpointed which exit you require before getting on to the ring-road system. Once on the *périphérique*, cross on to the central lanes allowing traffic to join from the right-hand side, and cross back on to the far right lane before leaving the ring road (may be hazardous for left-hand drive vehicles). Once inside Paris, a west-to-east motorway **(Georges Pompidou motorway)** runs along the Right Bank, facilitating the flow of cars.

SPEED LIMITS

Although liable to modification, speed limits are as follows:

- **Motorways** 130kph/80mph (110kph/68mph when raining);
- **Dual carriageways (divided highways)** 110kph/68mph (100kph/62mph when raining);
- **Main roads** 90kph/56mph (80kph/50mph when raining);
- **Built-up areas** 50kph/31mph unless otherwise indicated (Zones 30: 30kph/19mph) minimum speed limit of 80kph/50mph.

RENTAL CARS

Car rental agencies can be found at airports, air terminals and railway stations. European cars usually have manual transmission but automatic cars are available on request (*advance reservation recommended*). It is relatively expensive to hire a car in France; US citizens in particular will notice the difference and should consider booking a car from home before leaving or taking advantage of fly-drive schemes. If you rent a car in the UK, make sure to inform the car hire company that you intend to take the car to France, for insurance purposes. Most car rental firms will not hire out to under-21's and charge extra for any drivers aged between 21 and 25.

Avis	08 21 23 07 60
Europcar	08 25 35 83 58
Budget France	08 25 00 35 64
Hertz France	08 25 80 09 00
SIXT-Eurorent	08 20 00 74 98
National-CITER	08 25 16 12 12
Baron's Limousine	01 45 30 21 21

BY TAXI

Some 19 000 taxis cruising Paris streets park in the 745 ranks close to road junctions and other points beneath the signs labelled *Taxis*. Taxis may also be hailed in the street when the white taxi sign is fully lit. The rate varies according to the zone and time of day (higher rates 8pm–6.30am). The white, orange and blue lights correspond to the three different rates A, B and C and these appear on the meter inside the cab. A supplementary charge is made for taxi pick-up at train stations, air terminals and for heavy baggage or unwieldy parcels as well as for a fourth person and pets. **Taxis Bleus** 08 91 70 10 10, www. taxis-bleus.com; **Taxi G7** 01 41 27 66 99 (for English speaker) or 3607 (015€/min), www.taxisg7.fr; **Alpha Taxis** 01 45 85 85 85, www.alphataxis.fr.

Useful Words and Phrases

Sights

	Translation
Abbey	Abbaye
Belfry	Beffroi
Bridge	Pont
Castle	Château
Cemetery	Cimetière
Chapel	Chapelle
Church	Église
Cloisters	Cloître
Convent	Couvent
Courtyard	Cour
Fountain	Fontaine
Garden	Jardin
Gateway	Porte
Hall	Halle
House	Maison
Lock (Canal)	Écluse
Market	Marché
Monastery	Monastère
Museum	Musée
Park	Parc
Port/harbour	Port
Quay	Quai
Ramparts	Remparts
Square	Place
Statue	Statue
Street	Rue
Tower	Tour
Town hall	Mairie
Windmill	Moulin
Hello	Bonjour
Goodbye	Au revoir
Bread	Pain
Breakfast	Petit-déjeuner
Cheese	Fromage
Fish	Poisson
Ice cream	Glace
Meat	Viande
Vegetables	Légumes
Wine	Vin
Monday	Lundi
Tuesday	Mardi
Wednesday	Mercredi
Thursday	Jeudi
Friday	Vendredi
Saturday	Samedi
Sunday	Dimanche
Open	Ouvert
Closed	Fermé

USEFUL PHRASES

Do you speak English?
Parlez-vous anglais?
I don't understand
Je ne comprends pas
Talk slowly Parlez lentement
Where's…? Où est…?
When does the…leave?
A quelle heure part…?
When does the…arrive?
A quelle heure arrive…?
When does the museum open?
A quelle heure ouvre le musée?
When is the show?
A quelle heure a lieu la représentation?
When is breakfast served?
A quelle heure sert-on le petit-déjeuner?
What does it cost?
Combien cela coûte-t-il?
Where can I buy a newspaper in English? Où puis-je acheter un journal en anglais?
Where is the nearest petrol/ gas station? Où se trouve la station essence la plus proche?
Where can I change traveller's cheques? Où puis-je changer un traveller's chèque?
Where are the toilets? Où sont les toilettes?
Do you accept credit cards?…
Acceptez-vous les cartes de crédit?
Where is…? Où est?
Thank you Merci
Can you help me? Pouvez-vous m'aider?
How much/many? C'est combien?

Basic Information

BUSINESS HOURS

Admission to state-owned **museums** and historic monuments is free for travellers with special needs, such as people with disabilities – as well as those accompanying them – but the rules require that you show an identification card. Admission is free in most museums for children under 18; admission is free for all visitors on the first Sunday in every month. In Paris, national museums and art galleries are closed on Tuesdays; municipal museums are generally closed on Mondays.

Most of the larger **shops** are open Mon–Sat 9am–6.30pm/7.30pm. Smaller, individual shops may close during the lunch hour. Food shops – grocers, wine merchants and bakeries – are open from around 7am–7.30pm; some open on Sunday mornings. Open-air food markets close on Mondays. Hypermarkets usually stay open until 9pm/10pm.

Banks are usually open during the week 9am–4.30pm/5pm and are closed on Mondays or Saturdays; some branches open for limited transactions on Saturdays. Banks close early on the day before a bank holiday. A passport is required when cashing cheques. Commission charges vary and hotels usually charge more than banks for cashing cheques for non-residents. Most banks have **cash dispensers** (ATMs) which accept international credit or debit cards and are easily recognized by the logo showing a hand holding a card. Pads are numeric and PIN numbers have four digits in France. American Express cards can be used only in dispensers operated by the CLC Bank or by American Express. Detailed descriptions of Paris' museums are found within the *Discovering Paris* section. There is no admission charge for museums owned by the city of Paris (the catacombs are an exception).

COMMUNICATIONS

Public phones, rare in France, use prepaid phone cards *(télécartes)*, rather than coins. Some telephone booths accept credit cards (Visa, MasterCard/Eurocard). *Télécartes* (50 or 120 units) can be bought in post offices, branches of France Télécom, *bureaux de tabac* (cafés that sell cigarettes) and newsagents and can be used to make calls in France and abroad. Calls can be received at phone boxes where the blue bell sign is shown; the phone will not ring, so keep your eye on the little message screen.

NATIONAL CALLS

French telephone numbers have 10 digits. Paris and Paris region numbers begin with 01 (northwest France - 02; northeast - 03; southeast and Corsica - 04; southwest - 05).

TO USE YOUR PERSONAL CALLING CARD	
AT&T	☏ 0 800 99 00 11
Sprint	☏ 0 800 99 00 87
Verizon	☏ 0 800 99 00 19
Canada Direct	☏ 0 800 99 00 16

INTERNATIONAL CALLS

To call France from abroad, dial the country code (33) + nine-digit number (omit the initial 0). When calling abroad from France, dial 00, then dial the country code followed by the area code and number of your correspondent.

- **International information, USA/Canada:** 00 33 12 11
- **International operator:** 00 33 12 + country code
- **Local directory assistance:** 12
- **Special-rate numbers** in France begin with 0 800 (calls from within France only).

INTERNATIONAL DIALLING CODES *(00 + code)*			
Australia	☏ 61	**New Zealand**	☏ 64
Canada	☏ 1	**United Kingdom**	☏ 44
Ireland	☏ 353	**United States**	☏ 1

MOBILE PHONES

In France mobiles phones have numbers that begin with 06 or 07. The major networks are SFR, Orange, Bouygues and Free.

Some have their own pay-as-you-go services. Phones need to be GSM 90 or GSM 1800 to work in France. For mobile phone rentals (delivery provided):

♦ **World Cellular Rentals**
℘1 877 626 0216 (US and Canada)
www.worldcr.com

ELECTRICITY

The electric current is 220 volts/50Hz. Circular two-pin plugs are the rule. Adapters and converters (for hairdryers, for example) should be bought before you leave home; they are on sale in most airports.

If you have a rechargeable device (video camera, laptop, battery charger), read the instructions carefully or contact the manufacturer or shop. Sometimes these items only require a plug adapter; in other cases you must use a voltage converter as well or risk ruining your appliance.

EMERGENCIES

First aid, medical advice and chemists' night service rota are available from chemists/drugstores (*pharmacie* – identified by the green cross sign).

♦ **Useful numbers – SOS Médecins Paris Île-de-France** ℘01 47 07 77 77 (for emergencies).

♦ **Pharmacie Les Champs**
84 avenue des Champs-Élysées (Galerie des Champs-Élysées 75008), Ⓜ George V. Open 24hr a day, seven days a week.
℘01 45 62 02 41.

♦ **Pharmacie Européenne de la place de Clichy**, 6 place de Clichy, 75009. Open 24hr a day, seven days a week. ℘01 48 74 65 18.

♦ **American Hospital**, 63 boulevard Victor-Hugo, 93 Neuilly-sur-Seine (7.5km/4.6mi from central Paris). ℘01 46 41 25 25.

♦ **British Hospital**, 3 rue Barbès, 92 Levallois-Perret (7.5km/4.6mi from central Paris). ℘01 47 59 59 59.

LOST PROPERTY

Lost property office: Préfecture de Police, Objets trouvés, 36 rue des Morillons, 75015 Paris, Ⓜ Convention. ℘01 45 31 14 80 or 08 21 00 25 25. Open 8.30am–5pm Monday and Wednesday, to 5.30pm Friday, to 8pm Tuesday and Thursday.

MAIL/POST

Post offices generally open Mondays to Fridays 8am–7pm, Saturdays 8am–noon. Smaller branch post offices might close noon–2pm and at 4pm. Postage via air mail to:

♦ UK letter (20g) 0.95€
♦ US letter (20g) 1.20€
♦ US postcard 1.20€
♦ Australia and New Zealand letter (20g) 1.20€

www. tarifs-de-la-poste.fr. Stamps are also available from newsagents and tobacconists. Stamp collectors should ask for *timbres de collection* in any post office. *Poste Restante* (General Delivery) mail should be addressed as follows: Name, Poste Restante,

© Jeff Gynane /istockphoto.com

Poste Centrale, postal code of the *département* followed by town name, France. *Michelin Guide France* shows local postal codes.

MONEY

There are no restrictions on the amount of currency visitors can take into France; however, the amount of cash you may take out of France is subject to a limit, so visitors carrying a lot of cash should complete a currency declaration form on arrival.

NOTES AND COINS

Since February 2002, the **euro** has been the only currency accepted as a means of payment in France, as in the 14 member states participating in the monetary union. It is divided into 100 cents or centimes.

CREDIT CARDS

American Express, Visa (*Carte Bleue*), MasterCard/Eurocard and Diners Club are widely accepted in shops, hotels and restaurants and petrol stations. Before you leave home, learn your bank's emergency policies. Carry account numbers and emergency phone numbers separately from your wallet. Leave a copy with someone easily reachable. In the case of a lost or stolen credit card, ring one of the 24hr numbers in the box above.

These numbers are also listed at most ATM machines. Such loss or theft must also be reported to the local police, who will issue a certificate to show to the credit card company.

Traveller's cheques – Not widely accepted in France. Banks and post offices often give a better rate for traveller's cheques. Use Amex (dollars) or Visa (euro). You will not normally be able to pay directly with traveller's cheques, as in North America.

American Express	☎01 47 77 72 00
Visa	☎01 42 77 11 90
MasterCard/Eurocard	☎01 45 67 47 64
Diners Club	☎01 47 62 75 75

The cheapest and most convenient way to change money is to use ATMs, known in France as DABs. Money will be drawn from your home account at a better rate than offered by banks and money-changers. Most ATMs will give a cash advance using Visa or MasterCard but this option is more expensive.

Exchange bureaux – Bureaux can be found in many places in Paris. You can exchange without commission at the following bureau de changes: 101 boulevard Raspail, 70 boulevard de Strasbourg, Le Bureau de Change at 79 avenue de Champs-Élysées and at the Gare de l'Est.

PRICES IN PARIS

As a rule, the cost of staying in a hotel and eating in restaurants is significantly higher in Paris than in the French regions. However, by reserving a hotel room well in advance and taking advantage of the wide choice of restaurants, you can enjoy your trip without breaking the bank.

Restaurants usually charge for meals in two ways: a menu that is a **fixed-price menu** with two or three courses, sometimes a small pitcher of wine, all for a stated price, or **à la carte**, the more expensive way, with each course ordered separately.

Cafés have very different prices, depending on where they are located. The price of a drink or a coffee is cheaper if you stand at the counter (*comptoir*) than if you sit down (*salle*), and sometimes it is even more expensive if you sit outdoors (*terrasse*). ♨See also Food and Drink p400.

PUBLIC HOLIDAYS

Museums and other monuments may be closed or may vary their hours of admission on public holidays.

In addition to the usual school holidays at Christmas and in the spring and summer, there are long mid-term breaks (10 days to a fortnight) in February and early November.

1 January	New Year's Day
Mon after Easter Sun	Easter Day and Easter Monday (Pâques)
1 May	May Day (Fête du Travail)
8 May	VE Day (Fête de la Libération)
Thurs 40 days after Easter	Ascension Day (Ascension)
7th Sun-Mon after Easter	Whit Sunday and Monday (Pentecôte)
14 July	France's National Day (Fête de la Bastille)
15 August	Assumption (Assomption)
1 November	All Saint's Day (Toussaint)
11 November	Armistice Day (Fête de la Victoire)
25 December	Christmas Day (Noël)

REDUCED RATES

Significant discounts are available for senior citizens, students, youth under age 25, teachers, and groups for public transportation, museums and monuments and cinemas (at certain times of day). Bring student or senior identification cards with you, and bring along some extra passport-size photos for discount travel cards. A Paris Museum Pass is available from the Paris Tourism Office, participating museums and monuments.

PARIS MUSEUM PASS

This Museums and Monuments Pass allows free access, in many cases without queueing (except for security check), to more than 60 such sights in the capital. It may be purchased at participating museums and monuments, and at the Office du Tourisme or online. Cost: 42€, 56€ or 69€ for 2, 4 or 6 days respectively. www.parismuseumpass.fr.

SMOKING

Smoking is banned in all enclosed public spaces such as offices, universities and railway stations restaurants and cafés in France. The law now applies to e-cigarettes.

TAXES

In France a sales tax (TVA or Value Added Tax ranging from 2.1 percent to 20percent) is added to almost all retail goods – it can be worth your while to recover it.

RECOVERING VAT

VAT refunds are available to visitors from outside the EU only if purchases exceed 175€ per store. The system works in large stores which cater to tourists, in luxury stores and other shops advertising "duty free". Show your passport, and the store will complete a form which is to be stamped (at the airport) by customs. The refund is paid into your credit card account. Global Refund Tax Free Shopping is a service (www.globalrefund.com) that provides customers at participating stores with a check for the amount of refund which they must have stamped at the customs office at the airport, then send to the company or cash at one of the company's offices (Orly and Roissy-Charles de Gaulle airports). The service is not free, but it does simplify the process.

TIME

France is 1hr ahead of **Greenwich Mean Time** (GMT). When it is noon in France, it is: 11am in London, 6am in New York City, 3am in Los Angeles and 9pm in Sydney. France goes on **Daylight Saving Time** the last Sunday in March to the last Sunday in October. In France the 24-hour clock is used rather than "am" and "pm".

TIPPING

Since a service charge is automatically included in the prices of meals and accommodation in France, it is not necessary to tip in restaurants and hotels. If the service in a restaurant is especially good, an extra tip (this is the *pourboire*, rather than the *service*) of usually 2 to 4 euros is enough, but if the bill is big (a large party or a luxury restaurant), it is not uncommon to leave 7 to 8 euros or more.

Parc Monceau
© B. Merle /PHOTONONSTOP

Paris Today

The centuries-old capital of France is the centre of the country's political, administrative, economic and cultural life – and a vibrant, alluring metropolis in its own right. To an extent a global trendsetter, this city, poised at the crossroads of Europe, thrives on art and culture in every form and fashion. The lively mix of the people who live here keeps this dynamic European hub moving forward. A long-time magnet for tourists, artists and lovers, it has attracted many multinational corporations in recent years, and become an important international business centre; its reign as queen of gastronomy and fashion continues.

PORTRAIT OF A CITY

A map of Paris (♿ see the map on the inside front cover) reveals that the city is completely encircled by a great ring road, the boulevard Périphérique. Hemmed in by this visual boundary, the city within is roughly circular, yet slightly squashed, as it extends for 12km/7.5mi from east to west but only 9km/5.6mi from north to south. Flanked by two green lungs (the Bois de Boulogne and the Bois de Vincennes) and bisected by the River Seine, Paris is tiny compared to other capitals. These compact dimensions mean that everything is concentrated: the city packs in 20 000 inhabitants per square kilometre, compared to 3 300 in Marseille. And this small, enclosed space – home to more than two million people – is the beating heart of France.

THE RIVER AND THE ISLAND

Paris grew up around an island in the Seine, the **Île de la Cité**, an obligatory crossing point for anyone heading north from the Loire. The island's strategic position played a crucial role: the Seine was a channel for communication and the transport of goods, but it also provided natural defence.

The reason for Paris' existence in the first place, the river now meanders its way between the "mountains" that define its geography: the Buttes-Chaumont, Montmartre, Montparnasse, the Montagne Ste-Geneviève and the Butte-aux-Cailles. So it is fitting that the Seine is the source of the city's 16C motto: *Fluctuat nec mergitur* ("though buffeted by the waves, she never sinks").

The visage of Paris really has been shaped by the Seine, and the current logo (♿ see inside back cover) of the RATP (the major public transport operator) perfectly translates this image, with the course of the river tracing the outline of an upturned face in profile, encased within a circle symbolizing city limits.

THE QUARTIERS OF PARIS

Paris comprises 20 **arrondissements**, each with its own administration and characteristics. The *arrondissement* is then divided into four *quartiers*, or neighbourhoods, according to boundaries that were determined by their inhabitants, meaning that when you cross the road, you may not be in the same *quartier* or the same "village".

Different trades

From a historical point, different trades and occupations are associated with the various *quartiers*. The **Right Bank** has always been distinguished from the **Left Bank**, the former being dedicated to business and trade, and the latter the seat of learning with its universities and publishing houses. Political power, meanwhile, has spread out from its origins on the Île de la Cité, following the Voie Triomphale, the historic axis that cuts a straight line through the city from the Louvre to La Défense. Nowadays, **political institutions** are to be found on both the Right Bank (the president's Élysée Palace in the Faubourg St-Honoré) and the Left Bank (the **government ministries,** the Senate and the National Assembly in the Faubourg St-Germain).

Following the example of the medieval guilds, the various crafts and trades were grouped together in different *quartiers*, and the results of this differentiation can be seen to this day: haute couture in the Faubourg St-Honoré, avenue Montaigne

Rue Mouffetard market and église Saint-Médard

© Hervé HUGHES / hemis.fr

and the rue François-Ier, luxury-goods shops around the Opéra, jewellers in the rue de la Paix and the place Vendôme, publishers and bookshops around the Odéon, cabinet makers in the Faubourg St-Antoine (although their numbers are declining), clothing wholesalers in the Sentier and the Temple, antique dealers in the rue Bonaparte and the rue La Boétie, makers of religious supplies in St-Sulpice, crafters of stringed instruments in the rue de Rome, purveyors of crystal glass in the rue de Paradis, and seed merchants on the quai de la Mégisserie.

Finally, the massive influx of immigrants has created new districts specialising in goods from different parts of the world: Chinese in the Quartier des Arts-et-Métiers (3rd arr), Belleville (20th arr) and the 13th *arrondissement*; African and Caribbean in Château-Rouge (18th arr); North African in Barbès, the Goutte d'Or (18th arr) and Belleville; Jewish in the Marais (4th arr) and the Sentier (2nd arr); and Pakistani in La Chapelle (10th arr).

Different atmospheres

Each *quartier* has its own atmosphere The Butte-aux-Cailles with its wine bars is protected from the city's hustle and bustle by the steep little streets leading to it; the sights and smells of the market in the Rue Mouffetard, around the Église St-Médard; the Contrescarpe, with its cafés, where patrons idle away the hours

and put the world to rights. Place Maubert has its lopsided buildings and little squares with inviting outside tables; winding streets lead to the rue Maître-Albert, where you can turn a corner and suddenly be rewarded with a view of the delicate stonework of Notre-Dame, before browsing the second-hand books sold by the **bouquinistes** from their traditional green stalls.

The Île St-Louis exudes an intimate, peaceful atmosphere; it's a place to stop for an ice cream at Berthillon and take in the art galleries before a stroll beside the green waters of the Seine, surrounded by reminders of Paris' history, as a saxophonist leans against a plane tree and plays for his own enjoyment.

Around the place des Vosges and rue des Francs-Bourgeois, the Marais is an equally fascinating world: old mansions have a new lease on life as museums, shops selling antiques or designer clothes, bars and bookshops.

To the east, a more village-like style predominates: in Ménilmontant, rue St-Blaise runs downhill opposite the Église de Charonne, with its old-fashioned street lights, broad paving stones and white houses, home to creative types, artists and restaurants.

The traditionally minded should explore St-Germain-des-Prés, with its tangle of little streets between the Seine and St-Germain, taking in the market in the rue de Buci, Café Procope, the rue St-

45

André-des-Arts, the Cour St-Germain; or St-Sulpice with its fashion boutiques, or the Latin Quarter with its cinemas. Window shopping at the fashion boutiques of the avenue Montaigne and the rue du Faubourg-St-Honoré is a favoured pastime, while attending an international fashion show is a treat, as is a peek at the splendid jewellery on show in the place Vendôme and the rue de la Paix. Don't miss the colourful, double-decker macarons at Ladurée's shop on the Champs-Élysée.

PARISIAN LIFE

It might help to start off by asking who lives in Paris today. People born in the city with roots stretching back several generations are increasingly rare. Paris is a city that people leave or adopt, and these days, many of the city's inhabitants are not natives, but have become Parisians. They started off as newcomers from the provinces looking for work. Some came from overseas: Africans or Asians in search of a better life, which was not always what they found when they arrived. But ultimately, they have all become integrated into the city, each of them becoming Parisians in their own way and changing the face of the capital with their customs and lifestyles.

MÉTRO, BOULOT, DODO

How can you describe everyday life in Paris? The smell of croissants fresh from the oven, colourful displays of fruit and vegetables, café terraces ready to catch the sun from the first fine days of spring, the zinc-topped bars of the bistros where rows of half-asleep Parisians drink their early morning petit crème.

Unfortunately, everyday life in Paris is also about the daily grind of métro, boulot, dodo (metro, work, sleep): overcrowded public transport at rush hour, with some facing long journeys (it can easily take an hour to cross Paris), or traffic jams and the struggle to find a parking space. Parisians have to cope with regular surges in pollution, noise and stress, asthma, a sky that is often overcast, packed out public squares, and a relatively high cost of living.

A Sunday in Paris

From Monday to Friday, Parisians are hard at work. Saturday is set aside for shopping, so they are left with Sunday, the day when families go out for a stroll, descending on the city's parks and public gardens as soon as the sun shows its face; the banks of the Seine are closed to cars to be enjoyed by cyclists, roller-bladers and pedestrians. While a privileged few leave Paris for the surrounding countryside, the vast majority stay put and head for the city's green spaces to find a little room to breathe. Museums offer a welcome refuge on rainy days, and many of them try to attract families by offering activities suitable for children, not to mention the blockbuster exhibits enjoyed by locals and tourists alike, plus the huge array of cinemas showing films from around the world.

Paris in August

The image of Paris emptied of its inhabitants in August is an increasingly false one. Nowadays, many Parisians are happy to spend the summer months in the capital, because that's the period when they can reclaim their city: there are fewer cars on the roads and fewer people on the metro; life is less frenetic, and with Paris Plages transforming the banks of the Seine into a temporary beach, you can even laze in the sunshine and enjoy a whole host of special events.

From titi to bobo

Once upon a time, true Parisians were born in Paris, like their parents and grandparents before them, and nothing would have persuaded them to leave their native city. These inhabitants of Paris' working-class neighbourhoods were known as *titis*, and had a reputation for their cheeky, light-hearted nature and quick wits. You will find a wonderful portrayal of these characters in the films *Les Enfants du Paradis* (Children of Paradise) and *L'Hôtel du Nord*, starring the great actress Arletty.

These days, however, Paris is home to their polar opposites: the typical *bobo* (a combination of bourgeois and bohemian) lives in the east of the city – Oberkampf, Ménilmontant, Belleville, Bastille or the Canal St-Martin – in an old workshop transformed into an ultra-trendy loft apartment. Their busy social lives involve private views, independent cinemas, or stopping off for a drink by the Canal St-Martin; they buy their clothes from the designer boutiques of the Marais and eat exotic food, but are equally happy enjoying old favourites like *andouillette grillée*.

They live in a world of complex family arrangements with children from previous marriages, campaign for human rights and the environment, support cultural freedom and vote for the socialist party. They favour social diversity, want good schools for their children and have a soft spot for economic liberalism…

Unembarrassed by all their ideological contradictions, the *bobos* are the drivers of Parisian cultural life, the champions of the latest trends and have changed the face of neighbourhoods that used to be the domain of the *titis*…

Parisian, a nationality?

Being Parisian is not just about where you live. "Real" Parisians have a sort of dual nationality, and it might seem that the Parisian side takes precedence over the French. The director Sacha Guitry was right when he said that "Parisians don't live in Paris, Paris is their life."

You could even take this idea of nationality further and apply it to individual *quartiers*: Parisians are very much attached to their own neighbourhoods and to the favourite *quartiers* that they visit again and again, without ever setting foot in other parts of the city. People from the Bastille would not dream of going to Passy, and the denizens of Auteuil think that La Villette is somewhere lost in the wilds beyond the ring road.

It is not a case of "Paris for the Parisians", however. First, because people from the provinces are still trying to conquer Paris, admittedly in ever smaller numbers, and many international communities have adopted certain areas of the city (☸ *see Cultural Diversity below*).

GOING OUT IN THE CITY

One of the delights of Paris lies in its innumerable cafés, roughly 10 000 of them: cafés on the boulevards with their packed terraces, literary cafés keeping the Left Bank spirit alive, trendy cafés, little neighbourhood bistros. The best time to enjoy them is perhaps the early morning, the late afternoon or in the early evening for an aperitif, between the hours of 5pm and 7pm.

As the evening progresses, however, finding the right spot becomes more complex. Parisian nightlife is insular, and it can be hard to penetrate the layers of codes, word of mouth and selectivity that reserves hottest spots for a few people in the know and inveterate night-owls. Fashions change, and the honour of being the place to see and be seen passes from one *quartier* to the next: from the Marais to Bastille, Charonne and Ménilmontant to Oberkampf. All is not lost, however: when the hip crowd moves on, authenticity can resurface.

Paris is every bit as magical after dark: lights and shadow show it off to its best advantage. Take a boat trip on one of the *bateaux-mouches* and let the lights reveal the architectural beauty of the city's landmarks, highlighting details like friezes or pediments and enveloping places that you thought you knew with an air of mystery and poetry. Then pick a spot to spend the evening from the bewildering variety on offer: Montmartre and its cabarets (cancan at the Moulin Rouge for some, cosmopolitan musical choices at the Divan du Monde or La Cigale for others); Montparnasse and its cinemas, crêperies and famous brasseries; the Bastille with its opera house and wine bars; the Grands Boulevards and their string of theatres running from the Opéra to the Porte St-Martin; the Champs-Élysées, where Fouquet's and the Lido are just two of the wealth of options available; the Marais with its gay bars and cafés-théâtres; or the banks of the Seine, where former barges have been converted into venues. There are countless ways to spend an evening in Paris.

POPULATION

With some 2 240 621 inhabitants (2012), Paris is the country's most populated city as well as one of the most densely populated cities in the world. Although the inner-city population is declining slightly, figures show a constant influx from the provinces and abroad. Some minority groups have adopted particular neighbourhoods over the years: Russians in Montparnasse, Spaniards in Passy, North Africans in Clignancourt, La Villette, Aubervilliers, Asians in Belleville, the 13th *arrondissement*, etc.

But whatever their background, true Parisians are easy to distinguish from among the cosmopolitan crowd: tense, hurried, protesting, frivolous, quick-witted, even ready to poke fun.

CULTURAL DIVERSITY

Paris is a cosmopolitan city with a large number of communities from outside France: Caribbean, African, Slav, Far-Eastern, Latin-American, Jewish, Indian, Pakistani. It is a pleasure to eat an exotic meal, to search for ethnic music or find fabrics from the far corners of the world.

Afro-Caribbean community

African and West Indian communities (18th *arrondissement* or along the north side of the Paris ring road) have given us **zouk** music (a combination of African and West Indian musical rhythms), which evolved during the early 1980s. Radio Nova (on 101.5 FM) fashioned the concept of "world sono", which finally took off under the English name of **world music**.

Books and music – **L'Harmattan** at *16 rue des Écoles (5th arr)* and **Présence africaine** at *25 bis rue des Écoles (5th arr)*; Ⓜ*Maubert Mutualité, Cardinal Lemoine (5th arr)*. For tropical music, the **FNAC Forum** has a broader selection than other FNAC stores.

Art – **Musée du Quai Branly** at *37 quai Branly (7th arr)*; Ⓜ*Pont Alma*. Permanent collection and contemporary exhibitions. The **Musée Dapper**, at *50 avenue Victor-Hugo (16th arr)*; Ⓜ*Victor Hugo*, is a tiny, intimate museum that organizes biannual exhibitions of exquisite African

artefacts, painting, textiles, carvings… accompanied by excellent catalogues. Dealers specializing in African artefacts are grouped around Bastille (*rue Keller*) and St-Germain-des-Prés. For printed fabrics sold by weight or by the yard, try **Toto** at *49 boulevard Barbès (18th arr)*; the prices can't be beaten.

Special shops – **Izrael** at *30 rue François-Miron (4th arr)* is perhaps the best-known exotic grocery store in Paris; **Marché Dejean** at *rue Dejean, between rue des Poissonniers and rue du Poulet (18th arr)*, sells fish, meat and fresh or ready-prepared African specialities sold by women from their market stalls, Saturday mornings only; **Spécialités antillaises** at *14–16 boulevard de Belleville (20th arr)* has all the ingredients you need to make a fine Caribbean meal.

North African and Middle Eastern community

Many writers and journalists have made Paris their home, keeping abreast of both their indigenous culture and that of their adopted land: Tahar Ben Jelloun, the comedian Smaïn, and dramatists Moussa Lebkiri and Fatima Gallaire are all an integral part of the Parisian cultural scene.

The metro line linking Nation to Porte Dauphine (no 2) crosses several important concentrations of Mediterranean culture: **Barbès** and **Goutte d'Or** (*18th arr*), and **Belleville** (*19th and 20th arr*). The **Strasbourg-St-Denis** district between rue de Hauteville and passage Brady is predominantly Turkish, Indian and Pakistani.

La Grande Mosquée – 1–2 place du Puits-de-l'Ermite (*5th arr*); Ⓜ*Jussieu* has been used for countless films. Mint tea is served in the Moorish café annexe (Ⓒ*see Jussieu*); the baths are open on alternate days for men and women.

Art and culture – The **Institut du Monde Arabe** (*1 rue des Fossés-St-Bernard, 5th arr*; Ⓜ*Jussieu*), at the edge of the Latin Quarter, has a particularly useful library and reference section.

Books and theatre – **Avicenne** (*25 rue de Jussieu, 5th arr*) is the best Arabic bookshop.

Place de la Sorbonne

© Bertrand RIEGER / hemis.fr

Markets – Markets with produce and specialities dot the community: **Marché d'Aligre** on *place de l'Aligre* (largest of all the Arab markets; Tuesday–Sunday); **Marché de Belleville** (Tuesday and Friday mornings); **Marché de Barbès** (Wednesday and Saturday).

Jewish community

Historically, the **Marais** *(4th arr)* was the Jewish Quarter, a community that was decimated during the German Occupation, but whose numbers have swelled again with the arrival of North African immigrants; they have settled in the **Sentier** *(2nd arr)* and **Belleville** *(19th arr)*.

Synagogues – Liberal Synagogue, *24 rue Copernic, 16th arr,* ℰ 01 47 04 37 27. Synagogue La Victoire, *44 rue de la Victoire, 9th arr,* ℰ01 42 85 71 09 or *17 rue St-Georges, 9th arr,* ℰ01 40 82 26 26.

History and culture – The most significant commemorative monuments are the **Shoah Mémorial** *(rue G-L'Asnier, 4th arr)* and in the Père-Lachaise Cemetery, the **Monument à la mémoire des déportés de Buna, Monowitz, Auschwitz III** by Tim.

The **Musée d'Art et d'Histoire du Judaïsme** *(71 rue du Temple, 3rd arr)* is situated in the Hôtel St-Aignan in the Marais. The collection centres on North African religious articles, models and casts and includes paintings by Chagall, Lipschitz, Mané-Katz and Benn.

Pastries – Kosher and other speciality shops and restaurants abound on rue des Rosiers, in the Marais *(4th arr)*; try the strudel at Sacha Finkelsztajn's.

Chinese community

Until 1975, the predominant waves of immigrants came from southern China; the latter-day arrivals come from post-war homelands in Indo-China, Malaysia and the Philippines. Although not as famous as the Chinatowns of New York or San Francisco, the 13th *arrondissement* (in the high-rise triangle of avenue d'Ivry, avenue de Choisy and rue de Tolbiac) boasts 150 restaurants and shops piled high with exotic produce. The Chinese population, the largest concentration in Europe, is particularly busy around the Chinese New Year (end of January–beginning of February). In **Belleville**, there is a smaller group of Asian restaurants and stores. A plaque on the wall of no 13 rue Maurice-Denis in this neighbourhood pays homage to the 120 000 Chinese who came to France during World War I, 3 000 of whom decided to stay in Paris at the end of the war, forming the first Chinese community, near the Gare de Lyon.

Books – **Le Phénix** *(72 boulevard de Sébastopol, 3rd arr)* has generalist books on the Far East with a specialist section on China and Japan and **You Feng** *(45 rue Monsieur-le-Prince, 6th arr)* is the largest specialist bookshop on China.

Art – Paris is home to a number of pre-eminent collections of Oriental art, including the **Musée national des Arts asiatiques-Guimet**, *6 place d'Iéna*, and its annexe **Hôtel Heidelbach-Guimet**, *15 avenue d'Iéna* (Asian art from the Caucasus to Japan – ఓ*see ALMA*); the **Musée Cernuschi**, *7 avenue Velasquez* (Chinese antiques – ఓ*see MONCEAU*).

Shops – **Tang Frères**, *48 avenue d'Ivry (13th arr)* and at *168 avenue de Choisy (13th arr)*; **Paris Store**, *44 avenue d'Ivry (13th arr)* and at *12 boulevard de la Villette (19th arr)*; **Mandarin du marché**, *33 rue de Torcy (18th arr)*, **Hang Seng Heng**, *18 rue de l'Odéon (6th arr)*; **Odimex**, *17 rue de l'Odéon* (porcelain and ceramics); **Phu-Xuan**, *8 rue Monsieur-le-Prince (6th arr)* specialises in Chinese herbs, medicine and acupuncture.

Japanese community

The Japanese community (businessmen, employees of Japanese firms, students and artists) is concentrated around the **Opéra** and **rue Ste-Anne**, where opportunities abound to taste *sashimi*, *sushi* and *tempura*.

Art – The **Musée Guimet** houses a rich collection of Buddhas and Bodhisattvas brought back to France by Émile Guimet; the **Musée départemental Albert-Kahn**, *14 rue du Port, 92100 Boulogne-Billancourt* is also a must-see, with its Japanese garden, tea house and collection of autochrome plates.

Fashion – Japanese designers' boutiques are located around place des Victoires and in the St-Germain-des-Prés district: **Kenzo**, *3 place des Victoires (1st arr)*, *16–17 boulevard Raspail (7th arr)*; **Comme des garçons**, *40–42 rue Étienne Marcel (2nd arr)*; **Yohji Yamamoto**, *47 rue Étienne Marcel (1st arr)* and at *69 rue des St-Pères (6th arr)*; **Issey Miyake**, *201 boulevard St-Germain (6th arr)*, *17 boulevard Raspail (7th arr)*; **Irié**, *8 rue du Pré-aux-Clercs (7th arr)*.

Books – **Librairie Japonaise Junku** (*18 rue des Pyramides, 1st arr*) for all the Japanese newspapers or a selection from thousands of *bunko* (paperbacks) and *mangas* (comic books); **L'Harmattan** (ఓ*see Afro-Caribbean community*) also has books on Japan.

Food stores – **Kioko** (*46 rue des Petits-Champs, 2nd arr*) is brimming with multi-coloured bags of cocktail snacks, sauces, sake and frozen raw fish.

Home décor – There are several **Muji** stores in Paris, which sell clothes and household goods; visit the one at *47 Rue Francs Bourgeois, 4th arr*.

Indian and Pakistani subcontinent

Most immigrants from the Indian subcontinent are not actually Indian but Pakistani, Tamils from northern Sri Lanka or recently arrived Bangladeshis. India in Paris runs along rue St-Denis (between the Gare du Nord and Porte de la Chapelle, around rue Jarry, passage Brady and place du Caire). There are numerous food shops and restaurants in rue Gérando at the foot of the Sacré-Cœur, and beside the Lycée Jacques-Decours; Ⓜ*Anvers*.

Art and culture – **Centre culturel Mandapa** (*6 rue Wurtz, 13th arr*) stages some 100 or more Indian plays, dance shows and music concerts every year. **Maison des cultures du monde** (*101 boulevard Raspail, 6th arr*) features performances of traditional Indian, Pakistani and Bangladeshi music, dance and theatre.

Books – **Musée Guimet** bookshop has an excellent section on India, its civilizations, the arts from the Gandhâra (Greco-Buddhist art from Pakistan and Afghanistan) and from throughout the Far East.

Food – **Shah et Cie** (*33 rue Notre-Dame-de-Lorette, 9th arr*) is the oldest Indian grocery store in Paris; **Restaurant Yasmin** (*71 passage Brady, 10th arr*) serves Indian specialities.

NATIONAL GOVERNMENT

As the capital of France, Paris is home to the **Palais Bourbon**, or National Assembly, with 577 members. With 348 members, the **Senate** composes the other house of France's Parliament: it sits in the **Palais Luxembourg** in Paris. The **President** of France is Head of State, and is elected by the people, as is the National Assembly. Senate members are elected by a college of elected officials. The **Prime Minister**, who heads the goverment, is appointed by the President. Ministers are nominated by the President upon the recommendation of the Prime Minister. The country is governed by the French Republic's constitution enacted in 1958. The **Palais de l'Élysée** in Paris is the official residence of the President; weekly meetings of the Council of Ministers take place there.

LOCAL GOVERNMENT

Since March 1977, the **Mairie de Paris** has had an elected mayor, chosen by the 163 councillors who make up the municipal council; municipal elections are held every six years. With the exception of the police force, headed by a *préfet*, the mayor has the same status and powers of mayors of other municipalities.

The Paris municipal authority works closely with the town halls of the 20 *arrondissements*, which are the main units of local government. Paris being both a *commune* and a *département*, its council sits as a municipal authority and a general, or departmental, council.

The **Île-de-France** region comprises eight *départements*, each with its own prefecture, covering an area of 12 011sq km/4 637sq mi with an estimated population of 12 million in 2014 (Paris: 105sq km/40sq mi).

METAMORPHOSIS

In 1960, a century after Baron Haussmann's large-scale urban restructuring, steps were taken to resolve some of the capital's congestion problems, but much remains to be done.

Paris' historical, architectural and archaeological treasures have been safeguarded by the enlightened policy of **André Malraux** and his successors, who instituted a programme of cleaning, restoration and revitalization of whole areas such as the Marais and preservation of archaeological finds.

Meanwhile, structural engineers and planners wrestle with today's problems

– traffic and transport (ring road, motorway, RER), supply (Rungis, Garonor), cultural centres (G Pompidou Centre), sports facilities (Bercy), commercial property development (La Défense, Front de Seine, Maine-Montparnasse) and urban renewal (place d'Italie, Belleville, Bercy); the emphasis being on the preservation and restoration of historical heritage.

Major cultural and architectural achievements include the Cité des Sciences et de l'Industrie and the Cité de la Musique at La Villette, the Musée d'Orsay, the Grand Louvre, the Opéra-Bastille, the Grande Arche at La Défense and the Bibliothèque Nationale at Tolbiac.

The transfer of the wholesale markets from Les Halles to Rungis, the division of the university into 13 autonomous parts, the decentralization of the higher schools of learning, have all helped to relieve congestion in the city centre. Green spaces (La Villette, André Citroën) have been created, and old parks and gardens remodelled.

THE ECONOMY

The economy of Paris has been shaped over centuries by its location at the crossroads of Europe. Today **high-speed trains** from the city's seven train stations connect Paris to major capitals throughout Europe.

As the continent's second-ranked **airport hub**, Paris is served by Roissy-Charles de Gaulle (CDG), the largest airport in Europe and the eighth busiest in the world; and Paris-Orly (ORL), which handles a fifth of domestic flights. As Europe's number-one cargo hub, handling more than 2 million tonnes of cargo a year, CDG ranks fifth in the world.

Paris is the starting point of the country's main highways; six **major highways** radiate out from the city to reach the rest of the country.

TOURISM

The city's superb transportation network facilitates the arrival of international and domestic visitors. As the **most visited destination** in the world, France drew close to 85 million visitors in 2014. Paris saw 90 million passengers transit through its airports in 2013 alone, many of them tourists. Paris concentrates nearly 1 200 hotels – almost half of the region's accommodation capacity. Americans were the leading foreign clientele in Paris in 2013, with 1.6 million hotel arrivals.

In 2012, of the most-visited Parisian monuments, **Notre-Dame de Paris Cathedral** attracted some 13 650 000 visitors; the **Louvre Museum** regularly sees 10 million visitors come through its doors in a year.

Paris also draws **business tourism**. Rated as a top four international convention city, Paris hosted a total of 276 conventions in 2012. The Paris-Île de France region welcomed 407 **trade shows.** The Mondial de l'Automobile and the Salon international de l'Aéronautique et de l'Espace are the two largest events worldwide, respectively dedicated to the automobile industry and the aviation and space industry; the Foire internationale de Paris is Europe's biggest trade fair.

TRADE

Paris contributes 30 percent to the country's **GDP** (2012). It is Europe's second-ranked magnet for foreign investments. In 2012 the Ile-de-France accounted for one-quarter of French imports and 18 percent of French exports. The bulk of exchanges consist of **industrial goods**, such as mechanical or electrical devices. The European Union is the main client both for imports and exports, accounting for more than half of the exchange volume. Roughly a third of the region's industrial establishments – mostly manufacturers and builders – are located in Paris.

CORPORATE PARIS

More than 210 companies have corporate headquarters in Paris, including **Loréal**, LVMH, Hermes, Dior, Chanel, and industrial giants such as **Dassault** (aeronautics) and Bouygues (construction, telecoms, media). Movie industry player **Pathé,** advertising leader Publicis, spirits producer Cointreau and the iconic **Galeries Lafayette** also claim Paris as their home. French companies appearing on the Fortune 500 in 2014 included Société générale, Danone, Axa, Air France-KLM and SNCF, to name a few. Paris hosts the headquarters of the Organisation for Economic Co-operation and Development, an international organization that fosters cooperation among individual governments.

FASHION INDUSTRY

Fashion employs around 60 000 people in Paris and generates thousands of additional jobs indirectly. The city nurtures major **fashion schools**, such as the Duperré School created in the mid-19C, which has given birth to generations of famous designers. Today, some 70 leading designers are based in Paris. **Fashion Week** in Paris is the most important of the Big Four global shows, held also in New York City, London and Milan. Paris' greatest fashion houses can present up to six collections per year.

CENTRE OF LEARNING

Paris is home to eight main universities. The famous **Sorbonne**, with beginnings in 1257, is a gigantic complex in the Quartier Latin, accommodating 80,000 students. **Paris II Assas** is the major French university for legal matters (20 000 students). **Paris V Descartes** is the foremost French university for medical studies, with 40 000 students. **Pierre and Marie Curie University** offers students the best advanced physics, chemistry and mathematics training in France. As institutions of higher learning, postgraduate schools called **Grandes Ecoles** include Central, Polytechnique, the Ecole des Mines and the Ecole Nationale d'Administration, among the most prestigious ones.

GASTRONOMIC CAPITAL

French gastronomy is part of UNESCO's List of Intangible Cultural Heritage. Parisian chefs consistently rank among the world's greatest chefs. Based in Paris, the renowned **Le Cordon Bleu** provides culinary and hospitality instruction for thousands of future employees in the food industry world wide.

History

Paris has been forged throughout the centuries by the changing spirit and sensibility of each era, marked by the major events and upheavals that have occurred there during its long history.

TIME LINE
GALLO-ROMAN PERIOD

3C BC The Parisii, a Celtic fishing tribe, settle on Lutetia, now the Île de la Cité.

52 BC Labienus, Caesar's lieutenant, takes the city from the Gauls, who set fire to the Île de la Cité before fleeing.

1C AD The Gallo-Romans build the city of Lutetia.

c.250 The martyrdom of St Denis, first bishop of the city. Christianity takes hold and the first churches are built.

360 Julian the Apostate, Prefect of the Gauls, is proclaimed Emperor of Rome by his soldiers. Lutetia is known henceforth as Paris.

EARLY MIDDLE AGES

451 **Ste Geneviève** deflects Attila's attack on Paris.

508 Paris is taken over by Germanic tribes. Frankish King Clovis I makes it his capital, settling on the Cité.

8C Paris declines in importance when Charlemagne makes Aix-la-Chapelle (Aachen) his main capital.

885 Paris, besieged by the Normans for the fifth time, is defended by Count Eudes, who is made King of France in 888.

THE CAPETIANS

Early 12C Trade picks up on the Cité. The Watermen's Guild is at its peak. Suger, Abbot of St-Denis and minister under Louis VI and Louis VII, rebuilds the abbey.

1163 Maurice de Sully begins construction of Notre-Dame.

1180 During the reign of Philippe Auguste (reigned 1180–1223) a wall was erected around Paris and the Louvre was built.

1215 The University of Paris is founded, turning the city into an important cultural centre.

1226 Louis IX (reigned 1226–70), called St Louis, commissions the building of the Ste-Chapelle, Notre-Dame and St-Denis, and dispenses justice at Vincennes.

1253 Foundation of a college by Sorbon, later known as the Sorbonne.

1260 The Dean of the Merchants' Guild becomes Provost of Paris.

1307 Philip the Fair dissolves the Order of the Knights Templar.

THE VALOIS

1337 Beginning of the Hundred Years' War. Upon the death of Philip the Fair and his

Sainte Geneviève

The patron saint of Paris deflected the fearsome Attila the Hun's attack on Paris (he then went on to assault Orléans). She is also revered for two subsequent exploits.

Later when the city was besieged by Childeric, the King of the Salian Franks, she secretly crossed the siege lines and brought back grain to the city in a fleet of barges. She then went on to successfully intercede with Childeric regarding the treatment of prisoners, a feat which she was to repeat later with his successor Clovis I, who would eventually make Paris his capital.

Geneviève became Clovis' adviser and managed to convert him to Christianity. She persuaded him to build the first Christian church in Paris, which was later named in her honour.

Statue of Étienne Marcel, Hôtel de Ville

© Arap/Fotolia.com

three sons a problem of succession arises: the French barons prefer Philip the Fair's nephew, Philip de Valois, to his grandson, Edward III, King of England.

The following century is marked by battles between the French and the English, who lay claim to the French Crown, between the Armagnacs, supporters of the family of Orléans, and the Burgundians, supporters of the Dukes of Burgundy.

1358 Uprising under **Étienne Marcel**, Provost of Paris. The monarchs move to the Marais and the Louvre.

1364 **Charles V** (reigned 1364–1380) builds the Bastille and a new wall around Paris.

1382 During the troubled reign of Charles VI, the Parisians revolt against heavy taxes, but their loss strips them of earlier exemptions and severely weakens the provost's power.

1407 Duke Louis of Orleans is assassinated on the order of John the Fearless.

1408 Fighting breaks out between the Armagnacs and the Burgundians. The English take Paris.

1429 In vain Charles VII tries to lay siege to Paris; Joan of Arc is wounded at St-Honoré Gate.

1430 Henry VI of England is crowned King of France at Notre-Dame.

1437 Charles VII recaptures Paris.

1469 The first French printing works open in the Sorbonne.

1530 **François I** founds the Collège de France.

1534 Ignatius Loyola founds the Society of Jesus in Montmartre.

1559 Henri II is fatally wounded in a jousting tournament.

1572 The struggle between Protestant and Roman Catholic factions leads to the St Bartholomew's Day Massacre.

1578 Construction of the Pont Neuf (completed 1604).

1588 Paris strengthens its position as the centre of political power. The Catholic League turns against Henri III, and the citizens of Paris force him to flee after the Day of the Barricades (12 May).

1589 Returning to Paris with Henri of Navarre, Henri III is assassinated by a fanatical Dominican friar.

THE BOURBONS

1594 Paris opens its gates to Henri IV after he converts to Catholicism.

1594 Place des Vosges is created. La Charité and St-Louis Hospitals are founded (completed 1610).

1610 **Henri IV** is mortally wounded by Ravaillac (14 May).

1615 Marie de' Medici has Luxembourg Palace built (completed 1625).

1622 Paris becomes an episcopal see.

1629 The Palais-Royal is built.

1635 **Richelieu** founds the Académie Française.

1648 The **Fronde** (1648–53) foments a rebellion in Paris against the Crown.

1661 Mazarin founds the College of Four Nations, the future Institut de France.

1667 Colbert establishes the Observatoire and restructures the Gobelins Tapestry Works.

17C Louis XIV transfers the Court to Versailles, but increases royal control over Paris. Development of the Marais.

Late 17C The Louvre Colonnade and the Invalides are built.

Early 18C Construction of place Vendôme and development of the Faubourg St-Germain.

1717 **John Law's Bank** (failed 1720).

1760 Louis XV has the École Militaire, St-Geneviève (the future Panthéon) and place de la Concorde built (completed 1780).

1783 First balloon flights by Pilâtre de Rozier, Jacques Charles and Aîné Roberts.

1783 Versailles Treaty: independence of the 13 American States.

1784 Paris has nearly 500 000 inhabitants. To the discontent of the Parisians, the Farmers-General Wall is erected, including the gateways and toll-houses by Ledoux (completed 1791).

THE REVOLUTION AND THE FIRST EMPIRE

14 Jul 1789 Storming of the Bastille.

17 Jul 1789 Louis XVI at the Hôtel de Ville: the tricolore flag is adopted.

14 Jul 1790 Festival of Federation.

20 Jun 1792 A mob invades the Tuileries.

10 Aug 1792 Taking of the Tuileries and fall of the monarchy.

2–4 Sept 1792 September Massacres.

21 Sept 1792 Proclamation of the Republic.

21 Jan 1793 Execution of Louis XVI.

1793 Opening of the Louvre Museum and institution of the Natural History Museum.

1793 The Terror (ends 1794).

8 Jun 1794 Festival of the Supreme Being.

5 Oct 1795 Royalist uprising suppressed by Napoléon.

The Directory

Following the discredited Convention, executive power in France passed to the Directory in August 1795. Five "Directors" were made jointly responsible for the conduct of the government and assisted by a bicameral legislature consisting of the Council of the Ancients and the Council of the Five Hundred.

The first victories of the Napoléonic Wars were achieved during this period, but unfortunately many of the Directors proved to be corrupt. Chaos characterised provincial administration and soon people lost faith in the system. The Directory was overthrown on 18 Brumaire (9 Nov) 1799 by Napoléon who established the Consulate with himself as First Consul.

Taking of the Bastille on 14 July 1789 by Jean-Baptiste Lallemand

© Scala, Florence/Musée Carnavalet, Paris

9–10 Nov 1799 Fall of the Directory.

1800 Bonaparte creates the offices of Prefect of the Seine and of the Police.

2 Dec 1804 Napoléon's coronation at Notre-Dame.

1806 Napoléon continues construction of the Louvre and commissions the Arc de Triomphe and work begins on the Vendôme Column.

31 Mar 1814 The Allies occupy Paris. First Treaty of Paris.

1820 Gas lamps are used to light the city's streets.

THE RESTORATION

1815 Battle of Waterloo. Restoration of the Bourbons with Louis XVIII.

1824 Charles X (reigned 1824–30) mounts the throne, but his ultra-conservative policies displease the Parisians, who take to the streets to defend their freedom in the July Revolution. Fall of Charles X, who flees to the Palace of Holyroodhouse in Edinburgh and is succeeded by Louis-Philippe.

1832 A cholera epidemic kills 19 000 Parisians.

1837 The first French railway line links Paris with St-Germain.

1840 Return of Napoléon's ashes from St Helena.

1841 Construction of the Thiers fortifications (completed 1845).

Feb 1848 Fall of Louis-Philippe in the February Revolution; proclamation of Second Republic.

FROM 1848 TO 1870

Jun 1848 The suppression of the national workshops provokes socialist riots, signalling the failure of the Second Republic. Louis Napoléon is elected President of the Republic.

1852 Louis Napoléon becomes Napoléon III, creating the Second Empire. When the Parisians once again rise up in protest, the riots are violently repressed.

1852 Huge urban planning projects are undertaken by Baron Haussmann: Les Halles, the railway stations, the Buttes-Chaumont, Bois de Boulogne and Bois de Vincennes, the Opéra, the sewers, completion of the Louvre, and construction of the new boulevards. Paris is divided into 20 *arrondissements* (completed 1870).

1855 **World Exhibitions** (also 1867)

1870 Paris is besieged in winter 1870–71 by the Prussians and capitulates. Napoléon III goes into exile in England.

THE THIRD REPUBLIC

4 Sept 1870 The Third Republic is proclaimed.

Mar–May 1871 The Paris Commune is finally suppressed by the Men of Versailles during the Bloody Week (21–28 May); fire, destruction (Tuileries, Cour des Comptes, Hôtel de Ville, Vendôme Column) and massacres.

1879 Executive and legislative powers are returned from Versailles to Paris.

1882 Paris inaugurates its new Hôtel de Ville.

1889 World Exhibition at the foot of the new Eiffel Tower.

1892 First multi-storey building constructed of reinforced concrete.

1900 First metro line in operation between Maillot and Vincennes. The Grand and Petit Palais are built. Cubism is born at the Bateau-Lavoir. The Sacré-Cœur Basilica is erected on the Butte Montmartre.

1914 At the outset of the war, the government leaves Paris for Bordeaux. Paris, under the threat of German attack, is saved by the Battle of the Marne. A shell hits the church of St-Gervais.

1920 Interment of the Unknown Soldier under the Arc de Triomphe.

Roaring Twenties Paris is a cultural incubator where new literary and artistic movements are born.

1927 Inauguration of Monet's *Nymphéas* series at the Orangerie.

1930s The worldwide economic crisis hits Paris.

Feb 1934 Riots around the Chamber of Deputies end in a bloodbath.

Jun 1940 Paris is bombed, then occupied, by the Germans. Hostages and resistance fighters detained at Mont Valérien (Suresnes).

19–25 Aug 1944 Liberation of Paris.

27 Oct 1946 The Fourth Republic is proclaimed at the Hôtel de Ville.

THE FIFTH REPUBLIC

1958 Construction of the UNESCO, CNIT and Maison de Radio-France buildings (completed 1963).

1965 The Urban Development Plan for the greater Paris area is published.

May 1968 Strikes and demonstrations, triggered by students at the Sorbonne, spread to the whole of France within days, leading to the largest social movement in the country's history.

1969 Transfer of the wholesale markets from Les Halles to Rungis.

1970 The RER (Réseau Express Régional) is launched to extend the métro system.

1973 Completion of the boulevard Périphérique (ring road) and Montparnasse Tower.

25 Mar 1977 The first election of a mayor of Paris (J Chirac), 11 predecessors 1789–1871 having been appointed rather than elected.

1977 Opening of the Centre Georges-Pompidou.

1986 Inauguration of the Orsay Museum.

1989 Opening of the Louvre Pyramid, Grande Arche at La Défense and Opéra Bastille during bicentennial celebrations.

1995	Jacques Chirac is elected French president.
1996	The Bibliothèque Nationale opens at Tolbiac.
1999	Severe windstorms damage parks and monuments.
2001	Bertrand Delanoë becomes the city's first socialist mayor in over a century.
2003	Thousands of elderly die in a brutal summer heatwave.
2006	Opening of the Quai Branly Museum, the Simone de Beauvoir footbridge, and Josephine Baker swimming pool on the Seine.
2007	Opening of the Cité de l'Architecture et du patrimoine and election of Nicolas Sarkozy as president.
2012	François Hollande becomes the 24th president of the French Republic.
2013	Newly-renovated Tour Saint-Jacques, in central Paris, opens to the public for the first time since it was built in the early 16C.
2014	Anne Hidalgo is elected the first woman mayor of Paris. Opening of the Fondation Louis Vuitton dedicated to contemporary art.
2015	World leaders march with more than a million Parisians to pay tribute to journalists of French satirical magazine *Charlie Hebdo* murdered by terrorists.

URBAN GROWTH

The capital's site was carved out of the limestone and Tertiary sands by the Seine, which flowed at a level of 35m/115ft, above its present course.

GALLO-ROMAN WALL

The Parisii, taking advantage of the *Pax romana*, emerged from Lutetia, built by the Gauls and defended by the river and surrounding swamps, to settle along the Left Bank of the river. The Barbarians later forced them to retreat to the Cité (c. 276). On the island, they built houses, fortifications and a rampart wall to defend themselves against future invasions.

PHILIPPE AUGUSTE WALL

Between the 6C and 10C, the swamps were drained and cultivated, mona-steries founded and a river harbours established near the place de Grève. Between 1180 and 1210 Philippe Auguste ordered that a massive wall be built, reinforced upstream by a chain barrage across the river and downstream by the Louvre Fortress and Nesle Tower.

CHARLES V RAMPART

The town, which was on the Right Bank (as opposed to the university on the Left Bank, and the Cité), prospered as roads were built connecting it with Montmartre, St-Denis, the Knights Templar Commandery and the castle at Vincennes. By the end of the 14C, Charles V had erected new fortifications, supported in the east by the Bastille. The Paris ramparts enclosed just under 440ha/1 087 acres and protected 150 000 inhabitants. **Louis XIII Wall:** Throughout the 16C, the Wars of Religion and the siege by Henri of Navarre maintained a threat to the city, forcing Charles IX and Louis XIII to extend the 14C wall westwards to include the Louvre Palace.

FARMERS-GENERAL WALL

The monarchy moved to Versailles as Paris encroached upon the surrounding countryside, its population 500 000 strong. The Invalides, Observatory, Salpêtrière, St-Denis and St-Martin Gates were erected; new city confines were required, calling for a new wall (1784–91) complete with 57 **toll-houses** to be designed by **Ledoux**.

THIERS FORTIFICATIONS

During the Revolution many of the larger estates were broken up but little was built. Under the Empire, Paris faced problems of overcrowding and supply. The Restoration encouraged great industrial developments and social change: gas lighting was installed in the streets, and the railway allowed for growth and economic development in outlying villages (Austerlitz, Montrouge, Vaugirard, Passy, Montmartre, Belleville). Thiers determined the capital's perimeter with another wall (1841–45), reinforced at a cannon-ball's distance by 16 bastions, the official city confines from 1859. Subsequently, 20 *arrondissements* were created in the 77.7sq km/30sq mi, as Haussmann began his transformation of the city (population in 1846: 1 050 00; in 1866: 1 800 000).

THE PRESENT LIMIT

The forts remained intact (Mont Valérien, Romainville, Ivry, Bagneux), but the walls, after serving in the city's defence in 1871, were razed by the Third Republic in 1919. Between 1925 and 1930 the confines of the city were redefined to include the Bois de Boulogne and Bois de Vincennes, but not extending elsewhere beyond a narrow circular belt to give an overall surface area of 10 540ha/26 045 acres, for a population, in 1945, of 2 700 000.

BRITISH ASSOCIATIONS

Many an Englishman has harboured a secret admiration for Paris, while regretting that so many Parisians live there – the French might have a similar view of London.

London, England, is a mere 2hr 15min away by train. But in the realms of politics, the instinct for self-preservation has maintained a certain distance, commonly known as the *Entente Cordiale*. This relationship has been reiterated through history with many treaties – 1763 terminating the Seven Years' War, 1814 and 1815 ending the Napoléonic era, 1856 sealing the alliance at the end of the Crimean War, 1904–10 commercial treaties that concluded in the Entente Cordiale, and 1919 the Treaty of Versailles.

Since the 17C, Paris has been a major attraction for British travellers: artists on their way to Italy (Charles Dickens, John Ruskin), gentlemen on the Grand Tour (Lord Byron), public figures fleeing persecution at home (Oscar Wilde, Duke and Duchess of Windsor) or impov-erished journalists (WM Thackeray) and students (Orwell). By the mid-19C, Thomas Cook was organizing what he called package holidays. As he stated in Cook's Excursionist and Advertiser of 15 May 1863:

"We would have every class of British subjects visit Paris, that they may emulate its excellencies, and shun the vices and errors which detract from the glory of the French capital. In matters of taste and courtesy we have much to learn from Parisians…"
Lawrence Durrell wrote: *"the national characteristics… are the restless metaphysical curiosity, the tenderness of good living and the passionate individualism. This is the invisible constant in a place with which the ordinary tourist can get in touch just by sitting quite quietly over a glass of wine in a Paris bistrot."*

AMERICANS IN PARIS

The world's quintessential expatriate city, Paris has long held a special fascination for Americans. Offering an incomparable urban setting, a rich cultural legacy and a deep-rooted respect for artistic pursuits and individual freedom, the French capital has provided a stimulating environment for successive waves of celebrated American émigrés.

18C–19C

Franco-American ties developed out of shared conflict with the British and a steadfast commitment to Revolutionary ideals. Francophiles **Benjamin Franklin** and **Thomas Jefferson**, sent to France as official emissaries of the new Republic, contributed to establishing early political, cultural and scientific links between the two countries.

Throughout the 19C Paris reigned as the cultural capital of the Western world and as such, attracted numerous American artists including Whistler, Eakins and Impressionist Mary Cassatt. Many of America's leading architects – notably Richard Morris Hunt, Henry Hobson Richardson and Louis Sullivan – studied at the world-renowned **École des Beaux-Arts**, the supreme arbiter of Neoclassical 19C architectural trends.

Richard Wright: A Writer in Exile

American writer and intellectual Richard Wright lived at 14 rue Monsieur-le-Prince with his wife and two daughters from 1948 to 1959. Wright's novels *Black Boy, Native Son* and *American Hunger* and essays forcefully exposed racism in American society. Discontented with the racial and political climate in post-World War II America, Wright was finally granted an American passport thanks to the intervention of Gertrude Stein, who arranged to have the French Government extend him an official invitation. Among the haunts frequented by Wright and other members of the black intelligentsia was the nearby Café Tournon, 20 rue de Tournon. Martin Luther King visited the writer in his rue Monsieur-le-Prince apartment in 1959. Richard Wright died in Paris in 1960. His ashes are preserved in the Père-Lachaise cemetery (*see La PÈRE-LACHAISE*).

"WHERE THE 20C WAS"

Referring to the city's pivotal role in the birth and development of modern literary and artistic movements, **Gertrude Stein** asserted "Paris is where the twentieth century was". Like two other prominent lifelong expatriates – Natalie Clifford Barney and **Sylvia Beach** – Gertrude Stein was lured by the city's stimulating environment, which allowed a degree of artistic and sexual freedom unthinkable in early 20C America. Beach's **Shakespeare and Company** bookshop and the celebrated literary salons of Stein and Barney became important meeting places for the city's intelligentsia.

American expatriate life in Paris reached its heyday in the 1920s. World War I was over, the exchange rate was favourable, and Paris was the place to be. During that historic decade, the Left Bank was home to an astounding number of literary personalities: Ezra Pound, F Scott-Fitzgerald, Sherwood Anderson, Ford Madox-Ford and **Ernest Hemingway**, whose life and work is more intimately linked to Paris than any other American writer. This foremost Lost Generation novelist brilliantly captured the unbridled expatriate experience as played out in the legendary cafés, night spots and streets of Montparnasse and the Latin Quarter (*The Sun Also Rises* and *A Moveable Feast*). The period's unprecedented literary production gave rise to a proliferation of avant-garde expatriate reviews (*Little Review, Transitions*) and publishers (Black Sun Press, Black Manikin Press, and Hours Press founded by Nancy Cunard). The first uncensored edition of James Joyce's *Ulysses* was published in France in 1922 by Sylvia Beach.

Paris played host to an international colony of prodigious artists including Picasso, Chagall, Modigliani and Americans **Man Ray** and **Alexander Calder**. Among the expatriate performing artists were dancer **Isadora Duncan** and Revue Nègre star **Josephine Baker**, who cherished the racial equality and the international fame offered

Paris' coat-of-arms

© S. Sauvignier/Michelin

by France. The dizzying Paris scene was astutely observed by **Janet Flanner**, who, under the pseudonym Genêt, authored the "Letter from Paris" column in *The New Yorker* from 1925 to 1975. The 1930s were marked by the presence of **Henry Miller**. Like Hemingway, Miller came to Paris to become a writer and chose a Paris setting for his first novel. The quasi-autobiographical *Tropic of Cancer* (1934), banned in the USA until the 1960s, explicitly depicts a seedy Paris well off the beaten expatriate trail. During his Paris years, Miller met his American protector, muse and lover, **Anaïs Nin**.

POST-WORLD WAR II TO THE PRESENT

Expatriate life in Paris was interrupted by the outbreak of World War II: most of the American writers of the 1920s and 1930s had gone home or moved to safer havens. Shakespeare and Company, a Left-Bank institution, closed its doors in 1941 after 20 years of existence. During the late 1950s and 1960s, a new American-run bookshop and lending library opened in the Latin Quarter. This picturesque haunt (which took over the name Shakespeare and Company following Sylvia Beach's death in 1962) was frequented by Beat Generation writers Ginsberg and Burroughs, as well as by many of the newly arrived black writers, lured by France's reputation as a nation fostering a non-racist cultural climate. The most influential member of this group was acclaimed writer and intellectual **Richard Wright** (*Native Son*), whose self-imposed Paris exile began in 1947 and lasted until his death in 1960. Fellow-expatriate black American writers included **Chester Himes**, **William Gardner Smith** and **James Baldwin** (*Another Country, Giovanni's Room*). Although Paris' heyday as an avant-garde expatriate haven may be over, the City of Light continues to entice Americans.

The latest expat literary readings, writers' groups and related events are listed online at www.parisreadingsmonthlylisting.blogspot.com.

PARISIAN REVOLUTIONS

The history of Paris has been marked by a series of revolutions and great movements of social and political protest that have often had repercussions for the country as a whole.

ÉTIENNE MARCEL IN 1358

At the beginning of the 12C, Paris was able to take advantage of the political struggle between King Louis VI and his feudal lords, which was known as the Communal Revolution, to set up a municipal administration overseen by its merchant guilds. They attempted to meet the social and economic needs of the city's inhabitants that had resulted from its expansion on the left and right banks of the Seine. The most important guild was the guild of river merchants, which met at the **Parloir aux Bourgeois**, on the Left Bank. It was led by the provost of merchants, who combined the functions of municipal administrator and judge.

Étienne Marcel, a rich draper who became provost of merchants in 1355, had the Parloir aux Bourgeois relocated in 1357 to the Maison aux Piliers, on the place de Grève.

While King John II, known as John the Good, was being held captive in England, Marcel attempted to consolidate his power, but his actions were opposed by the heir to the throne, the future Charles V. With Paris under his control, Étienne Marcel responded angrily and incited the people of Paris to rise up.

On 22 February 1358, rioters led by Étienne Marcel burst into what is now the Palais de Justice, but was then the royal palace, and managed to enter the apartment of the future king. As the heir to the throne looked on, they cut the throats of his advisers, and the provost placed a hood in the red and blue colours of Paris on his head.

The attempted uprising ended in failure, however, and Étienne Marcel died an ignominious death at the hands of the Parisians, when he was about to open the city's gates to Charles the Bad, King of Navarre.

THE CATHOLIC LEAGUE (1588–94)

The bells of St-Germain-l'Auxerrois tolled on the night of 23–24 August 1572, marking the beginning of the Wars of Religion with the **St-Bartholomew's Day Massacre**.

Paris was a staunchly Catholic city and supported the anti-Protestant Catholic League: it adopted a theocratic regime led by a council of 16 members and reinforced its image as the centre of political power – the idea that the king could only rule if he was the master of Paris. King Henry III learned this lesson to his cost: the Parisians chased him out of the city for abusing his royal rights and shut the gates on him after the "Day of the Barricades", 12 May 1588.

Similarly, Henry IV only entered Paris, on 22 March 1594, after converting to Catholicism and buying the city from its governor, the Duke of Brissac, for the sum of 200,000 ecus.

THE FRONDE (1648–52)

The Fronde is one of the murkiest episodes in Paris' history. The uprising was fuelled by political discontent over centralized monarchical power and financial discontent over the creation of taxes. Although it was an uprising of the people for a time, the Fronde was essentially opposition of the rich Parisian bourgeoisie and the nobility to the ever-growing absolutism of the monarchy. Once again, Paris was a defender of liberties, even if its aims were not so noble. The regency of Anne of Austria was attempting to refill coffers depleted by foreign wars by raising already crippling levels of taxation. When a cloth merchant named Cadeau refused to pay the royal taxes, he was supported by his neighbours, and the riots began. This was how civil war returned to the streets of Paris in 1648, just as the Thirty Years' war in Europe was ending with the Peace of Westphalia. The "Day of the Barricades" of 26 August 1648 paved the way for an uprising that would last until 1653, spreading to the Parlement of Paris (an institution of the high bourgeoisie) and the Princes of France.

THE FRENCH REVOLUTION OF 1789

The popular unrest that took hold of Paris between 1789 and 1793, and led to the French Revolution, began in the east of the city, a stone's throw from the Bastille and the aristocratic mansions of the Marais.

On 5 May 1789, a meeting of the Estates General was held in Versailles. The Estates General was a general assembly representing the clergy, the nobility and the common people, known respectively as the first, second and third estates. The aim of the meeting was to find a solution to the country's bankruptcy, although many members wanted to bring about a reform of the monarchy. With the dispute over whether the voting system should give a vote to each member or to each estate still unresolved, the Estates General declared itself a National Assembly on 17 June 1789. On 20 June, members of the new assembly swore the Tennis Court Oath, vowing not to disband before providing France with a constitution.

On 12 July 1789, the fuse was lit when the popular finance minister Necker was dismissed by the king. The rebellious, frightened population of Paris rose up. In search of weapons, they looted the Hôtel des Invalides on the morning of 14 July, before moving on to the Bastille for arms and munitions. At the end of the afternoon, when the government saw that the French Guards had deserted their barracks and arrived on the scene, it agreed to back down. The Bastille was taken very quickly and its demolition began. The prison that had become a symbol of despotism was no more, and by the following year, people were dancing on its former site.

THE REVOLUTIONS OF 1830 AND 1848

The Revolution of 1830

The July Revolution, or the "Three Glorious Days", took place in Paris on 27, 28 and 29 July 1830. When the elections held in July went against him, King Charles X refused to submit to the chamber of deputies and decided to bolster his power. He drew up four ordinances that were a direct attack on the deputies, proclaiming the dissolution of the chamber elected less than one month earlier and setting a date for new elections. He abolished the freedom of the press and tried to exclude the bourgeoisie from elections. The population reacted violently. The next day, under the influence of Adolphe Thiers, journalists published calls for insurrection.

On 27 July, people took to the streets and blocked the roads with barricades. Less than ten days after the publication of his ordinances, Charles X was forced to abdicate. The July Revolution put an end to the Bourbon Restoration and proclaimed the July Monarchy on 29 July 1830.

The Revolution of 1848

Just like the Revolution of 1789, the 1848 Revolution was the result of an economic crisis affecting France's peasants and workers. The events unfolded in Paris on 23, 24 and 25 February 1848. On 22 February 1848, one of the political meetings known as *banquets des républicains* was banned, leading to riots. On the evening of 23 February, troops stationed outside the Ministry of Foreign Affairs opened fire on the demonstrators, and the riot turned into a revolt. The victorious insurgents invaded the Château des Tuileries, the residence of King Louis-Philippe and forced his abdication. The Republicans imposed a provisional government, putting an end to the July Monarchy, and created the Second Republic on 25 February 1848.

ⓔ *The Colonne de Juillet in the Place de la Bastille commemorates both the 1830 and the 1848 revolutions.*

THE COMMUNE (1871)

The Paris Commune was an extraordinary episode: from 26 March 1871 until the "Bloody Week" of repression, it set up a proletarian government run by workers opposing the government.

On 4 September 1870, after the disastrous defeat to the Prussians in the Battle of Sedan, Léon Gambetta, Jules Favre and Jules Ferry proclaimed a Republic at the Hôtel de Ville and set up a Government of National Defence. On 28 January 1871, however, the people of Paris were enraged when the capital was forced to capitulate to the Germans. They seized power and installed their own administration, the "Commune de Paris", at the Hôtel de Ville. From 21 to 28 May, during the bloody week of repression conducted by the Versaillais troops on behalf of the government of Adolphe Thiers, the Hôtel de Ville, the Tuileries Palace and several other major Parisian landmarks were burned down and the column in the Place Vendôme was toppled.

MAY 1968

In May 1968, the students of Paris were in revolt against an outmoded bourgeois society: the Latin Quarter was blocked off, the universities were on strike and paving stones were ripped up to be used as missiles. Before long, the students were joined by the workers and France was in crisis.

It all started on 22 March when a group of extreme left-wing students occupied the dean's office at the University of Paris in Nanterre. From 13 May, the students were joined by the young factory workers, and the trade union rallied to their support. The left-winger Pierre Mendès France went on the offensive, blaming the presidency of General de Gaulle.

On 20 May, the parliamentary left called on the government to step down and hold general elections, while publicly supporting the young demonstrators. The left's vote of no confidence was rejected, and General de Gaulle announced a referendum on workers' participation in company management and university reform. On 30 May, he announced his refusal to withdraw from political life to the people of France, dissolved the National Assembly and called on people to take "civic action": 100,000 demonstrated in support of the general. In early June, work resumed in state-run companies. On 30 June, the Gaullists won the elections. 1968 was over, but nothing would be the same again.

Architecture

The charm of the Parisian landscape is unquestionably due to its talented artists and craftsmen over the centuries; but it is also a result of its successful blending of styles from different periods, including contemporary buildings, almost all built in the ubiquitous beige limestone for a harmonious effect. Paris is a dynamic city whose contrasting faces never cease to astonish visitors and inhabitants alike.

MEDIEVAL PARIS

From the 6C to the 10C marshy areas were dried up and cultivated, while the city's port and trade activities developed around place de Grève. Walls were built around the city, and its first streets constructed – extensions of the town's few bridges. Traffic and hygienic conditions improved when Philippe Auguste had the streets paved. Soon, fountains began to dot the Parisian landscape, and springs – such as the one in Belleville – were tapped more frequently, providing a better water service.

Romanesque architecture, known as Norman style in England, didn't blossom in Paris as it did in the rest of France. Some rare examples include the chancel columns and bell-tower porch at St-Germain-des-Prés, the apse of St-Martin des Champs, and a few capitals in St-Pierre-de-Montmartre and St-Aignan Chapel.

Greater Paris was the cradle of **Gothic architecture**. Vast churches were built as tall and light as possible, using ogive or pointed arches and groin vaults (St-Germain-des-Prés chancel), whose thrust and weight are contained by side aisles and external buttressing (St-Julien-le-Pauvre apse).

Early Gothic (12C) architecture is best illustrated by Notre-Dame Cathedral, where the transition of building techniques and styles from the 12C to the early 14C can be seen in the vast chancel, slightly projecting transept and the dark triforium gallery. Capitals are decorated with motifs of plants and flowers from the greater Paris area. Sources of light are limited to narrow windows in the nave, topped by small round windows, or oculi, at the transept crossing.

High or Rayonnant Gothic (13C–14C) developed during the reign of Louis IX, when structural engineering reached new heights under architect Pierre de Montreuil. Walls are replaced by huge panels of glass, allowing light to flood in. Slender piers support the vault, reinforced externally by unobtrusive buttressing or flying buttresses (St-Martin-des-Champs refectory). With the new use of light, stained glass began to flourish. The *chevet* of Notre-Dame, Ste-Chapelle and the Royal Chapel at Vincennes are Paris' masterpieces of **High Gothic** architecture. The gargoyles were another innovation, designed as spouts to drain off rainwater. It is this style, in particular, that was assimilated in England at Canterbury and London (St Stephen's, Westminster).

In the 15C a trend emerged towards more exaggerated decoration during the **Late or Flamboyant Gothic period** (15C) with an increase in purely decorative vaulting (St Merri transept, St-Germain-l'Auxerrois porch) – flame motifs flourish on window tracery; the triforium gives way to ever taller clerestory windows; piers culminating in ribs without capitals run straight to the ceiling (St-Séverin ambulatory), from which hang monumental vault bosses (St-Étienne-du-Mont).

With the outbreak of the Hundred Years' War (1337–1453), civil architecture reverted to the sombre, massive style of feudal times (the Bastille and Men at Arms Hall in the Conciergerie).

Large residences with huge gardens such as the Hôtel St-Paul were built in the Marais district, along with many small half-timbered houses, a few of which can still be seen on rue François-Miron and on Île St-Louis.

In domestic architecture, defensive features – turrets, crenellations, wicket gates – blend with richly sculpted decorative elements such as balustrades and mullioned dormer windows.

Church of St-Germain-des-Prés

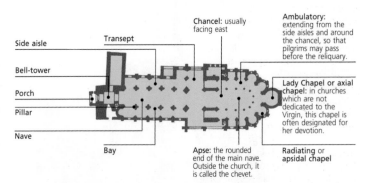

Chancel: usually facing east

Ambulatory: extending from the side aisles and around the chancel, so that pilgrims may pass before the reliquary.

Transept

Side aisle

Bell-tower

Porch

Pillar

Nave

Bay

Lady Chapel or axial chapel: in churches which are not dedicated to the Virgin, this chapel is often designated for her devotion.

Apse: the rounded end of the main nave. Outside the church, it is called the chevet.

Radiating or apsidal chapel

St-Séverin church: cross-section (from the east end looking towards the nave)

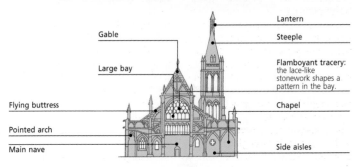

Gable

Large bay

Flying buttress

Pointed arch

Main nave

Lantern

Steeple

Flamboyant tracery: the lace-like stonework shapes a pattern in the bay.

Chapel

Side aisles

Church of St-Germain-des-Prés

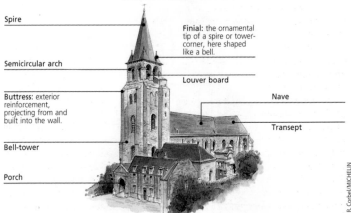

Spire

Semicircular arch

Buttress: exterior reinforcement, projecting from and built into the wall.

Bell-tower

Porch

Finial: the ornamental tip of a spire or tower-corner, here shaped like a bell.

Louver board

Nave

Transept

R. Corbel/MICHELIN

Chevet of Notre-Dame Cathedral

The cathedral is exquisite for its well-proportioned volumes, the purity of its lines and the craftsmanship of the decorative elements. The remarkable flying buttresses span the double ambulatory and the galleries inside.

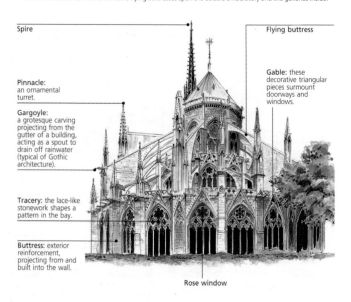

Spire

Flying buttress

Gable: these decorative triangular pieces surmount doorways and windows.

Pinnacle: an ornamental turret.

Gargoyle: a grotesque carving projecting from the gutter of a building, acting as a spout to drain off rainwater (typical of Gothic architecture).

Tracery: the lace-like stonework shapes a pattern in the bay.

Buttress: exterior reinforcement, projecting from and built into the wall.

Rose window

Church of the Sorbonne

The oldest part of the university, the church was built by Le Mercier between 1635-1642.

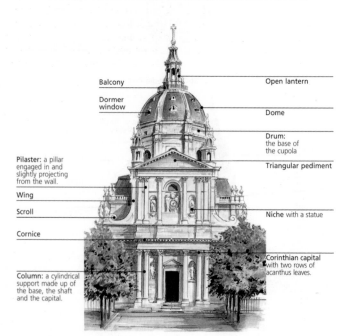

Balcony

Open lantern

Dormer window

Dome

Drum: the base of the cupola

Pilaster: a pillar engaged in and slightly projecting from the wall.

Triangular pediment

Wing

Scroll

Niche with a statue

Cornice

Corinthian capital with two rows of acanthus leaves.

Column: a cylindrical support made up of the base, the shaft and the capital.

R. Corbel/MICHELIN

THE RENAISSANCE

In the 16C, the war with Italy kindled the interest of French artists in Antiquity and non-religious decoration. Cradle or coffered ceilings (St-Nicolas des Champs) replaced ogive vaults, and architectural orders – especially Ionic and Corinthian – were reintroduced. The rood screen at St-Étienne-du-Mont and the stalls at St-Gervais are the finest examples of this style. However, Paris was not entirely loyal to the Italian influence. The capital preserved its own style, at least in terms of religious architecture.

A trio of Renaissance Parisian architects – The Renaissance in France is inextricably linked with the *châteaux de la Loire*. But Paris stands out for two majestic new edifices, the Louvre and the Tuileries, built by three men: Pierre Lescot (1515–78), Baptiste Androuët Du Cerceau (1560–1602) and Philibert Delorme (1517–70). All were influenced by Italian architecture. The former two introduced from Italy the continuous façade broken by projecting bays with semicircular pediments. The Cour Carrée in the Louvre combines the splendour of Antiquity with rich decoration: statues nestling in niches between fluted pilasters; a frieze and cornices above doorways; and inside, coffered ceilings (Henri II staircase in the Clock Pavilion of the Louvre).

Work on the first Hôtel de Ville was begun in 1533 by Le Boccador and Pierre Chambiges.

CLASSICAL ARCHITECTURE

Paris continued to expand, and new civil and religious edifices were always underway, despite the Wars of Religion and the siege of the city by Henri de Navarre. Charles IX and Louis XIII pushed the walls built by Philippe Auguste farther west. The right bank benefited from this dynamic urban development. Paris was transformed in the 17C with the rise of Classical art and architecture inspired by Antiquity. Rules were established by the Academy of Architecture, founded in 1671, and strengthened by an absolute monarchy, asserting the need to combine religion and Antiquity and leading Classical art to its pinnacle. Religious architecture was modelled on Roman churches, with columns, pediments and statues competing for space. The Jesuit style of the Counter-Reformation adopted for the design of St-Paul-St-Louis caught on and the Paris skyline was soon filled with domes. Lemercier built the Sorbonne and Val-de-Grâce (finished by Le Muet). The Sun King's architects demonstrated their progressive assimilation and mastery of the dome through the magnificent creations that beautified the city under Louis XIV:

Église du Val-de-Grâce

© Jopat/Fotolia

Some Buildings from the Past 30 Years

The Forum des Halles, Centre Georges-Pompidou, Cité des Sciences et de l'Industrie and the nearby Cité de la Musique (⏚see La VILLETTE), Institut du Monde Arabe, Opéra Bastille, Pyramide du Louvre, the CNIT and the Grande Arche (⏚see La DÉFENSE), Palais Omnisports, Ministère des Finances, and the Bibliothèque de France-site Tolbiac (BERCY), the Fondation Cartier near place Denfert-Rochereau (⏚see PORT-ROYAL), and the reflective plastic forms of the Le Ponant apartment block built on the site of the old Citroën car factory (⏚see VAUGIRARD).

Hardouin-Mansart (Invalides, St-Roch), Libéral-Bruant (Salpêtrière), Le Vau (St-Louis-en-l'Île), Soufflot (Panthéon). Public buildings were shaped by Classical symmetry and pure lines. Place des Vosges, place Dauphine and Hôpital St-Louis typify the Louis XIII style with the use of brick and stone; whereas Salomon de Brosse blended French and Italian features in the Luxembourg Palace built for Marie de' Medici. Mansart, Androuet Du Cerceau, Delamair and Le Muet created a new design in the Marais for the Parisian town house, or *hôtel particulier*, smaller than before and featuring a garden.

Classical architecture reached its height between 1650 and 1750 with magnificent buildings by Perrault (Louvre Colonnade), Le Vau (Institut de France) and Gabriel (place de la Concorde, École Militaire). Although originality was in vogue at the end of the 17C, the Rococo style (decorations on the Hôtel de Soubise) never was very popular in Paris. Under Louis XVI, taste gravitated towards the more elegant simplicity of Antiquity (Palais de la Légion d'Honneur) as epitomized by Ledoux (Farmers-General Wall toll-houses).

Urban development – Construction work was ongoing throughout the 17C in Paris. François Mansart (1598–1666) designed the Val-de-Grâce, the Hôtel de la Vrillière (Banque de France), and the façade of the Hôtel Carnavalet. His nephew, **Jules Hardouin-Mansart** (1646–1708), built the Invalides dome, place Vendôme, place des Victoires and the Hôtel Conti. Paris was fitted out with magnificent buildings and avenues. The Right and Left Banks tried to outdo each other. The Palais Cardinal designed by Jacques Lemercier, as well as the Cours de la Reine (Champs-Élysées), and place Royale – a model of Classical symmetry – were constructed on the Right Bank.

The Hôtel Lambert was built on Île St-Louis by **Le Vau** (1612–70), who also designed St-Sulpice and the Collège des Quatre Nations (now the Institut de France) on the Left Bank. The Manufacture des Gobelins and the Observatoire were erected in the late 17C.

The building frenzy continued into the 18C, when an impressive number of new monuments appeared on the Paris skyline: the Palais-Royal arcades, the Hôtel des Monnaies, the Palais de l'Élysée, the Palais Bourbon, the Théâtre de l'Odéon and the Palais de Bagatelle. After the Revolution, the city was divided into chic areas and the working-class districts west of the Marais, whose winding streets add a touch of charm from the past to present-day Paris (Latin Quarter and St-Merri Quarter).

Safety and cleanliness improved with the addition of lanterns that were lit until midnight, as well as a road maintenance service and fire brigade. Traffic problems were alleviated by ring roads built around the capital. The banks of the Seine were remodelled and new bridges constructed, allowing fresh supplies to be brought in by boat on a daily basis. Paris adopted its current system of street names and numbers with no 1 being the house closest to the Seine. Finally, the overcrowded cemeteries in the centre of Paris were emptied, their bones ceremoniously transferred to the quarry tunnels running beneath the city where they acted as stabilizers.

PONT-NEUF

Despite its name – "new bridge" – it is the oldest in Paris. The 12 arches are embellished with amusing mascarons.

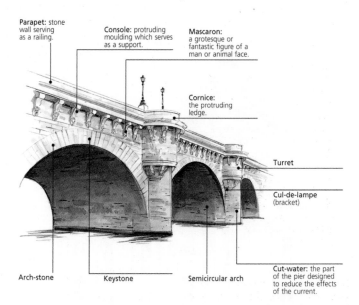

Parapet: stone wall serving as a railing.

Console: protruding moulding which serves as a support.

Mascaron: a grotesque or fantastic figure of a man or animal face.

Cornice: the protruding ledge.

Turret

Cul-de-lampe (bracket)

Arch-stone

Keystone

Semicircular arch

Cut-water: the part of the pier designed to reduce the effects of the current.

Pavillon de l'Horloge du Louvre

Also know as the Sully Pavilion, built by Le Mercier in the 17C.

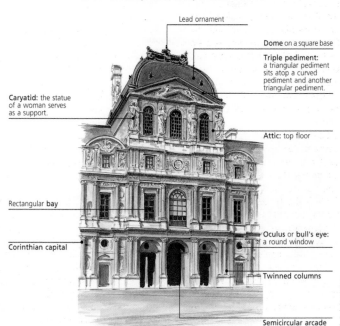

Lead ornament

Dome on a square base

Triple pediment: a triangular pediment sits atop a curved pediment and another triangular pediment.

Caryatid: the statue of a woman serves as a support.

Attic: top floor

Rectangular **bay**

Oculus or **bull's eye:** a round window

Corinthian capital

Twinned columns

Semicircular arcade

R. Corbel/MICHELIN

69

INSTITUT DE FRANCE

The chapel with its dome is set between two semicircular wings which lead to two square pavilions.

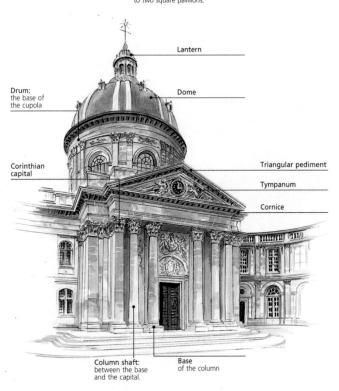

Lantern

Drum: the base of the cupola

Dome

Corinthian capital

Triangular pediment

Tympanum

Cornice

Column shaft: between the base and the capital.

Base of the column

PLACE VENDÔME

The magnificent architecture of this square is the work of Mansart. Arcades run along the ground level and pilasters adorn the upper floors; dormer windows are on the uppermost level.

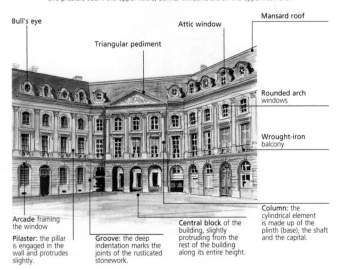

Bull's eye

Attic window

Mansard roof

Triangular pediment

Rounded arch windows

Wrought-iron balcony

Arcade framing the window

Pilaster: the pillar is engaged in the wall and protrudes slightly.

Groove: the deep indentation marks the joints of the rusticated stonework.

Central block of the building, slightly protruding from the rest of the building along its entire height.

Column: the cylindrical element is made up of the plinth (base), the shaft and the capital.

Building on rue de Seine
Louis XV façade with typical embellishments

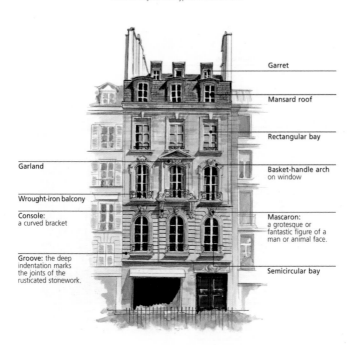

Garret

Mansard roof

Rectangular bay

Basket-handle arch
on window

Garland

Wrought-iron balcony

Console:
a curved bracket

Groove: the deep
indentation marks
the joints of the
rusticated stonework.

Mascaron:
a grotesque or
fantastic figure of a
man or animal face.

Semicircular bay

LA MADELEINE

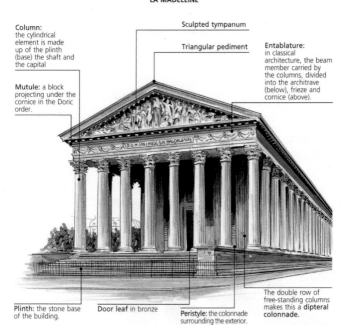

Column:
the cylindrical
element is made
up of the plinth
(base) the shaft and
the capital

Sculpted tympanum

Triangular pediment

Entablature:
in classical
architecture, the beam
member carried by
the columns, divided
into the architrave
(below), frieze and
cornice (above).

Mutule: a block
projecting under the
cornice in the Doric
order.

Plinth: the stone base
of the building.

Door leaf in bronze

Peristyle: the colonnade
surrounding the exterior.

The double row of
free-standing columns
makes this a dipteral
colonnade.

R. Corbel/MICHELIN

71

GARE DU NORD
Designed by the architect Hittorff, the train station was built between 1861-1868.

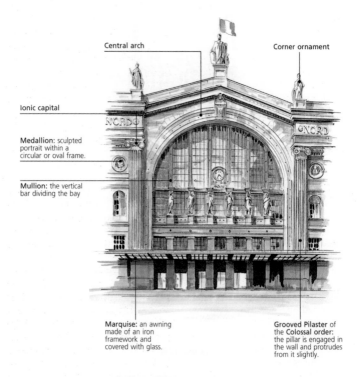

Central arch

Corner ornament

Ionic capital

Medallion: sculpted portrait within a circular or oval frame.

Mullion: the vertical bar dividing the bay

Marquise: an awning made of an iron framework and covered with glass.

Grooved Pilaster of the **Colossal order:** the pillar is engaged in the wall and protrudes from it slightly.

OPÉRA BASTILLE
Designed by Carlos Ott, 1989. The shiny, rounded surfaces seem to be pushing forward into the place de la Bastille. The main auditorium seats 2,700.

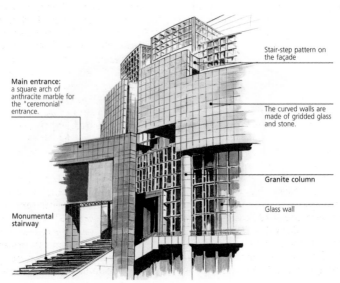

Stair-step pattern on the façade

Main entrance: a square arch of anthracite marble for the "ceremonial" entrance.

The curved walls are made of gridded glass and stone.

Granite column

Glass wall

Monumental stairway

R. Corbel/MICHELIN

SECOND EMPIRE AND INNOVATION

The Empire and Restoration were not marked by any significant architectural achievements. Napoléon I continued construction of the Louvre and built monuments such as the Madeleine, the Arc de Triomphe and the Arc de Triomphe du Carrousel. But the real transformation of Paris took place during the Second Empire, when **Baron Haussmann**'s massive urban planning programme and the new application of cast iron in construction irrevocably altered the city. The technique of cladding metallic sub-structures was refined by Baltard (St-Augustin, Pavillon Baltard at Nogent-sur-Marne), Labrouste (Bibliothèque Ste-Geneviève) and Hittorff (Gare du Nord), the most famous example of the new building method being **Gustave Eiffel**'s Tower.

Paris was enlarged to encompass some of its surrounding villages, and the current system of the 20 *arrondissements* was created. Haussmann's wide avenues enhance buildings such as the **Opéra Garnier**, one of the finer stone edifices of a period that was less preoccupied with monumental buildings.

Towards the end of the century, new trends developed that were different from the official style. Art Nouveau architects, the most well-known being Guimard, defined a new decorative vocabulary for façades, interiors and furniture featuring stylised floral motifs, asymmetrical designs and materials such as glass and ceramics.

THE 20C

The 20C marks a turning point in urban architecture. Architects and structural engineers collaborated on ever more economical and functional designs using industrially manufactured, thus cheaper, materials (cast iron, plate glass, artificial stone) and improved building methods.

Buildings in totally different styles have gone up side by side. While the Grand and Petit Palais, Pont Alexandre-III and Sacré-Cœur look to the past for their inspiration, the Théâtre des Champs-Élysées (Frères Perret), Palais de Chaillot and Palais de Tokyo, fashioned in reinforced concrete, look resolutely ahead to the modern age.

Late 20C – Since 1945, under the influence of **Le Corbusier** (Fondation, Cité Universitaire), architectural design has undergone a fundamental reappraisal. A wide variety of new forms, styles and lines strive to fit into the existing urban landscape, starting with social housing in the 1970s. Ricardo Bofill's buildings use elements of Classical architecture while employing modern materials such as glass and cement.

Glass has been used to cover most new constructions (La Défense, Institut du Monde Arabe, Bibliothèque de France, Palais de la culture du Japon), enabling architects to achieve stunning technical effects.

Blending past and future – Architecture today falls within the wider scope of town planning, with new buildings designed as part of a larger scheme of renovations in a district (Maine-Montparnasse, Les Halles, La Villette, Bercy) or of newly created areas (La Défense, Tolbiac). Green spaces, pedestrian zones and bicycle paths have also been designed as part of the restructuring of the city. The International Foundation for Human Rights in the Arche de La Défense, the Bibliothèque Nationale de France and the Palais Omnisports de Bercy are only a few examples of how the city's reputation as an important centre for culture and sports has been enhanced in recent years.

Paris has often chosen foreign architects to undertake its large-scale buildings. The Louvre Pyramide, one of the finest examples of a successful alliance of old and new, is the work of American architect **Ieoh Ming Pei**.

But the era of huge projects seems to be coming to an end. Today the accent is on improving and preserving existing monuments. Now, just a few years into the 21C Paris has experienced exciting contemporary developments such as Jean Nouvel's harmonious balance of glass and metal at Musée du Quai Branly.

Art

The City of Light has given birth to some of the world's most influential artists, artistic movements, and even new forms of art over the centuries.

PAINTING AND SCULPTURE

Painting and sculpture have always been closely interwoven into Parisian life. After centuries of working on commission from the monarchy, 19C and 20C artists began to reach levels of freedom and creativity acclaimed throughout the world.

IN THE MIDDLE AGES

Painting and sculpture appeared within a religious context during this period, as Gothic buildings were gradually decorated. Stained glass, the main medium, reached stunning heights (Ste-Chapelle, rose windows in Notre-Dame).

The palette of colours was broadened and became increasingly suffused with light. The realism of painting from the Middle Ages is striking through its expressive faces and minutely detailed clothing. Painters from this period were given the name Primitives.

Gothic sculpture also flourished. Realism and a sense of drama combined to transform what was until then mere decoration into a true art form. Churches were covered with statues: little sculptures adorn the balustrade and the sides of the chancel at Notre-Dame, whereas the Portal of the Last Judgement marks the beginning of a more sober style that developed in the 13C into French Gothic.

THE RENAISSANCE

At the beginning of the 14C the Parisian schools of painting chose a style that was still realistic but more subdued. Expressions became finer and details more important, leading to a Mannerist style.

Painting evolved and adopted new themes such as mythology and portraits, as well as humanist themes with Antiquity as the ideal. The influence of Italian art is omnipresent in French painting, whereas sculpture preserved its own character.

The art of stained glass was at its peak. Jean Cousin the Younger (1522–94) delved deeper into colour techniques. *The Judgement of Solomon* and the *Story of the Virgin* in St-Gervais and the *Story of St-Joseph* in St-Merri are like paintings made of stained glass.

Jean Goujon (1510–68) – The master of 16C French statuary. While he didn't reject Italian Mannerism, nature was his fundamental ideal. His works combine grace and elegance despite their complex composition. Fitting into the

Pilgrimage to the Island of Cythera (1717) by Jean-Antoine Watteau, Louvre

© Scala, Florence/Musée du Louvre

architectural design, they provide a preliminary idea of French Classicism. The Cariatides (Louvre) and bas-relief sculptures of the Fontaine des Innocents (1547–49) are his two greatest masterpieces.

THE 17C

Italian influence continued during the early 17C. Paintings were designed mainly as decoration for royal palaces such as the Louvre and Luxembourg. Sculpture also adopted the Italian style, becoming strictly decorative for the niches designated by architects.

But Classical French art asserts itself under the king's patronage in the second half of the 17C; and despite competition from Versailles, Paris was its main beneficiary. The main purpose of painting and sculpture became the glorification of the French monarchy, which enriches its 'great city' with magnificent monuments decorated by the Court's best sculptors: Girardon (Richelieu's tomb), Coysevox (Tuileries Gardens) and Coustou (The Marly Horses).

In 1648, the Academy of Painting and Sculpture was founded; it was to be the most important French art school until 1793. Quarrelling between the corporatists, represented by Vouet, and the independents, represented by Le Brun, kept things lively.

Pierre Mignard (1612–95) – Succeeding Le Brun as First Painter to the King, he was instrumental in the transition from the 17C to the 18C. His little paintings imitating Raphael are known as *mignardes*. By introducing a lighter, more elegant and realistic touch in his compositions, he started the quarrel between the Poussinists and the Rubenists similar to the literary spat between Ancients and Moderns. The modern painters gave nature the place of honour (the Le Nain brothers' landscapes), rejecting the Academy's sobriety.

BETWEEN BAROQUE AND CLASSIC

18C French painting was characterized by a surfeit of detail embellishing the themes of religious paintings (Boucher,

Pastoral Scene, Louvre) as well as by the humanization of mythology.

This Mannerist French style launched the "Fête Galante" genre illustrated by Watteau (1684–1721) in *Pilgrimage to the Island of Cythera* (1717, Louvre). Portraitists such as La Tour (*Portrait of the Marquise de Pompadour*, 1752–55, Louvre) preferred pastel techniques. Jean-Baptiste Siméon-Chardin (1699–1779), the great master of the French School, devoted himself to still-life paintings and portraits. Boucher's delicate landscapes heralded the pre-Romantic period.

The late 18C wavered between the pre-Romantic J-H Fragonard (1732–1806) and Neoclassicism, typified by J-L David and his *Oath of the Horatii* (1784–85, Louvre).

Monumental sculptures were as numerous as in the 17C: Robert le Lorrain (*Les Chevaux du soleil*, Hôtel de Rohan), Bouchardon (Quatre-Saisons Fountain) and Peigalle (St-Sulpice).

THE 19C AND 20C

Mirroring the era's political movements, painting and sculpture reacted violently to the new trends. Bright colours and fantasy came into fashion. Géricault (1791–1824) launched Romanticism: through its bold composition, dynamism and the characters' striking expressions, *Raft of the Medusa* (1819, Louvre) is in total opposition to the Classical style. Delacroix carried on in the same spirit. The official Salons were the scenes of battles between the two major trends: one advocating the superiority of drawing, the other that of colour. Ingres (1780–1867), taking his inspiration from Antiquity, lost the battle when he exhibited *The Apotheosis of Homer* at the 1827 Salon. However, the return to Academic art was successful at the 1863 Salon.

In reaction, Manet organized the 1863 Group featuring all of the painters rejected by the Salon. Fantin-Latour (1836–1904) and Manet portray everyday pleasures on their canvases, sometimes in a provocative manner in their drawings of women (*Olympia*, 1863,

Orsay). Like Courbet before them, they were the precursors of Impressionism.

From Impressionism to Expressionism – The Impressionists use the precepts of Realism (works based on nature) while adding a powerful luminosity to their paintings through the use of a chromatic palette. They also relied on the art of drawing. Edgar Degas' sketches of dancers show firm strokes. Above all, they had a strong penchant for landscapes (Claude Monet, *Argenteuil Bridge*, 1834, Orsay). Cézanne (1839–1906) and Pissarro (1830–1903) blended characters and landscapes or indoor scenes (Paul Cézanne, *The Card Players*, around 1890–95, Orsay).

The success of the genre opened up new possibilities: Seurat created scientific Impressionism in which characters are placed in a subtle balance; systematic juxtaposition of primary colours and their complementary tones gives rise to Pointillism. Nature becomes a symbol under the brushstrokes of Puvis de Chavannes (1824–98). Gauguin (1848–1903) and Van Gogh (1853–90) had a different reaction to Impressionism: while not breaking off from it, their explorations were directed towards expressive intensity through bright colours. The Expressionist movement was associated with a new concern over social problems prevalent at the beginning of the 20C, as illustrated by painters such as Rouault and Soutine.

From Fauvism to Cubism – The Fauvists were a new, modernist movement in the early 20C who had nothing left in common with the Realists or Symbolists. Their palette of colours and the shapes represented are often aggressive, which created a scandal at the 1905 Autumn Salon. Vlaminck, Matisse and Derain are the masters of this movement advocating freedom. They strove to free themselves of all constraints and conventions in their daily lives, living a bohemian existence in the Bateau-Lavoir in Montmartre.

Nevertheless, Matisse reintroduced the concept of rigour and constraints, with the idea that the emphasis on colour shouldn't lead to an overshadowing of form – however primitive – or composition. Picasso brought this trend to the fore with *Les Demoiselles d'Avignon* (1907). Braque applied it to landscape

Après le bain, femme nue s'essuyant la nuque (1898) by Edgar Degas

painting. But some preferred more creative impulses to this spirit of discipline. Modigliani, Soutine, Chagall, Zadkine and Léger settled in the La Ruche workshop in Montparnasse, where they gave free rein to their moods, reviving Expressionism. This was the golden age of the Paris School, which came to an end with World War II, when Surrealism burst upon the scene.

Sculpture – During the Second Empire and the Third Republic, Paris was gradually transformed into an open-air museum. Works by Carpeaux (Observatory Fountain) and Rude (*Marshal Ney, the Marseillaise on the Arc de Triomphe*) precede those of the great masters of the late 19C and the period between the two World Wars, including Rodin (*Balzac, Victor Hugo, Bronze Age),* Dalou (place de la Nation), Bourdelle (Palais de Tokyo, Théâtre des Champs-Élysées), Maillol (Tuileries Gardens) and Landowski (Ste-Geneviève on the Pont de la Tournelle, *Animals* at the Porte de St-Cloud).

The Art Nouveau style is epitomized by Hector Guimard's famous wrought-iron metro entrances, created around 1900. Abstract sculpture is also given its place: Calder's mobile (&see La Défense), Louis Leygue and Agam (&see La Défense). Renewing a 19C tradition, sculptures were erected in streets and gardens: of famous people (Georges Pompidou, Jean Moulin, Arthur Rimbaud) along with Symbolist works, and sculpture-fountains (Fontaine Stravinski, by Jean Tinguely and Niki de Saint-Phalle, next to Beaubourg).

PARIS IN PAINTINGS

Paris began to be the subject or background in paintings at the time of the Wars of Religion. During the reigns of Henry IV and Louis XIII, it was used as a theme by Jacques Callot (1592–1635) in his engravings and by Dutch landscape painters (De Verwer, Zeeman) fascinated by the light and atmosphere on the banks of the Seine.

The urban landscape of Paris really came into its own with the Impressionists, who preferred painting outdoors rather than in a studio. Corot painted the

Paris quaysides and Ville d'Avray a few miles away. Lépine, Monet (*St-Germain-l'Auxerrois, Gare St-Lazare),* Renoir (*Moulin de la Galette, Moulin Rouge),* Sisley (*Île St-Louis)* and Pissarro (*The Pont Neuf)* depict light effects in the capital at all hours and in all seasons. Paris is also an important focus in works by Seurat (*The Eiffel Tower),* Gauguin, Cézanne and Van Gogh (Montmartre scenes). Toulouse-Lautrec portrays a totally different view of Paris life in his witty, intimate sketches of cabaret artists. Among the Nabi artists, Vuillard captures the peace of Paris squares and gardens in a more poetic vein. In the early 20C, Paris figured prominently in the work of Fauve painters Marquet and Utrillo with their scenes of unfashionable neighbourhoods. Views of the capital by the naïve painters are sensitive, imaginative and highly colourful. Among more modern artists, Balthus (Paris between the wars), Yves Brayer and Bernard Buffet have cast Paris in a new light.

PHOTOGRAPHY

In 1825, French inventor **Nicéphore Niépce** became the first to produce a permanent photograph – an image produced on a polished pewter plate. Not long after this, Niépce teamed up with **Louis Daguerre** (born near Paris) and together they refined the process. However, the breakthrough in photography came when **William Henry Fox Talbot** in England invented the negative/positive photographic process in the 1830s, which led to the modern understanding of photography.

Eugène Atget, one of the fathers of modern photography, immortalized street scenes and tradesmen in a Paris that no longer exists (cabbies, street singers, rag merchants, lace sellers).

In more recent times, **Edouard Boubat**, **izis, Brassaï** (known as the "Toulouse-Lautrec of the camera lens") and **Marcel Bovis** captured the magic of Paris at night; **Jacques-Henri Lartigue** recorded the Roaring Twenties; **Cartier-Bresson**, the archetypal globetrotter and founding member of the Magnum agency, caught views of Paris that resemble watercolours *(Île de la Cité)*; **Willy Ronis** shot scenes of Belleville-Ménilmontant, now changed beyond all recognition.

Robert Doisneau (1912–94) – One of the great photographers of Paris, he specialized in humorous shots of ordinary people filled with depth and poetry: children playing, concierges, scenes of cafés and markets. *The Kiss*, taken in front of the Hôtel de Ville in 1950, remains his most famous work.

FILM

In the late 19C and early 20C, Paris encourages the development of the cinema by helping some of its pioneers, who were inspired by photography and theatre.

1892 – Émile Reynaud opens the Optical Theatre in the Musée Grévin, holding a total of 12 000 showings attended by 500 000 spectators.

28 December 1895 – The Lumière Brothers hold their first public showing of the cinematograph on boulevard des Capucines.

1896–97 – Georges Meliès (1861–1938) invents double exposure and presents his first films with scripts.

1898 – Charles Pathé creates his international firm and studios. First newsreels (Pathé-Journal).

1900 – The *cinéorama* (a 100m/110yd circular screen invented by Grimoin-Sanson) was presented at the Paris Exposition.

The Lumière Brothers and the cinematograph – In February 1895, Auguste (1862–1954) and Louis (1864–1948) Lumière registered the patent for the cinematograph, a machine that projects animated scenes at a speed of 18 frames per second. Their *Sortie des usines Lumière* (shot in 1894) was a success, and showings were held in the Salon Indien at the Grand-Café, boulevard des Capucines.

Léon Gaumont (1863–1946) – Pursuing the work begun by the Lumière Brothers with his *chronophone*, he added synchronized sound to films.

Early 20C – **Charles Pathé** created his studios on rue Francœur and turned the cinema into an industry.

POSTERS

Paris was the major source and beneficiary of this new art between painting and photography.

The French masters – Their goal was to depict the joys and sorrows of everyday life, and to combine Parisians' social and cultural demands. **Gavarni** (1804–66) evokes the seedier Paris in his black-and-white posters of street-walkers and poor neighbourhoods. He created posters based on *Selected Works* by Balzac, who also inspired Grandville's *Petites misères de la vie humaine*.

Chéret revolutionized the art of poster-designing in the second half of the 19C with his inflated, or Rococo, style and lively figures in colour.

Toulouse-Lautrec (1864–1901) – A lithographer, he adopted the principles of his teachers Chéret and Bonnat, but with a more cutting style. He portrayed the poverty in certain areas of Paris and frequented cabarets, where he created some of his greatest pieces such as *La Goulue at the Moulin Rouge*. His illustrations – verging on caricature and the grotesque – stirred up many a scandal.

Alphonse Mucha – Arriving in Paris in 1887 from his native Prague, Mucha lived in the city during a time of cultural blossoming. While Toulouse-Lautrec sought to bring out the truth of his subjects, Mucha created figures surrounded by great decorative verve and an abundance of motifs. Like Lautrec, he made poster designs for theatre openings, notably for Sarah Bernhardt.

Imprimerie Mourlot – Just before WWII, Fernand Mourlot took over the Imprimerie Bataille, a famous publicity printing press from the early 1900s.

He slowly became known for his art posters, and soon became the official poster printer for illustrious Parisian expositions at the Orangerie and Petit Palais for Delacroix, Monet, Rubens, Ingres, Gauguin, Matisse and Lautrec.

Literature

The story of Paris as a literary capital began with the creation of its university in the 12C, while the 18C saw the rise of the city's intellectual and cultural prestige. The history of French literature is closely linked with that of Paris and its legendary literary salons of the 17–20C. Many writers who were born in the city have celebrated it in their books, giving Paris a special place in literature.

MIDDLE AGES AND RENAISSANCE

12C–13C – The first Paris university opened its doors. It was the only university in northern France, and gave a boost to intellectual life. The Parisian dialect was adopted by the Court as its official language, putting Paris on the literary map.

15C–16C – Writers, and the heroes of their stories, "go up" to Paris, the former in order to write, the latter to study. Low life on the streets was portrayed in epic poems and mystery plays, whereas Rutebœuf and Villon wrote poems about individuals and everyday life. Although Rabelais criticized the Parisian character, he had Gargantua and Pantagruel attend the Sorbonne; and he himself lived and died in the Marais (d. 1553).

1530 – The Collège de France was founded by François I and Guillaume Budé. As the city grows into its role as capital, many writers choose to make it their second home, including Montaigne, Ronsard and the Pleiade poets, as well as Agrippa d'Aubigné, who witnessed the religious conflicts that overtook Paris and the rest of France in the late 16C.

THE 17C

As the city was embellished by Henri IV and Louis XIII, and agitated by the Fronde during Louis XIV's minority, writers and noted wits of the period developed the famous literary salons, first at the Hôtel de Rambouillet (17C) and later on in the homes of the Marquise de Lambert, Madame du Deffand and Madame Geoffrin (18C).

After its role as a centre of humanism in the 16C, Paris promoted Classicism in the 17C with the assertion of absolute monarchy. Writers during the reign of Louis XIV, such as Molière, went beyond prior conventions and were allowed to criticize society.

1634–35 – The Académie Française was founded by Richelieu. Paris became the centre of French literature. Contrary to the salons, where open discussion was encouraged, the Académie sought to standardize the French language and exert a restraining influence on all branches of literature.

1680 – The Comédie Française was created under the king's patronage.

Books for sale at Galerie Vivienne

©H. CHAJMOWICZ/Michelin

THE 18C – REVIVAL OF THE LITERARY SALONS

In the 18C, Louis XV and Louis XVI showed little interest in literature. Society resorted to philosophy salons and cafés (Procope, La Régence), where new ideas developed.

1710–80 – Prominent authors such as Marivaux and Montesquieu attended the salons, where Voltaire and Diderot also congregated.

Marivaux and Beaumarchais (*Barber of Seville* and *Marriage of Figaro*) tinged their light comedies about Paris society and lifestyle with irony, whereas Jean-Jacques Rousseau (1712–78), a precursor of Romanticism who was born in the provinces, expressed disdain for the place so full of "noise, smoke and mud!" Others concerned with the dichotomy between ethics and society include the Abbé Prévost (*Manon Lescaut*), Restif de la Bretonne (*Nights of Paris*), the Marquis de Sade and Choderlos de Laclos (*Dangerous Liaisons*). It is Voltaire (1694–1778), master social critic, historian, novelist (*Candide*), essayist, letter-writer, diarist, dramatist and humanist philosopher, who perhaps epitomizes the best of 18C writing in Paris: ironic and witty with a light touch and perfect turn of phrase.

During the Age of Enlightenment, Paris wielded a great deal of influence in international intellectual circles with emissaries such as d'Alembert and Diderot, who secured subscriptions to their 28-volume *Encyclopedia* from Catherine the Great of Russia among others.

THE 19C AND 20C

After the French Revolution, literature was no longer restricted to a small section of society. Writers were active in the social and political debates of their times through its major literary trends: Realism, Romanticism, Symbolism, Naturalism and Surrealism.

Paris has a double image, portrayed at times as rich and prestigious, and at others as a more popular city full of vices. Heroes in novels head for Paris, leaving behind their native provinces. In *Les Illusions perdues*, Lucien de Rubempré dies there. In *Les Misérables* and *La Comédie humaine*, by Hugo and Balzac respectively, the city is portrayed as a character with a personality of its own subject to moods and illness. Both Julien Sorel, the hero of Stendhal's *Le Rouge et le Noir*, and Léon the notary in Flaubert's *Madame Bovary* run away from Paris society; and some of Zola's novels depict certain circles and areas of the city as a kind of prison.

Parisian writers such as Dumas the Younger, Musset, the songwriter Béranger, Eugène Sue (*Mysteries of Paris*), Murger (*Scenes of Bohemian Life*) and Nerval vacillate between the two images of the city. Contrasts in humour and reflections on life's contradictions are explored, against the backdrop of Haussmann's upheavals, in verse by Baudelaire, the Parnassian and Symbolist poets, and in the emerging social-history, realist novel by Émile Zola (*Les Rougon-Macquart*).

Old Montmartre lives on in the **songs** of Bruant (1851–1925), the novels of Carco (1886–1958) and Marcel Aymé (1902–67), Montparnasse in the poems of Max Jacob (1876–1944) and Léon-Paul Fargue (1876–1947); still other writers and poets such as Colette and Cocteau, Simenon, Montherlant, Louise de Vilmorin, Aragon, Prévert, Sacha Guitry, Eluard, Sartre, Simone de Beauvoir and Beckett have celebrated Paris-as-muse in their many works.

Playwrights' reputations, like novelists', are made and broken in Paris. Vaudeville, the soul of boulevard theatre, was the 19C heir to the farces featuring dialogue and songs that were performed at the St-Germain and St-Laurent fairs in earlier days, as well as the bawdy tableaux and pastiches of scenes from well-known plays. Talented playwrights also wrote serious vaudeville. Light opera and revues emerged during the Second Empire, whereas dramas were another outgrowth of boulevard theatre.

One of the biggest events in Paris remains the annual *Salon du Livre*, highlighting France's top writers.

Music

Paris is rather like a grand orchestra where enchanting music is played. It has been both the theme and setting for a host of musical compositions, and its streets are often filled with the sounds of this art with its long-standing tradition in the city. From the classical master Berlioz to French chanson star Edith Piaf, Paris has given birth to many of the world's finest musicians.

IN THE MIDDLE AGES

Late 12C – A school of polyphony was established at Notre-Dame characterized by its refined expression of the deep religious faith of the period.

13C – Songs by aristocratic poet-composers, known as *Trouvères* (northern version of troubadours), inspire their kings and queens to greatness.

13C–14C – Musical works such as Machaut's masses and motets by contrapuntist Dufay are composed of several parts.

Under François I – A national musical printing works was created, illustrated by narrative ballads written by Janequin *(Les Cris de Paris)*. Madrigals and courtly songs with lute become popular.

1571 – The poet Baïf founded the Academy for Music and Poetry to revive Classical verse-form and poetic rhyme.

THE RENAISSANCE

"That most noble and gallant art" developed naturally at the Royal Court, first at the Louvre and later at Versailles, where sovereigns, their consorts and companions disported themselves in masques, ballets, allegorical dances, recitals, opera and comedy.

The first Parisian songs were published.

THE 17C: A MUSICAL HIGHLIGHT

Music, like literature, flourished under the renewed interest of the Court. Italian opera was welcomed, thanks to Mazarin, and major foreign operas such as the *Marriage of Orpheus and Eurydice* (1643) were staged in Paris.

Lully and lyric opera – Florentine composer **Jean-Baptiste Lully** (1632–87) settled in Paris, and Louis XIV appointed him to direct music first at Court, then at the Académie Royale de Musique (1672). He created operas and ballets *(Ballet des Bienvenus, Ballet de la naissance de Vénus)*, dominating every genre. In 1661, he collaborated with Molière, developing a new genre, *ballet-comédie (Les Fâcheux, Le Sicilien, Le Bourgeois gentilhomme)*.

Religious music was also part of his repertory (*Te Deum*, 1677), and he attained new heights in choral music at Notre-Dame (with *Campra*) and Notre-Dame-des-Victoires.

Fête de la Musique

NEW OPERATIC FORMS IN THE 18C

After the prestigious operas of the 17C, music was made more accessible to the general public in the comic operas given at the St-Germain and St-Laurent fairs. However, Jean-Philippe Rameau (1683–1764) carried on in the tradition of Lully, while accentuating the orchestra's role. His opera-ballets (Les Indes galantes), lyric tragedies (Castor et Pollux, Dardanus) and comedies (Platée) gave birth to the French style. Rameau moved away from the Italian tradition without renouncing it, prompting the so-called War of the Buffoons.

The Musical Wars – The War of the Buffoons was a quarrel over French and Italian opera in which Rameau was pitted against the Encyclopedists. The main protagonists in the quarrel were Diderot (Le Neveu de Rameau) and J-J Rousseau (Le Devin du village, Lettre sur la musique française), who enumerated all of the flaws in French music, which Lully still dominated.

The second war developed over the new genre, comic opera, which grew out of the Parisian fairs and was launched by Gluck and Puccini, two foreigners who had settled in Paris. Gluck stressed dramatic intensity in his operas, reformed the opera by reducing the action to three acts and replacing the harpsichord by the flute. His works (Orphée et Eurydice, Iphigénie en Aulide and Alceste) transformed the principles of French tragic opera.

1795 – The Conservatoire de Musique de Paris was founded in 1795 and directed successively by Cherubini, Auber and Ambroise Thomas.

THE 19C

1801 – The Théâtre de Feydeau and the Théâtre de Favart joined to form the Opéra-Comique de Paris.

Music in Paris was associated with the political and military events that were taking place there: the Revolution produced many popular songs, the most famous being La Carmagnole, a satirical song from 1792. In the 19C the city became the international capital of music, attracting the greatest masters of the century.

1830 – Berlioz composed the Symphonie Fantastique, which still resounds as the manifesto-opus of the young Romantic school.

1866 – Premiere in Paris of Offenbach's La Vie parisienne.

From **1870**, symphonic composition and opera evolved through the work of Bizet, St-Saëns, Charpentier and Dukas, Parisians by birth or adoption. France was the leader in ballet music, which draws inspiration from history and mythology.

Debussy and **Ravel** were the two major French Impressionist composers at the end of the 19C. Refusing all foreign influence (including Wagner) in symphonic music, they gave it a national character. Debussy and Ravel collaborated with Diaghilev's Ballets Russes.

1894 – The Schola Cantorum was founded by Bordes, Guilmant and d'Indy.

1885–99 – The Chat Noir was the chansonniers' favourite cabaret.

1899 – Premiere of La Prise de Troie by Berlioz at the Opéra.

The Garde républicaine – A description of Parisian musical life wouldn't be complete without mentioning the Garde républicaine, formed in 1871. Originating with the Garde de Paris, created in 1848, it is composed of 127 musicians. Its military marches (Sambre et Meuse, Marche lorraine, La Fille du régiment) are hymns to French victories.

THE 20C

Cabarets – These popular venues were all the rage at the beginning of the century. The chansonniers (singers) performing in Montmartre's cabarets are portrayed by Toulouse-Lautrec in his famous posters and lithographs.

1902 – Premiere of Pelléas et Mélisande by Debussy at the Opéra-Comique.

1903 – The Lapin Agile opens.

The Group of Six – Founded by Auric, Durey, Honegger, Milhaud, Poulenc and Tailleferre in 1920, the group created a new musical aesthetic rejecting Romanticism and Impressionism.

1936 – Writers such as Prévert, Aragon and Apollinaire flocked to the Bœuf

Opéra

sur le Toit, where their works were set to music. During World War I, Nadia Boulanger led a new Parisian movement known as the Neoclassical School, drawing inspiration from Stravinsky and Latin music. After 1920 Paris continued to nurture new forms of musical expression. From the *ondes martenot* to the Jeune-France Group and its humanist music, Schaeffer and his concrete sounds, Henry, Boulez, Xénakis and Messiaen, each one made important contributions to the musical scene. As major foreign musicians continued to arrive in Paris, the Paris School was created in 1951.

The piano sonatas, ballet (*Le Loup*, 1953), symphonies and orchestral pieces by composer Henri Dutilleux (b. 1916) are among the greatest works from the second half of the 20C.

National orchestras – Paris possesses some internationally renowned orchestras. The Orchestre National de France, Orchestre Philharmonique de Radio-France and its Maîtrise (Choir School created in 1981), the Ensemble Intercontemporain, the Orchestre de Paris and Université de Paris-Sorbonne choirs and the Petits Chanteurs de la Croix de Bois interpret major works.

Parisian organists – Marie-Madeleine Duruflé-Chevalier, Olivier Latry, Philippe Lefebvre, Jean-Pierre Leguay and Riccardo Miravet; each of these organ players – many known throughout the world – is connected to a particular church. Organ music is also featured at the Festival d'Art Sacré in the autumn.

Major venues for music – While the Opéra Garnier (inaugurated in 1875) continues to be a highly prestigious opera house (home of the Paris Ballet), the Opéra Bastille (designed by Carlos Ott) has become the main venue for staging operas since it opened in 1989. The **Théâtre des Champs-Élysées** has maintained its spirit of musical innovation since it was founded in 1913 by Gabriel Astruc. The Théâtre du Châtelet was a mecca for light opera fans from 1928 to 1970. Renamed the **Théâtre musical de Paris** in 1980, it presents prestigious concerts and opera productions.

The **Cité de la Musique** (Parc de la Villette), designed by Christian de Portzamparc, includes the Conservatoire National Supérieur de Musique, the Musée de la Musique, and the Institut National de Pédagogie Musicale, as well as a concert hall. **IRCAM** (Institute of Acoustic and Musical Research) is a department of the Centre Pompidou devoted to experimental music. Thanks to the fervour of composer Pierre Boulez and to sophisticated technology using computers, electronic laboratories and sound processors, IRCAM has won international acclaim.

View from Pont Alexandre III at dusk
© Paul Reid/Dreamstime.com

Arrondissements 1–4

La Cité★★★

Two islands dominate the Seine River in the geographic heart of the capital city: the Île de la Cité and the Île St-Louis. Considered the cradle of Paris, the Île de la Cité holds a most impressive monument, the Cathedral of Notre-Dame, closely followed by the exquisite Ste-Chapelle and the Conciergerie. The smaller Île St-Louis is largely a pleasant residential enclave.

> ⓘ **Info:** Paris Office du Tourisme, 25 rue des Pyramides. ℘08 92 68 30 00 (0.34€ per min). http://en.parisinfo.com.
>
> ▶ **Location:** The islands are in the centre of Paris, straddling the 1st and 4th arrondissements.
>
> 👁 **Don't Miss:** Flower market at place Lépine, view of Notre-Dame from square Jean XXIII and stained-glass windows of Ste-Chapelle.
>
> ⏱ **Timing:** Allow two hours to visit the two islands.
>
> 👪 **Kids:** Children's playground in the gardens of the square Jean XXIII.

A BIT OF HISTORY

Lutetia – Around 200 BC Gaulish fishermen and **boatmen** of the Parisii tribe discovered and set up their huts on the largest island in the Seine: Lutetia was born. The township was conquered by Roman legions in 52 BC and prospered from shipping. The boatmen's existence has been confirmed by the discovery beneath Notre-Dame of one of their pagan altars.

In AD 360 the Roman prefect, Julian the Apostate, was here proclaimed emperor by his legions. At the same time, Lutetia was renamed after its inhabitants and shortened to Paris.

Sainte Geneviève – In AD 451 Attila crossed the Rhine with 700 000 men; as he reached Laon, the Parisians began to flee. Geneviève, a young girl from Nanterre, who had dedicated her life to God, calmed them with the assurance that the town would be saved by heavenly intervention; the Huns approached, hesitated and turned away to advance on Orléans. Parisians adopted the girl as their protector and patron.

Ten years later when the island was besieged by the Franks and suffered famine, Geneviève escaped the enemy watch, loaded boats with victuals in Champagne and returned undetected as if by miracle. She died in AD 512 and was buried at King Clovis' side.

The Count of Paris becomes king – In AD 885, for the fifth time in 40 years, the Normans sailed up the Seine. The Cité – the name adopted in AD 506 when **Clovis** made it his capital – was confronted by 700 ships bearing 30 000 warriors bent on pillaging Burgundy. Siege proving unsuccessful, Eudes, Count of Paris and the leader of the resistance, was thereupon elected king.

Cathedral and Parliament – In the Middle Ages the population grew, spilling on to both banks of the river. The number of schools around the cathedral proliferated. Among the teachers were Alexander of Paris, creator of the 12-footed *alexandrine* line in poetry and at the beginning of the 12C, the

Île de la Cité and the Seine

© Jérôme Delaye/Fotolia.com

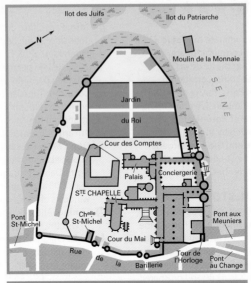

ILE DE LA CITÉ : DOWNSTREAM END IN THE 15C

philosopher **Abelard**, whose moving romance with Héloïse, the niece of the canon Fulbert, began in the cloisters of Notre-Dame. Chapels and convents multiplied on the island; by the close of the 13C, there were at least 22 bell-towers. The Cité, the seat of Parliament, the highest judiciary in the kingdom was, inevitably, involved in revolutions and uprisings such as that attempted in the 14C by **Étienne Marcel** and the **Fronde** in the 17C. During the Terror of 1793–94, the Conciergerie prisons were crowded, while next door the Revolutionary Tribunal continued to sit in the law courts, issuing merciless sentences.

Transformation – Under Louis-Philippe and to a greater extent, under Napoléon III, the centre of the island was demolished: 25 000 people were evacuated. Enormous administrative buildings were erected: the Hôtel-Dieu, barracks (now the police prefecture), the commercial courts; the Law Courts were doubled in size; place du Parvis before the cathedral was quadrupled in size; boulevard du Palais was built 10 times wider.

August 1944 – The Paris police barricaded themselves in the prefecture and hoisted the tricolour. For three days they held the Germans at bay until relieved by the French Army Division under Général Leclerc.

ÎLE DE LA CITÉ★★★

Ⓜ*Metro/Transport: Cité (line 4) – RER: St-Michel-Notre-Dame (line C). Buses: 21, 27, 38, 58, 70, 96.* Ⓟ*Underground parking can be found on rue de Lutèce and rue de la Cité.*

Notre-Dame Cathedral★★★

Ⓜ*Metro/Transport: Cité (line 4), St Michel (line 4) – RER: St-Michel-Notre-Dame (line B). Buses: 21, 38, 47, 85. Allow an hour for the tower, half-an-hour for the interior.* Ⓒ*Mon–Fri 8am–6.45pm, Sat–Sun 8am–7.15pm.* Guided tours in English Wed–Thu 2pm, Sat 2.30pm. Ⓟ*Underground parking right in front of the cathedral.* ℰ*01 42 34 56 10. www.cathedraledeparis.com.*

At the heart of Paris and in the heart of the Parisians, the cathedral of Notre-Dame has witnessed some of the greatest moments of the capital's history. This magnificent religious edifice is one of the supreme masterpieces of French art, and has been a source of visual and literary inspiration over the centuries.

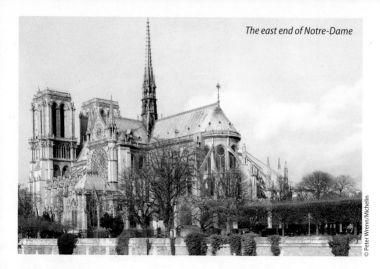

The east end of Notre-Dame

© Peter Wenn/Michelin

A Bit of History

Construction – For 2 000 years prayers have been offered from this spot. A Gallo-Roman temple, a Christian basilica, and a Romanesque church preceded the present cathedral founded by Bishop **Maurice de Sully** to rival the St-Denis basilica by Abbot Suger. Construction began in 1163, during the reign of Louis VII, under **Jean de Chelles** and **Pierre de Montreuil**, architect of the Ste-Chapelle. By about 1300 the building was complete. Notre-Dame is the last large galleried church and one of the first to be supported by flying buttresses.

Ceremonial occasions – Long before it was completed, Notre-Dame had become the setting for major religious and political ceremonies. **St Louis** entrusted it with the Crown of Thorns in 1239 pending the completion of the Ste-Chapelle. In 1302 **Philip the Fair** formally opened the kingdom's first Parliament. Celebrations, thanksgivings and state funerals have followed each other down the centuries: high points in French history include the coronation of young Henry VI of England (1430); the retrial of Joan of Arc (1455); the crowning of **Mary Stuart** (*see box p92*) as Queen of France following her marriage to François II; the unusual marriage ceremony of Marguerite of Valois to the Huguenot, Henri of Navarre (1572), when she stood alone in the chancel and he by the door, although he came later to agree that "Paris is well worth a mass", and attended subsequent ceremonies inside the cathedral; and the marriage of Henrietta Maria by proxy to Charles I of England (1625).

It has also been subjected to radical maltreatment: the destruction of the rood screen by **Mansart** and **Robert de Cotte** (1699), the replacement of the medieval stained glass by plain glass (18C), the vandalism of the main doorway by Soufflot to make way for an ever more grandiose processional dais (1771). During the Revolution, the statues of the Kings of Judea and Israel were decapitated; the building became a Temple of Reason and then of the Supreme Being. All but the great bell were melted down, and the church interior was used to store forage and food.

On 2 December 1804 the church, decked with hangings and ornaments to mask its dilapidation, received Pope Pius VII for the coronation of the emperor (*see the painting by David in the Louvre*).

Restoration – As a result of **Victor Hugo**'s novel *The Hunchback of Notre-Dame* (1831) and a general popular feeling roused by the Romantic Movement, the July Monarchy ordered in 1841 that the cathedral be restored.

Entrusted to **Viollet-le-Duc** and Lassus, the restoration programme lasted

89

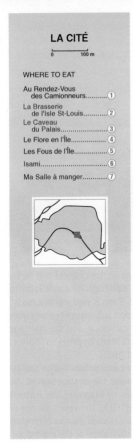

LA CITÉ

0   100 m

WHERE TO EAT

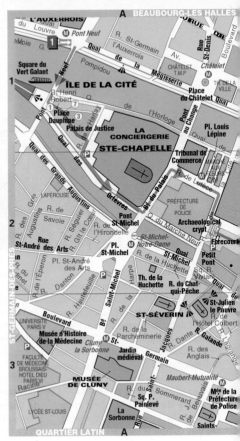

23 years: statuary and glass checked, extensions and appendages removed, the roof and upper sections repaired, doors and chancel restored, a spire added and a sacristy erected.

Today as before – Notre-Dame emerged virtually unscathed from the Commune of 1871 and the Liberation of 1944.

It continues to participate in major historical events, happy or sad: the magnificent *Te Deum* of 26 August 1944 during which an assassination attempt was made on **General de Gaulle**, the moving Requiem Mass in his honour on 12 November 1970, and the magnificat followed by a solemn mass celebrated on the parvis by Pope John-Paul II on 31 May 1980.

Exterior
Place du Parvis

In the Middle Ages, when religious plays were enacted before churches and cathedrals, the porch was used to represent the door to paradise *(paradis)* – hence the evolution of the name parvis. The square was quadrupled in size as cramped surrounding buildings were cleared away by Haussmann in the 19C, so today the cathedral can be seen in all its radiant glory.

A bronze plaque in the centre of the square marks the zero point from which all road distances in France are measured (&see box next page).

The **Crypte archéologique**★ (*Tue–Sun 10am–6pm; 7€; 01 55 42 50 10; www.crypte.paris.fr*) beneath the parvis displays traces of excavated buildings

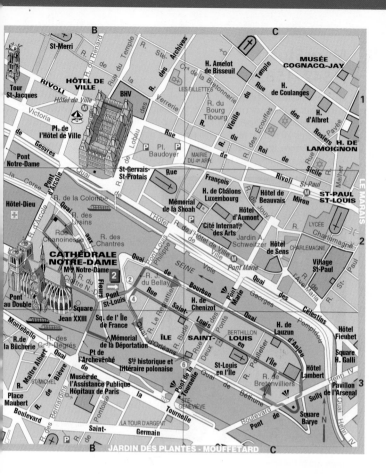

and monuments dating back to the 3C, including two Gallo-Roman rooms heated by hypocaust, fragments of the Late Roman Empire rampart, medieval cellars, and foundations of an orphanage.

The west front

The overall design is majestic and perfectly balanced despite being asymmetrical; the central doorway is the largest of the three, the left gabled. This medieval concept was iplemented to avoid monotony in design and symbolize the lack of perfect order on earth.

In the Middle Ages **the portals** would have looked completely different: brightly coloured statues stood out against a gold background. Designed to be read like a Bible in stone, the scriptures and the legends of the saints are graphically retold for an illiterate congregation. Legend has it that the locksmith who created the magnificent wooden door panels with the wrought-iron strap-hinges sold his soul to Satan. The central doors are 19C replacements.

Portal of the Virgin *(left)* – The fine tympanum has served as prototype to stonemasons throughout the Middle Ages. It shows the *Ark of the Covenant* flanked by three prophets speaking of Mary's destiny and three kings from whom she is descended; above, a depiction of the *Death of the Virgin* with Christ and the Apostles; at the apex, the *Coronation of the Virgin* with Christ handing a sceptre to his mother, crowned by an angel. Small low-relief carving representing the labours of the months and

91

Mary Stuart
(1542–1587)

The magnificent Cathedral of Notre-Dame was the setting for the crowning of Mary Stuart as Queen of France in 1559, following her marriage the previous year to the dauphin. A spectacular event, the coronation should have been the next step for Mary in fulfilling her destiny as queen of four realms, Scotland, France, England and Ireland. However, it was not long before events were to take an unfortunate turn and she was to lose everything.

© ImageState/Tips Images

She was crowned Queen of Scotland at less than a year old; her regents were, before long, keen for her to become betrothed to Henry VIII's son, Edward. However, as Henry became more and more difficult to deal with in his later years, the Scots abandoned the idea, preferring instead an alliance with France. This union was achieved by securing an agreement for her to marry the heir to the French throne, Francis, the son of the French King Henri II.

Five-year-old Mary was sent to France in 1548, rapidly becoming a favourite of the French king, who thought she was a perfect child, even giving her precedence over his own daughters, since she was already a queen in her own right. She soon met the dauphin and they quickly became friends, travelling everywhere together. An intelligent girl, Mary already spoke French and quickly learned Latin, Italian and some Greek. In addition she could sing, dance, play the lute and converse well – all important and necessary accomplishments for a future Queen of France.

She quickly adopted the French spelling of her name and signed documents as "Marie R", also using the French "Stuart" rather than the Scottish "Stewart". Every inch a queen, Mary was tall, beautiful and regal, but unfortunately her reign as Queen of France lasted only till the end of 1560 when Francis died. Mary was obliged to leave, returning to a troubled Scotland.

After two disastrous marriages, she became very unpopular and was dominated by Scottish nobles who eventually forced her to abdicate. She fled to England, where she hoped to seek refuge from her cousin Elizabeth I, but was considered too great a threat. As the granddaughter of Henry VIII's older sister, Margaret, Mary had considerable claims on the English throne; thus she was imprisoned and executed in 1587 at only 44 years of age. Few attending her splendid coronation in Notre-Dame so long ago could have imagined that her seemingly illustrious career would end as such tragic failure.

the signs of the Zodiac fill the sections on either side of the doorway. The statues in the embrasures were added by Viollet-le-Duc and include St Denis attended by two angels, John the Baptist and St Stephen.

Portal of the Last Judgement *(central)* – This sculptural composition of the struggle of Good over Evil is far removed from its original condition: the tympanum was breached by Soufflot in 1771, and Viollet-le-Duc has substantially restored the two lower lintels. Above a depiction of the *Resurrection* is the *Weighing of the Souls* in which the Good are led up to Heaven by angels, the Damned are led by demons to Hell; at the apex, a seated *Christ in Majesty* is flanked by the kneeling Virgin and St John, interceding for the lost souls. The six archivolts represent the celestial court. At the lowest level, Abraham receives the righteous *(left)* and condemned *(right)* symbolizing Heaven and Hell. The figures of the Wise and Foolish Virgins, differentiated by open *(left)* and closed *(right)* doors to paradise, are modern. In the embrasures, Viollet-le-Duc's Apostles stand over medallions representing the Virtues *(upper tier)* and Vices *(lower tier)*.

Portal to St Anne *(south)* – The cathedral's oldest statues fill the two upper levels of the tympanum. Created c. 1165, they pre-date the building by some 60 years and were evidently intended for a narrower door. A rather formal *Virgin in Majesty with the Infant Christ* draws on Romanesque prototypes; she is attended by two angels and the cathedral patrons: Bishop Maurice of Sully *(standing, left)* and Louis VII *(kneeling, right)*. The 12C lintel shows scenes from the Life of the Virgin. The central pier carries a 19C figure of St Marcellus, the 5C Bishop of Paris, who is meant to have delivered the capital from a dragon. Abutting the piers between portals are additional 19C statues *(from left to right)* of St Stephen, the Church, the Synagogue (blindfolded) and St Denis.

Gallery of Kings *(above the portals)* – The 28 Kings of Judea and Israel represent the Tree of Jesse, Christ's forebears. The original figures were destroyed in 1793 by the Revolutionaries who took them for the Kings of France.

Rose window – The central great rose, nearly 10m/32.8ft across, is so perfectly designed that its elements have not moved in more than seven centuries. From outside it provides the standing statue of the Virgin and Child. At the same level stand the figures of Adam *(left)* and Eve *(right)*, against stone masonry separating the window lights. Together, the group (restored by Viollet-le-Duc) portrays Redemption after the Fall from Grace.

Towers – The twin towers soar to a height of 69m/226.4ft, pierced by slender 16m/52.5ft lancets. Emmanuel, the **great bell** in the south tower, weighs 13t; its clapper weighs nearly 500kg/1 102lb. The perfect pitch of its toll (F-sharp) is said to be due to the gold and silver jewellery cast into the molten bronze by *Parisiennes* when the bell was re-struck in the 17C. Steep steps to a platform (◷*varying hours – phone for details; access at the foot of the north tower, 402 steps;* ◷*public holidays;* ✆*8.50€, under-18s free;* ✆*01 53 10 07 00)* in the south tower provide a splendid **view★★★** of the spire and flying buttresses, the Cité and Paris beyond. Note the famous chimeras (carved wild beasts) and large bell above the great gallery.

North side

The street is named after the cloister formerly flanked the north side. The magnificent **Cloister Portal** was built by Jean de Chelles (c. 1250), who applied experience gained from building the Ste-Chapelle (completed 1248) to maximize the amount of light permeating the interior.

The large intricate rose perfectly integrates with the clerestory to form an unexpectedly tall opening (18m/59ft high), slightly larger in diameter (13m/42.6ft). Below, the many-gabled, carved doorway is markedly more ornate than the doors of the west front, installed 30 years before. The three-tiered tympanum illustrates events from the *Life of the Virgin* and

Detail of the central great rose window

© patrickw/Fotolia.com

from the story of Théophile selling his soul to the Devil. The **Red Door**, built by Pierre of Montreuil, was reserved for members of the cathedral chapter. Its tympanum illustrates the Coronation of the Virgin attended by King Louis IX and his queen; the archivolts illustrate the Life of St Marcel. Seven 14C **bas-relief sculptures** inlaid into the foundations of the chancel chapels depict the Death and Assumption of the Virgin.

East end

At the beginning of the 14C, the cathedral's east end was reinforced by a series of flying buttresses to counteract the thrust of the vaulting. Splendid vistas of the east end and the Seine can be enjoyed from the small John XXIII Square. From here can be seen a 13C section of roof that retains the original timberwork, and the 90m/295.3ft-high spire reconstructed by Viollet-le-Duc, who included himself among the decorative copper figures of Evangelists and Apostles!

South side

Beyond the 19C sacristy is the magnificent **St Stephen's** doorway, similar to the cloister door but richer in sculpture. Initiated by Jean of Chelles (1258), and completed by Pierre of Montreuil, it has a remarkable tympanum illustrating the life and stoning of St Stephen, to whom

the former church that pre-dated the cathedral had been dedicated. At the base of the buttresses, eight small 13C low-relief sculptures depict street and university scenes.

Interior

Transitional Gothic – The sheer size (130m/426.5ft long x 48m/157.5ft wide) and soaring height (35m/114.8ft) mark a turning point in the development of Gothic architecture and building techniques on a grand scale. Besides the elevation, the floor plan also breaks new ground: the nave is given double aisles and the chancel a double ambulatory, separated in the middle by transepts that project only slightly from the outer aisles, thereby producing a unified space.

The windows – In the 13C and 14C, the clerestory windows were enlarged to allow extra light into the chapels. Not only was the wall mass reduced and lightened, the gallery was lowered; the weight and thrust of the vault therefore had to be diffused across the aisles and down to solid masonry at gallery level: the problem was ingeniously resolved with the invention of the flying buttress. A section of the 12C elevation can still be seen at the transept crossing. The medieval stained glass was replaced by clear glass inscribed with fleur-de-lis in the 18C and by *grisaille* glass in the

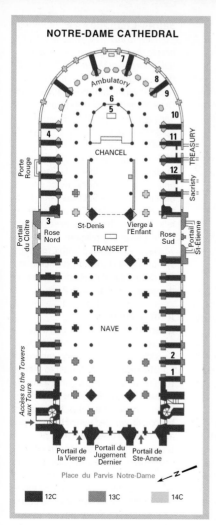

NOTRE-DAME CATHEDRAL

Ambulatory
Chancel
Porte Rouge
Portail du Cloître
Rose Nord
TRANSEPT
St-Denis
Vierge à l'Enfant
Rose Sud
Portail St-Étienne
TREASURY
Sacristy
NAVE
Access to the Towers / aux Tours
Portail de la Vierge
Portail du Jugement Dernier
Portail de Ste-Anne
Place du Parvis Notre-Dame

12C 13C 14C

1. *and* 2. *Mays by Le Brun.*
3. *May by Le Sueur.*
4. *Juigné, Archbishop of Paris, died 1811.*
5. *Pietà by Coustou.*
6. *Recumbant statue of 14C bishop.*
7. *Pierre de Gondi, ancestor of Cardinal de Retz. In one century, four archbishops would come from the Gondi family.*
8. *Darboy, executed as a hostage during the Commune of 1871.*
9. *Mausoleum of the Duke d'Harcourt, by Pigalle.*
10. *Jean Juvénal des Ursins and his wife.*
11. *Mgr Sibour, assassinated, 1857.*
12. *Mgr Affre, killed during the riots of 1848.*

endowed the cathedral with a work of art annually in May. Among the most beautiful are Mays by Le Brun (**1, 2**) and Le Sueur (**3**).

Transept – The **windows**, remarkable for their sheer size and weight, are testimony to the technical skill of the medieval masons. The north rose, which has survived almost intact since the 13C, depicts Old Testament figures around the Virgin; in the south rose, Christ is surrounded by saints and angels. On the southwest pier, a plaque commemorates British citizens lost in WWI, many of whom are buried in France.

19C. The modern glass by Le Chevalier, installed in 1965, returned to medieval manufacturing processes and colours. Massive piers measuring 5m/16.4ft across, support the towers, and the organ (restored in 1992), which boasts the largest number of pipes in France *(concerts on Sundays at 5.45pm).*

Chapels – Notre-Dame is edged with a continuous ring of chapels built between the buttresses in the 13C in response to demand from an increasing number of guilds and noble families. In keeping with a tradition renewed in 1949, the Goldsmith's Guild of Paris

Chancel – In front of the high altar lies Geoffrey Plantagenet, son of Henry II of England (d. 1186). The chancel was redecorated by Robert de Cotte (1708–25). Seventy-eight original stalls remain from the embellishment, as do a Pietà by Guillaume Coustou (**4**), Louis XIII by Coustou and Louis XIV by Coysevox. The only remarkable 14C **low-relief** scenes to survive pertain to the Life of Christ and His Apparitions, restored by Viollet-le-Duc. Tombstones for the bishops of Paris, who are buried in the crypt, line the ambulatory (**5–11**).

Point Zero

All roads may no longer lead to Rome, but do all roads in France lead to Paris? Point Zero, an eight-pointed bronze star with four stones laid around it to create a circle, appears to suggest that's the case.

The unusual symbol, located discreetly in the cobbles of the place du Parvis in front of the west façade of Notre-Dame Cathedral beside the main entrance, is the point from which all road distances in France are measured. Officially known as Point Zero des Routes de France, a marker was first placed here by the cartographers of the Ancien Régime in 1769, although the current star was not set into the pavement until 1924.

Point Zero also marks the geographic centre of the city. Many believe that visitors who stand at this spot will almost certainly return to Paris.

Treasury

🕐 *Mon–Sat 9.30am–6pm (Sat until 6.30pm), Sun 1.30pm–6.30pm.* ⊛ *4€.* ♿ 𝟁 *01 42 34 56 10.*

The sacristy, built by Viollet-le-Duc, contains the cathedral's treasury of liturgical manuscripts, ornaments and objects, mostly made of gold. Many objects date to the 17C and 18C. The treasury also holds the rings, stoles, copes and crucifixes that have belonged to bishops. The Crown of Thorns, the Holy Nail and a fragment of the True Cross are kept in a specially built reliquary shrine, the latest built in 1862. They are displayed on occasion to the public *(3pm mass every first Friday of the month, every Friday during Lent, and Good Friday 10am–5pm).* The relics of the Passion are guarded by the Knights of the Order of the Holy Sepulchre of Jerusalem.

Sainte-Chapelle★★★

4 boulevard du Palais, on Île de la Cité next to the Palais de Justice. Allow a half-hour to visit the chapel. Don't miss the intricate wooden spire, the fifth created over the centuries. 🕐 *Daily Mar– Oct 9.30am–6pm; Nov–Feb 9am–5pm; open Wed until 9pm May 15–Sept 15.* 🕐 *Mon–Fri 1pm–2pm; 1 Jan, 1 May, 1 and 25 Dec.* ⊛ *8.50€.* ♿ 𝟁 *01 53 40 60 80. http://sainte-chapelle. monuments-nationaux.fr.* 🅿 *Park underground on rue de Lutèce.*

Built in the 13C by **St Louis** (Louis IX) in the centre of Île de la Cité to house holy relics, the Ste-Chapelle comes as close to perfection as any religious edifice anywhere. The chapel is a Gothic marvel, a symphony of stone and stained glass. The deep glow of its windows is one of the great joys of a visit to Paris.

A Bit of History

A sacred shrine – Baudouin, a French nobleman who had been on the Fourth Crusade before becoming Emperor of Constantinople, was forced to pledge the Crown of Thorns against a loan of money from the Venetians.

Unable to meet his debts, he appealed to Louis IX, who redeemed the payment and retrieved the Crown in 1239.

Ultimately, the creation of suitable reliquaries would cost more than twice as much as the construction of the chapel This exceptional building, erected in only 33 months, is attributed to **Pierre of Montreuil** (known also as Pierre of Montereau); it was consecrated in 1248. Consisting of two superimposed chambers, the upper level was used by the sovereign and his court, the lower by his household.

Degradation and Restoration – During the Revolution the reliquary shrine was melted down; some of the relics were saved and are now in Notre-Dame. Between 1802 and 1837 the building was used to archive judiciary papers that were stacked high against the lancet windows; restoration was undertaken by Duban and Lassus (1841–67).

Upper chapel, Sainte-Chapelle

©Jeff Schultes/Dreamstime.com

Exterior

Completed just 80 years after Notre-Dame Cathedral, the Ste-Chapelle is perhaps the apogee of Gothic architecture. Its innovative great windows (15m/49.2ft high) make the walls appear to be built of glass rather than masonry; its vault is not reinforced with great flying buttresses, but rather anchored in place by a sculpted gable and balustrade. This remarkably delicate feat of balance and counter-balance was so perfectly engineered that no crack has appeared in seven centuries.
The spire soars to 75m/246ft.

Interior

In the **lower chapel**, 40 columns, decorated in the 19C, carry the central vault (only 7m/23ft high and 17m/55.8ft wide),

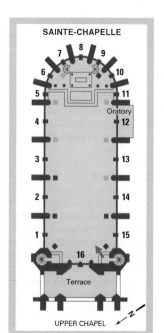

SAINTE-CHAPELLE

Oratory

Terrace

UPPER CHAPEL

1. *Genesis – Adam and Eve – Noah – Jacob (damaged by the storm of December 1999).*

2. *Exodus – Moses and Mount Sinai.*

3. *Exodus – The Law of Moses.*

4. *Deuteronomy – Joshua – Ruth and Boaz.*

5. *Judges – Gideon – Samson.*

6. *Isaiah – The Tree of Jesse.*

7. *St John the Evangelist – Life of the Virgin – The Childhood of Christ.*

8. *Christ's Passion.*

9. *John the Baptist – Daniel.*

10. *Ezekiel.*

11. *Jeremiah – Tobias.*

12. *Judith – Job.*

13. *Esther.*

14. *Kings: Samuel, David, Solomon.*

15. *St Helena and the True Cross – St Louis and the relics of the Passion.*

16. *15C Flamboyant rose window: the Apocalypse.*

Conciergerie along the Seine

©Patricia Grube/Michelin

contained by the external buttresses. The floor is paved with tombstones. A spiral staircase to the right leads to the **upper chapel**, a great bejewelled glass-house. The chamber is encircled by blind arcading, its capitals delicately carved with stylized vegetation; attached to each shaft is a figure of an Apostle holding one of the Church's 12 crosses of consecration – the six original ones *(pink on the plan)* are most expressive (the others are in the Musée Cluny). The painting is modern. Two deep recesses in the third bay were reserved for the king and his family. The oratory was added by Louis XI: a grille enabled him to follow the service unnoticed. The reliquary shrine would have stood at the centre of the apse on a raised platform surmounted by a wooden baldaquin. Of the two twisting staircases enclosed in the open-work turrets, the left one is original.

The **stained glass** is the oldest to survive in Paris. Of the 1 134 scenes represented over a glazed area of 618sq m/ 6 672sq ft, some 720 are original. The king summoned the best master-craftsmen from work recently completed at Chartres (1240) hence their similar treatments: roundel scenes, brilliant use of colour eclipsing simplicity of composition. The principal theme is the celebration of the Passion, as foretold by the Prophets and John the Baptist. The windows should be read from left to right and from bottom to top, with the exception of nos **6**, **7**, **9** and **11**, which read lancet by lancet.

Conciergerie★★

On the Île de la Cité next to the Palais de Justice. Entrance at 4 boulevard du Palais. ⊕*Don't miss the ancient clock on the Tour de l'Horloge (boulevard du Palais). Allow a half-hour for a visit of the Conciergerie.* ⏰*Call or check website for open hours.* 💶*8.50€ (combined ticket with the Ste-Chapelle 12.50€).* 📞*01 53 40 60 80. http://sainte-chapelle.monuments-nationaux.fr.* 🅿*Underground parking can be found on the rue de la Cité.*

The beauty of its medieval architecture conceals the bloody history of the Conciergerie. During the Revolution noblemen and ordinary citizens alike were imprisoned here.

A Bit of History

A noble keeper – The name *Conciergerie* was given to a section of the old palace precinct controlled by the *concierge* or keeper of the king's mansion. It served as a prison from the 14C.

The guillotine's antechamber – At the time of the Revolution, as many as 1 200 men and women were held at once in the Conciergerie; during the Terror the building became the antechamber to the Tribunal, which in nine cases out of 10 meant the guillotine.

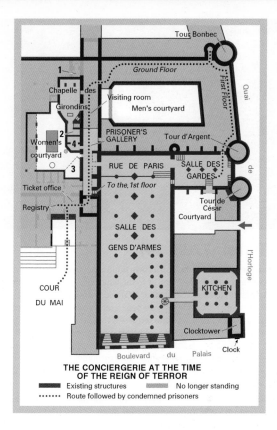

**THE CONCIERGERIE AT THE TIME
OF THE REIGN OF TERROR**

■■■ Existing structures   ▒▒▒ No longer standing
······· Route followed by condemned prisoners

Among those incarcerated here were Queen **Marie-Antoinette**; Madame Élisabeth, sister to Louis XVI; **Madame du Barry**, the favourite of Louis XV; Philippe-Égalité, father of the future King Louis-Philippe; and Revolutionaries **Danton** and **Robespierre**. In all, nearly 2 600 prisoners were guillotined between January 1793 and July 1794.

Exterior

The best **view★** of the exterior is from Mégisserie Quay on the Right Bank, with its four towers reflected in the Seine, which originally flowed right up to their base. This section is the oldest part of the palace built by the Capetian kings. The oldest tower is the crenellated one on the right, Tour Bonbec.

The square **Tour de l'Horloge** has, since 1370, housed the first public clock to be installed in Paris.

Interior
Salle des Gardes

Stout pillars with interesting capitals support the Gothic vaulting in this dark room.

Salle des Gens d'Armes★★ (Hall of the Men-at-Arms)

This magnificent four-aisled Gothic hall covers an area of 1 800sq m/2 153sq yd, on a par with those of the Mont-St-Michel and the Palais des Papes in Avignon. Above used to be the palace's Great Hall and royal apartments. On the first pillar in the central row, the level reached by the Seine in 1910 is marked. The Revolutionary Tribunal sat in this hall from 1793 to 1795.

The four huge fireplaces of the old **kitchens** were used to cook enough meat, to feed between 2 000 and 3 000 mouths, including the royal family.

Interior, Conciergerie

©H. Chajmowicz/Michelin

The Terror (1793–94)

The Conciergerie was to come into its own during the period of "The Terror", or more correctly the Reign of Terror, which took place during the French Revolution between September 1793 and the fall and execution of Robespierre in July 1794. Louis XVI had been executed in January, but among the first to be guillotined during the Terror was the Queen Marie-Antoinette. Subsequently many thousands of people were condemned to death after first being incarcerated in this building. While these figures included a number of aristocrats, there were many others from both the middle and working classes who in one way or another were thought to have transgressed against the notorious Committee for Public Safety.

Leading Revolutionaries feared a counter-revolution and a full restoration of the monarchy. They felt under threat from abroad as many foreign governments, including those of the United Kingdom and Austria, were hostile to the Revolution, fearing the spread of the concept to their own realms. In France there had been many attempts to overthrow the Revolution – in March, a peasant rebellion in the Vendée was viciously suppressed. Two thousand people were drowned in the River Loire at Nantes and hundreds executed by cannon fire at Lyons because it was thought that the guillotine was too slow.

The Committee for Public Safety was set up on 6 April 1793 with nine members, led unofficially by Georges-Jacques Danton. Gradually the supporters of Maximilien Robespierre gained control, and by the summer Danton had been voted off the Committee. Robespierre was voted on during July and for the next year ruled it with an iron fist. Anyone seen to oppose the Committee's work or offend Robespierre himself would be sent to the guillotine. The redoubtable Danton himself fell victim to the paranoia that gripped the Committee, and on 5 April 1794, he too was executed but not before predicting "Robespierre will follow me; I drag down Robespierre."

Although the Committee was apparently unified, this unity began to unravel as members worried that they may be the next to suffer the wrath of Robespierre. If Danton could be removed so easily, then lesser men must be vulnerable. And while the threat from both abroad and at home was beginning to subside, the number of executions was rising. Soon the tyrannical Robespierre was accused of seeking to become king. His colleagues moved against him and took matters into their own hands. Robespierre was sentenced without trial and executed on 28 July 1794 just as Danton had forecast. The Great Terror was finally at an end.

Prison

The Galerie des Prisonniers served as the main axis of the prison, where penniless prisoners slept on the bare ground while the rich paid for their own cell and better food. Prisoners were ushered from the Grande Chambre du Parlement down a spiral staircase hidden in the Bonbec Tower to the council room which on one side served as antechamber *(parloir)* to the men's prison yard (Préau des Hommes) and on the other, opened onto a staircase (**1**) up to the Tribunal.

The condemned crossed through the wicket gate *(guichet)* past the clerk of the court (*greffe* means register office) into the **May Courtyard** and out to the tumbrils.

Chapelle des Girondins

Ground floor.

The chapel was transformed into a collective prison where prisoners heard mass through the grille on the upper storey. From here, visit the cell occupied by Marie-Antoinette, which was converted to an expiatory chapel (**2**) in 1816.

Cour des Femmes

In the centre is a patch of grass and a lonely tree where women prisoners were allowed out of their cells each day. In the corridor known as the **Côté des Douzes** (**3**), prisoners of both sexes could talk through the bars. From here, the 12 inmates selected daily embarked for the guillotine. A door on the right leads to a reconstruction of **Marie-Antoinette's cell** (**4**). The furniture consisted of a cot, a chair and a table. Her letters were always opened and read.

Palais de Justice★

Next to La Conciergerie. Access via la cour du Mai, 4 boulevard du Palais.
🕐*Mon–Fri 8.30am–6pm.* 🕐*Public holidays.* 📞*01 44 32 52 52.* 🚫*Visitors are normally allowed to attend a civil or criminal hearing. General public not admitted to the Galerie des Bustes and Children's Court.*

To balance the power of the Church, the Île de la Cité also accommodated the Law Courts, the pre-eminent seat of the civil and judicial authorities.

King's Palace

The stone buildings erected by the Roman governors for their administrative and military headquarters were requisitioned first by the Merovingian kings, and then by the early Capetian kings, who fortified the palace with a keep and built a chapel in the precincts. Clovis died here.

The dauphin, the future **Charles V**, and regent while his father John the Good was being held in England, installed his Parliament in the palace. In 1358 a mob under **Étienne Marcel** entered the dauphin's apartments and compelled him to witness the bloody slaughter of his counsellors. When the troubles had subsided, Charles V moved out of the palace, preferring to live at the Louvre, at the Hôtel St-Paul or at Vincennes outside Paris.

Judicial Palace

Parliament was the kingdom's supreme court of justice. Originally its members were nominated by the king, until 1522 when **François I** sold the rights for money on condition that the position become hereditary; thus the highest dignitaries in the land (the chancellor, peers of the realm, royal princes) secured their position by right or privilege.

Fires were frequent, damaging the Grande Salle (1618), Ste-Chapelle spire (1630), the Cour des Comptes (Debtors' Court, 1737), and the Gallerie Marchande (1776).

In 1788 Parliament demanded the convocation of the States General, which was not a good idea, because the General Assembly announced its suppression and the Convention sent the members to the guillotine!

The Law Courts

The Revolution overturned the judicial system. New courts were installed in the old buildings, which took the name of Palais de Justice.

Restoration lasted from 1840 to 1914; the building was given its present

Palais de Justice

©H. Chaimowicz/Michelin

façade overlooking place Dauphine and its extension along quai des Orfèvres.

Cour du Mai

The Louis XVI wrought-iron grille is especially fine. The name *cour du Mai* is derived from an old custom by which the clerks of the court – an important corporation – planted in the courtyard a tree from one of the royal forests each year on 1 May.

The Galerie Marchande was once the most animated part of the building, bustling with plaintiffs, lawyers, clerks, court officials, souvenir peddlers and hangers-on.

The ornate Première Chambre Civile de la Cour d'Appel (Chamber of the Civil Court of Appeal) and the Cour de Cassation (Chamber of the Court of Cassation) are decorated with frescoes and tapestries.

Enter the **Salle des Pas-Perdus** (Lobby), formerly the Gothic Grand'Salle of Philip the Fair, twice destroyed, and reconstructed most recently after the Commune of 1871. Notice the monument to the 19C barrister, Berryer, on the right, with the tortoise – maligning the delays in the law.

At the end on the left is the former apartment of Louis IX, used as **Parlia-**

mentary Grand Chamber when Louis XII had it decorated with a fine ceiling, and then by the Revolutionary Tribunal under Fouquier-Tinville (1793–4). It is now the First Civil Court.

ÎLE SAINT-LOUIS★★

Ⓜ*Metro/Transport: Pont Marie (line 7) – Buses: 24, 63, 67, 86, 87, 89. Don't miss the famous ice cream at Maison Berthillon.* 🅿*Underground parking on the Right Bank at rue de l'Hôtel de Ville.*

Peaceful quays and unpretentious Classical architecture make Île St-Louis an attractive residential district right in the heart of Paris.

A Bit of History

Originally there were two islands on which, in the Middle Ages, judicial duels, known as the Judgements of God, were held. Early in the reign of Louis XIII, the contractor Christophe Marie joined the islets, constructed two stone bridges, and developed the land for resale in lots with a regular layout of intersecting streets and a homogenous Classical style of architecture.

Visit (👣*see Walking Tour* ②)

The island's central street is lined with tiny art galleries, quirky gift boutiques and gourmet food shops.

What makes Île St-Louis unique is its atmosphere of old-world charm and provincial calm. Bankers, lawyers and nobles accounted for the first residents, now replaced by writers, artists and lovers of old Paris. Behind massive panelled doors, studded with bosses and nails, lie secluded courtyards that have hardly changed since the 17C.

👣 WALKING TOURS

① ÎLE DE LA CITÉ

Pont Neuf★

Pont Neuf is the oldest of the Paris bridges. It was the first road in Paris to benefit from pavements separating pedestrians and traffic.

Built in two halves between 1578 and 1604, the bridge is on a broken axis. The 12 rounded arches each have a keystone carved with humorous grotesques. In the olden days, it used to be crowded with stallholders, tooth pullers, comic characters such as Tabarin and the Italian Pantaloon, Scarlatini, the all-time charlatan and a host of gawpers and pickpockets.

The original equestrian statue of **Henri IV** was melted down at the Revolution in 1792 and replaced during the Restoration with the present figure, made of bronze.

Square du Vert Galant

Down the steps behind the Henri IV statue, this serene stretch of green lies at its natural ground level, before the land was built up by **Henri III**. From the tip is a fine view of Pont Neuf, the Louvre and the Mint. The square's name derives from the nickname given to Henri IV, alluding to his reputation as an amorous gentleman despite his age.

Place Dauphine★

For a long time the western tip of the island gave way to a muddy marshy area broken by the river currents. In 1314, **Philip the Fair** had a stake erected on one of the mounds of ground. It was there that he ordered the execution by fire of the Grand Master of the **Order of Templars**, **Jacques de Molay**. The king watched him burn from his palace window. The gardens (Jardin du Roi), which extended from the Conciergerie into the river, became the first botanical garden under **Marie de' Medici**.

At the end of the 16C, Henri III decided to reorganize this untidy no man's land: the mud ditches were filled in, a great earth bank was amassed to support the future Pont Neuf, and the south bank was raised by some 6m/19.7ft. In 1607 a triangular square was built, surrounded by a series of houses constructed of brick, white stone and slate to a uniform design. The square was named after the dauphin, in honour of the future Louis XIII. Only a few façades such as no **14** retain their original features.

Quai des Orfèvres

During the 17C and 18C, the properties along the river front were the jewellers' quarter. Strass, inventor of the synthetic diamond, Boehmer and Bassenge who fashioned Marie-Antoinette's celebrated necklace, had their shops in place Dauphine and along the quay. No **36** is today well known as the headquarters of the CID (Police Judiciaire).

Place Louis-Lépine

A colourful **flower market** is held in front of the administrative offices of the Hôtel-Dieu, the police headquarters

Pont Neuf

©H. Chajmowicz/Michelin

103

and the commercial court, which have surrounded the square on three sides since the Second Empire. On Sundays a bird market replaces the flower stalls. First mentioned as early as the 9C, the **Hôtel-Dieu** hospice moved into its present premises between 1864 and 1877 (the old building stood on the opposite end of the Parvis by the statue of Charlemagne).

Ancien quartier du Chapitre

The area extending north of Notre-Dame to the Seine belonged to the cathedral chapter. Enclosed in a wall with four gates, it was populated by the cathedral canons, who each lodged their own students. Although considerably restored, the quarter is the only reminder of what the Cité looked like in the 11C and 12C when **Abelard**, St Bonaventure and St Dominic built up the reputation of the cathedral school that was later to merge with the **Sorbonne** (🖝see LE QUARTIER LATIN).

Rue Chanoinesse was the main thoroughfare of the former chapter. Numbers **24** and **22** are the last two medieval canons' houses; note the stone posts in the courtyard. In **rue de la Colombe** traces of the Lutetian Gallo-Roman wall of Lutetia remain; note the curious tavern at the top of some steps. In laying rue d'Arcole, the chapel of Ste-Marie was razed, where "de-flowered" brides could be married, sealing their vows with a ring made of straw. **Rue des Ursins** is level with the old banks of the Seine and Port St-Landry, Paris' first dock until the 12C when facilities on the Hôtel de Ville foreshore were established. At the end of the narrow street stand the last vestiges of the medieval chapel, St-Aignan, where priests celebrated mass secretly during the Revolution. At the picturesque corner with **rue des Chantres** stands a medieval mansion beyond which there is a fine view of Notre-Dame's skyline.

Quai aux Fleurs affords a **panorama** of St-Gervais and of the tip of the Île St-Louis.

Square Jean-XXIII

Until the beginning of the 19C, the area between Notre-Dame and the tip of the island was crowded with houses, chapels and the Archbishop's Palace. These structures were severely damaged in a riot and later razed to the ground (1831). The square opened as a formal garden with a neo-Gothic fountain, Fontain de la Vierge, in 1844. There's also a music bandstand and small play area for children.

Square de l'Île-de-France

Napoléon III built the Cité's municipal morgue on the upstream tip of the island, attracting until 1910 those with a morbid fascination. Today it's a peaceful park rarely discovered by the crowds at Notre-Dame, the perfect setting for the somber Deportation Memorial.

Mémorial de la Déportation

🕐Closed until May 2015. 📞01 46 33 87 56. www.cheminsdememoire.gouv.fr. A modern crypt accommodates a metal sculpture by Desserprit, funerary urns and the tomb of the Unknown Deportee from Struthof, to commemorate the suffering and loss of life in the Nazi camps.

2 ÎLE SAINT-LOUIS

Pont St-Louis

This modern metal arched bridge (which replaced the original Pont St-Landry in 1970) links the two Parisian islands. Closed to traffic, it's a peaceful place to appreciate the views of Notre-Dame, le Panthéon and the Hôtel de Ville.

Quai de Bourbon

From the picturesque tip of the island with chain-linked stone posts and canted 18C medallions, there is a delightful **view★** of the church of St-Gervais-St-Protais.

A little further on are two magnificent town houses (nos **19** and **15**) that once belonged to Parliamentarians. At no **19** the sculptress **Camille Claudel** had her studio (ground floor) between 1899 and 1913.

St Louis (1214–1270)

Île St-Louis was named after King Louis IX, the only French king to be made a saint. A member of the House of Capet, Louis ascended the throne in 1226 aged 12. At that time France was the foremost Christian country in Europe. It had the largest army and had, in Louis, the model Christian King, benevolent, devout and brave. He put an end to the Albigensian Crusade in 1229 and took part in two further crusades to the Middle East, the Seventh in 1248 and the Eighth in 1270. After some initial success, both ended in failure, but his reputation was untarnished. He died in Tunis during the Eighth Crusade, probably from dysentery, and by this time his reputation was such that Pope Boniface VIII canonized him in 1297.

Quai d'Anjou

At no **29**, in a former wine cellar, Ford Madox Ford established his journal *The Transatlantic Review* in collaboration with John Quinn, Ezra Pound and **James Joyce**.

The Marquise de Lambert, hostess of a famous literary salon, lived at no **27** (Hôtel de Nevers). The famous painter, sculptor, caricaturist and political satirist **Honoré Daumier** lived at no **9** between 1846 and 1863.

Hôtel de Lauzun

No 17 (⊶ Closed to the public).

The mansion was erected in 1657 by Le Vau for Gruyn, a military supplier who was imprisoned shortly afterwards for corruption. It belonged for only three years to the Duke of Lauzun, who nevertheless left it his name.

The poet Théophile Gautier lived there during the 1840s when he founded his Club des Hachischins, experimenting first with Baudelaire and later with Rilke, Sickert and Wagner. The house now belongs to the City of Paris.

Square Barye

This small garden at the tip of the island is the last trace of the terraced estate of a house that once belonged to the financier Bretonvilliers.

Pont de Sully

This bridge (1876) on the tip of Île St-Louis has a good **view**★ of Notre-Dame, the Cité and Île St-Louis.

In the 17C there was a bathing beach here that was popular with the Court and the aristocracy.

Hôtel Lambert★

No 2.

The mansion of President Lambert de Thorigny, known as Lambert the Rich, was built in 1640 by Le Vau and decorated by Le Sueur and Le Brun.

Église St-Louis-en-l'Île★

No 19 bis, rue St-Louis-en-l'Île. ◷*Mon–Sat 9.30am–7.30pm, Sun 9am–7pm.* ◷*Closed 1pm–2pm.* ✆*01 46 34 11 60.*

The church is marked outside by an unusual iron clock and its original pierced spire. Designed by Le Vau, who lived on the island, it was built 1664–1726. It is dedicated to King Louis IX, the only French king to be sainted.

The ornate interior, in the Jesuit style, is highly decorated: woodwork, gilding and marble of the Grand Siècle (17C), statuettes and enamels. The statues of Sainte Geneviève and Marie were spared during the Revolution when they represented Liberty and Equality.

Hôtel de Chenizot

No 51.

A very fine doorway surmounted by a faun mask and a majestic balcony mark this house which, in the middle of the 19C, accommodated the archbishop.

Quai d'Orléans

There is a splendid **view**★★ of the east end of Notre-Dame and the Left Bank.

Les Quais

The quays of Paris line the Seine River: Quays Henri IV, Célestins, Tournelle, Hôtel de Ville, Mégisserie, Grands-Augustins and Orfèvres – the list goes on. From one river bank to the other, between the bridges, from island to island, these wharves define the heart of Paris, with the best views and some of the best places to stroll in the city. Some are motorways, others are home to the bouquiniste stands. And from the month of May, they're prime locations for picnics, sunbathing, and the summertime Paris Plages. No visit to Paris would be complete without discovering the quays.

 WALKING TOURS

1 PONT MARIE–QUAI SAINT-MICHEL

▷ Start from Métro Pont Marie, on the Right Bank. Allow 1 hour. Cross the Pont Marie.

Pont Marie★

This bridge was built by Christophe Marie in 1635 and rebuilt in 1670. Not one crack has appeared since then, even though it's the oldest bridge in Paris after the Pont Neuf. Its simple structure also makes it one of the prettiest bridges in Paris.

On each side of the bridge are superb views of the façades of the Hôtels Particuliers on the quai de Bourbon (on your right) and the quai d'Anjou.

Quai de la Tournelle

Just before the Pont de l'Archevêché (1828), a line of old houses offers a splendid view★★★ of Notre-Dame from the bridge. Opposite Île St-Louis, the **Pont de la Tournelle** boasts a striking statue of Sainte Geneviève, the patron saint of Paris, by Landowski. Number 15, opposite the bridge, is the very old Tour d'Argent restaurant where Henri IV is said to have first

Info:
Paris Office du Tourisme, 25 rue des Pyramides. ℘08 92 68 30 00 (0.34€ per min). http://en.parisinfo.com.

▷ **Location:** Riverside quays surrounding the Île de la Cité and Île St-Louis.
M Metro/Transport: Cité, Châtelet, Hôtel de Ville, Pont Marie, Sully Morland, Maubert-Mutualité, St-Michel-Notre Dame.

P **Parking:** Underground parking can be found around the Hôtel de Ville.

Don't Miss: The imposing façade of the Hôtel de Ville and the Gothic architecture of St-Germain l'Auxerrois.

Timing: Allow three hours to do all three walks.

Kids: There's a carrousel on the square at the Hôtel de Ville and some play equipment in the square Réné Vivaldi.

used the fork, brought to France by his mother-in-law, Catherine de'Medici.

Quai de Montebello

In the Middle Ages, wood for building and heating was floated on rafts down to Paris and stored at the Port-aux-Bûches between the Petit Pont and the **Pont au Double**.

Square René Viviani

The small church garden contains one of the oldest trees in Paris, a Robinia or false acacia, planted in 1601. The **view★★★** is remarkable: the church of St-Julien itself stands out behind a curtain of trees; **rue St-Julien-le-Pauvre** bustles with life beneath a picturesque jumble of roofs; the Île de la Cité; and finally, above all, Notre-Dame is seen from its best angle in this square.

Quai St-Michel

No stroll along the Seine would be complete without a quick scan of the *bouquinistes,* the green stalls of the sellers of used books – an integral part of the Paris scene. The **view** of Notre-Dame across the river is particularly fine from here, while the narrow **rue du Chat Qui Pêche** on the left demonstrates the neighbourhood's medieval dimensions.

② QUAI DES CÉLESTINS– QUAI DE GESVRES

▶ Start at Métro Sully Morland. Allow 1 hour.

When exiting the metro, before joining the quai des Célestins, take a small detour to visit the Bibliothèque de l'Arsenal (on the square), a library in the heart of the old Arsenal district of Paris, whose history is intertwined with that of the quai des Célestins.

Quartier de l'Arsenal

In the Middle Ages, the quai des Célestins was part of the lands bordering the Seine that belonged to the Célestins Monastery. In 1512, the monks (who gave their name to the Republican Guard barracks on the boulevard Henri IV that remains to this day) had to give up their lands for what would become the municipal arsenal; under François I it became a royal arsenal until the time of Louis XIV, who, conscious of the risk of explosions, moved the manufacturing of gunpowder and cannons to the Left Bank.

Bibliothèque de l'Arsenal – The arsenal was the residence of the Duke de Sully, since he was the Grand Master of Artillery. Henri IV also built a residence there because he liked the neighbourhood so much. The boulevard and a small street still bear their names.

The nature of the district changed in the 18C: the Marquis d'Argenson, a scholar, started a collection of books that was continued by the Count d'Artois and then enriched, under the French Revolution, by the archives of the Bastille and diverse collections. It grew so large that the Arsenal became the national library in 1797.

It's possible to visit the manuscript room, the 18C music room, the bedroom and offices La Meilleraye (17C paintings).

Caserne des Célestins – *Entrance at 12 bd Henri IV.* Built in 1892, the barracks are part of the new neighbourhood housing the calvary and the Republican Guard. If you are fortunate, you might see the horseback guards on their way to the Bois de Vincennes.

Pavillon de l'Arsenal – *21 bd Morland.* ♿ ⏱ *Tue–Sat 10.30am–6.30pm, Sun 11am–7pm.* ☞ *Free entry.* ☎ *01 42 76 33 97. www.pavillon-arsenal.com.* Built in 1878, this structure in metal and glass is typical of the architecture at the end of the 19C. Today it's an exhibition space on Parisian architecture and urbanism from the time of the fortified city walls to today's contemporary creations (Bercy, Javel, La Villette and East Paris districts). There's a superb scale model of the city of Paris.

On the square outside you'll see the **statue of Arthur Rimbaud**, *Homme aux semelles devant,* which refers to what the poet Verlain wrote about Rimbaud, "The man with the wind in his heels".

Quai des Célestins

At no 2 bis of the quai des Célestins *(on the right)* is the **Hôtel Fieubet** (currently housing the École Massillon), richly decorated with cariatides, satyrs, fauns, and garlands of fruits and flowers.

At the top of the rue des Jardins-St-Paul rises the **Église St-Paul-St-Louis★★**; past the square Marie-Trintignant, you will enjoy a lovely view of the **Hôtel de Sens★** *(*☞ *see Le MARAIS).* The **Pont Marie★**, on your left, allows you to return to the Ile-St-Louis *(*☞*see Walk* ①*).* The green boxes of the *bouquinistes* overlook the Seine from the pavements. Continuing up the Seine, on the right of the quay, you'll see the gardens of the **Hôtel d'Aumont** and the Cité Internationale des Arts. When you reach the **Pont Marie**, the quai des Célestins turns into the quai de l'Hôtel de Ville. The **Pont Louis Philippe**, reconstructed

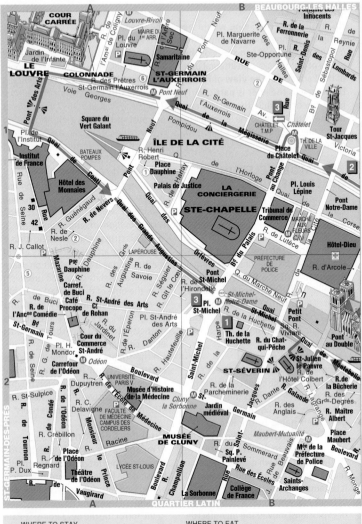

WHERE TO STAY		WHERE TO EAT	
Hôtel de Nesle	②	Au Rendez-Vous des Camionneurs	①
Hôtel Place du Louvre	⑥	Au Vieux Comptoir	②

under Napoléon III between 1860 and 1861, connects the Right Bank to the quai des Fleurs (on the Île de la Cité), just at the tip of the Île St Louis.

Église Saint-Gervais-Saint-Protais★

This edifice is constructed on a small hill, a fact that explains the steps leading up to it along the entrance and the rue François Miron. Since the 6C, it was a basilica dedicated to the saints Gervais and Protais, two brothers, Roman officers martyred under Néron. The bulk of the building, in Flamboyant Gothic style, was finished in 1657. The imposing Classical façade, the first in Paris (1616–21), attributed to Clément Métezeau, offers three styles of columns: Doric, Ionic and Corinthian. The elm planted on the square was, according to the medieval custom, a place of town meetings, pub-

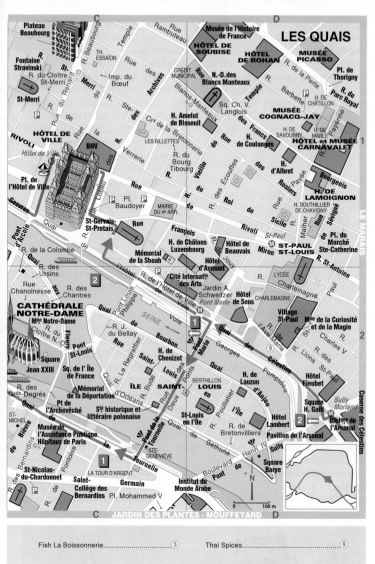

LES QUAIS

lic justice, job recruitment and a place to rendez-vous, . The chevet of the church is apparent from the rue des Barres; at **15** is a pretty gallery of the former cemetery.

From the original Flamboyant Gothic construction, the vaulting, the 16C stained glass and the woodens stalls carved with symbols representing different trades in the 16C and 17C remain intact. The organ, built in 1601 and restored in the 18C, is the oldest in Paris. It was maintained from 1656 to 1826 by eight generations of the Couperin family, a dynasty of organists. The front of the altar in the third chapel has a low-relief sculpture in stone representing the death of the Virgin (13C). To the left of the transept is a fine painting on wood from the Flemish School (16C) representing scenes from the Passion of Christ. On the left pillar in the transept is a stone statue of a Gothic Virgin and Child. In the Chapelle de la Vierge, a remarkable flamboyant keystone measuring 2.5m/8.2ft in diametre, juts out 1.5m/5ft. ⊕The church is continuously upgrading its clear stained glass for modern stained-glass windows designed by Sylvie Gaudin and Claude Courageux: *Moïse et Élie* in the north transept, and *La Jérusalem céleste* above the organ (2006).

Hôtel de Ville★

The city hall was entirely rebuilt from 1874 to 1882, following the fire during the fall of the Paris Commune in 1871. It was erected in the neo-Renaissance style by Ballu and Deperthes, its façades adorned with 146 statues of illustrious people and French towns.

A Bit of History

Maison aux Piliers – Paris was administered by a representative of the king until the 13C when municipal government was introduced, monopolized by the powerful watermen's guild that controlled the Seine. The municipal assembly, headed by a merchant provost (Étienne Marcel) and four aldermen, was based at the Pillared House on place de Grève (⊖*see below*) from 1357.

The Hôtel de Ville – Under François I, the dilapidated Pillared House was replaced by a mansion designed by Domenico Bernabei. The first stone was laid in 1533 but not finished until the early 17C. The central section of the present façade reproduces the original structure.

July 1789 – After the fall of the Bastille, the rioters marched on to the town hall for arms. Throughout the Revolution the town hall was controlled by the Commune. On 17 July 1789, Louis XVI appeared in the hall to kiss the newly adopted tricolour cockade. Between red and blue, the city colours since the provostship of Étienne Marcel in the 14C, La Fayette introduced the royal white.

The Second Republic – In 1848, when Louis-Philippe was dismissed, it was in the Hôtel de Ville that the provisional government was set up, and from there that the Second Republic was proclaimed on 24 February 1848.

The Second Empire and Commune of 1871 – Louis Napoléon proclaimed himself emperor in 1851 and charged his Prefect of the Seine, Baron Haussmann, with replanning the area around the Hôtel de Ville. He razed the adjoining streets, enlarged the square and built the two barracks in rue de Lobau.

On 4 September 1870, after the defeat of the French Army at the Battle of Sedan, Gambetta, Jules Favre and Jules Ferry proclaimed the Third Republic from the Hôtel de Ville and instituted a National Defence Government. The capitulation of Paris on 28 January 1871, however, roused the citizens to revolt against the government, installing in its place the Paris Commune. In May during its

Hôtel de Ville

©H. Chajmowicz/Michelin

final overthrow, the Hôtel de Ville, the Tuileries and several other buildings were set on fire by the Federalists. **25 August 1944** – It was from here that General de Gaulle made his famous speech "Paris! Paris outragé! Paris brisé! Paris martyrisé! mais Paris libéré! libéré par lui-même! libéré par son peuple avec le concours des armées de la France…" Since 1977, the Hôtel de Ville has been Paris' official reception and city government building.

Bazar de l'Hôtel de Ville

This store was founded in 1856 by Xavier Ruel, a street pedlar who had realized the commercial value of the site.

Place de l'Hôtel de Ville

Place de Grève, as it was known until 1830 as the Seine foreshore or *grève*, became a meeting place for those out of work, hence the expression *faire la grève*, meaning not working or on strike. During the Ancien Régime, it was the site where *bourgeois* and commoners were hanged and where gentlemen were beheaded by the axe or the sword; witches and heretics were burned at the stake; murderers were condemned to the wheel and punishment for treason consisted of being drawn and quartered.

Pont d'Arcole

Constructed in 1828 to connect the place de la Grève, today known as the place de l'Hôtel de Ville, to the Île de la Cité, this bridge, made entirely of iron, bears the name of a young man who was heroically killed during the Revolution of 1830.

Pont Notre-Dame

This bridge was the Great Bridge in Roman times. Burned down by the Normans and rebuilt on piles in 1413, it was the first to be given an official name; the houses built on it were the first to be numbered in Paris. It fell down in Louis XII's reign (1499), but was rebuilt and lined with houses with richly decorated façades, since it was on the royal route of solemn entries into Paris.

Pont au Change

The Money Changers' Bridge was established in the 9C by Charles the Bald. Louis VII instituted a money exchange here in 1141, where all foreigners and visitors to Paris bartered for the best rate of exchange. The present bridge dates from 1860.

3 CHÂTELET–SAINT-MICHEL

Place du Châtelet

The area gets its name from the Grand Châtelet, a large fortress that guarded the northern entrance into the city, over the Pont au Change. The fort in turn accommodated the city notaries, surrounded by the halls of powerful guilds (butchers, sausage makers, skinners and tanners). The Châtelet or **Palm Fountain** (1806–07) commemorates Napoléon's victories; the base was decorated with sphinxes in 1858.
The two theatres on either side were built by the architect Davioud in 1862.

Tour St-Jacques★

Fri–Sun 10am–5pm. Group visits only (online or telephone bookings). 01 83 96 15 05. www.parisinfo.com.
The tower is the former belfry of the church of St-Jacques-la-Boucherie, built in the 16C and one of the starting points for pilgrims journeying up rue St-Jacques and on to Santiago de Compostela in Spain. The church was pulled down in 1802 and the tower converted to a weather station.

Quai de la Mégisserie

This section of the embankment gets its name from the stinking public slaughterhouse (*mégisserie* meaning tawing) that lined the river until the Revolution. Now there are rows of garden and pet shops. An attractive **view★★** extends over the Law Courts, Conciergerie, and the old houses across the river.

La Samaritaine

Closed to the public.
This former department store overlooking the Pont Neuf is being converted into private residences.

Église St-Germain L'Auxerrois★★

In what is now place du Louvre, the Roman Labienus pitched his camp when he crushed the Parisii in 52 BC, as did the Normans when they besieged Paris in 885. Until the Second Empire, fine mansions stood between the Louvre and the church.

This church, named after St Germanus, Bishop of Auxerre in the 5C, spans five centuries of architectural development from the Romanesque (belfry) via High Gothic (chancel) and Flamboyant (porch and nave) to the Renaissance (doorway). Substantial restoration in the hands of Baltard and Lassus (1838–55) emphasized its composite nature further.

In the 14C when the Valois moved into the Louvre, St-Germain became the king's parish church. On the night of 24 August 1572, the bells rang for matins giving the signal for the **St Bartholomew's Day Massacre**, when thousands of Huguenots, invited to celebrate the marriage of Henri of Navarre to his cousin, Marguerite of Valois, were slaughtered according to a plan hatched by the Cardinal Duke of Guise, Catherine de' Medici, Charles IX and the future Henri III.

Many poets (Jodelle, Malherbe), painters (Coypel, Boucher, Nattier, Chardin, Van Loo), sculptors (Coysevox, the two Coustous), and architects (Le Vau, Robert de Cotte, Gabriel the Elder, Soufflot) are buried in the church.

On the exterior, the **porch** is the building's most original feature, dating between 1435 and 1439. The column-statues are modern. The outermost, lowest bays accommodate small chambers, covered with slate, in which the chapter placed the church archives and treasure. The three middle bays have multi-ribbed Flamboyant vaults, flanked by a plain Gothic bay. The most interesting, the central doorway is 13C. The figure in the right embrasure represents Sainte Geneviève holding a candle that a small devil tries to snuff out, while an angel nearby stands ready with a taper to rekindle it.

Inside, the restored 18C organ comes from the Ste-Chapelle. The **churchwarden's pew**, dating from 1684, is thought to have been used by successive kings and their families. In the fourth chapel is a fine early 16C Flemish **altarpiece**.

The **stained glass** in the transept and the two rose windows date from the 16C. The **chancel** is surrounded by an 18C grille before which stand 15C polychrome statues of St Germanus and St Vincent. The **Chapel of the Holy Sacrament** (on the right of the entrance) contains a 14C polychrome stone statue of the Virgin.

Passerelle des Arts

This bridge is the country's first cast-iron bridge. Reserved for pedestrians only since it was built in 1803, it's a pleasant place to stroll or to enjoy the **views★★★** from the wooden benches.

Quai de Conti A1

This quay runs along the Institut de France and La Monnaie (the Mint) on one side (& see SAINT-GERMAIN-DES-PRÉS), and the bouquinistes on the other, before ending at the Pont Neuf.

Quai des Grands-Augustins

Built in 1313 under Philippe le Bel, this quay is the oldest in Paris. It was named in 1670 after the convent of the Grands-Augustins, monks of Italian origins who were given the lands along the Seine by Saint Louis. Under the Revolution, it was here that the first paper bank notes were printed, called assignats. Two mansions on the quay date to the 17C: the restaurant Lapérouse at no 51 and the ancient Hôtel Feydeau-Montholon at no 35.

Place Saint-Michel

This place is a popular meeting spot for Parisians. The fountain by Davioud and the square date back to the 19C (& see Le QUARTIER LATIN). In August 1944, there was fierce fighting between the students of the Resistance and the Germans.

The Louvre★★★

For eight centuries the Louvre was the seat of kings and emperors. Constant alterations by successive rulers transformed it into a vast royal palace. Today it is famous as a major museum, with one of the richest collections of art and antiquities in the world that attracts some 10 million visitors a year.

A BIT OF HISTORY
The Buildings

Philippe Auguste (1180–1223) lived in the Palais de la Cité. In 1190 he had the Louvre fortress built on the north bank of the Seine, at the weakest point in his capital's defences against its English neighbours. This fortress was located on the southwest quarter of the present Cour Carrée. **Philip the Fair** (1285–1314) installed his arsenal and royal treasury in the Louvre, where they were to remain for the next four centuries.

Charles V (1364–80) transformed the old fortress into a comfortable residence, without changing its dimensions. He installed his famous **library** of 973 books, the largest in the kingdom. A miniature in the Duke of Berry's *Very Rich Hours* depicts an attractive Louvre, surrounded by new ramparts, its military career at an end. After Charles V, the Louvre was not to be inhabited by royalty for the next century and a half.

François I (1515–47) lived mainly in the Loire Valley or the Marais. In 1528, in desperate need of money, he prepared to demand contributions from the Parisian population. To soften them up, he announced his intention to take up residence in the Louvre. Rebuilding began: the keep, a bulky form that cast a shadow over the courtyard, was razed, and the advance defences were demolished; however, orders for a new palace for the King of France to be built on the foundations of the old fortress were not given to **Pierre Lescot** until 1546. Lescot's designs, in keeping with the style of the Italian Renaissance, which had found such favour on the banks of the Loire, were new to Paris. By 1547, at

🛈 **Info:** Paris Office du Tourisme, 25 rue des Pyramides. ✆08 92 68 30 00 (0.34€ per min). http://en.parisinfo.com. The Louvre,

🞂 **Location:** The Louvre stretches out along the centre of the Right Bank between the Seine and the rue de Rivoli.
For access, &see p118.

Ⓜ **Metro/Transport:** Palais Royal – Musée du Louvre (lines 1 and 7). Buses 21, 24, 27, 39, 48, 68, 69, 72, 81 or 95.

🅿 **Parking:** Underground parking along the rue de l'Amiral de Coligny.
&*See also Access p118.*

⊛ **Don't Miss:** The Greek and Egyptian Antiquities and the Italian paintings.

🕓 **Timing:** Allow a full day for an overview. If your time is limited, take the guided tour *(1hr30min)* that highlights the musem's most famous works.

the death of the king, construction was barely visible above ground level.

Henri II (1547–59) took up residence in the Louvre and retained Lescot as chief architect. The old great hall was transformed into the **Salle des Caryatides**; on the first floor, the Salle des Cent-Suisses, reserved for the Palace Guard, preceded the royal suite in the south wing (that of the queen was on the ground floor). The coffered vaulting over the Henri-II-style staircase leading to the two rooms was carved by Jean Goujon.

Catherine de' Medici (1519–89) withdrew to the Hôtel des Tournelles, her residence in the Marais, after the death of her husband Henri II. Once declared regent, she decided to take up residence in the Louvre, on the floor since known as the Logis des Reines (Queens' Lodg-

PRACTICAL INFORMATION

OPENING TIMES
&Open year-round daily 9am–6pm (Wed and Fri until 9.45pm). Closed 1 May, 14 Jul, 25 Dec.

ADMISSION CHARGES
Purchase tickets at the ticket booths *(payment in euros only or by credit card)* or automatic machines *(credit card only)* in the Hall Napoléon: permanent collection ⊜12€ *(under 18 years as well Europeans 18-25 years free; i.d. required); no charge the 1st Sun of the month Mar–Oct*; temporary exhibits ⊜11€. Tickets are valid all day long, even if you leave the museum. Ticket sales until 5.15pm (until 9.15pm Wed and Fri). Advance ticket purchase online (**FNAC** ☎08 92 68 46 94 (0.34€ per min), www.fnactickets. com, **Ticketnet** www.ticketweb.com and **TicketWeb** www.ticketmaster.fr) provide access with no waiting in line.

PASSES AND DISCOUNTS
Paris Museum Pass gives access to over 60 museums and monuments in Paris, with no waiting in line: valid 2 days 12€, 4 days 56€, 6 days 69€. Purchase it under the Pyramid, online (www.parismuseumpass.com), in metro stations or in Paris tourist offices. **Louvre Jeunes Pass Card** (valid one year; 18-26 years 15€, 26-29 years 35€) and **Adhérent Pass Card** (valid one year; 80€) allow unlimited access to permanent collections and temporary exhibits, cultural activities reserved for museum members, discounts on events and guided tours. For details ☎01 40 20 53 34 or www. amisdulouvre.fr.

SELF-GUIDED TOURS
Louvre Nintendo 3DS (5€) contain 700 comments and interactive floor plan in English. **Louvre audioguide for iPhone and Android** in English is available on App Store or Google Play (1.79€ to download in the Hall Napoléon on Louvre's Wi-Fi).

GUIDED TOURS
Guided tours are available in English. **Introductory tours** of the Louvre's most famous masterpieces *(1hr 30min)* daily at 11.15am and 2pm (except 1st Sun of month). Buy tickets on the same day as your visit at the booth marked **"Accueil des groupes"** under the Pyramid, ☎*01 40 20 52 63;* ⊜*12€ (museum entrance fee not included).* In many rooms, explanatory texts in several languages are placed for visitors' use in racks near the door.

ACCESS
The main entrance is via the **Pyramid**. Direct access to the **Carrousel du Louvre** shopping mall is possible via the **Palais Royal Musée du Louvre** metro station. Entrance at 99 rue de Rivoli is reserved for disabled visitors.

PARKING
The Carrousel-Louvre car park (open daily 7am–11pm) is accessed via the underground passage avenue du Général-Lemonnier, then enter the shopping mall through the old Charles V fortifications. Two public parking lots *(1 rue de Marengo and 6 rue de l'Amiral de Coligny)*, a 5min walk from Carrousel du Louvre, are open daily 24/7. Q-Park *(1 av. du Général-Lemonnier)* underground parking with direct access to Carrousel du Louvre is open daily 7am-11pm.

HALL NAPOLÉON
Under renovation until the second half of 2017. In this reception hall, under the Pyramid, visitors buy tickets, rent audioguides, get a museum floor plan and pay for a guided tour. Here also are the Le Café Grand Louvre, group facilities and an auditorium. From here you are immediately oriented to one of three wings of the museum: Denon, Richelieu or Sully *(&see collections opposite).*

INFORMATION

General information can be obtained by calling the following:

☎01 40 20 51 51 *(answering machine);* ☎01 40 20 53 17 *to speak to someone at the desk (six languages)* or going online to www.louvre.fr; interactive floor plans in English can also be found on www.louvre.fr/plan.

Video screens in the hall provide information about events on a daily basis in the museum.

GETTING AROUND

The collections are displayed in three wings: **Denon**, **Richelieu** and **Sully**. Each wing occupies four floors: –1 = Lower ground floor *(entresol)*; 0 = Ground floor *(rez-de-chaussée)*; 1 = 1st floor *(1er étage)*; 2 = 2nd floor *(2e étage)*. The maze can be incredibly confusing, so be sure to pick up a floor plan (available in English) at the information desk before entering the galleries.

It's best to check www.louvre.fr/en/hours-admission/schedule-room-closures to know which rooms may be currently closed for renovation, special events or loans of artworks.

SULLY WING

+ The model room Medieval Louvre: *Entresol.*
+ Near East Antiquities (including Antique Iran) *Ground floor.*
+ Pharaonic Egypt *Ground floor.*
+ Greek Antiquities *Ground floor.*
+ Rococco, Neoclassical, Louis XIV and Regency *1st floor.*
+ Pharaonic Egypt *1st floor.*
+ Greek ceramics *1st floor.*
+ Terra-cotta *1st floor.*
+ Bronze and precious objects *1st floor.*
+ Decorative Arts *1st floor.*
+ French paintings (14-18C) *2nd floor.*

DENON WING

+ Pre-classical Greece *Entresol.*
+ Coptic Egypt: *Entresol.*
+ East Mediterranean *Entresol.*
+ Islamic Art (7-19C): *Entresol.*
+ Italian sculpture (11-15C): *Entresol.*
+ North European sculpture (12-16C) Egypt: *Entresol.*
+ Spanish sculpture (11-15C) *Entresol.*
+ Etruscan and Roman Antiquities: *Ground floor.*
+ Jewellery collection *1st floor.*
+ Winged Victory of Samothrace *1st floor (Daru staircase).*
+ Italian paintings (13-18C) *1st floor.*
+ Spanish paintings *1st floor.*
+ Arts of Africa, Asia, Oceania and the Americas *1st floor.*
+ Large-format French paintings (19C) *1st floor.*

RICHELIEU WING

+ French sculpture (Cour Marly and Cour Puget): *Entresol.*
+ French sculpture (5-19C) *Ground floor.*
+ Near Eastern Antiquities (Mesopotamia) *Ground floor.*
+ Decorative Arts *1st floor.*
+ Napoléon III apartments *1st floor.*
+ July Monarchy *1st floor.*
+ Bourbon Restoration *1st floor.*
+ Middle Ages *1st floor.*
+ Renaissance *1st floor.*
+ 17C *1st floor.*
+ Germany (15-16C) *2nd floor.*
+ Netherlands (15-16C) *2nd floor.*
+ Flanders (17C) *2nd floor.*
+ German paintings (18-19C) *2nd floor.*
+ Holland (17C) *2nd floor.*

ing), but she was not at all happy living in the middle of Lescot's building site. In 1564 she ordered **Philibert Delorme** to build her a residence of her own on the site known as Les Tuileries, in which she would have greater freedom of movement.

Between the two palaces, the Queen Mother planned to have a covered passage built to enable people to walk the 500m/547yd unnoticed, under shelter from inclement weather. The connecting galleries – the **Petite Galerie** and the **Galerie du Bord de l'Eau** (or Grande Galerie), along the banks of the Seine – were duly begun, but work was brought to a halt by the Wars of Religion. The old Louvre was to keep its two Gothic and two Renaissance wings until the reign of Louis XIV.

Henri IV (1589–1610) continued work on his arrival in Paris in 1594. **Louis Métezeau** added an upper floor to the Galerie du Bord de l'Eau; **Jacques II Androuet Du Cerceau** completed the Petite Galerie and built the **Pavillon de Flore**, with another gallery leading off at right angles to link it with the Tuileries Palace, while seeing to the interior decoration of the Tuileries. The scale of construction on the Louvre site reflected the high status that the monarchy was once again enjoying at this time.

Louis XIII (1610–43) enjoyed living at the Louvre, but the Court endured very cramped conditions. Urged by Richelieu, Louis undertook to enlarge the Louvre

Statue of Henry IV

© S. Sauvignier/MICHELIN

fourfold. Lemercier built the Clock Pavilion, and the northwest corner of the courtyard, a Classical statement in response to Lescot's design. The Royal Mint and the Royal Press were accommodated in the Grande Galerie.

After the death of Louis XIII, Anne of Austria moved to the Palais-Royal with the under-age Louis. Nine years later, they moved to the Louvre, having found the Palais-Royal less than secure, and intimidated by the Fronde uprisings. **Louis XIV** (1643–1715) turned to **Le Vau** to resume work on the extension; he had him build the **Galerie d'Apollon** and requested a worthy façade be designed to close off the Cour Carrée (the **Colonnade**). In 1682, the king moved his court away from the capital to Versailles. Construction was brought to a halt; Le Vau's and Perrault's buildings were left without roofs.

By now, the Louvre was so run down as to prompt talk of pulling it down altogether. After the brief interval of the Regency (1715–22), Louis XV lived at Versailles, whence Louis XVI was brought to Paris on 6 October 1789, briefly occupying the Tuileries until his incarceration at the Temple prison.

The Convention used the theatre, and the Committee of Public Safety installed itself in the royal apartments of the Tuileries, until appropriated by Bonaparte, the Premier Consul.

Napoléon I (1799–1814), while living in the Tuileries, took great interest in the Louvre; his first undertaking was to expel its lodgers. The emperor commissioned the architects **Percier** and **Fontaine** to complete the Cour Carrée, to enlarge the place du Carrousel so that he might review his troops there, and to build the Arc de Triomphe du Carrousel. His fall as emperor stopped work in 1814.

Napoléon III (1852–70), also a resident in the Tuileries, oversaw completion of the Louvre. He entrusted first **Visconti**, then **Lefuel** with the task of closing off the Grande Cour to the north. The latter compensated for the difference in levels of the two arms of the Louvre by rebuilding the **Pavillon de Flore★** in

The Louvre, Centre for the Arts

The city of Paris gradually engulfed the area around the Louvre site.
In the late 17C the abandoned palace apartments were let to a wide variety of people. A bohemian colony of artists set up camp in the galleries, organising living quarters on the mezzanine level; the floor above was used as a passageway (in which the king touched those afflicted with scrofula on five occasions a year). Resident artists included **Coustou**, **Bouchardon**, **Coypel** and **Boucher**; the palace lanterns were tended by **Hubert Robert**'s wife. The space along the Colonnade was divided into apartments; rows of stove chimneys pierced the wonderous façade; shacks were erected in the courtyard; cabarets and taverns accommodated lean-tos along the outside façade.

The royal apartments became occupied by the *Académies* – the Académie Française, having been installed there in 1692, before Louis XIV moved out of the Tuileries. It attracted other academic bodies dedicated to writing and literature, architecture, science, painting and sculpture. The fine arts academy began organising exhibitions of members' work in 1699, an event held around the feast of St Louis (25 August) that was to become a regular feature in the Salon Carré from 1725, and which lasted until the 1848 Revolution. Diderot, followed by Baudelaire, became critics of these salons, at which taste in art during the 18C and early 19C was formulated.

an exaggeratedly grandiose style (note the high relief by **Carpeaux** titled **The Triumph of Flora★**) and by modifying the western section of the Galerie du Bord de l'Eau.

The uprising of the **Paris Commune** (a week of bloodshed in May 1871), which resulted in the proclamation of a new French Republic, the Tuileries Palace was, tragically, burned down; its collections were saved, at the last minute. In 1875 **Lefuel** undertook the restoration of the Louvre, proposing along with others that the Tuileries be rebuilt. In 1882 the Assembly had the ruins removed.

More than a century later, the **Grand Louvre** project was implemented by **François Mitterrand**, from 1981 onwards. Most of the work was finished by 1993, with the opening of the Richelieu wing.

The Collections

François I was the first eminent patron of Italian artists of his day. From his original collection, 12 paintings, including the *Mona Lisa* by Leonardo da Vinci, *La Belle Jardinière* by Raphael and a *Portrait of François I* by Titian, are among the most important works presently in State hands. By the time Louis XIV died, some 2 500 paintings hung in the palaces of the Louvre and Versailles.

The idea of making the collection accessible to the public, as envisaged by Marigny under Louis XVI, was finally realized by the Convention on 10 August 1793 when the doors of the Grande Galerie were opened to visitors.

Napoléon subsequently made the museum's collection the richest in the world by exacting a tribute in works of art from every country he conquered; many of these were reclaimed by the Allies in 1815.

In turn, Louis XVIII, Charles X and Louis-Philippe all further endowed the collections: scarcely had the *Venus of Milo* been rediscovered when she was brought to France by Dumont d'Urville. Departments for Egyptian and Assyrian art were opened.

Gifts, legacies and acquisitions continue to enrich the collections of the Louvre, with more than 460 000 works now catalogued; some 35,000 of those works are on display at any given time.

WALKING TOUR

PALACE EXTERIOR

Start from St-Germain l'Auxerrois church near the metro Ⓜ*Louvre-Rivoli.*

As well as being a museum, the Louvre is a palace steeped in history. A stroll around the outside helps one appreciate the scale of the buildings. The exhibit on the History of the Louvre and the excavations below ground also provides an understanding of the construction's evolution. *⟲An entrance ticket is needed to see the exhibit.*

▶ From rue de Rivoli, head towards the Seine. Opposite rises the immense colonnade of the Louvre Palace.

Cour Carrée

©Daniel Thierry/Photononstop/Tips Images

Colonnade★★

⟳Map p108. In 1662 Louis XIV decided that the palace exterior on the side facing Paris was still not quite grand enough for a royal residence. Three French architects – **Perrault**, **Le Vau** and **D'Orbay** – were commissioned. The true height and Classical harmony of the structure can be admired fully now that moats have been cleared to a depth of 7m/23ft around the rusticated base, in accordance with the original 17C plans.

▶ Head towards the river and turn right. Opposite the Pont des Arts, cross the Jardin de l'Infante to gain access to the Cour Carrée.

Cour Carrée★★★

⟳Map p108. The fine elegant Renaissance façade between the Clock Pavilion and the south wing is the work of **Pierre Lescot**. The graceful, expressive sculpture of the three avant-corps (projecting bay) and the upper storey are by the master **Jean Goujon**, depicting allegorical scenes in high relief, animated figures in niches, friezes of children and garlands. *⟲At night a system of illumination sets off the most impressive remnant of the old Louvre to full effect.*

▶ Leave the courtyard by passing under the Clock Pavilion.

Colonnade

© Miluxian/Dreamstime.com

Pavillion de Flore, along the Seine

© Peter Wrenn/MICHELIN

The **pavillon de l'Horloge** was built in 1640 under Louis XIII by **Lemercier**, who was also responsible for the northwest wing, a replica of Lescot's façade.

▶ Enter the Cour Napoléon and head for the Pyramid.

Pyramid★★

Designed by the architect **I. M. Pei**, the Pyramid, 21m/69ft high and 33m/108.3ft wide at the base, is built of sheet glass supported on a framework of stainless-steel tubes. From directly below the Pyramid, inside the museum reception area, over which it forms a huge see-through vault, visitors can fully appreciate the originality of design and materials used (&see photograph p10).

An **equestrian statue of Louis XIV**, a lead copy of a marble statue by Bernini, that stands on the axis leading to the Champs-Élysées, is slightly at an angle with the old medieval Louvre.

▶ Cross the road that traverses the place du Carrousel, in the direction of the **Jardins des Tuileries**.

Arc de Triomphe du Carrousel★

This delightful pastiche, inspired by the Roman triumphal arch of Septimus Severus, was built from 1806 to 1808. The six bas-relief sculptures commemorate the Napoléonic victories of 1805. On the platform, where Napoléon placed the four horses removed from the basilica of San Marco in Venice (until they were returned there in 1815), **Bosio** sculpted an allegorical goddess, representing the Restoration of the Bourbons, accompanied by Victories and driving a quadriga.

The square takes its name from the lavish equestrian and theatrical tournament held there in honour of the birth of the dauphin in 1662.

From directly beneath the arch, a magnificent **view★★★** unfolds along the axis that runs from the Louvre through the Tuileries, place de la Concorde, the Champs-Élysées and the Arc de Triomphe, as far as the Grande Arche at La Défense.

▶ Descend one of the flights of stairs near the Carrousel, or go through the Pyramid and the main entrance.

Galerie du Carrousel du Louvre

This light-filtered underground gallery acts as a luxury shopping mall leading to museum entry. A Printemps department store opened here in 2014.

▶ Pass Printemps, then through a museum security checkpoint to reach the Hall Napoléon with its information desk and ticket booth.

THE MUSEUM
History of the Louvre★

Decorated with stone reliefs by Jean Goujon, two galleries on each side of the rotunda present the architectural and decorative evolution of the Louvre building during its transformation from fortress to royal residence to museum.

▶ Carry on from the rotunda into the Sully crypt.

Medieval Louvre★★★

Here, a dark line on the floor indicates the location of one of the 10 towers that made up part of the old Louvre. Further on, visitors encounter the impressive surroundings of the **fortress** built by Philippe Auguste in the early 13C. The wooden walkway follows the line of the moat. On the east side, a trapezoidal construction indicates the

foundations of the residence added by Charles V in 1360. In the middle of the ditch, the supporting pier of the drawbridge is framed by the **east gate** towers of Philippe Auguste's castle.

A modern gallery leads to the moat around the circular keep or **Grosse Tour** built for Philippe Auguste between 1190 and 1202. The moat, with an average width of 7.5m/24.6ft, was once paved with enormous stones. Note the impressive **model** of the Louvre fortress at the beginning of the 15C. The tour of the medieval Louvre ends with two galleries. The first contains the earthenware items discovered during the excavation of Cour Carrée. The second, the **Salle St-Louis** with mid-13C vaulting, has a display of royal items found at the bottom of the well in the keep. These include a replica of Charles VI's parade helmet, the **chapel doré**.

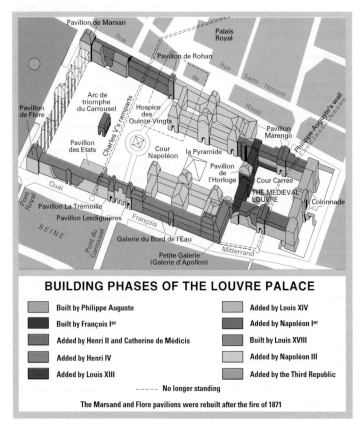

BUILDING PHASES OF THE LOUVRE PALACE

Built by Philippe Auguste	Added by Louis XIV
Built by François Ier	Added by Napoléon Ier
Added by Henri II and Catherine de Médicis	Built by Louis XVIII
Added by Henri IV	Added by Napoléon III
Added by Louis XIII	Added by the Third Republic

- - - - - No longer standing

The Marsand and Flore pavilions were rebuilt after the fire of 1871

EGYPTIAN ANTIQUITIES★★★

Enter by the Sully entrance (ground floor), through Medieval Louvre to the Crypt of the Sphinx, and follow the themed circuit.

The department of Egyptian Antiquities is the legacy of **Jean-François Champollion**, who drew on the work of the English physicist Thomas Young (1773–1829) for help in unravelling the mysteries of hieroglyphics in 1822, thus founding Egyptology. A consistent policy of purchasing, collecting and acquiring excavated material continued until World War II, endowing the Louvre with thousands of artefacts.

Crypt of the Sphinx

Sully wing, room 7.

This colossal monolith in pink granite, 4.8m/15.7ft long, was found at Tanis in the Nile delta, the capital of Egypt during its decline. Note the bas-relief of Ramses worshipping the Sphinx of Giza (c. 1279 BC).

Themed Circuit

19 galleries (ground floor) feature a thematic installation centered on major aspects of Egyptian civilization.

Nile River, field labor, animal husbandry, hunting and fishing – *Rooms 3–5*. Agricultural practices in ancient Egypt are evoked by means of statues and models for furnishing tombs, along with farming tools, and bas-relief sculptures, particularly those in the **Mastaba of Akhethétep★★**. See the fragments of a painting from Unsu's mortuary chapel portraying farm work from tillage through harvesting is worth a look.

Writing and scribes – *Room 6*. Exhibited are hieroglyphic writing along with the materials used by the scribes. Samples of ancient Egyptian texts illustrate the hieroglyphic script (typically found on tombs), the hieratic script (a simplified form of hieroglyphs used for everyday purpose) and the demotic script (mainly used for writing religious, scientific or legal documents).

Art and Crafts – *Room 7*. This section is devoted to highly skilled Egyptian artists and craftsmen who used a wide array of organic materials (wood, stone, clay, reed, hemp, linen) and dared audacious associations such as gold with bronze, glass with wood or stone with pottery, to produce the most delicate artefacts. Note a rare bronze of Horus on a pedestal, and an outstanding mummy's bead netting.

Domestic life – *Rooms 8-10*. A wooden chair inlaid with white ivory, its blue legs with lion's paws, and other furniture evoke the décor of wealthy homes. Pottery, baskets, jewels, containers of perfumed oil, wooden spoons carved in relief, harps, lyres, oboes, tambourines and other musical instruments, a tunic of pleated linen still in one piece dating back to 2033 BC, and hippopotamus-shaped board games with 58 holes are included.

Temples – *Rooms 11, 12 and 12 bis*. Processional avenues of sphinxes served as forecourts to Egyptian temples were reached via avenues of sphinxes, and this idea is evoked in the corridor leading to the Henri IV gallery. Visitors will see statues of gods and monumental columns adorned with intaglio-relief engraving. Note the statue of **Séthi II** (Karnak, c. 1200 BC) and reconstitution of Thutmosis III's **Chapel of the Ancestors** (Karnak, c. 1479 BC), which bears the names of 61 pharaohs.

Funerary rites, gods, animals – *Rooms 13–19*. Much has been learned of everyday life in Ancient Egypt from the reconstitution of the living world in tombs. The Crypt of Osiris and the pink granite cartouche-shaped box of **Ramses III** are among the shaped mummy cases. The **coffin of Madja** (c. 1550-1069 BC) stands out for its polychrome decoration. The mummy of a man from the Ptolemaic Period (c. 1069-30 BC), with a mask covering his head, perfectly illustrates embalming techniques. The role of magic and the animal kingdom in religion is also shown with mummified cats.

Chronological Circuit

At the end of the themed circuit, go up the stairs to explore rooms 20-30 located on the first floor of the Sully wing.

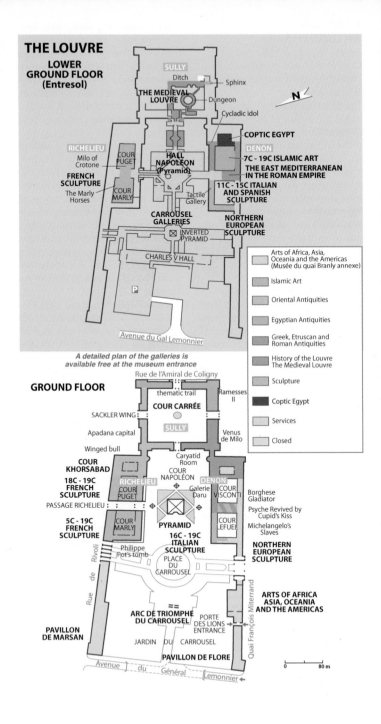

THE LOUVRE

LOWER GROUND FLOOR (Entresol)

SULLY
Ditch
Sphinx
THE MEDIEVAL LOUVRE
Dungeon
Cycladic idol
N

COPTIC EGYPT

DENON
7C - 19C ISLAMIC ART
THE EAST MEDITERRANEAN IN THE ROMAN EMPIRE

RICHELIEU
Milo of Crotone
COUR PUGET
HALL NAPOLÉON (Pyramid)

11C - 15C ITALIAN AND SPANISH SCULPTURE

FRENCH SCULPTURE
The Marly Horses
COUR MARLY
Tactile Gallery

NORTHERN EUROPEAN SCULPTURE

CARROUSEL GALLERIES

INVERTED PYRAMID

CHARLES V HALL

P

Avenue du Gal Lemonnier

	Arts of Africa, Asia, Oceania and the Americas (Musée du quai Branly annexe)
	Islamic Art
	Oriental Antiquities
	Egyptian Antiquities
	Greek, Etruscan and Roman Antiquities
	History of the Louvre The Medieval Louvre
	Sculpture
	Coptic Egypt
	Services
	Closed

A detailed plan of the galleries is available free at the museum entrance

GROUND FLOOR

Rue de l'Amiral de Coligny

thematic trail
COUR CARRÉE
Ramesses II

SACKLER WING
SULLY

Apadana capital
Venus de Milo

Winged bull
Caryatid Room

COUR KHORSABAD
COUR NAPOLÉON

18C - 19C FRENCH SCULPTURE
RICHELIEU
COUR PUGET
Galerie Daru
DENON
COUR VISCONTI

PASSAGE RICHELIEU
Borghese Gladiator

5C - 19C FRENCH SCULPTURE
COUR MARLY
PYRAMID
COUR LEFUEL
Psyche Revived by Cupid's Kiss
Michelangelo's Slaves

16C - 19C ITALIAN SCULPTURE
NORTHERN EUROPEAN SCULPTURE

Philippe Pot's tomb
PLACE DU CARROUSEL

Rue de Rivoli

ARTS OF AFRICA ASIA, OCEANIA AND THE AMERICAS

Quai François Mitterrand

ARC DE TRIOMPHE DU CARROUSEL
PORTE DES LIONS ENTRANCE

PAVILLON DE MARSAN

JARDIN DU CARROUSEL

PAVILLON DE FLORE

Avenue du Général Lemonnier

0   80 m

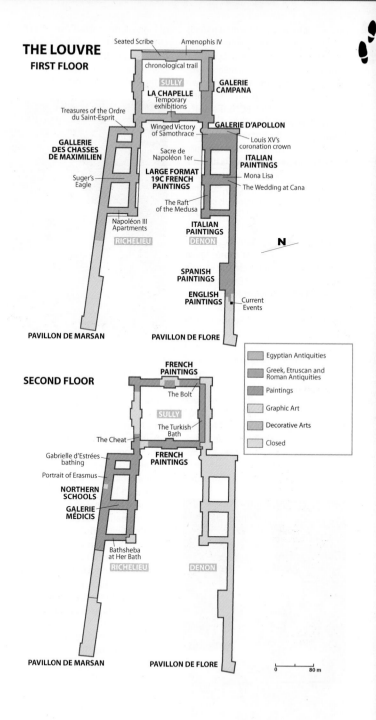

THE LOUVRE
FIRST FLOOR

Seated Scribe
Amenophis IV
chronological trail
SULLY
LA CHAPELLE
Temporary exhibitions
GALERIE CAMPANA

Treasures of the Ordre du Saint-Esprit
Winged Victory of Samothrace
GALERIE D'APOLLON
Louis XV's coronation crown

GALLERIE DES CHASSES DE MAXIMILIEN
Sacre de Napoléon 1er
ITALIAN PAINTINGS

Suger's Eagle
LARGE FORMAT 19C FRENCH PAINTINGS
Mona Lisa
The Wedding at Cana

The Raft of the Medusa

Napoléon III Apartments
RICHELIEU
ITALIAN PAINTINGS
DENON

N

SPANISH PAINTINGS

ENGLISH PAINTINGS
Current Events

PAVILLON DE MARSAN
PAVILLON DE FLORE

SECOND FLOOR

FRENCH PAINTINGS
The Bolt
SULLY
The Turkish Bath

The Cheat
FRENCH PAINTINGS

Gabrielle d'Estrées bathing
Portrait of Erasmus
NORTHERN SCHOOLS
GALERIE MÉDICIS

Bathsheba at Her Bath
RICHELIEU
DENON

PAVILLON DE MARSAN
PAVILLON DE FLORE

	Egyptian Antiquities
	Greek, Etruscan and Roman Antiquities
	Paintings
	Graphic Art
	Decorative Arts
	Closed

0   80 m

This circuit highlights historical periods and the development of Egyptian art, and includes a timeline of Ancient Egypt.

Naqaqa period (the end of prehistory) – Room 20. One of the earliest known silex tools to feature low-relief carving (prehistoric era c. 3200 BC) is the **Knife of Gebel-el-Arak★★**.

Thinite period (the first two dynasties) – *Room 21*. The highly stylised funerary **Stele of the Serpent King** (3100 BC), from Abydos, is one of the oldest examples of monumental hieroglyphs. King Djet, one of the first pharaohs, is symbolised by a cobra contained in a rectangle topped by the falcon god Horus.

Old Kingdom (2700–2200 BC) – *Room 22*. Some of the earliest examples of Egyptian statuary include the couple **Sepa and Nesa** (Third Dynasty) and the **Head of a Spinx of King Djedefre** (Fourth Dynasty, 2570 BC). The highlight is the **Seated Scribe★★★**, a famous limestone statue from the Fifth Dynasty (c. 2500 BC) that was excavated at Sakkara. Strikingly realistic, the facial expression is alert, the hands poised as if ready to commit to papyrus what he hears, his eyes, inlaid with coloured rock crystal and eyelids outlined in copper.

Middle Kingdom (c2033–1710BC) – *Rooms 23–24*. Note the life-size statue of chancellor Nakhti (c. 1900 BC), standing upright with his left hand clenched in a fist. It was made of a single trunk

of high-grade acacia. Covered in polychrome paint, the female offering-bearer is another classic of Egyptian craftmanship that came from a tomb of the Early Middle Kingdom.

Amenophis IV, New Kingdom, Eighteenth Dynasty

© Patricia Grube/Michelin

New Kingdom (1550–1069BC) – *Rooms 25–28*. One of the most famous pharaohs of the 18th Dynasty was **Amenophis IV** who changed his name to Akhenaton in deference to the sun god Aton. He and his queen, Nefertiti, introduced monotheism in Egypt, which prompted violent reactions from the dispossessed priesthood. After his death, his effigies were destroyed, as illustrated by a reconstituted bust on display of **Akhenaton★★**. His long face and enigmatic smile add to the mystery of his broken body. The famous sculpture of Akhenaton and Nefertiti shows them walking side by side, hand in hand. The collection includes the exquisite royal jewels, such as this delicate ring featuring ducks bearing the name of **Ramses IV,** and a bronze of a vanquished Libyan.

Final Pharaonic dynasties and the tolemaic period (1069–30 BC) – *Rooms 29–30*. The end of pharaonic Egypt was interspersed with intermediate periods when the kingdom was subject to exterior rule (Persians, Greeks). Dating from this period are the bronze statue of **Queen Karomama** inlaid with gold

Seated Scribe

© Zatac/Tips Images

and silver, and the precious **Osorkon Triad**, in gold and laps-lazuli, regrouping the holy triad of the Osiris family: Osiris seated on an altar, his wife and sister Isis and their son Horus, protector of the monarchy.

▷ For an-depth view of the Egyptian collections, go to the lower ground floor of the Denon wing. The following rooms provide insight into the art and culture of Roman and Coptic Egypt.

Funerary Art in Roman Egypt
Room 1 is now part of a new department called East Mediterranean in the Roman Empire (composed of 9 rooms) created in 2012 to exhibit artworks representative of the Late Antiquity in the East Mediterranean basin (which included Egypt). It sheds light on the religious beliefs of hellenized Romans, Greeks and Egyptians. Plaster death masks for men, women and children, mummies and funeral portraits demonstrate artistic adaptations to a population of mixed origins. Note the **mummified head** of a man with curly hair, his face coated with gold leaf.

▷ Walk through the room devoted to pre-Classical Greece and proceed to Coptic Egypt section.

Coptic Egypt: arts and civilisation 5-19AD
A rich collection of Coptic textiles and tapestries incorporates Egyptian, Roman, Greek, Byzantine and Ottoman motifs, icons (a masterpiece of the Coptic section being the Christ and Abbot Mena icon that dates to 6-7C), manuscripts, delicate wood reliefs, games, musical instruments, domestic objects, clothing and adornment, ceramics, liturgical objects (incense burner, etc.). A display is devoted to the Coptic language and writing.

Coptic Egypt : Southern Church of Bawit (Middle Egypt, 6-8C AD)
Most of the vestiges of this church, once influential monastery of Bawit (now in ruins), was donated to the Louvre in the early 20C. A life-size reconstruction of the monument, based on archives and photographs, brings to life Christian Egypt in the Byzantine period.

The decorated church, which assimilated oriental and hellenistic influences, illustrates the alternating use of sandstone blocks and wood characteristic of Coptic architecture. Columns, capitals, friezes, doors and window frames add embellishment.

GREEK ANTIQUITIES★★★
Start your tour of this section on the lower ground floor of the Denon wing.
The Greek Antiquities section is one of the jewels in the Louvre's collections.

Preclassical Greece
Room 1.

A set of white Cycladic idols called heads of female figures (c. 3000 BC) strangely evoke modern art. The artefacts from the Geometric Period (the first phase of Greek art, c. 900-750 BC), illustrated here by potteries decorated with basic motifs and plain bronze statuettes, exemplify Greek art's evolution in less than seven centuries from such simplicity to elaborate masterpieces like the Venus de Milo. The Orientalising Period (c. 720-620 BC) saw the birth of one of the earliest examples of Greek stone statuary: the Lady of Auxerre. Reminiscent of Ancient Egypt, the **Torso of a Kouros**, which features the nude standing figure of a young man in a frontal pose, belongs to the Archaïc Period (c. 620-480 BC).

Greek inscriptions
Room 2.
Dedicated to epigraphy, this gallery showcases architectural elements, stelae, statues and other votive objects from 6C BC to 4C AD bearing ancient Greek inscriptions on a variery of supports : stone, bronze, terra-cotta, lead. These engraved pieces (epitaphs, milestones, deeds of manumission, accounting documents, treaties or even poems) came from Lybia, Crimea, Afghanistan, Provence or any other part of the Antique World where Greek was spoken. Among the epigraphs on display,

one (5C BC) sadly lists the names of 108 citizens who died on the battlefied.

Severe style
Room 3.
The preferred material of many artists of the Severe Style generation (480-450 BC), which preceeded the Classical period, was bronze. Its softness was better suited to the expression of movement than marble, as illustrated by the **Victorious athlete** (c. 470 BC), a votive statuette that expresses stylistic innovations after the Archaic Period.

▷ Go to the Denon's wing ground floor.

Olympia Room
Room 4.
This room houses the fourth **metope** (space between two triglyphs of a Doric frieze, adorned with carved work) from the west façade of the Temple of Zeus (c. 460 BC) in Olympia. This three-dimensional relief, carved in Parian marble highlighted with red pigment, was sculpted at the apogee of the Early Classical style (480-450 BC). It features Heracles (son of Zeus) in a struggle with the Cretan bull that King Minos had refused to sacrifice to Poseïdon.

▷ Walk through room 5 (Rotonde de Mars) and room 6 (Salle de Diane) to see their refined décor.

Classical and Hellenistic Greece (450-30 BC)
Rooms 7-12.
On display are art pieces from Athens and central Greece *(7-8)*, "Great Greece" (coastal areas of Southern Italy on the Tarentine Gulf) and Sicily *(9)*, Macedonia *(10)*, Asia Minor and Middle East *(11)*, Egypt and Cyrenic Greece *(12)*. The plaque of the **Ergastines★★★** is a fragment from the frieze on the Parthenon portraying the procession of the Ergastines, young women from the aristocracy who, at the close of the Great Panathenaea Festival, would present the goddess Athena with a sacred embroidered peplos overgarment.

Replicas of statues, 5C–4C BC
Rooms 13-15.
Marble copies based on the cast of original pieces were made between 100 BC and 200 AD, often to satisfy the eclectic tastes of the Romans. A Roman copy in Paros marble of a monumental Greek statue is that of Athena known as the **Pallas of Velletri.** The copy dates from the Roman Imperial era (c. 1C AD), but the original bronze effigy (c. 430 BC) was attributed to a Cretan scupltor named Cresilas, known for his work on the Acropolis in Athens in late 5C BC. Important Greek sculptors were **Praxiteles** (400 BC-c. 326 BC), whose Aphrodite of Knidos became the most prized female statue of the Antiquity (a Roman copy of her head is on display); and **Lysippus** (c. 395 BC-c. 305 BC), official portraitist to Alexander the Great.

Venus of Milo★★★
Room 16.
The natural, serene beauty of this legendary statue (c.100 BC), twisted in a graceful spiral of movement echoed in the draperies around her body, make it one of the masterpieces of Antique statuary. The mutilated piece was discovered on the island of Melos in 1820. Her impassive face combined with the Hellenistic rendering of the body's nudity are indicative of the neoclassical style then in vogue among the Romans.

▷ At room 16, turn left and walk back to room 17.

Caryatides Room★★
Room 17.
This gallery was once the great hall of the old Louvre Palace, modified by the great Renaissance architect Pierre Lescot. It is named after **female figures** sculpted by Jean Goujon in 1550. The *Nymph of Fontainebleau* above the minstrels' balcony is a copy of the work by the Florentine **Benvenuto Cellini** (16C). The sculptures here are Roman copies of Greek Hellenistic originals, all of them now lost. They include *Hermes Tying his sandal, Crouching Aphrodite* of Vienna, *Artemis* known as **Diana of**

Winged Victory of Samothrace

© Photononstop/Tips Images

Versailles, *The Three Graces* and **Sleeping Hermaphrodite** (on a mattress by Bernini).

◗ The collection continues on the 1st floor, up the Daru staircase (Denon Wing).

Winged Victory of Samothrace★★★

In 2013-14 the impressive 18.3ft-tall, 29-ton representation of **Nike**, the Greek goddess of Victory, featured as a winged female figure standing on a base in the form of a ship, underwent much-needed restoration work. Majestically positioned at the top of the Daru staircase, this masterpiece of Hellenistic sculpture was discovered in shattered fragments on the island of Samothrace in 1863. The statue was carved out of white Paros marble around 2C BC; it was probably an offering to the gods after a naval victory at Rhodes around 190 BC.

◗ Pass left of the Winged Victory and go to 1st floor of the Sully wing.

Bronzes Room★★
Room 32.

Antique bronzes and jewellery are displayed alongside examples of Archaic pitcher handles with Gorgon head masks. Portrayals of infancy or old age, stunted growth and deformity are most characteristic of this period. Note *Eros and Psyche* with the faces of a black adolescent with his hands tied behind his back, a giant. The handsome **bust** of a young man from Beneventum draws inspiration from the works of Polyclitus.

Boscoreale Treasure★★
Room 33 (Salle Henri II).

Graced with a blue and black ceiling painted by Braque in 1953 *(The Birds)*, this room houses a collection that was found in Boscoreale, in the ruins of a Roman villa destroyed by the eruption of Mount Vesuvius in AD 79. The treasure trove consisted of coins, jewellery and **silver tableware**, put into a wine tank for safe keeping. Skeleton Goblets – two silver cups embellished with gold, bearing epicurian maxims – feature the skeletons of famous poets and Greek philosophers.

Antique glassware
Room 34.

In Louis XIV's former Grand Cabinet, designed by Le Vau, the ancient craft of glass-making is represented with pieces from the Greek, Hellenistic and Roman periods, made by **core-formed** technique (covering a prefabricated core of clay with glass, then decorating the object by winding) or by **moulding**. Delicate items illustrate the technique of **free-blown** glass: shaping glassware solely by inflation with a blowpipe.

Clarac Room
Room 35.

The attic red-figure vase known as the Niobid Krater (c. 460-450 BC) featuring Heracles and Athena is the centerpiece. Molded stucco reliefs (1C BC-2C AD) that decorated sarcophagi found in tombs in the city of Panticapeum (Crimean peninsula) are noteworthy.

Greek terra-cotta
Rooms 36-38.

These three rooms (note the ceilings) are devoted to terra-cottas in the Archaic, Classical, Hellenistic and Roman periods. Figurines, many of them roughly shaped, were the "ex-votos of the Poor".

Some were used as toys. Others of a grotesque nature feature crude subjects like the obese woman holding a vase (350-300 BC), satyre (5 BC).

Galerie Campana★★

Rooms 39-47 in the wing facing the Seine.
In 1861 Napoléon III bought most of the collection of the **Marquis de Campana**, who excavated the Etruscan necropolises of northern Latium. This gallery is a succession of nine halls exhibiting antique pottery vessels. Greek vases were made in specific shapes for storing wine and food (amphora), drinking wine or water (kantharos or kylix) and pouring libations in ritual occasions (lekythos). The final gallery displays the Greek hellenistic terracotta figures from Myrina and Tanagra.

▶ Go to the ground floor of the Denon wing.

Salle du Manège

Gallery A.
On display are Antiquity statues collected by Richelieu, Mazarin, the Borgheses and others as well as the French royal collections (16-18C). Striking pieces include a marble figure of Thetis (2C AD), a monumental statue of Emperor Titus (1 AD), a Barbarian captive (2C AD), and Eros and Psyche (2C AD).

Daru Gallery

Gallery B.
The Greek collection ends here with two masterpieces of the Roman Empire. The **Borghese Gladiator★★** (c. 100 BC) is a statue of the fighting warrior with an accented musculature thrusting his torso forward in a defensive movement. Another jewel of Hellenistic art dating from c. 40-30 BC is a monumental garden vase known as the **Borghese Vase★★** depicting a Bacchic procession, with dancing satyrs and maenads.

ETRUSCAN ANTIQUITIES★★

Start in Room 18, adjacent to the Olympia Room (Room 4).
The origins of the Etruscans are uncertain, but their civilisation is undisputed, drawn from Ancient Greece and absorbed by Ancient Rome. In 265 BC Etruria ceded its independence, becoming part of the Roman Empire. Artefacts have been recovered from tombs, including utensils in bronze and terra-cotta, jewels in gold, funerary urns, bronze toys and devotional objects. The terra-cotta **Sarcophagus of the Married Couple★★★** (c. 520-510 BC) found at Cerveteri (Italy) is the star exhibit. *Rooms 19 and 20* display Villanovian artefacts made of iron or bronze inscribed with geometric patterns. Bucchero Etruscan earthenware was characterized by a black, sometimes gray, shiny polish, typical of the Orientalizing period (mid-7C).

Sarcophagus of the Married Couple (6C BC)

© ImageState/Tips Images

Assyrian reliefs of Khorsabad

© Daniel Thierry/Photononstop/Tips Images

ROMAN ANTIQUITIES★★

Rooms 22-30.

Anne of Austria's (Louis XIV's mother) **private apartment★★**, (1658) comprises six interconnected rooms with ceilings painted by **Romanelli**. On display are three of the most original genres in Roman art: the portrait, relief carving, and **mosaics★** *(the latter are also displayed in Room 31)*. Pieces in *Rooms 28-30*, such as the black and white funerary mosaic of Nardus, Turassus and Restitutus from Tunisia (4C-5C AD), bearing various Christian symbols, illustrate the emergence of Christianity in Gaul, Africa and Syria. A fine example of paleochristian art is that of the marble **Sarcophagus of the Giving of the Law** (Rome, 4C AD). The outstanding **Cour du Sphinx★★** *(room 31)* has the largest group of architectural sculptures in the museum.

NEAR-EASTERN ANTIQUITIES★★★

Ground floors of Richelieu and Sully wings.

In 1843 **Paul-Émile Botta**, the French Consul in Mosul (Iraq), excavated the remains of the city built by Sargon II of Assyria, thereby discovering a lost civilisation. The Louvre galleries house the oldest treaties, laws and representations of historical scenes known to man. The collections are divided into three major geographical zones: **Mesopotamia** (the ancient region of southwestern Asia between the Tigris and the Euphrates corresponding to parts of modern-day Iraq and Syria); the **Levant** (bounded by the Mediterranean Sea to the west, Mesopotamia and the Arabian desert to the east and Anatolia to the north); and **Iran** all the way to Central Asia, each zone following a chronological order.

Antique Mesopotamia

Rooms 1-6, ground floor, Richelieu wing.

The Sumerian site of **Telloh** (Ancient Girsu) was home to the famous **vultures stele** (c. 2450 BC), immortalising the victory of King Eannatum of Lagash over the rival city of Umma. Fragments of this masterpiece greet visitors entering this section. Note the **votive relief** of King Ur-Nanshe (c. 2550-2500 BC, ancient Girsu), founder of the Lagash dynasty, and the silver and coppe**r vase** dedicated by King Entemena of Lagash to the god Ningirsu *(room 1A).*

The Sumerian culture spread northwards to present-day Syria (site of **Mari**). Worshippers would place votive figures in their own image in temples. The alabaster figure (c. 2400 BC) of **Ebih-II★**, Superintendent of Mari, depicts a man in with his hands clasped on his chest in prayer. Note his beautiful lapis-lazuli eyes. The Semitic dynasty of Akkad (2340–2200 BC) succeeded in uniting Mesopotamia around the Ancient Babylonian city of Agade. Artefacts dating from this dynasty include the **Victory stele of Naram-Sin** (c. 2250 BC) in pink sandstone, which depicts the triumph of the Akkadian king over mountain people called the Lullubi. The diorite representations of Gudea, prince of the independent kingdom of Lagash and those of his son **Ur-Ningirsu** were produced in Lagash c. 2120 BC.

Early in the 2nd millennium BC, the Babylonian king destroyed Mari and conquered Mesopotamia. In the centre of the gallery stands the famous **Code of Hammurabi★** (c. 1790 BC–1750 BC), the most complete legal compendium of antiquity, dating back to earlier than biblical law, written in cuneiform script and the Akkadian language. **Reliefs** feature servants, a war chariot carrier, a horse handler, a hero overpowering a lion, and the transport of timber from Lebanon *(room 4)*. After the 6C BC, Babylon reached the apex of its power under King Nebuchadnezzar.

Khorsabad Courtyard★★

The large Assyrian reliefs from the palace of Sargon II at Dur-Sharrukin (Iraq's modern Khorsabad) greet visitors at the same height as in the Assyrian era. Two **winged human-headed bulls** with five legs reconstitute part of the decoration of the third doorway of the palace. The wall opposite is a reconstruction of the façade of the throne room. The **Hittites**, who brought the Hammurabi dynasty to ruin, settled on the Anatolian plateau (Turkey) in the 2nd millennium BC. The **Stele of the Storm God Tarhunda** (c. 900 BC) is an example of Neo-Hittite art *(room 6)*. Conquered by Assyria in 9C BC, **Arslan-Tash** was an important provincial capital with sites that yielded spoils of war from Phoenician or Armenian cities, including ivories such as the **Cow Suckling Calf** (8C BC).

The **reliefs★★** from the palace of Ashurbanipal at **Nineveh** are counted among the masterpieces of world sculpture.

Antique Iran

Rooms 7-9, ground floor, Richelieu wing and 10-16, ground floor, Sully wing.
Transhumance between the **Fars mountains** (to the east, where Persepolis was later to be built) and the **Susa plain** perpetuated the Mesopotamian influence, and gave rise to the first Iranian state: **Elam**. From the end of the 5th millennium, Elamite potters were becoming renowned for highly stylized animal (large vase with ibex) or geometric decoration. The statue of the goddess **Narundi** (c. 2100 BC) illustrates the true extent of Mesopotamian influence on Elamite art; see as well the painted terra-cotta **secret-compartment vase** (labelled *vase à la cachette, room 8*).

Within the bounds of central Asia, a great civilisation was flourishing in **Bactria** (modern-day Uzbekistan and northern Afghanistan). The scar-faced statuette labelled **Le Balafré** features an anthropomorphic dragon-snake, an evil figure of the mythology of central Asia that symbolised primitive forces in nature *(room 9)*.

The art of bronze reached its apogee in the reign of King Untash-Napirisha, who had many statues made, including that of his own wife. Today the **Statue of Queen Napirasu** (1340-1300 BC) *(centre of the room)* indicates how elaborate Elamite metalworking techniques were. Bronze, copper and gold statuettes, jewellery and votive offerings *(rooms 10-11)* from the Middle Elamite Period were from the **Temple of Inshushinak cache**, found at Susa.

From 6C-4C BC Susa attained its apex under the Achaemenid kings. Gold- and silversmiths produced delicate works of art (bracelets and goblets, winged ibex), while architects built sumptuous palaces. The colossal **Apdana capital★★** (c. 510 BC) from the palace of Darius I at Susa gives some indication of the gigantic scale of the palaces of Persian rulers, which were decorated with enamel brick friezes. The floor **mosaics** (c. 260 AD) from the palace of Bichapur, featuring a dancer, harpist and satyr's head *(rooms 12-16)*, date from the Sasanian period and mark the transition to Islamic art.

Levant

The collection is divided between the west wing of Cour Carrée, (ground floor of the Sully wing, rooms A-D) and the north wing of the Cour Carrée, known as the "Sackler wing" (rooms 17a-17b, 18b and 21, ground floor of the Sully wing).

Cyprus
Room A.

Many artefacts here were found in the 20C by French archaeologist **Claude Shaeffer**, who led excavations at Vounous, a necropolis from the Ancien Bronze Period (3rd millenium BC). They yielded a number of feminine "red polished" terracotta figures, such as the Woman carrying a child in a cradle (c. 2000-1600 BC). Shaeffer also worked at Enkomi, site of a prosperous trading center towards the end of the 2nd millenium BC, where the Gold Band with sphinxes and stylised tree (c. 1400-1230 BC) on display was found; it would adorn the hair, chest or forehead of the deceased.

Coastal and Central Syria
Rooms B-C.

Excavations at the Canaanite city of **Ugarit** (present-day Ras Shamra), occupied as early as 6500 BC, revealed a flourishing capital that was to prefigure the Phoenician cities of Tyre and Sidon. Strategically located at the intersection of the maritime routes of the Mediterranean and the land routes of the Near East, Ugarit developed commercial and cultural exchanges with the Hittites, Egyptians Mesopotamians and Aegeans. Stelae were a major form of religious expression in the Levant, and the stele of the **storm god Baal** (18-15C BC), which was discovered in Ugarit, is an ideal example of it. The **gold dish** (14C–13C BC) features embossed decorations denoting the cosmopolitan mark of Egyptian, Aegean and Levantine traditions. Also on display are terracottas (vases, votive figurines, models of houses), a bronze figure of seated goddess from 15C BC, and cylinder seals bearing cuneiform inscriptions.

Palestine and Transjordania
Room D.

The basalt **stele of Mesha** (9C BC) commemorates the King of Moab's victory over the Omri dynasty and the Kings of Israel (the earliest known reference to the word "Israel"). The small steatite **scarabs** from c. 2000-1500 BC, found in tombs of Jericho, are worth noting.

Stele of Baal

© Scala, Florence/Musée du Louvre

Sackler Wing
Rooms 17-21.

The first section *(rooms 17-18b)* focuses on **Phoenician kingdoms** 8C to 2C BC. Great merchants and skilled craftsmen, the Phoenicians founded Tyr and Sidon in present-day Lebanon. They established colonies in North Africa, Spain, Sicily, Cyprus and elsewhere, but fell under Persian domination in 5-4C BC. Alexander the Great ended their civilisation around 333 BC.

Of the tombs on display, the Egyptian-style **Sarcophagus of Eshmunazar II★★**, King of Sidon (5C BC), is engraved with an epitaph that ends with of a curse. Marble sculptures from Sidon evoke the cult of Mithra, and bronzes that of Jupiter from Heliopolis (modern Baalbek) in Syria, during the Roman era. A section is devoted to **pre-Islamic Arabia** (7C BC-3C AD), essentially **Yemenite kingdoms** that gained wealth from trading frankincense and myrrh, and to **Palmyra** a caravan city at the crossroads of Syria. **Aphrodite with a Tortoise★** (2C-3C AD) and the votive relief known as **The Divine Triade** (1C AD) reveal a hybrid Palmyrene style *(rooms 19-20)*. The final section, on **Cyprus** (1st millenium BC), is structured around the monolithic **Vase from Amathus** (c. 7-5C BC), decorated with bulls on its handles; it was associated with the cult of Aphrodite *(room 21)*.

ISLAMIC ART★★

In the Visconti courtyard, lower ground floor, Denon wing.

The Visconti Courtyard houses Europe's largest collection of Islamic art (more than 15 000 items complemented by some 3 500 objects on loan from the Decorative Arts Department). Around 3 000 artefacts are showcased, including ceramics, textiles, metalwork and glasswork, stone and ivory objects and architectural elements. They illustrate the cultural reach of the Islamic world from Spain to India and its full chronological dimension, spanning 1 300 years of history. Selected iconic artefacts are placed within the context of their time.

Caliphate Period (8C-11C)

Area A, Rooms 1-7.

At the time of Prophet Muhammad's death in 632, Arabia was unified, and the new monotheistic religion known as Islam was rapidly spreading. A succession of four caliphates expanded their territory to the Persian and Byzantine empires and beyond. The museum's collection of **painted ceramics** from Western Iran and the Caucasus, and **metalware** from Eastern Iran, Afghanistan and Central Asia illustrates the true extent of the Conquest.

The *Coupelle au lièvre et au lion* (Egypt, 10C), featuring a hare and a lion, is a fine example of **lustreware**, use of lead-based glaze and silver and copper paint to create a golden shine.

Arabic was soon to become the dominant language in the Empire. The Arabic script started to appear on a variety of supports, such as on the white marble **fragment from Egypt** (2nd half of 9C) engraved with verses of the Quran.

Pictorial images that used to appear on coins were replaced by verses from the Quran. The pieces of stamped glass with Arabic script on display, along with **coins**, were actually used as weighing standards against a given quantity of struck gold or silver. The **Pyxide d'Al-Mughira**★★ (c. 968, Spain) is a surviving examples of the royal ivory carving tradition in Islamic Spain.

Turks and the Muslim West (11C-13C)

Area A, Rooms 1 and 2.

In the 11C Islam continued to spread to India, Anatolia and the kingdom of Ghana, but lost ground in Spain, Sicily and Jerusalem. After the fall of the Caliphate of **Cordoba** in 1031, the **Berber dynasties** that had established their empire in the Moroccan city of Marrakech tried to unify Islamic Spain and the **Maghreb**. Meanwhile, Seljuk Turks took control of Bagdad in 1055, and the Sunni leader of the Seljuks acquired the title of Sultan. In 1171 **Saladin** put an end to the Shiite Caliphate in Cairo, and captured Jerusalem in 1187.

Artefacts produced in these troubled times reflect a cosmopolitan culture inspired by Western and Oriental influences. The zoomorphic vessel known as the **Lion de Monzón**★★ (12-13C, Spain) exemplifies this period. Another outsanding piece from that period is the **Globe céleste signé Yunus b. al-Husayn al-Asturlabi**★★from Iran (c. 1144).

Mongols, Mamluks, Timurids (13C-15C)

Area C, Rooms 1-5.

In the mid 13C, **Genghis Khan** (1336-1405) unified the nomadic tribes of the Central Asian steppes and founded the **Mongol Empire**. He launched invasions throughout China, Central Asia, Iran and Iraq, spreading panic. **Baghdad** was captured in 1258. Most Muslim dynasties heavily relied on slaves for military purpose. In mid-13C, **Mamluks**, slave soldiers of mostly Turkish or Caucasian origin, emerged as a powerful military caste. During the **Mamluk Sultanate**, which ruled Syria and Egypt from 1250 until 1517, Cairo became the largest city of Islam. From 1347, the plague spread to the entire Islamic world. Timur the Lame, known as **Tamerlane** (1336-1405) became the ruler of a vast Central Asian empire, with **Samarkand**, located along the silk route, as capital. A great patron of the arts, he initiated a brilliant period in Islamic art, and his descendants, the

Timurids (1405-1507), perpetuated this tradition. Meanwhile, the **Ottomans** expanded to the Balkans and conquered Constantinople in 1453, putting an end to the Byzantine Empire. Granada was the last Spanish city to be reconquered by Catholic monarchs in 1492, sounding the death knell of Islamic Spain.

The hammered bronze **Baptistère de Saint Louis**★★★ (Syria or Egypt, c. 1320-1340) is a perfect example of an Islamic concept translated into an object aimed at Christian practice. Mosque lamps engraved with verses from the Quran, tableware and a **mosaic fountain basin** (Egypt, 14-15C) further exemplify the lavish life style of the Mamluk emirs. The **Plat à la ronde de poissons**★★ (Dish with a Swirl of Fish, Iran, late 13C-early 14C) is remarkable. Magnificent doors decorated with gilded interlacings reflect the **Mudéjar Style,** representing the fusion of Islamic and Christian artistic traditions.

Modern Empires (16C-19C)

Area D, Rooms 1-3.

By the 16C the Muslim world accounted for about a third of the world's population. The huge territory was divided into three main empires: the **Ottomans** to the west with Turkey, the Balkans, the Arabian Peninsula, Egypt and the Maghreb countries, except Morocco, under their control; the **Mughals** to the east, who dominated almost half of the Indian subcontinent by the 17C; and in Iran, the **Safavids** (1501-1722), who converted the country from Sunnism to Shiism. Threats of European expansion followed: in 1798, **Bonaparte** launched a scientific and military expedition in Egypt; a year later, the **British East India Company** would achieve a decisive victory over the Sultan of Mysore at Seringapatam, and get indirect control of his kingdom. Of the 17-18C Persian rugs on display, the best pieces have a foundation of silk with wool pile of a **high knot density**; they were exported towards Europe and India. Metal vessels, utensils and scientific instruments made of brass in Mughal India reveal

Arabic Calligraphy

The venerated art of calligraphy, strongly tied with the Koran, found its finest expression on a variety of supports. Arabic inscriptions could be written in the **Kufic style**, the oldest form of the Arabic script, characterised by rigid and angular strokes, or in the cursive style, called **Naskh style**, but many regions developed their own style. In Area A, room 7, a magnificent **Dish Adorned with calligraphy** (Iran or Central Asia, 10C) features black stylised vertical calligraphic stems on a white background converging toward a central motif that evokes Chinese yin and yang.

various techniques (inlays, etching, casting, hammered relief). Don't miss the **poignard à manche en tête de cheval**★★ (India, 17C), a curved dagger with a blade of damascened steel inlaid with gold, or the Mughal **sandstone partitions**★ called *jalis*. The **Mur du temps**★★★ (Wall of Time, 16-19C), with thousands of ceramic tiles from the Ottoman Empire, traces the evolution of Turkish ceramic art.

▶ Go back to Area B.

A new permanent exhibit in Area B is devoted to **The Book as Art.** On display are **Persian miniatures** and Iranian literary masterpieces such as **The Shahnameh of Ferdowsi** (a page is on view).

GALERIE D'APOLLON

Room 66, first floor, Denon wing.

The Apollo Rotunda leads to this long room, created by Le Vau under Louis XIV, where 28 tapestries, 118 sculpted figures and 41 paintings by Charles Le Brun and Delacroix are showcased. The French crown jewels are on display, including the **Regent diamond**★★★ weighing 140 carats. Other display cases contain Louis XIV's impressive collection of **semi-precious stone vases**★.

ITALIAN SCHOOL: PAINTING★★★

Denon wing; first floor, to the right of the Winged Victory of Samothrace.

The collection of Italian paintings, one of the glories of the Louvre, was carefully acquired as a result of a passion harboured by the Kings of France for the art of that peninsula. Renaissance masterpieces include such key works as the *Mona Lisa*, *The Wedding at Cana* and *The Man with the Glove*, but the Baroque pieces, favoured by Louis XIV, are unique. The collection is presented in chronological order.

Primitives and Quattrocento (15C)

In the *Salle Percier* and *Salle Fontaine,* by way of introduction to Italian painting, are the frescoes from the *Villa Lemmi* by **Botticelli** commemorating the marriage of Lorenzo Tornabuoni (surrounded by allegories of the Liberal Arts) with Giovanna degli Albizzi (offering her bridal veil to Venus and her attendants the three Graces). Fra Angelico's *Crucifixion* is found in the Salle Duchâtel.

Salon Carré

Thirty of the large-format Florentine **Primitives** hang where the former salons of the Académie des Beaux-Arts were held. It is **Giotto** who maintains the momentum to greater realism in the early 14C. Narrative scenes are reduced to the essentials: in the portrait of **Saint Francis of Assisi receiving the stigmata★★**, the saint is depicted in a rugged landscape of monumental proportions.

A Dominican monk, **Fra Angelico** the Blessed, the painter of the convent of San Marco in Florence, evoked life in Paradise as serenely mystical. Saints and angels crowd round in the *Coronation of the Virgin*, painted in 1435 for the church of San Domenico at Fiesole outside Florence. Intrigued by the problems of portraying perspective, **Paolo Uccello** painted the *Battle of San Romano*, in which the forces of Florence beat those of Siena in 1432 (the other panels, painted for the Medicis,

are in Florence (the Uffizi gallery) and London (the National Gallery): the captain Michelotto Attendoli's black charger suggests depth; the surging crowd of armed warriors in magnificent plumed helmets are depicted ready to advance or retreat, accentuating the theatrical effect of movement and action.

Salle des Sept-Mètres
Room 4.

In Siena the jewel-like art of **Simone Martini** (small panel of the *Way to Calvary*) recalls the art of illumination.

The Quattrocento was a period of quest and rationalization: how should space and volume be represented on a two-dimensional plane? Portraiture provided an opportunity for detailed observation and sensitive analysis: the medallion portrait in profile of *A Princess of the House of Este* by **Pisanello**; the authoritarian and enigmatic *Sigismondo Malatesta* by **Piero della Francesca**.

Grande Galerie

The immense cyma displays 13C to 15C works in its first part, as far as the famous Salle des États, and in the second part, 16C and 17C works. Subject matter, physiognomy and pose evolve. *Saint Sebastian* by **Mantegna** is so precisely observed as to be almost sculptural; note also the sorrowful *Resurrected Christ Giving Blessing* by **Giovanni Bellini**. The *Portrait of an Old Man and a Young Boy* by **Ghirlandaio** combines Florentine elegance with Flemish realism, featured also in the proud features of *Il Condottiere* and the face of *Christ at the Column* by **Antonello da Messina**.

The High Renaissance

Grande Galerie (second part devoted to the 16C and 17C).

The fulfilment of objectives and the successful application of ideal principles marked a new phase of the Renaissance, this time concentrated in Rome and nurtured by a reformed Papacy. When the city was sacked in 1527, Venice became the power-base and ultimate patron of the Arts, a possession guarded until the end of the 16C.

▷ From the Grande Galerie, turn right into the Salle des États (rooms 6–7).

Leonardo da Vinci (1452–1519) ranks in pride of place among the artists of this period. *The Virgin of the Rocks* is a mature work in which the play of the hands is particularly remarkable, strengthening the harmonious pyramidal arrangement of the figures against the rather menacing rocky crags of the background landscape. Brought up by his grandmother and then his mother, he suffered recurrent nightmares about being attacked by a ravening vulture, as seen in the folds of the Virgin's robes in *The Virgin and Child with St Anne*.

The portrait of **Mona Lisa★★★**, wife of the Florentine Del Giocondo, was finally moved here in 2006 after 55 years at the end of the Grand Galerie, with special lighting, protective glass and acoustics to absorb crowd noise.

The **Wedding at Cana★★★** by **Veronese**, executed in 1563 for the refectory of a convent in Venice, covers one entire wall (across from *La Joconde*). The painter uses the scene from the Gospel as a pretext for painting the Golden Age of Venice, *La Serenissima*.

The 130 figures in this enormous painting (66sq m/79sq yd) are mainly portraits of contemporary figures (Emperor Charles V, Suleiman the Magnificent, Titian, Bassano, Tintoretto and the artist himself, playing the viola).

▷ Return to the Grande Galerie (room 8).

Raphael (1483–1520), the pupil of Perugino, imbues his paintings with gentleness; his landscapes reflect the soft undulating countryside around his native Urbino. **La Belle Jardinière★★** portrays a gentle Virgin watching over the Infants Jesus and John the Baptist, combining humanity and harmony with religious faith. In the *Portrait of Balthazar Castiglione*, the temperament of the gentleman who was a close friend of Raphael is economically portrayed.

Correggio, who was a keen observer of women's sensibilities, developed in Parma a style combining a delicate and slightly self-conscious sensuality with a romantic elegance that was to influence painting into the 18C: *The Mystical Marriage of St Catherine, Antiope Sleeping*.

Counter-Reformation (late 16C) and Seicento (17C)

This section lies beyond the passage that leads to the Mollien wing, housing graphic works (drawings for tapestries by Lodi di Cremona, gouaches by Correggio).

This period is dominated by the Bolognese School, following the founding of the Accademia degli Incamminati (Academy of the Progressives) by the Carracci brothers. A *Circumcision* is on display by the revivalist **Barocci**.

The canvases of the Aemilian School (from the Emilia Romana region) are eclectic, fusing a tendency towards the

Wedding at Cana (1563) by Veronese

© Scala, Florence/Musée du Louvre

academic, a legacy from the study of the masters of the Renaissance (Domenichino's *Saints*) with forward-looking realism. The school's main exponents were **Annibale Carracci** (who often drew in the country; *Fishing* and *Hunting* might be said to be among the best landscapes in the Louvre), **Guido Reni** (who tended more to an aristocratic, decorative style: *Deianeira and the Centaur Nessus, David holding the head of Goliath*) and **Il Guercino** (painter of marvellously accurate human figures: *The Resurrection of Lazarus*). This realism was adopted even more forcefully by **Caravaggio**, who modelled his figures upon people drawn from the poorer walks of life (**The Fortune-Teller★★**). *The Death of the Virgin,* one of his most powerful works, was rejected by the chapter of the Roman church that had commissioned it because of its unorthodox use of an ordinary woman as the model for the Virgin.

At the end of the Grande Galerie, in the Pavillon des États, 17C works are exhibited in the Salle Salvatore Rossa: **Pietro da Cortona**, who practised in Rome (*Romulus and Remus Discovered by Faustulus*); **Domenico Fetti** of Venice (*Melancholy*); and **Luca Giordano** of Naples (*Portraits of Philosophers* dressed in the clothes of ordinary people).

Settecento (18C)

Paintings from this period are housed in the Piazzetta gallery and the small adjacent rooms. The opulent lifestyle of the noble classes during the Age of Enlightenment is reflected in the works of Pannini (*Concert Given in Rome on the Occasion of the Marriage of the Dauphin, Son of Louis XV*). **Guardi** captured the atmosphere of the lagoon of Venice in the dazzling series **Ascension Day Ceremonies★**, during which the doge, in a sumptuous state barge, celebrated the marriage of Venice with the Adriatic by throwing a ring into the sea. The luminous religious and mythological compositions of **Giambattista Tiepolo** contrast strongly with the scenes of street life painted by his son **Giandomenico Tiepolo** (*The Charlatan, Carni-*

val). The life of the common man is also portrayed in the work of **Pietro Longhi**, often with a humorous touch (*Presentation*). *The Flea*, by **Crespi** of Bologna, is reminiscent of Dutch painting.

SPANISH SCHOOL: PAINTING

Rooms 26 to 30.

Spanish painting is characterized by realism and mysticism. The collection of 15C **Spanish Primitives** includes *La lamentation sur le corps du Christ* (c. 1460) by Catalan painter Jaume Huguet and *La Flagellation de Saint Georges* (c. 1453). These two works precede the Mannerist Domenikos Theotokopoulos, an icon painter of Cretan origin, better known as **El Greco**. His **Christ en croix adoré par deux donateurs★★** pictures Christ dying on the Cross. His twisted figure, outlined against a dark, stormy background, confers an expressionist undertone, as if the artist were seeking to convey emotional experience rather than physical reality.

José de Ribera painted the reality of human cruelty, the social antithesis of the Spanish Golden Age. **Le Pied-Bot** (Club-footed Boy,1642) depicts the unfortunate cripple armed with his crutch and a note begging for charity. **Le Jeune Mendiant★★** (The Young Beggar) by **Murillo**, is in the same vein. The humane realism of such paintings contrasts with the spirituality of **Zurbarán** (*Funeral Ceremonies of Saint Bonaventura*), the Baroque exuberance of Carreño de Miranda (*Mass for the Founding of the Trinitarian Order*) and the stiff court Infanta portraits by **Velázquez**. The Madonnas painted by Murillo in muted colours, such as *L'Immaculée Conception* (c. 1650-1655). have the quality of pastels.

The **Beistegui Collection** (*Sully wing, 2nd floor, room A*) includes the portrait of the Marquesa de la Solana by **Goya**, along with *La Comtessa de Santa Cruz.*

FRENCH SCHOOL: PAINTING★★★ (14C-19C)

Second floor, Richelieu wing and second floor, Sully wing. Large-format 19C

French paintings are displayed on the first floor of the Denon wing. The Louvre museum houses the largest collection of French paintings in the world. They are arranged chronologically by genre: the Primitives, Fontainebleau Schools, Caravaggisti, 17C religious painting, etc. Among this profusion of masterpieces, works by artists such as Claude Lorrain, Poussin, Ingres, Fragonard, Chardin or Corot are truly outstanding.

14C

Rooms 1-2.

The anonymous depiction of King John II of France in profile, known as the **Portrait de Jean II le Bon★**, is believed to be the earliest known non-religious French portrait. It was painted prior to 1350, at a time when the subjects of painting were almost exclusively religious. Religious paintings here include *Le Parement de Narbonne,* painted in black ink on silk leaves.

15C

Rooms 3-6.

The International Gothic tradition of portraying vividly colored subjects on a gold background was maintained by the Court of Burgundy, as illustrated by *Le retable de Saint-Denis* by Henri Bellechose, *room 3*). In Southern France, the wealth of Provence attracted European artists, especially from Flanders. Marked by strong contrasts in light, a unique Provençal style came to life (*Pietà of Villeneuve-lès-Avignon* by **Enguerrand Quarton** *(room 4)*. Room 6 exhibits portraits by painters from central France, including Jean Hey, known as the **Master of Moulins,** who was trained in Flanders, but added a French predilection for elegance to his meticulous drawings. Jean Fouquet, a native of Tours, revolutionized European portraiture by using harmonious, golden number proportions (*Portrait de Charles VII, roi de France,* c. 1445 or 1450).

16C

Rooms 7-10.

Renaissance artists were passionately interested in humanism. Consequently, many works of art of this period focus on the individual, hence the profusion of portraits, such as those by **Jean Clouet** and the apprentices in his workshop *(rooms 7-8)*. The Italian artists summoned by François I during the construction of the Château de Fontainebleau introduced Mannerism into French decorative and applied arts. The First School of Fontainebleau *(room 9)* is illustrated with **Jean Cousin the Elder's** *Eva Prima Pandora* (c. 1550), featuring a sensual representation of Eve. Possibly painted to celebrate the birth of one of Henri IV's illegitimate children, *Portrait de Gabrielle d'Estrées et de sa soeur, la duchesse de Villlarsa* (c. 1594) is a fine example of the Second School of Fontainebleau *(room10)*.

17C

Rooms 11-34.

Deeply influenced by Caravaggio's unidealizing realism, French Caravaggisti *(room 11)* were known for their distinctive use of *chiaroscuro* (light and shade). They included **Valentin de Boulogne** (Concert au bas-relief) and **Simon Vouet** with his undated *Portrait de jeune homme.*

These painters imported the Italian Baroque style in France (*Italian Paintings, Denon wing)*. During the reign of Louis XIII *(room 12)*, luminous academic allegories such as Vouet's La Richesse (*Wealth* c.1640) contrasted with the austere, controlled style of **Philippe de Champaigne**, who emphasized in his **Portrait of Cardinal de Richelieu★** the dignity and unbending will of the statesman. **Georges de la Tour** (1593–1652) is a famous master of the illuminated figure on a black background, as exemplified in *Le Tricheur à l'as de carreau★*, in which the card players exchange intriguing glances, and *L'adoration des bergers* (c. 1640), a religious chiaroscuro scene lit by candlelight.

Nicolas Poussin (1594–1665), the artist-philosopher who settled in Rome, is regarded as the most Classical of French academic painters, drawing from the formal canons of Beauty and yet remaining sensitive to the sensuality of colour inspired by Titian. His platonic ideas of the cycles of life and time are seen in **Les Quatre saisons★★** (room 16). **Claude Gellée** (1602–82), otherwise known as **Le Lorrain**, provides another high point. He was perhaps the first painter to attempt to paint the sun as a direct light source, hence his influence upon the English painter Turner and later the Impressionists. Room 15 exhibits fine examples of his techniques, such as the *Port de mer au soleil couchant* (c. 1639) and *L'embarquement d'Ulysse* (1646).

Rooms 25-29

Genre scenes and small-format still-life works were executed by painters inspired by Flemish artists working in Paris, such as **Lubin Baugin**. Painting becomes a vehicle for portraying social reality in the works of the **Le Nain brothers**, in which sober realism hints at the moderate wealth of a middle-class patron: **Famille de paysans dans un intérieur★**. **Eustache Le Sueur** (1616–55), a painter of religious subjects, influenced by Raphael, painted a famous series of 22 paintings illustrating the life of Saint Bruno.

Rooms 31-32

Chancellor Séguier on Horseback is a solemn, official portrait by **Le Brun** of the artist's main patron during his youth, who enabled him to spend time in Italy. Another composition by Le Brun, *Entrée d'Alexandre le Grand dans Babylone* (1655), depicts Alexander the Great's triumphant entry into Babylon. **Philippe de Champaigne** displayed his talent for creating penetrating portraits of his contemporaries in *Le Prévôt des marchands et les échevins de la ville de Paris*, featuring the Provost of the merchants of Paris and the city's aldermen (1648).

18C

Rooms 34-54.

Leading portraitist at the court of Louis XIV in the latter half of his reign, **Rigaud** painted the sovereign, but also famous figures such as Bossuet, preacher of the Sun King and one of the greatest French orators ever. His stern figure dominates

rooms 34 and 35, along with a monumental *Passage du Rhin par les armées de Louis XIV* (1699) by Parrocel. Only a few years separate these paintings of the Grand Siècle from the dreamy, elegant canvases of **Watteau** (1684-1721). His iconic **Pélerinage à l'île de Cythère★★** depicts a merry crowd about to set sail for the mythical island… or are they actually returning from it? This touchy question hasn't been resolved yet. Watteau's artistic rendering of the birthplace of Venus and ideal island of Love inaugurated a trend for "fêtes galantes" (courtly scenes in an idyllic country setting) that was to blossom in the next decades *(room 36).*

Theatre was another source of inspiration for artists. Watteau himself painted a famous figure of Pierrot and his teacher **Claude Gillot** drew his inspiration from the Commedia dell'Arte. On his amusing street scene entitled *Les deux carrosses*, two carts pulled by servants block each other, as tempers flare out of control.

Room 38 contains hunting scenes by **Jean-François de Troy** and **Carle Vanloo** that were painted for the dining room in the Royal Suite at Fontainebleau. **Boucher** often drew his subjects from mythology, allowing him free licence to treat them with sensual delicacy. His **Diane sortant du Bain** and **Odalisque** *(room 38)*, both painted in fresh, shimmering tones, are examples of his exaltation of the female nude.

A more modest realism fashions the French arts in the second quarter of the 18C, as illustrated by **Chardin**'s still-lifes and genre paintings. Do not miss *Le Bénédicité*, *La Mère laborieuse*, and **La Raie★** in rooms 38 and 40.

Even Boucher joined in this gentle, intimistic movement. With his *Déjeuner* (Morning Coffee, c. 1739), he portrays a domestic happiness that illustrates daily life at the time of Louis XV.

Rooms 43-45

A collection of delicate pastels and miniatures by **Quentin de la Tour** (**Portrait of the Marquise de Pompadour★**), Chardin and others surrounds the great religious and mythological paintings found in room 43: *Pentecost*, a huge painting by **Restout** and *Le Repas chez Simon*, a seven-meter long painting by **Subleyras** that shows the influence of Veronese's large religious compositions.

Rooms 48-49

Fragonard's light touch and happy sense of movement are combined in *Les Baigneuses* (The Bathers, 1763-1764) and *L'Essaim d'Amours* (The Swarm of Cherubs, c. 1767). His energy and passion are further examplified in fantasy figures such as the *Portrait d l'Abbé de Saint-Nom*, painted in one hour, or a famed piece known as *Le Verroua* (The Bolt, 1777), full of sensuality, although more formal in its Neoclassical composition. Shortly before the Revolution, **Hubert Robert** undertook a series of canvases for the apartment of Louis XVI at Fontainebleau, depicting Romanticized Roman ruins that were arbitrarily juxtaposed, irrespective of topographical accuracy. A fine example of Robert's work is *La Maison Carrée, les Arènes et la Tour Magne à Nîmes* (1787).

Rooms 51-52

More paintings by Hubert Robert are on display in gallery 51. These depict the **Grande Galerie du Louvre** in two stages: one as a construction project, the other as a ruin. But the gallery is mostly dedicated to **Greuze** (1725-1805), who, following Diderot's advice, began painting scenes with moral subjects, thus formulating a new genre: *La malédiction paternelle ou Le Fils Ingrat* and *Le Fils Puni*. Room 52 is devoted to the delicate portraits of **Elisabeth Vigée-Lebrun**, regarded as the greatest French female painter of the 18C *(Portrait de Madame Rousseau et sa fille)*.

Room 54

Devoted to **Jacques-Louis David** and his apprentices, this gallery presents works *(Portrait de Madame Charles-Louis Trudaine*, 1791-92) by David himself or by **Antoine-Jean Gros** *(Bonaparte au Pont d'Arcole*, 1796*)*. The gallery marks the transition from the 18C to the 19C.

Masterful *Portrait d'une Femme Noire* (Portrait of a Black Woman, 1800) by **Marie-Guillemine Benoist** (1768-1826) is one of the first examples of a new trend that was to blossom during the 19C: looking at the exotic world with an aesthetical point of view.

19C

Rooms 55-73.

These galleries illustrate genre painting at the turn of the century. The highlights of this section are compositions attributed to **Prud'hon**: *Marie-Marguerite Lagnier, Venus Bathing or Innocence, Madame Jarre* (c. 1822) and Toulouse-born **Pierre-Henri de Valenciennes** (numerous landscapes, mainly from Southern France and Italy).

Ingres (1780-1867), pupil of David, epitomizes the softer Neoclassical taste of the empire. Clarity of line and form are the main concerns of this artist, who vigorously opposed those of the colourists Delacroix and Géricault, imposing a different interpretation of exotic subjects beloved to both factions of the Romantic School: **The Turkish Bath★**, painted 54 years after **The Valpinçon Bather★**, uses the same nude subject seen from behind. Ingres was director of the Académie de France in Rome when his pupil **Hippolyte Flandrin** painted his study *Young Nude Man by the Sea* (1836 – *gallery 63*).

Géricault regularly painted horses racing (**Epsom Derby★**). The artist was thrilled by the latent power of the horse: note his *Tête de lionne* (Head of a Lioness, c. 1819). His excellent portraits such as *La Folle Monomane du Jeu* (The Madwoman Obsessed with Gambling) show his propensity for studying the human character through facial features.

Delacroix's Romantic passion is apparent in his free and speedy brushwork notably in his **Self-Portrait★**; his *Mer vue des hauteurs de Dieppe* prefigures the Impressionists *(room 62)*. Other notable works include his *Young Orphan Girl at the Cemetery* (room 71);and the detail from Delacroix's study Head of a Woman (1823) from the Massacres at Chios; Greek Families Awaiting Death or

Slavery (♻see *19C Large-Format French Painting, below*). Room 63 is devoted to **Chassériau** (1819-1856), a pupil of Ingres and Delacroix with a unique style, full of a haunting sensuality, as illustrated by *La Toilette d'Esther* (1841). Located in a peaceful village near Paris that acted like a magnet for nature loving, pre-Impressionnist painters, the **Ecole de Barbizon** is evoked in room 64. The final galleries are devoted to **Corot**, who is recognized by his landscapes, often bathed in nostalgia, vibrant with scintillating light in the fresh, clear air (*Souvenir of Mortefontaine, Marissel Church, Bridge at Mantes*). *Douai Belfry* was painted during his stay in northern France.

Do not miss room 68 and its extraordinary **Salle de Bain de Corot**, decorated with travel scenes from Italy and Austria.

BEISTEGUI COLLECTION★
Gallery A.

The entire collection of **Carlos Beistegui** (1863, Mexico–1953, Biarritz) consisting above all of portraits, is displayed in a special gallery. Note **Fragonard**'s *Portrait d'un jeune artiste* and *Le Feu aux poudres* (a libertine nude scene that was painted before 1778); **David**'s famous *Le Général Bonaparte* (unfinished portrait of Napoléan); *The Duchess of Chaulnes as Hebe* by Jean-Marc Nattier; *La mort de Didon* by **Rubens**; and **The Marquesa de la Solana★** (1794), one of **Goya**'s best-known works.

PRINCESS LOUIS DE CROŸ DONATION
Gallery B.

This small collection mainly consists of portraits, still lives and landscapes by Dutch painters of the 16C, 17C and 18C.

HELENE AND VICTOR LYON DONATION
Gallery C.

Ranging from 16C Dutch painting to 19C French Impressionists, this collection includes works by Renoir, Boudin, Monet, Degas and Pissarro. The **Santa Maria della Salute** (c. 1735-1740) by

18C Italian painter **Canaletto** is the uncontested masterpiece of this gallery.

LARGE-FORMAT FRENCH PAINTING★★★ (19C)

Daru and Mollien Galleries (rooms 75 and 77), both on first floor of the Denon wing. These two galleries run parrallel to the Grande Galerie. They are separated from one another by the Salon Denon (gallery 76) whose extraordinary ceiling, painted by Charles-Louis Müller between 1863 and 1866, deserves a visit.

The museum's monumental works of the French Revolution, Empire and early 19C are on display in two galleries. As visitors enter room 75, the relief and truthfulness of the monumental painting by **David** (1748-1825) known as the **Sacre de l'Empereur Napoléon Ier et couronnement de l'Impératrice Joséphine dans la cathédrale Notre-Dame de Paris, le 2 décembre 1804★**. The artist met the challenge of producing a work that would glorify Napoléon and secure his imperial legitimacy; in the process, he earned himself a place in the history of painting. A preliminary sketch depicted the new Emperor crowning himself; in the final composition, however, Napoléon is shown in the act of crowning his spouse, Josephine.

In sharp contrast with the formal imperial scene, the opposite wall hosts David's delicate *Portrait of Madame Récamier* (1800). Extremely avant-garde for its time, it shows the famous socialite (and Bonaparte's opponent) dressed in the antique style, and gracefully reclined on a meridienne in a Pompeian décor (♻*see also Decorative Arts*).

The Oath of the Horatii, commissioned by Louis XVI, which **David** despatched from Rome for the Salon of 1785, was nothing less than the manifesto of Neoclassism. Based on an episode in Roman history that personified stoicism and patriotism, this "moral painting" was widely acclaimed by the public.

Ingres' overwhelming concern with the expressive and sensual use of line can be clearly seen in *La Grande Odalisque* and his three portraits of the Rivière family, particularly the *Portrait of Mademoiselle*

Rivière, wherein the aesthetic prevails over anatomical Realism.

Théodore Géricault gave artistic expression to current political issues; as illustrated by his portraits such as *Officier de chassseurs à cheval de la Garde impériale chargeant* (1812). His masterful **The Raft of the Medusa★★**(1819) drew its subject matter from a recent disastrous shipwreck thought largely to be the result of governmental incompetence. The effects of back-lighting and the positions of the unfortunate victims of the shipwreck of the Medusa evoke the wild fluctuations between hope and despair among the ragged survivors, who have just caught sight of the flag of the *Argus* (the ship that was to rescue them) on the horizon.

Eugène Delacroix, the leading exponent of Romanticism, expressed his support for the cause of Greek independence in *Scène des massacres de Scio; familles grecques attendant la mort ou l'esclavage,* inspired by the brutal repression imposed on the inhabitants of that island in 1822 by Ottoman rulers. His reaction to the days of violence in the 1830 Revolution was **La Liberté guidant le peuple★★**, which he exhibited at the Salon. *The Women of Algiers* was painted in the wake of his trip to Morocco and Algeria, and demonstrates Delacroix's use of contrasting colour (red for foreground, green for depth).

In **La Mort de Sardanapale★**, the Orient is portrayed in a mix of magnificence and barbaric decadence, as the sultan had ordered that everything and everyone he held dear should be destroyed in front of him, before he himself committed suicide.

The monumental illustrations by Baron Gros (1771-1835) of the Napoleonic wars add a political touch to Room 77.

NORTHERN SCHOOLS: PAINTING★★★

Second floor, Richelieu wing.

This section is devoted mostly to German, Flemish and Dutch paintings from 15-17C. However, rooms A-F also house Northern Schools paintings (Scandinavia and Russia included) 18C-early 19C.

Flemish Primitives (15C)

Room 5.

The Flemish Primitives masterfully capture lights and emotions. They also pay close attention to domestic detail, such as furniture, folds of clothing and textures. **La vierge du chancelier Rolin★★** by **Jan van Eyck** is the most famous work on display, a striking allegory of the impaired material world kneeling to Virgin Mary, herself a metaphor for the Church. The **Braque Family Triptych** is an intensely spiritual work painted by **Roger van der Weyden** in a revolutionary style inspired from Italian

The Raft of the Medusa (1819) by Théodore Géricault

© Scala, Florence/Musée du Louvre

painting. His *Annunciation* is depicted against the background of a luxuriously furnished interior.

Hans Memling, a German who moved to Flanders and eventually settled in Bruges, was greatly inspired by van der Weyden. He created a distinctive style that unified landscape and portraiture and became particularly popular with Italian patrons. The **Triptych of the Resurrection** and the *Portrait of an Old Woman* are examples of his serene touch. Set in a radiant landscape, the colorful *Déploration du Christ* (undated) of **Dirck Bouts** (c. 1415-1475) vividly illustrates the artist's emotional touch.

German School (15C-16C)
Rooms 7-8.

A rare known example of a 15C **painted table top** stands in the centre of the gallery. It was painted in 1534 by Hans Sebald Beham for the archbishop of Mainz, and depicts scenes from the life of David. Beham was to become the most important successor of Albrecht Dürer. Room 8 holds by Hans Holbein the Younger's portrait of **Erasme**, the greatest humanist of the northern Renaissance. Works by **Lucas Cranach the Elder** (c. 1472-1553)) feature graceful, almost naked female figures illustrating mythological scenes. First painter of the German Renaissance, **Albrecht Dürer** (1471-1528) portrayed himself in his *Portrait de l'artiste tenant un chardon*.

Flanders (16C-17C)
Rooms 9-26.

The impressive Retable de la Déploration du Christ was painted by **Joos van Cleve** (c. 1485-c. 1540). This magnificient work of art bears witness to the new artistic currents that influenced Flemish Renaissance art. In room 9, other highlights include **Jan Gossaert**'s *Dyptique Carondelet*, and Joachim Patinir's *Saint Jérôme dans le désert*.

The paintings by **Peter Paul Rubens** (1577-1640), master of the Baroque, seemed to exalt life itself with fleshy bodies and sumptuous attire. As the artist's reputation grew, various patrons commissioned him to paint historical or mythological subjects. These elements abound in the 24-panel cycle **Marie de' Medici★★**. A pupil of Rubens, **Jacob Jordaens**, cultivated a highly coloured realism that verged on earthiness; his style can be seen in *Le Roi boit! (room 19).*

Antoon Van Dyck was the portraitist to the Genoese and English aristocracy par excellence, catching the refined elegance of both courts: *Charles I, King of England, Portrait d'un homme de qualité avec son fils (room 24).*

Dutch School (17C)
Rooms 27-39.

The Netherlands, a maritime republic, fashioned its art to bourgeois taste depicting domestic scenes, portraiture and landscape.

Frans Hals pioneered the character portrait with paintings such as the *Gypsy Girl* and the *Lute-Player (room 38).* His robust style was to influence Fragonard and Manet. **Jacob van Ruisdael's** *Le Coup de soleil* (amusingly translated as The Ray of Sunlight, knowing that in French, a "coup de soleil" is actually a sunburn) may be seen in room 38. **Van Goyen**'s monochromatic *Paysage fluvial avec moulin et château en ruines* (1644) is a nostalgic evocation of a long-gone medieval past.

Rembrandt (1606-1669) gradually forsook *chiaroscuro* in favour of a more subtle palette ranging through warm, earthy tones of gold and brown; in his *The Philosopher in Meditation,* the artist's play of light and shadow makes Plato's famous allegory of the cave come alive. Other masters of this Golden Age include **Ter Borch**, **Pieter de Hooch**, **Gerrit Dou** and **Adriaen van Ostade**, who were principally genre painters. **Vermeer van Delft** imbues his contemplative scenes of domestic activity with peace through his use of indirect light and oblique shadows.

Northern Schools (18C-19C)
Galleries A to F. Access is through room 28.
This small collection showcases works from the Netherlands, Flanders, Russia, Scandinavia, Austria and Germany. Highlights include Flemish **Jan van Bredael**

Campement militaire in gallery A, and a Neoclassic, peaceful painting by Flemish painter **Balthasar Ommeganck** *Bestiaux dans une prairie près d'une rivière.*

ITALIAN SCHOOL: SCULPTURE★★
Lower level, Denon wing. The collection continues on the ground floor.

Donatello Gallery
Room 1.

13C Italian sculpture is stylised and static (*Virgin* from Ravenna), produced at a time of instability often coined as the Dark Ages. A century later, artists and sculptors learned to review Roman reliefs, reinterpreting their subject matter as Christian narrative. From Pisa (graceful *Virgin* by Nino Pisano) to 15C Siena (Jacopo della Quercia, *Seated Madonna*) and Florence, sculpture evolved to conform with Renaissance aesthetics, towards idealized form and calculated proportion (**Donatello** bas-relief of **The Virgin and Child★**, **Verrocchio**'s two delightful little angels). As you leave, take a look in room 2 dedicated to the **Della Robbia**, a prestigious family of Italian sculptors and potters whose famous workshop in Florence produced outsdanding tin-glazed terracotta sculptures in the 15C.

Michelangelo Gallery
The two marble **Slaves★★★** (1513–20) sculpted by **Michelangelo** for the tomb of Pope Julius II, although uncompleted, are famous masterpieces as expressions of strength apparently breaking out of the rough stone. The Neoclassical **Psyche Revived by the Kiss of Cupid★★** (1793) is quite exquisite, contrived by **Canova** to blend the Antique with a Rococo lightness of touch.

NORTHERN SCHOOLS: SCULPTURE★★
Denon wing: 12-16C (lower ground floor); 17-19C (ground floor, past the Italian sculptures from 16-19C).

Gallery A is mostly devoted to 15C sculpture from England, Belgium, the Netherlands, Germany, Austria and Switzerland,

The Dying Slave (1513–15) by Michelangelo

© Daniel Thierry/Photononstop/Tips Images

exhibiting minute, sometimes polychromic, religious reliefs in alabaster. Gallery B focuses on the 12-15C;15C statues of the Virgin with Child, mostly from the Holy German Empire, are displayed here. With their elegant attitudes and deeply folded drapery, these delicate statues are examples of the **International Gothic Style**. Gallery C is dedicated to 15C-16C Late Gothic Art from Flanders, the Netherlands and Germany, which departed from the stiffness of the Early Gothic era. Swabian sculptors imbue their figures with greater serenity (*Mary Magdalen* by Gregor Erhart), whereas the great Franconian master **Tilman Riemenschneider** produced more delicate pieces such as the marble **Virgin of the Annunciation★**.

Gallery D *(ground floor)* is dedicated to Baroque and Rococco sculpture 17C-18C. Neoclassicist sculptures from the 18C-19C are on display in the Thorvaldsen Gallery *(Gallery E, ground floor)*, named after the Danish sculptor (1770-1844).

FRENCH SCHOOL: SCULPTURE★★★
Ground floor, Richelieu wing: Cour Marly and Cour Puget.

The Renaissance collection is very comprehensive; any gaps in medieval sculpture may be filled by a visit to the Cluny Museum (&see Le QUARTIER LATIN).

High Middle Ages and Romanesque
Rooms 1-3.
The **Porte d'Estagel**, a monumental 12C stone portal from Languedoc, welcomes visitors ; 12C **capitals** from Burgundy and Poitou *(David Fights Goliath, Harvest Scene)*; and finally, the massive altarpiece **Carrières-sur-Seine** *(room 3)*, which marks the transition from Romanesque to Gothic art.

Gothic
Rooms 4-9.
The Gothic Middle Ages, the Age of Cathedrals, produced figurative sculpture imbued with such grace, poise, sophistication and serene beauty on the one hand and such expressive realism on the other as to bear comparison with the best creations from Antiquity. Towards the end of 12C, the iconography evolved towards humanization. The **statue** of King Childebert (c. 1240), in room 4, is an example of this new style.
Religious art soon followed the trend: delicate altarpieces in marble appeared in Northern France *(room 5)*.
Recumbent figures in stone, marble or wood became popular among the elite.

Late Gothic and Renaissance
Rooms 13-19.
Funerary monuments become much larger in the 15C: the **tomb of Philippe Pot★★**, Seneschal of Burgundy, is impressive with its famous hooded mourners. In gallery 11, the *Saint George Fighting the Dragon*, a famous bas-relief by **Michel Colombe**, heralds the Renaissance. The Mort-St-Innocent Gallery is named after the macabre effigy of death that stood at the centre of the Parisian cemetery of this name *(see Les HALLES)*. To the right of the entrance, note the **altarpiece of the Resurrection of Christ**, a delicately executed work in stone combining Flamboyant Gothic motifs with Renaissance ornamentation.
The **School of Fontainebleau** played a major role in the creation of a French-style version of Mannerism that had emerged from the Italian High Renaissance around 1520. Rooms14 and 15b house bas-reliefs by **Jean Goujon** (1510-1566). Those from the Fontaine des Innocents (Paris), featuring nymphs, children and fantastic creatures, and those from the Fontaine de Diane (château d'Anet, Loire Valley), exuding a distant sensuality, both echo these new tendencies. The **Longueville Pyramid** *(room 18)* is topped by an obelisk over four meters high. The 19C staircase, **Escalier Lefuel**, features an impressive array of arcades and banisters.

The 17C
French sculpture evolved little during the reigns of Henri IV and Louis XIII before enjoying a great vogue through the reign of Louis XIV.
The **Cour Marly★★** (the famous rearing **Marly Horses★★**), **Crypte Girardon★** (*The Grand Condé*, bronze by **Antoine Coysevox**), and the **Cour Puget★★** (**Milo of Croton★★** by **Pierre Puget**) display the best of French sculptures that once adorned the parks of royal residences at Marly, Versailles, Sceaux and the Tuileries.

18C-19C
Rooms 21-33 and Cour Puget's upper level. Rooms 21-24 run along Court Puget; 26-30 overlook Rue de Rivoli.
The exquisite **Cupid Putting a Finger to his Lips★** by **Falconet** *(room 22)* was commissioned by Madame de Pompadour to adorn the garden of her mansion, the Hôtel d'Évreux, now the Palais de l'Élysée. **Cupid Whittling a Bow from Hercules' Club★** by **Bouchardon** *(room 23)* was ill-received when presented to the Court in 1750, as Cupid was felt to be too realistic. Room 25 contains helter-skelter miniature sculptures that were used by the candidates to sculpture received by the Académie Royale de Peinture et de Sculpture: the version of **Pigalle**'s masterpiece *Mercury* is more sophisticated than that in bronze in the courtyard. *Psyche Abandoned* caused an uproar because of its complete nudity and stark realism *(room 27)*. The **gallery of great men** *(room 29)* regroups a series of marble effigies such as *Diana*

the Huntress by Houdon. Mythological figures by **Jean-Jacques Pradier**, the in favor in 19C French sculpture, as can be seen in *Three Graces*.

The final gallery *(room 33)* is devoted to the work of **François Rude**, author of the *Marseillaise* engraved on the Arc de Triomphe and **Antoine-Louis Barye**, famed for his observation of animals, sculpted in minute detail.

DECORATIVE ARTS★★★

1st floor, Richelieu wing, and 1st floor Sully wing (mostly northern side).
This department of the Louvre Museum has a long history dating back to the French Revolution. The most famous exhibits come from the Royal Abbey of St-Denis (ⓔ*see Excursions),* which served the French monarchy as a mausoleum.

Middle Ages★★★– *Rooms 1-11, Richelieu 1st floor.* The gold and silver plate and above all, the ivories, some of which are over 1 000 years old, are astounding. The entrance is flanked by pink porphyry columns with the bust of an emperor projecting from just above head level.
Charlemagne and High Middle Ages– *Room 1.* This gallery displays the spoils of Constantinople, pillaged by the Crusaders in 1204. Opposite the entrance is a 9C **equestrian statue of Charlemagne** or possibly of **Charles the Bald**, modelled on Antique equestrian statues. Also on view are artefacts discovered in 1959 in the tomb of Queen Arnegonde, wife of Clovis' son Clothair I (511–61), at St-Denis.
Romanesque and early Gothic Art – *Room 2.* Suger, the Abbot of St-Denis (1122–51), hoped to make his abbey one of the leading churches in Christendom. He experimented with a new type of construction, based on ogive vaulting, and enriched his treasury with liturgical vases. The most famous of these, the **Aigle de Suger★★**, was an antique Egyptian (or Roman) vase transformed into a precious chalice *(opposite the entrance).*
The central display case contains contains one of the oldest surviving examples of French regalia: the **coronation**

sword known as **Charlemagne**'s or the **Joyeuse**.
Gothic art – *Room 3.* Opposite the entrance stands the exquisite ivory statue of the **Virgin and Child** made for the chapel of the palace of St-Louis (now the Ste-Chapelle). It follows the Rayonnant Gothic style for large statuary. The real treasure is the silver gilt Virgin and Child group known as the **Virgin of Jeanne d'Evreux★** (c. 1324-1339).
Charles V Room – *Room 4.* As you enter, the magnificent altarpiece known as the **Retable de Poissy★★** made of wood and ivory was sculpted by the Venetian workshop of the Embriachi family in the early 15C. The **sceptre of Charles V** is embedded with pearls and rubies.
Display cases to the right hold a large, diamond-shaped **ornamental clasp**, and an **ivory diptych** (c. 1400).
Anne de Bretagne Room – *Room 6.* A corridor devoted to a collection of **Spanish earthenware** crockery from the 15C leads to this gallery. Apart from a few precious objects such as the so-called Saint-Louis **chess set** (15-17C), made of crystal, cedar wood, gilded bronze and silver, the room displays a collection of tapestries from the early 16C.
Saint Anatoile Room– *Room 8.* Another corridor housing **Italian majolica** (15C-16C) leads to gallery 8. You will find true masterpieces of the art of gold- or silversmithing here: incense burners, chalices, candlelights and other liturgical objets from the 15C-16C.
A gilded silver piece typical of the Gothic style, is actually displayed in the following room *(9),* among a profusion of 16C millefleur tapestries from Flanders.
Louis XII Room– *Room 11.* **Limoges painted enamels** on copper plaques are displayed here. A highlight is the *Vierge douloureuse* (The Sorrowful Virgin, c. 1500), a devotional medallion typical of the late medieval tradition.
Renaissance– *Rooms 12-31.* The Renaissance period is known for its paintings, yet the decorative arts are among its most sumptuous manifestation. Highlights include the azure blue **wedding gobelet** *(room 18),* 12 tapestries of **The Hunts of Maximilian★★***(room 19).*

The **Scorpio Gallery**★ *(room 20)* has painted enamel **tableware** from Limoges, as well as tapestries copied from one of the most famous series of tapestries from Renaissance Brussels, the **Great Scipio**, commissioned by François I. The **Jean Boulogne Rotunda**★ *(room 26)* houses bronzes by this master and his pupils. Gobelins tapestries hang on the walls. Room 31 houses the **Treasure of the Order of the Holy Spirit**★★, the most prestigious order of the Ancien Régime, founded by Henri III.

17C-18C
Room 32 (1st floor, Richelieu wing) and 33-35(1st floor, Sully wing).
The 17C collection largely comprises objects that had belonged to **Mazarin** and **Richelieu**, or had been collected by Louis XIV. The **Effiat Room**★ (32) is decorated with Louis XIII style furniture. Rooms 35-65 house the 18C collection. Note Marie-Antoinette's **travelling case**, seats by **Jacob**, and lacquer furniture by **Carlin**. The Gobelins **tapestries** were woven to designs by **Boucher**.

19C
Rooms 67-81 (first floor, Richelieu wing).
The Louvre's 19C collection spans the Restoration, Louis-Philippe and Empire periods. The sophisticated furniture of **Madame Récamier's Bedchamber**★ *(room 68),* probably designed by the **Jacob brothers** (1798), epitomizes Empire-style design, distinguished by elegant line. Most pieces, such as Joséphine's **jewelry cabinet** (1809) came from royal residences like the Tuileries.

Napoléon III Apartments★★★
Rooms 82-96 (first floor, Richelieu wing). Access via Cour Marly, up the Escalier du Ministre (towards the Pyramid).
The majestic staircase, decorated with a fine wrought-iron banister, leads to a stunning world of gold, crimson velvet and crystal. These apartments provide one of the few examples of great Second Empire décor to have survived complete with their original furnishings. They consist of an impressive maze of

Dining Room, Napoléon III Apartments

© Maurizio Bachis/Tips Images

private and formal rooms, antechambers, halls and corridors of all kinds. Specific attention should be given to the splendid **Grand Salon** *(room 87)*, a huge drawing room with lavish stucco decorations by Tranchan and a ceiling featuring Charles-Raphaël Maréchal's painting *The Reuniting of the Louvre and the Tuileries by Napoleon III*; the **Salon-théâtre** *(85)*; and the **Grande Salle à Manger** *(dining room) (83)*, with hunting scenes by Laurent-Godefroy Jadin and a remarkable ceiling by Eugène Appert featuring a luminous sky with birds.

ARTS OF AFRICA, OCEANIA, ASIA AND THE AMERICAS
Pavillon des Sessions; access is via the Porte de Lions.
This annex of the Musée du quai Branly is devoted to the indigenous art and cultures of Africa, Asia, Oceania and the Americas. It was created in 2000 to integrate masterpieces from non-European civilisations with the most respected icons of Western culture. Located on the south-west end of the Louvre palace, this exhibition space was subtly designed by Jean-Michel Wilmotte. It is conducive to a coherent and rewarding visit. Visitors will most definitely enjoy the selection of about 108 works of exceptional quality from all continents, carefully chosen for their artistic value and historical context. Works on display are rotated on a regular basis.

Beaubourg★★ and Les Halles★

Acrobats, jugglers and street artists of all kinds are attracted to the hub of the Georges Pompidou Centre, where the sound of music and the movement of the crowds create a festive feel. Inside this modern art centre is a fine collection of 20C art, as well as changing contemporary exhibitions. The urban renewal project for the Beaubourg plateau undertaken in the 1970s mingles zany, ultra-modern elements with medieval splendour – the Stravinski fountain and St-Merri. At Les Halles, the demolition and displacement of the city's main wholesale market has radically altered the area's character. Today, a busy shopping centre with a garden occupies the site of the old trade halls, once known as The Belly of Paris (the title of a novel by Émile Zola). Some of the old streets remain, as does one of Paris' most beautiful churches, St-Eustache.

A BIT OF HISTORY

The Old Halles – In 1135 there was already a twice-weekly market at Les Halles, where each street specialized in a particular trade. By the 16C, with a growing population of 300 000 in the capital, the trade in foodstuffs became of paramount importance, eventually replacing all other types of trade in the market. On the orders of Napoléon, the wine and leather markets were transferred to the Left Bank.

Until the Revolution, a pillory stood near St-Eustache crossroads; dishonest traders, thieves and prostitutes were publicly exposed there. By the 19C the great market was in urgent need of reconstruction. Wide avenues through the quarter were opened (rue de Rivoli, rue du Pont-Neuf, rue du Louvre, rue Étienne-Marcel), and 10 halls of iron girders and skylight roofs designed by **Baltard** and **Callet** were constructed (1854–74). The animated market scene

- **Info:** Paris Office du Tourisme, 25 rue des Pyramides. ☏08 92 68 30 00 (0.34€ per min). http://en.parisinfo.com.
- **Location:** On the Right Bank of the Seine, Beaubourg lies between Les Halles and the Marais. The Hôtel de Ville and rue de Rivoli mark its southern border.
- **Metro/Transport:** Les Halles, Louvre Rivoli, Rambuteau – RER: Châtelet-les-Halles (lines A, B and D). Buses: 29, 38, 47.
- **Parking:** There is underground parking at the Centre Pompidou and under the Forum des Halles. Most of Beaubourg is pedestrian only.
- **Don't Miss:** The panoramic city views from the top of the Centre Pompidou, and the food shops on rue Montorgueil.
- **Timing:** Beaubourg can be seen in less than an hour, longer if you decide to visit the museum. Allow one to two hours for Les Halles.
- **Kids:** The colourful, twirling water sculptures of the Stravinski fountain. The play areas in Jardin Nelson Mandela, and the Doll Museum– the Musée de la Poupée.

was rich with colours and smells. Locals enjoyed eating onion soup, snails and pig's trotters at 5am in simple but excellent restaurants with names like Le Chien qui Fume, Le Pied de Cochon. As the old buildings became inadequate, they were demolished and removed, and the market was relocated to the outskirts of the city at Rungis (1969).

Centre Georges-Pompidou

© S. Sauvignier/MICHELIN

CENTRE GEORGES-POMPIDOU★★★

Place Georges-Pompidou.
🕐*Wed–Mon 11am–9pm, Thu until 11pm (last admission 1hr before closing).*
🕐*1 May.* ♿ ☏*01 44 78 12 33.*
www.centrepompidou.fr.

This "inside out" building known as the Centre Georges Pompidou is easily spotted on the Parisian skyline with its bright red, blue and white pipes and beams. Built in 1977 on the grounds that were once the parking for the marketplace at Les Halles, it's home to a modern art museum, a public library, a music research centre, a café, several shops, an arthouse cinema and rooftop restaurant. The architects **Richard Rogers** (British) and **Renzo Piano** (Italian) achieved a totally futuristic building. The façade appears a tangle of pipes and tubes latticed along its glass skin, earning the establishment the nickname of "the inside-out museum".

The **Musée national d'Art moderne** occupies the 4th and 5th levels. The **Bibliothèque publique d'information**, the public library known as the BPI, resides on the 1st, 2nd and 3rd levels. The library is especially popular with Parisians, thanks to its late hours, open access and up-to-date collection of printed and other resources. The **IRCAM** (Institute for Acoustic and Musical Research) lies beneath place Stravin-

ski. The centre also houses **temporary exhibition halls** on the 1st (mezzanine) and 6th levels. In addition, it provides live entertainment, cinematic performances and spoken reviews. On level 0 is a bookshop, a design shop and a café (with a view over the main entrance) on level 1, and a restaurant on level 6.

Musée national d'Art moderne★★★

Place Georges-Pompidou.
🕐*Wed–Mon 11am–9pm, Thu until 11pm (last admission 1hr before closing). Atelier Brancusi 2pm–6pm.* 🕐*1 May. Museum and exhibits ☜10–13€, no charge 1st Sun in the month; 3€ for 6th-floor view only.* ♿ ☏*01 44 78 12 33. www.centrepompidou.fr.*

Ranking high among the most significant collections dedicated to modern art in the world (50 000 works and objects), the National Museum of Modern Art traces the evolution of art from Fauvism and Cubism to the contemporary art scene. The collection (1905–60) is housed on the fifth floor; contemporary exhibits from the 1960s onwards are held on the fourth floor.

Outside the museum, the Parisian sculpture workshop of **Constantin Brancusi** (1876–1957) has been reconstituted in its entirety in a small building in the square, and features the artist's tools and personal art collection.

Modern collection

Fifth floor.

Here, 40 galleries present around 900 works *(changed every 18 months)*. Throughout the exhibit, the juxtaposition of painting and sculpture with the design and architecture of the same decade enables the visitor to obtain an overview of 20C creativity. Galleries dedicated to a single artist (Matisse, Léger, Picasso, Rouault, Delaunay) alternate with thematic rooms. All the main movements of the first half of the 20C are represented here, such as **Fauvism** (1905–10; Derain, Marquet, Dufy and Matisse); **Cubism** (**Braque** and **Picasso** in 1907), **Dada** (from 1913; **Marcel Duchamp**), the **Paris School** (1910–30; **Soutine**, **Chagall**, **Modigliani**, Larionov, Gontcharova), the Abstract School (from 1910; **Kandinsky**, **Kupka**, **Mondrian**, **Klee**), and the **Bauhaus School**. **Surrealism** is represented by De Chirico, **Salvador Dalí**, Max Ernst, **Magritte**, Brauner, André Masson, Tanguy, Giacometti, Picasso and **Miró**.

During the 1950s Abstract art appealed to many French and foreign artists (Hartung, Poliakoff, De Staël, Dubuffet). The **Cobra** movement (1948–51) advocated spontaneous expression through the free use of bold colour and energetic brushstrokes (Alechinsky, Appel, Jorn). American art from the 1940s to the 1960s is represented by **Pollock**, **Rothko** and **Newman**. Colour and purity of line are all-important to **Matisse**, in his distinctive gouache cut-outs or "drawing with scissors", as the artist put it, whereas in sculpture, **Brancusi** and Calder pursue abstraction for its own sake.

Contemporary collection

Fourth floor.

These exhibits are regularly changed, representing the main artistic trends, together with major personalities, combining to create a world of colour, form and movement linking art with everyday life.

Major works include *Requiem for a Dead Leaf* (Tinguely), *Red Rhinoceros* (Veilhan).

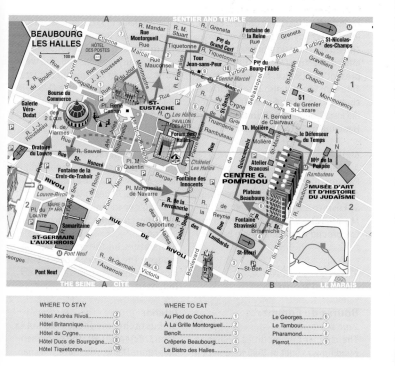

Église St-Eustache interior columns

©H. Chajmowicz/Michelin

Pop Art is represented by **Warhol** and Rauschenberg, **New Realism** by **Klein**, **Arman**, César, **Niki de Saint-Phalle**, **Op** and **Kinetic Art** by **Agam** (Antechamber of the Élysée Palace private apartments) and Vasarely, and there are installations by **Dubuffet** *(The Winter Garden)*, **Beuys** *(Plight)* and **Raynaud** *(Container Zero)*. Three rooms contain examples of design and architecture from the 1960s to the present day (Starck, Nouvel, Perrault, Toto Ito). Space is also devoted to the cinema (**Jean-Luc Godard**), multimedia installations (**Ugo Rondinone**) and Happening (**Gutaï** and **Fluxus**).

Sixth floor

A splendid **view★★** extends over the Paris rooftops – from right to left: Montmartre dominated by the Sacré-Cœur, St-Eustache, the Eiffel Tower, Maine-Montparnasse Tower, St-Merri in the foreground with Notre-Dame behind.

🐾 WALKING TOUR

Start from Ⓜ Louvre-Rivoli.

Bourse du Commerce

2 rue de Viarmes.
The circular Commodities Exchange building was built in 1889 to replace a wheat market built in Louis XVI's reign. Inside, the vast circular hall lit by a glass dome is now used by the Paris Chamber of Commerce.

Jardin Nelson Mandela

Honouring the former President of South Africa, this (4.3ha/10acre) garden is currently being transformed into a vast eco-sustainable space. Planted with trees, shrubs and grasses, and equipped with benches, children's play areas and tables for ping-pong and chess, it is re-opening in stages until late 2016.

Église St-Eustache★★

Place du Jour.
Gothic in plan and structure, but Renaissance in decoration, this edifice is one of Paris' most beautiful churches.
In 1214 a chapel dedicated to St Agnes was built on this spot. A few years later, the chapel was re-dedicated to St Eustache, a converted Roman general. But the Halles parish, which had become the largest in Paris, dreamed of a church worthy of its new status. Grandiose plans were made and the foundation stone was laid in 1532. Construction was slow, however, in spite of liberal gifts and the church was not consecrated until a century later, in 1640. The **west front** was never completed but later rebuilt in the Classical style (1754). In 1844 the edifice was badly damaged by fire and subsequently restored by **Baltard**.

North transept façade★

This fine Renaissance composition is flanked by twin staircase turrets ending in pinnacles. Beneath the gable point is a stag's head with a Cross between the antlers recalling St Eustache's conversion.
The statues on the door shafts are modern. The pilasters, niches, mouldings, grotesques and roses are delicately fashioned.

Interior

St-Eustache measures 100x44x 34m/328x144x111.5ft. The plan resembles Notre-Dame, with nave and chan-

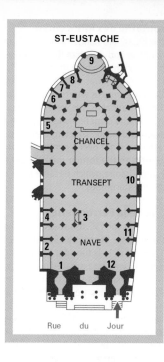

ST-EUSTACHE

CHANCEL

TRANSEPT

NAVE

Rue   du   Jour

1. *On the door; Martyrdom of St Eustace by Simon Vouet (17C).*

2. *Adoration of the Magi, Rubens copy.*

3. *Churchwarden's pew presented by Regent, Philippe of Orleans (1720).*

4. *Colourful naïve sculpture by R Mason commemorating the fruit and vegetable market's move out of Paris on 28 February 1969.*

5. *Tobias and the Angel, Santi di Tito (16C).*

6. *The Ecstasy of Mary Magdalene, a painting by Manetti (17C).*

7. *The Pilgrims at Emmaüs, Rubens.*

8. *Colbert's tomb by Le Brun; Coysevox carved the statues of the minister and of Abundance; Tuby that of Fidelity (left).*

9. *Statue of the Virgin by Pigalle. 19C chapel frescoes by Thomas Couture.*

10. *16C statue of St John the Evangelist.*

11. *Bust of the composer Jean-Philippe Rameau, who died in 1764.*

12. *Epitaph to Lieutenant-General Chevert.*

cel encircled by double aisles and flat transepts. The vaulting above the nave, transept and chancel is Flamboyant, adorned with numerous ribs and richly carved hanging keystones.

The elevation, however, is entirely different from the cathedral's. The aisles, devoid of galleries, rise very high, the arches being so tall that between them and the clerestory windows there is space only for a small Renaissance-style gallery.

The stained-glass windows in the chancel are after drawings by Philippe de Champaigne (1631). St Eustace appears at the centre, surrounded by the Fathers of the Church and the Apostles. The chapels are decorated with frescoes.

▶ Walk down the narrow rue du Jour.

No 4 once belonged to Montmorency-Bouteville, who was beheaded in 1628 for contravening Richelieu's ban on duelling.

▶ Then turn right onto rue Montmartre.

From nos 3 and 4 rue Montmartre, there are fine **views** of the church.

▶ At the end of rue Montmartre, turn left to rue Montorgueil.

Rue Montorgueil
This pedestrianized shopping neighbourhood, renovated in the 1990s, still retains some of its old-fashioned boutiques and food shops such as l'Escargot, Le Rocher de Cancale and Stroher, the latter a patisserie in Paris since 1730. The rue Montorgueil is crossed by some interesting side streets such as the **rue Mauconseil**, once home to theatre troupes, the **rue Tiquetonne**, with its historic façades, and the **rue Marie Stuart**, which leads to the shopping passage du Grand-Cerf.

▶ Go through the passage du Grand-Cerf (built in 1825 and restored in the 1980s, now home to modern boutique shops) and turn right onto the rue St-Denis to rejoin the rue Étienne-Marcel.

Tour de Jean-sans-Peur

20 rue Étienne Marcel. ○*Wed–Sun 1.30pm–6pm.* ∞*5€.* ℘*01 40 26 20 28. www.tourjeansanspeur.com.*

One of the last remaining visible examples of medieval architecture in Paris, this tower was built by John the Fearless for his own protection in 1409 following the assassination, on his orders, of the Duke of Orléans. The tower formed part of the **Hôtel de Bourgogne**. The vaulted ceiling above the original spiral staircase is a masterpiece of French sculpture. The tower is also home to the oldest toilets in Paris – dating from 1411.

Rue Saint-Denis

When it was created in the 8C, this street was one of the most important commercial streets in Paris; it was richly decorated since it was a royal processional road between Notre-Dame and St-Denis Basilica. The oldest profession in the world and sex shops are more apparent than anything royal these days.

A bit further on the right, the **rue de la Grande-Truanderie** refers to the historic "Courtyard of Miracles" where bandits and beggars sought refuge up until the 17C.

▶ Return to the Forum des Halles by the rue Lescot on the left.

Forum des Halles

Occupying the site of the capital city's former wholesale food market, this vast four-floor underground shopping centre and 27-screen cineplex is accessed via the world's busiest subterranean station, serving 750,000 passengers a day. The complex is currently being refurbished and fitted with a glass roof canopy by architect David Mangin, but remains open to the public during the overhaul.

▶ Return to the rue St-Honoré and continue to the place Marguerite-de-Navarre, which leads to the Fontaine des Innocents.

Fontaine des Innocents★

The 19C square stands on the site of the cemetery and church of the Holy Innocents, which date back to the 12C.

The cemetery was once encircled by a charnel house where bones from the communal graves were collected. In 1786, the cemetery was closed and nearly two million skeletons were transferred by night over a period of many months to the former quarries of La Tombe-Issoire, which became known as the Catacombes.

Rue de la Ferronnerie

Created in the 13C, this street bears the same name (Ironworks Street) since 1229. At no 11 is the spot where King Henri IV was assassinated on 14 May 1610. The king had left the Louvre to visit his ailing finance minister, Sully, at the Arsenal. His carriage was blocked by two smaller carts in the street, forcing it to stop. Ravaillac, who had followed the procession since the Louvre, saw his chance and jumped onto the carriage, stabbing Henri IV twice before the guards could reach him.

Rue des Lombards

This road is a typical medieval street where, in the Middle Ages, Lombardian loan sharks would sell their silver for the price of gold.

Église St-Merri★

Access to the church is through the main façade on rue St-Martin or through the St-Merri presbytery (76 rue de la Verrerie). ○*Call for hours.* ℘*01 42 71 93 93.*

St Merry or Medericus, who died here in the 7C, used to be invoked to assist in the release of captives. The former parish church of the Lombard usurers, although dating from 1520 to 1612, curiously conforms to the 15C Flamboyant Gothic style.

Outside, the west front stands directly on the narrow rue St-Martin, crowded in with small houses and shops.

The Flamboyant interior, remodelled under Louis XV, retains 16C stained-glass

windows in the first three bays of the chancel and transept, and fine ribbed vaulting at the transept crossing.
Don't miss the majestic 17C organ loft – the organ at one time played by **Camille St-Saëns** – and beautiful wood panelling by the Slodtz brothers (pulpit, sacristy and the glory at the back of the choir). One bell dating from 1331, probably the oldest in Paris, survives from the medieval chapel that stood on the site of the present church.

Fontaine Stravinski

The **Stravinski fountain**★ (place Stravinski), with black and coloured mobile sculptures by Tinguely and Niki de St-Phalle, respectively, illustrates the works of the great Russian composer (Rite of Spring, The Firebird) **Igor Stravinski** (1882-1971).

Rue St-Merri

On the north side of place Stravinski, across from rue du Renard.
Note nos 9 and 12 with their fine frontages and beyond, impasse du Bœuf, perhaps the oldest cul-de-sac in Paris.

Plateau de Beaubourg – place Georges Pompidou

The area takes its name from the old village included within the Philippe-Auguste wall at the end of the 12C. Run-down and derelict, the old quarter was cleaned up in 1939 and subjected to major redevelopment in 1968. In 1969, on the initiative of **Georges Pompidou** (1911–74), the then President of France, it was decided to create a multi-purpose cultural centre.

Rue Quincampoix

This is the site where the South Sea Bubble of the Scots financier **John Law** was situated. Law founded a bank here in 1719, attracting all kinds of speculators and expanding into the neighbouring houses. The frenzy lasted until 1720 when the bank crashed and the speculators fled. Law's house was razed when rue Rambuteau was built.

Several old houses (nos 10, 12, 13, 14) survive with unusual paved courtyards, mascarons (stone masks), intricate wrought-iron balconies and nailed or carved doors. Continue north on this narrow pedestrianised street to art galleries, boutiques and bars typifying the stylish urban atmosphere that has permeated the quarter since the construction of the Pompidou Centre.

Théâtre Molière – Maison de la Poésie

157 r. St-Martin. ©Tue–Sat 2pm–6pm. ℘01 44 54 53 00. www.maisondela poesieparis.com.
The Maison de la Poésie, created in 1983, and formerly housed in the Forum des Halles, is now situated in the Théâtre Molière. This theatre, established in 1791, had somewhat of a chaotic existence over the years until it was finally closed for good. Reopened to the public in 1994, it became both a theatre and the Maison de la Poésie, and exists to promote, through shows, concerts, readings and talks, the vast diversity of the world's poetic heritage.

Quartier de l'Horloge

Le Défenseur du Temps, an unusual brass and steel electronic clock with a Jack known as the Defender of Time, was designed by Jacques Monestier. On striking the hour, this life-size figure armed with a double-edged sword and shield, confronts one of three animals symbolising the elements: a dragon (earth), a bird (air) and a crab (water).

♟♙ Musée de la Poupée

22 rue Beaubourg. ©Tue–Sat 1pm–6pm. ©Holidays. ⊚8€; under-12s 4€. ♿ ℘01 42 72 73 11. www.museedelapoupeeparis.com.
Some 500 dolls from the 19C to today are presented with period furniture, accessories and toys. Temporary exhibits, a doll boutique and clinic.
Next to the museum is a small playground in the Jardin Anne-Frank.

Le Sentier and Le Temple

The Sentier Quarter is the centre of the rag trade, or textile wholesalers. It's a busy, noisy district devoid of retail shops, but nonetheless there are some interesting corners worth exploring. The Temple neighbourhood encompasses the bustling place de la République, on the periphery of the Marais and Beaubourg, the Temple, and the Oberkampf district which, with its many bars, is a popular place for an evening out.

A BIT OF HISTORY

Place de la République – In 1854 Haussmann incorporated this small square into his grand urban scheme, and it was named in honour of the First, Second and Third Republics. It is situated roughly on the site of the bastion and gateway to the Temple, once the stronghold of the Knights Templar in Paris. In 1879 the city authorities held a competition to design a monument to commemorate the proclamation of the new Republic. The Morice brothers won the contest: Léonard, who completed the sculpture and Charles, who produced the base. The Statue to the Republic was erected and inaugurated on 14 July 1883, with bronze low-relief sculptures around the base representing the great events in the history of the Republic from its inception to the first 14 July national celebration in 1880.

Quartier du Temple – This quarter was once the domain of the Knights Templar and the Benedictines from St-Martin-des-Champs. Their original impressive stronghold no longer exists, having been demolished by Napoléon and Napoléon III during the 19C. Constructed by the Templars in 1240 during the reign of King Louis IX, it was confiscated from them by King Philip the Fair after they fell from grace in 1307. There were a number of buildings on the site, which included a church, a huge keep called the Grosse Tour (the Great Tower) and the smaller Tour de César (Caesar's Tower). Today it is a busy district of

- **Info:** Paris Office du Tourisme, 25 rue des Pyramides. ℘08 92 68 30 00 (0.34€ per min). http://en.parisinfo.com.
- **Location:** On the Right Bank of the Seine, between the Marais and Canal St-Martin.
- **Metro/Transport:** For Le Sentier: Bourse (line 3), Sentier (line 3), Bonne Nouvelle (lines 8 and 9) – Buses: 67, 74, 85. For Le Temple: Temple (line 3), Réaumur Sébastopol (lines 3 and 4), Arts-et-Métiers (lines 3 and 11), République (lines 3, 5, 8, 9, 11) – Buses: 20, 54, 56, 65, 74.
- **Parking:** In Le Sentier there is underground parking on boulevard Bonne Nouvelle. In Le Temple there is underground parking on the avenue de la République.
- **Don't Miss:** The relief statues carved into the Passage du Caire entrance. The recently renovated Musée des Arts et Métiers.
- **Timing:** Allow an hour to explore this district, two if visiting the museum.
- **Kids:** There's a playground in the square du Temple.

jewellery and garment wholesalers, restaurants, and a renowned technical training school.

The Temple Prison – On 13 August 1792, the royal family were all imprisoned in the Temple Tower. On 20 January 1793, Louis XVI was condemned by the Convention and sent to the guillotine. On 2 August, the queen was transferred to the Conciergerie; she left only to go to the guillotine on 16 October.

Templar cross

The Knights Templar

In 1140 the religious and military order, known as the Order of Knights Templar, founded during 1118 in the Holy Land by nine knights to protect pilgrims, established a house in Paris. Independent of any ruling monarch, they were soon entrusted with great wealth that enabled them to create a substantial and unrivalled international banking system.

By the 13C their property investments amounted to almost one-quarter of the land area of Paris, including all the Marais neighbourhood *(see Le MARAIS)*.

King Philip IV, or as he was better known Philip the Fair, decided to suppress this state within a state. He was becoming more and more concerned about the increasing power of the Templars – who, as a religious order, were answerable only to the Pope – as well as being jealous of their great wealth, as the Crown was very much indebted to the order. He persuaded Pope Clement V – the Frenchman Bernard de Got – to support his intentions. On 13 October 1307, all the Templars in France were arrested, including the leader, Jacques de Molay, and 140 knights were imprisoned in Paris.

Having been granted the authority he needed by Clement V, the king dissolved the order and had de Molay together with 54 knights tortured and burned at the stake. Two-thirds of the estates were confiscated by the Crown; the rest was given to the Knights of St John of Jerusalem, later known as the Knights of Malta. According to legend, de Molay cursed both Philip and Clement as he was consumed by the flames, prophesying that they would both appear before God's Tribunal within the next year. As it transpired, both were dead within months of the execution – Clement in just over a month and Philip by the end of the year in a hunting accident!

Jacques de Molay and Geoffroy de Charnay burned at the stake, illustration from the Grandes Chroniques de France (14C)

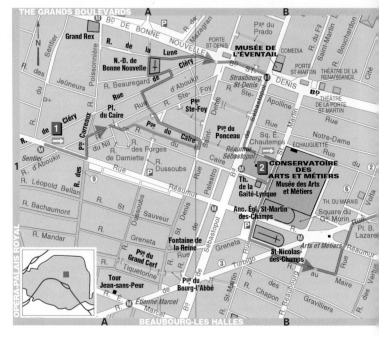

Other royal prisoners held here were Madame Élisabeth, sister of the king, who was guillotined in 1794; Princess Marie Thérèse, the daughter of the king, who was later exiled; and the young King Louis XVII, who died in the prison aged 10 years. Following the Terror, the prison became a place of pilgrimage for Royalists, and so it was demolished on the orders of Napoléon in 1808.

 WALKING TOURS

1 LE SENTIER
Start from Ⓜ *Sentier.*

◐ Take rue Réamur and turn left on to rue des Petits Carreaux.

Place du Caire
The former **cour des Miracles** (Courtyard of Miracles), a large courtyard, unpaved, stinking and muddy, lay hidden in a labyrinth of blind alleys, easily defensible passageways and darkened streets. Rogues, ruled by their own king, occupied the area that remained off-limits to any but their own. Victor

Hugo's novel *The Hunchback of Notre-Dame* is a depiction of this wayward life. The neighbourhood was cleared in 1667.

◐ From rue du Caire walk through passage du Caire.

Passage du Caire
A building decorated with Egyptian motifs (sphinx, lotus, hieroglyphs) marks the entrance of the passage intersected by three covered arcades. Napoléon's victorious campaign in Egypt in 1798 aroused great enthusiasm in Paris.
A taste for the Egyptian style influenced all the decorative and applied arts, architecture and fashion included. Here street names reflect the craze, borrowed from campaigns against the Turks and the Marmalukes (rue du Nil, rue du Caire, rue d'Aboukir).

◐ Walk to rue de Cléry via rue d'Alexandrie and rue St-Philippe.

Rue de Cléry
Fronted by clothes shops, this street is the old counterscarp of the Charles V perimeter wall.

SENTIER AND TEMPLE

▶ Turn left on to rue des Degrés, where a stairway gives access to the former ramparts and leads to the back of the church of Notre-Dame-de-Bonne-Nouvelle.

Église Notre-Dame de Bonne Nouvelle

The Classical belfry is all that remains of the church built by Anne of Austria; the rest of the building dates from 1823 to 1829. Note the painting by Mignard above the door in the south aisle of Anne of Austria and Henrietta-Maria, wife of Charles I of England; one at the end of the north aisle showing Henrietta of England and her three children before St Francis of Sales; an Annunciation by Lanfranco (centre of the chancel, light switch on the right), and a painting by Philippe de Champaigne (to the right). In the Lady Chapel there is a fine 18C Virgin and Child attributed to Pigalle. A small **treasury** contains a 17C alabaster statue of St Jerome, two depictions of the Deposition and an 18C silk garment worn by Abbot Edgeworth of Firmont, who accompanied Louis XVI on his way to the guillotine.

② LE TEMPLE
Start from Ⓜ*Réaumur-Sébastopol metro station.*

La Gaîté Lyrique
3bis rue Papin. ◐*Hours vary per exhibit.* ◉*Price varies per exhibit.* ✆*01 53 01 51 51. www.gaite-lyrique.net.*
Inaugurated in 1862, this venue was once one of the most beautiful Haussmann-era theatres. It became a circus and mime school in the 1970s, and lost most of its original interior architecture in 1986 when it was transformed into a children's amusement centre. Closed since 1990, it reopened in 2010 as a centre for digital arts, with reference library, concert hall and regular exhibitions.

Conservatoire national des Arts et Métiers★★
This former Benedictine priory became a conservatoire for technical studies under the Convention in 1794. Today it also houses a technology museum (&*see p158*).
In rue du Vertbois, a **watchtower** (*échauguette*) and fragments of the medieval (1273) priory wall can be seen.

In the courtyard, on the right, the former monastery **refectory★★** was designed by **Pierre de Montreuil** (13C).

▶ Turn left in rue de Turbigo to approach the **Ancienne Église St Martin des Champs★** with its Romanesque east end (1130 – restored), fine capitals, belfry and Gothic nave.

Église Saint-Nicolas-des-Champs★

The church was built in the 12C, rebuilt in the 15C, and enlarged in the 16C and 17C. The façade and belfry are Flamboyant Gothic, the south door is Renaissance (1581).

Inside hang a number of 17C, 18C and 19C paintings; on the double-sided altar are a retable by Simon Vouet (16C) and four angels by the 17C sculptor Sarrazin.

▶ Walk along rue au Maire, then turn left on to rue Volta and right on to rue de Turbigo, which leads to the back of Ste-Élisabeth; walk around the church.

Église Sainte-Élisabeth

This former monastic chapel (1628–46) dedicated to St Elisabeth of Hungary is now the church of the Knights of Malta. Of particular interest are the 100 early 16C Flemish low-relief sculptures depicting biblical scenes around the ambulatory.

Carreau du Temple

♿ ⏰ *Mon–Sat 1pm–7pm.* ⊞*Price varies per event.* ☎*01 83 81 93 30.* *www.carreaudutemple.eu.*
Next to the town hall and garden square, the Carreau is a centre for the performing arts, fashion and sport. It was converted into an open-air market after the Temple was pulled down during the Napoléonic era, specialising in second-hand clothing. It became known as the Carreau du Temple because the clothes were displayed on the *carreaux* or paving stones. In 1857 a covered market was constructed by Haussmann, and in 1904 the inaugural Foire de Paris or Paris Fair took place here.

MUSÉE DES ARTS ET MÉTIERS★★

⏰*Tue–Sun 10am–6pm (9.30pm Thu)* ⏰*1 May, 25 Dec.* ⊞*6.50€.* ☎*01 53 01 82 75. www.arts-et-metiers.net.*
The museum illustrates technical progress in industry and science. The visit begins with instruments used to explore the **infinitesimal** and **infinitely remote**. Next come **machines** and models showing **building techniques**. **Communication** is illustrated through printing, television, photography, computing, etc. The theme of **energy** is represented by a model of the Marly machine (1678–85), turbines, boilers and engines, whereas **locomotion** explores all means of transport: cycles, cars, aircraft (including Blériot's with which he crossed the channel) and 19C railways. The magnificent chapel is used to display the first steam buses, a model of the Statue of Liberty, of the engine of the European rocket Ariane and of Foucault's pendulum that proved the rotation of the earth. The finest exhibits include **Pascal's arithmetic machine** (1642), **Edison's phonograph** (1878), the **magic lantern** used by the **Lumière brothers** in 1895, Volta's battery (1800), an **automata theatre** that brings back to life Marie-Antoinette's dulcimer-playing puppet of 1784.

OBERKAMPF

11th Arr. From place de la République, walk up avenue de la République to rue Oberkampf (7th road on the left).
Rue Oberkampf and the surrounding streets (rue Saint-Maur, rue Jean-Pierre-Timbaud, rue Moret) hold a long string of bars and cafés, some styled to re-create the working-class atmosphere of Ménilmontant at the turn of the 19C, others with more modern décor.
One of the most famous along the street is the Café Charbon (no 109), with its retro dining room and contemporary nightclub, Nouvelle Casino, hidden in the back. The café is greatly in favour with young Parisians for its laid-back vibe and bars.

Le Marais★★★

The Marais district is unusual for its fine pre-Revolution residential architecture, including many illustrious mansions restored and converted into museums, and the place des Vosges, the city's oldest square. A popular district ever since its revival in the late 20C, today the Marais is home to the Jewish Quarter, hip and avant-garde fashion boutiques, contemporary art galleries and a lively gay community.

A BIT OF HISTORY

In the 13C marshland (*marais* in French) surrounding the raised rue St-Antoine, a highway since Roman times, was drained and converted into arable land. Philippe Auguste's defensive wall, which also served as a dike, and the Charles V wall ending in the formidable Bastille fortress in the east, brought the Marais within the city limits. Royal patronage began after the flight of **Charles V** from the royal palace to the **Hôtel St-Paul**. Charles VI also took up residence there. By the beginning of the 17C the then place Royale, now place des Vosges, built by Henri IV, had become the focal point of the Marais.

Splendid mansions were erected and decorated by the best contemporary artists. The *hôtel particulier*, a discreet Classically designed private residence, standing between the entrance court and garden, developed as a distinctive feature in French architecture. Women of the world attracted free-thinkers and philosophers through their *salons* – the brilliant conversational groups who frequented their houses. Two churches, St-Paul and St-Gervais, attracted famous preachers and musicians. Gradually, the nobility began to move west to Île St-Louis, then Faubourg St-Germain and Faubourg St-Honoré. After the taking of the Bastille, the quarter was virtually abandoned. In the 20C, the derelict quarter was essentially saved from complete destruction by **André Malraux**, Charles de Gaulle's Culture Minister.

Info: Paris Office du Tourisme, 25 rue des Pyramides. ✆08 92 68 30 00 (0.34€ per min). http://en.parisinfo.com.

Location: The Marais is on the Right Bank, bordered by the place de la Bastille and the Hôtel de Ville, the Seine and the Quartier du Temple.

Metro/Transport: Chemin-Vert (line 8), St-Paul (line 1). Buses: 20, 29, 69, 76, 96.

Parking: Underground parking only, at Hôtel de Ville, place de la Bastille.

Don't Miss: The free permanent collection of the Musée Carnavalet, the architecture of the place des Vosges, and the antique shops of the Village St-Paul.

Timing: At least a half-day, ideally a full day to visit the sights.

Kids: Musée de la Curiosité et de la Magie.

WALKING TOURS

See the highlights of the Marais with these two walking tours: the **St-Paul circuit** and the **Marais circuit**. The descriptions of museums and the collections housed in the most attractive of the hotels are found at the end of the chapter.

1 SAINT-PAUL CIRCUIT

This walk takes you through the southern part of the Marais. Start from St-Paul metro station.

Église Saint-Paul-Saint-Louis
99 rue St-Antoine.
In 1580 the Jesuits were given land by Louis XIII to build a church (1627–41) modelled on the Gesù Church in Rome. After the demolition of an old church

WHERE TO STAY

Croix de Malte........ ①
Grand Hôtel Amelot.................. ②
Grand Hôtel Malher.............. ④
Hôtel Acacias-Hôtel-de-Ville.... ⑧
Hôtel Bretonnerie.......... ⑯
Hôtel Campanile........... ⑳
Hôtel de la Place des Vosges.......... ㉔
Hôtel du 7e Art.............. ㉘
Hôtel Jeanne d'Arc, le Marais.............. ㉜
Hôtel Pavillon de la Reine.......... ㊱
Hôtel Saint-Louis Marais................ ㊵

WHERE TO EAT

Autour du Saumon... ①
Breizh Café.............. ②
Candelaria............... ③
Chez Marianne....... ④
L'As de Fallafel........ ⑤
L'Enoteca................ ⑥

Hôtel de Canillac.......... 4
Hôtel Duret-de-Chevry.. 8
Hôtel de Vigny............. 10
Hôtel de Croisilles...... 12
Hôtel de Sandreville..... 26
Hôtel d'Alméras......... 30
Maison parisienne de l'abbaye d'Ourscamp....... 44-46

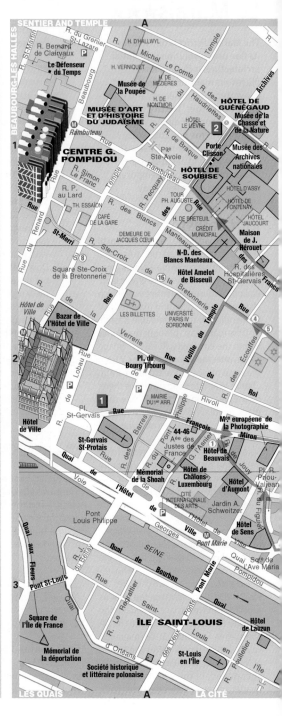

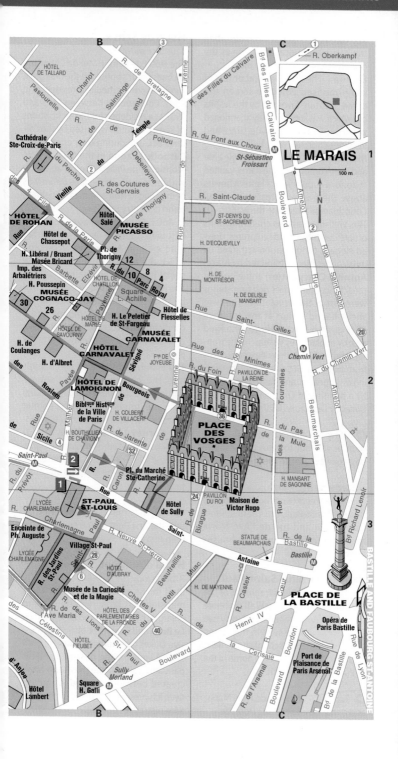

dedicated to St Paul, St-Louis absorbed the parish and became known as the church of St-Paul-St-Louis (1802).

Façade – The tall, Classical orders of superimposed columns screen the dome, a feature favoured by the Jesuits but which was subsequently abandoned when the Sorbonne, Val-de-Grâce and Invalides churches were built.

Interior – The Interior has a single aisle and inter-communicating barrel-vaulted chapels; a cupola with a lantern hovers above the transept crossing, and tall Corinthian pilasters line the walls.

This well-lit, spacious church, with its ornate decoration and sculptures, drew an elegant congregation attracted by musical excellence (directed by **Marc-Antoine Charpentier**) and eloquent preaching. Many of its rich furnishings were lost at the Revolution. The twin shell-shaped stoups at the entrance were given by **Victor Hugo**, who lived nearby in place des Vosges. In the transept three 17C paintings illustrate scenes from the life of St Louis. A fourth painting disappeared, and has been replaced by a painting of *Christ on the Mount of Olives* by Delacroix (1827).

▷ Leave the church by the left-hand door, as you look towards the altar. A passageway leads to rue St-Paul.

Village Saint-Paul

The maze of courtyards bordered by rue des Jardins-St-Paul, rue Charlemagne, rue St-Paul and rue de l'Avé-Maria has been restored and now houses antique shops.

Rue des Jardins–Saint-Paul

The largest surviving fragment of the **Philippe Auguste City Wall** (Enceinte de Philippe Auguste), intersected by two towers, can still be seen in this street, bordered by a high school sports field. To the north is a view of the dome of the St-Paul-St-Louis Church.

▷ Turn right on to rue de l'Avé Maria and continue into rue de l'Hôtel de Ville; walk on for c. 80m/87yd.

Hôtel de Sens★

1 rue du Figuier.

The Hôtel de Sens, Hôtel de Cluny and Jacques Cœur's house are the only great surviving private medieval residences in Paris. Constructed between 1475 and 1507 as a residence for the archbishops of Sens, the house was used by the Cardinal of Guise during the period of the **Catholic League** in the 16C. In 1594 Monsignor de Pellevé died of apoplexy within its walls while a *Te Deum* was being sung in Notre-Dame to celebrate Henri IV's entry into Paris.

In 1605, **Queen Margot**, Henri IV's first wife, came to live here after her long exile in Auvergne. At the age of 53, the former queen had a busy social life and many gallant callers. The house was subsequently occupied by several businesses, including the Lyons Stage Coach Company and a candy manufacturer before being purchased by the city and renovated in the early 20C.

The Flamboyant Gothic porch leads into the courtyard with a square battlemented tower enclosing a spiral staircase. Turrets and beautiful dormer windows adorn the external walls. The **Forney Library** (🕑*Tue, Fri–Sat 1pm–7.30pm, Wed–Thu 10am–7.30pm;* ⊜*6€;* ℘*01 42 78 14 60)* is devoted to the Decorative and Fine Arts, and industrial techniques.

▷ Return to rue de l'Hôtel de Ville; take the first right up rue de Fourcy, then first left.

Hôtel d'Aumont

7 rue de Jouy.

Built in the early 17C by Le Vau, this mansion was later remodelled and enlarged by Mansart, and decorated by **Le Brun** and Simon Vouet. Four successive Dukes of Aumont lived there until 1742. A large garden, obscured by a car park and ugly fencing, has since been created between the house and the river. It is presently occupied by the Paris administrative court.

▶ Return to rue de l'Hôtel de Ville; turn right at Cité Intern'l. des Arts.

Mémorial de la Shoah

17 rue Geoffroy l'Asnier. ◷*Sun–Fri 10am –6pm (10pm Thu).* ◷ *Jewish feast days and public holidays.* ☞*Guided tour in English 2nd Sun of the month at 3pm.* ♿*✆01 42 01 17 86. www.memorialdelashoah.org.*

Opened in 2005 on the site of Mémorial du Martyr Juif Inconnu, this centre devoted to the Holocaust houses permanent and temporary exhibitions, a documentation library, and the "Mur des Noms" with the names of the 76 000 Jews deported from France.

▶ Continue on rue Geoffroy l'Asnier.

Hôtel de Châlons-Luxembourg

26 rue Geoffroy l'Asnier.

Built in 1610, this mansion, once owned by a merchant named Châlons and Madame de Luxembourg, has a carved main gate and an interesting stone and brick façade.

▶ Walk back down rue Geoffroy-l'Asnier to rue de l'Hôtel de Ville; turn right on to rue des Barres.

Église St-Gervais-St-Protais★

Place St-Gervais.

The church stands on a low mound emphasized by steps leading up to the façade. A basilica dedicated to the brothers Gervase and Protase, Roman officers martyred by Nero, has stood on the site since the 6C.

The main part of the present building, in Flamboyant Gothic, was completed in 1657. The imposing façade (1616–21) with superimposed Doric, Ionic and Corinthian orders was the first expression of the Classical style in Paris. The elm in the square was, according to medieval custom, a place where justice was dispensed as well as a place for gambling, employment and rendezvous.

The Flamboyant vaulting, 16C windows and 16C and 17C fine stalls carved with misericords representing various trades are from the original building. Built in 1601 and enlarged in the 18C, the organ is the oldest in Paris. The position of organ-master was held successively by members of eight generations of Couperins between 1656 and 1826.

In the third chapel of the north aisle, a 13C low-relief altar-front depicts the Death of the Virgin. In the Lady Chapel a remarkable Flamboyant keystone hangs 1.5m/5ft below the vault, forming a circlet 2.5m/8.2ft in diameter.

▶ Exit the church on to rue François Miron.

Rue François Miron

This road, once a Roman highway through the marshes, still bears the name of a local magistrate of the time of Henri IV. In the Middle Ages it was lined with the town houses of several abbots of the Île-de-France. The half-timbered and much restored nos **13** and **11** date back to the reign of Louis XI (15C). The beautiful Marie Touchet, mistress of Charles IX, is said to have lived at no **30**. Behind the front building *(access via no 22 rue du Pont Louis Philippe, at the end of the corridor)*, a tiny Renaissance courtyard is decorated with carved wood panels.

The association for the preservation of Paris' historic buildings has uncovered

La Reine Margot

Marguerite de Valois, known affectionately as "La Reine Margot", was divorced from King Henri IV in 1599, but part of the agreement was for her to keep the title of queen. Henri quickly married Marie de' Médici, who persuaded her new husband to allow Queen Margot, with whom he remained on good terms, back to Court following her exile in the Auvergne. From 1605 she lived in the Hôtel de Sens in the Marais district and was able to continue her lavish lifestyle while conducting her many love affairs.

in the basements of nos **44–46** fine Gothic **cellars★**.

Hôtel de Beauvais★

68 rue François Miron.
In 1654 Catherine Bellier, known as One-Eyed Kate, first woman of the bedchamber to Anne of Austria, bestowed her favours on the 16-year-old Louis XIV and was rewarded with a fortune. In addition, for her services, she and her husband, Pierre Beauvais, were ennobled and acquired the site of the former (13C) town house of the abbots of Chaalis. They commissioned the architect Lepautre to build them a splendid mansion, from the balcony of which Anne of Austria, the Queen of England, Cardinal Mazarin and dignitaries observed the triumphal entry of Louis XIV and Marie-Thérèse into Paris in 1660. In 1763 seven-year-old Mozart stayed here with his father and sister, courtesy of the Bavarian ambassador.

◗ Continue along rue François Miron to rue de Fourcy.

Maison européenne de la Photographie

5–7 rue de Fourcy. ◷*Wed–Sun 11am–7.45pm.* ◷*Public holidays.* ⬤*8€.* ♿ ☏*01 44 78 75 00.* *www.mep-fr.org.*
This centre for contemporary photographic art exhibits in rotation works representing the cutting edge of photographic art (12 000 in all dating from 1958 onwards). The mansion between rue François Miron and rue de Fourcy was built in 1704 for Hénault de Contobre, the royal tax collector. Selected as the site for the photography museum, the building was restored and completed by an additional wing on rue de Fourcy. The façade overlooking the street, the period ironwork and the central staircase are fine examples of Classical architecture.
The centre houses an exhibition area, a large library, a video viewing facility and an auditorium. The Hénault-de-Cantobre hall is devoted to temporary exhibitions on historical and scientific themes. The basement contains a library, video library and an auditorium.

② MARAIS CIRCUIT

Starting from the St-Paul metro station, follow rue de Sévigné, then take the first right along rue d'Ormesson.

Place du Marché-Sainte-Catherine★

In the 13C a priory dedicated to Ste Catherine was built here. In the 18C the square was surrounded by large houses, harmonious in style, with mulberry trees planted in the middle. Today it's a pedestrian zone with outdoor cafés and restaurants.

◗ Follow rue d'Ormesson to the end; turn right on to rue de Turenne, which leads to rue St-Antoine.

Rue Saint-Antoine

From the 14C this unusually wide street became a popular setting for gatherings and celebrations. The area in front of the church was turned into a tilt-yard after the cobbles had been removed and the ground was covered with sand. It was here in 1559 that **Henri II** received a fatal blow to his eye in a tourney with his Scots captain of the guard, Montgomery. The king died in the Hôtel des Tournelles. Montgomery fled but was executed in 1574.
In the 17C rue St-Antoine was the city's most elegant thoroughfare.

Hôtel de Sully★

62 rue St-Antoine. ◷*Public access to the courtyard and gardens only, daily 9am–7pm.* ☏*01 44 61 21 50.*
This fine mansion was constructed in 1625 by Du Cerceau and bought 10 years later by the ageing Sully, former minister of Henri IV. Part of the building is used by the Caisse Nationale des Monuments Historiques et des Sites (Ancient Monuments and Historic Buildings Commission).
The main gate, between massive pavilions, has been restored and opens into the inner **courtyard★★**, an outstanding Louis XIII architectural composition with

ordered decoration, carved pediments and dormer windows; allegorical figures represent the Elements and the Seasons. The main building retains its original painted ceilings (1661, restored), which can be seen in the bookshop. Temporary photography exhibitions are held in the garden wing.

▷ At the far end of the garden, the Orangery (1625) opens on to place des Vosges.

Place des Vosges★★★

This is Paris' oldest square. Once the site of the **Hôtel des Tournelles**, acquired by the Crown in 1407 upon the assassination of the **Duke of Orléans**, the residence was pulled down by **Catherine de' Medici** after the death of Henri II. Subsequently named **place Royale**, Henri IV transformed it in 1605 into a vast square surrounded by houses built to a like symmetry. On its completion in 1612, the Royal Square became the centre of elegance, courtly parades and festivities. Duels were also fought there in spite of **Cardinal Richelieu**'s ban. From 1800 it took the name of place des Vosges after the Vosges *département*, the first to pay its taxes.

The 36 houses retain their original symmetrical appearance: two storeys with alternate stone and brick facings are built over the ground-level arcade rising to steeply pitched slate roofs pierced by dormer windows. The soberly decorated King's Pavilion, on the south side and the largest house in the square, is balanced by the Queen's Pavilion (Pavillon de la Reine) to the north.

Also of interest around the square are no **1 bis**, where Madame de Sévigné was born, no **21**, where Richelieu lived (1615–27), and no **6**, where Victor Hugo spent 16 years.

Today the square is a peaceful place to sit, either near the fountains in the central garden or under the cool arcades, where small orchestras play on Sundays.

▷ Walk through place des Vosges; turn left on to rue des Francs Bourgeois.

Rue des Francs-Bourgeois★

This old street was originally known as rue des Poulies after the pulleys *(poulies)* on the looms of the local weavers' shops. It took its present name in 1334 when almshouses were built in it for the poor, who were known as the men who pay no tax or *francs bourgeois*.

Place des Vosges

© Pi Ju Yang/Bigstockphoto.com

Hôtel d'Albret

Nos 29 bis and 31.

Built in the 16C for the Duke of Montmorency, Constable of France, this mansion was remodelled in the 17C. It was in this house that the widow of the playwright Scarron, the future **Marquise de Maintenon**, became governess to the children of **Mme de Montespan**, mistress of Louis XIV. The façade was altered in the 18C.

The restored mansion houses the city's Cultural Affairs Department.

Noteworthy Hôtels

Hôtel Barbes *(no 33)*, with its fine courtyard, was built around 1635. The **Hôtel de Savoury** *(4 rue Elzevir)* has an attractive courtyard. **Hôtel de Coulanges** *(nos 35–37)*, now Europe House, is 17C. **Hôtel de Sandreville** *(no 26)*, dating from 1586, has been converted into flats. **Hôtel d'Alméras** *(no 30)* has a brick and stone façade hidden behind a gateway featuring curious rams' heads. **Hôtel Poussepin** *(no 34)* now serves as the Swiss Cultural Centre. The **Maison de Jean Hérouet**★ *(54 rue Vieille du Temple)*, built around 1510, belonged to the treasurer to Louis XII; it still has its mullioned windows and an elegant corbelled turret. Nearby stood, in the 15C, the **Hôtel Barbette**, the discreet residence of Queen Isabella of Bavaria, who began the fashion for masked balls, while the king, Charles VI, resided at the Hôtel St-Paul.

Église de Notre-Dame-des-Blancs-Manteaux

The interior has remarkable woodwork: an inner door, organ loft, communion table and Flemish **pulpit**★ with marquetry panels inlaid with ivory and pewter, framed in gilded and fretted woodwork, typical of the Rococo style (1749).

Rue des Archives

This peaceful street houses the national archives behind the façades of its fine mansions.

Hôtel de Soubise★★ is the oldest of the mansions, dating from the 14C. The **gateway**★, known as the porte Clisson, is flanked by a pair of corbelled turrets *(no 58)*. From 1705 to 1709 the mansion was remodelled into an elegant palace with a majestic horseshoe-shaped **courtyard**★★. The Musée de l'Histoire de France is housed in the building (see Museums and Other Attractions). **Hôtel de Guénégaud**★★ at no 60, built c. 1650 by **Mansart**, was slightly remodelled in the 18C and beautifully restored in the 20C. With its plain harmonious lines, its majestic staircase and its small formal garden, the mansion is one of the finest houses of the Marais, now home to the Musée de la Chasse (see Museums and Other Attractions).

▶ Leave the hôtel and turn left on to rue des Quatre-Fils. Note the garden and rear façade of the mansion. Walk along rue Charlot.

Cathédrale Ste-Croix-de-Paris★

Sun 10am–1pm; weekdays by appointment. ℘01 44 59 23 50.

This much-restored church was erected in 1624 as a Capuchin monastery chapel and was attended by Mme de Sévigné. It is now an Armenian church.

The chancel is adorned with 18C gilded panelling from the former **Billettes Church**. To the left stands a remarkable **statue**★ of St Francis of Assisi by Germain Pilon (16C).

▶ Go back to rue de Quatre-Fils; continue until it meets rue Vieille du Temple.

Hôtel de Rohan★★

87 rue Vieille du Temple. Closed for renovation. ℘01 40 27 60 96.

In 1705 Delamair started work on the mansion simultaneously with the Hôtel de Soubise, for the Soubise's son, the Bishop of Strasbourg, who later became Cardinal de Rohan. It was successively the residence of four cardinals of the Rohan family, all of whom were Bishops of Strasbourg. The last one lived there in grand style until his disgrace in the affair of the queen's necklace (see box p165). It was occupied by the state press (Imprimerie Nationale) under Napoléon and

1785: Affair of the Diamond Necklace

Cardinal de Rohan had lost favour with Queen Marie-Antoinette. An unscrupulous adventuress, the Comtesse de la Motte devised an elaborate ruse to persuade Rohan to act as the purchaser of a diamond necklace worth 1 600 000 livres. She convinced him that the queen wanted to acquire the piece surreptitiously, even arranging a brief meeting in the gardens of Versailles one night with a prostitute playing the role of the queen! The plot came to light when the cardinal was unable to make the payments, and it was discovered that the necklace had been broken up and sold in London. Rohan was tried and acquitted, but deprived of his offices. The comtesse was sentenced to flogging, branding and life in prison, but fled to England and published her kiss-and-tell *Memoires*, vilifying the queen.

later in 1927 by the national archives. The main façade gives on to the garden, which serves both properties.

The interior decoration dates from 1750, with Gobelin tapestries in the entrance hall. A staircase leads to the Cardinals' **apartments★**. The first salons are adorned with Beauvais tapestries after drawings attributed to Boucher. Also of interest are the Gold Salon and the amusing small Monkey Room with animal decorations by Christophe Huet, and the delicate panelling and wall hangings of the smaller rooms.

▶ Follow rue de la Perle.

Place de Thorigny

This crossroads is a good place to sit and admire the façades of the **Hôtel de Chassepot** at 3–5 rue de la Perle, and at no 1 in the same street, of the **Hôtel Libéral Bruant**. This elegant mansion has been restored to its original appearance. In rue Thorigny, at no 5, is the **Hôtel Salé**, which contains the Picasso Museum (&*see Museums and Other Attractions*).

Rue du Parc-Royal

The 17C mansions lining the street opposite Léopold-Achille Square form a remarkable architectural ensemble notwithstanding remodelling: **Canillac** (*no* **4**), **Duret-de-Chevry** (*no* **8**, extensively restored), **Vigny** (*no* **10**, a national documentation centre) and **Croisilles** (*no* **12**), which houses the library and archives of France's historic buildings commission.

▶ Return to rue des Francs Bourgeois via rue Payenne or rue de Sévigné.

Rue Payenne

Lined by the orangery and the façade of the Hôtel St-Fargeau, square Georges-Cain is laid as a lapidary garden for the adjoining Musée Carnavalet. The neighbouring **Hôtel de Marle** or **de Polastron-Polignac** (*no* **11**) has a fine mask above the entrance and a keel-shaped roof attributed to Philibert Delorme; once owned by the Countess of Polignac, the governess of Marie-Antoinette's children, this house now accommodates a Swedish cultural centre. The architect François Mansart died at no **5**. The old gateway was uncovered during restoration.

Rue de Sévigné

Beyond the Hôtel Carnavalet, the **Hôtel Le Peletier de St-Fargeau** (*no* **29**) was built by Pierre Bullet (1686–90) and named after its owner, who voted for Louis XVI's death sentence. Number **52**, the much-restored **Hôtel de Flesselles**, bears the name of Paris' last provost.

Hôtel Carnavalet★★

23 rue de Sévigné.

Constructed in 1548 for Jacques des Ligneris, President of Parliament, the mansion was given its present appearance by **François Mansart** in 1655. Marie de Rabutin, the **Marquise de Sévigné**, author of the famous *Letters,* which give a lucid picture of day-to-day events, lived in the house from 1677 to 1696.

In 1866, the city of Paris acquired the mansion as a home for its historic collections, adding the buildings surrounding the garden courts. **Jean Goujon** carved the lions at the main entrance, which is 16C, and the keystone cornucopia. The supporting globe was later recarved into a carnival mask in allusion to the mansion's name.

In the courtyard the **statue** of Louis XIV by **Coysevox**, the only surviving pre-Revolution royal statue, was originally at the Hôtel de Ville.

▶ Follow rue des Francs Bourgeois to the right, and turn left on to rue Pavée.

Hôtel de Lamoignon★

24 rue Pavée.

The Hôtel d'Angoulême, which was built around 1585 for Diane of France, the legitimized daughter of Henri II, was bought in 1658 by Lamoignon, President of the first Parliament in Paris. There he entertained Racine, Mme de Sévigné, and Bourdaloue. In 1763 it became the **Bibliothèque historique de la ville de Paris**, a library rich in French Revolution documents.

The painted ceiling of its **reading room** is one of the finest in Paris.

▶ Follow rue Pavée south until it turns right into rue des Rosiers.

Rue des Rosiers

This street, together with the adjoining rue des Écouffes, which derives its name from a pawnbroker's shop sign, is the main axis of the **Jewish Quarter**, which has grown up in Paris' 4th *arrondissement*.

Rue Vieille du Temple and **rue du Roi de Sicile** are full of small shops selling the latest fashions, jewellery and decorative items. Rue du Roi de Sicile ends in a small, café-lined square, **place du Bourg Tibourg**.

MUSEUMS AND OTHER ATTRACTIONS
Musée d'Art et d'Histoire du Judaïsme★★

Hôtel de St-Aignan, 71 rue du Temple.
♿ ⏰ *Mon–Fri 11am–6pm (Wed until 9pm), Sun 10am–6pm.* ⏰ *1 May.* 💶 *8€.*
📞 *01 53 01 86 60. www.mahj.org.*

This ultra-modern museum within a historic setting presents both Ancient and contemporary exhibits. Accompanying explanatory notes provide the visitor with an in-depth view of Jewish culture.

Judaism and diaspora – The most important and unifying elements of the faith throughout the centuries are the Law (the Torah), religious teaching and cultural festivals. The history of the Jewish diaspora is one of journeys and exiles. Galleries illustrate the settlement of the Jews in France in the Middle Ages, and in Italy from the Renaissance to the 18C, showing the integration of the Jewish community, the problem of discrimination and their everyday life. There are also rooms dedicated to the two separately evolved communities, the Sephardic Jews from Muslim Spain and the Ashkenazic Jews from Eastern Europe.

Contemporary Judaism – Under the First Empire, the Age of Enlightenment in the early 19C favoured the emancipation of the Jews in France, but by the end of the century, modern anti-Semitism was all too present, with the Dreyfus affair and the Deportation leading to the creation of Zionism. This exhibition finishes in galleries 11 and 13 with an illustration of Jewish influence on 20C art and the contemporary Jewish world.

Musée Carnavalet-Histoire de Paris★★

Hôtel Carnavalet, 16 rue des Francs-Bourgeois. ⏰ *Tue–Sun 10am–6pm.*
⏰ *Public holidays.* 💶 *Fee (varies) for temporary exhibits only.* 📞 *01 44 59 58 58. www.carnavalet.paris.fr.*

Illustrating the history of Paris, the museum is housed in two separate mansions, the Hôtel Carnavalet and the Hôtel Le Peletier de St-Fargeau.

Paris from its tribal origins to the end of the Middle Ages is vividly depicted by means of archaeological finds such as the wooden **Neolithic canoes** found in Bercy in 1999; the oldest dates from 4 400 BC. The museum also brings back to life some of the main events of the capital's history, such as the French Revolution and the Commune.

It is particularly rich in decorative arts: painted and carved wood panelling and ceilings from other Parisian mansions have been reconstructed here (drawing rooms from the Hôtel de la Rivière painted by Lebrun, Belle-Époque décor of the Fouquet jewellery shop).

Literary history is illustrated by many portraits, pieces of furniture and souvenirs evoking famous writers (Marcel Proust's bedroom).

Musée Picasso★★

Hôtel Salé, 5 rue de Thorigny.
🕐*Tue–Fri 11.30am–6pm (3rd Fri/month until 9pm), Sat–Sun and holidays 9.30am–6pm.* 🕐*1 Jan, 1 May, 25 Dec.* 📞*01 85 56 00 36. www.musee-picasso.fr.*
Recently renovated by architect Jean-François Bodin and reopened in late 2014, the museum has doubled in size and now stretches from the vaulted cellar to the attic. The house was originally completed in 1659 for a salt tax collector, hence its name. Restored in the 1970s by the architect Simounet, the mansion became the Picasso Museum in 1985. Inside, the main **staircase★** with its spacious stairwell and splendid wrought-ironwork rises to the first floor and a profusely carved ceiling.

A dominant figure of 20C art, **Pablo Ruiz Picasso** (1881–1973) was born in Malaga, Spain. After studying art in Barcelona and Madrid, he settled in France at age 23, where he pursued his long

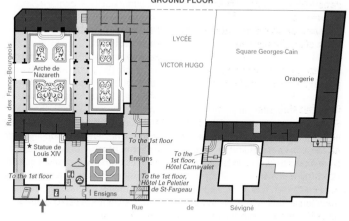

MUSÉE CARNAVALET
GROUND FLOOR

LYCÉE VICTOR HUGO

Square Georges-Cain

Orangerie

Rue des Francs-Bourgeois

Arche de Nazareth

★ Statue de Louis XIV

To the 1st floor

Ensigns

To the 1st floor, Hôtel Carnavalet

To the 1st floor

To the 1st floor, Hôtel Le Peletier de St-Fargeau

Ensigns

Rue   de   Sévigné

HÔTEL CARNAVALET   HÔTEL LE PELETIER DE SAINT-FARGEAU

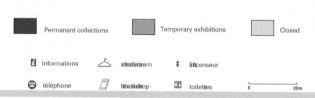

Permanent collections   Temporary exhibitions   Closed

ℹ informations   ⌂ vestiaire/cloakroom   ↕ lift/ascenseur

☎ téléphone   📕 bookshop/librairie   🚻 toilettes

0   20m

Musée Picasso

© Yoshimi Kanazawa/MICHELIN

Maison de Victor Hugo★

6 place des Vosges. ○*Tue–Sun 10am–6pm.* ○*Public holidays.* ○*Fee for temporary exhibits.* ✆*01 42 72 10 16. www.maisonsvictorhugo.paris.fr.*

Home to the writer **Victor Hugo** from 1832 to 1848 and turned into a museum in 1903, this residence overlooking the place des Vosges features drawings by Hugo himself as well as furniture and objects from his various residences in France and in exile abroad that show his talent as a decorator.

♣♣ Musée de la Curiosité et de la Magie★

11 rue St-Paul. ○*Wed and Sat–Sun 2pm–7pm. Call for information during school holiday periods.* ○*9€; 3-12 years 7€.* ✆*01 42 72 13 26. www.museedelamagie.com.*

This collection of ingenious accessories dispels some of the mystery from the art of magic, conjuring, legerdemain, prestidigitation and sleight-of-hand. Midway through the museum, a stage, a few seats and a number of tiers provide the setting for regular **magic shows** (*about 30min; included in the entry fee*).

Musée des Archives nationales★

Hôtel de Soubise, 60 rue des Francs-Bourgeois. ○*Mon–Fri 9am–4.45pm, Sat–Sun 2pm–5.30pm.* ○*3€.* ✆*01 40 27 60 96. www.archivesnationales. culture.gouv.fr.*

The building is a museum in its own right and has retained its original décor.

Apartments★★ – Delamair's Classical architectural style, typical of Louis XIV's reign (simple façade, vast courtyard and suite of rooms), contrasts with Boffrand's extravagant Rococo decoration under Louis XV, when formal décor gave way to more intimate interiors. Between 1735 and 1740 the most gifted painters (Boucher, Natoire, Van Loo) and sculptors of the period worked under Boffrand, a pupil of Mansart, to decorate with all the delicacy and flourish of the Rococo style as was fashionable at Versailles.

and active career. Between 1936 and 1955, Picasso lived at 7 rue des Grands Augustins (6th), where he painted *Guernica* (1937). Following his death at Mougins in 1973, Picasso's heirs donated an outstanding collection of the artist's works in lieu of estate duties, comprising more than 250 paintings, sculptures, collages, 3 000 drawings and engravings, and 88 ceramics.

Start by exploring Picasso's creative process through a display of studio photographs on the lower ground floor, or follow his long career in chronological order, starting on the ground floor with his *Self-Portrait* from the Blue Period. All the artist's styles and techniques are represented in his sketches for *Les Demoiselles d'Avignon*, *Still Life with Cane Chair* and *Pipes of Pan* and other favourite subjects such as female nudes, travelling acrobats and his own family. On the top floor, visitors will find Picasso's private collection of works by his friends and contemporaries such as Braque, **Cézanne** and **Rousseau**.

An unusual fountain by Simounet graces the formal public garden beyond the museum's garden.

Character of le Marais

This old district of Paris, saved by André Malraux, is the centre of Paris' Jewish community and the hub of its gay population. Hip, cool bars have sprung up everywhere *(crossroads of rue Vieille-du-Temple and rue Sainte-Croix-de-la-Bretonnerie)* and fashion shops line the pavements of rue des Francs-Bourgeois. Rue des Rosiers and the Rue de Ecouffes form the heart of the traditional Jewish neighbourhood, although its scruffy old charm is slowly giving way to upmarket fashion boutiques. The delightful place du Marché-Ste-Catherine is surrounded by restaurants, while the arcades of place des Vosges shelter restaurants, fashion shops, antique dealers and art galleries. The northern part of the Marais is quieter and home to many museums. Even further north is the old district of the Temple, traditional home of leather goods dealers and also, more recently, the contemporary art scene.

On the first floor, beside the Guise Chapel is the Salle des Gardes (guard-room), which served as the League headquarters during the Wars of Religion. The Assembly rooms, decorated with painted panels by Carl Van Loo and Boucher, contain a model of the Bastille made with stones from the fortress.

Chambre de la Princesse – This dazzling interior has survived intact. A large bed with baldaquin furnishes the room fitted with white and gold panelling. Two paintings by Boucher hang on either side of the bed. In the **Salon ovale de la Princesse**, the masterful display of Rococo is at its most refined, with the sky-blue ceiling contrasting well with Nattier's feminine hues in his depiction of the *Story of Psyche*. In the **Petite chambre de la Princesse** fine roundels illustrate the Elements, and panels by Van Loo, Restout, Trémolières and Boucher are set over the doors.

Musée de la Chasse et de la Nature

Hôtel Guénégaud, 62 rue des Archives. ⏱*Tue–Sun 11am–6pm (Wed until 9.30pm.* ⏱*Public holidays.* ⇔*8€.* ✆*01 53 01 92 40. www.chassenature.org.*
Housed in a magnificent 17C mansion designed by François Mansart, the collection includes arms from prehistory to the 19C and trophies and souvenirs from big-game expeditions. Tapestries, ceramics and sculptures on the theme of the hunt are also on view.

Cognacq-Jay Museum ★★

Hôtel Donon, 8 rue Elzévir. ⏱*Tue–Sun 10am–6pm.* ⏱*Public holidays.* ✆*01 40 27 07 21. www.cognacq-jay.paris.fr.*
This collection of 18C European art was bequeathed to the city of Paris by Ernest Cognacq, founder of the **Samaritaine** department store.

In the panelled ground-floor rooms are drawings by Watteau, paintings by Rembrandt, Ruisdael, Largillière and Chardin, and portraits of Louis XV's court: his queen, Marie Leczinska, their daughter Madame Adélaïde, and Alexandrine, the daughter of **Madame de Pompadour**, Louis XV's mistress.

On the second floor, watercolours by Mallet illustrate the life of the Bourgeoisie under **Louis XVI**. In the Oval Room Fragonard's portrayals of children and Rococo pastoral pictures contrast with terra-cottas by Lemoyen and paintings by Greuze. The sculpture gallery groups works showing a strong Italian influence (Falconet, Houdon and Clodion) with paintings by Hubert Robert and Boucher.

The third floor is dedicated to Mme Vigée-Lebrun: pastels include a self-portrait by La Tour, and British School paintings. In the carved oak-panelled salon are an oval table and *commode* signed RVLC by Roger Vandercruse, better known as Lacroix, and a pair of *commodes* by Martin Carlin. The study is hung with Venetian paintings, including Guardi's *St Mark's Square.* Showcases display Meissen and Sèvres porcelain, snuffboxes and *bonbonnières*.

Arrondissements 5-7

Jardin des Plantes-Mouffetard★★

Just beyond the Left Bank's Latin Quarter you'll find some of the city's oldest sites, including the historic rue Mouffetard with its medieval façades and bustling market, the ruins of the Roman arena known as the Arènes de Lutèce, and the former medicinal gardens of King Louis XIII, the Jardin des Plantes.

♟♟ MUSÉUM NATIONAL D'HISTOIRE NATURELLE★★

This is one of the world's greatest conservatories in the field of natural science. It comprises 14 sites in France, four of which are located in Paris.

At the Revolution Bernardin de St-Pierre was nominated curator of the Royal Botanic Gardens, renamed by the Convention (10 June 1793) the National Museum for Natural History. The same year a menagerie was instituted with animals from zoos, often privately owned by princes and circuses that Parisians had never seen: elephants, bears, giraffes, etc. In 1870, when Paris was under siege, citizens' hunger exceeded their curiosity and most of the animals were killed for food. With Goffroy-St-Hilaire, Lamarck, Lacépède, Cuvier, Becquerel and other great names, the institute won through its teaching and research in the 19C international recognition.

Grande Galerie de l'Évolution★★★

36 rue Geoffroy-St-Hilaire. ○*Wed–Mon 10am–6pm.* ○*1 May.* ∞*9€; under 26 years free.* ⑤ ☎*01 40 79 56 01. www.grandegaleriedelevolution.fr.*
The theory of evolution is one of the most important in scientific development. It draws together a large number of disciplines which, without it, would have remained isolated. Here, it serves as a constant theme throughout the Gallery presentations.

Info: Pyramides welcome centre, 25 rue des Pyramides. ☎08 92 68 30 00 (0.34€ per min). http://en.parisinfo.com.

Location: The gardens are on the eastern Left Bank overlooking the Seine.

Metro/RER: Gare d'Austerlitz (lines 5 and 10/C), Jussieu (lines 7 and 10), Cardinal Lemoine (line 10), Place Monge (line 7), Censier Daubenton (line 7). Buses: 24, 47, 57, 61, 63, 65, 67, 86, 87, 89, 91.

Parking: At the Gare d'Austerlitz. Street parking is possible on some of the smaller residential roads around Jussieu. In Mouffetard, underground parking is available near the Passage des Patriarches.

Don't Miss: The quiet Jardin Alpin. Notre-Dame seen from the 9th floor of the Arab World Institute. The interesting façades of the buildings along rue Mouffetard.

Timing: Enjoy the bustling rue Mouffetard in the morning (allow an hour for the Mouffetard walk ②) and the Jardin des Plantes in the afternoon. Allow at least a half-day to visit the Muséum National d'Histoire Naturelle. The Jussieu walk (①) takes around two hours.

Kids: At the Jardin des Plantes, the Menagerie and carrousel are popular with children. In Jussieu, the open-air sculpture garden along the Square Tino Rossi is particularly child friendly. In Mouffetard, there is a small playground in the St-Médard churchyard.

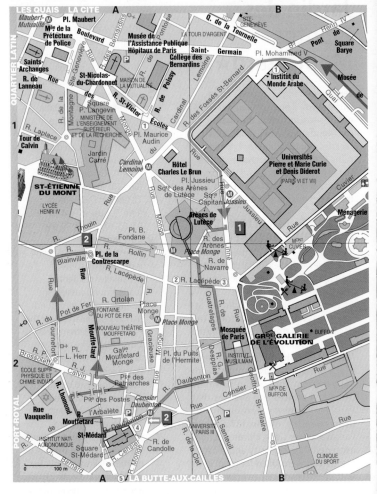

The ground and first levels feature the diversity of living species according to their environment. The polar regions are illustrated by polar bears, walruses and an enormous sea elephant; the African savannah by its famous caravan of zebras, giraffes, buffalo, lions and antelopes; the rain forest by display cases of insects, and a steel ladder as a perch for monkeys and birds.

On the first level there is a children's discovery room. Level two shows the effects of human action on evolution, illustrated by the **Galerie des Espèces menacées ou disparues★★** (Gallery of Endangered or Extinct Species). On the third floor is the museum's oldest

preserved animal, a rhinoceros from Asia that belonged to Louis XV and Louis XVI. A historical display introduces the scientists who questioned the origin of the diversity of living beings and whose ideas paved the way for the theory of evolution, spearheaded by Sir **Charles Darwin** (1809–82).

Galerie de Minéralogie et Géologie★

36 rue Geoffroy-St-Hilaire. ◑*Apr–Oct Wed–Mon 10am–6pm; rest of the year until 5pm.* ◑*1 May.* ⊛*6€; under 26 years 4€.* ♿ ✆*01 40 79 56 01. www.mnhn.fr.* This gallery has exceptional examples of **minerals**, meteorites and **precious**

JARDIN DES PLANTES
MOUFFETARD

WHERE TO STAY	WHERE TO EAT
Hôtel Familia................①	Café Littéraire................①
	El Picaflor........................②
	Le Jardin des Pâtes..........③
	Les Délices d'Aphrodite....................④
	Verse Toujours................⑤

stones and a collection of **giant crystals**, many of which come from Brazil. In the basement are shown the most precious stones, objets d'art and jewels from Louis XIV's collection.

Ménagerie

57 rue Cuvier. ⏱*Late Mar–Oct Mon–Sat 9am–6pm, Sun 9am–6.30pm; rest of the year call or go online for hours.* ⏺*13€; 4-16 years 9€.* ♿ ☏*01 40 79 56 01. www.mnhn.fr.*
Opened in 1794, this historic zoo houses some 1 800 animals, primarily large reptiles, birds and mammals in an old-fashioned setting. The rotunda, the oldest building in this section, contains a **Micro Zoo**, with microscopes to help visitors to discover the world of minute creatures in the zoo's collection of 900 insects.

Grande Galerie de l'Évolution

©H. Chajmowicz/Michelin

Galeries d'Anatomie comparée et de Paléontologie

2 rue Buffon. ⏱*Wed–Mon 10am–5pm, Sat–Sun 10am–6pm.* ⏱*1 May;* ⊚*7€; under 26 years free.* ♿ ☏*01 40 79 56 01. www.mnhn.fr.*

Housed in a brick building (1898, Ferdinand Dutert) on Rue du Buffon remaining from the 1890 World Exposition, the museum's 36 000 specimens present the **comparative anatomy** of vertebrates. **Fossils** are displayed on the first and second floors among reproductions of large prehistoric animals and extinct species.

JARDIN DES PLANTES★★

Entrance on place Valhubert. ⏱*Apr–Sept daily 7.30am–8pm; rest of the year, call or go online for hours.* ⏱*Public holidays.* ⊚*Free entry, except Serre 6€ and Alpin 2€ Sat–Sun.* ♿ ☏*01 40 79 54 79. www.jardindesplantes.net.*

In addition to hosting the Natural History Museum and a zoo, the Jardin des Plantes is a 24ha/59-acre expanse of greenery encompassing myriad botanic gardens. It consists of five major gardens and a botany school. A restaurant, cafeteria and snack kiosks can be found on its grounds as well as a carrousel.

A Bit of History

In 1626 Hérouard and Guy de la Brosse, physicians to Louis XIII, were granted permission to move the Royal Medicinal Herb Garden from the tip of the Île de la Cité to the St-Victor district. The garden evolved to encompass a school for botany, natural history and pharmacy. In 1640 the garden was opened to the public.

The gardens were at their greatest during the curatorship of **Georges-Louis Leclerc, Comte du Buffon** (1707–88), who published his 36-volume *Natural History*, extended the gardens to the banks of the Seine, planted avenues of lime trees and the maze, and built the galleries and the amphitheatre.

In the 17C a large accumulation of public waste occupied the site, over which Buffon laid a **maze**; at the heart of this labyrinth, a small gazebo overlooks the gardens from the highest point. The famous cedar of Lebanon is one of two planted by Bernard de Jussieu in 1734. Legend has it that he carried the plants in his hat after dropping and breaking the pots on his way back from Kew Gardens in England.

One of the oldest trees in Paris is a Robinia or false acacia, planted here in 1636, near allée des Becquerel.

Botanic gardens

The three winter garden glass hothouses of the **Grandes Serres du Jardin des Plantes** (⏱*Wed–Mon 10am–6pm, Sun until 6.30pm; winter Wed–Mon 10am–5pm;* ⊚*6€*), reopened in 2010 after extensive renovations, enclose four important collections: tropical forest plants, arid zone plants and cacti, a history of plants exhibition, and a greenhouse dedicated to the unique plantlife of New Caldonia.

The **School of Botany** (⏱*daily 7.30am–8pm; winter daily 8am–5.30pm;* ⏱*public holidays;* ♿) features some 10 000 species of flora, edible and/or medicinal herbs, classified by family in the botanic study beds.

The **Jardin Alpin** (⏱*Apr–Oct Mon–Fri 8am–3.50pm, Sat–Sun 1pm–6pm;* ⊚*2€ Sat–Sun, free Mon–Fri*) groups its high-altitude plants by soil type and orientation of the sun: Corsica, Morocco (south face), the Alps and the Himalayas (north face). Another garden has 180 varieties of antique and hybrid **roses**; a walled **iris garden** is combined with perennial and climbing plants, and beds of annuals on the **central alley** that change every season.

👣WALKING TOURS

① JUSSIEU★

Start at Ⓜ*Gare d'Austerlitz.*

Jussieu is the area bordered by the banks of the Seine, the Latin Quarter and the Gare d'Austerlitz.

Dominated by university buildings, this neighbourhood hosts a rich cultural diversity of Gallo-Roman ruins, science and natural history colleges, the Institute of the Arab World and the Paris Mosque.

Musée de la Sculpture en plein air

Square Tino-Rossi, Quai St-Bernard. ⚭ⓒ*Year-round, 24hrs a day.* ⚭*Free entry.*

This riverside garden was initiated by Gilioli César in 1980. It is an open-air museum graced with many contemporary sculptures by artists such as César, Brancusi, Stahly, Zadkine, Rougemont, and others.

Institut du Monde Arabe★

1 rue des Fossés St-Bernard. ⓒ*Tue–Thu 10am–6pm, Fri until 9.30pm, Sat–Sun until 7pm;* ⓒ*1 May. Free entry to the building; museum* ⚭*8€.* ⚭ ℘*01 40 51 38 38. www.imarabe.org.*

The aim of the Institute set up by France in conjunction with 20 Arab countries is to promote Islamic culture, cultural exchanges and cooperation. Enclosed in a mantle of glass and aluminium and covered by a sheath of translucent alabaster, the building was conceived by the architect **Jean Nouvel** and the Architecture Studio.

The permanent collection is exhibited throughout four floors in descending

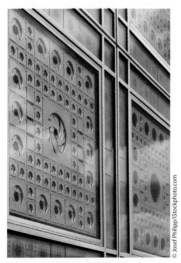

Window of Institute du Monde Arabe

© Josef Philipp/iStockphoto.com.

order from the 7th to the 4th. On display are works of art from the 9C to the 19C from countries ranging from Spain to India and illustrating Arab history: cut and over-painted glass, lustre ware, chased bronze, wood and ivory sculpture, geometric or floral carpets. Palace and mosque architecture and scientific achievements in the fields of medicine, astronomy and mathematics are also featured. There is a fine collection of astrolabes: these instruments were used to observe and calculate the position of heavenly bodies before the invention of the sextant.

On the ninth-floor **terrace**, a view of the east end of Notre-Dame, Île St-Louis and the Bastille neighbourhood unfolds.

Pierre and Marie Curie University (UPMC)

4 place Jussieu. ℘*01 44 27 44 27. www.upmc.fr.*

This modern university campus actually dates back to the 12C, with a brief turn as a wine market after the French Revolution. Part of the University of Paris since 1959, the imposing Zamansky tower was renovated in 2009, and the entire campus is getting a much-needed facelift. During term-time, this precinct in France's biggest university campus contrasts sharply with the quiet streets in the immediate vicinity.

The **Collection de Minéraux★**, the university's geology museum (ⓒ*Wed–Mon 1pm–6pm;* ⓒ*public holidays;* ⚭*5€; audio-guide 2€)* is worth a visit. Its study collection of stones, rocks and crystals ranks among the best in the world. Of the museum's 13 000 pieces, 1 500 are on display.

Hôtel Charles Le Brun

49 rue du Cardinal Lemoine.

Now used as offices, this fine building was built by Boffrand in 1700 for Charles II Le Brun, nephew of the famous painter at the Court of Louis XIV. Watteau lived here in 1718, as did **Buffon** in 1766; it was here that Buffon completed his treatise on natural history in several volumes. The fine Classical façade has a large carved triangular pediment.

Arènes de Lutèce

This, and the Cluny public bathhouse (ⓒsee Le QUARTIER LATIN, Hôtel de Cluny) are the only two Parisian monuments to survive from the Gallo-Roman period. The arena, the exact date of whose construction remains unknown, was destroyed in 280 by the Barbarians, and lay buried for 1 500 years before being rediscovered by accident when rue Monge was laid in 1869. The arena was used for gladiator battles and theatre; although many of its stone tiers have now vanished, the stage and layout of the dressing rooms survive.

Grand Mosquée de Paris★

Place du Puits-de-l'Ermite. ⓒ*Sat–Thu 9am–noon, 2pm–6pm.* ⓒ*Muslim feast days.* ⏪*Guided visits* ⊜*3€.* ✆*01 45 35 97 33. www.mosqueedeparis.net.*
This exotic walled compound of white Hispano-Moorish buildings overlooked by a minaret was erected between 1922 and 1926. Most of the interior decoration and courtyard design was entrusted to craftsmen from Muslim countries.

② MOUFFETARD★

Start at Ⓜ*Censier Daubenton. Follow rue Daubenton.*

Mouffetard lies at the southeastern end of the Latin Quarter. This area on the fringe of the quarter is dotted with small cafés and boutiques catering for the many students that permanently throng the neighbourhood.

▷ A gate and passage lead from no 41 rue Daubenton to a small side entrance to the church.

Église Saint-Médard

141 rue Mouffetard.
ⓒ*Mon 5pm–7.30pm; Tue–Fri 8am–12.30pm, 2.30pm–7.30pm; Sat 9am–12.30pm, 2.30pm–7.30pm; Sun 8.30am–12.30pm, 4pm–8pm.* ⓒ*1 and 8 May, Pentecost, 11 Nov.* ✆*01 44 08 87 00. www.saintmedard.org.*
Begun in the mid-15C, the church was completed in 1655. The Flamboyant Gothic nave has modern stained glass.

In 1784 the pillars were transformed into fluted Doric columns. There are paintings of the French School, a remarkable 16C triptych *(behind the pulpit)* and in the second chapel to the right of the chancel, a *Dead Christ* attributed to Philippe de Champaigne.

▷ Continue along rue Mouffetard.

Rue Mouffetard★

The *Mouffe*, as it is known, winds downhill to St-Médard, lined with old houses and crowded most mornings with food market shoppers; on Sundays, street musicians add further touches of colour to the area. Picturesque painted signs are a reminder of past times, like that at no 69 where a carved oak tree once topped the sign for *Le Vieux Chêne* and At the Clear Spring at **no 122**. The **Pot-de-Fer fountain**, like others in the district, runs with surplus water from the Arcueil Aqueduct, which **Marie de' Medici** had constructed to bring water to the Luxembourg Palace.

Other streets

Denis Diderot (1713–84) lived at **3 rue de l'Estrapade** between 1747 and 1754 while overseeing the publication of his famous *Encyclopedia*. There is a striking view to be caught over the dome of the Panthéon.
Rue Lhomond is lined with flights of steps – an indication of the former height of the hill. At no **30** stands the chapel serving the Séminaire du St-Esprit, built in 1780 by **Chalgrin**. **Passage des Postes** starts level with no 55. At **10 rue Vauquelin, Pierre and Marie Curie** isolated radium in October 1898 and discovered the principles of radioactivity.

Place de la Contrescarpe★

An inscription at no 1 recalls the Pinecone cabaret, La Pomme-de-Pin, described by Rabelais. René Descartes lived at **14** rue Rollin during his stay in Paris (1644–48).

Le Quartier Latin★★

Built on the Left Bank ruins of Roman Paris, the Latin Quarter gets its name from the common language spoken by theology students who came from all over Europe beginning in the 13C to study at local universities such as the Sorbonne. Although the Panthéon and the church of St-Étienne-du-Mont are the principal landmarks, the area is known for its lively, winding streets thronged by students and the bookshops and budget eateries that cater to them.

A BIT OF HISTORY

Gallo-Roman Lutetia – In the 3C Lutetia was a small town of some 6 000 inhabitants: Gauls occupied the Île de la Cité, while Romans settled around what is now known as Montagne Ste-Gene-viève, providing their community with an aqueduct stretching 15km/9.3mi, and a network of paved roads through the Latin Quarter.

The medieval Alma Mater – In the 12C teachers, clerks and scholars migrated to the monastic communities of Ste-Geneviève and St-Victor on the Left Bank. With authority from Pope Inno-cent III (1215), the group founded the University of Paris, the first in France. Latin, as the language of educated men and lingua franca among the different nationalities, continued to be spoken in the area until the Revolution in 1789.

From tutelage to autonomy – In 1806 Napoléon founded the Imperial Univer-sity of France, with academies being made responsible for education by the State. Gradually, the enormous influx of students made the system unwork-able, and new buildings were erected in order to decentralize the faculties, but this action did not prevent unrest. In **May 1968** the tension came to a head, provoked by the forced evacuation of the Sorbonne on 3 May (due to a sched-uled student protest against the Viet-nam War) and the closure of the main faculties on 6 May. Demonstrations and street violence left 945 injured as the area was barricaded and the students

Info: Office du Tourisme, 25 rue des Pyramides. ℘08 92 68 30 00 (0.34€ per min). ℘08 92 68 30 00 (0.34€ per min). http://en.parisinfo.com.

Location: The Latin Quarter is on the eastern end of the Left Bank.

Metro/Transport: St-Michel (line 4), Cluny la Sorbone (line 10), Cardinal Lemoine (line 10), Odéon (lines 4 and 10), Maubert-Mutualité (line 10). RER: St-Michel-Notre-Dame (lines B and C), Luxembourg (line B). Buses: 21, 27, 38, 47, 63, 82, 83, 84, 85, 86, 87, 89.

Parking: Look for underground parking at place Maubert or place Rostand, as well as under the Jardin du Luxembourg.

Don't Miss: The Ancient architecture at the Musée du Moyen Age. At the Jardin du Luxembourg, the espaliered fruit trees in the orchard and the Medici fountain. The medieval architectural remnants along rue Galande in the Maubert district.

Timing: Allow at least a half-day minimum to explore this area. The Jardin du Luxembourg can be visited in under an hour, but children may prefer to stay and play longer. You can spend an hour in Maubert's winding streets.

Kids: The Jardin Medieval. Playgrounds, a marionette show, and pony rides at the Jardin du Luxembourg. In Maubert, kids can stretch their legs in the square René Vivani.

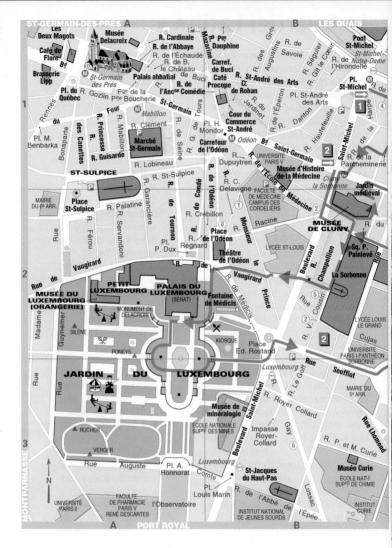

declared the Sorbonne to be a *commune libre*. Trade unions followed with large-scale strikes, bringing chaos to the nation. On 30 May President de Gaulle was forced to dissolve his government.

WALKING TOURS

1 QUARTIER LATIN CÔTÉ SEINE
Start at Ⓜ*/RER St-Michel.*

Quartier St-Séverin

This is perhaps one of the oldest quarters of Paris. **Rue de la Harpe** was the main north–south Gallo-Roman road; **rue de la Parcheminerie** (Parchment Street) was once lined with public scribes, letter-writers and copyists. Today, the bustle continues with local residents, students and tourists attracted by experimental cinemas and theatres such as the **Théâtre de la Huchette** *(23 rue de la Huchette)*, where **Ionesco**'s absurdist plays *The Bald Soprano* and *The Lesson* have been performed nightly since 1957.

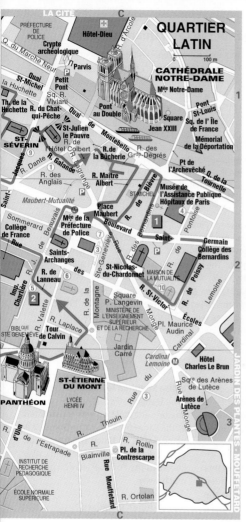

Église St-Séverin★★

1 rue des Prêtres-St-Séverin.

Building of the present church began in the first half of the 13C. The west door is from this era, while above, windows, balustrades and rose window are all 15C Flamboyant Gothic, as are the tower superstructure and spire. The width of the building compared to its length is immediately striking. The extra breadth dates from the 14C and 15C when expansion was possible only laterally. The first three bays of the nave are far superior to the rest with tracery typical of the Late Gothic Rayonnant style. In the later bays, columns are reduced to shafts devoid of capitals.

In the chancel, the five arches around the apse stand taller than those of the nave, reaching up to the well-articulated Flamboyant vaulting. The double **ambulatory★★** encircling the chancel is a spectacular further expression of Flamboyant architecture with its bouquets of ribs rising from elegant shafts, faceted with straight or spiralling surfaces. Piers in the chancel are faced with marble and wood. The beautiful **stained glass★** in

Colleges of the Latin Quarter

Whether ancient or more recent, the colleges represent the height of the academic humanist tradition in France. A bit of rivalry exists among them.

Collège des Écossais – *65 rue du Cardinal Lemoine*. The **Scottish College**, a building with a noble façade, which has belonged to the Roman Catholic Church of Scotland since the 14C. It is one of the oldest colleges of the University of Paris.

Collège de Navarre – *1 rue Descartes*. Several important academic bodies have been based at this address. First founded in 1304 by Jeanne of Navarre, wife of Philip the Fair, it was originally intended for 70 poor scholars, among whom, at different times, Henri III, Henri IV, Richelieu and Bossuet were numbered. In 1794 the Convention initiated the École Polytechnique to replace a deficit in engineers. The college was transferred to Palaiseau on the outskirts of Paris, in 1977.

Collège de Montaigu – *10 place du Panthéon*. This college was known for its teaching, its austere discipline and its squalor – its scholars were said to sleep on the ground amid lice, fleas and cockroaches.

Collège Ste Barbe – *rue Valette*. The last surviving building of the Latin Quarter colleges, dating from 1460.

Collège de France – *11 place Marcelin-Berthelot*. With its great past and an equal present-day reputation, this college offers free public lectures. 19C building reorganizations have been replaced in the 20C by vast additions. The college retains complete academic autonomy but has been dependent financially on the State since 1852.

the upper windows is late 15C; modern glass in the chevet is by Bazaine. Outside are the restored ruins of the **St-Séverin cloister** *(accessible Sun mornings only)*.

👤 Jardin medieval

This garden presents medieval plants and symbolism. A clearing has been designed for children. A path on the left side leads around to the entrance of the **Musée de Cluny**.

Maubert

This Latin Quarter neighbourhood is a fragment of medieval Paris, threaded with narrow, winding streets that have been the scene of mob assemblies and street barricades on more than one occasion. Its name is thought to be a corruption of Maître Albert or Albert the Great, who taught theology from the square in the 13C.

"La Maube" has recently been subjected to major restoration. French President Mitterrand (1916–96) lived in rue de Bièvre for many years.

Église St-Julien le Pauvre★

1 rue St-Julien le Pauvre.

The present building was constructed at the same time as Notre-Dame. It is named after St Julian the Confessor, the medieval Bishop of Le Mans, also known as the Poor because he gave so much away.

Rue St-Julien le Pauvre

No 14 dates from the 17C and used to be the house of the governor of the Petit Châtelet. The **view★★** of St-Séverin across the entrance to rue Galande is one of the most picturesque of old Paris, and still a popular subject for painters.

Rue Galande

At **nos 54–46** cellars and pointed medieval arches have been unearthed; a carved stone above the door of no **42** shows St Julian the Hospitaller in his boat. Note the 15C gable of no **31**. **Rue du Fouarre** was one of the places where, in the Middle Ages, public lectures were given by the university in the open air attended by students seated on bundles of straw *(fouarre)*. Dante is said to have attended lectures in this street in 1304.

Winding streets

The École d'Administration on the **rue de la Bûcherie** now occupies the premises of the first medical school founded in the 15C. **Impasse Maubert** was home to a Greek College founded in 1206 and the house where the infamous Marquise de Brinvilliers concocted her poisons in the 17C. The old houses of the **rue Maître Albert** rise above a network of underground passages down to the banks of the Seine that sheltered rogues and conspirators up until the 20C.

Since the early Middle Ages, the **place Maubert** has been a traditional rallying point for students, with barricades at times. The **rue de Bièvre** is a paved-over tributary of the Seine, once used by tanners and boatmen.

Rue de Poissy

This street was laid through the gardens of the historic **Bernardins College** (*20 rue de Poissy*) founded in 1246 to educate monks and taken over by the Cistercians in the 14C.

From 1845 until 2010 the buildings served as a fire station. Newly restored as a Catholic educational and research institute under the direction of Notre-Dame Cathedral, the Grande Nef (nave) with its ancient vaulted aisles and sacristy can be visited (🕐 *Mon–Sat 10am–6pm, Sun 2pm–6pm;* ✆*free;* 𝄞*01 53 10 74 44; www.collegedesbernardins.fr).*

Église Saint-Nicolas-du-Chardonnet

23 rue Bernardins.

A chapel was constructed in what was a field of thistles *(chardons)* in the 13C. In 1656 it was replaced by the present building; the façade was completed only in 1934. In 1977 the church was taken over by an ultra-conservative group of "traditionalist" Catholics known as the Fraternité Sacerdotale Saint-Pie X, who continue to run the church to this day.

Église des Saints-Archanges

9 bis rue Jean de Beauvais.

Purchased by the Romanian Orthodox Church in 1882, this much-restored chapel is dedicated to the archangels Michael, Gabriel and Raphael.

② QUARTIER LATIN CÔTÉ JARDIN

Boulevard Saint-Michel

Boul' Mich, as it is known, is the heart of the area with its café terraces, publishing houses and bookshops. It leads past the ruins of Cluny's Roman baths.

Place Saint-Michel

This is a popular meeting point for students and night revellers. The present square and fountain by Davioud date from the reign of Napoléon III.

There are many cafés around place St-Michel and along the lower part of boulevard St-Michel.

Rue des Écoles

Dating from the 19C, this street takes its name from the Quartier des Écoles. The main entrances of the **Collège de France** and **Sorbonne** are found here.

Place de la Sorbonne

Lined with cafés, bookshops and other shops, this square serves as the courtyard for the Sorbonne, watched over by the statue of philosopher Auguste Comte. In springtime, place de la Sorbonne with its lively pavement cafés is the favourite haunt of students and lecturers of the nearby university.

La Sorbonne

47 rue des Écoles. ✆*Guided tours (90min) available by appointment Mon–Fri and one Sat per month;* ✆*9€ (for tour)* 𝄞*01 40 46 23 48.*
www.sorbonne.fr.

In 1257 a college for 16 poor students who wished to study theology was founded by King Louis IX, at the instigation of his confessor, Robert de Sorbon (named after his native village of Sorbon in the Ardennes). From such a simple beginning was to develop the

Sorbonne, the centre of theological study in pre-Revolutionary France and the seat of the University of Paris.

Under pressure from Philip the Fair, the theological faculty condemned the Knights Templar, who were burned at the stake in 1314. During the Hundred Years War, the Sorbonne sided with the Burgundians and the English, sending their most eminent bishop to Rouen as prosecutor in the trial of Joan of Arc. The Sorbonne steadfastly opposed all Protestants in the 16C and all philosophers in the 18C. Originally restored under Richelieu in the 17C, the Sorbonne was rebuilt and expanded to become the most important university in France between 1885 and 1901.

The complex accommodates 22 lecture halls, 2 museums, 16 examination halls, 22 seminar rooms, 37 tutorial rooms for teaching staff, 240 laboratories, a library, a physics tower, an astronomy tower, administration offices and the chancellor's lodge.

The renovated **Église de la Sorbonne★** was designed by **Lemercier** between 1635 and 1642 in the Jesuit style. In the chancel is the white-marble **tomb★** of Cardinal Richelieu, designed by Le Brun, and magnificently carved by **Girardon** (1694). The cupola pendentives painted with Richelieu's coat of arms and Church Fathers are by Philippe de Champaigne.

Luxembourg Palace★★

The historic gardens of Luxembourg Palace, seat of the French Senate, are a magnificent oasis of greenery in the heart of the Latin Quarter, making it a popular place where locals and visitors alike can sit and absorb the atmosphere of Paris.

Religious beginnings – In 1257 a community of Carthusians, with the help of St Louis, laid claim to the area and built a vast monastery with extensive grounds.

Marie de' Medici's Palace – After the death of her husband Henri IV, Queen Marie de' Medici, who disliked living at the Louvre, built her own palace on lands purchased from the Duke de Luxembourg. It was modelled on the Palazzo Pitti in Florence, where she had spent her childhood.

Construction started in 1615, with a commission in 1621 for **Rubens** to paint 24 large allegorical pictures representing the queen's life (these paintings are now in the Louvre).

The Palace As Parliament – In 1790 when the monastery was suppressed, the palace gardens were extended to the avenue de l'Observatoire. After serving as a prison during the Terror, the palace successively became home to a parliamentary assembly for the Directory, the Consulate, the Senate and its successor the Peers' Chamber. The Germans occupied the building during World War II.

To give a Florentine quality to his design for the palace, architect Salomon de Brosse used bosses, ringed columns and Tuscan capitals, while keeping the typically French ground plan of a central block built around an arcaded courtyard, with a central domed gateway-pavilion.

The Palace Today – Today the palace is the seat of the **Sénat** (the French Upper House), composed of 348 members. The **Petit Luxembourg**, now the residence of the President of the Senate, comprises the original Hôtel de Luxembourg given to Richelieu by Marie de' Medici and also the cloister and chapel of a convent founded by the queen.

The **Musée du Luxembourg** *(enter at 19 rue de Vaugirard; during exhibitions daily 10am–7.30pm, Mon and Fri until 10pm; 12€; 01 40 13 62 00; www. museeduluxembourg.fr)* houses temporary exhibitions in the former orangerie.

Jardin du Luxembourg★★

The gardens are in the centre of the Left Bank, straddling the 5th and 6th arrondissements. The park is open until dusk and entry is free.

Luxembourg Gardens exert a great draw on Parisians ever since Napoléon decreed that they should be dedicated to children. They attract students and young mothers or nannies with children who stop to watch the tennis or *boules*, to see the *marionnette* puppet shows or listen to the free concerts, to sail boats on the *grand bassin*, or ride miniature ponies. Overall the gardens conform to

Fontaine de Médicis (1624)

©H. Chajmowicz/Michelin

Marie de' Medici (1573–1642)

Born in Florence in 1573, Marie was the daughter of Francesco de' Medici, the Grand Duke of Tuscany. The Medicis were for a time one of the wealthiest and most powerful families in Europe and helped to launch the Italian Renaissance, which spread to France. Very pretty in her youth, she did not marry until the age of 27 and became the second wife of Henri IV of France. It was not a successful marriage as she had to compete with Henri's various mistresses, often shocking the Court with her rather colourful language. However, she bore him several children. Her eldest son became Louis XIII of France following the assassination of his father in 1610.

Although Marie had hitherto shown little interest in politics, she become regent to the infant Louis, and during this time the Palace and Gardens of Luxembourg were created for her. Unfortunately for her, she was unable to enjoy this beautiful 25ha/62-acre estate for very long because when the regency came to an end in 1617, she was exiled by her son to Blois before the palace and garden were actually finished. The period of her regency had not been a success. Thought by many to have been aware of the plot to kill her husband, she was considered to be not very bright and was certainly very stubborn. She had been too easily influenced by her maid's husband, the pro-Habsburg and pro-Spanish Concini, who was eventually assassinated on the orders of Louis. She had, however, introduced to Court the very able Cardinal Richelieu, who was soon to become the king's Chief Minister, and it was he who was instrumental in bringing her back from exile in 1622. By 1625 Marie had installed herself in the recently completed palace, but was to spend only six years in her magnificent new home and garden because she made the fatal mistake of trying to persuade her son to get rid of Richelieu. Louis promised to do so, but secretly had no intention of losing such an able minister. The day it happened, 12 November 1630, was to become known as the Day of Deceit or, as the French call it, the Journée des Dupes. The result was that the by now obese Marie was exiled again in 1631, spending her last years scheming against Richelieu in Brussels, Amsterdam and Cologne where she died penniless in 1642.

A reminder of Marie today is the Baroque Fontaine de Médicis created in 1624 and set at the end of an oblong pool in a shady corner of the garden leading towards the boulevard St-Michel. It acts as a reminder of the woman who was once Queen of France and ended her life as a pauper but nevertheless bequeathed to Paris a wonderful garden to be enjoyed by all.

Jardin du Luxembourg

© J.-P. Clapham/MICHELIN

a formal layout, with the only serpentine lines of the more English-style garden along rue Guynemer and rue Auguste-Comte. The spirit of the monks lives on in the serious tending of trees and bees in the southern end of the park.

Statues of the queens of France and other illustrious women line the terraces, while the **Medici fountain** (1624) has a leafy setting at the far end of a long pool shaded by plane trees, showing its obvious Italian influence.

Rue Soufflot

Notice the niches in the façade at no 3, with its mythological statues. The pharmacy below retains its ancient apothecary style.

The imposing **Panthéon**★★ (ⓖsee p187) dominates the street, surrounded by the semicircular square lined with the symmetrical block of the former Law Faculty (by Soufflot, 1772) – now used as university offices – and the city hall for the 5th *arrondissement*.

Rue Saint-Jacques

This street got its name from the pilgrims on their way to Compostela in Spain, who were lodged in a hostel on this site in the 14C. To the left, the street is bordered by the austere façades of the Sorbonne and the Lycée Louis-Le-Grand. To the right the street becomes narrower, with older buildings.

Further down is the **Centre de la Mer et des Eaux** and past rue Gay-Lussac, the **Église St-Jacques du Haut Pas** *(252 rue St-Jacques)*. The church, built in the Classical style between 1630 and 1685, became a Jansenist centre.

Tour de Calvin

19–21 rue Valette.
Looking north from the square you can see a hexagonal tower (1560), all that remains of Fortet College where, in 1585, the Duke of Guise founded the Catholic League, which was to expel Henri III from Paris.

Église Saint-Étienne du Mont★★

Place Ste-Geneviève. ⓞ *Tue–Fri 8.45am –7.30pm; Sat 8.45am–noon, 2pm–7.45pm; Sun 8.45am–12.15pm, 1.30pm–7.45pm;* ✆*01 43 54 11 79.*

It is in this unique church, known for its **rood screen**★★, the only one in existence in Paris, that Ste Geneviève is venerated. The current church was constructed between 1492 and 1626 to accommodate the growing abbey of St Geneviève and parish of St Stephen. The **façade**★★ is highly original. Three superimposed pediments stand at the centre, their lines emphasized by the upward sweep of the belfry.

Despite its date, the structure is Gothic. Tall aisle walls allow for large windows; an elegant line of balusters cuts the height of the tall pillars. The Flamboyant vaulting above the transept is most eye-catching. The stained glass, which for the most part dates from the 16C and 17C, is particularly unusual in the ambulatory and chancel.

1) 1650 **pulpit**★ supported by a figure of Samson.
2) **Stained-glass window**★ of 1586 illustrating the parable of those invited to the feast.
3) 17C Entombment.
4) The epitaphs of Racine (by Boileau) and Pascal.

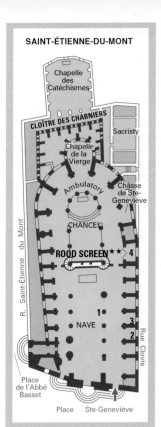

SAINT-ÉTIENNE-DU-MONT

Chapelle des Catéchismes

CLOÎTRE DES CHARNIERS

Sacristy

Chapelle de la Vierge

Ambulatory

Châsse de Ste-Geneviève

CHANCEL

ROOD SCREEN ★★ 4

R. Saint-Étienne du Mont

1
NAVE
3
2

Rue Clovis

Place de l'Abbé Basset

Place   Ste-Geneviève

Cloisters

At one time the church was bordered to the north and east by two small burial grounds. Also known as the Charnel Cloisters, the cloisters are built off the right side of the ambulatory at the church's east end, and may at one time have been used as a charnel house. The **stained-glass windows**★ date back to the 17C. A small Catechism Chapel was added by Baltard in 1859.

▶ From rue de la Montaigne St-Geneviève, turn left on the rue École Polytechnique, and follow rue de Lanneau to rue des Écoles and the square Paul Painlevé.

LE PANTHÉON★★

Place du Panthéon. ◐*Apr–Sept daily 10am–6.30pm; Oct–Mar daily 10am–6pm.* ☙*Guided tours in French* *Apr–Oct.* ◐*Public holidays.* ⊛*7.50€.* ☎*01 44 32 18 00. http://pantheon. monuments-nationaux.fr.*

The Panthéon's distinctive silhouette on the hilltop and its role as the necropolis of France's greatest citizens make it a popular national monument.

Louis XV vowed, when desperately ill in 1744, that should he recover he would replace the semi-ruined church of the abbey of Ste-Geneviève with a magnificent edifice. The project was given to the architect Jacques **Soufflot**. A lack of funds and cracks in the structure caused by ground movements delayed completion until after Soufflot's death (1780), in 1789.

In April 1791 its function as a church was suspended by the Constituent Assembly in order to "receive the bodies of great men who died in the period of French liberty" – thus it became a Pantheon. Voltaire and Rousseau are buried here, as were Mirabeau and Marat for a short while. Successively the Panthéon served as a church under the empire, a necropolis in the reign of Louis-Philippe, a church under Napoléon III, the headquarters of the Commune and finally as a lay temple to receive the ashes of Victor Hugo in 1885.

Exterior

The **dome**★★, strengthened with an iron framework, can be best surveyed from a distance. Eleven steps rise to the peristyle composed of fluted columns supporting a triangular pediment, the first of its kind in Paris. It is inscribed with its dedication "To the great men, the nation is grateful" in gold letters.

Interior

Greek-cross in plan, the nave is divided from the aisles by a line of columns supporting a frieze, cornice and balustrade, roofed with flattened domes. The upper section has a fresco by Baron Antoine Jean Gros (1771–1835) depicting *St Geneviève's Apotheosis*. Stairs lead up to the dome from a place where there is a fine **view**★★ over Paris.

Crypt

Access from the east end.

Although eerie and empty, the crypt contains the tombs of great men throughout France's history: La Tour d'Auvergne, Voltaire, Rousseau, Victor Hugo, Émile Zola, Marcelin Berthelot, Louis Braille, Jean Jaurès, the explorer Bougainville.

More recent heroes to be so honoured are the Nobel Prize winners Pierre and Marie Curie (who was also the first female Nobel Prize winner), and the Resistance leader Jean Moulin.

Foucault's Pendulum

In 1851 **Léon Foucault** took advantage of the dome's height to repeat publicly his experiment that proved the rotation of the earth – a discovery he had made in 1849 using a brass pendulum (28kg/62lb) hung from a steel cable (67m/220ft), which deviated from its axis during oscillation in a circular movement. The pendulum can now be seen at the Musée des Arts et Métiers (&see *LE SENTIER AND LE TEMPLE*).

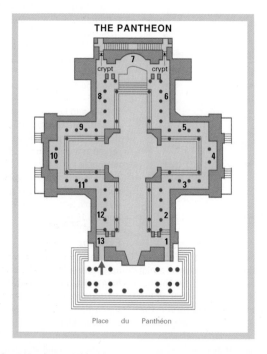

THE PANTHEON

Place   du   Panthéon

1. *Saint Denis' Prediction (Galand).*

2. *Scenes from the Life of St Geneviève (Puvis de Chavannes).*

3. *Charlemagne Crowned Emperor, and Protector of the Humanities (H Lévy).*

4. *Miraculous Cure of Quiblinf and Procession of the Reliquary of St Geneviève (Maillot).*

5. *Battle of Tolbiac and Baptism of Clovis (J Blanc).*

6. *Death and Funeral of St Geneviève (J-P Laurens).*

7. *Towards Glory (E Detaille).*

8. *St Geneviève Watching over Paris and St Geneviève Bringing Food to the Town (Puvis de Chavannes).*

9. *Story of Joan of Arc (J-E Lenepveu).*

10. *The Concept of Fatherland, Plenty, Home and Plague (Humbert). Monument to the Unknown Heroes (Landowski).*

11. *The Life of St Louis (Cabanel).*

12. *St Geneviève Encourages and Reassures the Parisians (Delaunay).*

13. *Martyrdom of St Denis (Bonnat).*

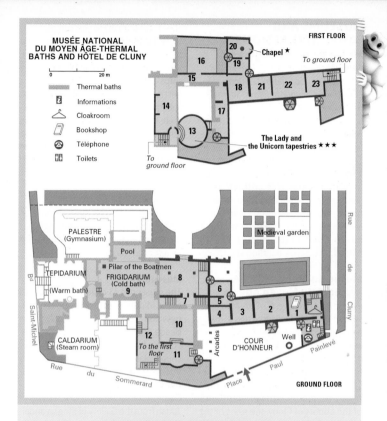

MUSÉE NATIONAL DU MOYEN ÂGE-THERMAL BATHS AND HÔTEL DE CLUNY

FIRST FLOOR

- Thermal baths
- ℹ Informations
- △ Cloakroom
- 📄 Bookshop
- ☎ Téléphone
- 🚻 Toilets

20
16
19
Chapel ★
To ground floor
15
18 21 22 23
14
17
13
To ground floor
The Lady and the Unicorn tapestries ★★★

PALESTRE (Gymnasium)
Medieval garden
Pool
Pilar of the Boatmen
TEPIDARIUM
FRIGIDARIUM (Cold bath)
8
(Warm bath)
9
6
7
5
4 3 2 1
Bd Saint-Michel
CALDARIUM (Steam room)
12
10
To the first floor
11
Arcades
COUR D'HONNEUR
Well
Rue du Sommerard
Place Paul Painlevé
Rue de Cluny
GROUND FLOOR

Abbots' Residence to Museum

About 1330, Pierre of Châlus, Abbot of Cluny-en-Bourgogne, the influential Burgundian abbey, bought the ruins and the surrounding land to build a residence for abbots visiting Paris. Jacques of Amboise, Bishop of Clermont and Abbot of Jumièges in Normandy, rebuilt the house to its present design between 1485 and 1500. Hospitality was offered to many guests, including in 1515 Henry VIII's sister, Mary, widowed at 16 by the death of Louis XII of France, a man in his fifties who survived the marriage only three months. The white queen – as royal widows endured their period of mourning dressed in white – was closely watched over by Louis' cousin and successor, François I, lest she should bear a child, an act that might cost him his throne. When Mary was discovered one night in the company of the young Duke of Suffolk, the king compelled her to marry the Englishman in the chapel there and then before despatching her to England. In the 17C the house accommodated the papal nuncios, the most illustrious being Mazarin. At the Revolution the residence classed as State property was sold, passing to a variety of owners including a surgeon who used the chapel as a dissecting room, a cooper, a printer and a laundress. The City of Paris acquired the baths in 1819 and agreed to cede their rights to the land on condition that the whole be opened as a museum. In 1833 Alexandre du Sommerard came to live in the house, installing his substantial collection of artefacts from the Middle Ages and the Renaissance. At his death in 1842, the mansion and its contents were purchased by the State; Edmond du Sommerard, son of the former owner, was appointed as curator in 1844.

MUSEUMS AND OTHER ATTRACTIONS
Musée de minéralogie★★

60 boulevard St-Michel. Tue–Fri 1.30pm–6pm, Sat 10am–12.30pm, 2pm–5pm. Public holidays, Sat mid-Jul–mid-Aug. 6€. 01 40 51 91 39. www.musee.ensmp.fr.

The museum is situated within the École Supérieure des Mines. It was founded in 1783 and installed in the former hôtel de Vendôme in 1815. The 100 000-specimen **mineralogical collection** is among the world's richest and includes precious stones, minerals, crystals and meteorites displayed in 9 rooms. Don't miss the meteorites illuminated with black lights, a truly dazzling sight.

Musée de Cluny – Musée national du Moyen Âge★★

6 place Paul Painlevé. Wed–Mon 9.15am–5.45pm (last admission 45min before closing). 1 Jan, 1 May, 25 Dec. 8€; no charge 1st Sun of the month. 01 53 73 78 00. www.musee-moyenage.fr. See floor plan p190.

This National Museum of the Middle Ages encompasses the old residence of the abbots of Cluny, the ruins of the Roman baths and an outstanding collection of medieval arts.

Hôtel de Cluny

This mansion, together with the Hôtel de Sens, is one of only two 15C private houses in Paris. Despite much restoration, original medieval details survive in features such as the wall crenellations and turrets. The left wing is articulated with arches; the central building has mullioned windows; a frieze and Flamboyant balustrade, from which gargoyles spurt, line the base of the roof, ornamented with picturesque dormer windows swagged with coats of arms. A pentagonal tower juts out from the central building. *Concerts of medieval and Baroque music are often held here.*

Les Thermes★

Excavations have determined the plan of these **Gallo-Roman public baths** dating from AD 200. The present ruins cover about one-third of the vast complex ransacked in the 3C by the barbarians. The best-preserved area is the **frigidarium**. Vault ribs rest on consoles carved as ships' prows – an unusual motif suggesting the idea that the building was constructed by the Paris guild of boatmen. It was this same guild that, in the reign of Tiberius (AD 14–37), dedicated a pillar to Jupiter, known as **le pilier des Nautes★** (Boatmen's Pillar); it is Paris' oldest existing sculpture.

Chapel★

The chapel, on the first floor, was designed as the abbots' oratory. It has an elegant Flamboyant vault supported by a central column.

Museum★★

The museum's 23 galleries are devoted to the Middle Ages, displaying the richness and skill of the applied arts of the period. These include illuminated manuscripts, furniture, arms and armour, church plate, ironwork and stained glass. Room 8 contains fragments of figurative sculpture from the façade of Notre-Dame: notably 21 heads of the Kings of Judah from the Gallery of Kings, vandalized during the Revolution. Some of the finest masterpieces of the late Middle Ages are grouped in room 14: the Tarascon *Pietà*; a tapestry depicting the story of the Prodigal Son; and sculptures in stone, marble and wood including two Flemish altarpieces.

In room 13 *(1st floor)* **La Dame à la Licorne★★★** (The Lady and the Unicorn) panels are the most exquisite examples of 15C and early 16C tapestries of the *mille-fleurs* or thousand flower design, woven in the south of the Netherlands. The six tapestries, armorial bearings of the Le Viste family from Lyon, portray the lion (chivalric nobility) and the unicorn (bourgeois nobility) on either side of a richly attired lady. Five are thought to be allegories of the senses with the sixth, to my heart's desire, showing the young woman depositing a necklace in a casket, symbolizing a renouncement of such earthly, sensual pleasures.

Saint-Germain-des-Prés★★

On the Left Bank, the old quarter of Saint-Germain-des-Prés is known for its beautiful church, famous cafés, narrow streets and antique shops. Post-war jazz clubs and an intellectual spirit have mostly made way for upmarket fashion and home décor boutiques. Bordering the Latin Quarter and the St-Germain-des-Prés neighbourhood, Odéon brims with cafés, bookshops and cinemas permanently animated by young students, university staff, publishers and night revellers. The Saint-Sulpice district has long been famous for selling religious trinkets that became known as St-Sulpice art and often reached heights of kitsch. It has come under the influence of neighbouring St-Germain-des-Prés and its shops now include bookshops and upscale fashion boutiques.

 WALKING TOURS

1 ST-GERMAIN-DES-PRÉS TO SAINT-SULPICE

Start at M *St-Germain-des-Prés.*

Place du Québec

Charles Daudelin's **fountain** reproduces the effect of the snow-melt breaking up great layers of ice, reminiscent of Canadian winters. Famous jewellers (Cartier) and fashion houses (Armani) replaced older bookshops and boutiques in 1998.

Église St-Germain-des-Prés★★

Founded in the 8C, the Benedictine abbey of St-Germain-des-Prés became sovereign ruler of its domain, answerable in spiritual matters to the Pope alone. The monastery was sacked four times in 40 years by the Normans, then rebuilt and enlarged each time. In the 14C, when Charles V enclosed the city, the abbey fortified itself with crenellated walls, towers and a moat linked

Info: Pyramides welcome centre, 25 rue des Pyramides. 08 92 68 30 00 (0.34€ per min). http://en.parisinfo.com.

Location: The quarter sits in the centre of the Left Bank along the Seine, at the northeast end of the 6th arrondissement.

Metro/Transport: For Saint-Germain: St-Germain des Prés (line 4) – Buses: 39, 63, 70, 86, 87, 95, 96. For the Institute de France: Pont Neuf (line 7), Odéon (lines 4 and 10) – Buses: 24, 27, 58, 70. For Saint-Sulpice: St-Sulpice (line 4), Mabillon (line 10) – Buses: 48, 63, 70, 84, 95, 96. For Odéon: Odéon (lines 4 and 10), Mabillon (line 10) – Buses: 58, 70, 86, 96.

Parking: Underground parking throughout the district: at Odéon, at place St-André des Arts, near St-Michel, at place St-Sulpice, near the Institute de France, on rue Bonaparte and boulevard St-Germain.

Don't Miss: In St-Germain, the pleasant square in rue de Furstemberg. In Odéon, the charming boutiques of the Cour du Commerce St-André. The Delacroix mural paintings in the Église St-Sulpice. The view of the Institut de France from the Pont des Arts.

Timing: Allow one to two hours for the St-Sulpice walking tour (1), two hours for the Institut de France area walk (2) and a further 90 minutes for the Odéon neighbourhood walking tour (3).

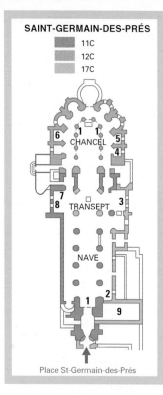

SAINT-GERMAIN-DES-PRÉS

- 11C
- 12C
- 17C

CHANCEL

TRANSEPT

NAVE

Place St-Germain-des-Prés

1. *Modern wrought-iron grille by Raymond Subes.*

2. *Our Lady of Consolation (1340).*

3. *Tomb by Girardon (17C).*

4. *Mausoleum of James Douglas, a 17C Scottish nobleman attached to the Court of Louis XIII.*

5. *Descartes' and the learned Benedictines, Mabillon's and Montfaucon's tombstones.*

6. *Boileau, the poet and critic's tombstone.*

7. *Statue of St Francis Xavier by N Coustou.*

8. *Tomb of John Casimir, King of Poland, who died in 1672, Abbot of St-Germain-des-Prés.*

9. *St Symphorian Chapel.*

to the right of the cradle vaulted porch is the Merovingian sanctuary with the tomb of St Germanus, known as **St Symphorian's Chapel** (◯*daily 8am–7.45pm; ℘01 55 42 81 18).*

Rue de l'Abbaye

Homage to Apollinaire, a Picasso sculpture, has been placed in a small square on the corner of place St-Germain-des-Prés. The impressive brick and stone former **Abbatial Palace** at no 5 was built in 1586 by the Cardinal-Abbot Charles of Bourbon. The palace was remodelled in 1699 by Abbé de Fürstenberg and sold in 1797 as State property. The angle pavilion and the Renaissance façade have been restored to their original appearance.

Rue de Furstenberg★

This old-fashioned street with its square shaded by paulownia and white-globe street lights was built by the cardinal of the same name through the former monastery stableyard. Nos **6** and **8** are the remains of the outbuildings.

The **Musée Eugène Delacroix** (*6 place de Furstenberg;* ◯*Wed–Mon 9.30am–5.30pm;* ◯*1 Jan, 1 May, 25 Dec;* ◉*6€; free 1st Sun/month and 14 Jul;* ℘*01 44 41 86 50; www.musee-delacroix.fr)* is in the colourist's last studio-home; he lived here from 1858 to 1863. Dedicated to Delacroix, leader of the Romantic painters, it features works by the artist and his friends, with changing exhibitions.

to the Seine. From 1674 the abbey was used as a State prison, and at the Revolution it was completely destroyed: the library was burned, the royal tombs disappeared, the church turned into saltpetre works, and the rest of the buildings demolished.

The church and the abbatial palace are all that remain of the famous Benedictine abbey. The 11C Romanesque church, the oldest in Paris, has altered considerably in appearance. The chancel flying buttresses are contemporary with Notre-Dame; of the three original belltowers only one remains; it was restored in the 19C when it was crowned with its present pitched roof. The original porch is hidden by an outer doorway added in 1607.

The church's small dimensions are explained by the fact that it was built as a monastery chapel and not as a parish church. Grand-scale restoration work in the 19C left vaults, walls and capitals painted in garish colours. Off

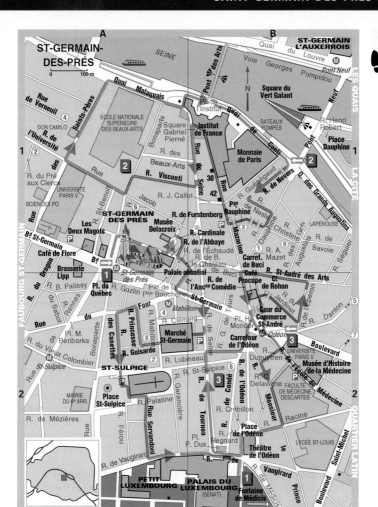

WHERE TO STAY

Hôtel St-Thomas-d'Aquin... ②
Hôtel Verneuil................... ④
Millésime Hôtel................. ⑥

WHERE TO EAT

Azabu................................. ①
Bar à Soupes et Quenelles... ②
L'Heure Gourmande............. ③
La Table d'Erica................... ④
La Tourelle.......................... ⑤
Le Marco Polo..................... ⑥
Maison de la Lozère........... ⑦
Ristorante da
Alfredo Positano......... ⑧
Rôtisserie d'en Face........ ⑨

Rue Cardinale

Twisting and turning, this street was created in 1700 by the Abbe de Fürstenberg through the long monastery tennis
court.

Still partially lined by old houses (nos
3–9) it extends to a picturesque crossroads with rue de l'Échaudé (1388) and
rue de Bourbon le Château.

◯ Take rue de l'Échaudé to reach
boulevard St-Germain then turn right.

Boulevard Saint-Germain

Just off place St-Germain-des-Prés are
the **Café des Deux-Magots** and the
Café de Flore, the famous meeting
spots for Left-Bank intellectuals and
artists in the 1950s and 1960s.

Opposite, the **Brasserie Lipp** (no 151) is a popular venue with politicians, writers and celebrities. Further on, two 18C mansions survive (nos **159** and **173**).

▶ Take rue de Seine towards the Odéon to rue Toustain, turn right.

Marché Saint-Germain

Rue de Montfaucon at one time gave access to the St-Germain fairground. The fair, founded in 1482 by Louis XI for the benefit of the abbey, had until the Revolution (1790) a considerable effect on Paris' economy: it was a forerunner of international exhibitions and world-trade fairs today.

In 1818 the covered **St-Germain market** was built on part of the site. It combines a food hall and commercial clothing boutiques.

Rues Guisarde and Princesse

Pedestrians rule these small streets of old Paris. In summer the flowering window boxes decorate the façades. Pubs, bars and restaurants give the neighbourhood a lively atmosphere until dawn.

Rue du Four

It was at no 48 on this street that, on 27 May 1943, the National Council of the French Resistance, united under Jean Moulin, recognized General de Gaulle as its official leader.

Rue des Canettes

Duckling Street takes its name from the low relief at no **18**. It is a lively place to go out in the evening, with many bars, restaurants and nightclubs.

Place Saint-Sulpice

Initiated in 1754, the square was designed as a semicircular space defined by uniform façades of the type at no **6** (at the corner of rue des Canettes), designed by Servandoni. But the plan's implementation did not materialize.

The central fountain, erected by Visconti in 1844, is known as the Fontaine des Quatre Points Cardinaux after the sculpted portraits of Bossuet, Fénelon, Massillon and Fléchier, facing the cardinal points of the compass. Shops bearing famous names such as Yves Saint Laurent and Christian Lacroix are found along the northern side of the square.

Église de Saint-Sulpice★★

The church, dedicated to the 6C Archbishop of Bourges, St Sulpicius, was founded by the abbey of St-Germain-des-Prés as a parish church for peasants living in its domain. Rebuilding began in 1646 with the chancel. A succession of six architects took charge over a period of 134 years.

Exterior – In 1732 a competition was held for the design of the façade and won by a Florentine, **Servandoni**, who proposed a fine façade in the Antique style, in contrast to the rest of the edifice. The final façade differs considerably from Servandoni's original concept. The colossal pediment has been abandoned; the belfries are crowned not by Renaissance pinnacles but by balustrades; the towers are dissimilar, the left one being

Église de Saint-Sulpice

© Yoshimi Kanazawa/MICHELIN

taller and more ornate than the other one, which was never completed.

Interior – The interior is extremely impressive by its size. Of the 20 artists who worked on the internal paintings, Delacroix, and his genius, dominate. His **murals★**, painted between 1849 and 1861, illustrate *St Michael Killing the Demon* (ceiling), *Heliodorus Being Driven from the Temple*, and *Jacob Wrestling with the Angel* (left wall).

The **Lady Chapel★** in the apse was painted under the personal supervision of Servandoni. The Virgin and Child group behind the altar is the work of **Pigalle**. The **organ loft★** was designed by Chalgrin in 1776. Rebuilt in 1862, the organ is the largest in France and considered one of the finest. Two stoups abutting the second pillars of the nave are made from giant shells given to François I by the Venetian Republic and by Louis XV to the church of St-Sulpice in 1745.

In the transept, a copper band inlaid in the floor stretches from a plaque in the southern *(right)* transept to a marble obelisk in the northern *(left)* arm. At noon at the winter solstice, a ray of sunlight, passing through a small hole in the upper window in the south transept, strikes marked points on the obelisk in the far transept. At the spring and autumn equinoxes, the ray is caught by the metal plaque at noon.

Rue Servandoni
This charming little street, with its cobblestones and old houses with heavy wooden doors (the French economist Condorcet lived at no 5 in 1793–4), leads to the rue de Vaugirard and the Jardin du Luxembourg (&see *Le QUARTIER LATIN*).

2 INSTITUT DE FRANCE
Start beside the Pont Neuf (&see La Cité).

Quai des Grands Augustins
The oldest quay in Paris dates from 1313, and derives its name from the Great Augustine monastery established by St Louis in the 13C on a nearby site. Note,

as you pass, two 17C mansions: no **51**, now the famous Lapérouse Restaurant, and no **35**, the former Hôtel Feydeau-Montholon.

Rue de Nevers
This curious, picturesque alley created in the 13C maintains its medieval character. It abuts a fragment of the old wall built by Philippe-Auguste around the city.

Rue Mazarine
This narrow street contains small art galleries. As you leave the passage, look at the building opposite: it is decorated with statues perched on stilts. Opera was presented for the first time in France, in 1671, at the **Guénégaud Theatre** (no **42**), which was formerly an indoor tennis court. At no **30**, the first Paris **fire station** was home to the capital's first fire brigade in 1722. At no **12**, beyond place Gabriel Pierné, stood a theatre in which **Molière** made his first appearance as an actor.

Rue de Seine
With the rue Mazarine running parallel, this street lies in the heart of the Association Art à St-Germain-des-Prés, a factor that explains the impressive number of art galleries. At no 53, at the back of the courtyard, the **Galerie Jeanne Bucher** was founded in 1925. At nos 35–37, another must-see gallery, **Galerie Visconti**, promoted the painter Bernard Buffet.

Rue Visconti
This narrow alleyway was known in the 16C as Little Geneva because of its Protestant community. At no **26** the sign of a 17C cabaret (Le Petit Maure) remains. The playwright **Racine** died at no **24** in 1699. Two hundred years later, **Balzac** founded a printing house at no **17** (1826) that soon went bankrupt. Later still, **Delacroix** had his studio here from 1836 to 1844.

▶ Take rue Jacob to rue des Sts-Pères; turn right on the quai Malaquais.

The Academy

Founded by Cardinal Richelieu in 1635, the Académie Française exists to regulate French grammar, spelling and literature. Suppressed during the Revolution, the Académie was fully restored by Napoléon Bonaparte in 1816; it has been in operation ever since. The Académie has 40 members called Les Immortels; its motto is "À l'immortalité" or "To immortality". While there is not a bar on non-French members, there have been very few, and the Académie appears not to be an equal opportunity organisation, since only four women have ever been members – the first being Marguerite Yourcenar in 1980.

Strangely, the recommendations of the Académie carry no legal power, but they do produce a dictionary of acceptable French usage, entitled *Le Dictionnaire de l'Académie Française*. Looked upon as official in France, the dictionary is often ignored even by government departments; strangely, it is not on sale to the general public.

Increasingly the problem for the Académie is that French culture and language have come under pressure from the widespread use of English as the main international language and also the parallel growth of the Internet. Words borrowed from English, while widely understood by the French, are discouraged by the Académie. Email should be referred to as *courriel,* while computer software should be *logiciel* and the computer has to be *l'ordinateur.*

Much more controversial, however, is the issue of what to call a female in an occupation that has a masculine noun as the job title. Lionel Jospin's government, for example, used the form *la ministre* to refer to a female colleague following the example set by the Swiss, Canadian and Belgian governments. Greatly frowned upon by Les Immortels, such usage remains a matter unresolved.

While the concept of protecting the Culture and Language of La Belle France is admirable, there is perhaps an echo of King Canute. Even the most ardent supporters of the French language may eventually have to concede the inevitable.

Quai Malaquais

The École nationale supérieure des Beaux-Arts *(on the right)* has stood here since 1816. On the corner with rue Bonaparte at no **9** stands a 17C stone and brick house, visited by Manon Lescaut in the story by Abbé Prévost. The writer Anatole France (1844-1924) was born at no **19** (plaque on no **15**), which also served George Sand between 1832 and 1836, when she wrote *Lélia.*

Institut de France★★

23 quai de Conti. ↻ *Closed to the public except by guided group tour (see below). The Centre des Monuments Nationaux (National Monuments Centre) organizes guided tours of the Institut de France the 2nd Sun of the month for groups of 30 people. Fee. Call or go*
online for details. The tour includes the interior courtyards, the dome and Mazarin's tomb. Reservations: 01 44 41 44 41. www.institute-de-france.fr.

The Institut is one of the gems of the Left Bank; among the academies housed within its walls is the renowned **Académie Française**. Open only to visitors with a guide, this seat of learning is not easy to get into. The building is best admired from the bridge, the **Pont des Arts**; surrounding streets evoke memories of Molière, Racine and Balzac.

The building seen today came into being as a result of a bequest by the Cardinal Mazarin, three days before he died in 1661, for a college of scholars from France's newly acquired provinces. The Institute was founded in 1795 and consists of five academies: the Académies des Inscriptions et Belles Lettres,

Sciences, Beaux-Arts, Sciences morales et Politiques, and the famous Académie Française, best known by linguists for safeguarding the French language from franglais. The main activity of the "40 Immortels" is the constant revision of the definitive Dictionary of the French Language (&see box The Academy).

A magnificent dome distinguishes the building from afar. The central chapel is flanked by two pavilions by **Le Vau**, architect of the Louvre. In the courtyard, to the left of the dome, is the **Mazarin Library**★.

Inside, the former chapel is now the formal audience chamber where members are sworn in, with a Mazarin commemorative monument by **Coysevox**. A second courtyard is surrounded by the buildings in which the scholars once lived.

Monnaie de Paris★

11 quai Conti. &*Closed for renovations until late 2016. Temporary art exhibits on view, free of charge.* &*01 40 46 57 57. www.monnaiedeparis.fr.*

In the 18C Louis XV installed the Mint here, selecting the architect **Jacques-Denis Antoine** to design the workshops, which were built between 1768 and 1775. The simplicity of line, sober rustication and restrained decoration was praised by the contemporary public, tired of excessive Classical orders and colonnades. Before being transferred to Pessac, all of France's currency was minted here. Collection pieces, medals and decorations are still produced here. The **Coin Museum** *(back of the main courtyard)* occupies the refurbished minting and milling halls.

Exhibits retrace the history of French coin making and minting from 300 BC. A fine collection of coins, medals, banking documentation, paintings, engravings and drawings illustrate various political, social and financial developments.

Pont des Arts

The bridge dating from 1803 was the first in Paris to be built of iron and the first pedestrian bridge. Access was subject to a toll, as it was for most of the

Pont des Arts leading to the Institut de France

© Olivier Nicolas/Photononstop/Tips Images

bridges, levied until 1849. Its success was immediate: 65 000 Parisians paid to cross it the day it opened. The present construction is steel and has seven arches instead of the original eight.

The **view**★★★ is outstanding, encompassing the full length of Pont Neuf and the Île de la Cité, including Notre-Dame; downstream the Louvre, the Grand Palais and the Carrousel Bridge.

③ QUARTIER DE L'ODÉON★

Start at Ⓜ *Odéon.*

Carrefour de l'Odéon (place Henri-Mondor)

This great junction is dominated by a bronze statue of **Georges-Jacques Danton** (1759–94), erected at the end of the 19C on the site of the famous Revolutionary leader's house (&*see box p198*).

Cour du Commerce St-André★

Entrance via 130 boulevard St-Germain, opposite Danton's statue.

This courtyard was opened in 1776 on the site of an actual **tennis court** *(jeu de paume)* used for an archaic form of the game. It was here in a loft in 1790 that Dr Guillotin demonstrated his humane decapitating machine by using sheep as the victim. At no **8, Jean-Paul Marat** printed his Revolutionary paper *L'Ami du Peuple (*The People's Friend). In the first alleyway (gated) to the right, a tower of the Philippe Auguste city wall can be seen on the corner.

Cour de Rohan

A series of three courtyards formed part of a mansion in the 15C owned by the archbishops of Rouen (Rohan is a corruption of Rouen). The middle one is overlooked by the fine Renaissance house where Diane de Poitiers lived. The peaceful rue du Jardinet, built on the site of former gardens, runs on to rue de l'Éperon, home to Paris' first girls' school (1893), the Lycée Fénelon.

Carrefour de Buci

In the 18C the Buci was the liveliest spot on the Left Bank – and a place of ill-repute. It had palaquins (enclosed chairs for carrying people of rank), sentries in the area, a pillory with an iron collar for miscreants and a gallows.

Today the area around the Buci cross-roads is particularly animated on Satur-days (*rue Grégoire-de-Tours, rue de Bourbon-le-Château*); there are many fashion boutiques and restaurants as well as antique shops along rue Mazarine and rue Dauphine leading to the river.

Rue de l'Ancienne-Comédie

Formerly rue des Fossés-St-Germain, this street was renamed in 1770, the date the Comédie-Française moved out. On the brink of financial ruin, the company went to the Tuileries Palace Theatre before finally moving to the Odéon.

Rue de l'École de Médecine

At no **5** the long-gowned Brotherhood of Surgeons, founded by St Louis in the 13C, performed anatomical operations of every kind until the 17C. At no **15** stood the **Couvent des Cordeliers** – a Franciscan monastery of high reputation in the Middle Ages for its teaching. In 1791, the Revolutionary group formed by Danton, Marat, Camille Desmoulins and Hébert, known as the Cordeliers, took over both the monastery and its name; opposite lived Jean-Paul **Marat** (1743–93), the pamphleteer who was stabbed in his bath by Charlotte Corday on 13 July 1793. The present buildings, now part of the university (*6th arr*), were built between 1877 and 1900 to house the School of Practical Medicine. The central part of the former medical school (*no 12*), now known as the **René Descartes University** (*5th arr*), dates back to 1775.

Danton

Dominating the Carrefour de l'Odéon is the bronze statue of **Georges-Jacques Danton** (1759–94) on the site of his former house. One of the leading figures in the drama of the French Revolution, Danton is often thought of as a more normal human being than his cold dispassionate colleague Robespierre, his eventual nemesis. Unlike many Revolutionaries, he was pragmatic rather than idealistic, well educated (he could speak five languages) and liked "the good life". Born in 1759 at Arcis-sur-Aube, Danton was a robust child. He studied law at Reims and qualified as a lawyer, seemingly destined for an ordinary middle-class existence until he became involved in Revolutionary politics.

Often referred to as "the man of August 10th" for his part in the Tuileries uprising of 1792, he became Minister of Justice and later, the first President of the Committee of Public Safety. Unlike Robespierre, he regretted many of the excesses which took place during this period and eventually became disillusioned with politics. Accused by Robespierre of venality and leniency towards the enemies of the Revolution, he suffered the inevitable result: he was executed on 5 April 1794.

René Descartes (1596–1630)

Often referred to as "the father of modern philosophy", Descartes was also a prominent mathematician and scientist. He was most well known for his statement "I think, therefore I am"; his tomb is in the Church of Saint-Germain-des-Prés.

The **Musée d'Histoire de la Médecine** (*Université René-Descartes, 12 rue de l'École de Médecine;* ⏱*mid-Jul–Aug Mon–Fri 2pm–5.30pm; rest of the year Mon–Wed and Fri–Sat 2pm–5.30pm;* ⏱*20 Dec–4 Jan, public holidays;* ⚭*3.50€;* ✆*01 40 46 16 93; www.univ-paris5.fr)* features the College of Surgeons' collections of surgical instruments from Ancient Egypt to modern times.

Rue Monsieur Le Prince

The door at no 4, formerly of the Hôtel de Bacq, is typical of the 18C style. At no 10 is the apartment where the philosopher **Auguste Comte** lived from 1841 until his death in 1857. Now open to the public, the **Maison Auguste Comte** (⏱*Wed 2pm–5pm;* ⏱*public holidays;* ⚭*4€;* ✆*01 43 26 08 56; www.augustecomte.org)* presents the residence as it looked when the philosopher died.

Place de l'Odéon

This semicircular square has remained essentially unchanged since its creation in 1779. At no **1**, the Café Voltaire was frequented by the Encyclopedists and at the turn of the 19C, by famous writers and poets such as Barrès, Bourget, Mallarmé, **Verlaine**, **Gide**, **Hemingway** and others.

Théâtre de l'Odéon

In 1782 a theatre was built in the gardens of the former Condé mansion to accommodate the French Comedians who had been confined to the Tuileries Palace Theatre. The new theatre, built in the popular Antique style of the day, was given the name Théâtre Français.

Beaumarchais' *Le Mariage de Figaro* was particularly well received in 1784. With the advent of the Revolution, the actors split between Royalists and Republicans, and disbanded in 1792.
In 1797 the theatre was taken over and renamed the Odéon, after the building used by the Greeks to hold musical competitions. In 1807 the building was rebuilt to its original plans after a fire. In spite of the great success of Alphonse Daudet's play, *L'Arlésienne,* set to music by **Bizet**, the audiences dwindled, migrating to theatres on the Right Bank. Between 1946 and 1959, known first as the Salle Luxembourg and then as the Théâtre de France, it began to specialize in 20C plays, achieving pre-eminence in 1968 under Jean-Louis Barrault and Madeleine Renaud. In 1983 the theatre became the **Théâtre de l'Europe** *(place de l'Odéon;* ✆*01 44 85 40 40; www.theatre-odeon.eu),* first on a part-time basis, then completely assuming this identity in 1990.
Inside, the ceiling is painted by André Masson (1963).

Rue de l'Odéon

Sylvia Beach opened the original Shakespeare & Co. bookshop at no 12, where she published James Joyce's *Ulysses* in 1922. At no 9 the Arts et Autographes gallery sells letters signed by de Gaulle, Monet, Freud and Matisse.

Rue de Tournon

Leaving the place Pierre-Dux, at no 27 *(on the right when going down)* is the house of the Chevalier d'Airain, Jacques Casanova de Seingalt, in place of the house given to the 17C poet Clément Marot. Further down at no 17 is the house where the popular French theatre actor Gérard Philipe (*Le Cid, Fanfan la Tulipe*) died in Novembre 1959. On the pavement to the left, at no 8, is an old carriage doorway where the musician and orchestra conductor Gabriel Pierné lived in 1900–37, and at no 6, the Hôtel de Brancas, the carriage door hides a lovely interior courtyard in this charming *hôtel particulier.*

Faubourg Saint-Germain★★

The Faubourg Saint-Germain was originally the aristocratic suburb *(faubourg)* of the abbey of St-Germain-des-Prés. The Revolution closed its sumptuous town houses, and today the district is known more for its government ministries. Only through a half-open door will you catch glimpses of the 18C atmosphere. Curious travellers who wander outside the well-known St-Germain and St-Sulpice districts will find the elegant residential neighbourhood of Sèvres-Babylone dotted with interesting shops and lively cafés.

A BIT OF HISTORY

At the end of the 16C, the university acquired a strip of meadow at the river's edge from the abbey of St-Germain-des-Prés, known as the Pré aux Clercs (Scholars' Meadow).

Marguerite of Valois, first wife of Henri IV, took the east end of the meadow in the 17C from the university and built a vast mansion with a garden running down to the Seine. On her death in 1615, the university tried to reclaim the land but succeeded only in having the main street of the new quarter named rue de l'Université.

The district was at its most fashionable in the 18C. Noble lords and rich financiers built houses that gave the streets an individual character: one monumental entrance followed another, each opening on to a courtyard closed at the far end by the façade of a handsome mansion, beyond which lay a large garden. The Revolution closed many of the mansions, and more were pulled down when boulevard St-Germain and boulevard Raspail were opened in the late 19C. The finest houses remaining now belong to the State, such as the National Assembly and the Hôtel Matignon, while others serve as ambassadorial residences.

Several noteworthy museums include the Musée Rodin, where the artist

Info: Pyramides welcome centre, 25 rue des Pyramides. ✆08 92 68 30 00 (0.34€ per min). http://en.parisinfo.com.

Location: This Right-Bank quarter overlooking the Seine sits between the Hôtel des Invalides and the Musée d'Orsay.

Metro/Transport: For Faubourg St-Germain: Assemblée Nationale (line 12), Solférino (line 12), Varenne (line 13) – RER: Musée d'Orsay (line C) – Buses: 73, 83, 84, 94. For Sèvres-Babylone: Rue-du-Bac (line 12), Sèvres Babylone (lines 10 and 12), Vaneau (line 10); Buses: 39, 68, 70, 83, 87, 94.

Parking: Underground parking in Faubourg St-Germain off the boulevard St-Germain, or side streets; in Sèvres Babylone in front of the Bon Marché department store.

Don't Miss: The Musée Rodin gardens, the views from the Musée d'Orsay. Fashionable people-watching from the cafés on rue de Sèvres.

Timing: Allow a half-day for the walk and museum visits around Faubourg St-Germain. Allow two to three hours to visit all of the sights in Sèvres-Babylone.

Kids: Playground in the Musée Rodin gardens. The square Boucicault in Sèvres-Babylone has a large playground.

once lived and worked, and the Musée d'Orsay, which occupies a former train station overlooking the Seine.

🐾 WALKING TOURS
Start from the Ⓜ Varenne.

1 HÔTELS AND MINISTÈRES
This walk takes in the buildings that house the French Government head-quarters, the Assemblée Nationale and several sumptuous 18C residential houses, now serving official functions.

Musée Rodin★★
79 rue de Varenne. ⏰Tue–Sun 10am–5.45pm (Wed until 8.45pm). ⏰1 Jan, 1 May, 25 Dec. ⊜7€; garden only, 2€; free 1st Sun of the month. ℘01 44 18 61 10. www.musee-rodin.fr.

Since 2005 a visitors' entrance, gift shop, library, auditorium, research room, workshops, and a temporary exposition room have occupied the 5 000sq m/5 980sq yd of space within chapel of the Rodin Museum. The architect in charge of the renovations, Pierre-Louis Faloci, wanted to turn this already popular place into a "must-see Parisian museum". Visitors enter via the chapel. With its 12m/13yd-high glass skylight, it's the perfect setting for temporary exhibitions.

Don't miss the superb **gardens** (and the pleasant café), where some of the artist's most important works are displayed, including **The Thinker**, **The Burghers of Calais** (made in 1884 with the help of Camille Claudel), the **Gates of Hell** and **Ugolino**.

Inside the house with its parquet floors and wood-panelled walls are some of Rodin's most expressive works, **The Cathedral**, **The Kiss**, **The Walking Man**, **The Man with a Broken Nose**, **Eve** and the **Age of Bronze** and others. Creation, in the guise of restless figures emerging from the roughly hewn rock, was a favourite theme (**Hand of God**) although it was his renderings of the nude that demonstrated his true technical genius (**St John the Baptist**) and won him public acclaim in 1879.

One room is devoted to drawings by the artist that are exhibited in rotation. Upstairs are plaster *maquettes* for the large groups and for the statues of **Balzac** and **Victor Hugo**, **The Wave**.

The personal collections of the artist are also on display, including **Le Père Tanguy** by Van Gogh, a female nude by **Renoir**, and *Mother and Child* by **Eugène Carrière**.

Hôtel Biron★★ – *Under renovation until fall 2015 (Camille Claudel's works are not on display)*. This 18C mansion belonged to the poet Rainer Maria Rilke, before being converted into a convent for the education of wealthy girls. After convents were disbanded in 1904, part of the property became the Lycée Victor-Duruy. The State loaned the house to Rodin, who lived there until his death in 1917, in exchange for his artworks.

Rue de Varenne
Several attractive old houses occupy this street: at no 73 the great **Hôtel de Broglie** (1735); no 78 and no 80, the **Hôtel de Villeroy** (1724), now the Ministry of Agriculture; no 72, the large **Hôtel de Castries** (1700). At no 56, the **Hôtel de Gouffier de Thoix** has a magnificent doorway ornamented with a shell carving. No 47, the **Hôtel de Boisgelin**, is now the Italian Embassy.

The most famous house, of course, is the **Hôtel Matignon** at no 57, built by Courtonne in 1721 but since considerably remodelled. Talleyrand, diplomat and statesman to successive regimes, owned it from 1808 to 1811, then Madame Adelaïde, sister to Louis-Philippe. Between 1884 and 1914, it housed the Austro-Hungarian Embassy; in 1935 it became the office of the President of the Council of Ministers (as the prime minister was known at the time); in 1958 it became the Paris residence of the prime minister.

The American writer **Edith Wharton** (1862–1937), author of *The Age of Innocence*, lived at both no 53 and no 58 rue de Varenne for 13 years (1907–20) before moving north to the Pavillon Colombe near the Montmorency Forest. At the heart of literary circles including Morton Fullerton, Henry James, André Gide, she entertained the upper-class Faubourg society in the manner of a Belle-Époque salon hostess. She is buried in the city of Versailles.

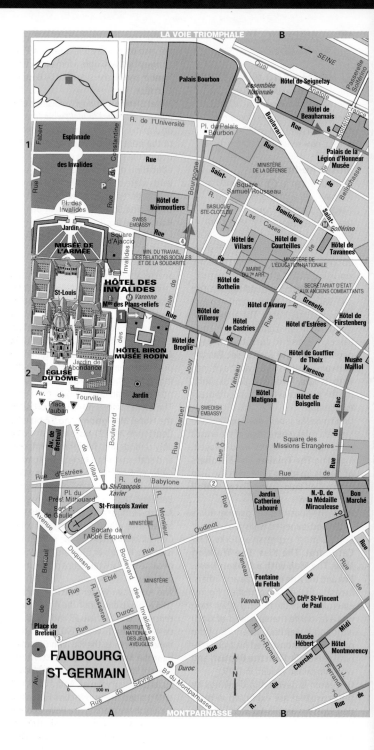

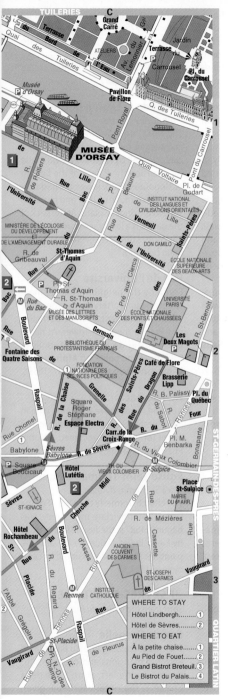

Hôtel Matignon

Built in 1721, this mansion is considered one of the most beautiful buildings of the *faubourg*. It belonged to the statesman Tallyrand (1808–11). It later became the Austro-Hungarian Embassy (1884–1914) and finally the prime minister's official residence in 1958.

▶ Double-back to rue de Bellechasse, then turn left on to the rue de Grenelle.

Rue de Grenelle

Many old mansions survive on this street: at no 79 stands the **Hôtel d'Estrées** (1713); no 85 is the **Hôtel d'Avaray** (1728); no 110, the **Hôtel de Courteilles** (1778), dominating the street with its massive façade, is now the Ministry of Education; no 118 is the **Hôtel de Villars**, built in 1712 and extremely elegant with twin garlanded, oval windows; no 136, the **Hôtel de Noir-moutiers** (1722), at one time the army staff headquarters, was the house in which Marshal Foch died on 20 March 1929. It is now the official residence of the préfet of the Île-de-France region.

▶ Turn right on to rue de Bourgogne and follow it to the Palais de Bourbon.

Palais Bourbon★

33 quai d'Orsay. ⊶*No public tours.* ℘*01 40 63 60 00.*
www.assemblee-nationale.fr.
In 1722 the Duchess of Bourbon, daughter of **Louis XIV** and **Mme de Montespan**, bought land to build a house on rue de l'Université. Louis XV later bought the property, and in 1764 Louis XVI sold it to the Prince of Condé, who enlarged and embellished it. Ultimately, the adjoining **Hôtel de Lassay**

was added and renamed Le Petit Bourbon. The palace was confiscated during the Revolution for the Council of the Five Hundred. Next it was used to house archives, before serving as accommodation for the École Polytechnique. In 1807 Napoléon commissioned Poyet to design the present façade overlooking place de la Concorde in harmony with the Greek plan of the Madeleine Church. At the Restoration the palace was returned to the Condé family, only to be bought back in 1827 and converted for use by the Legislative Assembly.

Exterior – The Antique-style façade is decorated with an allegorical pediment by Cortot (1842), statues *(copies)*, on high, of Minerva by Houdon and Themis by Roland. The allegorical low-relief sculptures on the wings are by Rude *(right)* and Pradier *(left)*.

Interior – Among the most impressive of the many rooms decorated with paintings and sculpture, are the lobby, with its ceiling by Horace Vernet, and the semicircular Council Chamber (**Salle des Séances**) where the President of the **National Assembly** presides over 577 deputies, arranged left to right according to party. The **Library**★★ is magnificently decorated with a History of Civilization, painted by **Delacroix** between 1838 and 1845.

Rue de Lille

This street, named after the town of Lille, is typical of the old noble *faubourg*. The mansions at no 80 and no 78 were designed by the architect Boffrand in 1714. The first, the **Hôtel de Seignelay**, was owned originally by Colbert's grandson, then by the Duke of Charost, tutor to the young Louis XV and aristocrat philanthropist who was saved from the guillotine by his own peasants. The **Hôtel de Beauharnais**, next door, was purchased and lavishly redecorated by Napoléon's daughter Hortense and son-in-law Eugène in 1803. Since 1818 the house has been the seat of first the Prussian, and later, the German diplomatic missions to France. Now restored, it is the residence of the German ambassador. Other buildings

of interest include no **71** the Hôtel de Mouchy (1775), and no **67** the Hôtel du Président Duret (1706). The **Hôtel de Salm** at no 64 houses the Palace and Museum of the Legion of Honour, facing the **Musée d'Orsay**.

Palais de la Légion d'Honneur

2 rue de Bellechasse.

The **Hôtel de Salm** was built in 1786 and owned by various people until it was acquired by Napoléon, who made the mansion the Palace of the Legion of Honour in 1804. It was burned during the Commune of 1871 and rebuilt in 1878 to the original plans. At the back of the palace is a lovely semicircular pavilion contrasting the severe lines of the main building.

Rue de l'Université

Formerly the neighbourhood's main street, this long artery crosses the entire 7th *arrondissement*, from St-Germain-des-Prés to the Eiffel Tower. At no 51 is the **Hôtel de Soyecourt**, built in 1707; poet and politician **Alphonse de Lamartine** lived at no 82 (1837–1853).

Rue du Bac

At no 44 lived **André Malraux**, who in 1933 wrote *La Condition humaine*, the novel for which he received a Nobel Prize for Literature.

Église Saint-Thomas d'Aquin

Place St-Thomas d'Aquin.

The church, formerly the chapel of the Dominican noviciate monastery, was begun in 1682 in the Jesuit style to plans by Pierre Bullet. Inside are 17C and 18C paintings and a ceiling painted by Lemoyne in 1723.

② SÈVRES-BABYLONE★

Start from the Ⓜ Rue du Bac.

Rue de Grenelle

This street crossing Rue du Bac is lined with old mansions and couture boutiques. On the left, at no 5 rue de la Chaise, is the Hôtel Vaudreuil, given by Napoléon to the Borghese family, in-laws of his sister Pauline. Next door *(no 7)* stood the Abbaye aux Bois, where Mme Récamier and her mentor, the novelist Chateaubriand, held salons between 1819 and 1849. The beautiful **Fontaine des Quatre Saisons**★ carved by **Bouchardon** between 1739 and 1745 stands outside no 59 and no 61. Behind the fountain is the house where **Alfred de Musset**, the Romantic poet, lived from 1824 to 1839.

Musée Maillol★ (Foundation Dina Vierny)

61 rue de Grenelle. ⓧ*Closed for renovations.* ♿ ♪*01 42 22 59 58. www.museemaillol.com.*

This museum draws from the private collection of Dina Vierny, once an eminent art dealer and model of Maillol. It comprises not only the paintings and sculptures of her Catalan mentor, **Aristide Maillol** (1861–1944), but those of several of his contemporaries: Bonnard, Cézanne, Degas, Duchamp, Gauguin, Kandinski, Renoir, Rousseau.

Rue du Bac

The rue du Bac and the rue de Babylone, are home to several religious congregations. At no 120 is the **square des Missions Étrangères**. This beautiful French-style garden, 1ha/2.5acres in size, was originally created in the 17C for Chateaubriand, who lived here for 10 years. The **Maison des Soeurs-St-Vincent-de-Paul** (no 140) welcome religious pilgrims who come to pray at the reliquary of Ste Catherine Labouré (**Chapelle Notre-Dame de la Médaille Miraculeuse**). It's believed that the Virgin appeared to this young nun in 1830.

▶ Retrace your steps and take a left on the rue de Babylone.

For a pleasant break, take a stroll in the **Jardin Catherine Labouré** *(29 rue de Babylone).* Open to the public thanks to the generosity of the sisters at St-Vincent-de-Paul, who gave up part of their kitchen garden, it is shaded by a long pergola planted with vines. The garden is surrounded by lawns and trees.

Le Bon Marché

Corner of rue de Bac and rue de Sèvres.
This department store, founded on the site of three former leprosy clinics, was the venture of Aristide Boucicault and his wife (1852). Success was achieved by several new practices now taken for granted such as undercutting of competitors, permitting an exchange of unwanted goods, and discount sales. A tour of the *Épicerie* is a must.

Boulevard Raspail

Dominating the intersection at rue de Sèvres, the **Hôtel Lutétia** *(no 45)* was built in 1907 by the architects Boileau and Tanzin; the façade was sculpted by Binet and Belmondo. Roughly hewn square blocks of rock at nos 52–54 mark the site of the former Prison du Cherche-Midi (1853–1954). Captain Dreyfus was imprisoned here in 1894. Later, the prison served as a World War II interrogation centre.

Rue de la Chaise

At no 5, the Borghese family profited from the generosity of Napoléon, who offered them the old **Hôtel Vaudreuil**. Mme Récamier and her mentor, Chateaubriand, hosted a literary salon here from 1819 to 1849 in the convent of **l'Abbaye-aux-Bois** *(no 7).*

Rue des Saints-Pères

The name is a distortion of St-Pierre to whom a chapel *(no 51)* was dedicated in the 17C. It is now the Ukrainian Catholic church of St Vladimir the Great. Among the fashion boutiques are two prestigious institutions: the National Foundation for Political Sciences, and the French Protestant Library at no 54.

Rue du Dragon

With its lopsided and misaligned mansions, this street has maintained the charm of old Paris. Explore side streets rue Bernard-Palissy and rue du Sabot.

Carrefour de la Croix-Rouge

Intersection of rue de Sèvres and rue du Cherche Midi.

This crossroads was likely the site of a pagan temple dedicated to Isis pre-dating the abbey of St-Germain. A red cross would have been installed in the 16C to rid the place of impious associations: hence the name. The present bronze Centaur statue is by the sculptor César.

Rue du Cherche Midi

This long street links Montparnasse with Sèvres-Babylone. At no 85 is the **Hôtel de Montmorency**, which today houses the Musée Hébert (*see opposite*). At no 86, the Cour des Vieilles-Tuileries, an example of architecture from the 18C and 19C. Former artists' studios are nestling in narrow, flowered culs-de-sac. On the corner of rue de l'Abbé Grégoire is the Maison de Laënnec, once owned by René Laënnec (1781–1826), inventor of the stethoscope. The **Hôtel de Rochambeau** at no 40 was home to Count Rochambeau, who, in 1780, was sent by Louis XVI to lead the French allied army in the American War of Independence against the British.

Musée Hébert

85 rue du Cherche Midi. Closed for renovations. 01 42 22 23 82. www.musee-orsay.fr.

The grand **Hôtel de Montmorency**, acquired in 1808 by the Maréchal Lefebvre, houses the works by the painter **Ernest Hébert** (1817–1908), official artist of the Second Empire who modelled himself after Ingres: Italian landscapes, many portraits, especially of women, and sketches.

▶ Turn left on to rue Jean-Ferrandi, with its former artist ateliers. Then turn left on to rue de Vaugirard to reach the metro St-Placide.

Musée d'Orsay★★★

Since 1986, the immense space of the former Gare d'Orsay has served as a fine arts museum, whose collection covers the years 1848 to 1914. It's an impressive place, for both the setting and the masterpieces it contains. A footbridge across the Seine links the museum with the Tuileries Gardens opposite.

A BIT OF HISTORY

From railway station to museum – At the end of the 19C, the Orléans rail company acquired the site of the ruined Orsay Palace, which had been set ablaze in 1871 during the Commune.

Designed to harmonize with the buildings of this elegant quarter, the iron and glass structure is screened on the outside by a monumental façade modelled on the Louvre across the Seine and on the inside by a coffered ceiling with stucco decoration. The building was inaugurated two years later on 14 July 1900. For nearly 40 years Orsay station

- **Info:** 1 rue de la Légion d'Honneur, 75007. 01 40 49 48 14. www.musee-orsay.fr.
- **Hours and Fees:** Tue–Sun 9.30am–6pm (until 9.45pm Thu). 1 Jan, 1 May, 25 Dec. 11€ for the permanent collection and temporary exhibits; free 1st Sun of the month.
- **Location:** 62 rue de Lille. By the Seine, opposite the Tuileries.
- **Metro/Transport:** Solférino (line 12) – RER: Musée-d'Orsay (line C) – Buses: 24, 73.
- **Parking:** Underground parking outside.
- **Don't Miss:** The scale model of a cross-section of the Opéra Garnier.
- **Timing:** Allow two hours.

Musée d'Orsay seen across the Seine

© Camille Moirenc/Photononstop/Tips Images

handled about 200 trains daily on the Paris–Orléans route. As electrification spread to the rest of the network, longer trains came into service, outgrowing the platforms at Orsay station.

In 1939 progress outpaced the building's capabilities; the mainline station functioned briefly for suburban traffic before succumbing to closure. It was put to a number of uses: as reception centre for prisoners at the Liberation, a film-set for Kafka's *The Trial* filmed by Orson Welles in 1962, and temporary **auction-rooms** during the refurbishment of the Hôtel Drouot in 1974.

In 1977 President Valérie Giscard d'Estaing entrusted the architect Gae Aulenti to transform the station into a museum of 19C art, and the Musée d'Orsay was inaugurated nine years later by President François Mitterrand. Today it includes a restaurant, two cafés, a take-out kiosk, and museum shops.

Permanent Collection

A free floor plan of the museum, available at the reception desk, shows the exact content of the galleries. It will help the visitor relate to the main artistic movements described here.

The works are presented in chronological order and by theme. Each major artistic movement from the period 1848 to 1914 is represented, and the collection is divided into four major categories: painting, sculpture, architecture and decorative arts.

The permanent collections begins on the ground floor, continues on the uppermost level, and finishes on the middle floor.

😊 Touring Tips 😊

Making the most of the Musée d'Orsay – Either consult the theme cards at the entrance to each room or request a guided tour (general, theme, monographic, etc.): detailed programme at the information desk. Audio-guides can also be rented.

Shopping in the Musée d'Orsay – Free access to the book-, card and gift shops, *open Tue–Sun 9.30am–6.30pm (until 9.30pm Thu).*

PAINTING AND SCULPTURE
Neoclassicism

This movement, which was inspired by the works of Antiquity, dates from the end of the 18C and reached its height in the early to mid-19C. Artists include the sculptors Cavelier, Guillaume and **Pradier**, and the painter **Jean-Auguste-Dominique Ingres** (1780–1867).

Romanticism

Running parallel with Neoclassicism, Romanticism developed first in England and Germany and concentrated on colour and movement. Still popular in 1860, Romanticism lists among its artists the sculptors Barye, Rude and Préault, and the painters Chassériau and **Eugène Delacroix** (1798–1863).

Realism

From 1830 until the end of the 19C, the Realists started painting from their observations of everyday life and of nature, abandoning contemporary aca-

Girl in Pink Dress (1860–65) by Camille Corot

© Scala, Florence/Musée d'Orsay

by Carrier-Belleuse, in the central alley, as well as Carpeaux's *Ugolin* (1862) and *The Dance* (1869), created for the façade of the Opéra Garnier. Other eclecticism works are by the sculptors Debois, Clésinger, Cordier and Jean-Baptiste Carpeaux (1827–75); and the painters Winterhalter, Fromentin and Guillaumet.

Academism

This label regroups all the artists who continued to work in the established academic tradition throughout the second half of the 19C, including the sculptors Fremiet, Mercié and Albert Carrier-Belleuse (1824–87), and the painters Blanche, Cabanel, Duran and Gérôme.

Symbolism

Between 1855 and 1900 there was a reaction towards Expressionism and against Naturalism and Impressionism. The Symbolists rejected reality and sought to explore hidden worlds by graphic means. Sculptors include Bartholomé, Camille Claudel and **Auguste Rodin** (1840–1917), who felt that *Balzac* (1897) was a true expression of his own art, representing the great novelist in an abstracted pose that contrasts with the brilliance of his creative genius. Symbolist painters include Burne-Jones, Hodler, Homer, Mucha, Doré, Detaille, Levy-Dhurmer, Munch, Klimt, Carrière, Puvis de Chavannes, and Gustave Moreau (1826–98), whose poetic mysterious vision is suffused with languid sensuality (*Orpheus*, 1865).

Origins of Impressionism

The new generation of artists, in reacting against the sombre shades used by their predecessors, set out to render the vibrations of light and to capture impressions of colour; hence their choice of subjects: sunlit gardens, snow, mist and flesh tones.

The early **Impressionists** include Boudin, Bazille, Cézanne, Renoir, Monet, Edgar Degas (1834–1917) and Edouard Manet (1832–83), who broke with studio convention by the boldness of their colours and compositions.

demic practice. Artists include the sculptor Meissonnier, the painters Antigna, Rosa Bonheur, Fantin-Latour, **Honoré Daumier** (1808–79), Jean-François Millet (1814–75) and Gustave Courbet (1819–77), whose paintings caused a scandal, especially *The Origin of Life. The Burial at Ornans* (1849) is perhaps the first real expression of Realism. Likened to his contemporary Émile Zola, who developed the Realist novel, Courbet depicts the real life of ordinary people from his home village, full of dignity and reverence while attending the funeral of a working man.

Barbizon School

The development of industrial towns prompted some artists to rediscover the countryside. **Camille Corot** (1796–1875) moved to Barbizon in 1830, favouring dark, earthy hues of colour, muted tones of twilight, inspired by the wooded landscapes around Fontainebleau. Théodore Rousseau (1812–67) is considered the leader of the Barbizon School of painters, skilfully catching the effect of fleeting light.

Eclecticism

This broad movement, covering the second half of the 19C, and corresponding to the Second Empire in France, was followed by official painters. It no longer favoured only Antiquity, but a mixture of all previous styles. Note the harmonious marble sculpture *Sleeping Hebe* (1869)

Detail of La table de cuisine (1888–90) by Paul Cézanne

©Scala, Florence/Musée d'Orsay

Le Déjeuner sur l'herbe was shown at the 1863 Salon des Refusés. Manet's naked bourgeois figures depicted in a harsh uncompromising light scandalized contemporary audiences. Two years later, Manet further affronted his public with *Olympia*, who unlike her idealized nude Renaissance counterparts, is depicted with realism, unashamedly naked.

Impressionism

The 1870 war prompted artists to disperse and to regroup in the Île-de-France region: Pontoise, Auvers-sur-Oise. As the official Salons repeatedly rejected their paintings, they decided to show their work independently: the first exhibition was held in 1874 at the studio of the photographer **Nadar**, where the contemptuous term Impressionists was first coined after Monet's *Impression-Sunrise* (*see PASSY, Musée Marmottan-Monet*). **Artists** include the sculptors Degas and Rosso, the painters **Degas**, **Sisley**, **Cézanne**, **Manet**, **Berthe Morisot**, **Pissarro**, Gustave Caillebotte (1848–94; also renowned as a patron of the arts), **Pierre-Auguste Renoir** (1841–1919) and **Claude Monet** (1840–1926), whose work epitomized this new relationship between the artist and nature. Among the best-known works from this group of artists are *Planing the floor* (1875) by Caillebotte (*gallery 30*), Renoir's *Le Moulin de la Galette* (1876), and the bronze *Little 14-Year-Old Dancer* (1881) by Degas.

Naturalism

This movement lasted from 1870 to 1920 and continued the tradition of Realism, this time as expressed by official or academic artists such as the sculptors Aubé, Dalou and Constantin Meunier (1831–1905), and the painters Breitner, Bashkirtseff, Bastien-Lepage and Cormon.

The Pont-Aven School

The charming Breton village of Pont-Aven attracted artists from 1885 to 1895, who together formulated a new style by eliminating detail, simplifying forms and using flat, bright colours. **Paul Gauguin** (1848–1903), who later moved to Tahiti in search of a mythical Eden, painted his *Self-Portrait with the Yellow Christ* (1889) at Pouldu, in Brittany.

The Crib (1872) by Berthe Morisot

© Scala, Florence/Musée d'Orsay

Post-Impressionism

The year 1886 marks the official end of Impressionism, but research into the nature of light continued with Divisionism or Pointillism. Here small dabs of pigment are painstakingly juxtaposed to evoke shimmering light. Artists of this style include **Matisse**, Renoir, Cross, Paul Signac (1863–1935), Paul Cézanne (1839–1906), **Georges Seurat** (1859–91), **Henri de Toulouse-Lautrec** (1864–1901), and **Vincent Van Gogh** (1853–90), whose tormented temperament was reflected in the anguished movement of his work (*Self-Portrait*, 1889).

The Nabis

This group of painters, whose name is derived from the Hebrew for prophet, devised the Nabis pictorial manifesto under the direction of Gauguin in October 1888 at Pont-Aven. The movement continued until 1910. All the artists involved were concerned as much with easel paintings as with large decorative panels, book illustration, prints and stage sets, including the painters Roussel, Vallotton, **Édouard Vuillard** (1868–1940), **Pierre Bonnard** (1867–1947), who was strongly influenced by Japanese prints, and **Maurice Denis** (1870–1943), who published pamphlets outlining the group's aspirations. Note Bonnard's *Game of Croquet* (1892), *The Muses* (1893) by Denis and Vuillard's *Public Garden* (1894).

ARCHITECTURE

This section is limited to the architecture of the Second Empire period (1852–70). Among the architectural models is a study of the Opéra district, with a cross-section through the Opéra Garnier showing the stage and its machinery.

DECORATIVE AND APPLIED ARTS 1850–80

The key quality inherent in the exhibits of this period is versatility, as fashion and taste succumbed to the influence of colonization, foreign travel, the universal exhibitions, in particular that of 1867, which revealed Japanese art. New industrial businesses employed artists who combined good design with practicality, able to produce one-off pieces as well as the mass-produced. **Christofle** radically changed their orientation as electro-plating processes enabled mass production of silver-plate without losing the fine art of crafting quality. The **medal cabinet**, regarded as one of the most original pieces of the 1867 exhibition, is decorated with scenes from Merovingian history (low relief in silver-plated bronze by Frémiet).

French Art Nouveau

A desire for change and for a new form of expression away from the past swept through Europe in around 1890. Art Nouveau, or the Modern Style, is characterised by serpentine lines and organic decoration. Art in everything, a fundamental concept to the style, broke down distinctions between artist and craftsman, painter and decorator, to achieve the most complete design. In France Art Nouveau was launched by the Nancy School. After studying sculpture and painted wallpapers, Lalique (1860–1945) turned his hand to glass and jewellery, inspired by the organic shapes of plants. Other artists include Majorelle, Gruber, Carabin and Charpentier.

International Art Nouveau

From 1880 the first examples of Art Nouveau appeared in England and soon spread to other parts of Europe, such as Vienna, and to the US. Artists include the Belgians Van de Velde and Horta, the Austrians Loos and Thonet, known for his wooden furniture, the American Frank Lloyd Wright and the Scot Rennie Mackintosh, pioneer of Functionalism.

PHOTOGRAPHY

The most recent addition to the museum, the photography galleries are consecrated to about 50 000 images: slides, negatives and albums. Anonymous photos and works by Stieglitz, Nadar and Le Gray, among others, make up the collection, which showcases the evolution of the medium from 1839 to 1920.

Les Invalides★★★

This fine neighbourhood elbowing the Faubourg St-Germain is endowed with elegant buildings that include the most outstanding single monumental group in Paris: the noble Dôme church that houses the tomb of **Napoléon** and the adjacent Army Museum, endowed with its rich and spectacular collections.

A BIT OF HISTORY

Barracks for 4 000 men – Before Louis XIV's reign, old or invalid soldiers were, in theory, looked after in convent hospitals. In reality, most were reduced to beggary. In 1670 the Sun King founded the Invalides on the edge of what was then the Grenelle Plain. The dome was added in 1706, lifting the overall effect from strictly utilitarian to monumental.

Pillage – On the morning of 14 July 1789, rebels on the way to the Bastille advanced on the Invalides in search of arms. They crossed the moat, disarmed the sentries and entered the underground rifle stores, making off with 28 000 rifles.

Napoléon's return – In 1793 the Revolution transformed the two churches, which were still adjoined, into a Temple to Mars. The captured enemy standards were transferred there from Nôtre-Dame. When Napoléon had Marshal Turenne (d. 1675) interred in the church

Info: Pyramides welcome centre, 25 rue des Pyramides. ℘08 92 68 30 00 (0.34€ per min). http://en.parisinfo.com.

Opening: The Invalides comprise three museums: Army, Relief Maps and the Order of Liberation. The ticket provides access to all three, the Dôme Church and Napoléon's tomb.

Location: Les Invalides overlooks the Seine from the Left Bank, between the Eiffel Tower and St-Germain-des-Prés.

Metro/Transport: Invalides (line 13), Varenne (line 13), St-François Xavier (line 13) – Buses: 28, 48, 49, 69, 82, 92, 93.

Parking: There is above and below ground parking along the esplanade.

Don't Miss: The intricate suits of armour of King François I and Henri II in the Army Museum.

Timing: Allow at least three hours to visit the museums.

Kids: Playground in the square Santiago du Chili.

Église du Dôme, Hôtel des Invalides

© Y. Kanazawa/Michelin

DÔME DES INVALIDES

ÉGLISE SAINT-LOUIS DES INVALIDES

1. *High altar with corkscrew columns and baldaquin (designed by Mansart) by Visconti, under the vaulted ceiling decorated by Coypel.*

2. *Tomb of Général Duroc.*

3. *Tomb of Général Bertrand.*

in 1800, it became a military mausoleum, receiving further countless trophies from the imperial campaigns. In 1840 Napoléon's remains were brought back to Paris and finally placed beneath the Dôme on 3 April 1861.

The institution's revival – After the two World Wars, the institution reverted to its original role in offering shelter and care to the war-wounded with modernized hospital facilities. The buildings are now occupied by military administration and the Army Museum. To celebrate the bicentenary of the French Revolution in 1989, the Dôme was re-gilded.

⚏ HÔTEL DES INVALIDES★★★

Access from esplanade des Invalides.
Apr–Oct daily 10am–6pm; rest of the year until 5pm. Last admission 30min before closing. 1st Mon of the month, 1 Jan, 1 May, 1 Nov, 25 Dec. ⚏ 9.50€; under 18 years free; one ticket is valid for admission to all museums and Dôme). 01 44 42 38 77. www.invalides.org.

Garden – Fronting the Invalides is a series of gardens, bordered by a wide dry moat, ramparts lined with 17C and 18C bronze cannon and an 18-piece triumphal battery used to fire salutes on such occasions as the Armistice (11 November 1918) and the Victory March (14 July 1919).

Façade★★ – The façade is majestic in style and line, and in proportion and size – 196m/643ft long. The central block is dominated by a magnificent doorway, which features an equestrian statue of Louis XIV supported by Prudence and Justice.

Cour d'honneur★*(access through the gate)* – Napoléon took great pleasure in reviewing his veterans here. At the centre is his statue by Seurre. An impressive series of cannon are laid around the courtyard: note the *Catherina* (1487) and the *Württemberg* culverin (16C); near the stairs is a Renault tank and one of the Marne taxis used to carry soldiers to the front in World War I.

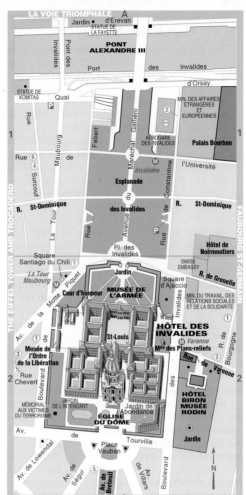

LES INVALIDES

0 ___ 100 m

WHERE TO STAY

Hôtel du
Palais-Bourbon............(1)
Hôtel L'Empereur............(2)
Hôtel Muguet..................(3)

WHERE TO EAT

Café de l'Esplanade.........(1)
Chez Françoise................(2)
Café du Musée Rodin.......(3)
Le Petit Bordelais............(4)
Le Vauban.......................(5)
Miyako............................(6)

Musée de l'Armée★★★

The galleries of one of the world's richest army museums, containing more than 500 000 exhibits, lie on either side of the main courtyard, on several floors. Displays focus on five main themes.

Arms and armour *(west side)* illustrate the evolution of methods of defence and attack with real weapons and suits of armour from prehistoric times to the 16C. The Ancien Régime and 19C *(east side)* section presents the collection of weapons and uniforms from the 17C to the Second Empire, including many uniforms and souvenirs relating

to Napoléon. Banners and artillery are displayed around the courtyard, on different floors, including 200 cannons in the **Salle Gribeauval** *(west side)* and French banners dating from 1619 to 1953 in the **ground-floor galleries**.

World Wars I and II sections *(west side)* feature animated maps showing troop movements. Displays show the development of World War I and three floors are devoted to World War II, the Free French forces, and the Resistance movement. The displays follow a chronological order from the 1940 defeat and General de Gaulle's radio appeal to the

213

Napoléon – Artillery Officer to First Consul

Arguably the most famous Frenchman of all time, Napoléon Bonaparte was not actually French but Corsican with Italian antecedents. He became a professional soldier at the age of 16, and after the Revolution of 1789 he returned to Corsica where he sided with the Jacobins against the Royalists and Corsican Nationalists.

Napoléon's exploits during various battles led to his becoming friendly with Robespierre's brother. This connection proved to be a bit of a setback when Robespierre was guillotined and Napoléon spent a short period in jail.

As commander of the Revolutionary forces in Paris, Bonaparte impressed Barras, leader of the new Directory, and was soon appointed commander of the Army of Italy. He led a successful campaign against the Austrians and his feats in Italy made him popular in France, where he sought unsuccessfully to become a member of the Directory.

There followed the campaign in Egypt against the Ottomans, which was very successful on land but much less so at sea. The British, not keen to see the expansion of French power in the Mediterranean, deployed the Royal Navy led by Nelson, which destroyed the French Fleet during the battle of the Nile.

With political instability at home, Napoléon was recalled by the Directory, which was rapidly losing popularity. He seized his opportunity, and on 9 November he dispersed the Legislative Council in the Coup de Brumaire and emerged as joint First Consul. In 1802 he became First Consul in his own right, becoming first Consul for Life. The stage was now set for him to later become Emperor of France – the young artillery officer was now reaching the pinnacle of his career.

French people on 18 June 1940 to the concentration camps and the capitulation of Japan in 1945. Personal objects, weapons, models, video films, photos and documents illustrate the role each party played in this worldwide conflict.

Musée des Plans reliefs★★
4th floor, west side.
A collection of scale models of towns, harbours and fortresses (1:600) from the time of Vauban (17C) to the present chronicles the evolution of fortifications in France over the last 300 years.

Église du Dôme★★★
The church is one of the major masterpieces of the age of Louis XIV, reaching new heights in the French Classical style. Louis XIV commissioned **Hardouin-Mansart** to design a church that would complement the Invalides buildings of Libéral Bruant. In 1677 work began on the royal church, joined to the Soldiers' Church by a common sanctuary. It was completed by Robert de Cotte in 1735.

Decorated with trophies, garlands and other ornaments, the dome is capped by a gold lantern. The dome roof was first given its golden splendour in 1715.
Interior – The decoration is sumptuous: painted cupolas, walls adorned with columns and pilasters framing low-relief sculptures by the greatest contemporary artists. In 1842, two years after the return of Napoléon's body, Visconti enlarged the high altar (**1**), replaced the original baldaquin and had the crypt dug to receive the "Eagle's" sarcophagus. By the entrance to the crypt are the tombs of Generals Duroc (**2**) and Bertrand (**3**).
Napoléon's tomb – The majesty of the setting befits the emperor's image. To preserve the design of the church and a view of the altar, **Visconti** dug a circular crypt for the red porphyry sarcophagus on its base of green granite from the Vosges. Two massive bronze statues stand guard at the crypt entrance, one bearing an orb, the other the imperial sceptre and crown; 12 statues by Pradier surround the crypt.

Musée de l'Ordre de la Libération★

www.ordredelaliberation.fr.
The Order of Liberation, created by Général de Gaulle at Brazzaville in 1940, honoured as companions those who made an outstanding contribution to the final victory. The list includes service personnel and civilians, and a few overseas leaders including King George VI, Winston Churchill and General Eisenhower. The museum also perpetuates the memory of French heroes from the African campaigns, major operations of the Resistance and the concentration camps. Displays include documents, trophies and relics.

Église de Saint-Louis des Invalides★

The church was designed by Libéral Bruant and built by Mansart. Captured enemy banners overhang the upper galleries. A window behind the high altar provides a glimpse of the baldaquin in the Dôme Church. The 17C organ is enclosed in a loft designed by Hardouin-Mansart. It was here that **Berlioz**'s *Requiem* was first heard, in 1837.

PONT ALEXANDRE III★★

This bridge was built for the 1900 World Exhibition and is an example of the popular steel architecture and ornate style of the period. The armorial bearings of Russia and France evoke the memory of Alexander III, father of Nicholas II of Russia, who laid the foundation stone. It has a splendid single-span, surbased arch.

Eiffel Tower★★★
Trocadéro★★

The best-loved monument in Paris, if not in the entire world, straddles gardens once used for military parades. Nearby is a fine example of Classical French architecture, the École Militaire. The tower is the perfect place for a bird's-eye view of the city. Over the river, set in the Trocadéro Gardens, the Chaillot Palace, with its broad terrace and powerful fountains, provides a raised view over the Seine, the Champ de Mars and the Eiffel Tower. This imposing architectural monument of the early 20C also houses rich and diverse museum collections.

EIFFEL TOWER★★★

Visitors can climb steps to the first floor or go higher by lift. Lift: ⊙daily mid-Jun–early Sept 9am–12.45am (last lift to the summit 11pm); mid-Sept–early Jun 9.30am–11.45pm (last lift to the summit 10.30pm). ⊛5€ (1st floor via stairs), 9€ (2nd floor), 15.50€ (third floor). ℘08 92 70 12 393. www.tour-eiffel.fr.

- ℹ **Info:** Tourisme Office, 25 rue des Pyramides. ℘08 92 68 30 00 (0.34€ per min). http://en.parisinfo.com.
- ▶ **Location:** The Eiffel Tower and Trocadéro straddle the Seine in west Paris.
- Ⓜ **Metro/Transport:** Eiffel Tower: Bir-Hakeim (line 6), École Militaire (line 8). RER: Champ de Mars Tour Eiffel (line C) – Buses: 82, 92. Trocadéro (lines 6 and 9) – Buses: 22, 30, 32, 63, 82.
- 🅿 **Parking:** Street parking in front of the École Militaire.
- 🖘 **Don't Miss:** The Peace Wall; views from Palais de Chaillot's esplanade.
- ⏱ **Timing:** Allow two hours for the Tower, and two hours for Palais de Chaillot.
- 👫 **Kids:** There are several play areas around the Champ de Mars.

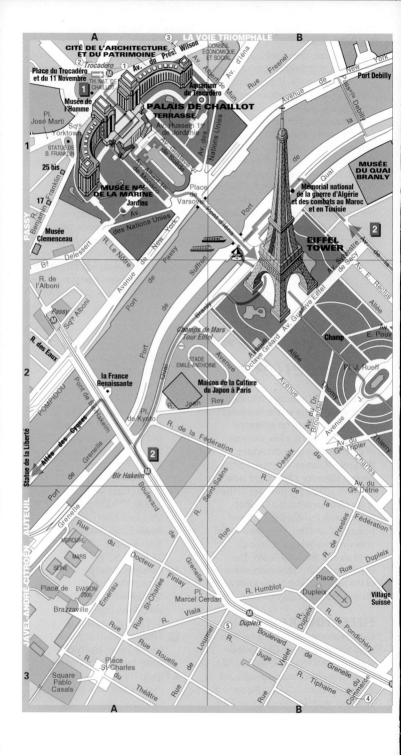

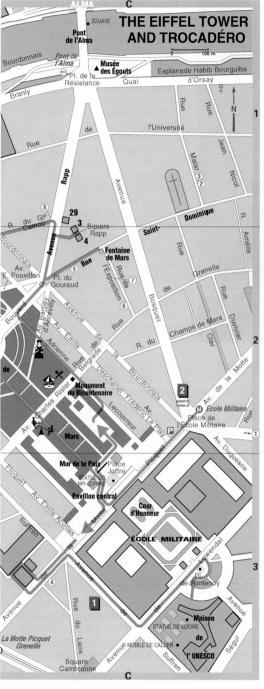

THE EIFFEL TOWER AND TROCADÉRO

WHERE TO STAY

Hôtel de France............①
Hôtel de la Tulipe.........②
Hôtel Malar..................③
Saphir Grenelle Hôtel....④
Timhotel Tour Eiffel......⑤

WHERE TO EAT

Brasserie Le Coq..........①
Carette.......................②
Essaouira....................③
Le Père Claude.............④
Les Cocottes................⑤
P'tit Troquet.................⑥
Philippe Excoffier..........⑦
Sancerre......................⑧

Eiffel Tower

Gustave Eiffel (1832–1923)

Engineer and entrepreneur in equal measure, Eiffel was to enjoy both success and failure during his long life. Mostly remembered today for his Tower, he was also responsible for several other massively impressive structures both in France and further afield. The Garabit Viaduct, the Pest Railway Station and the internal structure of the Statue of Liberty are just three examples of his fine work still in use. Unfortunately, Eiffel became embroiled in the scandal caused by the French Panama Canal Company, a scheme seriously mismanaged by Ferdinand de Lesseps that failed, causing severe financial losses. Although not involved in the finances of the enterprise, Eiffel was found guilty of fraud, a decision that was later reversed. Forced to retire, he spent the rest of his life as a scientist, using his Tower for wind resistance experiments, as an aerial mast and a weather station.

©Mark Soskolne/iStockphoto.com

Controversial to Acclaimed

Built for the Exposition Universelle of 1889, the Eiffel Tower was the tallest construction in the world when it was erected, rising 300m/984ft. The addition of television aerials has increased its height by 20.75m/68ft.

The engineer **Gustave Eiffel** (🔗*see box above*) began the project in 1884; between 1887 and 1889 some 300 sky-jacks pieced the tower together using 2.5 million rivets. Eiffel, in his enthusiasm, exclaimed "France will be the only country with a 300m (984ft)flagpole!" Artists and writers, however, were appalled; the "Petition of the 300" was signed in protest by artists, writers and even **Charles Garnier**, the architect of the Opéra.

Despite the critics, the tower's very boldness and novelty brought it also great acclaim. By the beginning of the new century it had become a subject for celebration – now recognized the world over – by a new generation of poets, dramatists and painters. In 1909, when its permit expired, the tower was saved because its huge antennae were so vital to French radio.

Visit

The sway at the top in the highest winds has never been more than 12cm/4.7in – while its height can vary by as much as 15cm/6in – depending on the temperature. There are three platforms – the first is at 57m/187ft, the second at 115m/377ft, the third at 276m/905.5ft. From the third platform, the **view★★★** over Paris and the suburbs can extend across 67km/42mi in ideal conditions (*viewing tables*).

🕙The best light is usually 1hr before sunset. At night the illuminated tower has a jewel-like quality, sparkling for the first 5 minutes of every hour. At level 3, Eiffel's sitting room can be seen through a window. The second floor houses a restaurant, brasseries and boutiques. On the first floor is a museum, a gift shop, a post office and a restaurant.

⚓ WALKING TOURS
Start from the Ⓜ Trocadéro.

① TROCADÉRO– L'ÉCOLE MILITAIRE

Place du Trocadéro et du 11 Novembre
Named after a fort the French army captured near Cadiz in 1823, the semicircular square is dominated by an equestrian statue of Marshal Foch.

Palais de Chaillot★★
Built in 1939, the low-lying palace of white stone consists of twin pavilions linked by a portico and extended by wings curving to frame the wide terrace. It was the design of architects Carlu, Boileau and Azéma. Eight gilded figures line the terrace along the wings – *Flora* by Marcel Gimont being the most famous. Before the left pavilion stands a monumental bronze of Apollo by **Bouchard** balanced on the Passy side, with *America* by Jacques Zwoboda. From the **terrace** a **view★★★** of the Seine and the Eiffel Tower is afforded; at the end of the Champ de Mars is the 18C École Militaire. The **gardens★★★** were designed for the 1937 Exhibition. A long rectangular pool follows the slope down Chaillot Hill to the Iena Bridge. The pool, bordered by stone statues (*Youth* by Pierre Loison and *Joie de Vivre* by Léon Divier), is at its most spectacular at night when the fountains are floodlit.
Théâtre National de Chaillot – Beneath the palace terrace is one of the capital's largest theatres. Firmin Génier created the Théâtre National Populaire in 1920. In 1988 Jérôme Savary, of Grand Magic Circus fame, became the prolific and provocative director of the newly baptized Théâtre National de Chaillot.

👥 Aquarium Paris
5 Avenue Albert de Mun. ⊙*Daily 10am–7pm. Last admission 1hr before closing.* ⊛*20.50€, 13-17 years 17€, 3-12 years 13€.* ⊙*14 Jul.* ♿ ℘ *01 40 69 23 23. www.cineaqua.com.*
This ancient quarry at the base of the Chaillot Hill houses an aquarium opened

for the Universal Exposition of 1878. Closed since 1985, it reopened in 2006 with a renovated interior combining an aquarium with a cinema: see 10 000 fish and the shark tunnel, or catch the latest animated films.

▷ Cross the Seine on the Pont d'Iéna.

Champs de Mars
Once used for military parades, fairs and world exhibitions, this vast formal garden stretches from the Eiffel Tower to the École Militaire. On your right, as you walk towards the École Militaire, is the **Village suisse** (*avenue de la Motte Picquet;* ⊙*Thu–Mon 10.30am–7pm;* ♿ ℘*01 73 79 15 41; www.villagesuisse.com*), a conglomeration of 80 antiques and bric-a-brac shops.

École Militaire★
1 place Joffre.
Thanks to prompting by **Mme de Pompadour**, Louis XV's favourite mistress, a Royal Military Academy was built in 1751, wherein young gentlemen without means might be trained to become accomplished officers.
Designed by the architect **Jacques-Ange Gabriel**, the impressive building is fronted by 10 superb Corinthian columns, with displayed trophies and allegorical figures. Facing the central pavilion is the equestrian statue of Marshal Joffre by Real del Sarte (1939). At age 15, the young cadet Bonaparte was formally sworn-in in the Academy chapel in 1784; his final report stated that he would "go far in favourable circumstances".
The buildings have retained their status as both a military quarters and a training centre for French and foreign officers attending the School of Advanced War Studies, and the School for National Defence.

Maison de l'UNESCO★ (United Nations Educational, Scientific and Cultural Organization HQ)
7 place de Fontenoy. ⊙*By reservation.* ℘*01 45 68 10 00. www.unesco.org.*
Behind the École Militaire, the headquarters of UNESCO was opened in

1958. It is the most truly international undertaking in Paris: the membership by 195 states and the construction of the buildings jointly by Breuer, Nervi and Zehrfuss, American, Italian and French architects respectively, demonstrate unique cooperation. A monumental statue, *Fiure in Repose* by **Henry Moore**, can be viewed from avenue de Suffren.

2 L'ÉCOLE MILITAIRE–BIR-HAKEIM

Start from the Ⓜ *École Militaire.*

Mur de la Paix

Created to commemorate the year 2000 by the painter Clara Halter and the architect Jean-Michel Wilmotte, the Peace Wall was inspired by Jerusalem's wailing wall. Touch screens allow visitors to read and send their own messages of peace in all languages around the world. It was meant to be a temporary exhibition but the Parisians decided to keep it in place, and others have followed around the world (St Petersburg and Hiroshima).

At the intersection of allée Adrienne Lecouvreur and avenue Charles Risler is a **monument** celebrating the bicentennial of the French Revolution. Designed by Yvan Theimer, it features an abundance of bronze figures.

Rue Saint-Dominiqiue

At no 129 is the **Fontaine de Mars** by François-Jean Bralle (1750–1832), who also designed the fountain at place du Châtelet. Stop on the rue du Champ de Mars to see the elegant floral façade at no 33, designed by Raquin in 1900.

Avenue Rapp

At no **29** is an Art Nouveau building designed by Jules Lavirotte in 1901 for the ceramicist Alexandre Bigot. Its elaborate ceramic façade was awarded a prize from the City of Paris the same year. Nearby, at no 3, is the home of Lavirotte himself, constructed two years earlier in the Art Nouveau noodle style.

Musée du Quai Branly★★

37 quai Branly. ⊙*Tue–Sun 11am–7pm (until 9pm Thu–Sat). Last admission 1hr before closing.* ⊛*9€.* ♿ ☏*01 56 61 70 00. www.quaibranly.fr.*

Designed by the architect Jean Nouvel, this fairly new primitive arts museum opened in the summer of 2006. The setting is remarkable: undulating leather-clad low walls lead visitors through the glass and metal structure to the different sections dedicated to the arts and civilizations of Africa, Asia, Oceania and the Americas. Video and multimedia installations are interspersed throughout.

The surrounding gardens enhance the feeling that the city is far, far away. Other museum facilities include a multimedia gallery, a themed exhibition gallery, and an anthropology gallery, as well as a café and an upmarket glass-domed restaurant, Les Ombres, that overlooks the Seine.

Musée du Quai Branly

Maison de la culture du Japon à Paris

101 bis quai Branly. ◑*Sept–Jul Tue–Sat noon–7pm (until 8pm Thu).* ◑*Aug, 21 Dec–5 Jan, public holidays.* ✆*01 44 37 95 01. www.mcjp.fr.*
Inaugurated in 1997, the Year of Japan in France, the Maison de la culture du Japon à Paris was built by two young architects, Yamanaka Masayuki of Japan and Kenneth Armstrong of the UK.

On the programme are concerts, theatre, cinema, music recitals, and poetry set to music, as well as Japanese floral art *(ikebana)*, calligraphy and Go, an ancient board game. On the ground floor, a boutique has books, postcards, tea sets, lacquered bowls and incense.

◒The Maison de la Culture hosts presentations of *Chanoyu* (tea ceremony) in the tea pavillion *(5th floor)*. Reservations at least one month in advance are necessary.

Allée des Cygnes

From halfway across the Bir-Hakeim Bridge, there is access down to the manmade islet in the Seine. Allée des Cygnes, or Swans' Walk, provides a good view of the Maison de Radio-France *(see AUTEUIL).* The figure of *France Renaissante* looking upstream was completed by the Danish sculptor Wederkinch (1930); a bronze replica of the **Statue of Liberty** faces downstream in the direction of the USA.

TROCADÉRO MUSEUMS
Musée National de la Marine★★

Palais de Chaillot, 17 place du Trocadéro et du 11 Novembre. ♿◑*Wed–Mon 11am–6pm (until 7pm Sat–Sun).* ◑*1 Jan, 1 May, 25 Dec.* ◉*8.50€, under 18 years free.* ✆*01 53 65 69 69. www.musee-marine.fr.*
The Maritime Museum was founded in 1827 by order of Charles X. Scale models and important artefacts from the naval dockyards trace maritime history. The models of galleys and sailing ships date from the 17C. The **Ports of France**★ is a series of canvases by the 18C artist Joseph Vernet. The *Royal Louis* is a rare

model from the Louis XV period. From the Revolution and the First Empire, there is the *Emperor's Barge* (1811). The history of merchant shipping, steam ships and the navy is accompanied by film shows. The visit ends with two modern French warships: the nuclear submarine *Le Triomphant* (1996) and the *Charles-de-Gaulle* (1999).

Cité de l'Architecture et du Patrimoine★★

Palais de Chaillot, 1 place du Trocadéro et du 11 Novembre. ◑*Wed–Mon 11am–7pm (until 9pm Thu).* ◉*8€.* ✆*01 58 51 52 00. www.citechaillot.fr.*
The museum of France's monumental art and mural painting was the brainchild of the Gothic Revival architect and restorer of medieval monuments Viollet-le-Duc. First opened in 1879, it was restored and reopened in 2007.

Comprising casts and replicas of the greatest examples of French architecture, the collection includes partial casts of the most famous Gothic cathedrals, stained-glass windows from Chartres, and even modern constructions by Le Corbusier.

The modernization of the space includes interactive videos with joysticks that allow visitors to see 360° images of the monuments. Video-guides in English help bring it all to life.

Musée de l'Homme★★

Palais de Chaillot, 1 place du Trocadéro et du 11 Novembre. ◑*Closed for renovations until fall 2015.* ✆*01 44 05 72 72. www.museedelhomme.fr.*
Part of the National Natural History Museum *(see p172)*, this museum houses prehistoric anthropology and palaeontology galleries, with a focus on temporary expositions.

Its collections are arranged mainly according to geographical region. Included is the brain of scientist, mathematician, physicist and philosopher René Descartes as well as the Inca mummy that inspired Edvard Munch's painting *The Scream*.

Arrondissements 8–10 & 17

Alma★

The area around **place de l'Alma** is one of the most luxurious quarters of Paris, with something for all tastes: a concert at the Théâtre des Champs-Élysées, an evening at the Crazy Horse, an exhibition at the Musée d'Art moderne, or a stroll among the couturiers and perfumers at the heart of the world of fashion.

WALKING TOUR

Start from Ⓜ *Alma-Marceau.*

Place de l'Alma

On the southern side of the square, at the beginning of avenue de New York, stands a life-size gilded **model** of the flame held by the Statue of Liberty in New York, a gift to the city for the 100th anniversary from the *International Herald Tribune*.

The original stone bridge, the **Pont de l'Alma** dating back to 1856, was replaced in 1970 by an asymmetrical steel structure with a 110m/361ft span. Only the **Zouave** (upstream by the single pile) remains of the four Second Empire soldier statues that decorated the old bridge; it serves as a high-water marker and is much loved by Parisians – in January 1910, the water reached the chin of the statue.

André-Louis Gody, a resident of Gravelines, in the north of France, served as the model for the Zouave's sculptor, Georges Diebolt. At the western entrance of the Cours Albert I is a statue by **Bourdelle** of the Polish poet and patriot **Mickiewicz** (1798–1855). At no 40, note the fine René Lalique façade.

Avenue Montaigne

Formerly known as allée des Veuves (Widows' Alley), this disreputable area focused on the Mabille Dance Hall, which closed in 1870. Today this street exudes wealth and chic, lined with elegant buildings accommodating banks, art galleries and exclusive luxury boutiques like YSL, Prada, Céline, Versace and Dior.

Info: Paris Office du Tourisme, 25 rue des Pyramides. ☏01 49 52 42 63 (0.34€ per min). http://en.parisinfo.com.

Location: From the Left Bank, the Pont de l'Alma brings you right into the heart of the Alma district. From here, its main streets (the avenues Iéna, Marceau, George V and Montaigne) all lead to the Champs-Élysées. To the right is the embarkment for the *bateaux-mouches*.

Parking: Underground parking can be found just off the place de l'Alma, the avenue Montaigne and along the Champs-Élysées.

Don't Miss: The Musée d'Art moderne and the Buddhist Panthéon annexe at the Musée Guimet.

Timing: Allow at least two hours to visit Alma's many museums.

Kids: Tours of the Paris sewer system (Musée des Egouts) are particularly fascinating to youngsters.

The **Théâtre des Champs-Élysées**, designed by the Perret brothers, is one of the first major monuments built in reinforced concrete (1912). The façade sculptures are designed by Antoine Bourdelle. The main auditorium, with its ceiling decorated by **Maurice Denis**, is one of the finest in Paris; it has a seating capacity of 2 100. It was here that **Igor Stravinski** first directed his *Rite of Spring* (1913), scandalizing the audience with its tonal audacity; it caused such a furore that the composer had to flee the auditorium. Since then, the theatre has welcomed many stars: Richard Strauss, Paganini, **Diaghilev** with his Ballets Russes and **Jean Cocteau**. In 1925 the *Negro Review* introduced **Josephine Baker** dancing half-naked

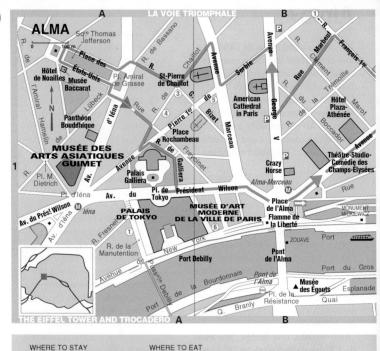

THE EIFFEL TOWER AND TROCADERO

WHERE TO STAY		WHERE TO EAT			
Hôtel Powers	①	Aux Marches du Palais	①	Gusto Sardo	③
		Thiou	②	Oscar	④

Zouave stands below the Pont de l'Alma

© S. Sauvignier/MICHELIN

to a Charleston and rhythms played on the saxophone by Sidney Bechet.
At no 25, the **Hôtel Plaza-Athénée** welcomes heads of State, princes and ambassadors.

▶ Go back up the avenue Montaigne, taking a right down the rue François I to the square of the same name.

Place François I

On this charming little square with its own central fountain, the Hôtel de Vilgruy, at no 9, was built by Henri Labrouste in 1865.

At no 23 rue Jean Goujon *(the street intersecting the square)* is the Armenian church and Notre-Dame-de-Conso-lation. The latter was built in 1900 in memory of the victims of a fire at the Charity Bazaar in 1871, an annual ball frequented by high society.

At 22 **rue Bayard** watch for the Radio-Télé-Luxembourg (RTL) station; note that the façade of the building is deco-rated by Vasarely.

Opposite is the Scottish Kirk (church).

Avenue George V

This street is famous for its grand **Hotel George V** at no 31; the neo-Gothic **American Cathedral in Paris**, which was consecrated at the same time as the Statue of Liberty, was unveiled in New York Harbor (1886); the **Crazy Horse** music hall at no 12, with its renowned programme of topless stage shows.

Église Saint-Pierre de Chaillot

31 avenue Marceau, on the corner of rue de Chaillot.

The church was rebuilt in the neo-Romanesque style in 1937. Overlooking its façade, on which the life of St Peter has been carved by Bouchard, is a 65m/213ft-high belfry.

Place des États-Unis

It was under the pressure of the American State department that this square received its current name. In fact, when the American delegation moved its offices into no 3 in 1882, the square was called place de Bitche (a French town near the Belgian border). Feeling that this address was inappropriate, the American diplomats appealed to the Parisian authorities to change it.

Several commemorative monuments decorate the gardens in the centre of the square: on the avenue d'Iéna side is the *Monument to the American Volunteers Who Died for France during the Great War* (by Boucher); at the other end of the square is a statue (a bronze by Bartholdi) of Lafayette and Washington, heroes of America's Revolutionary War.

Surrounded by impressive mansions, most of which were used as embassies, the square is now devoted to crystal. Following the Cristallerie d'Arques at no 6, the **Galerie-Musée Baccarat** opened at no 11 in the beautiful Hôtel de Noailles, also known as the "Trianon" built in 1880 by the architect Paul-Ernest Samson for the art collector Ferdinand Bischoffsheim.

Also along the avenue Marceau, no 5 was the address of legendary haute-couture designer Yves Saint Laurent, who died in 2008; it is now transformed into the **Fondation Pierre Bergé-Yves Saint Laurent**, open to the public for temporary expositions *(3 rue Léonce-Raynaud; ⊙Tue–Sun 11am–6pm; ⊙closed public holidays; ⊗7€; ₺; ℘01 44 31 64 00; www.fondation-pb-ysl.net).*

MUSEUMS AND OTHER ATTRACTIONS
Musée Guimet – Musée national des Arts asiatiques★★★

6 place d'Iéna. ⊙Wed–Mon 10am–6pm. ⊙1 Jan, 1 May, 25 Dec. ⊗7.50€. Audio-guide no extra cost. ₺; ℘01 56 52 53 00. www.guimet.fr.

This museum, founded by Émile Guimet, a successful 19C industrialist from Lyon, contains superb Oriental works of art.

Southeast Asia *(ground floor)* – A colossal statue of Nâga, a seven-head stone serpent from Angkor, sets the scene on the way to the area dedicated to **Khmer art★★** (Cambodia). Indian divinities are displayed in the room on the left. The journey continues through Vietnam,

Indonesia, Burma and Thailand with its splendid **heads of Buddha**.

First floor – The art of **India**, Pakistan and Afghanistan is of special interest. The collection of Ancient Chinese art includes a collection of Han and Tang **funerary objects★★** from northern China, displayed in a glass case.

Second floor – Classical Chinese arts include **Ming porcelain★** (1368–1644) with polychrome or blue-and-white motifs. Korean works are represented by the Celadon pottery, 18C theatre masks and an imposing **portrait of Cho Man-Yong**, a 19C dignitary. Examples of Japanese art include the gilt-lacquer screens dating from the Edo period and the collection of etchings by Utamaro (18C), Sharaku (actors' portraits – late 18C), Hiroshige (19C) and Hokusai (**Wave off the Coast of Kanagawa★★**).

The third and fourth floors exhibit **Chinese porcelain** from the Qing period and house the lacquer rotunda.

Galeries du Panthéon Bouddhique – This annex (Hôtel Heidelbach, 19 avenue d'Iéna; ⊙Wed–Mon 10am–5.45pm; ⊙1 Jan, 1 May, 25 Dec; ⊛free entry; ℘01 40 73 88 00) of the Guimet Museum is housed in a superb Neoclassical mansion. It is dedicated to Chinese and Japanese Buddhism from the 5C to the 19C, with statues and idols from temples and private chapels. Don't miss the extraordinary Japanese Garden.

Musée d'Art Moderne de la Ville de Paris★★

11 avenue du Président Wilson, in Palais de Tokyo. ⊙*Tue–Sun 10am–6pm.* ⊙*Public holidays.* ⊛*Free (charge for temporary exhibits).* ℘*01 53 67 40 00. www.mam.paris.fr.*

This municipal collection illustrates the main trends of 20C art, including major works such as: *France* by Bourdelle (on a terrace), *Les Disques* by Léger (1918), *L'Équipe de Cardiff* by Robert Delaunay (1912–13), **Danse de Paris★** by Matisse (1932), *Évocation* by Picasso and *Rêve* by Chagall. Dufy's **Fée Électricité★** *(The Good Fairy Electricity)* is the largest picture in the world (600sq m/6 460sq ft).

Palais de Tokyo

13 avenue du Président-Wilson. ⊙*Wed–Mon noon–midnight.* ⊙*Public holidays.* ⊛*10€.* ℘*01 47 23 54 01. www.palaisdetokyo.com.*

Housed in one of the wings of the Palais de Tokyo, built for the 1937 World Exhibition, this centre, opened in 2001, is devoted to exhibits and events relating to contemporary culture and arts.

Palais Galliera (Musée de la Mode de la ville de Paris)

10 avenue Pierre 1 de Serbie. ⊙*Tue–Sun 10am–6pm (Thu until 9pm).* ⊙*Public holidays.* ⊛*9€.* ℘*01 56 52 86 00. www.palaisgalliera.paris.fr.*

The Duchess of Galliera, wife of the Italian financier and philanthropist, had this structure built (1878–94) in the Italian Renaissance style. Restored and reopened in 2013, the mansion now hosts temporary exhibitions on themes of **fashion** and costume, drawn from a vast collection of men's, women's and children's clothing from 1735 to the present day.

♿ Musée des Égouts

Entrance at the corner of quai d'Orsay and Pont de l'Alma. ⊙*May–Sept Sat–Wed 11am–6pm; Oct–Apr Sat–Wed 11am–5pm.* ⊛*4.40€.* ℘*01 53 68 27 81. www.paris.fr.*

The Paris **sewer** system was constructed at the time of Napoléon III. Today it incorporates 2 100km/1 305mi of underground tunnels. Guided visits include historic images and technical models.

♿ Galerie-musée Baccarat

11 place des États-Unis. ⊙*Mon, Wed–Sat 10am–6pm.* ⊙*Public holidays.* ⊛*7€; under 18 years free.* ♿ ℘*01 40 22 11 00.*

Opened in 2003 in a mansion once owned by art collector Marie-Laure de Noailles, this Baccarat museum and gallery was designed by Philippe Starck. It displays historical and modern crystal pieces in a magical setting.

La Voie Triomphale★★★

The most famous thoroughfare in Paris is at once an avenue with a spectacular view, a place of entertainment and a street of smart luxury shops. The vista extending down the Champs-Élysées, with the Arc de Triomphe silhouetted against the sky, is known the world over. To Parisians it is the Voie Triomphale or **Triumphal Way**. At times of great patriotic fervour, the triumphal avenue continues to be the spontaneous rallying point for the people of Paris. La Voie Triomphale is peppered with some of France's greatest monuments: the Louvre Pyramid, the Arc du Carrousel, the Arc de Triomphe, Concorde and l'arche de La Défense.

WALKING TOUR
Maps p230 and pp228–229.

Begin at the Arc de Triomphe du Carrousel, near the Louvre.

Arc de Triomphe du Carrousel★
This delightful pastiche, inspired by the Roman triumphal arch of Septimus Severus, was built from 1806 to 1808.

Location: The Champs-Élysées stretches from the the place de la Concorde to the Arc de Triomphe.

Metro/Transport: Concorde (lines 1, 8 and 12), Champs-Élysées Clemenceau (lines 1 and 13), Franklin D Roosevelt (lines 1 and 9), Georges V (line 1), Étoile (lines 1, 2 and 6), Tuileries (lines 1 and 7).

Info: Paris Office du Tourisme, 25 rue des Pyramides. ℘08 92 68 30 00 (0.34€ per min). www.parisinfo.com.

Parking: Parking is possible underground at place de la Concorde and along the Champs-Élysées.

Don't Miss: The view from atop the Arc de Triomphe.

Timing: The walk alone takes 2hr 30min, so leave a half-day, and a full day if visiting the museums.

Kids: The playground and toy boat rentals in the Tuileries. The marionnette theatre near the Rond-Point des Champs-Élysées and the Palais de la Découverte.

Arc de Triomphe

©H. Chajmowicz/Michelin

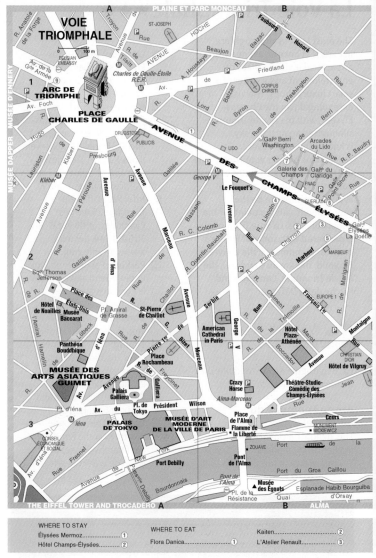

WHERE TO STAY
Élysées Mermoz.....................①
Hôtel Champs-Élysées............②

WHERE TO EAT
Flora Danica.....................①

Kaiten...............................②
L'Atelier Renault..................③

Jardin du Carrousel

Burned down by the rioters of the Paris Commune in 1871, the ruins of the Tuileries were razed in 1883 and replaced by the Carrousel Garden, named after an equestrian parade, or carrousel, that took place here in the 18C. Two flowerbeds frame the yew hedges radiating out from the Arc de la Carrousel. Within the hedges are placed 18 **statues★** of female nudes by the sculptor Maillol,

which are framed by the two wings of the Louvre Museum.

Jardin des Tuileries★

Stretching between the Louvre and place de la Concorde, the Tuileries Gardens, with their elegant statues and fountains, make it easy for weary museum-goers and shoppers to forget that this haven witnessed some of the most turbulent events in Paris' history.

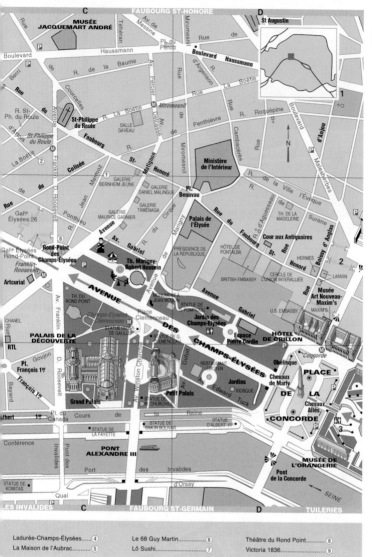

The lost château – Named after the clay dug up here for making tiles – or *tuiles* – the land was purchased in 1563 by Catherine de' Medici for a château adjoining the Louvre, a project she entrusted to **Philibert Delorme**. Work was abruptly halted when the Queen Mother learned that her horoscope predicted that she would die near St-Germain (the Tuileries was in parish St-Germain-l'Auxerrois).

In 1594 Henri IV ordered work to proceed, and the Pavillon de Flore was built with a riverside gallery linked to the Louvre. In 1664 Le Vau revamped the exterior and constructed the Pavillon de Marsan for Louis XIV, who spent three winters at the Tuileries while building progressed on the Louvre.

The 18C – In 1715, on the death of the Sun King, the regency installed the young Louis XV in the Tuileries. In

Bassin Octogonal, Jardin des Tuileries

© David Hughes/Dreamstime.com

1722 he moved the court back to Versailles. The palace was abandoned as a residence, and Paris' first public concert-hall was set up in the Salle des Suisses in 1725. It drew many major composers and musicians, including **Mozart** (1778). The Comédie Française moved here in 1770, staging **Beaumarchais'** *Barber of Seville* and Voltaire's *Irène* before 1782.

Troubled times – On 17 October 1789 the royal family were forced by an angry mob back to Paris. On 20 June 1792 the palace was invaded by rioters and two

months later, on 10 August, the palace was attacked: 600 of the defending 900 Swiss guards were slaughtered (*see box opposite*), and the palace was ransacked while the king took refuge in the Legislative Assembly.

During the Convention, the buildings served as ministry offices.

Final decline – **Napoléon I** (Bonaparte) took up residence in 1800, and under him, the architects **Visconti** and Lefuel completed the Galerie Rivoli, thereby completing the union of the Tuileries

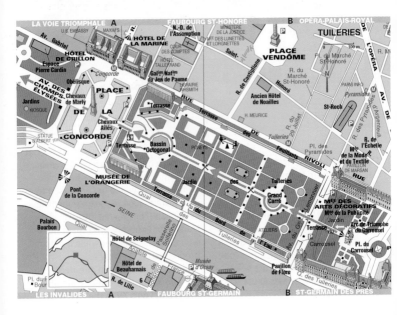

and the Louvre. During the Commune uprisings (1871), the Tuileries Palace was burned down. In 1883 the stone ruins were purchased by a Corsican family who used the stones to build a replica palace in Ajaccio (this palace too was burned down, in 1978).

The gardens – Catherine de' Medici envisaged an Italian-style park, complete with fountains, a maze, a grotto, populated with terra-cotta figures by **Bernard Palissy**, and a menagerie for her palace next to the Louvre. Henri IV later added an orangery and a silkworm farm. In 1664 Le Nôtre raised two terraces lengthways and of unequal height to level the sloping ground, creating the magnificent central axis; he created the pools and designed formal flower beds, quincunxes and slopes. Colbert was so delighted that he intended the gardens to be kept for the royal family, but was subsequently persuaded by the author, Charles Perrault, to allow access to the public. In the 18C chairs were made available for hire and toilets installed. Louis-Philippe reserved a part of the gardens for the royal family.

The Tuileries today – The gardens have recently undergone a substantial restoration programme. Parts designed by Le Nôtre remain unaltered, although some sculptures have been moved and oth-

Walks

Tuileries Garden covers 25ha/62 acres, from the two sphinxes that mount guard opposite the Pavillon de Flore (brought back from Sebastopol after the city was seized in 1855) to the national gallery of the Jeu de Paume, opposite the Hôtel Talleyrand on rue de Rivoli.

ers added, including the fine collection of **nudes★** by **Maillol**, Rodin's *The Kiss*, and works by Dubuffet, Ernst, Calder, Giacometti, Arp and Picasso. Steps and ramps afford access at several points to the terraces (the **Feuillants** on the north side, the **Bord de l'Eau** on the south) which run the length of the gardens and culminate in the Jeu de Paume and Orangery pavilions.

From the riverside terrace there is a splendid **view★★** over the gardens, the Seine and in the background, the Louvre. This setting was the playground of the royal princes, including the sons of Napoléon I and III.

Below, an underground passage running the length of the terrace to place de la Concorde enabled Louis-Philippe to escape from the palace in 1848. The **central alley** affords a magnificent **vista★★★**.

Massacre of the Swiss Guards

Louis XVI and his family were expelled from Versailles following the fall of the Bastille in 1789 and went to live at the Tuileries Palace. Sensing the danger they were in, the king and his family tried to escape in June 1791, but were arrested after being discovered at Varennes near the border with Germany.

They were brought under escort back to the Tuileries, where they were confined and protected only by the king's faithful Swiss Guards. There they remained for the next year, but by the summer of 1792 there was no longer a desire to retain the monarchy. On 10 August the Tuileries Palace was stormed by the people of Paris led by Danton and others. The royal family had already escaped to the General Assembly Hall, but the Swiss Guards set about defending the palace unaware of the family's departure. At first they threw cartridges out of the windows as a gesture of peace but fighting soon broke out. A note arrived from the king ordering the Swiss Guard not to fire on the insurgents, but they were heavily outnumbered and had no choice.

The result was a massacre in which 600 of the 900 Swiss Guards died in the fighting. A further 60 were killed after being taken prisoner and many died in prison. It is estimated that only about 100 survived.

Octagonal pool – Around the huge basin of water, statues, terraces, slopes and stairways are arranged in a single architectural whole. Works are listed *(below)* counter-clockwise, starting from the eastern side of the basin:

♦ *The Seasons* (Coustou and Van Clève)
♦ Arcade from the Tuileries Palace
♦ Bust of Le Nôtre (Coysevox) – the original is in St-Roch *(see Palais Royal)*.
♦ *The Tiber* copied from the Antique
♦ *The Seine* and *The Marne* (Coustou)
♦ *The Loire* and *The Loiret* (Van Clève)
♦ *The Nile* copied from the Antique
♦ *Fame* on a winged horse after Coysevox *(on the left of the main gate)*
♦ *Mercury* on a winged horse after Coysevox *(on the right of the main gate)* – originals in the Louvre.

👥 **Fair** – Every year a carnival is held in the gardens from 21 June to 25 Aug. The Ferris wheel and other attractions can be seen from afar.

Place de la Concorde★★★

Everything about this square – site, size, elegance – is impressive, particularly the obelisk *(see opposite)*, which dominates the scene. Place de la Concorde is one of the most beautiful squares in Paris, but also one of the busiest.

Wanting to find favour with Louis XV, Paris aldermen commissioned the sculptor Bouchardon to carve an equestrian statue of Le Bien-Aimé (the beloved, as he was known), and organized a competition to find an architect for the square. **Ange-Jacques Gabriel** won for his design for an octagon bordered by a dry moat and balustrade. Work began in 1755 and continued until 1775.

In 1792 the royal statue was toppled, and the name of the square was changed from place Louis-XV to place de la Révolution. On 21 January 1793, a guillotine was erected in the northwest corner (near the spot where the Brest statue now stands) for the execution of **Louis XVI**. On 13 May, "the national razor", now installed near the grille to the Tuileries, began to claim a further 1 343 victims, including Marie-Antoinette. The Directory, hopeful of a better future,

Rue de Rivoli

Rue de Rivoli crosses the site of the former Tuileries **Riding School**. In 1789 the school was hastily converted into a meeting place for the Constituent Assembly. Sessions were subsequently held there by the Legislative Assembly and the Convention. On 21 September 1792, the day following the French victory over the Prussians at Valmy (see the commemorative tablet on a pillar in the Tuileries railings opposite no **230**), it became the setting for the proclamation of the Republic and the trial of Louis XVI.

In 1944 the German General von Choltitz, Commandant of Paris, who had his headquarters at the **Hôtel Meurice** (no **228**), made a momentous decision in the capital's own history by refusing to follow Hitler's orders to blow up the capital's bridges and principal buildings when the tanks of General Leclerc's division and the Resistance were known to be approaching. He surrendered on 25 August and Paris was liberated intact. At the far end, by place de la Concorde, several commemorative plaques record the heroism of those who fell during the Liberation.

👥 Along rue de Rivoli, the Tuileries Garden has a wide range of activities for children: merry-go-rounds, donkey rides *(Wednesdays and weekends)* and several play areas. Small toy sailing boats can be rented *(in the summer)* for the pond in the middle of the garden.

Place de la Concorde

© S. Sauvignier/MICHELIN

renamed the blood-soaked area place de la Concorde.

Under Louis-Philippe, the square's decoration was completed by the neutral symbol of an obelisk, two fountains inspired by those in St Peter's Square in Rome, and eight statues representing eight French cities: Brest, Rouen, Lille, Strasbourg, Lyon, Marseille, Bordeaux and Nantes.

Two mansions★★ – The colossal mansions on either side of the opening to rue Royale are among the finest examples of the early Louis XVI style. Their architect, Ange-Jacques Gabriel, succeeded his father, Jacques Gabriel, at the head of the Academy of Architecture. The right pavilion, the **Hôtel de la Marine**, was until 1792 the royal store; it then became the Admiralty Office. Today it houses the navy headquarters.

The **Hôtel de Crillon**, across the street, was at first occupied by four noblemen. It now accommodates the French Automobile Club and a famous hotel and is flanked on the left by the American Embassy. To the right of the Hôtel de la Marine is the Hôtel Talleyrand (today home to the American Consulate), where the statesman and diplomat **Talleyrand** died in 1838.

Obelisk★ – In the centre of the square stands an obelisk from the ruins of the temple at Luxor, given to France in 1831 by Mohammed Ali, Viceroy of Egypt. It reached Paris via the Seine four years later and was erected on 25 October 1836. The pink granite monument is 3 300 years old and covered in hieroglyphics; it is 23m/75.5ft tall, and weighs more than 220t. The point of the obelisk indicates international time, making it the largest sundial in the world.

Views★★★ – The obelisk provides the best point from which to get a view of the Champs-Élysées, framed by the **Marly Horses** (commissioned from **Guillaume Coustou** for Marly, Louis XIV's superb château near Versailles) looking up the avenue towards the Arc de Triomphe. Coysevox's Winged Horses frame the view across the Tuileries towards the Louvre. Replicas have replaced the two original marble groups of horses, which are now in the Louvre.

Pont de la Concorde – The bridge was designed in 1787 by the civil engineer Perronet. It was completed by 1791 with the stones from the Bastille prison used in its construction so that, it was said, "the people could forever trample the ruins of the old fortress". The bridge is classified as a UNESCO World Heritage Site, and offers a spectacular **view★★★** of the Seine and place de la Concorde, towards La Madeleine.

Baron Haussmann

More than anyone else, **Georges-Eugène Haussmann** (1809–1891) was responsible for the appearance of Paris today. Born in Paris, and a lawyer by training, he went on to become a professional civil servant and was appointed Prefect of the Seine by Napoléon III in 1852. He set about demolishing the filthy crowded streets of the medieval city, which were thought to have caused the cholera epidemic of 1832, in which about 20 000 Parisians perished. His vision was to create a well-ordered, airy city within a geometrical pattern, and he set about widening the existing Grand Boulevards in addition to building new ones such as the Boulevard Richard Lenoir. His work can be best appreciated from the viewing platform of the Arc de Triomphe. Although not responsible for the Arc itself, which had been finished by Louis-Philippe in 1836, Haussmann completed a star of 12 magnificent avenues, radiating from the place de l'Étoile in which the world-famous monument is located.

Jardins des Champs-Élysées

Landscaped with trees and bordered by avenues with grand horse-chestnuts, the gardens contain theatres **L'Espace Pierre Cardin** and **Théâtre Marigny**, designed by **Charles Garnier** in 1853, and used almost exclusively by Jacques Offenbach from 1855 to amuse the Parisian public with his operettas.

Four monuments evoke heroes of past wars; a bronze statue of the statesman **Georges Clemenceau**, *The Father of Victory*, by François Cogné (1932) stands in place Clemenceau. Across avenue Winston Churchill rises the statue of **Général Charles de Gaulle** by J Cardot (2000). The monument on the corner with avenue de Marigny honours Resistance leader **Jean Moulin**. Near Cours de la Reine is the statue of **Sir Winston Churchill**, looking resolute.

Shaded gardens on the northern side of **avenue Gabriel**, running parallel to the Champs-Élysées, stretch along the back of smart mansions lining the Faubourg St-Honoré: the **Elysée Palace** (fine wrought-iron gate with gilded cockerel, 1905), the British Embassy, the United States Embassy (in the former home of the gastronome Grimod de la Reynière).

Avenue des Champs-Élysées★★★

Today, the Champs-Élysées is lined with restaurants and cafés, car showrooms and banks, cinemas and nightclubs. Most of the shops are international chains, with the majority of the luxury fashion boutiques found along the side streets like avenues George V and Montaigne.

The Second Empire private houses and amusement halls that once lined it have vanished; the only exception is no **25**, a mansion built by La Païva, a Polish adventuress whose house was famous for dinners attended by philosophers, painters and writers, and for its unique onyx staircase. **Le Colisée**, an amphitheatre built in 1770 to hold an audience of 40 000, has left its name to a street, a café and a cinema.

Arc de Triomphe★★★

The arch commemorates Napoléon's victories and the fate of the Unknown Soldier, whose tomb lies beneath.

In 1806 **Napoléon** commissioned **Jean-François Chalgrin** to construct a giant arch. It wouldn't be finished until 1836, under **Louis-Philippe**. In 1840 the carriage bearing the emperor's body passed beneath the arch. On 14 July 1919, the victorious Allied armies, led by the marshals, marched in procession. The Unknown Soldier killed in the Great War was laid to rest in 1921. On 26 August 1944, Paris was liberated from German occupation, and Général de Gaulle marched through the arch.

The arch, and **place Charles de Gaulle★★★**, which surrounds it, form one of Paris' most famous landmarks. Twelve avenues radiate from the arch, and explain why it is also called **place de**

Sculptures of the Arc de Triomphe

Facing the Champs-Élysées:

1 – *The Departure of the Volunteers* in 1792, commonly called
La Marseillaise★★, Rude's sublime masterpiece represents the Nation leading her people to defend their independence.
2 – *General Marceau's Funeral.*
3 – *The Triumph of 1810* (by Cortot) celebrating the Treaty of Vienna.
4 – *The Battle of Aboukir.*

Facing avenue de Wagram:

5 – *The Battle of Austerlitz.*

Facing avenue de la Grande Armée:

6 – *Resistance* (by Etex).
7 – *The Passage of the Bridge of Arcola.*
8 – *Peace* (by Etex).
9 – *The Capture of Alexandria.*

Facing avenue Kléber:

10 – *The Battle of Jemmapes.*

Beneath the monument, the flame of the Unknown Soldier is rekindled each evening at 6.30pm. Lesser battles are engraved on the arch's inner walls together with the names of 558 generals – the names of those who died in the field are underlined.

235

l'**Étoile** (*étoile* means star). **Haussmann** redesigned the square in 1854, creating a further seven radiating avenues in addition to the original five, while Hittorff planned the uniform façades that surround it.

Chalgrin's undertaking is truly colossal, measuring 50m/164ft high by 45m/147.6ft wide, with massive high reliefs. **Rude** was commissioned to carve the four main panels, but Etex and Cortot managed to steal work for three of the four groups; Rude's is the only inspired one. Pradier's *Fames*, four trumpet-blowing figures, abut the main arches. A frieze with hundreds of figures, each 2m/6.6ft tall, encircles the arch.

Arch platform

Access by tunnel on east and on west side, or inside de Gaulle-Etoile metro station (follow signs to Arc de Triomphe). ◷*Apr–Sept daily 10am–11pm; Oct–Mar daily 10am–10.30pm; last admission 45min before closing.* ◷*Public holidays.* ◉*9.50€; under 18 years free.* ✆*01 55 37 73 77; http://arc-de-triomphe. monuments-nationaux.fr.*

From the platform, a **panorama★★★** of the capital is obtained: in the foreground are the 12 avenues radiating from the square; in the distance, the Louvre and at the other end of the Champs-Élysées, La Défense can be seen.

Assembled in a small museum are mementoes of the arch's construction and the ceremonies it has hosted.

MUSEUMS AND OTHER ATTRACTIONS

Musée de l'Orangerie★★

In Jardin des Tuileries. ◷*Wed–Mon 9am–6pm.* ◷*1 May, 14 July, 25 Dec.* ◉*9€.* ♿ ✆*01 44 50 43 00.* *www.musee-orangerie.fr.*

Tuileries Garden's two pavilions, the **Orangerie** and the **Jeu de Paum**, were built during the Second Empire; they have served as art galleries since the beginning of the 20C.

Reopened in 2006 after extensive renovations, the two oval rooms on the ground floor of the Orangerie are hung with panels from the water-lily series known as the **Nymphéas★★★** painted by **Claude Monet** of his garden at Giverny, in Normandy. The lower-level galleries accommodate the **Walter-Guillaume Collection** (Impressionists to 1930) of works by Soutine, Picasso, Modigliani, Cézanne, Renoir, Matisse, Rousseau and other artists.

Galerie nationale du Jeu de Paume

◷*Tue–Sun 11am–7pm (until 9pm Tue).* ◷*1 Jan, 1 May, 25 Dec.* ◉*10€.* ♿ ✆*01 47 03 12 50. www.jeudepaume.org.*

Since 2004 this converted "old tennis court" is home to the Galerie nationale du Jeu de Paume, the Centre national de la photographie, and the Patrimoine Photographique. It includes collections of photography, film, video and installations.

Nymphéas by Claude Monet, Musée de l'Orangerie

© Francesco Tomasinelli/age fotostock

Musée du Petit Palais★

Avenue Winston Churchill. ⏰*Tue–Sun 10am–6pm.* ⏰*Public holidays.* ♿📞*01 53 43 40 00. www.petitpalais.paris.fr.* 💶*Free (charge for temporary exhibits).*

The **Petit Palais**, **Musée des Beaux-Arts de la ville de Paris**, features a diverse collection of fine arts. On display are the Dutuit (antiques, medieval and Renaissance art objects, paintings, drawings, books, enamels, porcelain) and Tuck (18C furniture and objets d'art) bequests. The city of Paris' collection of 19C paintings includes works by **Ingres**, **Delacroix**, Courbet, Dalou, **Barbizon School** and the Impressionists. Note *The Good Samaritan* (1880) by Morot and *Ascension* (1879) by **Gustave Doré**.

Grand Palais★

This immense exhibition hall is formally fronted by an Ionic colonnade running the length of the building, before a mosaic frieze. Enormous quadrigae punctuate the corners; elsewhere turn-of-the-19C modern-style decorative elements are scattered. Inside, a single glazed space is covered by a flattened dome. With an exhibition area of nearly 5 000sq m/5 980sq yd, the **Galeries du Grand Palais** *(3 av. du Général Eisenhower; hours and prices vary per exhibit;* ⏰*1 May, 25 Dec;* 📞*01 40 13 48 00 ; www. rmn.fr)* have become a cultural centre for exhibitions from around the world.

👥 Palais de la Découverte★★

Inside the Grand Palais; entrance on avenue Franklin D Roosevelt. ⏰*Tue–Sat 9.30am–6pm, Sun and public holidays 10am–7pm.* ⏰*1 Jan, 1 May, 14 Jul, 25 Dec.* 💶*9€; under 25 years 7€; Planetarium 3€.* 📞*01 56 43 20 20. www.palais-decouverte.fr.*

Founded by a physicist in 1937, this museum is dedicated to scientific discovery; it is a centre for higher scientific study and for popular enlightenment. Many interactive attractions are specially intended for children, particularly in the field of biology. Other themes (mathematics, nuclear physics) are geared to visitors who are already competent in these fields.

The domed **planetarium**★ *(level 2)* introduces the heavens, including the course of the planets in the solar system.

Musée Art Nouveau – Maxim's

Maxim's de Paris, 3 rue Royale. 🗣️*By guided tour (1hr), in English, Wed–Sun 2pm.* 💶*15€.* 📞*01 42 65 30 47. www. maxims-musee-artnouveau.com.*

Maxim's is a Paris legend. This intimate museum allows visitors to see the 1900 collection of the owner and fashion designer **Pierre Cardin**: Art Nouveau furniture and objects by Majorelle, Guimard, Gaudi, Gallé and Tiffany.

Musée Dapper

35 bis rue Paul Valéry. ⏰*Open during expositions Wed, Fri–Mon 11am–7pm.* 💶*6€; free under 18 years and last Wed of the month.* 📞*01 45 00 91 75. www.dapper.fr.*

This museum organizes temporary exhibits dedicated to Africa. It also houses a bookshop and a performance space for the promotion of African culture: literature, dance, theatre, storytelling and music. A café is located under the elevated bridge at the entrance.

Musée arménien – Fondation Nourhan Fringhian

59 avenue Foch. 🚫*Closed indefinitely for restoration.* 📞*01 45 56 15 88. www.le-maf.com.*

This museum, housed in a historic Parisian mansion, displays Armenian objects.

Musée d'Ennery

59 avenue Foch. ⏰*Guided tours (1hr) mid-Sep–Jun Sat 11.30am by reservation only.* 💶*Free.* 📞*01 56 52 53 45. www.guimet.fr.*

An annex of the Guimet Museum of Asian Arts, this museum houses a collection of 17C–19C Far East objects gathered at the end of the 19C by Madame Clémence d'Ennery.

There is an impressive collection of **netsukés**★, little wooden buttons, sculpted and painted to resemble humorous human or animal figures. The Japanese would attach these to the centre of their kimono.

Monceau★★

In 1778 the Duke of Chartres, the future Philippe-Égalité, commissioned the painter-writer Carmontelle to design a garden inspired by the romantic English and German style of the day. A century later elegant mansions were built around it, several of which are now museums, in which art is the focus.

SIGHTS
Parc Monceau★
Entrance outside metro Monceau.
Two fine gates frame the entrance. Trees in the park include maples, plane trees and ginkos. The Pavillon de Chartres, known as "La Rotonde", was designed by Ledoux as a tax booth built into city fortifications. White marble statues, an oval basin, a small lake and the Renaissance arcade grace the park.

Cathédrale Saint-Alexandre Nevski
12 rue Daru. ◷*Tue, Fri, Sun 3pm–5pm.* ℘*03 86 91 97 88.*
This Russian Orthodox church was built in 1860 in the neo-Byzantine style.

Rue du Faubourg St-Honoré★
This elegant artery connects the rue Royale to the place des Ternes. At no 252 is the **Salle Pleyel**, a theatre built in 1927 (restored in 2006), which is renowned for its acoustics. Home to the Orchestre de Paris, it also houses an exhibit room

Info: Paris Office du Tourisme, 25 rue des Pyramides. ℘08 92 68 30 00 (0.34 per min). http://en.parisinfo.com.

Location: North of the Champs-Élysées district.

Metro/Transport: Monceau (line 2) – Buses: 30, 84, 94.

Parking: Plenty of street parking.

Don't Miss: The beautiful café of the Jacquemart-André Museum.

Timing: Allow a half day.

Kids: Parc Monceau has large play areas for kids.

of historical instruments, a café and art gallery. The entryway is decorated in mosaics, wrought iron, and a cupola finished in pure Art Deco style.

At the corner of rue Berryer (no 11) are the gardens of the former Hôtel Salomon de Rothschild. Completed in 1878, it is now home to the Fondation Nationale des Arts Graphiques et Plastiques.

MUSEUMS
Musée Jacquemart-André★★
158 boulevard Haussmann. ◷*Daily 10am–6pm.* ⌐*12€.* ⌂ ℘*01 45 62 11 59. www.musee-jacquemart-andre.com.*
This elegant late-19C house contains outstanding 18C European Renais-

Musée Nissim de Camondo

© Y. Kanazawa/MICHELIN

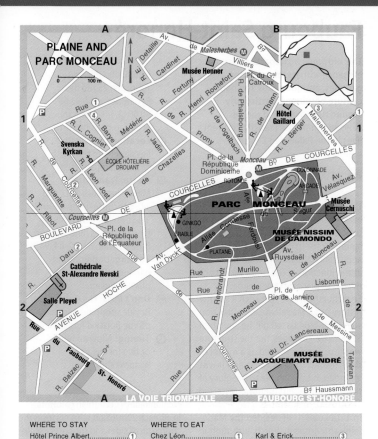

PLAINE AND
PARC MONCEAU

N

0   100 m

Av. Detaille

de Malesherbes

B⁴

Villiers

Cardinet

R. Fortuny

Musée Henner

Pl. du Gᵃˡ
Catroux

R. Henri Rochefort

de R. Henri

R. de Phalsbourg

R. de Thann

Hôtel
Gaillard

Rue

R.

P

R. Barye

Médéric

R. L. Cogniet

R. Jadin

de Chazelles

Prony

R. de Logelbach

R. de Thann

R. G. Berger

Malesherbes

Svenska
Kyrkan

ÉCOLE HÔTELIÈRE
DROUANT

Pl. de la
République
Dominicaine

Monceau

B⁴ DE COURCELLES

COLONNADE

Av.
Vélasquez

R. Léon Jost

de

R.

COURCELLES

ROTONDE

ARCADE

Musée
Cernuschi

Marguerite

de

Courcelles

DE

Allée Comtesse Fabdoui

PARC   MONCEAU

Sagut

R. T. Ribot

BOULEVARD

Courcelles M

GINKGO

ÉRABLE

Allée Comtesse

MUSÉE NISSIM
DE CAMONDO

Pl. de la
République
de l'Équateur

Daru

PLATANE

Av. Ruysdaël

Av. de Monceau

Cathédrale
St-Alexandre Nevski

Rue

Av. Van Dyck

Rue

Murillo

de

Lisbonne

R.

Salle Pleyel

HOCHE

Rue

Rembrandt

R.

de

Pl. de
Rio de Janeiro

Av. de Messine

Téhéran

AVENUE

Rue

du

Monceau

Av. de Messine

R.

P

Faubourg

St-Honoré

Rue

de

Courcelles

Rue

du Dr. Lancereaux

MUSÉE
JACQUEMART ANDRÉ

R. Balzac

P

Bᵈ Haussmann

LA VOIE TRIOMPHALE   FAUBOURG ST-HONORÉ

sance art. It was formerly owned by art collectors Edouard André and Nélie Jacquemart, banker and painter respectively, who married in 1881 and travelled in Europe and Asia. Works displayed are by Boucher, Nattier, Chardin, Houdon, Canaletto and others. Nélie's first-floor studio features Renaissance sculpture.

Musée Nissim de Camondo★★

63 rue de Monceau. ○*Wed–Sun 10am–5.30pm.* ○*1 Jan, 1 May, 25 Dec.* ○*9€ (includes audio guide).* ℘*01 53 89 06 50. www.lesartsdecoratifs.fr.*
In 1936 the banker Moïse de Camondo bequeathed his handsome mansion and collection of 18C French arts and furnishings to Les Arts Decoratifs. It's fully preserved in its original condition.

Musée Cernuschi★

7 avenue Vélasquez. ○*Tue–Sun 10am–6pm.* ○*Public holidays.* ○*Free entry.* ℘*01 53 96 21 50. www.cernuschi.paris.fr.*
The banker Henri Cernuschi bequeathed his house and extensive collection of Oriental art to the City of Paris in 1896.

Musée Jean-Jacques Henner

43 avenue de Villiers. ○*Closed for renovation until Nov 2015.* ℘*01 47 63 42 73. www.musee-henner.fr.*
This 19C mansion houses the collections of **Jean-Jacques Henner** (1829–1905), one of the finest French Impressionist artists of the early 20C.

Faubourg Saint-Honoré★

This old *faubourg* imparts a leisured elegance with its luxury shops, art galleries, antique shops and haute-couture boutiques, particularly around rue Royale and rue de l'Élysée, where the French president lives in the Palais de l'Élysée.

🐾 WALKING TOUR

La Madeleine★★

La Madeleine, the church dedicated to St Mary Magdalene, is a distinctive landmark for its striking Greek temple appearance and its convenient position at the junction of the boulevards connected to place de la Concorde.

Few churches have had such a stormy history as La Madeleine. Construction started in 1764 based on the church of St-Louis des Invalides, but the structure was razed and restarted as a model of the Panthéon. Under Napoléon it was intended to be a temple to the glory of the Great Army, but then was restarted again as a Greek temple.

In 1814 Louis XVIII decided the Madeleine should be a church, although in 1837 the building was nearly selected for use as Paris' first railway terminal. The church's vicissitudes ended with its consecration in 1842, although its priest was shot by the Commune in 1871.

> 🛈 **Info:** Paris Office du Tourisme, 25 rue des Pyramides. ☏08 92 68 30 00 (0.34€ per min). http://en.parisinfo.com.
>
> ▶ **Location:** This quarter lies directly to the north of the Champs-Élysées.
>
> Ⓜ **Metro/Transport:** Madeleine (lines 8, 12 and 14), Concorde (lines 1, 8 and 12) St-Philippe du Roule (line 9), Ternes (line 2) – Buses: 24, 42, 52, 80, 84, 94.
>
> 🅿 **Parking:** Underground parking off the place Beauvau.
>
> ⊘ **Don't Miss:** The Galerie Royale shopping passage off rue Boissy d'Anglas.
>
> 🕐 **Timing:** Allow an hour or two for leisurely window shopping.

A colonnade of Corinthian **columns** – 52 in all, each 20m/65.6ft tall – encloses the church on all sides and supports a sculptured frieze. A monumental flight of 28 steps leads to the imposing peristyle giving on to place de la Madeleine and provides a fine **view**★ down rue Royale, the obelisk at the heart of place de la Concorde and beyond to the Palais Bourbon and the Invalides dome. Reliefs on the bronze doors represent the Ten Commandments.

The single nave church has a dark vestibule, decorated with works by Pradier and Rude. The nave is crowned by three domes. Chopin's funeral took place here in 1849. In 1858, Camille Saint-Saëns was hired to play the organ, where he composed some of his most remarkable pieces.

Place de la Madeleine

Next to the church is a flower market and surrounding it, famous epicure *épiceries* or food stores, upmarket fashion houses and gourmet restaurants.

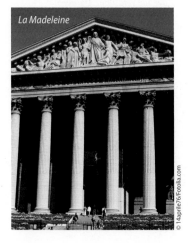

La Madeleine

© 14aprile76/Fotolia.com

Camille Saint-Saëns (1835–1921)

The great composer Camille Saint-Saëns was the organist at La Madeleine from 1857 to 1876, when he composed many of his best-known pieces.

An infant prodigy, Saint-Saëns was taught music by his mother, Clémance, and a great-aunt, having lost his father at the age of two. His first public piano performance was given at the tender age of five and by seven he had already begun to compose his own music. Admitted to the Paris Conservatoire by the age of thirteen, he studied organ and composition. Very soon his work was being admired by such musical talents as Schumann, Berlioz, Gounod and most importantly, Liszt, with whom he enjoyed a close working and personal relationship.

In 1853 he was appointed as organist at Saint Merry and then in 1857 he moved to the same post at La Madeleine. In 1875 he married Marie-Laure Truffot, a young lady of 19 who bore him two sons – both boys died in unfortunate circumstances and Saint-Saëns left, blaming her for the deaths.

© Photoshot

One of Saint-Saëns' best-known pieces is *The Carnival of the Animals,* a satire written in 1886 in which his fellow musicians are portrayed as animals. He would not allow the composition to be performed in public during his lifetime, and it was premiered only in 1922. He also wrote poetry, scientific papers and essays about music in which he was not afraid to criticize his contemporaries.

After the death of his mother in 1888, he withdrew from life in Paris and travelled the world performing and composing. He visited Asia, South America and North Africa; it was in Algiers in 1921 that he died of pneumonia. His body was brought back to Paris and buried at Montparnasse Cemetery.

Below: Camille Saint-Saëns playing the piano at Salle Gaveau, Paris

© Albert Harlingue/Photoshot

241

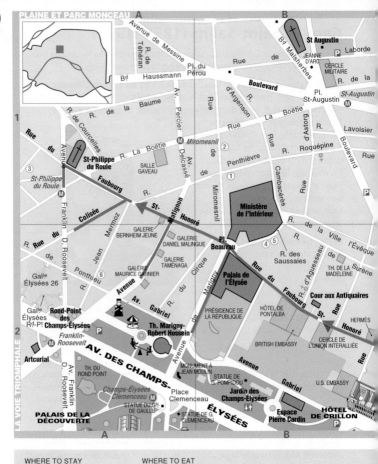

WHERE TO STAY

Hôtel d'Albion......................①

WHERE TO EAT

Chez Cécile la Ferme
des Mathurins...............①

Granterroirs.........................②

L'Arôme................................③

Le Griffonnier.......................④

Rue Royale★

The street runs from the Madeleine to place de la Concorde. The restaurant **Maxim's** (no **3**), was once the Hôtel de Richelieu. In the 18C the writer Mme de Staël lived at no **6**, and Gabriel at no **8**.

Église Notre-Dame de l'Assomption

Place Maurice-Barrès.

This Polish church, once part of the Convent of the Sisters of the Assumption, has an Annunciation by **Vien** (18C) and an Adoration of the Magi by **Van Loo**. In

Paul Poiret once occupied 107 rue du Faubourg St-Honoré. This couturier (1879–1944) banned the whale-bone corset and launched a taste for strong theatrical styles and colours. He integrated exotic features into dress design (harem-inspired *jupes-culottes,* Japanese-style kimono sleeves, and long, ankle-clinging hobble skirts) and may have been responsible for the revival of huge plumed hats. After World War I he employed **Raoul Dufy** to paint his fabrics; his fashion house was the first to launch its own perfume.

Swoon's .... ⑤
Village d'Ung et Li Lam .... ⑥

the dome is a fresco of the Assumption by **Charles de la Fosse** (17C).

Rue du Faubourg Saint-Honoré★

Starting from the rue Royale, this street of luxury boutiques and art galleries is bordered by elegant mansions.
Empress Eugénie was superstitious: the street bears no number 13. Her sister-in-law Pauline lived at the **Hôtel de Charost** (no 39), now home to the British Embassy.
At no 41, the Hôtel Edmond de Rothschild was built in 1835 by Visconti.

Palais de l'Élysée

55 rue du Faubourg St-Honoré.
○━ *Closed to the public.*
The mansion was constructed in 1718 for the Count of Évreux. It was acquired for a short time by the Marquise de Pompadour. During the Revolution it became a dance hall. It was home to Caroline Murat, Napoléon's sister, then Empress Josephine, who redecorated it; Napoléon signed his second abdication here after his defeat at Waterloo, on 22 June 1815. It was also the home of the future **Napoléon III**, who planned his successful *coup d'état* of 1851 here. Since 1873 the Élysée Palace has been the Paris residence of France's president.

Place Beauvau

A fine wrought-iron gate (1836) marks the entrance to the 18C aristocratic mansion now occupied by the Ministry of Home Affairs since 1861.

Avenue de Marigny

On the right, at no 23, is the former Hôtel de Rothschild and its park, now used by the Elysée Palace for visiting dignitaries. Just before the Champs-Élysées is the **Théâtre Marigny**, built by Charles Garnier in 1883.

Avenue Matignon

This street is lined with art galleries dedicated to contemporary Fine Art: Maurice Garnier, Taménaga, Daniel Malingue, Bernheim-Jeune. The auction house Christie's is located in a 1913 mansion designed by René Sergent.

Rue du Colisée

Named after a Roman-style 40 000-seat theatre built in 1770 by Le Camus, this street is home to the mythical Art Deco establishment *Boeuf sur le Toit (no 34)*.

Église Saint-Philippe du Roule

154 rue du Faubourg St-Honoré.
The church designed by **Chalgrin** in imitation of a Roman basilica was erected between 1774 and 1784. The ambulatory was added around the apse in 1845.
A fresco over the chancel of *The Deposition* was created by Chassériau.

Opéra★★ and Palais Royal

With its long avenue of the same name stretching to the Palais Royal, Opéra encompasses the distinctive Palais Garnier Opera House and the splendid place Vendôme. The district is at the hub of theatreland, and home to many contemporary fashion designers and banks.

WALKING TOURS

1 PLACE VENDÔME – OPERA
Start from Ⓜ *Tuileries.*

Rue de Rivoli★
It was Napoléon who, in 1811, had the part of the avenue between rue de Castiglione and place des Pyramides constructed, although it was not to be completed until nearly the middle of the century. The houses facing the Tuileries are of uniform design above arcades lined with both souvenir and luxury shops.

Rue de Castiglione
Formerly known as passage des Feuillants after the Benedictine monastery which it skirted, the rue de Castiglione affords a view of the place and Colonne Vendôme.

Place Vendôme★★
Place Vendôme epitomizes the full majesty of 17C French design. It is named after the Duke of Vendôme, the illegitimate son of Henri IV. In 1680 the Superintendent of Buildings conceived the idea of designing a square lined with splendid buildings around a monumental statue of Louis XIV, and commissioned **Jules Hardouin-Mansart** to design it.

The column – During the Revolution the royal statue was destroyed, and in 1810 **Napoléon** erected the column at its centre. The original statue mounted on the column was of Napoléon as Caesar; in 1814 it was replaced by one

- ℹ️ **Info:** Pyramides welcome centre, 25 rue des Pyramides. ✆08 92 68 30 00 (0.34€ per min). http://en.parisinfo.com.
- ▷ **Location:** This district straddles the 1st and 9th *arrondissements*.
- Ⓜ **Metro/Transport:** Opéra (lines 3, 7 and 8) – Buses: 20, 21, 22, 27, 42, 52, 53, 66, 81, 95. Place des Victoires: Étienne Marcel (line 4) – Buses: 29, 67, 74, 85. Palais Royal: Musée du Louvre (lines 1 and 7) – Buses: 21, 27, 69, 76, 81, 95.
- 🅿 **Parking:** Underground parking available at the place Vendôme, La Bourse and rue des Pyramides.
- **Don't Miss:** The grand marble staircase of the Opéra Garnier. Boutiques of the Passage Vivienne.
- **Kids:** The Palais Royal gardens have a sandbox playground.
- 🕐 **Timing:** Allow four hours to visit this neighbourhood, a day if you plan to visit museums.

of Henri IV, removed for the 100 Days (1815) when Napoléon attempted to regain power. Louis XVIII then had a colossal fleur-de-lis hoisted there; Louis-Philippe re-established Napoléon, this time in military uniform, and Napoléon III substituted a replica of the original. The Commune tore down the column in 1871, an incident for which the painter Gustave Courbet was blamed and exiled.

The Residents – No **15** now houses the **Ritz Hotel**; no **13** and no **11**, occupied by the Ministry of Justice, were formerly the Royal Chancellery – the official measure for the metre was inlaid in the façade in 1848; no **9** was the house of the military governor of Paris at the end of the 19C; **Chopin** died at no **12** in 1849; no **16** was the home of the Ger-

Place Vendôme

© Jose Ignacio Soto/iStockphoto.com

man Dr Mesmer, founder of the theory of Mesmerism.

The square and its surrounding area collect together all the great names in jewellery design: Van Cleef & Arpels, Boucheron, Mauboussin and others. At a stone's throw, in rue Cambon, is the house from which **Coco Chanel** reigned over the fashion world for half a century, while living at the Ritz.

Rue de la Paix

In the French version of Monopoly, this rue is the most expensive street in Paris. Jewellers and goldsmiths, **Cartier** (no **11**) among others, have brought it international fame, making its name synonymous with elegance and luxury.

Place de l'Opéra★★

Haussmann envisaged place de l'Opéra not simply as a setting for the National Music Academy but also as a circus from which a number of roads should radiate. This vision was criticized for being too grandiose: the square seemed enormous at that time, whereas today, choked with traffic, it barely seems big enough.

The square is presently lined with luxurious shop windows proffering elegant leather goods (Lancel) and jewellery (Maty), whereas the Café de la Paix terraces provide an enticing break for the foot-weary.

Boulevard des Capucines

This street takes its name from a Capuchin monastery that once stood here. No 27 has a splendid façade embellished with brass and copper panels by Frantz Jourdain, maestro of the Art Nouveau decorative style.

Rue Scribe

This street is named for Eugène Scribe (1791–1861), who directed the Théâtre Comique Français for 30 years. At no 4, **Le Grand-Hôtel** is a grand vestige from the era of Napoléon III (1862); the Opéra salon is now a restaurant.

Place Gaillon

Erected in 1707, this fountain was remodelled by Visconti in 1827.

Avenue de l'Opéra★

One of the main arteries of the city, this luxurious thoroughfare was begun simultaneously at either end by Haussmann in 1854 and completed in 1878. For the tourist the avenue is the ideal centre for perfumes, scarves, gifts and *articles de Paris* (fancy souvenirs).

Rue de l'Échelle

The rue is so called after the ladder or flight of steps leading to a scaffold that stood on the site in the Ancien Régime, used to publicly humiliate polygamists, perjurers and blasphemers.

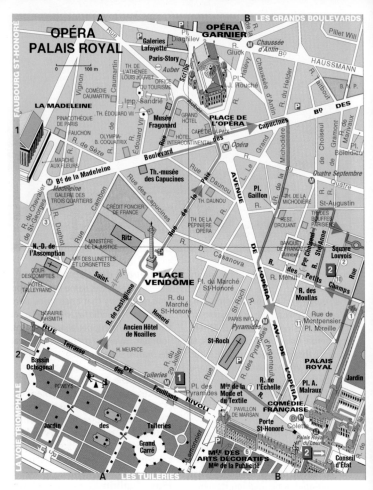

Rue Saint-Honoré★

The windows of the section of rue St-Honoré between rue Royale and rue de Castiglione are a window-shopper's paradise. Under the Ancien Régime, before rue de Rivoli was laid, this road was the main route out of Paris towards the west. The members of the royal court, nobility and financiers all came to do their shopping here.

Place des Pyramides

The equestrian statue of **Joan of Arc** by the 19C sculptor Frémiet marks the site where she was wounded in September 1429 when leading her attack on the capital.

② PALAIS ROYAL AND BIBLIOTHÈQUE NATIONALE

Place du Palais Royal

The façade of the Palais Royal overlooking the square consists of a central block (occupied by the Conseil d'État) with two recessed lateral wings, the whole decorated with restrained 18C carvings of military trophies and allegorical figures by Pajou. The **Louvre des Antiquaires** consists of 250 antique shops.

Comédie-Française

2 rue de Richelieu.

The best way to appreciate the interior of one of the finest theatres in Paris is to attend a performance. The repertoire is

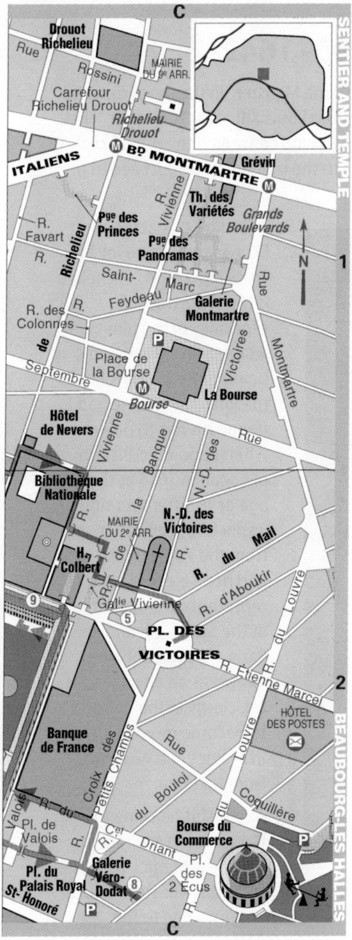

SENTIER AND TEMPLE

Map labels (clockwise/as shown):
Drouot Richelieu, Rue, Rossini, MAIRIE DU 9e ARR., Carrefour Richelieu Drouot, Richelieu Drouot, ITALIENS, Bd MONTMARTRE, Grévin, R. Favart, Pge des Princes, R. Richelieu, Pge des Panoramas, Th. des Variétés, Grands Boulevards, Saint-, R. Vivienne, Marc, R. Feydeau, Rue, Galerie Montmartre, Rue Montmartre, R. des Colonnes, de, Septembre, Place de la Bourse, P, Rue Vivienne, des, Victoires, La Bourse, Bourse, Hôtel de Nevers, Rue, N.-D. des, Bibliothèque Nationale, R. de la Banque, MAIRIE DU 2e ARR., N.-D. des Victoires, R. du Mail, Hr Colbert, Gale Vivienne, R. d'Aboukir, PL. DES VICTOIRES, R. Étienne Marcel, Banque de France, Rue, des, Petits Champs, du Bouloi, Rue, Coquillière, HÔTEL DES POSTES, BEAUBOURG-LES HALLES, R. du, Croix, des, Pl. de Valois, Cdrant, Bourse du Commerce, Galerie Véro-Dodat, Pl. du Palais Royal, St-Honoré, Pl. des 2 Écus, P

mainly classical, although the works of more modern authors are now included. In the foyer are Houdon's famous bust of **Voltaire**★★ and the chair in which **Molière** was sitting when taken fatally ill on stage in 1673 in a performance of *Le Malade imaginaire*.

Place André Malraux★

From this crossroads there is a splendid view up avenue de l'Opéra. Created in the time of Napoléon III and ornamented with modern fountains, the square was formerly known as place du Théâtre-Français, taking its present name from the writer and Minister of Culture under De Gaulle.

Palais Royal★★

In this part of Paris, the grandiose setting of the Palais Royal and the church of St-Roch vividly evoke the city's past, in contrast to rue de Rivoli and rue St-Honoré, which seem to epitomize the present with their bustling shops.

A Bit of History

The Cardinal's Palace – In 1624, **Richelieu**, having just become prime minister, acquired a mansion near the Louvre and commissioned the architect **Jacques Lemercier** to build the huge edifice, known as the Cardinal's Palace. On his deathbed in 1642, the cardinal left his mansion to Louis XIII, who soon followed him to the grave.

The Royal Palace – The king's widow, Anne of Austria, left the Louvre for the mansion, which was smaller and more comfortable, with her young son, the future Louis XIV. It was henceforth known as the Royal Palace. The Fronde in 1648 forced their hasty departure. When Louis XIV returned to Paris, he settled back into the Louvre, lodging various royal family members in the Palais Royal, including **Queen Henrietta Maria** of France, widow of Charles I of England.

The Orléans – In 1780 the palace passed to Louis-Philippe of Orléans, who, being forever short of money, undertook to redevelop the site: around three sides of the garden, he commissioned the architect **Victor Louis** to build uniformly fronted blocks of apartments over arcades of shops at ground level. Three new streets were called after the younger Orléans brothers: Valois, Montpensier and Beaujolais.

Cardinal Richelieu (1585–1642)

Cardinal Richelieu is often called the first "Prime Minister" in the modern sense of the term, because he was referred to by King Louis XIII as his "Chief" or "First" Minister. Richelieu was a formidable politician who controlled the power of the nobility by suppressing internal opposition to the monarchy. He succeeded in turning France into a strong centralized state.

Cardinal Richelieu - 19C engraving by Richard Woodman

© Georgios Kollidas/iStockphoto.com

A leading character in Dumas senior's novel *The Three Musketeers*, Richelieu is often portrayed, especially in the film adaptations of the book, as being more powerful than the king himself. He had begun his rise to power when appointed Bishop of Luçon in 1606 at the age of 19, after securing a special dispensation from the Pope; by 1614 had been elected as a representative of Poitou at the States-General in Paris. He soon became known as an advocate for the clergy in their efforts to become more involved in politics and be exempt from taxation.

As a result he came to the notice of the regent Marie de' Medici, who introduced him to Anne of Austria, the new wife of King Louis XIII. Richelieu was appointed as her almoner, one who distributes alms (money) to the poor. Soon the influential Concini, then the most powerful minister in France, recognized his talents and appointed him Secretary of State for War and Foreign Affairs.

Richelieu's burgeoning career received a setback in 1617 when Concini was murdered. He accompanied the king's mother, Marie de' Medici, when she was exiled to Blois for apparently siding with her son's enemies – a very wise move as it turned out. During this period Richelieu acted as a go-between for mother and son, leading finally to her reinstatement at Court in 1622. In 1622 Marie persuaded her son to appoint Richelieu as an adviser, and by the year 1622 he had been made a cardinal. The path was now clear for Richelieu's almost inevitable rise to power, and he was appointed "First Minister" in 1624 – a position he held till his death in 1642.

During his ministry, he reformed the French navy and its army, and became known for his severe tactics that crushed rebellions, attacked the Huguenots, and carefully crafted merciless foreign policies that would make France the most powerful country in Europe. Richelieu used somewhat unlikeable means to raise money for the State (aside from taxing the clergy, of course), and paved the way for the royal absolutism that would peak under the reign of Louis XIV.

The Théâtre Français (now the Comédie-Française; *see p246)* and the Palais Royal Theatre at the corner of rue de Montpensier and rue Beaujolais (also still in operation) were added in 1786 and 1790.

After the Revolution, the palace became a gambling house. In 1801 Napoléon converted it into offices, and in 1807 into the Exchange and Commercial Court. Louis XVIII returned the mansion to the Orléans family and it was from there that Louis-Philippe set out for the Hôtel de Ville, in 1830, to be proclaimed king. Richelieu's palace now accommodates the Ministry of Culture, Constitutional Council, and the Council of State (⚷ *closed to the public).*

Visit

Pass through the covered passage into the **main courtyard** enclosed within a continuous arcaded gallery. An impressive central façade surmounted by allegorical statues overlooks the controversial modern composition (280 black and white columns of unequal height) by **Daniel Buren**. Separating the courtyard from the garden is a double colonnade, the Orléans Gallery, built at the time of the Restoration (1814–30) and formerly covered by an iron and glass roof. The Valois side gallery is known as the Prow Gallery because of its nautical decoration (Richelieu was minister for the navy).

Take a detour through the passage leading out of the arcades to the place de Valois, following the rue Montesquieu to the Galerie Véro-Dodat.

Galerie Véro-Dodat

Created in 1826 by two butchers Véro and Dodat, it was one of the first Parisian streets with gas lamps. The interior décor of the covered passage is Neoclassic in style, housing many charming arts and antiques boutiques.

Jardin du Palais Royal★★

The quiet garden has retained its 18C atmosphere, surrounded by the elegant façades designed by the architect Victor Louis. The shops along the gallery are a mix of upmarket couture and art, and dusty stamp and medal collectors. The writer Sidonie **Colette** (1873–1954) died at the age of 81 at 94 Galerie de Beaujolais. **Jean Cocteau** (1889–1963), poet, playwright and film-maker, lived for 20 years in an apartment overlooking the gardens at 36 rue de Montpensier.

Rue de Richelieu

The 19C **Molière** fountain by Visconti with statues by Pradier stands just before no **40**, the site of Molière's house, to which he was taken after collapsing on stage in 1673 at the age of 51. No **61** served as home to Henri Beyle (1783–1842), more commonly known as **Stendhal**, where he wrote his novels *Le Rouge et le Noir* and *Promenades dans Rome*.

A Turbulent History

In 1680 Louis XIV combined Molière's company with the troupe at the **Hôtel de Bourgogne** and granted it the sole right of performance in the capital. The new company took the name Comédie-Française. Caught up in endless quarrels with the authorities at the Sorbonne, the company was constantly on the move. During the Revolution a dispute broke out in the company between players who supported the Republicans and those favouring the Royalists. In 1792 the former, led by Talma, took over the present theatre. Napoléon showed a great interest in the Comédie-Française, and also in the leading lady, Mlle Mars. In 1812 he decreed that the company should consist of an association of actors, active associates, apprentice players and retired players on pension. Today the theatre continues to be managed by a director nominated by the State.

Rue Sainte-Anne

No **47** is the house the composer **Lully** had built in 1671, borrowing 11 000 *livres* from Molière to do so. Note the music masks and motifs ornamenting the façade.

Passage Choiseul

Open since 1827, this passage connects the rue des Petits Champs and the rue St-Augustin. Louis-Ferdinand Céline grew up at the residence at no 64 and no 67. In *Mort à Crédit* (1936) he describes the passage in dazzling language, with a humorous and biting description.

Square Louvois

The square accommodates a fine fountain by Visconti (1884), whose four allegorical sculptures represent France's major four rivers: the Seine, the Rhône, the Loire and the Garonne.

Bibliothèque nationale de France: site Richelieu

58 rue de Richelieu.

The present national collection was founded on François I's library from Fontainebleau, endowed with a copy of every book subsequently printed in France. As of 1998, when printed works and periodicals were transferred to the new buildings at the François Mitterand site (*see BERCY*), this part of the library has kept the specialized collections from Antiquity.

In the 17C the Hôtel Tubeuf was enlarged by Mansart and named after Cardinal Mazarin, whose art collection it housed. The **Mazarin Gallery★** by Mansart is magnificent *(first floor)*. The great staircase leads to the **Medals and Antiques Museum★** *(mezzanine level;* ⊙*Mon–Fri 1pm–6pm, Sat 1pm–5.45pm;* ⊙*1 Jan, 15 Aug, 25 Dec;* ⊛*free entry;* ℘*01 53 79 83 30; www.bnf.fr).*

The arcades

The galleries Vivienne and Colbert date to 1823 and 1826. Vivienne, with natural lighting from the vast glass atrium, is lined with fashion boutiques, old shops and a tearoom. It has retained its original décor of nymphs and goddesses.

Vidoq, the prince of thieves who became a crime writer, lived at no 13. Colbert, restored with its Pompei-style décor, belongs to the National Library; it is open only during expositions or conferences. Be sure to see the elegant Grand Colbert brasserie, dating back to 1900.

Basilique de Notre-Dame des Victoires

The basilica (built 1629–1740) served as the Petits-Pères monastery chapel, dedicated in honour of the king's victories. It served as the Stock Exchange from 1795 to 1809.

Place des Victoires★

In 1685 Marshal de la Feuillade commissioned a statue of the king from the sculptor **Desjardins**. The statue, unveiled in 1686, showed the king, crowned with the laurels of victory, standing on a pedestal adorned with six low-relief sculptures and four captives representing the vanquished Spain, Holland, Prussia and Austria.

The statue was melted down in 1792 and the present equestrian statue of the Sun King was sculpted by Bosio in 1822.

OPÉRA GARNIER★★

Place de l'Opéra, entrance around the back of the rue Scribe. ⊙*Mid-Jul–Sept, daily 10am–5.30pm (except during matinée or special event); Sept–mid-Jul, 10am–4.30pm.* ⊶*Guided tours of the public foyers and museum Wed, Sat, Sun 11.30am, 2.30pm (daily Jul–Aug).* ⊛*10€; 14.50€ with tour.* ⊙*1 Jan, 1 May.* ℘*08 92 89 90 90. www.operadeparis.fr.*

The celebrity of France's first home of opera, the prestige of its ballet company, the architectural magnificence of the great staircase and foyer and the sumptuous decoration of the auditorium make attending a performance here a gala event. It is worth taking the tour of the Opéra, which has recently been completely restored, inside and out.

The Opéra company – The Paris Opéra has been based successively at the Palais Royal Theatre (1673), at the Salle des Machines in the Tuileries Palace (1764),

Façade, Opéra Garnier

© S. Sauvignier/MICHELN

then back at the Palais Royal for great performances of Rameau and Gluck, the Salle Favart (1820), the Salle Le Peletier (1821) and the present Palais Garnier (1875) before being partly transferred to the Opéra Bastille in 1990. Since 1994 the **Palais Garnier** and the **Opéra Bastille** (1989 Carlos Ott) have been collectively known as the **Opéra National de Paris** (ONP).

The opera house – Under Napoléon III the idea for a purpose-built opera house was born. **Charles Garnier**, a 35-year-old unknown architect, was awarded the contract. The large theatre has a vast stage that holds up to 450 performers.

The building – The opera house is considered the most brilliant monument of the Second Empire; its main façade, overlooking the place de l'Opéra, shows off a series of sculpted figures.

Interior★★★ – A feature of the building's originality is Garnier's use of multicoloured marbles quarried in different parts of France: white, blue, pink, red and green. The magnificent **Great Staircase** and the **Grand Foyer** are conceived for sumptuous occasions.

MUSEUMS
Musée des Arts décoratifs★★
111 rue de Rivoli. ○*Tue–Sun 11am–6pm (9pm until Thu).* ○*1 Jan, 1 May, 15 Aug, 25 Dec.* ⊚*11€ (combined ticket with Fashion and Textiles museum).* ♿ ℘*01 44 55 57 50. www.lesartsdecoratifs.fr.*

This museum holds one of the world's leading collections of decorative and applied arts, with 150 000 items. The numerous period rooms provide a broad cross-section of the evolution of design and taste in France from the Middle Ages to the 20C: sculpture, painting, ceramics, furniture, jewellery, glass and tableware. Most of the paintings and sculptures come from churches and monasteries.

Musée de la Mode et du Textile★
107 rue de Rivoli. ○*Tue–Sun 11am–6pm (until 9pm Thu).* ○*1 Jan, 1 May, 15 Aug, 25 Dec.* ⊚*11€ (combined ticket with the Museum of Decorative Arts).* ♿ ℘*01 44 55 57 50. www.lesartsdecoratifs.fr.*

The collection at this museum of fashion and textiles encompasses some 20 000 outfits, 35 000 accessories and 21 000 fabric samples dating from the 18C to the present day, displayed in changing exhibitions. Famous names include Poiret, Lanvin, Schiaparelli, Dior and Paco Rabanne.

Musée de la Publicité
107 rue de Rivoli. ○*Same as for the Musée de la Mode et du Textile.* ♿ ℘*01 44 55 57 50. www.lesartsdecoratifs.fr.*

The museum showcases permanent and changing temporary exhibitions. A **database★** composed of thousands of posters and advertising films is available for consultation.

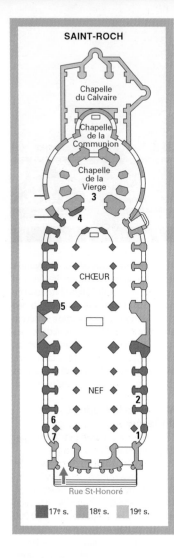

SAINT-ROCH

Chapelle du Calvaire

Chapelle de la Communion

Chapelle de la Vierge

3

4

CHŒUR

5

NEF

2

6

7

1

Rue St-Honoré

17e s.   18e s.   19e s.

1. *Tomb of Henri of Lorraine, Count d'Harcourt by Renard (17C) and bust of the 17C Marshal de Créqui by Coysevox (17C).*

2. *Tomb of Duke Charles de Créqui.*

3. *The Triumph of the Virgin – painted by J B Pierre on the dome. The Nativity at the altar, by the Anguier brothers, was brought from the Val-de-Grâce.*

4. *Resurrection of the Son of the Widow of Naïm by Le Sueur (17C).*

5. *Le Nôtre bust by Coysevox and funerary inscription.*

6. *Baptism of Christ by Lemoyne.*

7. *Baptismal Chapel: frescoes by Chassériau (19C).*

General Napoléon Bonaparte, who was in charge of the defence, mowed down with gunfire the men massed on the church steps and perched on its façade. The bullet holes can still be seen.

The foundation stone of the church was laid by Louis XIV in 1653. Funds quickly ran dry, but work was able to continue as a result of a lottery organized in 1705. Instead of completing the nave, however, a series of chapels was constructed beyond the apse, so that the church's original length (80m/262.5ft) was extended to 125m/410ft. It effectively destroyed the unity of design.

In 1719 a gift of 100 000 *livres* from **John Law**, who had recently converted to Catholicism, enabled the nave to be completed. Robert de Cotte's Jesuit-style façade dates from 1736.

The **Lady Chapel★** by Jules Hardouin-Mansart, with its tall, richly decorated dome, leads into a Communion Chapel with a flat dome and finally a Calvary Chapel, rebuilt in the 19C.

Among those buried in St-Roch in the Lady Chapel and side chapels are the playwright Corneille, the garden designer **Le Nôtre**, the philosophers **Diderot** and d'Holbach, and **Mme Geoffrin**, hostess of a famous 18C salon.

ÉGLISE ST-ROCH★

Some idea of the scale of Baron Haussmann's earth-moving undertakings can be gained from the fact that to enter the church nowadays you have to walk up 13 steps, whereas before the construction of avenue de l'Opéra, you had to go down just seven steps.

On 5 October 1795 St-Roch was the scene of bloody fighting. A column of Royalists leading an attack on the Convention, then in the Tuileries, aimed to march through rue St-Roch. A young

Les Grands Boulevards

The grand boulevards succeeded the ancient walls surrounding Paris. Thronged today with pedestrians hurrying on business or idly window gazing, the broad tree-lined avenues are full of cars, café tables spilling on to the pavement, innumerable cinemas, theatres, brasseries, and a thousand shops, a profusion of signs, advertising slogans and glowing flashing neon at night: the atmosphere lives on. Nearby neighbourhoods include Opéra, Faubourg Poissonnière and République.

A BIT OF HISTORY

The ramparts transformed – In 1660 **Louis XIV** had the city's obsolete fortifications – built between the Bastille and the Madeleine under Charles V, Charles IX and Louis XIII – dismantled and filled in. The land was terraced with a broad carriageway and double rows of trees; triumphal arches replaced the fortified gates. At first the area surrounded by open countryside remained deserted; safe for the odd game of *boules* by day, unsafe after dark.

Around 1750 the boulevard became a fashionable place for fancy carriages and gentry on horseback. Under the Directoire, **boulevard des Italiens,** then **boulevard Montmartre,** were frequented by members of High Society, who built themselves fine town houses and became known as *Boulevardiers* – an epithet for ephemeral, superficial people who flirted with fad and fashion. The roads were paved in 1778, and gas lamps appeared in passage des Panoramas in 1817, and along the boulevards in 1826. The first omnibus appeared in 1828 linking the Madeleine to the Bastille.

The modern boulevards – Hauss-mann's radical urban planning transformed the area by inserting broad avenues between place de l'Opéra and place de la République. The area boasts

Info: Paris Office du Tourisme, 25 rue des Pyramides. ☎08 92 68 30 00 (0.34€ per min). http://en.parisinfo.com.

Location: The Grands Boulevards district is at the centre of the Right Bank, the heart of the boulevards that run from Madeleine to Bastille.

Metro/Transport: Richelieu Drouot (lines 8 and 9), Strasbourg St-Denis (lines 4, 8 and 9), Grands Boulevards (lines 8 and 9) – Buses: 20, 38, 39, 47, 48. Gare de l'Est, Poissonnière, Cadet, Buses: 30, 31, 32, 38, 39, 46, 47, 56, 65.

Parking: There is street parking on the side streets of the boulevards, and underground parking on the rue du Havre, place de Budapest and rue du Faubourg Poissonière.

Don't Miss: The covered shopping passages off the boulevard Montmartre, food shops along the rue du Faubourg St-Denis.

Timing: Allow three hours for the walk, more if you visit the sights and cafés.

Kids: The Grévin Wax Museum fascinates kids of all ages.

a number of famous theatres and night-spots today.

WALKING TOUR

Start from metro Ⓜ *St-Lazare. Maps p243 and pp254-255.*

Quartier Saint-Lazare

Those who dislike crowds should avoid this district. Every morning and evening, thousands of commuters pass through the Gare St-Lazare, northwest of the St-

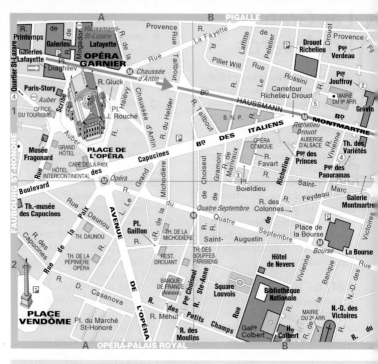

WHERE TO STAY

Hôtel Paradis...............................①	Hôtel Favart.................................③	
Hôtel Chopin...............................②	Hôtel Vivienne.............................④	

Lazare Metro Station, on their way to and from the suburbs.

The major department stores in the area attract yet more people, and the café terraces are a good place to sit and watch the world go by.

The neighbourhood – The St-Lazare mainline **railway station** links northwest France (Dieppe, Caen, Le Havre) with Paris, shuttling people from the suburbs to town or out to the coast and seaside.

The exciting development of the railway was especially well captured by the Impressionist painter **Claude Monet**. The area around it was developed in the 19C to accommodate a middle-class society in standardized, comfortable apartment blocks served by large, convenient department stores.

Place de l'Europe – The major intersection of six important roads straddles the railway lines north of St-Lazare. It also marks the boundary between the bourgeois neighbourhood to the west and a more working-class quarter to the east, as defined at the time of the Restoration and the Second Empire.

▷ Walk east along Bd Haussmann, home to major department stores.

Boulevard Haussmann

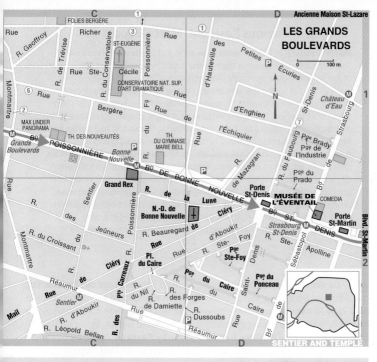

SENTIER AND TEMPLE

Boulevard Haussmann

Printemps (no. 64 ♿ see SHOPPING p444) department store was founded in 1865 and owed its immediate success to its proximity to the train station. It was the first to install lifts. At Christmastime it creates magical window displays for children.

Galeries Lafayette. (no. 40 ♿ see SHOPPING p444) was originally a tiny haberdashery founded in 1895 by Alphonse Khan. Its dome and balustrades were designed by Ferdinand Chanut in 1910. In 1919, the aviator Védrines landed his Caudron G3 on the shop's roof terrace.

Boulevard des Italiens

The history of this thoroughfare, which intersects with Boulevard Haussman, is inextricably linked to that of fashion. At the time of the Directoire, the area was haunted by *Muscadins* – bow-legged and hunched fops in exaggerated garb;

Merveilleuses dressed in high-waisted, transparent dresses in the style of Antiquity or with huge extravagant Turkish-style hats. During the Restoration, such characters were followed by the *Gandins*, moustachioed with side-whiskers, in top hat, cravat and jacket with broad turned-down collar. Under **Louis-Philippe**, the *Dandys* and the *Lions* followed the fashion from across the Channel: they began to smoke in public (1835). The Second Empire was a more sober age; waxed moustaches and close-cut goatee beards appeared, ladies sported crinolines and café society flourished. The boulevard got its name from the acting troupe of the **Opéra-Comique** (along rue Favart), known as the Italians.

Today the area is popular for the proliferation of cinemas and chain restaurants At the western end of the boulevard, the 1889 **Théâtre-Musée des Capucines**

Famous Resident: Marcel Proust

Marcel Proust (1871–1922) spent 12 years at **102 boulevard Haussmann**. The second-floor bedroom is open to the public by appointment. The author of *À la recherche du temps perdu (Remembrance of Things Past)* chose to live in his aunt's flat for the macabre reason that he had witnessed his uncle die there, and this memory might provide inspiration for his writing. Being very susceptible to noise, Proust tended to work at night and struggled to sleep by day through the noise of the boulevard below; to this end he had the bedroom muffled with cork tiles and heavy curtains. There he would spend days on end shut-up in bed, brewing various vapours to help his chronic asthma. His main distraction, other than occasionally venturing out to socialize with the upper classes at the **Ritz**, was the *théâtrephone*, which relayed live performances of opera down an early version of the telephone, at some exorbitant expense. When *Du côté de chez Swann*, the first volume of the collection, was submitted to the Gallimard publishers, it was turned down by André Gide, who subsequently admitted that his decision had been the "gravest mistake ever made".

(no 39 bd des Capucines; ◷*by guided tour Mon–Sat 9am–6pm;* ⊜*free entry; 01 47 42 04 56; www.fragonard.com)* now houses Fragonard's perfume museum, including a display of perfume bottles and distilling equipment. The company's additional **Musee du Parfum** resides at no 9 rue de Scribe *(same hrs, but also open Sun 9am–5pm).*

▶ At the intersection of bds des Italiens and Haussman, detour left on to rue Drouot.

Hôtel des Ventes Drouot Richelieu

9 rue Drouot. ◷*call or go online for hrs.* ☏*01 48 00 20 20. www.drouot.com.* Since 1980, antique dealers, collectors, and experts have conducted business in a lively way in this **auction house,** one of the world's oldest. But furniture, silver service, jewellery, art and other collectibles are first displayed for future sale. Rue Drouot is also the haunt of stamp collectors.

Boulevard Montmartre

In 1836 the famous Jockey Club was located on the corner of rue Drouot. At no 7 is the **Théâtre des Variétés**, built in 1807 for the actress and theatre director Mlle Montansier; Offenbach's opera *La Belle Hélène* was performed here.

Behind is the **passage des Panoramas**, which was opened in 1799 and leads to the Stock Exchange (La Bourse). At no 10 is Musée Grévin (◉*see MUSEUMS).* Nearby **Passage Jouffroy** has small cafés and interesting shops.

Boulevard Poissonnière

At no 1, the **Cinéma Grand Rex** is a temple to the glory of the silver screen. Its Baroque décor and large screen make the building one of Europe's landmark cinemas. ♟♟ **Les Étoiles du Rex** *(*◷*Wed–Sun 10am–6pm;* ⊜*11€; under-18 years 9€;* ☏*08 25 05 44 05; www. legrandrex.com),* a 50min interactive tour in French, reveals the backstage legends and stars of Europe's most famous film theatre.

Side street **rue du Faubourg Poissonnière** was the last leg of the fish-traders' journey from the coast to the wholesale markets at Les Halles.

Just before Porte St-Denis, the **view★** of the crossroads of **rue de Cléry**, rue Beauregard and **rue de la Lune** gives an idea of what Paris looked like in the 19C.

Porte St-Denis★

This impressive gate, 24m/78.7ft high, was erected in 1672 by the architect and military engineer Nicolas François Blondel to celebrate Louis XIV's victorious campaigns on the Rhine. Said to be the inspiration for the Arc de Triomphe, it has on its southern façade a bas relief that represents the crossing of the Rhine. On the northern façade, the king is shown taking control of Maastricht. The kings would return to their capital from attending mass at the Basilica at St-Denis along Rue St-Denis and through the arch – the same route followed by Napoléon's troops after a victorious campaign in 1816. The last monarch to pass through the arch was Queen Victoria in 1855, when she visited the Grand Exposition Universelle.

▶ Detour left on to rue du Faubourg St-Denis.

Ancienne maison Saint-Lazare
107 rue du Faubourg St-Denis.
In the Middle Ages this was the capital's leper house. St Vincent de Paul died here in 1660. It's been a hospital since 1935.

Porte St-Martin★
Like the nearby Porte St-Denis, this gate was commissioned by Louis XIV and erected in 1674 to commemorate the capture of Besançon and the defeat of the German, Spanish and Dutch armies. A mere 17m/55.8ft high, the arch was designed by Pierre Bullet. On the southern façade, an inscription in Latin

Staires on Boulevard St-Martin

© S. Sauvignier/MICHELIN

states, "To Louis the Great, for having vanquished the German, Spanish and Dutch armies: the Dean of the Guild and the Aldermen of Paris."

Boulevard St-Martin
This street leads down to place de la République. The area was built up on an old rubbish dump, hence the undulations and the need for laying the road at a different gradient and level from the pavements.

MUSEUMS
👥 Musée Grévin★
10 boulevard Montmartre. ◷Mon–Fri 10am–6.30pm, Sat–Sun 10am–7pm (last admission 1hr before closing). ◉24.50€; 15-17 years 21.50€; 6-14 years 17.50€. ♿ ℘01 47 70 85 05. www.grevin.com.
Grévin, a caricaturist, founded the museum in 1882. In addition to **waxen effigies** of famous politicians, artists and sportspeople and re-creations of momentous historical and contemporary events in the form of tableaux, there is a hall of mirrors. Live conjuring sessions also add to the magical entertainment on offer.

Musée de la Franc-Maçonnerie★
16 rue Cadet. ◷Tue–Fri 10am–12.30pm, 2pm–6pm; Sat 10am–1pm, 2pm–7pm;. ◉6€. ♿ ℘01 45 23 74 09. www.museefm.org.
A large room in this modern building accommodates a collection of documents (Constitution of Anderson from 1723), badges, and portraits that encapsulate the history of the main Masonic lodge of France.

Musée de l'Éventail
2 boulevard de Strasbourg. ◷Sept–Jul Mon–Wed 2pm–6pm. ◷Aug and public holidays. ◉6.50€. ℘01 42 08 90 20. www.annehouget.fr/musee.htm.
Occupying an 1893 exposition hall with interior décor of the period of Henry II, this museum is dedicated to fans and fan-making. Grouped by theme, some 2 000 examples date from 17C to 20C.

Pigalle

A century ago, Pigalle was home to painters' studios and literary cafés such as the influential Nouvelle Athènes Café. Today, the cosmopolitan crowd is attracted by the neon lights of cabarets, nightclubs, bars and sex shops: a milieu at once racy and romantic.

👣 WALKING TOUR

Place de Clichy

Restaurants, cinemas, theatres and clubs make Pigalle a hub of Paris nightlife. The bustling **square** was the site of one of Ledoux's toll-houses, defended by Marshal Moncey in 1814 against the Allies.

▶ Follow **boulevard de Clichy** to **place Blanche**, the site of a former plaster quarry now famous for the neon red windmill of Moulin Rouge.

Moulin Rouge

Opened in 1889, this famed cabaret and its legendary **cancan** were immortalized by the painter Toulouse-Lautrec in 1891, and continue to attract visitors from around the world today.

▶ Take rue de Bruxelles to the **place Adolphe-Max**, with its artist ateliers and the superb gated residence at no 10. Continue down rue de Ventimille to rue Ballu, lined with elegant mansions and courtyard gardens and the **Villa Ballu** passageway.

Emile Zola lived at **no 23** rue Ballu, with its pretty Art Nouveau balcony, in 1867.

▶ Take rue Blanche to rue Chaptal.

Rue Chaptal

The **Théâtre du Grand-Guignol** at the end of the Cité Chaptal was known for its gruesomely realistic horror plays, now home to the Théâtre 347. At no 16 is a hidden cottage and artist atelier of the **Musée de la Vie Romantique** (*Tue–Sun 10am–6pm; free entry; 01 55 31*

Info: 72 bd Rochechouart. 08 92 68 30 00 (0.34€ per min). http://en.parisinfo.com.

Location: Pigalle lies at the foot of Montmartre's southern hillside.

Metro/Transport: Place de Clichy (lines 2 and 13), Pigalle (lines 2 and 12), Blanche (line 2) – Buses: 30, 54, 67.

Parking: Along the boulevard de Clichy.

Don't Miss: The garden tearoom at the Musée de la Vie Romantique.

Timing: Allow 90 minutes for this neighbourhood.

95 67; www.vie-romantique.paris.fr), former home of the painter **Ary Scheffer** (1795–1858), who hosted a salon frequented by Delacroix, Liszt and the writer **George Sand** *(her manuscripts and personal objects on the ground floor)*.

▶ Follow the rue Henner, where the poet **Apollinaire** lived at no 9 in 1907, then rue La Bruyère to rue J B Pigalle.

On the left is the cobblestoned **Cité Pigalle**, where a plaque in the back on the right notes that **Van Gogh** lived on the fourth floor.

▶ At the top of J B Pigalle, take rue N D de Lorette to **rue de la Rochefoucauld.**

Gustave Moreau National Museum★

14 rue de la Rochefoucauld. Mon, Wed, Thu 10am–12.45pm, 2pm–5.15pm; Fri–Sun 10am–5.15pm. 6€. 01 48 74 38 50. www.musee-moreau.fr.
The 19C painter bequeathed his house and collection of 50 paintings, 7 000 drawings, 350 watercolours and wax sculptures to the State in 1895.

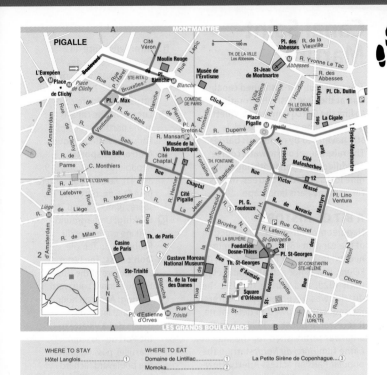

▶ Turn right on **rue de la Tour des Dames**, lined with mansions in which theatre stars, painters and writers lived in the late 19C. Continue to the neo-Renaissance **Église de la Trinité** (1867, Théodore Ballu). Follow rue Blanche to rue St-Lazare and rue Taitbout.

At no 80 the London-style buildings of the **square d'Orléans** were home to Alexandre Dumas Père, Chopin and George Sand in the 19C.

▶ Backtrack and turn left on rue St-Georges, past **Théâtre St-Georges** with its trompe l'œil façade.

Place St-Georges

The statue is of *Puech et Guillaume*, two characters popularized by the satirical cartoonist Gavarni (1804–66). The **Fondation Dosne-Thiers**, at no 27, is part of the Institut de France, housing a history library open to the public. At no 28 the **Hôtel de la Païva** is a neo-Renaissance

mansion (1840) built for Thérèse Lachmann, Marquise de Païva.
Continue to **place Gustave-Toudouze**, turn right on to **rue de Navarin**, with its neo-Gothic façades at no 9, then a left on the **rue des Martyrs**, named for the first Christian martyrs of the Butte Montmartre. The **Cité Malesherbes** at no 59 has some lovely mansions.
Turn left on **rue Victor Massé**, a street of musical instrument shops. Avenue Frochot was once home to Alexandre Dumas, Jean and Auguste Renoir, and Toulouse-Lautrec. Next door is the Art Nouveau stained glass of the historic **Théâtre en Rond**, now a billiards hall.

Place Pigalle

Named for the sculptor Baptiste Pigalle (1714–85), the square was a centre of literary cafés and artists. It and boulevard de Rochechouart are now lined with sex shops, bars and nightclubs such as the **Élysée-Montmartre** (*no 72*) and **La Cigale** (*no 120*).

Canal Saint-Martin★

This peaceful, old-fashioned canal, dug at the time of the Restoration to link the Ourcq Canal at La Villette with the Seine via the Arsenal, is still navigated by numerous barges. The raised level of the watercourse straddled with iron footbridges, its nine locks and rows of trees, makes for a serene Paris landscape.

A BIT OF HISTORY

Napoléon ordered the construction of the canal in 1802 to provide much-needed fresh water from the Canal de l'Ourq. It was not actually completed until 1825, and during the 19C the district was occupied by labourers. Subsequently allowed to deteriorate, it received a boost in 1938 when the area was refurbished for the Marcel Carné film *Hôtel du Nord*, starring the popular Parisian actress Arletty. However, during the 1960s the canal began to fall into disuse. New boutiques and trendy cafés opened in the past 10 years have renewed interest in the canal, now popular with strolling tourists who like to watch the barges navigate the locks, locals with their picnics, and "bourgeois bohemian" professionals who snap up the canalside apartments.

Info: Paris Office du Tourisme, 25 rue des Pyramides. ℘08 92 68 30 00 (0.34€ per min). http://en.parisinfo.com.

Location: The canal is in the northeast end of Paris, above République.

Metro/Transport: République (lines 3, 5, 8, 9 and 11), Jacques Bonsergent (line 5), Goncourt (line 11), Jaurès (lines 2, 5 and 7B).

Parking: Underground parking on the rue du Faubourg du Temple.

Don't Miss: The historic architecture of the Hôpital St-Louis' inner courtyard.

Timing: Allow an hour. The canal links the Bassin de La Villette to the Port de l'Arsenal (Bastille), passing under the boulevard Richard Lenoir. After walking along the canal from the République to La Villette, you can return by boat.

Kids: Kids of all ages enjoy the canal cruises to La Villette.

Strolling along the Canal Saint-Martin

© Y. Kanazawa/MICHELIN

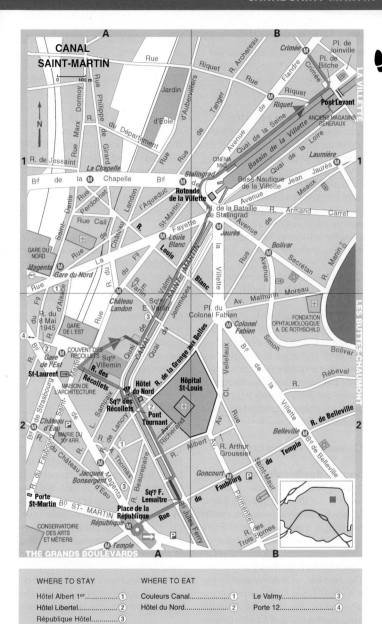

WHERE TO STAY

Hôtel Albert 1er...............①
Hôtel Libertel..................②
République Hôtel.............③

WHERE TO EAT

Couleurs Canal...................①
Hôtel du Nord....................②

Le Valmy...........................③
Porte 12............................④

Arletty – The vivacious Arletty was one of the most famous actresses of the 1930s, representing the typical *Parisienne* with her cheeky humour and tough-girl accent. Born in the Paris suburbs of Courbevoie as Léonie Bathiat in 1898, she got her start in theatre before taking on roles in *Hôtel du Nord*, *Les Visiteurs du soir* (1942) and *Les Enfants du paradis* (1944) under director Marcel Carné. After some lesser rolls, she retired from acting in 1963 and died in 1992.

WALKING TOUR

Start from place de la République, take rue du Faubourg du Temple as far as boulevard Jules Ferry. Turn left on to square Frédéric Lemaître.

Square Frédéric Lemaître

From here there is an attractive **view** of one of the canal's locks. The canal disappears into an underpass, resurfacing beyond place de la Bastille as the Arsenal Basin (*see BASTILLE). Follow the canal, climbing with it as it passes through nine locks. The tiny squares give way to metal footbridges.* When a barge gliding along the still waters has to negotiate a lock, the canal comes to life.

◯ Take avenue Richerand to visit the Hôpital St-Louis via rue Bichat.

Saint-Louis Hospital

Built in the early 17C, this hospital pioneered the science of dermatology. The brick and stone buildings of the **central courtyard★** are reminiscent of place des Vosges and place Dauphine. Flower-decked courtyards separate the buildings of steeply pitched roofs and dormer windows.

◯ Return to St-Martin Canal.

Square des Récollets

A **swing bridge** crosses the canal, connecting rue de Lancry and rue de la Grange aux Belles. Between two smaller footbridges is the square named after a Franciscan convent that stood nearby.

Montfaucon Gallows

This area was once dominated by gallows that could hang up to 60 condemned people at a time. After the assassination (1572) of Admiral Coligny, his body was displayed here. Although already in disuse in the 17C, the gallows were not dismantled until 1760.

Hôtel du Nord

102 quai de Jemmapes.
This building lent its name to the film by Marcel Carné (*see A Bit of History, above*), who reconstructed the canalside setting in his studio. Today it is a trendy café-restaurant.

◯ Continue along the canal to place Stalingrad.

Rotonde de la Villette

Place de la Bataille de Stalingrad.
The rotunda, one of the ring of tollhouses designed by Ledoux, serves as a storehouse for archaeological finds.

◯ Follow the left-hand quay of the Bassin de la Villette.

The walk finishes with the impressive sight of the **transporter bridge** in rue de Crimée, which opens to let boats pass from the Bassin de la Villette to the Canal de l'Ourcq.

◯ The Crimée metro station is a few steps away to the left. It is also possible to walk back along the other side of the Bassin as far as the Jean-Jaurès metro station.

BOAT TRIPS★

Beginning at the Canal de l'Arsenal at the place de la Bastille, boat trips pass through the nine locks for a 2.5-hour tour to the Bassin de la Villette. The boats pass through the tunnel built by Baron Haussmann in 1860, which is 1 854m/6 082ft long, lit and ventilated by openings at street level. Underneath place de la Bastille, it is possible to see the grilles of the crypt where those killed in the uprisings of 1830 and 1848 are buried.
The boat resurfaces after the place de la République, and continues along the peaceful canal shaded by plane trees.

Paris Canal Cruises

Cruises on the Seine and Canal St-Martin between the Musée d'Orsay and the Parc de la Villette depart mid-Mar–mid-Nov daily 10.30am and 2.30pm at Parc de la Villette, and 9.45am and 2.45pm from the Musée d'Orsay; 19€, children 12€. Reservations required. ℘01 42 40 96 97. www. pariscanal.com.

Arrondissements 11-12

Bastille and Faubourg Saint-Antoine

Scene of the historic revolutions of 1789, 1830 and 1848, the place de la Bastille remains a symbolic rallying point for demonstrations, marches and public celebrations, dominated by the commemorative July Column and the Opéra Bastille. It's also a popular student nightspot, with a lively bar and club scene. Nearby, the old, densely populated streets around the Faubourg St-Antoine have been the centre of the cabinet-making industry for centuries; today they retain the charm of their former days despite the influx of high-street shops and bars.

☙ WALKING TOURS
Start from the Arsenal marina.

① BASTILLE

The Bastille prison – Charles V built this fortified residence in the 14C using forced labour recruited by press-gangs from passers-by. Besieged seven times in periods of civil strife, it surrendered six times. Political prisoners included the Man in the Iron Mask and Voltaire.
The taking of the Bastille – On 14 July 1789 a militant crowd rallied and marched first to the Invalides to capture arms, then on to the Arsenal and the Bastille. By late afternoon the Bastille was seized and the seven remaining prisoners were freed. The fortress was immediately demolished, 83 of its stones being carved into replicas and sent to the provinces. The following year there was dancing on the site.

Place de la Bastille

Paving stones mark out the ground plan of the former Bastille, best seen from the corner where rue St-Antoine meets the place. **Colonne de Juillet**, a bronze column (52m/171ft high) crowned by the figure of Liberty, serves as a memorial crypt for the Parisians killed during the uprisings of July 1830 and 1848.

ℹ️ Info: Paris Office du Tourisme, 25 rue des Pyramides. ℘08 92 68 30 00 (0.34€ per min). http://en.parisinfo.com.

Ⓜ Metro/Transport: Bastille (lines 1, 5 and 8), Ledru Rollin (line 8), Faidherbe Chaligny (line 8) or Nation (lines 1, 2, 6 and 9) – RER: Nation (line A) – Buses: 20, 65, 69, 76, 86, 87, 91.

▶ Location: Located on the eastern edge of the Marais, the place de la Bastille sits at the crossroads of the boulevards Richard Lenoir and Beaumarchais, the rues du Faubourg St-Antoine and St-Antoine, and the Port de l'Arsenal. The area of Faubourg St-Antoine lies east of place de la Bastille.

🅿 Parking: Underground parking can be found along the Port and the rue St-Antoine, avenue Daumesnil and avenue Ledru Rollin. Street parking is available along the boulevards.

🐾 Don't Miss: Tours of the Opéra Bastille, or the colourful open-air and covered markets at the place d'Aligre.

👫 Kids: The Port de l'Arsenal has a small playground in the gardens overlooking the houseboats.

🕐 Timing: Allow an hour to visit the Bastille area and another two hours for Faubourg St-Antoine.

Opéra de Paris Bastille★

☙*By guided tour (1hr 15min)only, call for go online for hours. ⊕12€ cash only. ℘01 40 01 19 70. www.operadeparis.fr.*

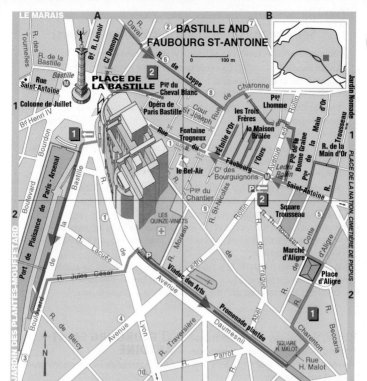

WHERE TO STAY		Grand Bleu........................③		Les Sans-Culottes...............⑧
Hôtel Paris Bastille.......①		La Biche au Bois...............④		Swann et Vincent...............⑨
WHERE TO EAT		La Gazzetta.....................⑤		Traversière.........................⑩
Barrio Latino................①		La Pirada.........................⑥		
Blue Elephant..............②		Le Café Moderne..............⑦		

Designed by Carlos Ott, this massive glass and marble building is often likened to a ship. The curvilinear, utilitarian structure accommodates a 2 700-seat auditorium with several revolving stages for quick scene changes, workshops housing 74 different trades and rehearsal rooms.

Port de Plaisance de Paris-Arsenal

This pleasure port, a former moat of Charles V's fortifications, connects the Seine to the Canal St-Martin, which runs beneath the boulevard Richard Lenoir and resurfaces at République.

Note the cannon and mortar on the rooftop balustrade of **L'Arsenal** (*entrance: 1 rue de Sully*), recalling

the original function of the building. In 1512 the city set up a cannon foundry, which Henri II later converted to a royal arsenal producing gunpowder among other things. Destroyed in an explosion (1563), the Arsenal was rebuilt and inhabited by Sully, until Louis XIII finally closed the cannon works.

Viaduc des Arts★

The stone and pink-brick viaduct that used to carry the old suburban railway has also been put to new and better use. The 60 restored vaulted archways house a variety of businesses – silver- and **goldsmiths**, cabinet makers, fine art and sculpture restorers, and craft boutiques.

265

Some of the Great Ébénistes (Cabinet Makers)

Associated with the Louis XV and Louis XVI style are the following:

André Boulle (1642–1732): furniture supplier to the court, the most distinctive feature is the exquisite quality of brass and tortoiseshell inlay. His style enjoyed a revival during the Second Empire.

Charles Cressent (1685–1768): his bureaux and commodes are perhaps the most elegant of the Regency style, embellished with curvilinear ornamental ormulu (gilded bronze) mounts.

Jean-François Oeben (1720–63): the master of Riesener and Leleu; marks the transition between the Louis XV and Louis XVI styles. His intricate geometric marquetry and furniture with hidden mechanisms are particularly famous.

Jean-François Leleu (1729–1807): the master of the Louis XVI style at its most grandiose, rich in ormolu *appliqués* to complement overall design.

Jean Riesener (1734–1806): 30 workshops and retail outlets on rue St-Honoré. Highly successful, he was one of the innovators of the Louis XVI style. His mahogany chests of drawers and *bureaux* with bronze mounts are distinctively sober in form and line.

Georges Jacob (1739–1814): established near Porte St-Martin, he dominates furniture design between Louis XVI and the First Empire. Renowned for his armchairs, he is credited with the invention of the *fauteuil à la reine*.

Above, the railway has been transformed into a pedestrian promenade (🐾*see below*) with trees, gardens and shaded arbours.

▶ Follow the route marked on the map to visit **Place d'Aligre** and the **marché d'Aligre**, its vegetable stalls and flea market.

👥 Promenade plantée★

Enter via the stairs at av Daumesnil.

Train service came to a standstill; the grass grew tall, then the train tracks that connected the Bastille to the suburbs from 1859 to 1969 (giving Parisians a chance to breathe the country air in the Bois de Vincennes or the riverbanks of the Marne) were replaced by a pedestrian walkway measuring 4.5km/14.8mi long.

Lindens, hazelnut trees, climbing vines and aromatic plants line the promenade, while the distant sound of traffic down below makes it clear you're still in Paris. The promenade offers a unique perspective on Paris as you walk between the residential buildings, with an up-close view of architectural details that are missed on street-level.

② FAUBOURG SAINT-ANTOINE

Start from rue du Faubourg St-Antoine.

Craftsmen's Liberties – In the 12C Louis XI allowed the fortified Royal Abbey of St-Antoine to dispense justice locally and exempted the craftsmen from the rules of the powerful and restrictive guilds. From 1657 the cabinetmakers of St-Antoine were licensed by Colbert to replicate pieces from the royal workshops, to use exotic woods instead of being bound to oak, and to develop the decorative use of bronze and marquetry. These freedoms helped create the independent spirit of the *faubourg*.

National workshops – At 31 rue de Montreuil, **Réveillon** pioneered the production of painted wallpapers, but the crowded conditions in his workshops provoked social unrest that erupted into violence on 28 April 1789, forcing the industrialist to flee.

The Revolution soon followed, and incorporated guilds were abolished. In the face of mechanization and labour-saving industrial processes, traditional multi-skilled craftsmen had to evolve specialized trades to survive. Small workshops abounded, but still in June 1848 when the national workshops were disbanded, the unemployed rallied to build numerous barricades in protest, leading to further Revolutionary violence in the *faubourg*.

Rue du Faubourg St-Antoine

The street is lined with furniture shops and the surrounding area honeycombed with courtyards and arcades, often with picturesque names, such as **Le Bel-Air★** (no 56), **l'Étoile d'Or** (no 75), **les Trois Frères** (no 83) and **l'Ours**. On the corner with rue de Charonne, **Fontaine Trogneux** is an attractive fountain from 1710.

Cour Damoye

🕐*Closed Sunday morning.*

Ateliers of sculptors and painters, a boutique selling festival posters, silk painting and a tea shop are a few of the businesses here. In the middle of the charming passage decorated with flowerpots and ivy, an old iron freight lift from the 1920s used to service a concrete factory.

Rue de Lappe

This street was the legendary Parisian street of the *bals populaires*, or **dance halls**, until World War II. Le Balajo is the only survivor of these dance halls frequented by the *apaches*, or street gangs. Its name comes from Jo, who created his own *Bal à Jo*.

▷ Enter the doors at no 24, no 26 (Cour St-Louis with its little statue at the entry) or no 34 (you'll have to enter through the café); they lead to a leafy courtyard.

Passage Lhomme

If the weather is nice, you may see the furniture artisans working in their ateliers in this flowered courtyard. In the centre are some of the last fireplaces made in the 18C to power steam engines.

Passage de la Bonne Graine

This passage "of the Good Grain" was once occupied by grain merchants. In the middle of the alley is the shiny sign of the cabinet maker Rinck, founded in 1934. Across from it is the atelier of the embroiderers (tassels for curtains and decorative braiding) Boulet Frères. Further on is the Maison Dissidi, who have specialized for centuries in the reproduction of fine furnishings.

Rue Trousseau

At no 22, sunflowers and daisies adorn the building's floors.

At the corner of rue Trousseau and rue Delescluze, the **Jardin Nomade** is a community garden of individual plots that welcomes children.

NEARBY
Place de la Nation

This square was originally named the Throne Square in honour of the throne erected for the official entry into Paris by Louis XIV and his bride, the Infanta Maria-Theresa, in 1660. It was renamed place du Trône Renversé (the Overturned Throne) by the Convention in 1794, and a guillotine was set up. It was given its present name on 14 July 1880, the first anniversary celebrations of the Revolution.

Dalou (1838–1902) took 20 years to perfect his monumental bronze group, **Le Triomphe de la République★** (11m/36ft high and 38t in weight). The two columns on either side of avenue du Trône represent Philippe Auguste and St Louis.

Cimetière de Picpus

🕐*Mid-Apr–mid-Oct Mon–Sat 2pm–6pm; rest of the year Mon–Sat 2pm–4pm.* ✆2€. ☎01 43 44 18 54.

In 1794, the guillotine in place de la Nation claimed 1 306 lives. The bodies were placed in two communal graves located in a sand quarry nearby. Later on, the families of the victims bought the surrounding ground and turned it into a cemetery. The *champ des martyrs* (martyrs' field), planted with cypress trees, can be seen through a railing.

Bois and Château de Vincennes★★

Vincennes is known for its vast woodland with its natural attractions, its famous zoo, beautiful flower garden and racecourse, making it one of the capital's most popular recreation areas. It also boasts a mighty fortress, once a royal residence that witnessed some of the most dramatic events in French history.

A BIT OF HISTORY

The forest – Philippe Auguste enclosed the wood as a royal hunt with a wall 12km/7.4mi long and stocked it with game in the 12C. **Charles V** built a small château within it on a low hill. In the 17C the forest became a fashionable place to walk. A military firing range was opened in 1798, the first of a series of enclaves in the forest made exclusively for military purposes. Napoléon III ceded the estate at Vincennes – excluding the château and military installations – in 1860 to the City of Paris, to be made into an English-style park, after London's Hyde Park.

The château – (♿see p272) This medieval Versailles has two distinct features within its walls: a tall forbidding keep and majestic 17C buildings. Mazarin, appointed governor of Vincennes in 1652, had symmetrical **royal pavilions** built by Le Vau to frame the main courtyard facing south over the forest. In 1660 the young Louis XIV spent his honeymoon in the King's pavilion.

Other uses – From the beginning of the 16C to 1784, the keep, no longer favoured as a royal residence, was used as a State prison. The disgrace of detention in Vincennes was far less than at the Bastille. Among the most famous were the Great Condé, the Prince de Conti, Fouquet (guarded by d'Artagnan), **Diderot** and Mirabeau. In 1738 part of the château became a porcelain factory, transferred to **Sèvres** in 1756.

Info: Paris Office du Tourisme, 25 rue des Pyramides. ☎08 92 68 30 00 (0.34€ per min). http://en.parisinfo.com.

Location: The park lies at the southeastern border of Paris.

Parking: Street parking possible outside the Parc Floral.

Don't Miss: Sign up for a tour of the recently restored château keep (donjon).

Timing: Allow an entire day to enjoy the Bois de Vincennes.

Kids: The Parc Floral has train rides, mini-golf and jungle gyms. Also the zoo, aquarium and farm.

The military establishment – Under **Louis-Philippe**, Vincennes was incorporated into the Paris defence system: a fort was built beside the château, the ramparts were reinforced with massive casemates, and the complex virtually buried below glacis. Under Napoléon the château had been converted to a formidable arsenal. The towers were reduced to the height of the perimeter wall and mounted with cannon, the rampart crenellations were removed, and the keep reverted to a prison.

On 24 August 1944 the Germans, before their departure from the castle, shot 26 resistance fighters, exploded three mines, breaching the ramparts in two places and damaging the King's Pavilion, and set fire to the Queen's Pavilion.

Restoration – The first restoration of Vincennes was entrusted by **Napoléon III** to **Viollet-le-Duc**. Repair work carried out sporadically has lasted over a century and has only recently been completed. The main courtyard looks again much as it did in the 17C, the moat around the keep having been redug, the 19C casemates removed and the pavilions and keep restored.

King Charles the Wise (1337–80)

Although Kings Philippe Auguste and St Louis of the House of Capet were the first to have a manor house on the site of Vincennes, it was not until the next century that King Charles V of the Valois dynasty actually had a château built there.

Born at Vincennes in 1337, Charles became Dauphin of France in 1350 on the accession to the throne of his father King Jean II the Good. He was, in fact, the first heir to the French throne to use the title, derived from the Dauphiné region, which had belonged to his grandfather. He was regent from 1356 until 1360 (and again in 1364) during the captivity of his father in England following the end of the disastrous (for the French) first phase of the Hundred Years War, in which a large part of western France was ceded to the English by the Treaty of Brétigny.

On becoming king in 1364, he set about recovering the lost territories and had the good sense to recognize the military talents of the minor Breton nobleman du Guesclin. A great part of the lands conceded under the treaty were eventually regained under the generalship of du Guesclin, with the added bonus that he was able to rid France of the Tard-Venus, or mercenary soldiers who had terrorized the southwest following the end of the hostilities. He simply hired them and took them to Spain, where they became engaged in the civil war then raging.

Not all of Charles' policies were quite so successful. For example, towards the end of reign his support for the anti-Pope Clement VII over the legitimately elected Urban VI, brought about the Papal Schism, which was to split Europe for 40 years. However, the sobriquet "Wise" remained with him due to his many astute decisions, among which he managed to stabilize the currency, create a standing army and a powerful navy. Also, he was a patron of the arts and amassed a large library of books, having many classic texts translated into French to enable his advisers to read them.

THE WOODS

The vast woodlands incorporate many walking, cycling and equestrian trails as well as three lakes: the **Lac Daumesnil★** *(to the west),* the **Lac des Minimes** *(to the east)* and the **Lac de Gravelle** *(to the south),* all popular focal points for walkers and boaters alike.

The islands are accessible across bridges: **Île de Reuilly** has a café and **Île de la Porte Jaune** has a restaurant. There are usually bike rental stands and pony rides on weekends near the Porte Dorée end of Lake Daumesnil.

The thousand-year-old **Foire du Trône** (Throne Fair), formerly known as the Foire aux Pains d'Epice or **Gingerbread Fair**, is held each spring *(Palm Sunday–Easter)* on the Reuilly Lawn near Lake Daumesnil. The fair recalls a con-cession obtained in 957 by the monks of St Antoine's Abbey to sell a piglet-shaped rye, honey and aniseed bread in memory of their saint during Holy Week. Nowadays the yearly fun fair is better known for its flashy midway and stomach-churning rides.

Centre bouddhique du Bois de Vincennes

40 bis route de Ceinture du Lac Daumesnil. ◷*Apr–Oct call or go online for hours.* ✆*001 43 41 02 49. www.bouddhisme-france.org.*

South of Lake Daumesnil, the Buddhist Temple of Paris is housed in a 1931 Colonial Exhibition building. The roof has 180 000 tiles carved with an axe out of a chestnut tree. Inside is a monumental gilded statue of Buddha (9m/29.5ft).

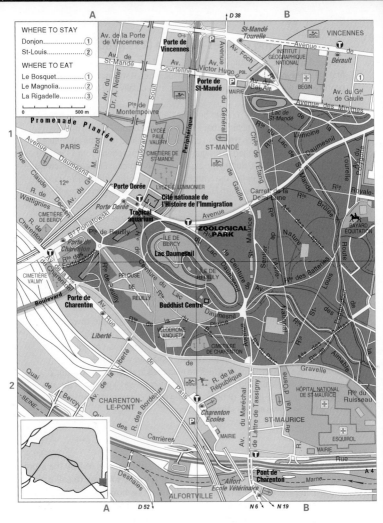

Duc d'Enghien

From the bridge over the moat can be seen, at the foot of the Tour de la Reine on the right, the column marking the spot where the Duc d'Enghien, Prince of Condé, was executed by a firing squad on 20 March 1804, accused of plotting against Napoléon (his body was exhumed on the orders of Louis XVIII and reburied in the Royal Chapel).

♟♟ Palais de la Porte Dorée★★

293 avenue Daumesnil. ◷*Tue–Fri 10am–5.30pm, Sat–Sun 10am–7pm.* ℘*01 53 59 58 60. www.palais-portedoree.fr.*

This palace has housed a **tropical aquarium** (*⊚5€; children 3.50€*) since 1931. Thousands of aquatic creatures are housed here, from Asia, Africa, South America and elsewhere, including crocodiles, sharks and piranha fish. The Palais also hosts the **Cité nationale de l'histoire de l'immigration** (*⊚6€, under 18 years free*), a museum on the history and culture of immigration.

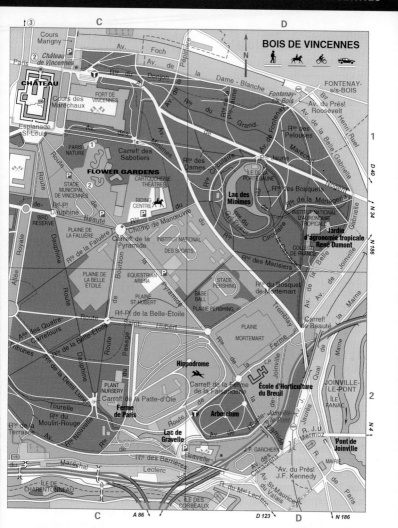

👥 Parc zoologique de Paris★★

53 avenue Daumesnil. 🕐*Mar–mid-Oct Mon–Fri 10am–6pm, Sat–Sun 9:30am–7:30pm; rest of the year daily 10am–5pm.* 💶*22€; 12-25 years 16.50€, 3-11 years 14€.* 📞*08 11 22 41 22. www.parczoologiquedeparis.fr.*

To the west of the park, 535 mammals and 600 birds of some 82 different species live in natural surroundings close to their familiar habitat at this zoo. Around 120 births take place every year. At the centre is an artificial rock 65m/213ft high inhabited by wild mountain sheep.

Arboretum de l'École du Breuil

Route de la Ferme. 🕐*Daily Apr–Sept 9.30am–8pm; Oct and Mar 9.30am–6.30pm; Nov–Feb 9.30am–5pm.* 💶*Free.* 📞*01 53 66 14 00.*

Created in 1867, the school specializes in horticulture and landscape design; it has lovely gardens. The arboretum extends over 12ha/29.6 acres and includes 2 000 trees of 80 different species.

Hippodrome

Route de la Ferme.

This former royal racecourse, created in 1863, spans 42ha/104 acres. It is one of the most modern of tracks, still in use.

Daumesnil's Refusals

In 1814 when the Allies called for the surrender of Vincennes, the then governor, **General Daumesnil**, known as Peg Leg having lost a leg at the Battle of Wagram, retorted "I'll surrender Vincennes when you give me back my leg". At the end of the Hundred Days, the castle was again called to surrender, and there came a second refusal. Five months later, however, the doors were opened to Louis XVIII.

In 1830 Daumesnil was still governor as insurgents attempted to attack Charles X's ministers imprisoned in the keep. The governor refused them entry, announcing that before surrendering he would blow himself and the castle sky-high.

🧑‍🤝‍🧑 Ferme de Paris

Route du Pesage. ⊙*Jul–Aug and Easter vacation Tue–Fri 1.30am–5.30pm, Sat–Sun 1.30am–6.30pm; Apr–Jun and Sept Sat–Sun 1.30am–6.30pm; rest of the year call for hours.* ✆*Free entry.* ☏*01 71 28 50 56.*

This is a working farm, with cows, sheep, pigs, fruit trees and wheat fields to help educate children about food production. There are demonstrations of cow milking and sheep shearing.

PARC FLORAL★★

Route de la Pyramide. ⊙*summer daily 9.30am–8pm; winter 9.30am–6.30pm.* ✆*5.50€; free entry Sept–Jun.* ♿☏*01 43 28 39 75. www.paris.fr.*

The flower gardens, landscaped by Collin in 1969, extend over 30ha/75 acres and include hundreds of species.

The **Vallée des Fleurs** is delightful all year round. The pavilions tucked away amid pine trees around the lake, together with the Hall de la Pinède, house exhibitions and shows (art, dance and horticulture). Alleyways lined with modern sculpture (*The Tall Woman* by **Giacometti**, *Stabile* by **Calder**, the polished-steel *Chronos* by Nicolas

Schöffer) suggest an open-air museum. The **Dahlia Garden** from Sceaux, south of Paris, has been re-created near the Pyramid *(in flower Sept–Oct)*. The water garden with its water-lilies and lotus is at its best Jul–Sept. There is also a **Four Seasons Garden**, as well as gardens growing medicinal plants *(best seen May–Oct)*, irises *(May)* and bamboo. Flower shows are held throughout the year: orchids *(early Mar)*, tulips *(from Apr)*, rhododendrons and azaleas *(from May)*. In summer an outdoor jazz festival is held *(weekends)* in the Delta pavilion.

CHÂTEAU DE VINCENNES★★

⊙*May–Aug, 10am–6pm, Sept–Apr, 10am–5pm. Tickets and audio-guides at the Accueil Charles V.* ⊙*1 Jan, 1 May, 1 and 11 Nov, 25 Dec.* ✆*8.50€.* ☏*01 48 08 31 20. www.chateau-vincennes.fr.*

Philippe Auguste built the first manor house in the 12C, to which Louis IX added a chapel. The king was known to receive his subjects quite unceremoniously at the foot of an oak. Construction of the castle began under Valois Philippe VI, and in Charles V's reign, it was completed, in 1396.

Outside the walls

A walk round the outside of the château, following the embankment around the moat, provides a good sense of scale. The **Tour du Village★**, a massive tower 42m/138ft high, which survived the 19C alterations, served as the governor's residence in the Middle Ages, where he could survey the drawbridge entrance. Continue down the **Cours des Maréchaux** along the perimeter wall. It was in the penultimate of the five truncated towers along the east wall, the Tour du Diable, that the porcelain factory was established. The arcades of the Classical Vincennes portico, overlooking the forest and closing the perimeter wall on the south side, come into view as you reach the château esplanade. The **Tour du Bois** in the middle was reduced by Le Vau in the 17C when he transformed the gate into a state entrance (appearing as a triumphal arch from inside).

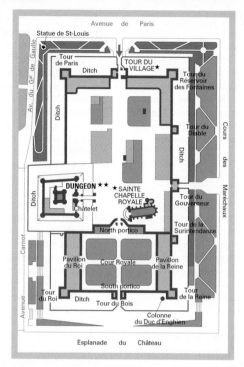

Cour Royale

The main courtyard is closed to the north by a portico, framed by the two royal pavilions. Anne of Austria and Louis XIV's brother lived in the Pavillon de la Reine, where the governor, Daumesnil, died of cholera in 1832; the last royal occupant was the Duke of Montpensier, Louis-Philippe's youngest son. Mazarin died in the Pavillon du Roi in 1661.

Donjon★★

On the western side, the walls are dominated by the impressive **keep** *(donjon)*, erected in 1337, a fine surviving example of medieval military architecture. The 52m/170.6ft-tall tower is enclosed by a fortified wall and a separate moat. The base of the stone wall was reinforced to protect against sapping (breaching defences by undermining a wall), and turrets defended the corners. At sky level, a roofed sentry path, complete with battlements, and machicolations with gun embrasures below, ran right around the inner tower.

The ground floor served as the kitchens. The main room on the first floor originally served as a royal reception room hung with tapestries.

Mirabeau was imprisoned for three years in one of the towers, where he wrote a scathing condemnation of royal warrants.

A wide spiral staircase leads to the second floor and the royal bedchamber. Henri V of England, Charles VI's son-in-law, died of dysentery in this room in 1422.

Chapelle Royale★

The Royal Chapel, begun by Charles V in the 14C in place of the one built by **St Louis**, was completed only in the 16C during the reign of Henri II.

The building is pure Gothic; the façade with its beautiful stone rose windows is Flamboyant.

The windows in the chancel are filled with unusually coloured mid-16C **stained glass★** featuring scenes from the Apocalypse.

273

Bercy★

Once the historic centre of the wine-bottling industry, Bercy was transformed in the 1990s into an entertainment district, with a 13ha/32-acre riverside park, a large stadium, shops and cinemas. The massive premises of the Ministry of Finance dominate the whole area.

⚡ WALKING TOUR

The Ministry of Finance
Transferred from its former home in the Rivoli wing of the Louvre, the Ministry occupies a massive modern structure straddling the embankment expressway with a foothold in the Seine.

Palais omnisports de Paris-Bercy
This sports complex was built in 1994 to stage international indoor sporting events. Outside, grass-covered walls slope down at 45°.
In the square to the east of the stadium, an fountain with a gully, the Canyoneaustrate by Gérard Singer, recalls geological formations in the North America.

Cinémathèque française
51 rue de Bercy. Ⓜ*Bercy.* Ⓜ*Museum Mon, Wed–Sat noon–7pm, Sun 10am–8pm.* ≋*5€.* ✆*01 71 19 33 33. www.cinematheque.fr.*

🄸 **Info:** Paris Office du Tourisme, 25 rue des Pyramides. ✆08 92 68 30 00 (0.34€ per min). http://en.parisinfo.com.

▶ **Location:** Bercy stretches along the Right Bank of the Seine in southeast Paris, with the Ministry of Finance at one end and Bercy Village at the other.

🅿 **Parking:** There are several underground parking garages around the stadium, park and Bercy Village cinemas.

🚫 **Don't Miss:** The Cinémathèque française within the renovated Frank Gehry building, and the historic Maison du jardinage in the park.

🕐 **Timing:** The main sights can be seen in about an hour or two.

👪 **Kids:** There are several play areas within the Parc de Bercy.

Designed by architect Frank Gehry, the Cinémathèque houses both a cinema **museum**, with a permanent collection as well as temporary exhibits, and a **theatre** for regular screenings *(Wed–Mon; call or go online for prices)* that

Passerelle Simone-de-Beauvoir over the Seine

© athor/Fotolia.com

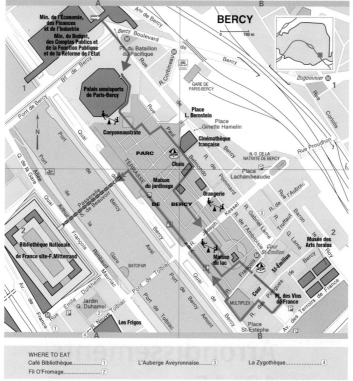

showcase directors, periods, and styles from France and around the world. A cinema library and research centre are also on-site.

Parc de Bercy★

A few old wine storehouses have been left standing as historical landmarks. There are three sections to the Parc de Bercy: a vast expanse of grass lawns at the northwest end, and two gardens divided by the rue J Kessel. The eastern one (named in honour of the assassinated Israeli President Yitzhak Rabin) includes an orchard, a vegetable garden, a vineyard and a rose garden. The romantic garden to the east has a small lake and a hilltop labyrinth.

Cour Saint-Émilion – Bercy Village★

The former stone warehouses have been converted and now house boutiques, wine bars and a cinema.

Musée des Arts forains

53 avenue des Terroirs-de-France.
℘01 43 40 16 22. www.pavillons-de-bercy.com.
The Museum of Fairground Art has a remarkable collection of merry-go-rounds, barrel organs, and other colourful objects of fun fairs of bygone days.

Bibliothèque nationale de France: site F. Mitterrand★

○Tue–Sat 10am–7pm (lower level 8pm), Mon 2pm–7pm (lower level 8pm), Sun 1pm–7pm (lower level closed Sun).
○Public holidays and 2nd–4th Mon in Sept. ∞3.50€, free after 5pm.
℘01 53 79 59 59. www.bnf.fr.
Designed by Dominique Perrault, the library is set atop a vast rectangular esplanade planted with trees. The tall buildings represent the shapes of four open books, framing the central esplanade and sunken gardens. A cineplex and cafés line the western edge.

Arrondissements 13–15

La Butte-aux-Cailles

This charming hillside neighbourhood popular with students and locals is known for its tiny garden houses, natural hot spring pool, and cobblestone streets lined with laid-back cafés and bars.

LES GOBELINS

You may have admired Gobelins tapestries hanging in many of the great museums and great houses, but the history of their manufacture is less well known. An opportunity to see these national treasures being made in the traditional style should not be missed.

In about 1440 the dyer, **Jean Gobelin**, who specialized in scarlet, set up a workshop beside the River Bièvre. The work continued through the generations until the reign of Henri IV, when it was taken over by two Flemish craftsmen summoned by the king (early 17C).

Under Louis XIV the tapestry and carpet-weaving industry around the Gobelins workshops became, in 1662, the Manufacture Royale des Tapisseries de la Couronne (Royal Factory of Tapestry and Carpet Weavers to the Crown). The artist **Charles Le Brun** was appointed as director. Five years later it became associated with the Manufacture Royale des Meubles (Royal Cabinet Makers).

Info: Paris Office du Tourisme, 25 rue des Pyramides. ✆08 92 68 30 00 (0.34€ per min). http://en.parisinfo.com.

Location: The district sits on the south edge of the Latin Quarter.

Metro/Transport: Place d'Italie (lines 5, 6, 7) – Buses: 27, 47, 83, 91.

Parking: Underground parking is available at the Italie 2 commercial centre.

Don't Miss: The Bièvre river running through square René Le Gall.

Timing: Allow two hours to visit the neighbourhood.

Kids: A large play area can be found at the Square René-Le-Gall.

The greatest craftsmen, including goldsmiths and gilders, thus worked side by side to decorate and furnish the sumptuous palaces of the Sun King and create a Louis XIV style.

Today the work continues within the walls of buildings as old as the 17C.

The Four Great French Tapestry Workshops

Aubusson: producing hangings for the lesser 17C and 18C aristocracy and bourgeoisie; subject matter includes floral and organic compositions, animals and beasts, Classical mythology and landscapes. Rococo chinoiseries and pastoral scenes (after Huet) are also common.

Beauvais: very finely woven often with vivid coloured silks which, unfortunately, have faded. Motifs include grotesques, Fables after La Fontaine (by Oudry), Boucher's figures from the Commedia dell'Arte, Classical mythology, chinoiseries, and pastoral scenes (after Huet). The use of 18C designs continued into the 19C.

Felletin: coarser-weave hangings with rustic subject matter.

Gobelins: sumptuous hangings often interwoven with gold. Renowned for the originality of design, series include The Seasons and Elements, The Life of the King, The Royal Residences, Louis XV at the Hunt, as well as paintings by Oudry and Boucher (*Loves of the Gods*). Their most influential weaver during the late 18C was Neilson, a Scot.

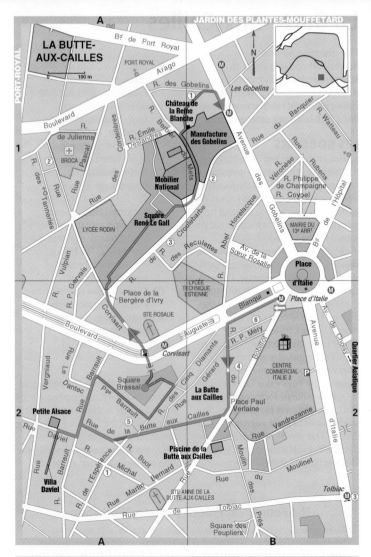

Manufacture des Gobelins★

42 avenue des Gobelins. Workshops: 🚶🚶*By guided tour (1.5hr) only, Tue– Thu (except holidays) 1pm.* 🎫*9€ (includes Galerie). Galerie des Gobelins* 🕐*Tue–Sun 11am–6pm.* 🎫*6€ (free last*

Sun of month). 🕐*1 Jan, 1 May, 25 Dec.* 📞*01 44 08 53 49. www.mobiliernational.culture.gouv.fr.* On the tour, visitors observe working methods that have changed little since the 17C: warp threads are set by daylight, the colours being selected from a range of more than 14 000 tones.

Each weaver, working with mirrors, completes up to 8sq m/1.2 to 9.6sq yd per year depending on the design.

Tapestry exhibitions take place regularly in the **Galerie des Gobelins**, the 400-year-old building with its handsome brick and stone façade.

☁ WALKING TOUR

Start from place d'Italie and end at the Gobelins workshops.

Place d'Italie

This square stands on the edge of an area bristling with high-rise buildings. The 19C local council building *(mairie)* stands opposite the contemporary Italie 2 commercial centre.

▶ Take boulevard A Blanqui, then follow rue du Moulin des Prés (first left) as far as place Paul Verlaine.

La Butte-aux-Cailles

In 1783, after taking off from the vicinity of La Muette, the physicist **Pilâtre de Rozier** landed his hot-air balloon on this mound, then occupied by several solitary windmills. His was the first free-flight in a hot-air balloon.

Today the hilltop is one of surprising contrasts as old cobblestone streets and low-lying houses slowly give way to modern blocks of flats with new urban development. The brick Art Deco brick building houses a municipal **swimming pool** (piscine) opened in 1924. Its water comes from a natural hot-water spring.

▶ Take rue de la Butte aux Cailles to its end, turn left then right on rue Daviel.

At no 10, **Petit Alsace★** is an ensemble of timbered houses dating back to 1912 that frame a courtyard and a garden. At no 7, opposite, the **Villa Daviel★** aligns its brick pavillons with gardens in the front.

▶ Retrace your steps and turn left on to rue Barrault. Cross boulevard Aug. Blanqui and take rue Corvisart.

Square René Le Gall

Rue de Croulebarbe and rue Berbier du Mets drive the River **Bièvre** (seen in the corner of the park) underground.

Up to the 17C the willow-bordered stream was sparkling clear water, and ice taken from the surrounding marshes in the winter was packed into wells and then covered with earth. This activity gave the locality its name, **Glacière**, meaning ice house. Dyeing, tanning and bleaching turned the river murky and foul-smelling; in 1910 it was filled in.

▶ Exit via rue de Croulebarbe.

The **Mobilier National** building was designed by Auguste Perret (1935); the two concrete hounds are the work of André Abbel.

▶ Follow the first street on the left, rue Berbier du Mets, then continue along rue G Geffroy.

The **Château de la Reine Blanche** *(no 17)* was probably named after Blanche de Bourgogne, the unfaithful wife of Charles IV. It was here in 1393 that Charles VI was almost burned alive at one of the festivities organized on his physicians' orders to cure his insanity.

▶ Rue G Geffroy leads to avenue des Gobelins and the Gobelins factories.

QUARTIER ASIATIQUE

In the 1960s the underdeveloped part of the City known as the "Triangle de Choisy" consisted of the area around avenue de Choisy, **avenue d'Ivry** and the boulevard Masséna south of the place d'Italie. Authorities built several tower blocks and by the early 1970s immigrants from Southeast Asia settled in the area. The Tang Frères shop *(av de Choisy at av Edison)* is a good introduction to this "Chinatown". Chinese, Thai and Vietnamese restaurants are nearby.

Port-Royal

The Port-Royal neighbourhood is centred on the crossroads of boulevard de Port Royal and avenue de l'Observatoire, where traffic lanes are separated by a pretty garden. Underground in Denfert-Rochereau lie the disused quarries that became the catacombs, now filled with several million skeletons, while above ground is a pleasant district with residential and commercial avenues refashioned by Haussmann.

🐾 WALKING TOUR
Start from place C. Jullian.

Avenue de l'Observatoire
The wide avenue with its central flower borders is lined with university buildings. The **Observatory Fountain★** (1873) by Davioud is known for its famous four quarters of the globe by Carpeaux.

▶ Take rue du Val de Grâce, to the right off the boulevard St-Michel.

Val de Grâce★★
1 place Alphonse Laveran.
In the early 17C Mother Angélique Arnauld ordered the construction of Port-Royal, the dependency of the Jansenist Port-Royal-des-Champs. Anne of Austria visited the community frequently to pray and discreetly to plot against Richelieu. At age 37 Anne, who had been married 23 years, was still childless; she promised the gift of a magnificent church if her prayers were answered; she kept her vow on the birth of Louis XIV in 1638.
Plans for the Val de Grâce church were drawn by **François Mansart**, and the foundation stone laid by the young king himself in 1645. Val de Grâce became a military hospital in 1793. On-site is the Musée de Service de Santé des Armées. The **church★★** *(free access Sun 11am for mass)*, probably the most Roman-looking in France, was erected in the Jesuit style.

ℹ Info: Paris Office du Tourisme, 25 rue des Pyramides. ✆08 92 68 30 00 (0.34€ per min). http://en.parisinfo.com.

▶ Location: Port-Royal lies below Luxembourg Gardens on the Left Bank. Denfert Rochereau sits at the intersection of boulevards Raspail and St-Michel.

Ⓜ Metro/Transport: RER: Port Royal (line B) – Buses: 38, 83, 91. Denfert Rochereau (lines 4 and 6) – RER: Denfert Rochereau (line B) – Buses: 38, 68.

Ⓟ Parking: Underground on the boulevard du Montparnasse and beneath Place Denfert Rochereau.

⊘ Don't Miss: The impressive architecture of Val de Grâce. The typically Parisian cafés and shops of the rue Daguerre.

Kids: Older kids tend to enjoy the creepy Catacombes.

Ⓣ Timing: Allow an hour to visit this area, a further two to visit all the sights.

The **dome★★** is frescoed by Mignard with 200 figures three times life-size. In the former convent, beyond the porch *(right of the church)* is the Classical cloister, with two superimposed tiers of bay and a mansard roof. The pavilion used by Anne of Austria is distinguished by its porch with ringed columns.

▶ Follow rue St-Jacques across bd de Port Royal.

Ancienne Abbaye de Port-Royal
✆01 39 30 72 72.
The convent became, in turn, a prison, a home for abandoned children and finally the Baudelocque maternity hospital in 1818. All that remains of the

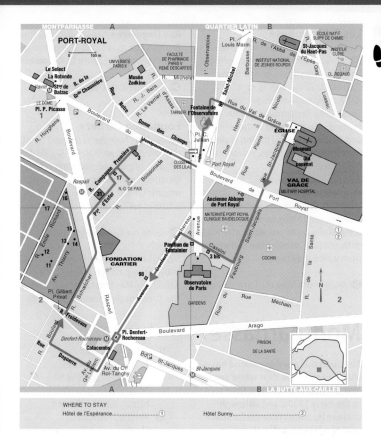

former abbey are the Hôtel d'Atry, the cloisters, the chapel and the chapter-house, which has retained its period woodwork.

▶ Follow Avenue Denfert-Rochereau.

Observatoire de Paris★

℘01 40 51 22 21. www.obspm.fr.
On orders from **Colbert** and to plans by **Claude Perrault**, construction was begun at the summer solstice in 1667, and completed in 1672.

Important **discoveries** at the Observatory include the calculation of the true dimensions of the solar system (1672), the exact determination of longitudinal meridians (Louis XIV remarked that the Academician's calculations had considerably reduced the extent of his kingdom), a calculation of the speed of light, the production of a large map of the moon (1679) and the discovery by mathematical deduction of the planet Neptune by **Le Verrier** (1846).

The four walls face the cardinal points of the compass, the south side of the building determines the capital's latitude, and its median plan is bisected by the **Paris Meridian**, calculated by the astronomer Arago in 1667. It determined 0° longitude until 1884, when Greenwich Mean Time was adopted.

Place Denfert-Rochereau

The reduced bronze version of Bartholdi's Lion in the middle of place Denfert Rochereau commemorates Colonel Denfert-Rochereau, who defended Belfort in 1870–71. The two elegantly proportioned buildings adorned by sculpted friezes are examples of Ledoux's city gates and toll-houses that punctuated the city's fortified wall, built 1784–91.

Les Catacombes★

Entrance: 1 place Denfert-Rochereau.
🕐*Tue–Sun 10am–8pm (last admission 7pm). 130 steps down, no restrooms.*
🕐*Public holidays.* 💶*10€.* ✆*01 43 22 47 63. www.catacombes.paris.fr.*

These Gallo-Roman quarries were transformed into ossuaries between 1785 and 1810 with several million skeletons from Parisian cemeteries, notably of the Innocents.

After walking down 130 steps and through long access tunnels, visitors come to the entrance of the Catacombes, where femurs, skulls and tibias are artfully arranged along the walls with plaques naming the cemeteries from which they came.

▶ Walk south from the Catacombes.

Montparnasse★

Although this neighbourhood has changed since the days when artists and philosophers made it their own in the early 1900s, and although chain restaurants now vie for space with the famous cafés, it is still a great place to spend an evening, have a drink, see a film, enjoy a meal and feel the energy of the crowd.

A BIT OF HISTORY

Mount Parnassus – The debris from age-old quarries formed a deserted, rough grass-covered mound. Students came to freely declaim poetry, naming this wild place Mount Parnassus after the sacred mountain where Apollo entertained his Muses.

A pleasure ground – At the time of the Revolution, cafés and cabarets mushroomed on the city's outskirts, and the polka and the cancan were first introduced to Paris. As the sprawl continued, Haussmann intervened, organizing the area into neighbourhoods around the villages Plaisance, **Vaugirard** and Montrouge, accessed by rue de Rennes, boulevard Arago and boulevard d'Enfer (now boulevard Raspail).

Rue Daguerre★ has small shops. **Rue Froidevaux** runs along Montparnasse Cemetery; nos 21–23 are 1920s ateliers.

▶ Take rue Victor-Schoelcher to boulevard Raspail.

Fondation Cartier★

🕐*Tue–Sun 11am–8pm (Tue until 10pm).*
🕐*1 Jan, 25 Dec.* 💶*10.50€.* ♿✆*01 42 18 56 50. http://fondation.cartier.com.*

Devoted to contemporary art, Cartier mounts temporary exhibits of budding artists as well as those well-known.

▶ Go to rue Campagne Première.

Modigliani (no 3), Man Ray (no 31 bis), and, at the passage at **no 17**, Picasso, Kandinsky, Max Ernst and Miró lived on this street, as did other artists.

> 🛈 **Info:** Paris Office du Tourisme, 25 rue des Pyramides. ✆08 92 68 30 00 (0.34€ per min). http://en.parisinfo.com.
>
> Ⓜ **Metro/Transport:** Montparnasse Bienvenüe (lines 4, 6, 12 and 13), Edgar Quinet (line 6), Vavin (line 4), Gaîté (line 13) and Raspail (lines 4 and 6) – Buses: 28, 48, 58, 82, 89, 91, 92, 94, 95, 96.
>
> Ⓟ **Parking:** Street and underground parking on boulevards and the Tour.
>
> ⊚ **Don't Miss:** The charming Musée Bourdelle, views from Tour Montparnasse.
>
> 🕐 **Timing:** Allow two hours to half a day.
>
> 👪 **Kids:** The Jardin Atlantique is popular with kids of all ages.

Bohemian Montparnasse – At the turn of the 19C, avant-garde artists, poets and writers moved to Montparnasse

View from Tour Montparnasse

© William Fawcett/iStockphoto.com

following a lead set by **Henri Murger**, who had already described the lifestyle in his *Scenes of Bohemian Life*. Newcomers included **Apollinaire**, Max Jacob and Jean Moréas.

The former Wine Pavilion from the 1900 Exhibition was reconstructed at no 52 **rue de Dantzig**. The main pavilion, circular in shape, with a cubist roof, accommodated 24 painters in narrow cells or "coffins" on two floors, thereby earning its name **La Ruche**, meaning Beehive. It replaced the **Bateau Lavoir** (*see MONTMARTRE*) by providing lodging and studios to impoverished, often foreign, artists, notably Modigliani, **Soutine**, Chagall, **Zadkine** and Léger. From such cramped quarters emerged the Expressionist movement.

Discussion and debate were animated by Russian political exiles (Lenin, Trotsky), composers (Stravinsky, Satie and the Six), foreign artists and writers (Hemingway, Foujita, Picasso, Eisenstein, Blasco Ibañez, **Man Ray**, Cendrars, Fargué, André Breton, **Cocteau**). This was the golden age of the **Paris School**, lasting into the mid-1930s, and ending with the outbreak of war in Spain and Western Europe.

This former international bohemian quarter became entirely Parisian in the post-war materialistic age, frequented by the trendy set and sporty "stylish" hatchback cars. Cocktail bars began to replace the old-time cafés, late-night opening stretched ever further into the morning – such was the American influence of the 1950s. During the 1960s, the pace became too much; Aragon, Cocteau, **Braque**, **Sartre**, de Beauvoir continued to be glimpsed, but already the likes of Foujita, Picasso, Chagall had moved on.

Today there are still quiet patches of traditional Parisian streets, but the busy Maine-Montparnasse complex has become the nucleus of a neon-lit business area where locals and out-of-towners are drawn to the shops, cafés, cinemas and nightclubs. Montparnasse has two faces: the modern tower, train station and place de Catalogne, and the traditional cafés and theatres reminiscent of the area's bohemian past.

WALKING TOUR

Start on bd du Montparnasse at pl du 18 Juin 1940.

Place du 18 Juin 1940

Until 1967 this site was occupied by a railway station, remembered as Général Leclerc's headquarters during the liberation of Paris, and where, on 25 August 1944, the German military governor surrendered. Today the square is lined with cinemas and cafés. The Centre Commercial houses department stores and luxury boutiques.

Tour Montparnasse★★

33 avenue du Maine. ○Apr–Sept daily 9.30am–11.30pm; rest of the year Sun–Thu 9.30am–10.30pm, Fri–Sat and day

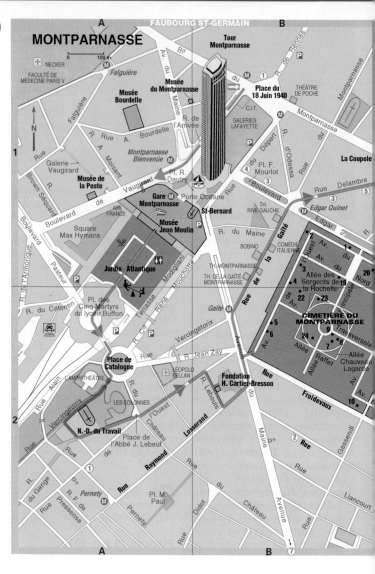

before public holidays 9.30am–11pm. Last admission 30min before closing. ⊙15€. ℘01 45 38 52 56. *www.tourmontparnasse56.com.* Completed in 1973, this 209m/685.7ft-high tower dominates the whole quarter, adding a very tall, modern landmark to the Paris skyline. The foundations are sunk to a depth of 70m/229.7ft, bearing 120 000t of masonry and shafts.

It takes 40 seconds to reach the 56th floor observatory, from which a magnificent **panorama★★★** of Paris and its suburbs unfolds, including the Eiffel Tower in the distance.

Also at the observatory level is a bar and a panoramic restaurant. From the open roof terrace *(59th floor)*, the view can extend as far as 50km/31mi in clear weather.

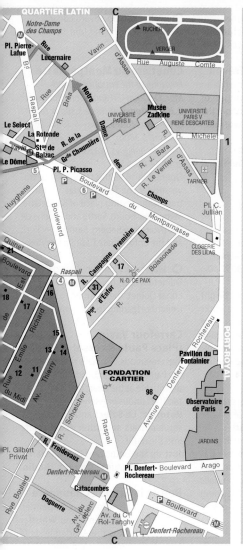

Gare Montparnasse

This immense 18-storey glass, steel and concrete block **train station** on five levels connects with the metro and supplies every amenity, even a small chapel to **St-Bernard** (*entrance at no 34*) – the lectern was carved from a railway sleeper.

A massive concrete slab suspended over the tracks has been laid with a large expanse of garden, the **Jardin Atlantique**★. Typical of Paris' modern green oases, it appeals to all the senses, with textured walkways, fountains and colourful flowers.

Place de Catalogne

The two six-storey, strikingly modern yet Neoclassical buildings were designed by Ricardo Bofill around oval squares. The continuous semicircular façades of the stone Amphithéâtre surround a vast sunken disc-shaped fountain in the centre.

▷ Walk beneath the arch formed by the façade. Continue down rue Vercingétorix and past the park.

Église Notre-Dame du Travail

This unusual church (1900) with an audacious metal interior structure of bare iron girders is meant to honour the combined ideals of work and worship.

▷ Turn left and go behind the church; continue along rue l'Ouest and turn right on to rue Lebouis.

Fondation Henri Cartier-Bresson

2 Impasse Lebouis. ◷*Tue–Sun 1pm–6.30pm (Wed until 8.30pm), Sat 11am–6.45pm. Last admission 30min before closing.* ∞*7€.* ℘*01 56 80 27 00. www.henricartierbresson.org.*

Installed on several levels in a bright atelier, the foundation houses the works of the famous and prolific photographer **Henri Cartier-Bresson** (1908–2004). There are also regularly scheduled projections, videos, debates and conferences on photography.

▷ Turn right on to rue R. Losserand.

Rue Raymond Losserand

Once the main road from the village of Vanves into Paris, this market street was renamed in 1945 after a local municipal representative executed by the Germans in 1942. Be sure to note the charming cobblestone passage, rue Thermopyles (*no 91*).

▷ Walk to avenue du Maine, turn left, then turn right on to rue de la Gaîté.

Rue de la Gaîté

Lined with cabarets, restaurants, dance halls and other places of entertainment, this road has been synonymous with pleasure since the 18C. Its reputation is maintained today by the **Montparnasse** Theatre (no **31**), the **Gaîté Montparnasse** Theatre (no **26**), the famous **Bobino** Music Hall (no **20**), the **Comédie Italienne** (no **17**) and the **Rive Gauche** Theatre (no **6**).

▷ Walk along boulevard Edgar Quinet, away from the Tour, to the cemetery.

Cimetière du Montparnasse

Free map at the entrance. ◷*Mid-Mar–Oct Mon–Fri 8am–6pm, Sat 8.30am–6pm, Sun 9am–5.30pm; rest of the year Mon–Fri 8am–5.30pm, Sat 8.30am–5.30pm, Sun 9am–5.30pm.* ◷*Public holidays.* ∞*Free entry.* ℘*01 44 10 86 50.*

Opened in 1824, this tranquil spot traversed by shaded avenues of linden trees is the resting place of Baudelaire, Serge Gainsbourg, Sartre and Simone de Beauvoir, Jean Seberg, Samuel Beckett, and the unfortunate Captain Dreyfus.

▷ Walk back along boulevard Edgar Quinet towards the Tour as far as place Edgar Quinet, then turn on to rue Delambre leading to carrefour Vavin.

Carrefour Vavin (Place Pablo Picasso)

This crossroads, originally the summit of the Parnassus Mound, continues to bustle with life at the heart of the old quarter. The famous brasseries **Le Dôme**, **La Rotonde**, **Le Sélect** and **La Coupole** serve oysters and other delights late into the night.

Just up the boulevard Raspail stands the famous statue of **Balzac** by **Rodin**.

Rue de la Grande Chaumière

At no 10 is the Académie Charpentier, where Gauguin, Manet and Whistler worked; no 14 is the Académie de la Grande Chaumière, open since 1904, where the Russian and Polish artists of the Paris School worked.

A bit further, the Sennelier boutique sells its art supplies, including the oil pastels that Henri Sennelier developed especially for Picasso.

Rue Notre Dame des Champs

Note the interesting sculptures on the façade of no 82. Fernand Léger lived in the atelier at no 86 at the end of his life. In the other direction, at no 53, is the **Lucernaire**, an experimental theatre with two cinemas, a restaurant and the popular Avant-Scène café.

Place Pierre-Lafue

On this tiny island between boulevard Raspail and rue Notre-Dame des Champs is the statue by Louis Mitelberg (aka "Tim", 1919–2002) called *Hommage au Capitaine Dreyfus*.

MUSEUMS

Musée Bourdelle★★

18 rue Antoine Bourdelle. ◷*Tue–Sun 10am–6pm (last admission 30min before closing).* ◷*Public holidays.* ◉*Free for permanent collection; fees vary for temporary exhibits.* ✆*01 49 54 73 73. www.bourdelle.paris.fr.*

The house, garden and studio of **Antoine Bourdelle** (1861–1929) have been converted to display the artist's sculptures, paintings and drawings. Having studied under Rodin, he found his work evolving from an animated naturalistic figurative style to a more stylized and archaic one modelled on Romanesque, Byzantine and Gothic examples. In the great hall are the original plaster prototypes for his large sculptures cast in bronze, including **Heracles the Archer★★**. Outstanding items among his immense output include the huge bronzes now in the garden and his portrait busts of his contemporaries (**Rodin**, Anatole France). The bronze **Head of Apollo★**, *Rodin Working* and the 21 **portraits of Beethoven★** are in the second series of studios.

The 1992 extension to the museum, designed by Christian de Portzamparc, presents all the studies and fragments relating to the *Monument to Adam Mickiewicz*, erected near place de l'Alma, and the 1870 *War Monument* in Montauban.

Musée de la Poste★

34 boulevard de Vaugirard. ◷*Mon–Fri 10am–6pm.* ◷*Public holidays.* ◉*5€.* ✆*01 42 79 24 24. www.ladressemuseedelaposte.com. Permanent exhibit closed in Oct 2014 for renovation; reopening 2017.*

The museum presents an attractive account of the postal services through the ages, from incised clay tablets from 2500 BC, medieval manuscripts on parchment and carrier pigeons to the 18 000 French post offices of today. Of particular note are the stamp printing and franking machines displayed, a complete collection of French stamps since the first issue in 1849 and exhibits of other national collections.

Musée du Montparnasse

21 avenue du Maine. ◷*Tue–Sun 12.30pm–7pm (last admission 15min before closing).* ◷*1 May, 14 July.* ◉*6€.* ✆*01 42 22 91 96. http://en.parisinfo.com.*

The ivy-covered artists' studios, former studio of the Russian painter Maria Vassilieff, exude a charm from another era. Exhibits recounting the history of the district and its artists are changed every four months.

Musée du Général Leclerc de Hautecloque et de la Libération de Paris – Musée Jean Moulin

Jardin Atlantique. ◷*Tue–Sun 10am-6pm (last admission 15min before closing).* ◷*Public holidays.* ◉*Free for permanent collection.* ✆*01 40 64 39 44. http://museesleclercmoulin.paris.fr.*

Exhibits are dedicated to documents, photographs and artefacts commemorating two French heroes of World War II, one a symbolic figure for the Free French, the other a hero of the Resistance.

Musée Zadkine

100 bis rue d'Assas. ◷*Tue–Sun 10am–6pm.* ◷*Public holidays.* ◉*Free entry.* ✆*01 55 42 77 20. www.zadkine.paris.fr.*

This tiny cottage atelier tucked between the large surrounding buildings features 300 sculptures in stone and wood by **Ossip Zadkine** (1890–1967), a Russian-born French artist; they span Cubism to abstraction. Zadkine was a talented artist to the extent that he has been likened to Picasso. The small museum is often quiet, so it makes a pleasant stop on a walk around Montparnasse.

Parc Montsouris★

The Montsouris Park forms a large green open space to the south of the city, a real haven of peace with a lake, open lawns, century-old trees and colourful flowerbeds. The surrounding streets are lined with quaint small houses, while the Cité Universitaire explores the many styles of international architecture.

A BIT OF HISTORY

Vast Transformation– Following Haussmann's instructions, **Jean-Charles Adolphe Alphand** began work on the area, undermined as it was by quarries and capped by dozens of windmills in 1868. By 1878 he had turned it into a 16ha/39-acre English-style park with paths snaking up the mounds and circling the cascades, and a large artificial lake (the engineer directly involved in the construction committed suicide when the lake suddenly dried out on opening day).

At the turn of the 19C, painters attracted by the park's peace and its proximity to Montparnasse came to live here, notably **Douanier Rousseau** and Georges Braque.

THE PARK

🕑*Mon–Fri from 8am, Sat–Sun from 9am; closing hours vary.* 🆓*Free entry.* ✆*01 46 57 70 18.* http://equipement.paris.fr. The park is decorated with sculptures, including the **South bearing** *(mire Sud)* of the Paris **meridian**. The city's mete-

- 🛈 **Info:** Paris Office du Tourisme, 25 rue des Pyramides. ✆08 92 68 30 00 (0.34€ per min). http://en.parisinfo.com.
- ▶ **Location:** Montsouris is in southeastern Paris, on the Left Bank.
- Ⓜ **Metro/Transport:** Porte d'Orléans (line 4) – RER: Cité Universitaire (line B) – Buses: 21, 67, 88, PC.
- 🅿 **Parking:** Street parking is possible on the side streets around the park.
- 🚫 **Don't Miss:** The scenic waterfall in the Parc Montsouris.
- 🕑 **Timing:** Allow an hour or two to visit the area.
- 👪 **Kids:** There are several playgrounds in the park.

orological observatory is housed in a building in the park, with weather predictions posted on the door. The Pavillon Montsouris, an exclusive restaurant in the park, has an inviting terrace.

Beyond the park, take time to explore **rue de Parc Montsouris**, **rue Braque** and **square de Monsouris** before heading north along rue Saint-Yves to **Villa Seurat**. During the inter-war period, famous residents of the this villa included Gromaire, Lurçat, Orloff

Villa Seurat

18 Villa Sourat, just off rue de la Tombe Issoire.

In the 1930s American novelist **Henry Miller** (1891-1980) immortalized this tranquil cul-de-sac (fictionalized as the Villa Borghese) in his controversial novel *Tropic of Cancer*, which was published in Paris in 1934 and banned in the USA and England until the 1960s.

> *The whole street is given up to quiet, joyous work. Every house contains a writer, painter, musician, sculptor, dancer or actor. It is such a quiet street and yet there is such activity going on, silently….*

Miller Walks (www.millerwalks.com) offers walks around Montsouris, including one which incorporates 18 Villa Seurat, where Miller lived from 1934 to 1939.

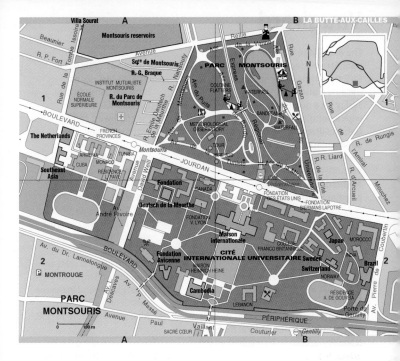

the sculptor, Henry Miller (installed in Artaud's studio at no 18 by Anaïs Nin), Dalí and **Soutine**. No **2** avenue Reille was designed by Auguste Perret and no **53** by Le Corbusier.

The avenues Reille and René Coty are overlooked by the grass-covered **Montsouris reservoirs**, where half the city's water supply is collected in the 100-year-old reservoirs from the Vanne, Loing and Lunain Rivers.

CITÉ INTERNATIONALE UNIVERSITAIRE★

Main entrance: 19–21 boulevard Jourdan. ◐*Daily 7am–10pm.*
Guided tours Sun; call or check website to confirm meeting place.
≋*10€.* ✆*01 40 44 16 64 00.*
www.ciup.fr.

The city on the edge of Montsouris Park spreads over an area of 40ha/100 acres; it houses more than 5 500 students from 120 different countries in its 37 halls of residence. Each hall forms an independent community, its architecture and individual character inspired by the country that founded it.

The first hall to be built was the **E-and-L-Deutsch-de-la-Meurthe Foundation**, inaugurated in 1925. The Maison internationale (1936) with a swimming pool, theatre and vast rooms was sponsored by John D Rockefeller Jr. The Fondation Suisse and Fondation Franco-Brézilienne were designed by **Le Corbusier**.

Cité internationale universitaire

© Franck Guiziou/hemis.fr

Vaugirard

The old village of Vaugirard was a small rural dependency of the St-Germain-des-Prés abbey until it became a district of Paris in 1860. Today it's a quiet residential area, with a popular book market in Parc Georges-Brassens and an open-air flea market on weekends. The southern border is at the Porte de Versailles, where major trade fairs are held year-round including the popular Foire de Paris in May.

SIGHTS
Institut Pasteur
25 rue du Dr-Roux. Museum visit by guided (45min) only, Mon–Fri 2pm, 3pm, 4pm. Aug and holidays. 7€. 01 45 68 82 83. www.pasteur.fr.

Louis Pasteur (1822–95) is hailed as one of the greatest scientists ever to have lived. At 25, in his laboratory at the École Normale Supérieure, he established the principle of molecular dissymmetry; at 35, that of fermentation; at 40, he laid the foundations for asepsis, and he studied the ruinous diseases affecting beer and wine production and of the silkworm; at 58, he studied viruses and vaccines. He isolated the rabies virus, researching its prevention and delivered an antidote for the first time on 7 July 1885.

The tour includes his vast apartment, filled with his furnishings and personal objects, both family and professional; the scientific souvenir room; and the mosaic-tiled **neo-Byzantine crypt★**, where he and his wife are buried.

♣♣ Parc Georges-Brassens★
Rue des Morillons.

This park was created in the 19C on the site of the old Vaugirard abattoirs. A few vestiges survive: the horse hall, two bronze bulls by the animal sculptor Cain at the main entrance, and the auction belfry reflected in the central basin. A wooded hill dominates the park with its children's play areas, a belvedere, a climbing rock and a vineyard harvested in early October with great fanfare.

ⓘ Info: Paris Office du Tourisme, 25 rue des Pyramides. 08 92 68 30 00 (0.34€ per min). http://en.parisinfo.com.

▶ Location: Located in the southwest corner of the Left Bank.

Ⓜ Metro/Transport: Vaugirard (line 12) – Buses: 39, 70, 80, 88, 89.

ⓟ Parking: Street parking is possible around the Parc Georges-Brassens.

Don't Miss: The old artist ateliers of the passage de Dantzig.

Ⓣ Timing: Allow at least an hour for this large district.

♣♣ Kids: Playground in the Parc Georges-Brassens.

Also See: MONTPARNASSE.

Rue Santos-Dumont★ and Villa Santos-Dumont★
Access via rue des Morillons.

Zadkine, Fernard Léger and Georges Brassens found inspiration for their work in the discreet charm of this corner of Paris.

Passage Dantzig
The three-storey wine pavilion, designed by Eiffel for the Exposition Universelle, of 1900 was salvaged from scrap by the sculptor Boucher, and adapted for use as artists' lodgings and studios, known as **La Ruche★**. Among its most famous lodgers were Fernand Léger (1905), Chagall (1910), Soutine, **Modigliani** and the Swiss novelist Blaise Cendras. The second generation included the sculptors **Zadkine**, **Brancusi** and Kisling.

Rue de Vaugirard
This is Paris' longest street, running between the Latin Quarter and the Porte de Versailles. Shops tend to cluster around intersections of rue de la Convention and rue de Vaugirard, rue Lecourbe, rue du Commerce and rue St-Charles.

Javel–André-Citroën

This former industrial quarter was famous for manufacturing Citroën cars and bleach *(eau de javel)*. **Today a magnificent contemporary garden named after André Citroën has replaced the factories.**

SIGHTS
👤👤 Parc André-Citroën★★

As you come out of the Javel metro station (facing the river), turn left along the Port de Javel Bas.

André Citroën (1878–1935) went into manufacturing during World War I when he built a factory here for producing shells. It was converted into a Citroën manufacturing plant in 1919; it operated here until the mid-1970s.

The vast 14ha/35-acre site left by the closure of the Citroën factory has been transformed into a modern park with open lawns where vegetation merges with stone, glass and above all water, which is omnipresent.

Visit

Jardin blanc – *On the other side of rue Balard, at the entrance to the park.*

High walls enclose a small square planted with white-flowering perennials. To the north, water tumbles over a series of striated granite blocks.

Jardin noir★ – Here, connoisseurs will recognize spirea, reeds, bear's breech, rhododendrons, poppies, irises, amid the vegetation. A path leads into an open space with 64 fountains.

Jardins sériels ★ – Six beds are bisected by stretches of cascading water. Ramps and walkways provide a bird's-eye view over the whole area. Each garden is a concept: yellow is associated with gold and the sixth sense, silver with sight, red with bauxite and taste, orange with rust and touch, green with oxidized copper and hearing, blue with mercury and smell. Paths paved in stone or over wooden ramps thread their way through open space or dense foliage, under a pergola or through the air.

Restless garden – Clumps of rustling bamboo and random trees punctuate

> ▶ **Location:** Located on the western end of the Left Bank, overlooking the Seine.
>
> Ⓜ **Metro/Transport:** RER: Javel (line 10/C) – Bus: 42.
>
> 🅿 **Parking:** Along rue Leblanc.
>
> 🕐 **Timing:** Allow half an hour to visit the park.
>
> 👤👤 **Kids:** Aquaboulevard.
>
> 👁 **Don't Miss:** Views from anchored Eutelsat hot-air balloon.
>
> 🕯 **Also See:** EIFFEL TOWER.

this man-made wilderness where apparently wind-sown plants are left to grow in the uncut grass, ever changing with the seasons.

Beaugrenelle–Front de Seine

The towers of this vast complex of skyscrapers were built between 1967 and 1985 with lodgings, offices, public services and the Beaugrenelle commercial centre. A raised flagstone walkway allows pedestrians access to the complex without having to worry about the traffic below. Vast renovations are underway to modernize the buildings and surroundings.

👁 *Amid all the towers, don't miss the* **Tour Dexia**, *nos 7–11, or the* **Tour de Cristal** *and its 100sq m/119.6sq yd bronze glass façade (by the architects Penven and Le Bail, 1990), two of the most recent constructions of the Front de Seine.*

From the Pont de Grenelle is a view of the small replica of the **Statue of Liberty**. At 61 quai de Grenelle is a red building with round windows that look like television screens, housing the Hôtel Novotel Paris Tour Eiffel (formerly the Hôtel Nikko), also by Penven and Le Bail, 1976. At no 55 the angular Tour Totem was finished in 1978 by architects Andrault and Parat.

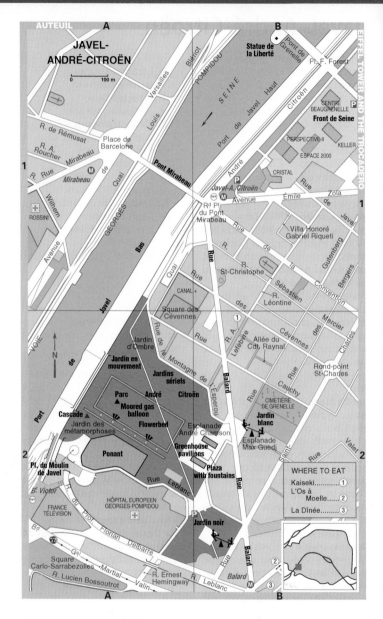

ADDITIONAL SIGHT
👥♿ Aquaboulevard

4–6 rue Louis-Armand (Porte de Sèvres). Ⓜ*Balard.* 🕐*Mon–Fri 9am–11pm (Fri until midnight), Sat 8am–midnight, Sun 8am–11pm (last admission 9pm).* 🕐*Two weeks in Jan.* 🎫*23–29€; 3-11 years 15€; under 3 years not admitted.* 📞*01 40 60 10 00. www.aquaboulevard.fr.*

This indoor water-world complex, set among trees and greenery, includes a swimming pool with jacuzzi, a wave machine and a giant slide.

Additional fun is provided by mini-golf, bowling lanes, tennis and squash courts, exercise and body-building rooms as well as restaurants and shops.

Arrondissement 16

Auteuil

It was only at the turn of the 19C that the last vineyards disappeared from Auteuil, although it became part of the City of Paris during the Second Empire. It still enjoys a village atmosphere, in contrast to the modern development and high-rise blocks across the river. Many of the houses of this desirable residential area have retained good-size gardens, and the streets named after famous composers and writers recall the era of Salon society.

🐾 WALKING TOUR
Start from the Ⓜ Église d'Auteuil.

Place d'Auteuil
The **Church of Notre-Dame** (1880) is a Romano-Byzantine pastiche. The obelisk opposite the chapel of Ste-Bernadette is the last remaining tomb from the one-time cemetery.

Rue d'Auteuil
At no 11 bis, the 17C château is now occupied by a school. Admire at no **16** the main front of the Hôtel de Puscher; nos **43–47** is an 18C mansion. The modern building at no **59** marks the site of a literary Salon of Madame Helvétius, which was frequented by philosophers and writers from 1762 to 1800, includ-

Auteuil "village"
© S. Sauvignier/MICHELIN

- **ⓘ Info:** Paris Office du Tourisme, 25 rue des Pyramides. ☎08 92 68 30 00 (0.34€ per min). http://en.parisinfo.com.
- **Ⓒ Location:** Auteuil sits on the Right Bank just west of the Seine; two bridges give access to the Left Bank: Pont de Grenelle and Pont Mirabeau. To the northwest is the Ranelagh quarter, and the Passy Village to the northeast.
- **Ⓟ Parking:** There is plenty of parking in this residential district, and underground parking at Radio-France.
- **Don't Miss:** The beautiful Art Nouveau villas designed by Guimard.
- **Ⓞ Timing:** Allow at least two hours if you're on foot and don't go into any of the museums. This is an ideal district to visit by bicycle.
- **Kids:** The Tenniseum at Roland-Garros includes a behind-the-scenes tour of the famous tennis stadium and its red-clay courts.

ing the Americans Thomas Jefferson, **Benjamin Franklin** and John Adams.

Ⓒ Continue to the place de la Porte d'Auteuil, cross the intersection to the avenue de la Porte d'Auteuil and follow it past the Périphérique road.

Jardin des Serres d'Auteuil
3 avenue de la Porte d'Auteuil. ⓞDaily 8am–8.30pm (summer); rest of the year 9am–5.30pm; public holidays 9am–5pm. ⊕Free entry. www.paris.fr.
The formal garden, which still retains its 19C charm, is surrounded by hot-houses cultivating azaleas, palm trees and ornamental plants for public build-ings and official occasions. The central building contains a palm house and a tropical house with banana trees,

papyrus plants and giant strelitzias. The azalea and chrysanthemum displays draw large crowds. When leaving the Serres d'Auteuil, take a short cut through the small **square des Poètes** next door. Beyond the garden is the **Stade Roland-Garros** (*see below*), where the French Open Tennis Championships are held.

○ Retrace your steps, turn right at place Jean Lorrain and follow the rue Michel-Ange to rue Molitor (first left). Turn right on the rue Boileau, then a left on rue Jouvenet.

Promenade des villas d'Auteuil★

The Villa Boileau (no 18 rue Molitor), **Hameau Boileau** (no 38 rue Boileau) and **Villa Molitor** (at rue Jouvenet and Chardon-Lagache) are havens of peace and greenery.

○ Cross boulevard Exelmans by rue Chardon Lagache, then turn right along rue Charles Marie Widor and continue on rue Claude Lorrain, turning left on to avenue G Risler.

The **Villa Mulhouse** is a group of small houses reminiscent of late-19C workers' housing in the city of Mulhouse.

○ Head north back along rue Michel-Ange to place Jean-Lorrain. Detour via rue Leconte de Lisle and the picturesque **rue des Perchamps** (*left*) before rejoining rue La Fontaine.

Rue La Fontaine

As in rue Agar, several buildings are by **Hector Guimard**, the famed Art Nouveau architect. His best-known block of flats, **Castel Béranger**, is at no 14. No **60**, also by Guimard, was built in 1911. Avenue Léopold II leads to place Rodin, the setting for Rodin's allegory **L'Âge d'Airain** (*The Age of Bronze*), admired for its precision at the Salon of 1874.

○ Go towards the Maison de Radio-France, via avenue du Recteur Poincaré, rue La Fontaine and rue de Boulainvilliers.

MUSEUMS AND OTHER ATTRACTIONS
Maison de Radio-France★

116 avenue du Président Kennedy.
One concentric building and a tower 68m/223ft tall make up the Maison de Radio-France. Designed by Henri Bernard in 1963, it houses the studios and auditorium in which national radio programmes have been produced since 1975. *Free tickets for classical concerts are available in the entrance hall.*

Fondation Le Corbusier

8–10 square du Dr Blanche. Mon *1.30pm–6pm, Tue–Sat 10am–6pm.* Guided tours (1hr) in English Tue 2pm, call to reserve. *First week Aug and public holidays.* 8€. 01 42 88 41 53. www.fondationlecorbusier.asso.fr. Two buildings dating from 1923 serve as a documentation centre for the work of the famous architect **Charles Édouard Jeanneret** (1887–1965), known as Le Corbusier. Maison La Roche houses a permanent exhibition, a library and photographic collection.

Stade Roland-Garros/ Musée de la Fédération Française de Tennis★

2 avenue Gordon Bennett.
Wed, Fri–Sun 10am–6pm. Mon public holidays and 1 Jan, 1 May, 25 Dec. *Museum 8€; under 18 years 4€.* Guided tours in English 11am and 3pm; reservations required. 01 47 43 48 48. www.fft.fr.
Host of the annual French Open Tennis Championships (*late May–early Jun*), the Roland-Garros tennis stadium opened its grounds to the public in 2003. Today the complex is open year-round and offers visitors a tennis boutique, multimedia museum and behind-the-scenes tours of the players' lockers and the famous red-clay courts. The museum features the history of the sport as well as a video library of modern matches and player interviews. There are regular expositions and contemporary art shows on tennis themes.

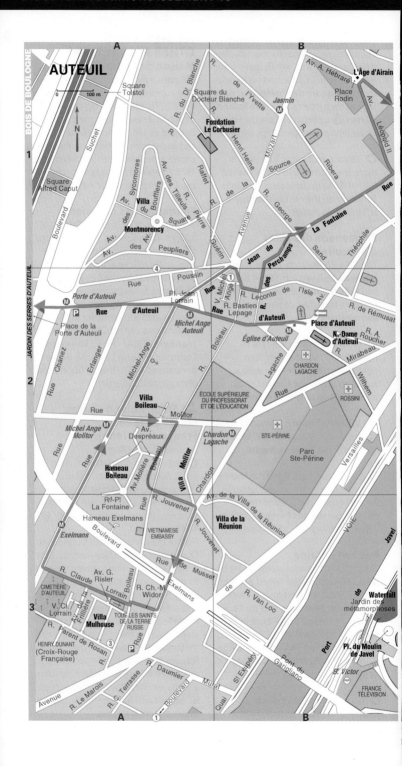

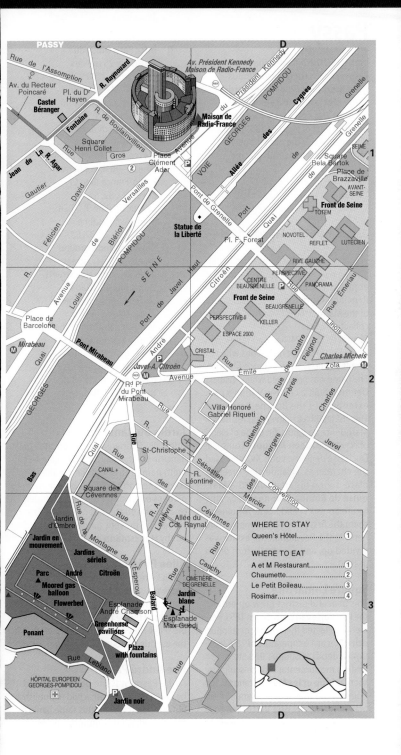

PASSY

Rue de l'Assomption

Av. du Recteur Poincaré

Castel Béranger

Pl. du Dr Hayen

Fontaine

R. de Boulainvilliers

Square Henri Collet

Gros

Rue

La R. Agar

Jean de

Gautier

Féticien

David

de

Blériot

Versailles

R.

Louis

Avenue

Place de Barcelone

Mirabeau

Quai

GEORGES

Bas

R. Raynouard

AVENUE   GEORGES

VOIE

Place Clément Ader

Pont de Grenelle

Statue de la Liberté

S E I N E

Port

de

Javel

POMPIDOU

Pont Mirabeau

Javel-A. Citroën

Rd Pt du Pont Mirabeau

Av. Président Kennedy
Maison de Radio-France

POMPIDOU

du

Allée

des

de

Maison de Radio-France

Port

de

Grenelle

Quai

Citroën

Haut

André

Avenue

Rue

Villa Honoré Gabriel Riqueti

R.

R. St-Christophe

CANAL +

Square des Cévennes

Jardin d'Ombre

Jardin en mouvement

Jardins sériels

Parc   André   Citroën

Moored gas balloon

Flowerbed

Ponant

Rue   Leblanc

HÔPITAL EUROPEEN GEORGES-POMPIDOU

Jardin noir

Rue de la Montagne de l'Esperou

Lefebvre

R. A.

des

Rue

Allée du Cdt. Raynal

R. Sébastien Léontine

des

Cévennes

Rue

Cauchy

Rue

Mercier

Convention

la

Esplanade André Chamson

Greenhouse pavilions

Plaza with fountains

Balard

CIMETIÈRE DE GRENELLE

Jardin blanc

Esplanade Max Guedj

Cygnes

Grenelle

Grenelle

SEINE

Square Bela Bartok

Place de Brazzaville

AVANT-SEINE

Front de Seine

TOTEM

NOVOTEL

REFLET   LUTECIEN

RIVE GAUCHE

PERSPECTIVE

CENTRE BEAUGRENELLE

Front de Seine

BEAUGRENELLE

PERSPECTIVE-II   KELLER

ESPACE 2000

CRISTAL

Rue   Émile   Zola

Charles Michels

de   Rue   des   Quatre   Frères

Gutenberg

Bergers

Peignot

Linois

Rue   Émeriau

PANORAMA

Charles

Javel

WHERE TO STAY

Queen's Hôtel .... ①

WHERE TO EAT

A et M Restaurant .... ①
Chaumette .... ②
Le Petit Boileau .... ③
Rosimar .... ④

297

Passy

In the 18C the hillside village of Passy, known for its ferruginous waters, was covered in vineyards. Large blocks of flats replaced the gardens and cottages when Passy became part of Paris in 1859, but a few vestiges of the old village still survive in this peaceful quarter.

🦶 WALKING TOURS

Start from the Ⓜ *Rue de la Pompe.*

1 LA MUETTE-RANELAGH★

The original Muette Estate was developed as an elegant quarter. Today it enjoys the green open space of the Ranelagh Gardens and the attraction of the Marmottan Museum with its rich collection of art.

Charles IX (1550–74) had a hunting lodge here where he kept his falcons when in moult (French *en mue,* hence Muette). The name was preserved when Philibert Delorme built a château within a park extending to the Bois de Boulogne. The château had many royal residents: Marguerite de Valois, first wife of Henri of Navarre (**Queen Margot**); Louis XIII; Duchesse de Berry; Louis XV, who used the château as a clandestine meeting place during his affair with the **Marquise de Pompadour** (⚑*see box*); the future Louis XVI and Marie-Antoinette spent the first years of their married life here. At the Revolution the estate was divided up, and eventually torn down in 1920.

Square Lamartine

This peaceful district grew up around the Passy artesian wells dug in 1855. Residents collected their supply of sulphur-rich water at a temperature of 28°C/82°F from a depth of 600m/1 968.5ft.

Rodin's monumental bronze sculpture **Victor Hugo et les Muses** stands at the point where the elegant avenue Henri Martin meets **avenue Victor Hugo**, a street lined with prestigious jewellery and fashion houses.

ℹ️ **Info:** Paris Office du Tourisme, 25 rue des Pyramides. ☎08 92 68 30 00 (0.34€ per min). http://en.parisinfo.com.

▶️ **Location:** This southwestern district is on the Right Bank.

Ⓜ **Metro/Transport:** Passy (line 6) – RER: Kennedy Radio-France (line C) – Buses: 22, 32, 52, PC. La Muette (line 9) – RER: Boulainvilliers (line C) – Buses: 22, 32, 52.

🅿️ **Parking:** Underground on rue de Passy, street parking on the side streets.

😊 **Don't Miss:** Balzac's cottage house; the caves of the Musée du Vin; Monet's paintings at the Musée Marmottan.

🕐 **Timing:** Allow 3–5hrs.

👪 **Kids:** The Parc de Passy has a playground, as does the Jardin du Ranelagh.

Jardin du Ranelagh

Originally, Parisians came to the area to dance in the open air. In 1774 a café was built, named the Petit Ranelagh after Lord Ranelagh's fashionable pleasure gardens outside London, and extended to accommodate a dance-hall-with-stage. The present gardens were laid out by **Haussmann** in 1860.

Allée Pilâtre de Rozier

In 1783, the famous aeronaut, for whom the walkway is named, accomplished the first free flight in a hot-air balloon, witnessed by the royal family. The marble relief *The Poet's Vision* at the end of the avenue honours Victor Hugo.

Rue André Pascal

André Pascal was the pen-name used by Baron Henri de Rothschild to publish his writings; it was for this same banker that the adjacent sumptuous mansion was built.

Madame de Pompadour (1721–1764)

Arguably one of the best-known royal mistresses in history, **Jeanne-Antoinette Poisson**, later to be known as the Marquise (and later still, Duchesse) de Pompadour, was to become the mistress of King Louis XV. Married to the nephew of her guardian at 19 and wealthy due to receiving a wedding gift comprising the estate at Étoiles, she became known for her Salon, to which the eminent writer **Voltaire** was a regular visitor.

Étoiles happened to be on the edge of the royal hunting ground at Sénart, and she engineered an encounter with the king one day in the royal forest. Impressed by her beauty, the king invited her to a masked ball at Versailles, and within two months she was installed as a royal mistress. Now legally separated from her husband, she was given the estate of Pompadour and the title of Marquise by Louis. During this period the Château at La Muette was used as a secret meeting place between the two.

Although not as politically influential as many believed, she was undoubtedly very powerful behind the scenes and was certainly approached by foreign dignitaries who believed she had the ear of the king. Later, she was blamed by her enemies for the disastrous Seven Years' War, but was probably guilty of nothing more than comforting the king with the phrase "Après nous, le déluge" meaning "I don't care what happens when we're dead and gone". Although there were other royal mistresses, Louis remained devoted to her until her death in 1764 and mourned her passing. Voltaire himself wrote: "I am very sad at the death of Madame de Pompadour. I was indebted to her and I mourn her out of gratitude. It seems absurd that while an ancient penpusher, hardly able to walk, should still be alive, a beautiful woman, in the midst of a splendid career, should die at the age of forty-three."

Since 1948 the mansion has been classified as international territory and houses the seat of the Organisation for Economic Co-operation and Development (⚭ *closed to the public*).

Rue du Ranelagh

Running straight to the Seine, this street holds several charming 19C mansions (no 123-no 90). Note especially the red-brick house at no **94**, built in 1885, with gargoyles and a pepperpot turret.

② LA MUETTE TO PASSY

Start at Ⓜ La Muette.

Ancienne Gare de la Muette

19 Chaussée de la Muette.
Built in 1864, this ornate station provided train services until the mid-1980s, when it was turned into an upmarket 250-seat restaurant, Restaurant La Gare, now in the heart of a busy intersection (⚜ *see Where to Eat at the back of the guide*).

Rue de Passy

This commercial street is home to luxury shops and upmarket department store **Franck et Fils** (no 80). Previously known (1575) as the road to the Bois de Boulogne, then *la Grande Rue* (the road ended where it met La rue de la Pompe), this road is a principal artery for the urban village of Passy.

▶ At **place de Passy**, lively with shops and cafés, bear right on to rue de l'Annonciation.

Rue de l'Annonciation

Before rue Lekain, this street is quite commercial and pedestrianized. Beyond it, the street's low-lying houses retain a village appearance. Overlooking the place du Père Marcelin Champagnat, the 17C **Eglise Notre-Dame-de-Grace de Passy** has three Annunciation paintings by Corot. *Exit by the door on the left behind the chancel to get back to rue de l'Annonciation.*

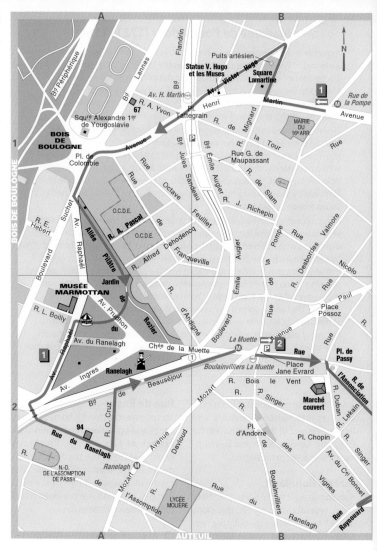

Rue Raynouard

Many famous people have lived in this street, including the Enlightenment philosopher **Jean-Jacques Rousseau**. The cottage (Maison de Balzac) on the left, at no 47, belonged to the prolific writer Honoré de Balzac. The modern residences in reinforced concrete at nos 51 to 55 show a confident application of the new material by architect Auguste Perret, who lived here from 1932 until his death in 1954.

Benjamin Franklin resided at no 66 while negotiating the alliance between Louis XVI and the new Republic of the United States; he erected France's first lightning rod over his house.

Maison de Balzac★ *(47 rue Raynouard;* **⊙***Tue–Sun 10am–6pm;* **⊙***public holidays;* ⊜*free enry;* ☏*01 55 74 41 80; www. balzac.paris.fr),* half-hidden in a garden, is the house occupied illicitly by **Honoré de Balzac** (1799-1850) between 1840 and 1847; often on the run from creditors, he used back route out of the

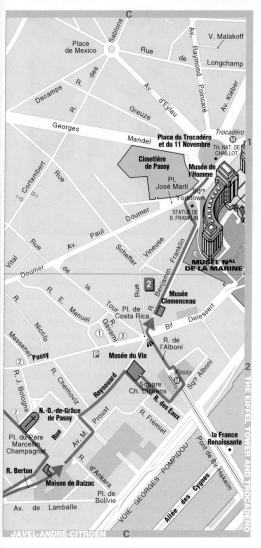

house. Manuscripts, caricatures and engravings pertaining to the author of *La Comédie Humaine* described in his novels complement an adjoining library.

Rue Berton★

Rue Berton is one of the most unusual streets in Paris, its ivy-clad walls and gas-light brackets giving it an old country atmosphere. No 24 was the back entrance to Balzac's house, where he would go to escape from creditors.

Rue des Eaux

Named for the natural spring discovered here in 1650, this street now leads to the Musée du Vin (⟨see MUSEUMS).

Cimetière de Passy

2 rue du Commandant-Schloesing. ◷*Mid-Mar–early Nov Mon–Fri 8am– 6pm, Sat 8.30am–6pm, Sun and public holidays 9am–6pm; rest of the year until 5.30pm.* ⬩*Free entry.* ⬩*Guided tours (2hrs) cost ⬩6€.* ℘*01 40 72 16 16.*

Musée Marmottan-Monet

© Sylvain Sonnet/hemis.fr

Passy Cemetery contains the somewhat extravagant graves of local residents as well as famous writers and artists: Manet, Giraudoux, Berthe Morisot, Claude Debussy, Gabriel Fauré and Madeleine Renaud among them. The most impressive tomb is that of Ukrainian poet and painter Marie Bashkirtseff.

MUSEUMS

Musée Marmottan-Monet★★

2 rue Louis-Boilly. ◷*Tue–Sun 10am– 6pm (until 8pm Thur).* ◷*1 Jan, 1 May, 25 Dec.* ⊚*10€.* ✆*01 44 96 50 33.* *www.marmottan.com.*

The art historian **Paul Marmottan** bequeathed, in 1932, his private house, Renaissance tapestries and sculpture, Consular and First Empire portraits (26 of Boilly), medallions, paintings (Vernet) and furniture (Desmalter) to the Académie des Beaux-Arts. In 1950 Mme Donop de Monchy donated a part of her father's collection, including works by the Impressionists befriended and treated by Dr de Bellio (*Impression – Sunrise*). In 1971 Michel Monet left 65 of his father's painted canvases to the museum, further endowed by the Wildenstein legacy of 13C–16C illuminated manuscripts from European schools.

This collection of **Claude Monet** paintings, probably the most important known body of work by the Master of Impressionism, is accommodated in a purpose-built underground gallery;

many of the works were painted at the artist's Normandy home at Giverny. Other panels show the painter's preoccupation with light (*The Houses of Parliament – London, Rouen Cathedral*).

The Duhem Bequest of some 60 paintings, drawings and watercolours includes **Gauguin**'s *Bouquet of Flowers* painted in Tahiti and a pastel by **Renoir**: *Seated Girl in a White Hat*. Exceptional pictures by Albrecht Bonts, Fragonard and Renoir provide comparison.

Musée Clemenceau

8 rue Benjamin Franklin. ◷*Tue–Sat 2pm–5.30pm.* ◷*Aug, public holidays.* ⊚*6€.* &✆*01 45 20 53 41.* *www.musee-clemenceau.fr.*

The apartment of **Georges Clemenceau** (1841-1929), in which he spent 34 years, remains as it was when he died. His career as a journalist, writer, politician and prime minister of France are well documented in the displays. Note his horseshoe-shaped desk.

Musée du Vin Paris

5 square Charles Dickens. ◷*Tue–Sun 10am–6pm.* ⊚*10€.* &✆*01 45 25 63 26. www.museeduvinparis.com.*

No 5 rue des Eaux marks the original entrance to the former quarries, now housing a wine museum with waxwork figures and implements recalling the days when monks produced wine there. A restaurant is open for lunch.

Bois de Boulogne★★

This vast 19C park (846ha/2 090 acres) is cut by wide shaded roads, paths for pedestrians and cyclists, and trails for horses. There are lakes and waterfalls, gardens, lawns and woodland, cafés and restaurants. Horse races are held at Longchamp and Auteuil, and music concerts take place in the Bagatelle and Pré Catelan gardens. A victim of its own popularity on the weekends, the park is a pleasant place for a stroll on weekday mornings.

A BIT OF HISTORY

A royal forest – In Merovingian times the forest was hunted for bear, deer, wolves and wild boar. Later, the royal forest became a refuge for bandits, and in 1556 Henri II enclosed it with a wall pierced by eight gates. In the 17C Colbert adapted it for hunting with a crisscross of straight roads. Louis XIV opened the wood to the public as a place for country walks, but its reputation soon left a lot to be desired. According to one chronicle, "marriages from the Bois de Boulogne do not get celebrated by the priest".

Decline – During the Revolution the forest again provided refuge to those on the run, the destitute and poachers. In 1815 the English and Russian armies set up camp in the forest, devastating a great section. In the replanting, oaks were replaced by horse chestnuts, acacias, sycamores and maples, though sadly many of these trees were uprooted in the great storm of 1999 and the heatwave of 2003.

The woods today – When Napoléon III gave the forest to the city in 1852, his urban planner Haussmann demolished the curtain wall and landscaped the area, creating paths, ornamental lakes and ponds, the Longchamp racecourse, restaurants, kiosks and pavilions. The Auteuil racecourse was built after 1870. The 20C saw the construction of

Info: Paris Office du Tourisme, 25 rue des Pyramides. ✆08 92 68 30 00 (0.34€ per min). http://en.parisinfo.com.

Location: Located on the western edge of the city, the park is bordered on the west by the Seine, with the Port Maillot and the suburb of Neuilly to the north, Porte d'Auteuil and the suburb of Boulogne-Billancourt to the south.

Parking: There is parking near the Lac Inférieur and the Porte d'Auteuil.

Don't Miss: The world-famous roses at the Parc de Bagatelle, the Shakespeare Garden at the Pré Catelan and the picturesque Lac Inférieur.

Timing: Allow a half-day to visit all of the sights. The best way to get around is by bike.

Kids: The Jardin d'Acclimatation amusement park.

the Paris ring road, Jardin des Serres, **Roland-Garros** and **Parc des Princes**.

THE PARK
Avenue Foch

This imposing avenue completed by Haussmann is 120m/394ft wide and lined on both sides by lawns and side alleys. As soon as it was inaugurated in 1854, it became the fashionable haunt of carriages on their way to the Bois de Boulogne. Private mansions and luxury blocks of flats were gradually built along the grass borders.

The Lakes★

Lac Supérieur is a pleasant recreation area, as is the larger **Lac Inférieur**, which is popular on Sundays. It has a motorboat service to the islands *(café-restaurant)* and rowing boats for hire.

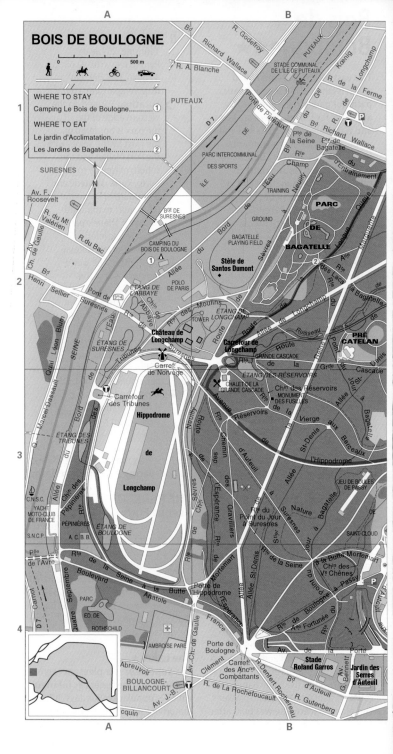

BOIS DE BOULOGNE

WHERE TO STAY

Camping Le Bois de Boulogne............①

WHERE TO EAT

Le jardin d'Acclimatation...................①

Les Jardins de Bagatelle.....................②

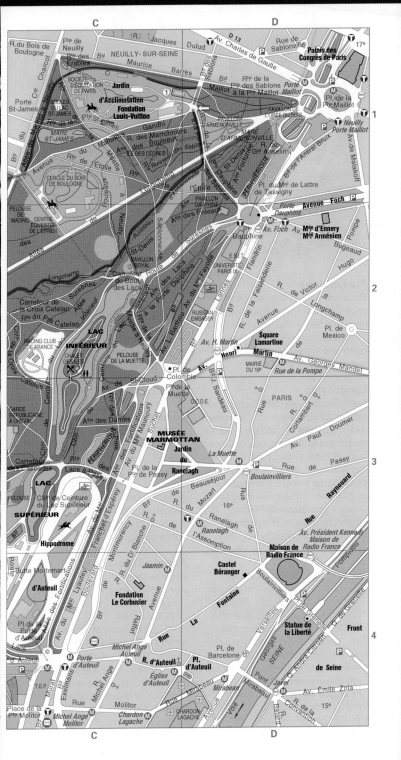

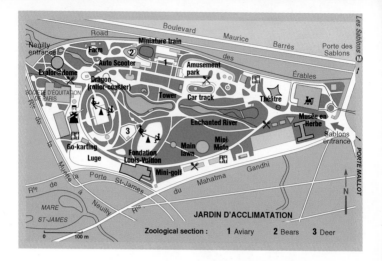

Zoological section : **1** Aviary **2** Bears **3** Deer

Pré Catelan★

This attractive well-kept park is named after a court minstrel from Provence murdered here in the reign of Philip IV. It includes a luxurious café-restaurant, lawns and shaded areas and a copper beech nearly 200 years old.

Longchamp

A man-made waterfall (Grande Cascade) graces the crossroads (**carrefour de Longchamp**). Beyond the pond is a monument to 35 young people shot by Nazis in 1944; a nearby oak is still visibly scarred by gunshot. **Château de Longchamp** was given to Haussmann by Napoléon III, and now houses the Centre International de l'Enfance. The famous racecourse, **Hippodrome de Longchamp**, opened by Napoléon III in 1857, hosts a number of racing events.

Jardin d'Acclimatation

🕐Daily May–Sept 10am–7pm (Fri until 10pm); Oct–Apr 10am–6pm (Fri until 10pm, Sat–Sun 7pm). ⊛3€. ♿𝄞01 40 67 90 82. www.jardindacclimatation.fr. This park, primarily arranged as a children's amusement park, includes a small zoo with a pets' corner, a typical Norman farm and an aviary.

The **Musée en Herbe** (🕐daily 10am–7pm, until 9pm Thu; ⊛10€; children 6€–10€ plus 4€–6€ adult. 𝄞01 40 67 97 66; www.musee-en-herbe.com) is a

museum-plus-workshop designed for youngsters.

The **Explor@dome** (🕐Tue, Thu–Fri 10am–noon, 1.30pm–5pm; Wed, Sat 10am–6pm, Sun 1pm–6pm. During summer months: Mon–Sat 10am–6pm; 🕐1 Jan, 1 May, 25 Dec; ⊛6€; 𝄞01 43 91 16 20; www.exploradome.com) is a science and multimedia centre.

Fondation Louis Vuitton

8 Av. du Mahatma Gandhi. 🕐Mon, Wed–Fri noon–7pm (until 11pm Fri), Sat–Sun 11am–8pm. ⊛14€. 𝄞01 40 69 96 00. www.fondationlouisvuitton.fr. Designed by Frank Gehry, the latest major Parisian museum is topped by 12 curved glass "sails", houses 11 galleries and hosts temporary exhibits of 20-21C contemporary art.

Parc de Bagatelle★★

Route de Sèvres à Neuilly. 🕐Daily Apr–Oct 9.30am–8pm; rest of the year 5pm (Mar until 6.30pm). ⊛8€. 𝄞01 53 64 53 80.

In 1775 the Count of Artois – future Charles X – waged a bet with his sister-in-law, **Marie-Antoinette**, that he would have a house built and a garden landscaped within three months. He won. Bagatelle survived the Revolution and was passed to Napoléon, the Duc de Berry, the Hertford family and finally sold to the City of Paris in 1905.

Arrondissements 18-20

Montmartre★★★

The Butte (or hillock), as it is known locally, is the part of Paris most full of contrasts – anonymous boulevards run close to delightful village streets and courtyards, steep stone steps lead to open terraces, pilgrims tread the streets beside nightclub revellers. On the southern side, a funicular provides access to one of city's most famous landmarks, the Sacré-Cœur.

A BIT OF HISTORY

Martyrs' Mound – In Roman times, Montmartre had two hilltop temples dedicated to Mercury and Mars. It was known as martyrs' mound from the 8C after **St Denis**, first **Bishop of Lutetia**, was beheaded here by the Romans. According to legend, St Denis picked up his head and walked to the place now known as St-Denis.

Early days of the Commune – In 1871, after the fall of Paris, the working-class people of Montmartre collected 171 cannons on the hill to prevent their capture by the Prussians. The new royalist government (that had officially capitulated) tried to seize the cannons from the "rebels" on 18 March, but the crowd seized the generals and shot them. This bloody episode was to mark the beginning of the Commune: a civil war that lasted until the Communards' defeat three months later.

Bohemian life – Throughout the 19C, artists and men of letters were drawn to the free-and-easy way of life as lived on the Butte. Composers, writers, painters and poets made up the great 1871–1914 generation of young artists seeking inspiration on place Pigalle, where artists' models and seamstresses led a bohemian existence. In the early days, poets congregated at Le Chat Noir, enlivened with poems by Charles Cros and Jehan Rictus, songs by **Aristide Bruant**, drawings by André Gill and **Toulouse-Lautrec**. The **Moulin Rouge** opened in 1889 with cancan star Louise Weber, nicknamed *La Gou-*

- 🛈 **Info:** 21 pl. du Tertre. ☎08 92 68 30 00 (.34€ per min). http://en.parisinfo.com.
- ▶ **Location:** Montmartre is at the far north edge of the city, in the 18th arrondissement.
- Ⓜ **Metro/Transport:** Anvers (line 2), Abbesses (line 12), Lamarck Caulaincourt (line 12) – Buses: 30, 54, 67, Montmartrobus.
- 🅿 **Parking:** Best along the boulevards from Anvers to Blanche metro stations.
- 😊 **Don't Miss:** The adorable houses around the Clos du Montmartre vineyard.
- 🕐 **Timing:** Allow a half-day to explore the Butte.
- 👫 **Kids:** The carrousel in the square Willette.

lue. The Butte, thanks to the **Lapin Agile** café and **Bateau Lavoir** studios, remained until the outbreak of the Great War the capital's artistic centre. As the next generation of artists and émigrés congregated in Montparnasse, Montmartre abandoned itself to its nocturnal entertainments. Today Montmartre draws tourists from far afield in search of the spirit of the Belle Époque, or more simply to enjoy the view over the city.

👣 WALKING TOUR

Start from the Ⓜ Anvers.

▶ From boulevard de Rochechouart take rue de Steinkerque to rue d'Orsel for a view of Sacré-Coeur; turn left.

Place Charles-Dullin

On this attractive shady little square, the small theatre nestling among the trees was founded in the early 19C as the Théâtre de Montmartre; it grew to fame between the wars when Charles Dullin founded the **Théâtre de l'Atelier** in 1922.

◯ Take rue des Trois Frères; turn left on to rue Yvonne Le Tac.

Martyrium
11 rue Yvonne Le Tac.
A chapel has replaced the medieval sanctuary built to mark the site where St Denis is presumed to have been decapitated. It was here in the former crypt, on 15 August 1534, that **Ignatius Loyola** founded the Jesuit Order.

Place des Abbesses★
This animated little square is the very heart of the community, with its distinctive **Hector Guimard** Art Nouveau entrance to the metro station (the only other is at Porte Dauphine).

Église St-Jean-de-Montmartre
South side of the square.
This unusual church, designed by Baudot, was the first to be built of reinforced concrete (1904); it continues to impress structural engineers on account of its audacious use of the material.

◯ Leave square Jean Rictus by rue des Abbesses and turn right on to rue Ravignan.

Place Émile-Goudeau★
This high point in artistic and literary realms was frequented from 1900 by the pioneers of modern painting and poetry. **Picasso**, Van Dongen, Braque and Juan Gris evolved Cubism – with Picasso's famous *Demoiselles d'Avignon*; whereas Max Jacob, **Apollinaire** and Mac Orlan broke away from traditional poetic form and expression. They met at no 13, Le **Bateau Lavoir**, a rickety wooden building that was rebuilt after burning down in 1970; it still houses artists' studios and apartments.

◯ Continue up rue Ravignan to place **Jean-Baptiste-Clément** and along rue Norvins past a former watertower.

Carrefour de l'Auberge-de-la Bonne-Franquette
The **crossroads** with rue Norvins, rue des Saules and rue St-Rustique was often painted by **Utrillo**, who evoked Old Montmartre. In the late 19C, this haunt was frequented by Pissarro, Sisley, Cézanne, Toulouse-Lautrec, **Renoir**, **Monet** and **Émile Zola**.

◯ Take rue Poulbot on the right to place du Calvaire, which commands an exceptional **view** over Paris.

Espace Dalí-Montmartre
9-11 rue Poulbot. ◷*Daily 10am–6pm, (until 8pm Jul–Aug).* ◉*11.50€.* ✆*01 42 64 40 10. www.daliparis.com.*
Down in an old cellar, the sculptures, prints and drawings of Surrealist artist **Salvador Dalí** (1904-1989) are on view.

Place du Tertre★★
This shaded square with small houses is a peaceful in the morning hours; later, invaded by sightseers, it becomes a busy tourist attraction animated by cafés, and street artists offering personalized charcoal portraits or paper cut-outs. No **21** is the seat of the Free Commune, founded in 1920 to preserve the traditions of the Butte. No **3**, once the local town hall, is now Poulbot House, commemorating local children (*P'tits Poulbots*), popularized in the illustrations of artist **Francisque Poulbot** (1879-1946).

Église Saint Pierre-de-Montmartre★
2 rue du Mont-Cenis.
Dating to 1134 the church of St Peter is the last surviving vestige of the great abbey of Montmartre. The nave was revaulted in the 15C; the west front dates from the 18C. The three bronze doors are by the Italian sculptor **Gismondi** (1980). The oldest pointed arches in Paris (1147) meet in the single bay of the apse.

◯ Go down on to rue St-Eleuthère; turn left on to rue Azais; follow it until you see the basilica.

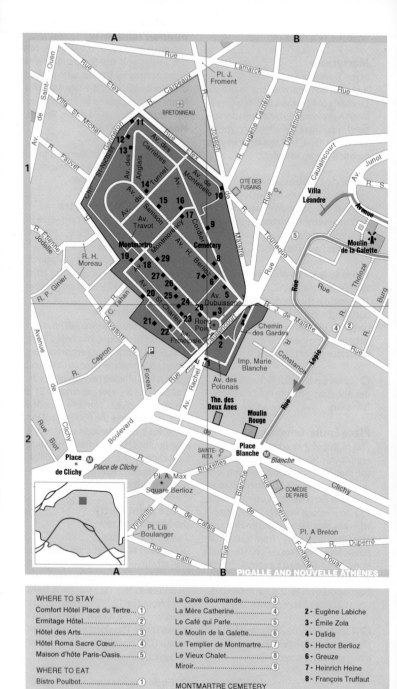

WHERE TO STAY

Comfort Hôtel Place du Tertre... ①
Ermitage Hôtel.........................②
Hôtel des Arts..........................③
Hôtel Roma Sacre Cœur...........④
Maison d'hôte Paris-Oasis........⑤

WHERE TO EAT

Bistro Poulbot..........................①
L'Été en Pente Douce...............②

La Cave Gourmande..............③
La Mère Catherine..................④
Le Café qui Parle....................⑤
Le Moulin de la Galette...........⑥
Le Templier de Montmartre.....⑦
Le Vieux Chalet.....................⑧
Miroir....................................⑨

MONTMARTRE CEMETERY
1 - Lucien et Sacha Guitry

2 - Eugène Labiche
3 - Émile Zola
4 - Dalida
5 - Hector Berlioz
6 - Greuze
7 - Heinrich Heine
8 - François Truffaut

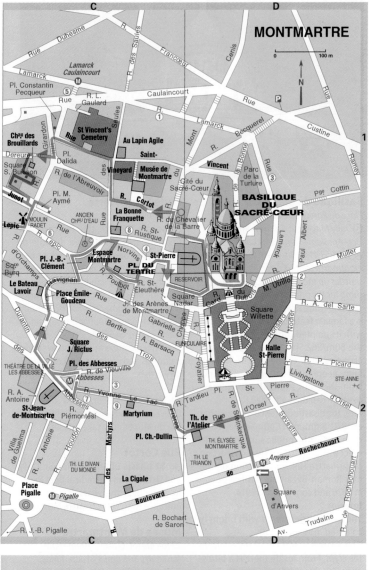

MONTMARTRE

0   100 m

N

Basilique du Sacré-Cœur atop Montmartre

© S. Sauvignier/MICHELIN

Basilique du Sacré-Cœur★★

Place du Parvis-du-Sacré-Cœur.
Daily May–Sept 8.30am–8pm;
Oct–Apr 9am–5pm. fee varies (call).
01 53 41 89 00. www.sacre-coeur-montmartre.com. A funicular train shuttles up the steep hill saving a steep climb for the price of a metro ticket.
The tall, white silhouette of the basilica is a familiar feature of the Paris skyline, with its pointed cupolas dominated by the 80m/262.5ft campanile. The travertine exterior exudes calcite when it rains, keeping the stone façade white. From the steps a remarkable **view★★** over the capital is afforded.

After the disastrous Franco-Prussian War of 1870, a group of Catholics vowed to raise money by public subscription to erect a church to the Sacred Heart on Montmartre Hill. Construction on the neo-Roman-Byzantine basilica began in 1876 and concluded in 1914.

Interior

The inside is decorated with bright ly coloured mosaics.
The Dome – *300 steps; access from the crypt.* From inside there is a bird's-eye view down into the church. From the external gallery a **panorama★★★** stretches 30km/18.6mi on a clear day. Hanging in the belfry, **la Savoyarde** is one of the heaviest bells in the world (19t). Cast in 1895 at Annecy, it was a gift from the dioceses of Savoy.

Crypt – The church plate is visible in the crypt; an audio-visual display recounts church history.

Halle Saint-Pierre

2 rue Ronsard.
Off square Willette, this 19C cast-iron textile market, built by a disciple of Baltard, has been transformed into an exhibit hall. The ground floor hosts temporary year-long exhibits. On the first floor, the **Musée d'Art naïf Max Fourny** (*Mon–Fri 11am–6pm, Sat 11am–5pm, Sun noon–6pm; public holidays and 2 weeks in Aug; 8€; 01 42 58 72 89; www.hallesaintpierre.org*) displays naïve paintings and sculpture by contemporary artists.

▶ Pass Sacré-Coeur; follow rue du Chevalier de la Barre; turn right on to rue du Mont Cenis; take first left.

Rue Cortot

No **12** boasts of tenants Renoir, Dufy and **Utrillo**, and the radical poet Pierre Reverdy over the years. It is now the entrance to the Montmartre Museum.

Musée de Montmartre

12 rue Cortot. Daily 10am–6pm (last entry 5:15pm). 1 Jan, 1 May, 25 Dec. 9.50€. 01 49 25 89 37. www.museedemontmartre.fr.
The museum houses a rich collection of mementoes evoking the quarter's bohemian life, its nightclubs and its personalities.

▶ Continue on rue Cortot until rue des Saules on the right.

The Vineyard

On the first Saturday in October, the grapes are harvested for the Clos du Montmartre wine.

Rue Saint-Vincent

The junction with rue des Saules is one of the most delightful corners of the Butte: flights of steps drop away mysteriously straight ahead, while another road rises steeply beside the **cemetery**; the picturesque charm is further enhanced by the famous **Lapin Agile**, a traditional cabaret that attracted a host of often penniless writers and artists between 1900 and 1914. It still draws a crowd (⏱Tue–Sun 9pm–1am; show and a drink 28€; ℘01 46 06 85 87; www.au-lapin-agile.com). **Hector Berlioz** once lived in the house on the corner with rue du Mont Cenis, where he composed Harold in Italy and Benvenuto Cellini.

Cimetière Saint-Vincent

This modest cemetery is the resting place of the musician Honegger, the painter Utrillo, the writer Marcel Aymé, and Émile Goudeau, the founder of the Club des Hydropathes.

Nearby (52 rue Lamarck), the most fashionable restaurant in Montmartre, the Beauvilliers, was named after **Antoine Beauvilliers**, a famous chef at the court of Louis XVIII; note the exuberant late 19C décor (sculptures, paintings).

▶ Walk up the steps on the left then turn right on to a narrow lane.

Château des Brouillards

This mansion was built in the 18C as a folly; it was later used as a dance hall. Its grounds have become square Suzanne Buisson (a statue of St Denis stands on the spot where he is said to have washed his decapitated head).

▶ Go through Square S Buisson and down on to avenue Junot.

Avenue Junot

This peaceful thoroughfare is home to artists' studios and private houses: the **Hameau des Artistes** (no 11) and the

Villa Léandre★ (no 25). There is a view of the windmill from no 10.

▶ Stay on avenue Junot; take a sharp right at rue Lepic.

Moulin de la Galette

This dance hall, which enjoyed such a rage at the turn of the 19C, inspired many painters including **Renoir**, **Van Gogh** and Adolphe Willette. The windmill, which has topped the hill for more than six centuries, is the old Blute-fin, which was defended against the Cossacks in 1814 by the heroic mill-owner Debray, whose corpse was finally crucified upon the sails.

Rue Lepic

The old quarry road that winds gently down the steep hill is the scene each autumn of a veteran car rally. Van Gogh lived with his brother at no **54**.

Cimetière de Montmartre

20 Avenue Rachel. ⏱Daily 8am–5.30pm (9am Sun); winter, 8.30am–5.30pm (8.30am on Sat; 9am on Sun). ☞Guided tours by appointment. ℘01 53 42 30 30.

Split in two by the elevated road, this small cemetery has many famous people buried here, among them artists and writers, including the dramatist Labiche, painter Edgar Degas, the great dancer Nijinski, actor Louis Jouvet, composer Jacques Offenbach, and film director François Truffaut. 💡see Montmartre Cemetery map key for a fuller list.

▶ Go down rue Lepic, which joins boulevard de Clichy at place Blanche.

Moulin-Rouge

82 boulevard de Clichy. ☞From 77€ (show only) to 170€ and up (dinner, show, champagne). ℘01 53 09 82 82. www.moulinrouge.fr.

Since 1889 this famous nightclub has presented lavish revues (with lots of plumes, sequins and rhinestones) to spectators from around the world. The French cancan dance was immortalised here by the art of Toulouse-Lautrec.

La Villette★★

The largest park within city limits stretches between the Porte de la Villette and the Porte de Pantin, a vast green space that's home to two modern museum complexes, concert venues, cinemas, and play areas specially designed for children.

CITÉ DES SCIENCES ET DE L'INDUSTRIE★★★

30 avenue Corentin Cariou. Ⓜ*Port de la Villette.* Ⓞ*Tue–Sat 10am–6pm, Sun 10am–7pm* Ⓞ*1 Jan, 1 May, 25 Dec.* *Prices vary per venue (see below).* &*01 40 05 80 00 (recording).* *www.cite-sciences.fr.*

Designed by architect Adrien Fainsilber and opened in 1986, this modern interactive complex has three aims: to inform, to teach and to provide enjoyment. It succeeds in all three, in a contemporary setting interwoven with elements of water, vegetation and light. Below are highlights of a visit.

Explora★★

Levels 1 and 2. *9€; under 25 years 7€; under 6 years free. Planetarium 3€.*

Explore today's and tomorrow's world by means of a variety of exhibitions and interactive shows, models and hands-on activities.

On **Levels 1** and **2** are the permanent exhibits on **space and the universe** (with satellite images of Earth and an exploration of the origins of the universe on two levels), **images** (how to transform what we see: photography, cinema, television, video films, digital images), **sounds** (listen to a multitude of sounds, from a rubbing noise to a buzzing noise, a whistling noise and others), an **innovations lab**, and displays on **mathematics**, and **current events**. These two levels also host temporary exhibits with themes such as biodiversity, counterfeiting, food and flavours, and building with natural materials.

Level 2's north mezzanine presents the immensely popular **Planétarium** (astronomical phenomena are described with projections of actual real-life

Info: Paris tourism office, 25 rue des Pyramides. &08 92 68 30 00 (0.34€ per min). http://en.parisinfo.com.

Location: La Villette is located in the far northeast corner of the city.

Ⓜ **Metro/Transport:** Porte de La Villette (north: Cité des Sciences et de L'Industrie – line 7) and Porte de Pantin (south: Cité de la Musique – line 5) – Buses: 75, 139, 150, 152

Parking: Underground parking at the Porte de Pantin.

Don't Miss: The excellent temporary exhibitions at the Cité des Sciences.

Timing: Allow a half day for this vast park complex.

Kids: The Dragon slide and Cité des Enfants are kid favourites.

images, a simulator and triphonic sound), **Man and health**, **Medicine** (take a trip through the human body and learn that drugs are not the only means of curing people), **Biology** and **Light effects**.

Cité des Enfants★★

Ground floor. Ⓞ*Tue– Fri 10am, 11.45am, 1.30pm, 3.15pm; Sat–Sun 10.30am, 12.30pm, 2.30pm and 4.30pm.* *7€ per child for 1hr 30min. Reservations advised.* &*08 92 69 70 72 (0.34€ min).*

This hands-on interactive section is reserved for children age 2-7 and 5-12. The younger kids learn in five themed rooms: I Discover, I Can Do It, I Figure It Out, I Experiment, and All Together. There is plenty to keep older children intrigued, as they find the answers to scientific and technical questions.

This Cité allows kids more independence in six zones: The Body, Communication, TV Studio, Water Games, The Garden, and The Factory.

La Géode

©H. Chajmowicz/Michelin

Bibliothèque

Levels 1 and 2 for adults, ground floor for children. ⏱*Tue–Sun noon–6.45pm.* 🎫*Free entry.*

This library provides not only books and printed data, but also access to externally held computerized published information in the form of video, CD-ROM and other educational material.

👥 Géode★★

In the park just outside the Cité des Sciences. The most comfortable viewing is from the top of the hall. ⏱*Hourly sessions Tue–Sun 10.30am–8.30pm (check online for Mon hours).* ⏱*1 May, 25 Dec.* 🎫*12€-16€ per projection. Reservations online. www.lageode.fr.*

The shining steel globe, 36m/118ft in diameter, seems to hover over a sheet of water. Inside, the auditorium is equipped with a hemispherical aluminium 1 000sq m/10 765sq ft screen, perforated for sound. The wide-angle lens encompasses a 180° field of vision. The multimedia system projects films with scientific and cultural themes.

L'Argonaute

Outside, next to the Géode. ⏱*Tue–Sat 10am–5.30pm (until 6.30pm Sun).* 🎫*3€.*

This submarine was launched on 29 June 1957 at Cherbourg, France. Since then it has covered336,000km/210 000mi, and was submerged a total of 32 700hr before finally coming to rest beside the Géode.

👥 Cinaxe

Outside. ⏱*Tue–Sun 11am–5pm; film every 15min.* 🎫*4.80€ at the Cinaxe ticket window. Children under age 4 years not allowed; not advisable for pregnant women, heart patients, etc. Reservations* ✆*01 40 05 12 12.*

The Cinaxe simulator enables up to 56 people to physically experience a particular film action – a flight through outer space, or driving round a motor-racing track – during a 4 to 5min ride. This sensation is in part achieved by the capsule's actual hydraulic motion, and partly through wearing 3-D glasses *(provided).*

Taking a Break

The Cité des Sciences et de l'Industrie has several snack bars, cafés, and restaurants that are located on levels 0, 1 and -2. The **gift shop** *(ground floor)* sells games, gifts and other souvenirs, including lots of fun toys for children that demonstrate scientific principles, as well as catalogues of the exhibitions, guidebooks, postcards and scientific reviews and books.

Musée de la Musique

© Directpck/age fotostock

FREE ACTIVITIES

In addition to many activities that have an admission or participation fee, the City of Sciences and Industry offers several activities that are free of charge, including an aquarium.

Here are a few:

Cité des métiers: *Tue–Fri. 10am–6pm, Sat noon–6pm. Closed public holidays.* Level –1.

Bibliothèque: Levels –1 and –2 for adults; ground floor for children.

Salle Louis Braille: Computerized reading room for the blind. Level 1, inside the Bibliothèque, by appointment.

Cinéma Jean-Bertin: Documentaries, scientific and technical films. Ground floor; projection times on location.

Mediterranean aquarium: Level – 2

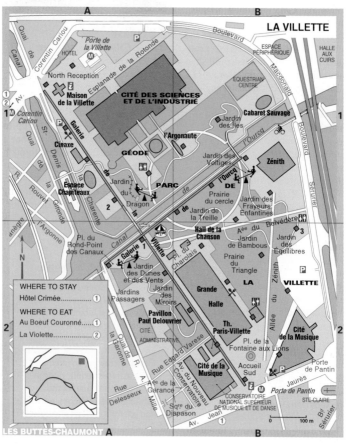

WHERE TO STAY
Hôtel Crimée...............①

WHERE TO EAT
Au Boeuf Couronné......①
La Violette...................②

👥 CITÉ DE LA MUSIQUE

221 avenue Jean Jaurès. Ⓜ *Port de Pantin.* ♿ ℘*01 44 84 44 84.*
www.citedelamusique.fr.

Located at the southern entrance to the park, near the Porte de Pantin, this Music City, designed by Christian de Portzamparc, houses all the facilities needed to study dance and music in France today. The western building contains the **Conservatoire national supérieur de musique et de danse de Paris** (Paris National Conservatory of Music and Dance), whereas the eastern building houses a concert hall and a music museum.

Musée de la Musique★

🕐*Tue–Fri noon–6pm, Sat–Sun 10am–6pm.* 🕐*Public holidays.* ◉*7€ (additional 5€ for temporary exhibits).*

The museum contains around 900 **musical instruments** dating the 17C to the present time.

An audio-visual tour, taking the visitor through the history of Western music, includes exhibits of Stradivarius and Amati violins, some 50 spinets, harpsichords, and pianos, guitars, recorders, bass viols and lutes.

Also on display are instruments once owned by famous musicians (Berlioz, Chopin and Fauré, Adolphe Sax and others).

👥 PARC DE LA VILLETTE★

211 avenue Jean Jaurès. Ⓜ *Port de Pantin. Information/ticket office* 🕐*daily 9.30am–6.30pm.* ℘*01 40 03 75 75. www.villette.com. Chairs and mats are available for hire. Check the programme in any events magazine, such as Pariscope, or go online.*

This immense, 55ha/136-acre park, which lies between the Cité des Sciences et de l'Industrie and the Cité de la Musique, was designed by **Bernard Tschumi** around three principal sets of features: follies, galleries and play areas. It has become a favourite place to spend a summer evening in the park watching films projected on a giant outdoor screen. The ambience is friendly and relaxed.

Red pavilions, built of enamelled iron over a concrete frame, punctuate the park every 120m/393.7ft on a grid pattern. Some 26 **follies**, more usually denoting 18C fanciful pavilions, are here designed with a particular function, be it a slide, weather vane or viewing platform.Trees and grassy areas abound.

La Grande Halle

This former cattle market auction hall has been skilfully converted into a space for a variety of activities: concerts, circuses, theatre and dance productions, trade fairs and other assemblies. It was inaugurated in 1985 on the occasion the the Paris Biennale and restored in 2007.

Playing fields

One is triangular, one is circular; both fields are large, flat grassy spaces, eminently suitable for all kinds of ball games, sunbathing, open-air concerts and cinema.

👥 Gardens

There are 12 gardens in all in the park, with delightful play equipment for children. One favourite area, the **Jardin des Dunes**, is designed around the theme of wind and dunes; children run, climb and swing in the different sections, according to their age group. The vast **bamboo garden**, with some 30 varieties, has been laid out in a 6m/19.7ft pit to create a micro-climate. The Dragon and the garden of Acrobats are popular too.

Buttes-Chaumont★

Known as the *mont chauve*, the denuded (literally **"bald"**) rise of Chaumont, riddled with open quarrying and full of dumped rubbish, used to be a sinister place until **Haussmann** and Napoléon III transformed the area by creating the very first park on the northern edge of Paris, between 1864 and 1867.

VISIT
Buttes-Chaumont Park★
Built along the contours of the original quarry, the park is known for its dramatic hills and cliffs. In the centre is a man-made **lake**, landscaped with an island and huge rocks 50m/164ft high (half natural, half artificial). Access was pro-

ℹ Info: Paris Office du Tourisme, 25 rue des Pyramides. ☏08 92 68 30 00 (0.34€ per min.) http://en.parisinfo.com.

◐ Location: The Buttes-Chaumont are in the northeastern corner of the city (19th *arrondissement*), between La Villette and Belleville.

🅿 Parking: There is plenty of parking in this predominantly residential area, and underground parking on the avenue Secretan.

⊘ Don't Miss: Views from the park's temple.

🕓 Timing: An hour for the park and streets.

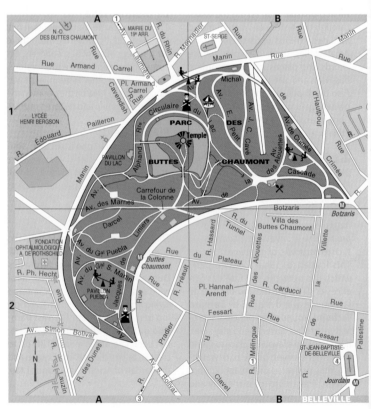

vided by two bridges: one in brick, nick-named the suicide bridge, the other a footbridge. The Corinthian-style Sybille **temple** on the island, modelled on the Roman temple of the same name in Tivoli, Italy, commands a good **view★** over Montmartre and St-Denis.

Other features include a **waterfall** and a **cave★** encrusted with stalactites. There are 5km/3mi of walking paths past lawns and indigenous and exotic trees such as Cedars of Lebanon, Byzantine Hazelnut and Siberian Elm.

Quartier d'Amérique★

To the east of the park.

Hidden behind modern buildings, the charming area of **Mouzaïa** – the name of an Algerian town – consists of flower-decked 19C villas built for the workers of eastern Paris. It's also called the American quarter, since the gymsum mined here was exported overseas.

Parc des Buttes-Chaumont

©H. Chaimowicz/Michelin

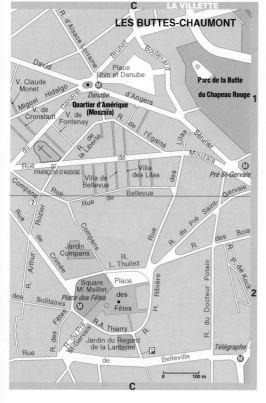

LES BUTTES-CHAUMONT

WHERE TO STAY

Laumière......................... ①

WHERE TO EAT

L'Hermès........................... ①
L'Heure Bleue................... ②
Le Fleuve Rouge.............. ③
Nakagawa........................ ④

Belleville★

Built on the highest hill in Paris after Montmartre (128m/420ft), this district owes part of its charm to the unexpectedly steep paths and winding streets. Despite the mushrooming of modern buildings, Belleville has, on the whole, kept its traditional atmosphere, its quiet streets and their secluded life, vacant spaces and little snatches of greenery. The main streets, however, are full of popular ethnic restaurants and food shops (Chinese, Vietnamese). Belleville also has the highest number of artist ateliers, over 250, open to the public during the annual Portes Ouvertes in May.

A BIT OF HISTORY

An old village – Once the country retreat of the Merovingian kings, then the property of several abbeys and priories, the hill and particularly the ancient hamlet of **Ménilmontant**

- **Info:** Paris Office du Tourisme, 25 rue des Pyramides. ✆08 92 68 30 00 (0.34€ per min.) http://en.parisinfo.com.
- **Location:** Belleville straddles the north end of the 20th *arrondissement*, bordered by the wide boulevard de Belleville and the narrow rue de Belleville.
- **Parking:** Street and underground parking along the boulevard de Belleville.
- **Don't Miss:** The view of Paris from the rue Piat, above the Parc de Belleville.
- **Timing:** Allow two to three hours for this hilly neighbourhood.
- **Kids:** The Parc de Belleville and Maison de l'Air.

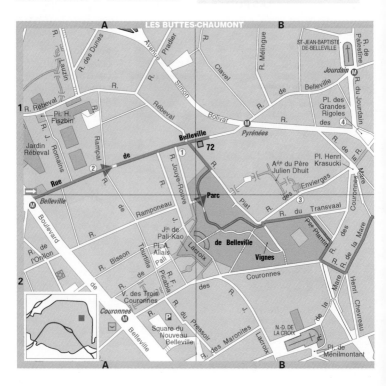

Stars of Belleville

On 19 December 1915, Giovanna Gassion was born to abject poverty on the steps of 72 rue de Belleville. She later sang in the streets, before becoming a radio, gramophone and music hall success in 1935 under the name of **Édith Piaf**. Beloved for the instinctive but deeply moving inflexions of her voice, she came to embody the spirit of France *(La Vie en rose, Les Cloches)*. A small private **museum** in rue Crespin du Gast contains souvenirs of the great singer.

Another famous figure to come from this neighbourhood was **Maurice Chevalier** (1888–1974), film star, entertainer and *chansonnier*. He paired with Jeanne Mistinguett at the Folies-Bergère (1909) and sang at the Casino de Paris between the wars. Before attaining fame on Broadway in black-tie and boater, he was known at home for songs that were rooted in Belleville: *Ma pomme Prosper* and *Marche de Ménilmontant*.

were, for a long time, inhabited only by quarry workers and a handful of wine growers. In the 18C, it became known as Belleville, probably a corruption of *belle vue* or beautiful view, becoming a commune in 1789. In 1860 the village, whose population had grown at an increasing pace, was annexed to Paris and allocated between the 19th and 20th *arrondissements*.

A succession of different immigrant populations and artists has resulted in a lively, popular place to live, particularly among the young. Streets between the metro Jourdain and metro Pyrénées are full of trendy boutiques, art galleries and bistros, while night owls find many bars and late-night cafés along rue de Ménilmontant.

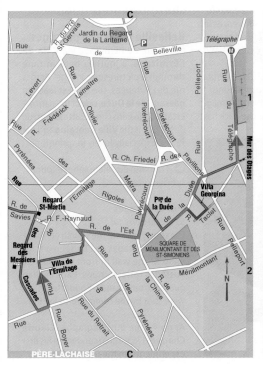

BELLEVILLE

0   100 m

WHERE TO EAT

▪▪ WALKING TOUR
Start from the Ⓜ*Belleville station.*

◉ Follow rue de Belleville uphill to appreciate the particularly lively character of the neighbourhood.

As you walk, be sure to look up to catch the many examples of street art, murals and whimsical grafitti decorating the walls and street corners.

Rue de Belleville
This lively shopping street lined with Chinese food shops stretches from Belleville metro station to the Porte des Lilas. Édith Piaf was born at no 72.

◉ Retrace your steps and turn left along rue Piat.

♟ Parc de Belleville★
Ⓢ*Daily from 10am, closing hours vary.*
Passage Julien Lacroix, with its stone steps, is the main thoroughfare through this 4.5ha/11-acre park, converted from a quarry on Belleville Hill to a contemporary park in 1988. The differences in ground level have been used to create tiered gardens, with cascades and waterfalls.
The **Aire de Jeux** (*closes 30min before park*) is a new adventure playground. From the top of the park, there is a magnificent **view★★** of Paris. The park has

View of Paris from Parc de Belleville

© S. Sauvignier/MICHELIN

several other play areas for children, a small vineyard and grassy lawns.

◉ Leave via rue du Transvaal, take the passage Plantin on the right, then turn right on to rue des Couronnes, by the old railway line. Take rue de la Mare, then rue de Savies.

Rue des Cascades, narrow, winding and paved, is among the quaintest in the neighbourhood, reminiscent of a small provincial town. There is a magnificent **view** over Paris from the corner of the steps of rue Fernand-Raynaud.
Regard St-Martin at no 42, opposite rue de Savies, is one of four buildings of its kind constructed in Belleville to channel the supply of water to the capital by means of underground aqueducts. At no 17 is the **Regard des Messiers** (*descend the steps*). The Messiers were the guards who kept watch over the vines and fields.

◉ Go to the end of rue des Cascades; turn left on to rue de Ménilmontant, then right on to rue de l'Ermitage.

Belleville villas and passages
Leave rue de l'Ermitage via **Villa de l'Ermitage**, a journey back in time through a picturesque village. Across rue des Pyrénées, rue de l'Est leads to **passage de la Duée**, one of the narrowest streets in Paris (1m/3.28ft). Along rue de la Duée is the **Villa Georgina** and rue Taclet, especially lovely in springtime.

◉ From rue du Télégraphe detour to rue du Borrégo.

Mur des Otages
53 rue du Borrégo.
In a courtyard near the church of Notre-Dame des Otages can be seen a fragment of the wall in front of which 52 hostages (priests, nuns, Paris civilian guards) from Grande-Roquette prison were shot by the *communards* in 1871.

At no 40 rue du Télégraphe, **Claude Chappe** (1763–1805) conducted his first experiments on the telegraph in 1793.

Le Père-Lachaise★★

Paris' largest cemetery spreads over 40ha/99 acres of sloping ground; it is the final resting place of many famous figures. A pleasant place for a stroll, Père-Lachaise is exceptional, not only for its size, but also for the quality of its statuary.

A BIT OF HISTORY

In 1626 the Jesuits bought a piece of land in the open countryside to build a retreat for retired priests. One frequent visitor to the place was Louis XIV's confessor, Father La Chaise, who gave funds generously to the house's reconstruction in 1682.

Forty years after the Jesuits' expulsion in 1763, the city purchased the land for a cemetery to be designed by Brongniart. When it was first opened, Parisians thought it was too far from the city, so in 1817 the authorities moved the tombs of several well-known people to Père Lachaise to make it more popular. Its success was immediate. Among those moved were La Fontaine, Molière and the medieval lovers Abélard and Héloïse. By 1830 there were more than 30,000 tombs, so the cemetery had to be expanded six times between 1824 and 1850.

Today, at its present size, there is space for 70,000 burial plots.

ℹ Info: Pyramides welcome centre, 25 rue des Pyramides. ☏08 92 68 30 00 (0.34€ per min). http://en.parisinfo.com.

▶ Location: The cemetery is in the northeast end of Paris' Right Bank.

Ⓜ Metro/Transport: Père Lachaise (lines 2 and 3) – Buses: 26, 60, 61, 69.

Ⓟ Parking: Along the boulevard de Ménilmontant and avenue Gambetta.

Don't Miss: The Mur des Fédérés and the houses of La Campagne à Paris.

🕐 Timing: Allow two hours for the cemetery and walking tour.

CEMETERY★★

🕐 *Mid-Mar–Oct Mon–Fri 8am–6pm, Sat 8.30am–6pm, Sun and public holidays 9am–6pm; Nov–early Mar Mon–Fri 8am–5.30pm, Sat 8.30am–5.30pm, Sun and public holidays 9am–5.30pm.* ✆*Guided tour possible Sat–Sun.* ✆*Free entry.* ☏01 55 25 82 10.

An Américaine in Paris

"Paris was where the twentieth century was."

American expatriates **Gertrude Stein** and **Alice B Toklas** lived just minutes from the Luxembourg Gardens at no 27 rue de Fleurus.

From 1903 to 1937, their courtyard apartment and atelier, with its famed collection of paintings by contemporary masters, hosted Paris' most avant-garde expatriate Salon. Their guest list reads like a Who's Who of the early 20C art and literary world: Picasso, Juan Gris, Matisse, Erik Satie, Hemingway, Pound, Sherwood Anderson and others. Although Gertrude Stein significantly influenced numerous expatriate writers (the term Lost Generation is attributed to her), international recognition for her own experimental works came only in 1933 with the publication of *The Autobiography of Alice B Toklas*.

In 1938 the two women moved nearby to no 5 rue Christine (in the Odéon Quarter). Stein died in 1946 and was buried in Père-Lachaise Cemetery. Toklas joined her in 1967 (her name is on the back of the tombstone).

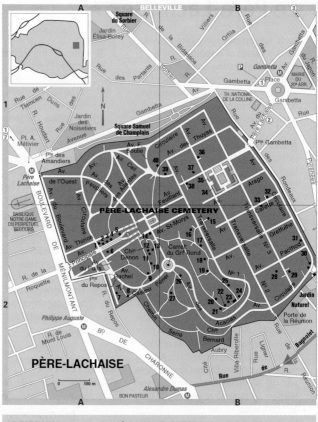

WHERE TO STAY

Hôtel Palma.................................①
Hôtel Paris-Gambetta..............②
Mama Shelter.............................③

WHERE TO EAT

Café Charbon............................①
Café Justine..............................②
Le Bistrot des Soupirs
    "Chez les On".......................③
Les Allobroges.........................④

PÈRE-LACHAISE CEMETERY

1 - Colette
2 - Rossini (cénotaphe)
3 - A. de Musset (sous un saule,
    selon son vœu)
4 - Baron Haussmann
5 - Généraux Lecomte et Thomas
6 - Arago
7 - James de Rothschild.
8 - Abélard, Héloïse
9 - Miguel Angel Asturias
10 - Chopin

11 - Cherubini
12 - Boieldieu (cénotaphe)
13 - Bellini
14 - Thiers
15 - Sarah Bernhardt
16 - Corot
17 - Molière et La Fontaine
18 - Alphonse Daudet
19 - Famille Hugo
20 - Famille Bibesco
     (Anna de Noailles)

Maps are available at Porte des Amandiers and Porte Gambetta.

Full of romantic funerary statues, this national heritage site is graced with more than 3 000 trees, creating an attractive setting for the tombs. Wealthy Parisiens erected Baroque monuments, like the lighthouse of Felix Beaujour. Chopin, Édith Piaf, Balzac, Proust, Oscar Wilde, Colette and Jim Morrison can be found in this stunning setting (&see numbered key below the map above).

Le Mur des Fédérés

On the evening of 27 May 1871, the last insurgents of the Paris **Commune**, having shot their hostages in Belleville, rallied in the cemetery, fighting the Versailles troops among the tombstones.

At dawn the 147 survivors were shot against what is now known as the **Federalists' Wall** in the southeast corner and buried where they fell in a communal grave. Their burial ground has

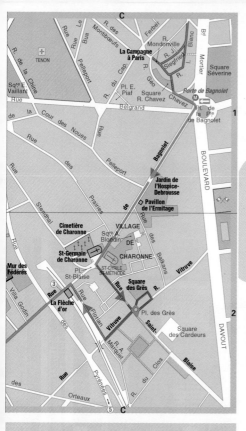

WALKING TOUR

Start at M Porte de Bagnolet. (From the cemetery, walk to place Gambetta, then go east on rue Belgrand.)

CHARONNE VILLAGE

▶ From the metro, walk to the northeast corner of the square with the same name, then take the steps in rue Géo Chavez.

The village of Charonne kept its country atmosphere until recently, but still provides a haven of peace and quiet, not far from the busy Paris ring-road. The garden houses of **La Campagne à Paris★** were built for working-class families at the end of the 19C atop a former quarry dump. A pleasant stroll can be enjoyed around the more working-class area along rue du Père Prosper Enfantin, rue Irénée Blanc, rue Mondonville and rue Jules Seigfried.

▶ Retrace your steps and walk southwest on rue de Bagnolet.

Place St-Blaise and the **Église Saint-Germain-de-Charonne** were the focal point of the village. The church's stunted bell-tower has interesting carved capitals. Pushing south from the square, take the **Rue St-Blaise★**, which was formerly the main thoroughfare of the village. St-Blaise is now a pretty little street, partly pedestrianized. The carefully restored 19C houses at **square des Grès★** and **rue Vitruve** mingle with modern buildings.

▶ Take rue de Bagnolet west to end the tour at M Alexandre Dumas.

become a place of pilgrimage for many ever since.

Perhaps the most moving monuments are the ones next to the wall, dedicated to the Resistance movement and deportees of World War II. All along the avenue Circulaire are the heartachingly grim statues created by artists to remember the men, women and children killed in the Nazi concentration camps of Sachsenhausen, Buchenwald-Dora, Ravensbrück, Auschwitz.

View of La Défense from the Seine
© Raga Jose Fuste / age fotostock

Outer Paris

La Défense★★

The modern business district of La Défense, juxtaposing traditional office space with experimental housing developments, is a truly exceptional environment. The Grande Arche stands at the extreme west of an axis along the Champs-Élysées, which starts at the Louvre and passes through the Arc de Triomphe. As for the business sector, the Esso building first opened in 1964, and since then more than 40 towers have been completed, providing office space for 1 500 companies.

LA GRANDE ARCHE★★

🕐 *Daily Apr–Aug 10am–8pm; rest of the year until 7pm.* ⊛*10€.* 📞*01 49 07 27 55. www.grandearche.com.*
Designed by Otto von Spreckelsen, the arch is one of the most controversial of the *Grands Projets* instigated by President François Mitterrand. This gigantic open cube (110m/361ft wide) weighs 300 000t on 12 piles sunk below ground. (The cathedral of Notre-Dame could fit inside the arch.) The top part of the arch is occupied by a computer museum, art gallery, restaurant and belvedere (⊶ *access to the rooftop closed to the public indefinitely*) offering exceptional **views ★★★** of the Arc de Triomphe, the Louvre and other parts of the city.

🛈 **Info:** Espace Info Défense, Place de la Défense.
📞01 47 74 84 24.
www.ladefense.fr.
▶ **Location:** This western business district is divided into 11 zones; the 130ha/321-acre site falls in the Puteaux, Nanterre and Courbevoie districts.
Ⓜ **Metro/Transport:** Esplanade de la Défense (line 1), RER E: La Défense Grande Arche – Buses: 73, 141, 144, 161, 174, 178, 258, 262, 272.
🕐 **Timing:** Allow two hours.
🅿 **Parking:** Underground.
👁 **Don't Miss:** Views from the Grande Arche's platform.

👣 WALKING TOUR

Esplanade de la Défense

This pedestrian promenade is a splendid place for a **walk★★** to admire the modern architecture and 20C sculptures exhibited in this open-air gallery.
At place Carpeaux is César's *Thumb* (**1**), whereas to the right of the Great Arch is a metal sculpture by the Japanese artist Miyawaki (**2**). For an optional detour,

La Grande Arche

© Michal Bednarek/Dreamstime.com

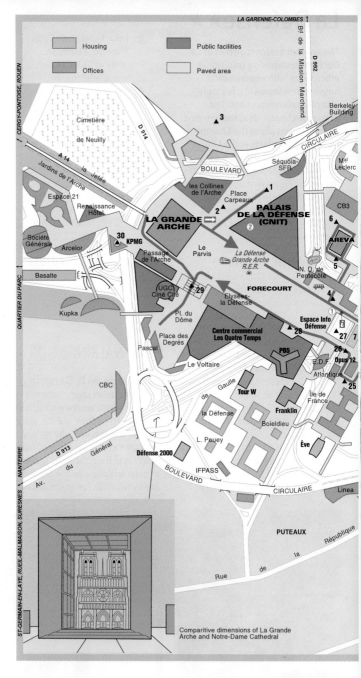

Comparitive dimensions of La Grande Arche and Notre-Dame Cathedral

take the small footbridge over the circular boulevard towards the Faubourg de l'Arche and the Léonard de Vinci university for a view of the *Colosse* (**3**) in the distance, by Igor Mitoraj.

The **Palais de la Défense** (**CNIT**)★, the first construction (1958), is remarkable

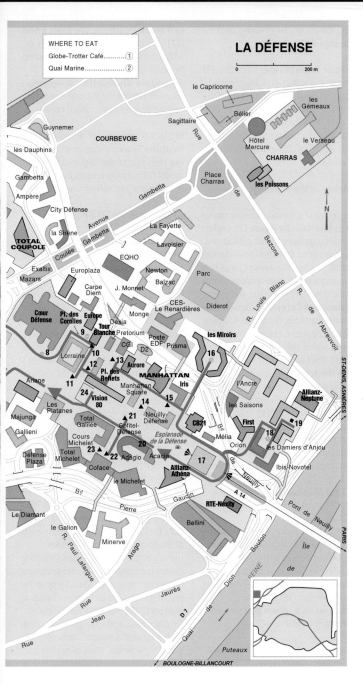

LA DÉFENSE

0   200 m

WHERE TO EAT
Globe-Trotter Café...........①
Quai Marine....................②

for the boldness of its architecture. Its record-breaking concrete vault (220m/722ft span) has only three points of support.

Further on, to the left, on place de la Défense, is **Alexander Calder**'s last work, a red stabile 15m/49.2ft high (**4**).

331

▷ Walk through the opening on the left to the Fiat Tower.

The **Tour Framatome**, with the **Elf Tower**, is the tallest building, rising 45 storeys to 178m/584ft. At the foot of the tower, *The Great Toscano* (**5**), a bronze bust by Mitoraj, evokes an antique giant. Pass round the tower to the left to see *Les Lieux du Corps* (**6**), in polyester resin, by Delfino.

▷ Return to the esplanade.

In the centre of the esplanade is a monumental **fountain by Agam** (**7**); underground is a **gallery** for art exhibitions. Pass in front of the *Midday-Midnight* pond (**8**), where the artist Clarus has decorated a ventilation shaft to represent the trajectory of the sun and moon. The **place des Corelles** is named after its copper fountain, *Corolla* (**9**), sculpted by Louis Leygue. A ceramic fresco *The Cloud Sculptor* (**10**) by Attila adorns a low wall. Philolaos' *Mechanical Bird* (**11**) graces the terrace, as it carefully folds its immense steel wings.

Beyond the Vision 80 Tower, built on stilts, **place des Reflets** (**12**) is overlooked by and reflected in the shimmering **Aurore Tower**, in contrast to its neighbouring rose-coloured Manhattan Tower and the green GAN Tower. Note the allegory by Derbré of *The Earth* (**13**). The **Tour Manhattan** is designed as a series of curves and counter-curves that mirror the sky.

In the distance on the right is the **Moretti Tower** (**14**), an aeration chimney that has been transformed into art with 672 coloured tubes of fibreglass. In **place de l'Iris** the slender silhouette of the *Sleepwalker* (**15**) by Henri de Miller is balanced on a sphere poised on the ridge of a cuboid.

▷ Turn left in front of the **Tour GAN** shaped like a Greek cross.

Les Miroirs (**16**) is the work of Henri La Fonta: the fountain in the courtyard consists of 10 cylinders decorated with mosaics.

East of the esplanade, the **Takis pond** (**17**) consists of a stretch of water on which the reflection of 49 multicoloured flexible light-tubes seem to play.

On **square Vivaldi** the *Conversation Fountain* (**18**) by Busato represents two bronze figures in animated conversation.

In place Napoléon-I at the foot of the **Neptune Tower**, a monument shaped like the Cross of the Légion d'Honneur medal (**19**) commemorates the return of the emperor's remains from St Helena.

▷ Return to the Takis pond.

The **Tour Hoechst-Marion-Roussel**, an attractive blue-green, steel and glass high-rise, was built in 1967.

Straight ahead is a fountain *The Frog* (**20**) with drinking water, by Torricini, and a bronze low-relief *Ophelia* (**21**) by the Catalan sculptor Apel les Fenosa. Go around the Sofitel Hotel on your left. From the terrace overlooking the square cours Michelet, you can see Venet's 14m/46ft-high painted-steel sculpture (**22**), and further on, to the right, Jakober's assemblage of welded iron resembling an American footballer's mask (**23**).

In the square below the esplanade, 35 flower-planters (**24**) interspersed with faces and clasped hands are the work of Selinger. A white-marble sculpture, *Lady Moon* (**25**) by Julio Silva, rises between the Atlantique and Crédit Lyonnais Towers. Barrias' bronze group *La Défense* (**27**), for which the district is named, is at the foot of the Agam fountain.

In front of the **Quatre Temps** shopping centre is a brightly coloured sculpture (**28**) of two figures by Miró. Steps to the left of the Élysées-La Défense building lead up to the UGC Ciné Cité cineplex. On place des Degrés, the sculptor Kowalski has created a *mineral landscape* (**29**): parts of pyramids, wave of granite, etc.

▷ Back on the esplanade, take the passage de l'Arche to the **KPMG building**, which forms a glass arc around the monumental head *Tindajo* (**30**) by Mitoraj**.**

Marché aux Puces de Saint-Ouen★

Looking for old furniture, medals, uniforms, dolls or a hat that was once fashionable? The Saint-Ouen flea markets are a source of never-ending interest. They are open at weekends and on Mondays all year round, but beware pickpockets and fake Rolexes from street vendors.

VISIT

🕐 *Sat–Sun 10am–6pm and Mon 11am–5pm.* 👣 *Organized guided group and individual tours (2hrs) are available; call for info* 📞 *01 40 11 77 36.* The most famous flea market in Paris is located on the northern edge of the city on the avenue de la Porte de Clignancourt. Flea markets are starting to look more like shops these days, although the neighbourhood retains the atmosphere of an unusual and picturesque village. There are between 2 500 and 3 000 stalls in total and 12 markets open to the public. If you search long enough and bargain carefully, you may find something to treasure among the assorted bric-a-brac; the place is a real collector's paradise. *The markets that follow are arranged geographically from the right side of the Rue des Rosiers down to the Warehouse and then back up the other side of the Rue des Rosiers. All 12 markets are described.*

ℹ️ **Info:** Espace Accueil et Information du Marché aux Puces, 7 Impasse Simon, 93400 St-Ouen. 📞 01 58 61 22 90. www.marchesauxpuces.fr.

▶ **Location:** The flea market is actually just outside Paris, in the suburb of St-Ouen, a five-minute walk from the metro Clignancourt (go north under the boulevard Périphérique to reach the markets).

🅿 **Parking:** There is underground parking at the markets along rue des Rosiers.

😊 **Don't Miss:** The lively atmosphere at the flea market bistros.

🕐 **Timing:** Allow at least three hours to wander the market stalls and soak up the atmosphere.

Marché Vernaison

The oldest market in the *Puces* goes by the name of its proprietor. In about 1885 he rented a part of his property to dealers, known as *chiff-tir* or *biffins* (rag-pickers), who resold objects they had collected, a practice true today: knick-knacks, furniture, vintage fabrics.

Saint-Ouen shopping

©H. Chalmowicz/Michelin

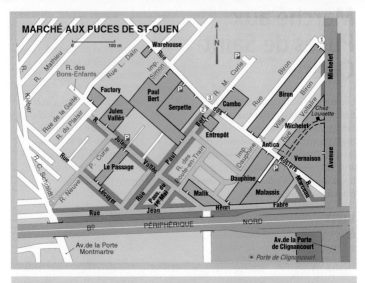

MARCHÉ AUX PUCES DE ST-OUEN

WHERE TO EAT

Brasserie Biron.................①   Le P'tit Landais...............③
Café Le Paul Bert.............②

Temporary markets

Streets closed to traffic
on market days

Marché Antica
This tiny market mainly has antique furniture lamps, ornaments, pictures.

Marché Biron★
Founded in 1925 by 70 antique dealers, Biron is the smartest of the flea markets, with a friendly atmosphere.

Marché Cambo
Extending over two floors, Cambo has furniture and art objects of the 18C-19C.

Marché l'Usine (18 rue des Bons-Enfants) and **Marché Lécuyer** (27 rue Lécuyer) are open to dealers only.

Marché le Passage
Along its central aisle, stalls brim with old clothing, books, furniture, trinkets.

Marché Jules Vallès
This bric-a-brac market has a reputation for the most affordable prices.

Marché Paul Bert
This open-air market features retro and rustic furniture, garden accessories and oversize architectural remnants.

Marché Serpette
This fairly recent market offers country furniture, knick-knacks, old weapons.

Marché de l'Entrepôt
Large-scale objects are on the spacious site: mansion gates, garden gazebos, paneling from private houses, etc.

Marché Malik
Browse for trendy designs and sports-wear here. Opposite is the Café A. Picolo.

Marché Dauphine★
Specializing in old books, prints and paintings, Dauphine is the most up-to-date market, not only in the setting, but also in its trading: a certificate is provided for buyers who request it (there is an independent valuation office in rue des Rosiers). There's furniture and brick-a-brac to suit every taste and from all periods.

Marché Malassis
This gallery-style market is home to high-end antiques and collectibles. The adjoining streets hold temporary stalls filled with clothing on sale.

Saint-Denis★★

In 1840 the village of Saint-Denis numbered a few thousand inhabitants; the Industrial Revolution brought this number to 100 000 and made the town one of the main manufacturing centres of the northern suburbs. Most of the town was razed and rebuilt in the 1970s, the unattractive results still apparent today. The inauguration of the Stade de France in 1998 gave the town new hopes for future prosperity, although it remains a densely populated suburb of recent immigrants from Francophone Sub-Saharan and North African countries. For visitors, however, the most interesting sight in Saint-Denis remains its basilica, which houses the mausoleum of the kings and queens of France.

A BIT OF HISTORY

Monsieur St-Denis – Legend has it that after his beheading in Montmartre, the Evangelist St Denis, first Bishop of Lutetia, got to his feet, picked up his severed head and walked north out of the city; he is said to have been buried where

🛈 **Info:** 1 rue de la République, 93200 St-Denis. ✆01 55 87 08 70. www.saint-denis-tourisme.com.

▶ **Location:** Located north of Paris on the way to Roissy-CDG Airport.

Ⓜ **Metro/Transport:** Metro station Saint-Denis Porte de Paris (line 13). RER D stop: Gare de Saint-Denis.

🅿 **Parking:** Place Jean-Jaurès near the basilica.

👁 **Don't Miss:** Louis XVIII's funeral robes.

🕐 **Timing:** Allow two hours.

he was found. The place soon attracted pilgrims from near and far. In AD 475 a large village church was erected on the site. Dagobert I had it rebuilt and offered it to a Benedictine community who took charge of the pilgrimage. This abbey was to become the wealthiest and the most celebrated in France. Towards AD 750 the church was dismantled a second time and rebuilt by Pepin the Short, who set up a shrine under the chancel to receive the sacred remains of saints.

Basilique St-Denis

© Franco Di Meo/Fotolia.com

BASILIQUE ST-DENIS★★★
Mausoleum for the kings of France

This monument of Gothic art is a treasured repository of some 70 recumbent sculptures and 12C and 19C stained-glass windows. Over a remarkable span of 12 centuries, all but three of the Kings of France, from Dagobert I to Louis XVIII, were buried at St-Denis. In 1793, during the French Revolution, Barrère asked the Convention for permission to destroy the tombs. They were opened and the remains thrown into unmarked graves. Alexandre Lenoir salvaged the most precious tombs and moved them to Paris, entrusted to the Petits-Augustins, later to become the Museum of French Monuments. In 1816 Louis XVIII returned the tombs to the basilica.

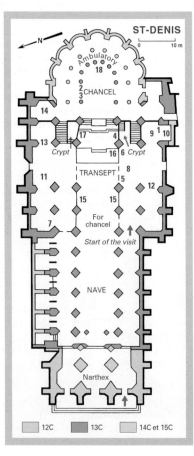

Construction of St-Denis

This basilica marks a turning point in the development of French architecture: it was the first large church to feature a unity of design in plan and style. This element, combined with its significance as a centre of pilgrimage, proved to be the springboard for subsequent late-12C cathedrals and the evolution towards the Gothic style (Chartres, Senlis and Meaux). Abbot Suger supervised construction in 1136–1147 on the west front, the first two bays of the nave, the chancel, crypt and the Carolingian nave. The amazing rapidity of the whole operation was due to his dedication and help from parishioners in transporting the stone from the Pontoise quarries. In the early 13C the north tower was crowned by a magnificent stone spire. In 1247 **Pierre de Montreuil** was appointed master mason by St Louis and remained in charge of the work until his death in 1267.

Decline and restoration

The basilica subsequently fell into disrepair. The French Revolution caused further ravages, and in his *Genius of Christianity*, Chateaubriand lamented the sorry state of the church. Napoléon gave orders to repair the damage and reinstated public worship in 1806. The architect Debret aroused a wave of public indignation on account of his poor knowledge of medieval methods. He was succeeded by **Viollet-le-Duc**, who studied a number of original documents that guided him in his work. From 1858 up to his death (1879), he toiled relentlessly and produced the basilica that stands today. The choir and west front (although much restored) provide some idea of the original.

Exterior

The absence of the north tower mars the harmony of the west front. In the Middle Ages the building would have been fortified, from which some crenellation survives at the base of the towers. All three doorways have been restored. The columnar figures of the doorways feature the Wise and Foolish Virgins *(centre)*, the labours of the months *(right)* and the signs of the Zodiac *(left)*. On the north side of the basilica, the nave is supported by double flying buttresses.

Interior

Apr–Sept Mon–Sat 10am–6.15pm, Sun and public holidays noon–6.15pm; Oct–Mar Mon–Sat 10am–5pm, Sun noon–5.15pm (last admission 30min before closing). Guided tours (90min) are possible. 1 Jan, 1 May, 25 Dec and during some religious services. 8.50€. 01 49 21 14 87. http://saint-denis.monuments-nationaux.fr.

The basilica is marginally smaller than Notre-Dame: 108m/354ft long, 38m/125ft wide in the transept and 29m/95ft high. The elegant nave is attributed to Pierre de Montreuil.

Tombs★★★

St-Denis Basilica houses the remains of kings, queens and royal children, as well as those of leading personalities who served the French Court, such as Bertrand du Guesclin (1). It is possible to date most monuments simply from their appearance, thus they serve as a chronological chart of French funeral art through the Middle Ages and into the Renaissance. Up to the Renaissance, the only sculpture to adorn tombs was in the form of **recumbent figures**. Note the 12C funeral slab of Clovis (2) and Fredegonde (3), worked in mosaic and copper, from the abbey of St-Germain-des-Prés. Around 1260 St Louis commissioned a series of effigies of all the rulers who had preceded him since the 7C. The figures were mere allegories, but they provide a telling example of how royalty was portrayed towards the mid-13C. They include the imposing tomb of Dagobert (4), with its lively, spirited scenes, the recumbent statues of Charles Martel (5) and Pepin the Short (6), and the female effigy carved in Tournai marble (7). The tomb of Isabella of Aragon and

Philippe III the Bold (8), who died in 1285, shows an early concern for accurate portraiture imbued with a strong sense of personality. Towards the middle of the 14C, the wealthy oversaw the building of their tomb in their own lifetime. The effigies of Charles V by Beauneveu (9), Charles VI and Isabella of Bavaria (10) are therefore extremely lifelike.

During the Renaissance, **mausoleums** took on monumental proportions and were lavishly decorated. They had two tiers, representing life and death, each contrasting sharply with the other. On the upper level, the king and his wife are featured kneeling in full regalia; on the lower level, the deceased were pictured lying down as naked cadavers. Admire the twin monument built for Louis XII and Anne of Brittany (11), and that of François I and Claude de France (12).

After commissioning the royal tomb, **Catherine de' Medici**, who survived her husband Henri II by 30 years, actually fainted in horror on seeing herself portrayed dead according to the standard convention; she therefore ordered a new effigy to be made showing her asleep. Both, by Primaticcio (13), and Germain Pilon (14), are here displayed.

Chancel

The beautiful pre-Renaissance stalls (15) in the pre-chancel were taken from the Norman château at Gaillon. The splendid Romanesque **Virgin★** in painted wood (16) was brought from St-Martin-des-Champs. The episcopal throne opposite (17) is a replica of Dagobert's royal seat (the original lies in the Medals and Antiquities Gallery at the Bibliothèque Nationale in Paris – *see Place Des Victoires*). At the far end, the modern reliquary of Saints Denis, Rusticus and Eleutherius (18) stands at the edge of Suger's **ambulatory★**, with its wide arches and slim columns.

Crypt★★

The lower ambulatory was built in the Romanesque style by Abbot Suger (12C) and restored by Viollet-le-Duc. In the centre stands a vaulted chapel known as

Tomb of Louis XII and Anne of Brittany

Hilduin's Chapel. Beneath its marble slab lies the burial vault of the Bourbon family, including the remains, among others, of Louis XVI, Marie-Antoinette and Louis XVIII. The communal grave in the north transept received in 1817 the bones of around 800 kings and queens, royal highnesses, and princes of the blood.

MUSEUMS AND OTHER ATTRACTIONS
Musée d'Art et d'Histoire de Saint-Denis

22 bis rue Gabriel-Péri, in the town of St-Denis. ◖Mon, Wed, Fri 10am–5.30pm, Thu 10am–8pm, Sat–Sun 2pm–6.30pm. ◖Public holidays. ☜5€. ✆01 42 43 05 10. *http://ville-saint-denis.fr.*

The museum is set up in the former Carmelite convent, founded by Cardinal de Bérulle in 1625 and occupied by Louis XV's daughter Madame Louise de France between 1770 and 1787.

The refectory and kitchen contain archaeological finds from St-Denis or from the old hospital. On the second floor are drawings, paintings and documents relating to the Paris Commune of 1871.

Stade de France★

Other than attending a concert or sports event, visit by ☜ guided tour (1 hr) only, Apr–Aug daily (including school holidays) 11am, noon, 2pm, 3pm, 4pm (in French) and at 10.30am, 2.30pm (in English); Sept–Mar daily 10am, noon, 2pm, 4pm (in English and French; no tours Mon during school holidays). ☜15€. ✆08 92 700 900. *www.stadefrance.com.*

This huge yet elegant stadium was designed by four architects: Zublena, Macary, Regembal and Costantini. It was the last major construction project of the 20C, built in a record 31 months, and inaugurated with great ceremony on 28 January 1998. It was the setting for the 1998 World Cup, which the French team won for the first time.

The elliptical arena can be adapted to accommodate all kinds of events; thanks to a system of movable seats, the number of spectators can be increased from 80 000 for matches to 100 000 for concerts.

The Golden Age

The Time of the Pilgrims

To the north of Lutèce developed, from the 1C, a Roman city, Catulliacus. A large street cut through the city towards the future city of Rouen. St Denis was buried here, around AD 250, in a Gallo-Roman cemetery. It's traditionally believed that Ste Geneviève built the first churcharound 475 in the place, which had become a popular pilgrimage destination. In 630, King Dagobert became the benefactor of the monastery that established itself there. He transformed it into a royal abbey, and set up a Benedictine community to take care of the pilgrims.

"The Cemetery of Kings"

Dagobert was the first sovereign buried at St-Denis. In 754 Pépin le Bref was crowned king there by the Pope. Under the choir he had a "martyrium" constructed where the faithful could come and see the relics of St Denis and his martyred companions, Éleuthère and Rustique. The ties between the abbey and the crown were strengthened: the Merovingian kings, for the most part, were buried in Paris, but starting with Hughes Capet, all of them would henceforth be buried at St-Denis, except for five of them.

Precious Relics

The kings were buried at St-Denis because of the relics. The relics were believed to protect the bodies and spirits of the deceased, but also the sacred royal objects such as the king's sceptre, the hand of justice, and the king's war banner.

Suger, Monk and Statesman

An exceptionally gifted man, Abbot Suger (c. 1081–1151) gave St-Denis its illustrious reputation. Born to a poor family, he was "placed" in the abbey at the age of 10, and studied alongside the future Louis VI, who called him to his court to be his adviser and ambassador to the Pope. Elected Abbot of St-Denis in 1122, he redesigned the architecture of the church in Gothic style. As minister under Louis VII, he was named regent while the king was fighting the Second Crusade. His wisdom and care for the public good were so renowned that upon his return to Paris, Louis VII named him "Father of the Homeland".

Since the Revolution

Revolutionary Anger

In 1793 the abbey was transformed into a Temple of Reason. Barrère asked the Convention if he could dismantle the statues, symbols of the monarchy. Some tombs, such as Hugh Capet's, were destroyed, the bodies thrown into a communal grave. Lenoir, from the Commission des Monuments, took the most precious tombs to Paris, to the Petits-Augustins warehouse, which eventually became the Museum of French Monuments. In 1817, under the reign of Louis XVIII, these tombs were returned to the basilica. Two years earlier the bodies of Louis XVI and Marie-Antoinette were transferred there from the Madeleine Cemetery.

Industrial Wasteland

Renamed Franciade during the Revolution, St-Denis got its name back in 1800, the beginning of the Industrial era. It was soon surrounded by printers and dyers, then heavy industry on the Plaine. Today, the city remains transformed.

Fontainebleau
©H. Chajmowicz/Michelin

Excursions

Château de Versailles★★★

Symbol of absolute monarchy and the apogee of the arts in France during the reign of the Sun King, Versailles became the residence of the Court and seat of government from May 1682 until the Revolution.

A BIT OF HISTORY

Birth of the Sun King's palace – The original château was a small hunting lodge around the present Marble Court, built in 1624 for **Louis XIII**, who had Philibert le Roy reconstruct it in brick and stone in 1631. The young **Louis XIV** saw Versailles as the perfect place to build his own château far from the mobs of Paris, a magnificent palace of immense proportions and opulence never seen before. He wanted to demonstrate the glory of the French arts as well as establish the absolute power of the Sun King. He commissioned a renowned team to realize his dream: the architect **Louis Le Vau**, the landscape architect **Le Nôtre**, and the decorator **Le Brun**.

Construction began – and continued to some extent for almost a century – in 1661 with the gardens, embellished for Louis XIV's splendid festivals. In 1668 Le Vau constructed stone façades around the original château, creating an "envelope" that concealed the old façades.

Height of the French monarchy – **Jules Hardouin-Mansart** succeeded Le Vau, adding the Galerie des Glaces (Hall of Mirrors) and two wings in the south (1682) and the north (1689). Under Colbert and Le Brun, the Gobelins factory and the artists of the Académie Royale designed the main furniture and decoration with the remarkable stylistic unity that defines Versailles Classicism. Court life at Versailles revolved around a complex system of etiquette and feasts.

Revolution and Restoration – Under **Louis XV** changes to the interior included the creation of the Petits Cabinets. He added the Petit Trianon and gardens in the park next to the Grand Trianon, which was eventually given to **Louis XVI**'s queen, Marie-Antoinette, who would expand it with a private

theatre and hamlet. A century of royal occupation came to a close when the **Revolution** drove Louis XVI from Versailles. The artworks were placed in the Louvre and the furnishings auctioned off.

In the 19C **Louis-Philippe** transformed part of the palace into a museum dedicated to French history, including its fallen monarchy and Napoléon's empire. Since 1914 the State, supported by private patronage (including that of John D Rockefeller), has carried out important restoration work and refurbished the palace, which is listed as one of UNESCO's World Heritage Monuments.

THE CHÂTEAU★★★

Tue–Sun Apr–Oct 9am–6.30pm; Nov–Mar 9am–5.30pm. Trianon Palaces and Antoinette Estate open at noon.
1 Jan, 1 May, 25 Dec. Palace ticket 15€. Passport ticket 18€/1 day, 25€/2 days. Trianon and Antoinette Estate ticket 10€. Musical Fountains shows 9€; under-18 years free. 01 30 83 78 00. www.chateauversailles.fr.

Info: 2 bis avenue de Paris, 78000 Versailles. 01 39 24 88 88. www.versailles-tourisme.com.

Location: The town of Versailles lies 22km/13.7mi southwest of Paris.

Parking: Street parking at the château; underground on avenue de l'Europe.

Don't Miss: The restored Domaine de Marie-Antoinette in the château park.

Timing: Allow two days to fully appreciate Versailles.

Kids: Boats and bicycles can be rented in the château park.

Also See: CHARTRES, FONTAINEBLEAU.

A complete tour of the palace, gardens, park and the Marie-Antoinette's Estate takes two days. If you have only one day it is recommended that you begin with the interior of the château, where the most magnificent apartments are to be found. The park and gardens are best enjoyed at leisure.

For an unforgettable experience, visit them on one of the Jours des Grandes Eaux Musicales in summer, when all the fountains are turned on to a musical accompaniment.

Entrance

Beyond the palace's wrought-iron railings, created under Louis XVIII, lie three courtyards. In the centre is the forecourt, the **Cour des Ministres** (Ministers' Court), newly separated from the **Cour royale** (Royal Court) with a restored gold-leaf gate that only persons of high rank were permitted to cross in horse-drawn carriages. In this courtyard is the statue of Louis XIV commissioned by Louis-Philippe.

The two bordering wings were furnished with a colonnade under Louis XV. Finally there is the **Cour de Marbre★★** (Marble Court) with its black and white marble pavement, the heart of Louis XIII's château.

Across from the château entrance is the semicircular **Place d'Armes★★**, framed by **La Grande Ecurie★** (Royal Stables) by Jules Hardouin-Mansart.

The north wing houses the **Academy of Equestrian Arts** (℘01 39 02 62 75; www.acadequestre.fr) and the **Coach Museum** (⊙closed through 2015; ℘01 30 83 78 00), which presents a collection of magnificent coaches used at Versailles, including Louis XVIII's funeral hearse and Charles X's Coronation coach.

STATE APARTMENTS, CHAPEL

🛈 *Ticket office in the South Ministers Wing where there are restrooms, coatcheck and audio-guides; if you have a Passport ticket, you are eligible for free admission; proceed to Entrance A.*

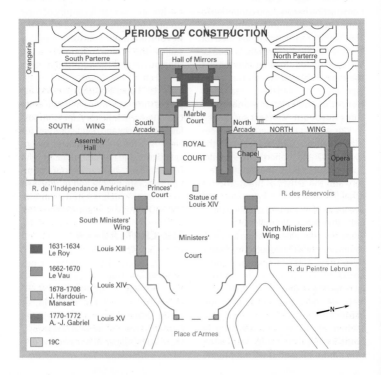

Cour de Marbre

© Terraxplorer/iStockphoto.com

▶ Begin at the Chapel Room (a).

Chapelle royale★★★

The two-storey palatine chapel with a royal gallery is dedicated to St Louis. It was constructed by Jules Hardouin-Mansart, and finished in 1710 by his brother-in-law Robert de Cotte. The ceiling is the work of the painters Jouvent, Coypel and La Fosse. The marble altar sculpted by Van Clève is decorated in front with a gilded bronze low relief representing a Pietà by Vassé.

▶ The tour continues upstairs, with a view of the upper level of the chapel.

Grands Appartements★★★

The six-room suite with decoration by Le Brun was the king's apartment from 1673 to 1682. Then Louis XIV took up residence definitively at Versailles and had a new apartment designed around the Marble Court. Three times a week on Mondays, Wednesdays and Thursdays from 6pm to 10pm the king held court in the Grand Apartments.

Salon d'Hercule★★★

Known as Hercules' Salon, this room, begun in 1712 and completed in 1736, owes its name to the ceiling painted by Lemoyne. The artist needed three years to cover the 480sq m/5 167sq ft ceiling with a painting of Hercules entering the Kingdom of the Gods. The artist committed suicide in 1737 shortly after finishing it.

Two Veronese canvases occupy their original places: **Christ at the House of Simon the Pharisee★**, and *Eliezer and Rebecca*.

Salon de l'Abondance (b)

When the king held court during the time of Louis XIV, there were three buffets, one for hot drinks and two for cold. The ceiling by Houasse portrays the royal magnificence and the goldware collections of Louis XIV in *trompe-l'œil*.

Salon de Vénus (c)

The ceiling was painted by Houasse and, like the ceilings of the next rooms, it features decorated panels with gilt stucco borders. The courtiers entered the rooms via the Royal Court by the Ambassadors' Staircase, sumptuously designed to impress visitors. It was torn down by Louis XV in 1752.

Salon de Diane (d)

This salon served as the billiard room under Louis XIV. Notice the bust of Louis XIV by Bernini (1665), a striking example of Baroque workmanship. Paintings by La Fosse and Blanchard can also be seen.

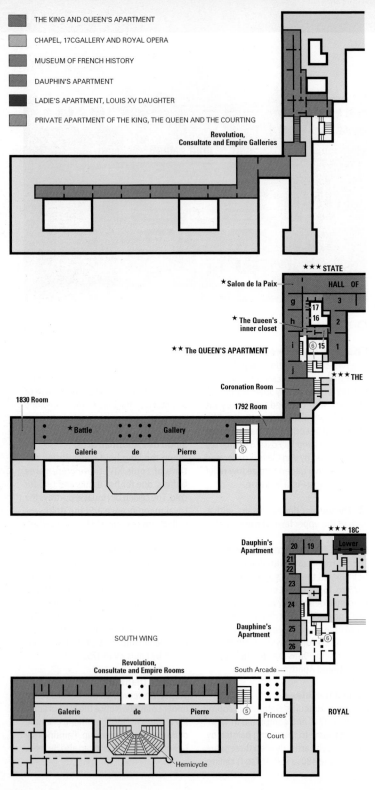

THE KING AND QUEEN'S APARTMENT

CHAPEL, 17C GALLERY AND ROYAL OPERA

MUSEUM OF FRENCH HISTORY

DAUPHIN'S APARTMENT

LADIE'S APARTMENT, LOUIS XV DAUGHTER

PRIVATE APARTMENT OF THE KING, THE QUEEN AND THE COURTING

Revolution, Consulate and Empire Galleries

★★★ STATE

★ Salon de la Paix

HALL OF

g | 17 | 3
h | 16 | 2

★ The Queen's inner closet

★★ The QUEEN'S APARTMENT

i | ⑥ 15 | 1

j

★★★ THE

Coronation Room

1830 Room

1792 Room

★ Battle   Gallery

Galerie   de   Pierre   ⑤

★★★ 18C

Dauphin's Apartment

20 | 19 | Lower
21
22
23
24
Dauphine's Apartment
25
26 | ⑥

SOUTH WING

Revolution, Consulate and Empire Rooms

South Arcade

Galerie   de   Pierre   ⑤

ROYAL

Princes'

Court

Hemicycle

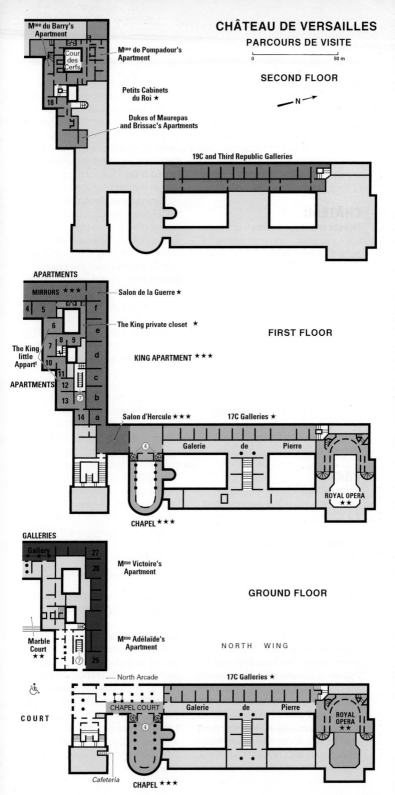

CHÂTEAU DE VERSAILLES
PARCOURS DE VISITE

0 ——— 50 m

SECOND FLOOR

N →

Mme du Barry's Apartment

Mme de Pompadour's Apartment

Cour des Cerfs

Petits Cabinets du Roi ★

18

Dukes of Maurepas and Brissac's Apartments

19C and Third Republic Galleries

APARTMENTS

MIRRORS ★★★

Salon de la Guerre ★

4 5 f

The King private closet ★

6 e

FIRST FLOOR

The King little Appart.

7 8 9
d

KING APARTMENT ★★★

10
11 c
12
13 ⑦ b

APARTMENTS

14 a

Salon d'Hercule ★★★

17C Galleries ★

④ Galerie de Pierre

ROYAL OPERA ★★

CHAPEL ★★★

GALLERIES

Gallery 27

Mme Victoire's Apartment

28

GROUND FLOOR

Mme Adélaïde's Apartment

NORTH WING

Marble Court ★★

⑦ 29

North Arcade

17C Galleries ★

♿

COURT

CHAPEL COURT

④ Galerie de Pierre

ROYAL OPERA ★★

Cafeteria

CHAPEL ★★★

347

GETTING THERE

BY RER: (line C) Versailles Rive-Gauche – Château de Versailles. By **commuter trains** from St-Lazare (Versailles Rive-Droite) and Montparnasse (Versailles-Chantiers) rail stations.By **car** from the Porte de St-Cloud, take **Motorway A13 to exit 1** and follow signs to Versailles-Château (16km/10mi). Time: 30-45min.

CHÂTEAU

Tickets and Information – Entrance tickets, passports and reservations for guided tours are available from this office in the South Ministers' Wing.
Entrances – The various tours of the château start from different entrances:
Entrance **A:** State Apartments (except groups, use entrance **B**)
Entrance **H:** Access reserved for visitors with disabilities
Guided tours meet at the North Ministers Wing, Cour d'Honneur
Music – Concerts of works by 17C and 18C French composers given by the Baroque Music Centre (*Oct–Dec*) in the Opéra Royal, Chapelle Royale, Salon d'Hercule or Galerie Basse. ℘01 39 20 78 10. www.cmbv.com.

PARK

Fêtes de Nuit – These shows take place seven times in summer around the Bassin de Neptune; they end with a fireworks display.
Grandes Eaux Musicales – In summer, water displays recall those

that took place in the reign of Louis XIV. Spectators are given an itinerary starting from the Bassin de Latone and ending at the Bassin de Neptune and Bassin du Dragon, where a breathtaking finale takes place. ℘01 30 83 78 00. www.chateauversailles.fr.
Tourist train – Tour of the grounds (50min) with stops at the Trianons and Grand Canal. Departure from the Terrasse Nord of the château. High season: 11am–6.15pm; low season 11.30am–5pm. ☜7.50€; children 11–18 years: 5.80€. ℘01 39 54 21 47. www.train-versailles.com.
Bicycle hire – Rental points: near the Petite Venise and St-Antoine Grille daily (except rainy weather) Apr–Oct 10am–6.45pm; Feb–Mar 10am–5.30pm; Nov 10am–5pm. ☜7.50€ per hour, 17€ half day. ℘01 39 66 97 66.
Electric-vehicle hire – Daily Feb–Mar 10am–5.30pm; Apr–Oct 10am–6.45pm; Nov–Dec 10am–5pm. ☜30€ 1st hour, 8.50€ each additional 15min. ℘01 39 66 97 66.
Boat hire – Mar Mon–Fri 1pm–5.30pm, Sat–Sun 11am–6.30pm; Apr Mon–Fri noon–5.30pm, Sat–Sun 10.30am–6.30pm; May–Jun Mon–Fri 11am–6.45pm, Sat–Sun 10.30am–6.45pm; Jul–Aug daily 10am–6.45pm; Sept–Oct Mon–Fri 1pm–6.45pm, Sat–Sun 10.30–6.45pm; Nov Mon–Fri 1pm–5pm, Sat–Sun 10.30am–5pm. ☜16€/1hr (boat for 4 people). ℘01 39 66 97 66.

Salon de Mars (e)

The guard-room before 1682, this room was later used by Louis XIV for balls, games and music. Two paintings have been restored to their 18C places: *Darius' Tent* by Le Brun and *The Pilgrims of Emmaüs* after Veronese. On the side walls, *Louis XV* by Rigaud and *Maria Leczczynska* by Van Loo occupy their original places. The ceiling with its martial scenes is by Audran, Jouvenet and Houasse. Above the fireplace hangs one of Louis XIV's favourite paintings, *King David* by Domenichino, in which he

is pictured playing the harp. It originally hung in the King's Bedchamber.

Salon de Mercure (f)

Formerly the antechamber, this room served as a place where kings were laid in state. In 1715 Louis XIV was kept here an entire week in his coffin, with 72 ecclesiastics keeping vigil to ensure that four masses could be said simultaneously every day from five in the morning until noon without interruption. The ceiling is the work of JB de Champaigne.

Salon d'Apollon or Salle du Trône (g)

The throne stood on a central platform beneath a large canopy. The three hooks would have supported a canopy. It was here that ambassadors were received, and that dances and concerts were put on when the king held court. The ceiling features *Apollo in a Sun Chariot* by La Fosse.

Galerie des Glaces★★★

Crossing the **Salon de la Guerre★** (War Salon), which links the Grand Apartment and the Hall of Mirrors, notice the large oval low relief by Coysevox representing Louis XIV triumphing over his enemies. Designed by Jules Hardouin-Mansart in 1687, the **Hall of Mirrors** was the showpiece under Louis XIV, in which court celebrations and elaborate receptions for foreign potentates took place.

The hall measures 75m/246ft long, 10m/33ft wide, and 12m/40ft high. It is illuminated by 17 large windows echoing 17 glass panels on the opposite wall. Completely restored in 2008, the 578 mirrors of glass that compose these panels are the largest that could be manufactured at that time. The hall enjoys the last rays of the setting sun. On the ceiling **Le Brun** executed the most important cycle of his career as the king's chief painter. The cycle illustrates the life of Louis XIV and his military victories until the Treaty of Nijmegen in 1678. The Hall of Mirrors was abundantly decorated with solid-silver furniture cast under Louis XIV.

The German Empire was proclaimed in this room on 18 January 1871, and the **Treaty of Versailles** was signed on 28 June 1919. From the central windows there is a good **view★★★** of the Grand Perspective.

▷ Detour from the Hall of Mirrors into the King's Apartments.

Appartement du Roi or Appartement de Louis XIV★★★

The king's suite stretches around the Marble Court. Designed between 1682 and 1701 by Mansart in Louis XIII's château, the decoration marks a clear break in the evolution of the Louis XIV style. The ceilings are not coffered but painted white; the white and gold panelling replaces the marble tiling; large mirrors adorn the fireplaces. After the guard-room (**1**), an antechamber (**2**) leads to the Salon de l'Œil de bœuf (**3**). Here gentlemen attended the ceremonious king's rising *(le lever)* and retiring *(le coucher)*. The decoration marks the first flowering of the Louis XV style.

Chambre du Roi (4)

This was the bedroom of Louis XIV from 1701, and it was here that he died. Above the bed, the alcove decoration represents France watching over the sleeping king and was sculpted by Coustou. The wall hangings are faithful reproductions of the summer furnishings of 1705. The paintings belonged to the King's personal collection.

Salle du Conseil (5)

Characteristic of Rococo, the Council Chamber was created under Louis XV by uniting two rooms. In this room decisions were made that involved the destiny of France, among them the decision to participate in the American War of Independence.

▷ Return to the Hall of Mirrors and continue to the Queen's Apartments.

Appartement de la Reine★★

Entrance to the Queen's Suite is through the **Salon de la Paix★**, which is decorated with a canvas by Lemoyne of Louis XV presenting peace to Europe. The Queen's suite was constructed for Louis XIV's wife Queen Marie-Thérèse, who died here in 1683.

Chambre de la Reine (h)

Le Brun's original decoration for Marie-Thérèse was redone for Queen Maria Leczczynska between 1729 and 1735. The white and gold woodwork, the greyish tones of the ceiling by Boucher, and the doors decorated by Natoire and De Troy demonstrate the inclination towards the Rococo under Louis XV. Marie-Antoinette had other reno-

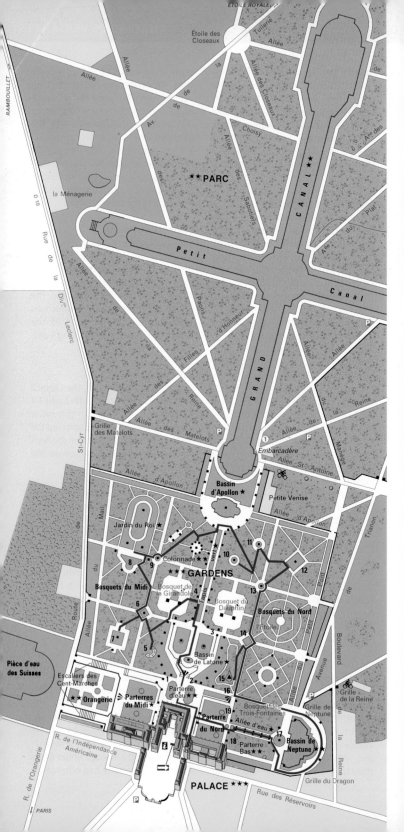

PARC ★★

RAMBOUILLET ➞

la Ménagerie

D 10

Rue de la Div⁻ⁱᵉ Leclerc

Allée

de

Allée

Étoile des Closeaux

Tuilerie Allée

la Allée des Closeaux

Av. de Choisy

des

des Sabotiers

Allée

CANAL ★★

de l'An de Plat

Petit Canal

Canal

GRAND

Allée des Paons

Allée d'Honneur

Allée des Filles

Allée des Reine

du Plat

Allée

Allée de la Reine

de

St-Cyr

Grille des Matelots

Allée d'Apollon

Allée des Matelots

P

Embarcadère ①

Allée ·St·-Antoine

de la Mariage

P

🚲

Bassin d'Apollon ★

Petite Venise

Allée d'Apollon

Trianon

de Mail

du

Route

Allée

Jardin du Roi ★

Colonnade ★★

8 9

★★★ GARDENS

Bosquets du Midi

6

Bosquet de la Girandole

4

Bosquet du Dauphin

Bosquet du Nord ★

l'Étoile

10

11

13

12

Bosquets du Nord

14

3

Bassin de Latone ★

5

Pièce d'eau des Suisses

Escaliers des Cent-Marches

1

Bassin d'eau

15 ▲

16

Boulevard

P

Grille de la Reine

Allée de la Reine

★★ Orangerie ≥ **Parterres du Midi** ★

Parterre d'eau ★★

Parterre du Nord ★

19

17

Bosquet des Trois-Fontaines

Allée d'eau

Grille de Neptune

R. de l'Orangerie

R. de l'Indépendance Américaine

P

18 Parterre Bas ★★

Bassin de Neptune ★

Avenue

↓ PARIS

PALACE ★★★

Grille du Dragon

Rue des Réservoirs

Reine

la

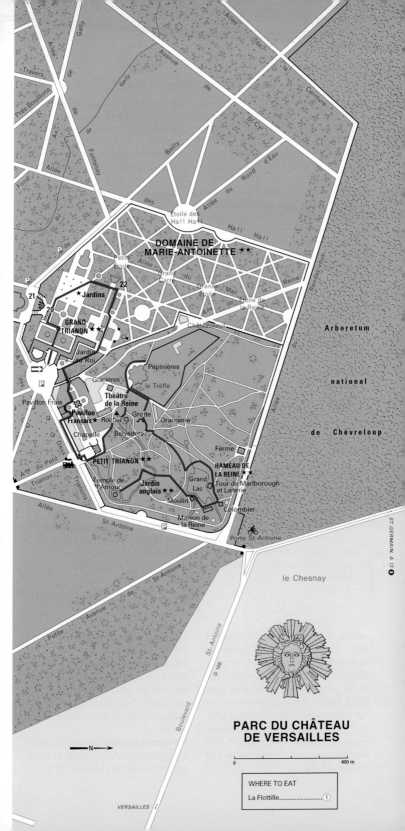

Travers
de Gally
Allée
de
Allée
de la
Ceinture
Prés Bouillons
Gally
Avenue
de
St-Cy'
Fontenay
Bailly
de
Allée
Fond
Rû
des
du
Rond
d'Eau
Ha!!

Etoile des
Ha!! Ha!!
Ha!!
Ha!!

**DOMAINE DE
MARIE-ANTOINETTE ★★**

Petite
Etoile
Allée

Grand
Carre'
du
Reine

★ **Jardins**
22
21
20
Grand
Mail
Etoile de
la Reine

Grand
Etoile

**GRAND
TRIANON ★★**

Chateauneuf

Arboretum

Jardin
du Roi

Pépinières
le Trèfle

national

Glacières
le Trèfle

Allée

Pavillon Frais

**Théâtre
de la Reine**

**Pavillon
Français★**
Rocher
Grotte
Orangerie

de Chèvreloup

Chapelle
Belvédère

Ferme

PETIT TRIANON ★★

**HAMEAU DE
LA REINE ★★**

Allée
de
Temple de
l'Amour

**Jardin
anglais ★★**
Grand
Lac

Tour de Marlborough
et Laiterie

Moulin

Colombier

Allée
St-Antoine

Maison de
la Reine
P
Porte St-Antoine

le Chesnay

Ae' du Petit
Trianon
Deux
Trianons

Allée
St-Antoine

de

Avenue

Petite

St-Antoine

D 186

Boulevard

ST GERMAIN, A 13 ●

**PARC DU CHÂTEAU
DE VERSAILLES**

→N→

0 — 400 m

WHERE TO EAT
La Flottille.....................①

VERSAILLES ↓

Versailles and the Sun King

Born in 1638 Louis XIV succeeded to the throne of France in 1643 and reigned until 1715, the longest reign of any European sovereign. Although Louis was not the only monarch to live at the Palace of Versailles, he will forever be the one most associated with it. The building was begun in 1624 during the reign of Louis XIII, his father, although at first it was a simple hunting lodge. While still the dauphin, Louis took possession of the building in 1632 and began a programme of minor improvements.

It was not until well into his reign, however, that Louis began to develop Versailles into the building we know today. He became increasingly convinced that the way to avoid the unrest, which had troubled his father's reign, was to move the Court away from Paris to Versailles. He was determined to centralize the government and reduce the power of the nobility. Following the death of his First Minister Mazarin in 1661, Louis assumed absolute power and began to rule without resort to advice from anyone. Although he probably did not utter the phrase "L'État, c'est moi", ("the State, it is me"), he certainly embodied the sentiment. It was no coincidence that he became known as the "Sun King", because everything had to revolve around him.

Louis employed the services of the best-known architects and landscape designers of his day. There began a programme of works that was to transform the old hunting lodge into a palace that would eventually become the largest in Europe. The idea was to build a palace so huge that he could keep all his potential opponents in one place and thus stifle any rebellious rumblings – in fact, he believed that they would be so consumed by their personal rivalries that they would not have the time or the inclination to trouble the monarch.

Although some building works had taken place between 1664 and 1668, these were mainly to prepare the palace for a party known as the Plaisirs de l'Île enchantée, which Louis held to celebrate the two queens, Anne of Austria, the Queen Mother, and Marie-Thérèse, his wife. Much more extensive work took place during the period 1669–72 with the construction of the Grand Appartement du Roi and the Grand Appartement de la Reine. In 1682 Louis officially installed the Court at Versailles, finally accomplishing what he had set out to achieve – the creation of a small town consisting of government buildings that allowed him to exercise the absolute power he craved.

The Bourbon monarchy was to remain at Versailles until they were compelled to leave during the Revolution, ironically a state of affairs brought about, in part at least, by the absolute power which the Sun King had insisted upon having 100 years before, and which now was leading to the downfall of his heirs.

vations made in 1770; the two-headed eagle and the portraits of the house of Austria recall the queen's origins. The floral wall hangings were rewoven to the original pattern in Lyon, matching exactly the original hanging of the queen's summer furnishings of 1786. In France, royal births were public events: in this room 19 children of France were born, among them Louis XV and Philip V of Spain.

Salon des Nobles de la Reine (Peers' Salon) (k)
In this one-time antechamber, presentations to the queen took place. This room was also the place where queens and dauphins of France lay in state. The room has been restored to the way it looked in 1789.

In the **antechamber (m)** note the painting by Madame Vigée-Lebrun of *Marie-Antoinette and Her Children* (1787).

Salle de gardes de la Reine (Queen's Guards-room) (n)

This room protected the queen against intrusions such as that which occurred on the morning of 6 October 1789, when a rioting mob tried to invade the Queen's Suite and had to be fought off by the royal guard in a prolonged and bloody scuffle.

Salle du Sacre

The Coronation room was initially used as a chapel from 1676 to 1682; otherwise this large guard-room housed the sessions of Parliament, which passed laws here. Louis-Philippe had the room altered to accommodate three enormous paintings: *Murat at the Battle of Aboukir* by Gros, *Champ de Mars Eagles* and *The Consecration of Napoléon* by **David**.

Salle de 1792 (p)

The walls of this large unfurnished room, situated at the angle of the central part of the palace and the south wing, are covered with portraits of warriors and battle scenes. Note Coignet's *The Paris National Guard Departs to Join the Army*, in which Louis-Philippe appears in the uniform of a lieutenant-general.

Galerie des Batailles★ (Battle Gallery)

🕐*Open sporadically, call to confirm hours.* 📞*01 30 83 78 00.*
Designed in the south wing in 1836 under Louis-Philippe, the History of France Galleries created a sensation. The 33 vast pictures evoke France's greatest military victories and include works by **Horace Vernet**, **Eugène Delacroix** and **Baron Gérard**.

At the end of the gallery is the **Salle de 1830**, devoted to Louis-Philippe's accession to the throne.

DAUPHINE'S AND MESDAMES' APARTMENTS

▶ Start from Entrance (C2), on the ground floor.

Dauphin's Apartments – Heir to the Throne

These rooms are the private rooms of the Dauphin Louis, son of Louis XV, restored in the 20C by Pierre de Nolhac. After his first wife, Marie-Therese Raphaelle of Spain, died, he moved here with his second wife, Marie Joseph of Saxony, who gave him seven children, including the future Louis XVI.

The apartments consisted of a first anteroom and a second anteroom with windows overlooking the Parterre d'Eau. The bedchamber (**29**) has the original wainscotting by Verberckt, and a brown marble fireplace decorated with bronzes by Caffieri representing *Flora* and *Zephyr*. The corner salon (**28**), with four windows overlooking the gardens to the south and east, is decorated by paintings by Jean-Baptiste Oudry. The large writing desk was made for the room by Bernard Van Riesen, a Dutch cabinet maker who signed his furnishings with BVRB. Louis' library (**27**) has decorations over the doors by Vernet.

Dauphine's Apartments

The Dauphine's apartments were connected to her husband's, with a small office (**25**) separating her bedchamber (**26**) from the library. The last three kings of France – Louis XVI, Louis XVIII and Charles X – were born in the bedchamber. The original wainscotting has disappeared in the large salon (**23**), but there are two paintings of Louis XV by **Rigaud** and **Van Loo** in the Dauphine's two antechambers (**21**, **22**).

Mesdames' Apartments

🕐*Sat–Sun only.*
Of Louis XV's 10 children with Marie Leszczyska, eight were girls. The three eldest grew up at Versailles in the south wing's apartments known as the Enfants de France, whereas the others were educated at the Abbey of Fontevrault. As adults, the princesses finally settled into the ground-floor apartments across the Marble Courtyard from their brother, the dauphin.

The apartments of Madame Victoire and Madame Adélaïde have been restored

353

to look the way they did before Louis-Philippe, including the bedrooms, antechambers and salons; however, most of the furnishings were lost during the Revolution. A few personal effects have been recovered, including the intricately designed organ that belonged to Adélaïde.

KING'S PRIVATE APARTMENTS

Guided tour by reservation. 7€.
01 30 83 78 00.

Appartement intérieur du Roi★★★

The King's Private Suite served as private apartments to Louis XV, reserved for those closest to him. Here the king removed himself from the constraints of the Court. The rooms were designed by Gabriel and are decorated with carvings by Verberckt: shells, foliated scrolls and Rococo flower motifs are scattered everywhere.

Chambre à coucher (6)

Louis XV, and then Louis XVI, retired to this bedroom after they had performed the rising and retiring ceremonies, which took place in the Grand Apartment. It was here that Louis XV died of smallpox on 10 May 1774.

Cabinet de la Pendule (7)

The Clock Room served as a gaming room when the king held court. Until 1769 it owed its name to the astronomical clock whose works were built by Passemant and Dauthiau with bronze embellishments by Caffiéri.

When crossing the **Antichambre des Chiens** (Dogs' Antechamber) (**8**) note the Louis XIV panelling. In the dining room called **Retours de chasse** (Hunters' Dining Hall) (**9**) Louis XV gave private dinners on hunting days.

Cabinet intérieur du Roi (10)

The Corner Room became a workroom in 1753. As an example of Verberckt's Rococo style, the furniture is remarkable; the medal cabinet is by Gaudreaux (1739), corner cupboards by Joubert

(1755) and a roll-top **desk★** by Oeben and Riesener (1769).

Salles neuves

The new rooms were designed under Louis XV in the place of the Ambassadors' Staircase. In the **Cabinet de Mme Adélaïde** (**12**), the child **Mozart** played the harpsichord. The medal cabinet by Benneman is a masterpiece.

The following rooms, Louis XVI's **Library** (**13**) and the **Porcelain Salon** (**14**) show the evolution of Versailles style towards sober Neoclassicism. The most notable is the **Salon des Jeux** (Louis XVI's Gaming Room) (**15**) as it appeared in 1775, with corner cupboards by Riesener (1774), chairs by Boulard and gouache landscapes by Van Blarenberghe.

OPERA ROYAL★★

Guided tour by reservation. 7€.
01 30 83 78 00.

The opera house begun by Gabriel in 1768 was inaugurated in 1770 for the marriage celebrations of the dauphin, the future Louis XVI, and Marie-Antoinette. The first oval hall in France, it received other exceptional technical touches from the engineer Arnoult: for festivals, the floor of the stalls and circle could be raised to the level of the stage. The balconies' low-relief sculptures, executed by **Pajou**, represent the gods of Olympus and the children and their signs of the Zodiac.

Initially reserved for the court, the opera hosted sumptuous receptions on the occasion of visits from the King of Sweden in 1784, of Emperor Joseph II in 1777 and 1781, and of **Queen Victoria** in 1855. The National Assembly held session here from 1871 until 1875. On 30 January 1875 the adoption of the Wallon Amendment here laid the foundation of the Third Republic. A reception for **Queen Elizabeth II of England** in 1957 coincided with completion of the final restoration.

Other tours include the Queen's Private Suite, The milestones of the French Parliament's history, and Madame de Maintenon's Apartments.

GRAND PARK AND GARDENS★★★

See map. *Daily Apr–Oct 8am–8.30pm; Nov–Mar 8am–6pm. Free access Nov–Mar and Apr–Oct, Mon–Fri; 9€ Sat–Sun (for Musical Fountains event; free with Passport ticket). Free access daily to the Grand Park for pedestrians. 01 30 83 78 00.*

Laid out principally by **Le Nôtre** during the years 1660 to 1670, the park and gardens are masterpieces of the art of French landscape gardening, in which nature is ordered geometrically according to the principles of Classicism. The basins, fountains and statues are perfectly integrated with nature. A fine view is obtained from the **Parterres du Midi★** (**1**) of **l'Orangerie★★** and **Pièce d'eau des Suisses**. On either side of the Orangery, descend the **Escaliers des Cent-Marches** (100 steps).

Louis XIV's favourite view was from the **Parterre d'eau★★** (**2**), where the grand perspective or east–west axis symbolically retraces the path of the sun, from the **Latona Basin★** and fountain to the **Apollo Basin★**, continuing along the **Grand Canal★★**.

3) **Bosquet du Dauphin**
4) **Bosquet de la Girandole**
5) **Bosquet des Rocailles**
6) **Bassin de Bacchus**
7) **Bosquet de la Reine**
8) **Bassin du Miroir**, overlooking the **Jardin du Roi★**
9) **Bassin de Saturne**, leads to the **Colonnade★★**.

10) **Bosquet des Dômes**
11) **Bosquet de l'Encelade**
12) **Bosquet de l'Obélisque**
13) **Bassin de Flore**
14) **Bassin de Cérès**
15) **Basquet des Bains d'Apollon**
16) **Parterre du Nord**
17) The **Bassin du Dragon** overlooks the **Bassin de Neptune★★** and **Parterre Bas★★**.
18) **Allée d'eau★**
19) **Bosquet des Trois Fontaines**

DOMAINE DE MARIE-ANTOINETTE★★

Tue–Sun Apr–Oct noon–6.30pm (7.30pm gardens); Nov–Mar Grand Trianon and gardens of the Petit Trianon noon–5.30pm. Entry Apr–Oct 10€; free with Passport ticket. 01 30 83 78 00. www.chateauversailles.fr.

No trip to Versailles would be complete without visiting the **Marie-Antoinette's Estate** located on the northern edge of the Grand Park. It started with the **Grand Trianon★★**, built as a personal retreat for Louis XIV in 1687, with its own **gardens★** overlooking the **Petit Canal** (**21**) and romantic **groves** (**22**). Next door is the **Petit Trianon★★** (1768), where Marie-Antoinette spent much of her time with her children. She had a private theatre, an English-style **garden★** with lakes and folies, and a replica village, **le Hameau de la Reine★★**, complete with thatched-roof houses, animals and mill.

L'Orangerie, adjacent to the Château

© Cosmo Condina/Tips Images

Disneyland Resort Paris★★★

Opened in 1992 under the name EuroDisney, **Disneyland Paris** is an enormous holiday resort outside Paris with two theme parks, Disney Village entertainment and shopping complex, hotels, a 27-hole golf course and a campsite. The Disney Studios opened in 2002, and other new developments are planned through to 2017.

A BIT OF HISTORY

Born in Chicago in 1901, **Walter Elias "Walt" Disney** showed great ability in drawing. After World War I, in which he served as an ambulance driver in France, he returned to the US where he met a young Dutchman called Ub Iwerks, who was also passionate about drawing.

In 1923 the pair produced in Hollywood the **Alice Comedies,** a series of short films, and in 1928 Mickey Mouse was created. There next followed the era of the Oscar-winning, full-length animated cartoon films such as The **Three Little Pigs** (1933), **Snow White and the Seven Dwarfs** (1937), **Dumbo** (1941). Disney productions also developed to include films starring real people, such as **Treasure Island** (1950), and some mixing of the two, for instance in **Mary Poppins** (1964), which won six Oscars. **Theme parks** followed in the US and Japan, attracting crowds by the thousands year around.

▷ **Location:** The resort, consisting of two theme parks, is located 30km/18.6mi east of Paris in Chessy.

🅿 **Parking:** Parking on-site, 15€/car, 10€/motorcycle, 20€/camping-cars.

🚫 **Don't Miss:** The daily parade on Main Street.

🕐 **Timing:** Allow two days to visit the entire resort.

👥 **Kids:** "Meet & Greet" Disney characters at specific restaurants.

DISNEYLAND PARK★★★

This theme park is a realization of Walt Disney's dream of creating an enchanted park filled with rides and shows where children and adults can enjoy themselves together.

The large Disneyland Paris site (more than 55ha/136 acres) is surrounded by trees and comprises five territories or lands, each with a different theme.

Every day at 4pm down the Main Street there's a procession of floats carrying all the favourite Disney cartoon characters called **Disney Magic on Parade★★**, an event that adds even more delight to the fairy-tale setting, especially for young ones.

Disneyland Resort Paris

© Tim Oram/age fotostock

GETTING THERE

BY TRAIN to Marne-la-Vallée-Chessy station: Eurostar from England, TGV from Lille, Lyon, Avignon, Marseille, Bordeaux, Nantes and Toulouse; RER line A from Paris. By shuttle from Orly and Roissy-Charles de Gaulle Airports. **BY CAR** via motorway A4 direction Metz; **exit at junction 14** and follow signs to Disneyland.

GENERAL INFORMATION

Entry – Hours vary daily (check website). Mid-Jul–Aug: 10am–11pm; Sept–mid-Apr 10am–7pm, Sat–Sun and holidays 10am–10pm; mid-Apr–early Jul 10am–10pm, Sat 10am–11pm.
Disney Studios: high season and weekends 10am–7pm; low season 10am–6pm. ✆ 01 60 30 60 30. For **guided tours**, contact the City Hall (Disneyland Park) on Town Square in Main Street, USA: ⊚25€ (children 15€). Admission varies per season, if one or both parks, and where/when tickets are purchased: 1day/1park ⊚53€ (children 3–11 years: 48€), 2-park passes/1-4 days ⊚65€–170€ (children 3–11 years: 60€–154€), Ticket usually valid for one year.
Hotel reservations – ✆ 01 60 30 60 53.
Website – www.disneylandparis.com.
Booking a show – Entertainment programmes and booking facilities are available from City Hall, located in Town Square, inside Disneyland Park.
Currency exchange – Facilities are available at the parks' main entrance.
Disabled guests – A guide detailing special services available can be obtained from City Hall (Disneyland Park), from the information desk inside Walt Disney Studios Park or online.
Baggage storage – At the entrance of Disneyland Park.
Rental – Guests can rent pushchairs and wheelchairs in Town Square Terrace (Disneyland Park) and in Front Lot (Walt Disney Studios Park).

Animals – They are not allowed in the theme parks, in Disney Village or in the hotels. The Animal Care Center is located near the visitors' car park.
Baby Care Center, Meeting Place for Lost Children, First Aid – Near the Plaza Gardens Restaurant (Disneyland Park) or at Studio Services (Walt Disney Studios Park).

MAKING THE MOST OF IT

Tips – To avoid long queues at popular attractions, visit these attractions during the parade, at the end of the day or get a **Fast Pass** issued by distributors outside the most popular attractions in both parks; this ticket assigns a time slot during which the bearer may enter without waiting in line.
Disneyland Park: Indiana Jones (Adventureland); Space Mountain (Discoveryland); Buzz Lightyear Laser Blast (Discoveryland); Peter Pan's Flight (Fantasyland); Big Thunder Mountain (Frontierland); Star Tours (Discoveryland).
Walt Disney Studios Park: Rock'n Roller Coaster (Backlot); Flying Carpets (Toon Studio); The Twilight Zone Tower of Terror (Production Courtyard), Ratatouille: the Adventure (Toon Studio).
Where to eat – Park maps include a list of eating places, with symbols indicating those offering table service and vegetarian meals. For quick meals go to **Bella Notte**, **Colonel Hathi's** or **Plaza Gardens** in Disneyland Park, or to the **Backlot Express Restaurant** in Disney Studios. Take time and go to one of the following table service restaurants to enjoy a fine meal enhanced by an original décor (booking recommended, ✆ 01 64 74 28 82 or call at City Hall): **Silver Spur Steakhouse**, **Blue Lagoon Restaurant**, **Walt's Restaurant** and **Auberge de Cendrillon** in Disneyland Park or **Café des Cascadeurs** in Walt Disney Studios Park.

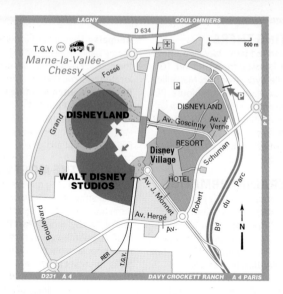

Main Street USA

Enter the park on to the main street of an American town at the turn of the 19C, bordered by shops with Victorian-style fronts. Horse-drawn street cars, double-decker buses, fire engines and Black Marias transport visitors from Town Square to Central Plaza while colourful musicians play favourite ragtime, jazz and Dixieland tunes.

From Main Street station, a small steam train, the **Disneyland Railroad★**, travels across the park with stops at Frontierland, Fantasyland and Discoveryland.

Frontierland

The conquest of the West, the gold trail and the Far West with its legends and folklore are brought together in Thunder Mesa, a typical Western town. In the bowels of **Big Thunder Mountain★★★** lies an old gold mine, which is visited via the mine train: this train turns out to be a runaway train that hurtles out of control to provide a thrilling ride.

A tour of the dilapidated **Phantom Manor★★★** overlooking the rivers of the Far West is a spine-chilling house of hundreds of mischievous ghosts. The horseshoe-shaped **Lucky Nugget Saloon★** – every Western town had its saloon – presents the dinner show **Lilly's Follies**.

Adventureland

Access this land of exotic adventure from the Central Plaza, through Adventureland Bazaar. In the tropical Caribbean seas, marauding pirates attack and loot a coastal fort and village in the famous action-packed encounter **Pirates of the Caribbean★★★**.

Courageous archaeologists brave the ruined temple deep in the jungle in **Indiana Jones et le Temple du Péril… à l'envers★★★**, while the giant tree **La Cabane des Robinson★★** (27m/89ft high) offers panoramic views from the ingeniously furnished home of the ship-wrecked Swiss family Robinson from JD Wyss' novel.

Fantasyland

Based on Walt Disney's familiar trademark, Sleeping Beauty's castle, this land recalls favourite fairy tales by authors such as Charles Perrault, Lewis Carroll and the Brothers Grimm. **Le Château de la Belle au bois dormant★★**, with its blue and gold turrets crowned with pennants, is at the very heart of Disneyland. Inside, Aubusson tapestries recount episodes from this famous story. Below, in the depths of the castle, a huge scaly dragon appears to be sleeping.

It's a Small World★★ is a delightful musical cruise in celebration of the innocence and joy of children throughout the world, while **Alice's Curious Labyrinth**★ is a maze leading to the Queen of Hearts' castle.

Fly in a boat through the skies above London and in Never-Never Land on **Peter Pan's Flight**★★ or visit the lovable puppet Pinocchio and his friends on **Les Voyages de Pinocchio**★.

Enjoyable tours in mining cars from the dwarfs' mine lead through the mysterious forest with **Blanche-Neige et les Sept Nains**★.

Discoveryland

This land is the world of past discoveries and future dreams of great visionaries such as Leonardo da Vinci, Jules Verne and HG Wells and their wonderful inventions.

Space Mountain★★★ – **Mission 2** is a fantastic journey through space, while **Star Tours**★★★ presents a breathtaking inter-planetary experience full of special effects inspired by the film *Star Wars*. Zap alien invaders in **Buzz Lightyear's Laser Blast**, or zoom around **Autopia**. Michael Jackson as **Captain EO** is back, mixing music and special effects.

WALT DISNEY STUDIOS PARK

Opened in 2002, this park is dedicated to the wonders of the cinema. It offers guests an opportunity to explore backstage and discover the secrets of filming, animation techniques and television.

Front Lot

The park entrance is overlooked by a 33m/108ft-high water tower, a traditional landmark in film studios. In the centre of the Spanish-style courtyard, planted with palm trees, a fountain is dedicated to Mickey. **Disney Studio 1** is the reconstruction of a famous film set, Hollywood Boulevard.

Toon Studio

This area offers a tribute to Walt Disney's invaluable contribution to the development of animation. **Animagique**★★★ celebrates Disney's full-length animation films; spectators find themselves

at the centre of a 3D cartoon, next to Mickey, Donald Duck, Dumbo's pink elephants, and Pinocchio. The **Art of Disney Animation**★★ is an interactive discovery of the secrets of animation. **Flying Carpets**★★ is a film set where Aladdin's Genie guides guests on to flying carpets!

Production Courtyard

Here spectators are allowed to see what happens in the usually out-of-bounds backstage areas of cinema and television studios. **Cinémagique**★★★ is the place where fiction meets reality, as spectators literally go through the screen and become the actors and heroes of the film.

Dare to step aboard the Twilight Zone's **Tower of Terror**, or participate in a production of **Stitch Live!** Sit back and enjoy the **Studio Tram Tour**★★ through amazing film sets until you reach **Catastrophe Canyon!**★★★

Backlot

Here you'll find action, thrills and special effects. Set on a meteorite-threatened space station, **Armageddon**★★ is a thrilling (and particularly loud) experience. At a similar decibel level, the **Rock'n Roller Coaster**★★★ is a unique musical experience inside a recording studio; be prepared to be propelled at full speed on a breathtaking journey that is not for the faint-hearted.

DISNEY VILLAGE★

Across from the theme parks is Disney Village. In the main street of this American town it's always party time. On summer evenings there are plenty of events and entertainment going on in the shops, restaurants and bars.

The famous adventures of pioneer William Frederick Cody (1846–1917), alias Buffalo Bill, are the inspiration for **La Légende de Buffalo Bill**★★, a cabaret dinner spot that evokes the story of the Wild West, complete with horses, bison, cowboys and Indians.

Château de Chantilly★★★

The name Chantilly brings to mind a château, a forest, a racecourse and the world of horse racing in general. Because of its remarkable setting, its park and the treasures in its museum, the Château de Chantilly is considered one of the major sights in France. Chantilly is also rapidly becoming an important cultural centre, thanks to the activities of the Centre des Fontaines, with its library boasting 600 000 titles (philosophy, art, religion, etc).

Info: Office de Tourisme, 73 rue du Connetable, 60500 Chantilly. ☎03 44 67 37 37. www.chantilly-tourisme.com.

Location: Chantilly is about one hour's drive north of Paris. Take junction 7 from the Autoroute du Nord.

Parking: At the château.

Don't Miss: The facsimile of *Les Très Riches Heures du Duc de Berry*.

Timing: Allow half a day to see the Château and Park.

A BIT OF HISTORY

Cantilius to the Montmorency – Over the past 2 000 years, five castles have occupied this part of the Nonette Valley. Above the ponds and marshes of the area rose a rocky island where **Cantilius**, a native of Roman Gaul, built the first fortified dwelling. His name and achievement gave birth to Chantilly.

In the Middle Ages the building became a fortress belonging to the Bouteiller de France, named after the hereditary duties he carried out at the court of the Capetians; originally in charge of the royal cellars, the Bouteiller was one of the king's close advisers.

In 1386 the land was bought by the chancellor, d'Orgemont, who had the castle rebuilt. The feudal foundations bore the three subsequent constructions. In 1450 the last descendant of the Orgemont married one of the Barons of Montmorency, and Chantilly became the property of this illustrious family. It remained in their possession for 200 years.

Anne, Duc de Montmorency – Anne de Montmorency was a devoted servant to a succession of six French kings from Louis XII to Charles IX. This formidable character gained a reputation as warrior, statesman, diplomat and patron of the arts. For 40 years, apart from a few brief periods, he remained the leading noble of the land, second to the king. Childhood friend and companion-in-arms to François I, close adviser to Henri II, he even had some influence

Château de Chantilly

© Jose Fuste Raga/age fotostock

over Catherine de' Medici, who looked favourably upon the man who had advised her on cures for her infertility. Constable Anne owned 600 fiefs, some 130 castles and estates, four mansions in Paris and numerous posts and offices. He was immensely wealthy. When he went to court, he was escorted by 300 guards on horseback. Through his five sons and the husbands of his seven daughters, he controlled most of the country's highest positions and had connections with Henri II, as well as with all the other most distinguished French families.

The feudal castle of the Orgemont was demolished in 1528, and the architect Pierre Chambiges replaced it with a palace built in the French Renaissance style. On a nearby island Jean Bullant erected the charming château that still stands today: the Petit Château. It was separated from the Grand Château by a moat – now filled in – that was spanned by two superimposed bridges. An aviary was set up in the tiny garden on the island. Constable Anne ordered great loads of earth and built the terrace that bears his statue.

Last love of Henri IV – Henri IV often stayed at Chantilly, with his companion-in-arms Henri I de Montmorency, the son of Constable Anne. At the age of 54, the king fell in love with his host's ravishing daughter Charlotte, only age 15. He arranged for her to marry Henri II de Bourbon-Condé, a shy and gauche young man, whom the king hoped would prove an accommodating husband. The day after the wedding, however, Condé left the capital with his wife. Henri IV ordered them to return to Paris. The young couple fled to Brussels, where they stayed under the protection of the King of Spain. Henri IV raged, implored, threatened and even went as far as to ask the Pope to intervene. Only when he was murdered by Ravaillac did the two fugitives return to France.

Henri de Montmorency – Encouraged by Louis XIII's brother, the scheming Gaston d'Orléans, Henri II de Montmorency plotted against Richelieu. He was defeated at Castelnaudary near Toulouse and made a prisoner after receiv-

Statue of Henri IV

© S. Sauvignier/MICHELIN

ing 18 wounds, including five by bullets. By way of an apology, he bequeathed to Cardinal Richelieu the two *Slave* statues by Michelangelo, now in the Louvre; those at Chantilly and Écouen are replicas.

The Great Condé – Charlotte de Montmorency and her husband, the Prince of Condé (the couple persecuted by Henri IV) inherited Chantilly in 1643. The château remained family property until 1830. Descendants of Charles de Bourbon, like Henri IV, the Princes of Condé were of royal blood, and the heir apparent to the title was called the Duke of Enghien.

The Great Condé was the son of Charlotte and Henri II. He applied himself to renovating the Château de Chantilly with the same energy and efficiency he had shown in military operations. In 1662 he commissioned Le Nôtre to redesign the park and the forest. The fountains at Chantilly were considered the most elegant in France, and Louis XIV made a point of outclassing them at Versailles. The work lasted 20 years and the result was a splendid achievement, part of which still stands today.

Last of the Condés – The Prince of Condé died at Fontainebleau (&see *FONTAINEBLEAU*) in 1686, to the king's great dismay. During the religious ceremony preceding the burial, Bossuet delivered a funeral oration that became famous.

The great-grandson of the Great Condé, Louis-Henri de Bourbon, alias "Monsieur le Duc", was an artist with a taste for splendour, who gave Chantilly a new

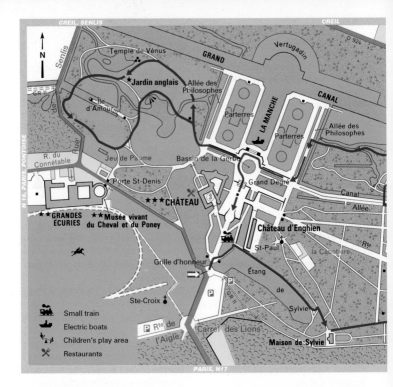

Map legend:
- Small train
- Electric boats
- Children's play area
- Restaurants

lease of life. He asked Jean Aubert to build the Grandes Écuries, a masterpiece of the 18C, and set up a porcelain factory (it closed down in 1870).

The Château d'Enghien was built on the estate by Louis-Joseph de Condé in 1769. His grandson the Duke of Enghien, who had just been born, was its first occupant. The father of the newly born baby was 16, his grandfather 36. The young prince died tragically in 1804; he was seized by the French police in the margravate of Baden and shot outside the fortress of Vincennes on the orders of Bonaparte.

During the French Revolution the main building was razed to the ground, though the smaller château was spared. Louis-Joseph was 78 when he returned from exile. His son accompanied him back to Chantilly and the two of them were dismayed: their beloved château was in ruins and the park in a shambles. They decided to renovate the estate. They bought back the plots of their former land, restored the Petit Château,

and redesigned and refurbished the grounds. The prince died in 1818, but the duke continued the work. He was an enthusiastic hunter; at the age of 70, he still hunted daily. Thanks to his efforts, Chantilly became the lively, fashionable place it had been in the years preceding the Revolution.

As in former times, the receptions and hunting parties attracted crowds of elegant visitors. The renovation and restoration work was a source of income for the local population.

The duke was worried by the Revolution of 1830, which raised his cousin Louis-Philippe to the throne, and considered returning to England. A few days later, he was found hanging from a window at his castle in St-Leu. He was the last descendant of the Condé.

The Duke of Aumale – The Duke of Bourbon had left Chantilly to his great-nephew and godson the Duke of Aumale, the fourth son of Louis-Philippe. This prince gained recognition in Africa when he captured Abdel-

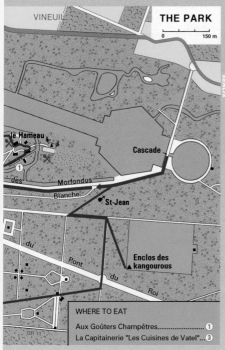

THE PARK

0   150 m

VINEUIL

SENLIS

le Hameau

Cascade

des

Morfondus

Blanche

St-Jean

du

Enclos des
▲ kangourous

Pont

du

Roi

GR 11

WHERE TO EAT

Aux Goûters Champêtres.........................①
La Capitainerie "Les Cuisines de Vatel"...③

the lower road and into the Route de l'Aigle, which skirts the racecourse. The road from Senlis through Vineuil offers a good view of the château and its park; leaving Vineuil, turn left at each junction.

From Chapelle-en-Serval, crossing Chantilly Forest, the château suddenly rises into view from the carrefour des Lions; it appears to floating on the water in a superb setting of rocks, ponds, lawns and trees. Picture the Château de Chantilly at the time of the Condé, when the two main buildings were still divided by an arm of water: the 16C Petit Château (or barbican) and the Grand Château, for which Daumet used the foundations of the former stronghold.

◗ Cross the constable's terrace that bears the equestrian statue of Anne de Montmorency, and enter the main courtyard through the main gateway (Grille d'Honneur), flanked by the two copies of Michelangelo's *Slaves*.

The Duke of Aumale did not intend to establish a museum for educational purposes; he merely wanted to build up a fine art collection. He therefore hung the works in chronological order of purchase, though favourite ones were sometimes placed in a separate room. The curators have respected his layout. According to the terms of the duke's legacy, the Institute must agree "to make no changes to the interior and exterior architecture of the château". Moreover, it is not allowed to lend any of the exhibits.

◗ *The reception hall is the starting point for guided tours of the chapel and the various apartments as well as for unaccompanied tours of the collections. It is advisable to interrupt a visit to the collections if the custodians announce a guided tour of the apartments.*

Kader and his numerous relations. The Revolution of 1848 forced him into exile, and he returned only in 1870; in 1873 he presided over the court martial that sentenced Marshal Bazaine.

From 1875 to 1881 the duke commissioned Daumet to build the Grand Château in the Renaissance style. This castle, the fifth, still stands today. Back in exile between 1883 and 1889, he died in 1897, and the Institute of France inherited his estate at Chantilly, together with the superb collections that constitute the Condé Museum.

THE CHÂTEAU★★★

◷*Apr–Oct daily 10am–6pm (grounds until 8pm); Nov–Mar Wed–Mon 10.30am–5pm (grounds until 6pm). Château and park with audioguide ⊚16€. Grounds only ⊚7€. ☎ Guided tours (45min) 3€. ☏03 44 27 31 80. www.domainedechantilly.com.*

◗ From Paris, take N 16; do not drive through the town but turn right after

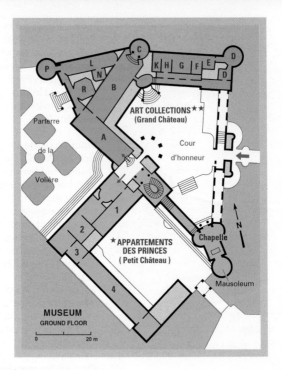

ART COLLECTIONS★★
(Grand Château)

Parterre

de la

Volière

Cour
d'honneur

★ APPARTEMENTS
DES PRINCES
(Petit Château)

Chapelle

Mausoleum

MUSEUM
GROUND FLOOR

0   20 m

Appartements des Princes★

♿ Situated in the **Petit Château**, this suite, occupied by the Great Condé and his descendants, was embellished with Regency and Rococo **wainscoting★★**, especially in the 18C thanks to the Duke of Bourbon. It was not occupied by the Duke of Aumale, who had taken up residence on the ground floor.

The antechamber and part of the library, the work of the Duke of Aumale, are located on the site of the old moat.

Cabinet des Livres★ (Library) (1)

This room contains a splendid collection of manuscripts, including **The Rich Hours of the Duke of Berry** (*Les Très Riches Heures du Duc de Berry*) with 15C illuminations by the Limbourg brothers. This extremely fragile document is not permanently exhibited, but visitors may see a facsimile by Faksimile Verlag of Luzern.

Another interesting reproduction is the psalter of Queen Ingeburge of Denmark. Among the ornamental motifs feature the monogram of the Duke of Aumale

(HO for Henri d'Orléans) and the Condé coat of arms (France's "broken" coat of arms with a diagonal line symbolizing the younger branch of the family).

Chambre de Monsieur le Prince (2)

This title referred to the reigning Condé Prince, in this instance the Duke of Bourbon (1692–1740), who installed a wainscot at the far end of the room, into which were embedded panels painted by C Huet in 1735. The famous Louis XVI commode was designed by Riesener and made by Hervieu.

Salon des Singes (3)

A collection of monkey scenes *(singeries)* dating from the early 18C is a masterpiece by an anonymous draughtsman; note the fire screen depicting the monkeys' reading lesson.

Galerie de Monsieur le Prince (4)

The Great Condé had ordered his own battle gallery, which he never saw completed (1692). The sequence was interrupted from 1652 to 1659 during

Galerie des Batailles

©H. Chajmowicz/Michelin

his years of rebellion. A painting conceived by the hero's son portrays him stopping a Fame from publishing a list of his treacherous deeds and asking another Fame to issue a formal apology.

Chapelle

An **altar★** attributed to Jean Goujon and 16C wainscoting and stained-glass windows from the chapel at Écouen were brought here by the Duke of Aumale. The apse contains the **mausoleum** of Henri II de Condé (bronze statues by J Sarrazin taken from the Jesuit Church of St-Paul-St-Louis in Paris) and the stone urn that received the hearts of the Condé princes. Up to the Revolution, the Condé necropolis was at Vallery in Burgundy, where another sepulchral monument celebrating Henri II still stands.

▶ Cross the **Galerie des Cerfs (A)** with its hunting theme; note the 17C Gobelins tapestries.

The Collections★★

Galerie de Peinture (B) – The variety of paintings here reflects the eclectic tastes of the Duke of Aumale. Military events are illustrated on huge canvases (*Battle on the Railway Line* by Neuville, Meissonnier's *The Cuirassiers of 1805*). Orientalism is well represented with Gros' work *The Plague Victims* of Jaffa,

H Vernet's *Arab Sheikhs Holding Council*, and *The Falcon Hunt* by Fromentin. Note, too, the famous portrait of *Gabrielle d'Estrées in Her Bath* (16C French School), the portraits of Cardinals Richelieu and Mazarin by Philippe de Champaigne, and *The Massacre of the Holy Innocents* by Poussin.

Rotonde (C) – The *Loreto Madonna* by **Raphael**, **Piero di Cosimo**'s portrait of the ravishing Simonetta Vespucci, who is believed to have been Botticelli's model for his *Birth of Venus*, and Chapu's kneeling statue of Joan of Arc listening to voices are exhibited here.

Salle de la Smalah et Rotonde de la Minerve (D) – Family portraits of the Orléans (17C, 18C and 19C) and of Louis-Philippe's relations in particular: Bonnat's picture of the Duke of Aumale at the age of 68.

Cabinet de Giotto (E) – This room is devoted to Italian Primitives: *Angels Dancing in the Sun* (Italian School, 15C).

Salle Isabelle (F) – Numerous 19C paintings here include *Moroccan Guards* by Delacroix, *Horse Leaving the Stables* by Géricault, and *Françoise de Rimini* by Ingres.

Salle d'Orléans (G) – The glass cabinets contain soft-paste **Chantilly porcelain** manufactured in the workshops founded in 1725 by the Duke de Bourbon (armorial service bearing the Condé coat of arms or the Duke of Orléans' monogram).

Salle Caroline (**H**) – 18C painting has pride of place here, with portraits by Largillière and Greuze, *Young Woman Playing with Children* by Van Loo, *The Worried Lover* and *The Serenade Player* by Watteau, or *Snowstorm* by Everdingen.

Cabinet des Clouet (**K**) – Here, find a collection of small and extremely rare **paintings**★★ executed by the **Clouets**, Corneille de Lyon, and others portraying François I, Marguerite of Navarre (stroking a little dog) and Henri II as a child.

Galerie de Psyché (**L**) – The 44 **stained-glass windows** (16C) that tell the story of the loves of Psyche and Cupid came from Constable Anne's other family home, Château d'Écouen.

Santuario★★★ (**N**) – This room houses the museum's most precious exhibits: Raphael's *Orléans Madonna*, *The Three Ages of Womanhood*, also known as *The Three Graces*, by the same artist; *Esther and Ahasuerus*, the panel of a wedding chest painted by Filippino Lippi and 40 miniature works by Jean Fouquet, cut out of Estienne Chevalier's book of hours, an example of French 15C art.

Cabinet des Gemmes (**P**) – Jewels of stunning beauty are on display. The Pink Diamond, alias the Great Condé (a copy of which is permanently on show), was stolen in 1926. but later found in an apple where the thieves had hidden it. The room also boasts an outstanding collection of enamels and miniatures.

Tribune (**R**) – Above the cornice of this polygonal room are painted panels representing episodes from the life of the Duke of Aumale and the house of Orléans. The paintings include *Autumn* by **Botticelli**, *Love Disarmed* and *Pastoral Pleasures* by **Watteau**, a portrait of Molière by **Mignard**, and on the "Écouen Wall", three superb works by **Ingres**: a self-portrait, *Madame Devaucay* and *Venus*.

Petits Appartements★ – *Access by the stairway off the reception hall*. The Duke of Aumale had these private apartments designed by painter Eugène Lami specially for his marriage in 1844.

THE PARK★★

🕐 *Apr–Oct daily 10am–8pm (last admission 6pm); Nov–Mar daily 10.30am–6pm (last admission 5pm).* 🎫7€. 🚻 ☎03 44 27 31 80.

Jardin anglais★ –The landscaped English-style garden was laid out on the surviving relics of Le Nôtre's park in 1820. Its charm derives from the pleasant groves (plane trees, swamp cypresses, weeping willows) rather than from the symbolic monuments: remains of a Temple of Venus and of Love (Île d'Amour).

Chapelle St-Jean – The chapel was erected on the estate by Constable Anne in 1538, with six other chapels, in memory of the seven churches of Rome he had visited in order to gain the indulgences granted to those who undertook this pilgrimage. He obtained from the Pope the same privileges for the chapels at Chantilly. Two other chapels still stand on the estate: St Paul's, located behind the Château d'Enghien, and Ste-Croix, on the lawns of the racecourse.

▷ Take allée Blanche along the banks of the Canal des Morfondus.

La Chute – These tiered waterfalls mark the start of the Grand Canal.

▷ Return along allée Blanche; cross Canal des Morfondus at the footbridge.

Le Hameau – Dating from 1775, this hamlet was built before the Trianon at Versailles. Under the influence of Jean-Jacques Rousseau, French princes used to seek new horizons by creating miniature villages. The mill and a few half-timbered buildings used to accommodate a kitchen, a dining room and a billiard room are on-site. The barn provided a drawing room that was restored by the Duke of Aumale. All the big parties included supper in this charming spot in the park.

▷ Skirt the brook by the small village.

Grandes écuries, Musée Vivant du Cheval et du Poney

© Arnaud Chicurel/hemis.fr

Parterres – The parterres are framed by two avenues of lime trees, called "The Philosophers' Path" because the great writers who visited Chantilly used to pace up and down the shaded avenue, exchanging their views and ideas.

The circular Vertugadin lawns lie along the line of La Manche, flanked by delightful stretches of water. Between La Manche and the round basin (Bassin de la Gerbe) stands Coysevox's statue of the Great Condé, framed by the effigies of La Bruyère and Bossuet (statues of Molière and Le Nôtre, seated, may be seen in the near distance). A monumental stairway (Grand Degré) leads from the parterres up to the terrace; on either side of these imposing steps are grottoes, their carved decoration representing rivers.

Le Potager des Princes

17 rue de la Faisanderie. ⏱*Mid-Mar–Oct daily 10pm–7pm.* ✎*9€.* ✆*03 44 57 39 66. www.potagerdesprinces.com.*
Originally designed by André Le Nôtre and Jean-Baptiste de la Quintinie, this garden includes an area reserved for farmyard animals, an orchard, a rose garden and a vegetable garden where medicinal and culinary herbs grow next to traditional vegetables.

Grandes écuries★★ (Stables)

Jean Aubert's masterpiece constitutes the most stunning piece of 18C architecture in Chantilly. The St-Denis Gateway – built astride the road leading to town – marks the site of an uncompleted pavilion. The most attractive façade of the stables overlooks the racecourse.

Musée Vivant du Cheval et du Poney★★

⏱*Call or check website for the show schedule;* ✎*21€ includes museum visit and 1hr equestrian show.* ✆*03 44 27 31 80. www.domainedechantilly.com.*
This museum is brought to life by saddle and draught animals (horses and ponies bred in France or in the Iberian Peninsula) that occupy the stalls built in the days of the Duke of Aumale. Well-choreographed equestrian shows combine music and expert horsemanship.

FORÊT DE CHANTILLY

The vast wooded area has been reshaped by hunting enthusiasts over 500 years. The network of paths through the forest is suitable for country walks, and the light soil favours riding activities; training sessions take place at carrefour du Petit Couvert. The forests of Coye, Orry and Pontarmé are reserved for walkers.

Chartres★★★

Chartres is the capital of Beauce, France's famous corn belt, but for tourists the town is known mainly for the Cathedral of Our Lady, a magnificent edifice, now a UNESCO World Heritage Site, which reigns supreme over a picturesque setting of monuments and old streets.

A BIT OF HISTORY

A town with a destiny – Since ancient times Chartres has always had a strong influence over religious matters. It is believed that a Gallo-Roman well on the Chartres plateau was the object of a pagan cult and that in the 4C, this well was transformed into a Christian cult by the first Evangelists. Adventius, the first known bishop of Chartres, lived during the middle of the 4C. A document from the 7C mentions a bishop Béthaire kneeling in front of Notre-Dame, which suggests the existence of a Marian cult. In 876 the chemise said to belong to the Virgin Mary was given to the cathedral by Charles the Bald, confirming that Chartres was already a place of pilgrimage. Up to the 14C the town of Chartres continued to flourish.

The pilgrimage – Chartres Cathedral was consecrated to the Assumption of the Virgin Mary in 1260; in the Middle Ages it attracted many pilgrims.
In 1912 and 1913 the writer and poet **Charles Péguy** (1873–1914) made the

Info: 8 rue de la Poissonerie, 28008 Chartres. ☎02 37 18 26 26. www.chartres-tourisme.com.

Location: Chartres lies off the A11. The town is situated on a knoll on the left bank of the River Eure, in the heart of the Beauce. The cathedral dominates the Old Town, known as the Quartier St-André.

Parking: There is a large underground car park at Le Boeuf Couronne, and street parking (paid) along the boulevard de la Résistance and the boulevard Maurice Violette.

Don't Miss: For a bird's-eye view of the cathedral, stand behind the Monument aux Aviateurs Militaires, a memorial to the French Air Force high above the east bank of the river.

Timing: Allow 90min to 2hrs to visit the cathedral and at least another 2hrs to visit the Old Town and Central District.

pilgrimage to Chartres. The strong influence it had on his work inspired a small group of enthusiasts after World War I to

Old Town Chartres

Chartres Cathedral

© Raga Jose Fuste/age fotostock

follow suit and led, in 1935, to the establishment of the "Students' Pilgrimage" (*during Whitsun*).

An exceptional man – In the **Église St-Jean-Baptiste** in the Rechèvres district to the north of the town lies the body of the abbot **Franz Stock**, whose tomb is still a place of pilgrimage. This German priest, chaplain to the prisons of Paris from 1940 to 1944, refused to retreat with the Wehrmacht and was taken prisoner. At the Morancez prison camp near Chartres, he founded a seminary for prisoners of war and was the Superior there for two years. He died in February 1948 at the age of 43.

THE CATHEDRAL★★★

🕐 *Open daily 8.30am–7.30pm. www.cathedrale-chartres.org. Allow 1hr 30min.*

The illustrious cathedral, which Rodin referred to as "the Acropolis of France" on account of its aesthetic and spiritual value, stands today as a monument of Gothic glory and popular pilgrimage.

A Bit of History

The building rests upon the Romanesque cathedral erected by Bishop Fulbert in the 11C and 12C: there remain the crypt, the towers and the foundations of the west front, including the Royal Doorway, and fragments of the Notre-Dame-de-la-Belle-Verrière stained-glass window.

The remaining sections of the cathedral were built in the wake of the Great Fire of 1194; princes and dignitaries contributed generously to the work, while the poor offered their labour.

These combined efforts made it possible to complete the cathedral in 25 years, and to add on the north and south porches 20 years later, with the result that the architecture and decoration of Notre-Dame form a harmonious composition almost unparalleled in the history of Gothic art.

By some miracle, the Wars of Religion, the French Revolution and the two World Wars spared the famous basilica. Only the cathedral's "forest" – the superb roof timbers – were destroyed by flames in 1836, and subsequently replaced by a metal framework.

The 4 000 carved figures and the 5 000 characters portrayed by the stained-glass windows demanded a lifelong commitment from the specialists who studied them.

Beneath the cathedral close, where it is planned to build an international medieval centre, archaeological excavations covering an area of some 1 200sq m/ 12 919sq ft are currently in progress. The remains of two 13C houses have been uncovered.

Exterior

West front

The two tall spires and the Royal Doorway form one of the best compositions encountered in French religious art. The **New Bell-Tower** on the left was built first; the lower part dates back to 1134. Its present name dates from the 16C, when Jehan de Beauce erected a stone spire (115m /377ft high) to replace the wooden steeple that had burned down in 1506. The Old Bell-Tower (c. 1145–64), rising 106m/348ft, is a masterpiece of Romanesque art, forming a stark contrast to the ornate Gothic construction. The Royal Doorway and the three large windows above date from the 12C. Everything above this ensemble was built at a later date: the rose window (13C), the 14C gable and the king's gallery featuring the Kings of Judah, the ancestors of the Virgin Mary. On the gable, the Virgin Mary is depicted presenting her son to the Beauce area.

The **Royal Doorway★★★** (Portail Royal), a splendid example of Late Romanesque architecture (1145–70), represents the life and triumph of the Saviour. The Christ in Majesty on the central tympanum and the statue-columns are famous throughout the world.

The elongated features of the biblical kings and queens, prophets, priests and patriarchs study the visitors from the embrasures. While the faces are animated, the bodies remain rigid, in deliberate contrast to the figures adorning the arches and the capitals. The statues were primarily designed to be columns, not human beings.

▷ Leave the west front on your left and walk round the cathedral, stepping back for a view of its lines.

North porch and doorway

The nave is extremely high and unusually wide. The problem of how to support it was brilliantly resolved with the construction of three-tiered flying buttresses; the lower two arcs were joined together by colonnettes. The elegant **Pavillon de l'Horloge** near the New Bell-Tower is the work of Jehan de Beauce (1520). The ornamentation of the north porch is similar to that of the doorway, executed at an earlier date. Treated more freely than those on the Royal Doorway, the characters are elegant and very lively, illustrating a new, more realistic approach to religious art. The statue of St Modesta, a local martyr who is pictured gazing up at the New Bell-Tower, is extremely graceful.

Once again, the decoration of the **three doors** refers to the Old Testament. The right door pays tribute to the biblical heroes who exercised the virtues recommended in the teachings of Christ. The central panel shows the Virgin Mary and the Prophets who foretold the coming of the Messiah. The door on the left presents the Annunciation, Visitation and Nativity, together with the Vices and Virtues.

In the **bishop's garden**, the raised terrace commands a view of the town below lying on the banks of the lower River Eure. Before reaching the garden gate, look left and note the archway straddling a narrow street. It used to open into the Notre-Dame cloisters.

East end

The complexity of the double-course **flying buttresses** – reinforced here with an intermediate pier as they cross over the chapels – and the succession of radiating chapels, chancel and arms of the transept are stunning. The 14C St-Piat Chapel, originally separate, was joined to Notre-Dame by a stately staircase.

South porch and doorway

Here, the upper stonework is concealed by a constellation of colonnettes. The perspective of these planes, stretching from the arches of the porch to the gables, confers to this arm of the transept a sense of unity that is lacking in the north transept.

The theme is the Church of Christ and the Last Judgement. In the Middle Ages, these scenes would usually be reserved for the west portal, but in this case the Royal Doorway already featured ornamentation. Consequently, the

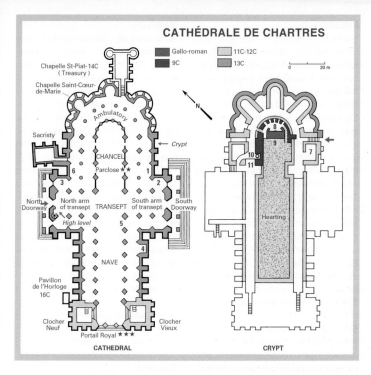

CATHÉDRALE DE CHARTRES

Gallo-roman
9C
11C–12C
13C

0   20 m

Chapelle St-Piat- 14C
(Treasury)

Chapelle Saint-Cœur-
de-Marie

Ambulatory

Sacristy

CHANCEL

Crypt

Parclose ★★

North
Doorway

6

3

1

2

North arm
of transept

TRANSEPT

South arm
of transept

South
Doorway

High level

5

N

4

NAVE

Pavillon
de l'Horloge
16C

Clocher
Neuf

Clocher
Vieux

Portail Royal ★★★

CATHEDRAL

8

9

10

7

11

Hearting

CRYPT

scenes portraying the Coming of a New World, prepared by the martyrs, were destined for the left-door embrasures, while those of the Confessors (witnesses of Christ who have not yet been made martyrs) adorn the right door.

Christ reigns supreme on the central tympanum. He is also present on the pier, framed by the double row of the 12 Apostles with their lean, ascetic faces, draped in long, gently folded robes.

Among the martyrs, note the **statues** standing in the foreground: St George and St Theodore, both admirable 13C representations of knights in armour. These figures are quite separate from the columns – the feet are flat and no longer slanted – and are there for purely decorative purposes.

The most delightful feature of the sculpted porch is the display of **medallions**, grouped in sets of six and placed on the recessed arches of the three doorways: the lives of the martyrs, the Vices and Virtues, and so on.

Returning to the west front, note the **Old Bell-Tower** and its ironical statue of

a donkey playing the fiddle, symbolizing man's desire to share in celestial music.

◉ At the corner of the building, stop to admire the tall figure of the sundial Angel.

Access to the Bell-Tower★

◷*May–Aug Mon–Sat 9.30am– 12.30pm, 2pm–6pm, Sun 2pm–6pm; Sept–Apr Mon–Sat 9.30am–12.30pm, 2pm–5pm, Sun 2pm–5pm (last ascent 30min before closing).* ◷*1 Jan, 1 May, 25 Dec.* ✆*7.50€.* ✆*02 37 21 22 07. www.monuments-nationaux.fr.*

The tour *(300 steps)* leads round the north side and up to the lower platform of the New Bell-Tower. Seen from a height of 70m/230ft, the buttresses, flying buttresses, statues, gargoyles and Old Bell-Tower are most impressive.

It is still possible to recognise the former Notre-Dame cloisters, thanks to the old pointed roof. Enclosed by a wall right up to the 19C, this area was frequented by clerics, especially canons.

Interior

The nave (16m/52ft) is wider than any other in France (Notre-Dame in Paris 1.2m/40ft; Notre-Dame in Amiens 14m/46ft), though it has single aisles. The vaulting reaches a height of 37m/121ft and the interior is 130m/427ft long. This nave is 13C, built in the style known as early or lancet Gothic. There is no gallery; instead, there is a blind triforium. In a place of pilgrimage of this importance, the chancel and the transept had to accommodate large-scale ceremonies; they were therefore wider than the nave. In Chartres, the chancel, its double ambulatory and the transept form an ensemble 64m/210ft wide between the north and south doorways.

Note the gentle slope of the floor, rising slightly towards the chancel; the slope made it easier to wash down the church when the pilgrims had stayed overnight.

Stained-glass windows★★★

The 12C and 13C stained-glass windows of Notre-Dame constitute, together with those of Bourges, the largest collection in France. The Virgin and Child and the Annunciation and Visitation scenes in the clerestory at the far end of the chancel produce a striking impression.

Detail of the stained-glass window of Notre-Dame-de-la-Belle-Verrière

© Ingrid Klimbek-lebedev/Dreamstime.com

West front

These three 12C windows used to throw light on Fulbert's Romanesque cathedral and the dark, low nave that stood behind, a feature that explains why they are so long. The scenes *(bottom to top)* illustrate the fulfilment of the prophecies: *(right)*, the Tree of Jesse *(centre)*, the childhood and life of Our Lord (Incarnation cycle) and *(left)* Passion and Resurrection (Redemption cycle).

You can feast your eyes on the famous 12C "Chartres blue", with its clear, deep tones enhanced by reddish tinges, especially radiant in the rays of the setting sun. For many years, people believed that this particular shade of blue was a long-lost trade secret. Modern laboratories have now established that the sodium compounds and silica in the glass made it more resistant to dirt and corrosion than the panes made with other materials and in other times. The large 13C rose window on the west front depicts the Last Judgement.

Transept

This ensemble consists of two 13C rose windows, to which were added a number of lancet windows featuring tall figures. The themes are the same as those on the corresponding carved doorway: Old Testament (*north*), the End of the World (*south*).

The **north rose** (*rose de France*) was a present from Blanche of Castille, mother of St Louis and Regent of France, and portrays a Virgin and Child. It is characterised by the fleur-de-lis motif on the shield under the central lancet and by the alternating Castile towers and fleurs-de-lis pictured on the small corner lancets. The larger lancets depict St Anne holding the infant Virgin Mary, framed by four kings or high priests: Melchizedek and David stand on the left, Solomon and Aaron on the right.

The centre roundel of the **south rose** shows the risen Christ, surrounded by the Old Men of the Apocalypse, forming two rings of 12 medallions. The yellow- and blue-chequered quatrefoils represent the coat of arms of the benefactors, the Comte de Dreux Pierre Mauclerc and his wife, who are also featured at the bottom of the lancets.

The lancets on either side of the Virgin and Child depict four striking figures – the Great Prophets Isaiah, Jeremiah, Ezekiel and Daniel – with the four Evangelists seated on their shoulders.

The morality of the scene is simple: although they are weak and lacking dignity, the Evangelists can see farther than the giants of the Old Testament thanks to the Holy Spirit.

Notre-Dame-de-la-Belle-Verrière★ (1)

This stained-glass window is very famous. The Virgin and Child, a fragment of the window spared by the fire of 1194, has been mounted in 13C stained glass. The range of blues is quite superb.

Other stained-glass windows – The aisles of the nave and the chapels around the ambulatory are lit by a number of celebrated stained-glass windows from the 13C verging on the sombre side. On the east side, the arms of the transept have received two works of recent making, in perfect harmony with the early fenestration: St Fulbert's window *(south transept)* (**2**), donated by the American Association of Architects (from the François Lorin workshop, 1954), and the window of Peace *(north transept)* (**3**), a present from a group of German admirers (1971).

The Vendôme Chapel (**4**) features a particularly radiant 15C stained-glass window. It illustrates the development of this art, which eventually led to the lighter panes of the 17C and 18C.

Parclose★★

The screen was started by Jehan de Beauce in 1514 and finished in the 18C. This fine work consists of 41 sculpted compositions depicting the lives of Christ and the Virgin Mary. These Renaissance medallions, evoking biblical history, local history and mythology, contrast sharply with the Gothic statues of the doorways.

Chancel

The marble facing, the Assumption group above the high altar and the low-relief carvings separating the columns were added in the 18C.

Organ (5)

The case dates from the 16C.

Vierge du Pilier (6)

This wooden statue (c. 1510) stood against the rood screen, now sadly disappeared. The richly clothed Virgin is the object of a procession celebrated annually.

Treasury

◦━ *Closed to the public.*

Chapelle St-Piat was built to house the cathedral treasury. It is linked to the east end of the cathedral by a Renaissance staircase. The interior holds some superb items of church plate.

Chapelle des Martyrs

This chapel has been refurbished and now contains the **Virgin Mary's Veil**, laid out in a glass-fronted reliquary. Pilgrims used to pray to this veil, calling it a tunic or "Holy Chemise".

Crypt★

🔊 *Visit by guided tour (30min) only: English tour Mon–Sat noon and 2.45pm departs from gift shop. Tours in French Apr–Oct Mon–Sat 11am, 2.15pm, 3.30pm, 4.30pm; Nov–Mar Tue–Sat 11am, Wed–Sun 4.15pm. ⊚2.70€.* 📞02 37 21 59 08.

The entrance is outside the cathedral, on the south side (⑂ *see floor plan above*). This is France's longest crypt (220m/722ft long). It dates largely from the 11C and features Romanesque groined vaulting. It is a curious shape; the two long galleries joined by the ambulatory pass under the chancel and the aisles give on to seven chapels. Of the seven radiating chapels, only three are Romanesque. The other four were added by the master architect of the Gothic cathedral to serve as foundations for the chancel and the apse of the future building.

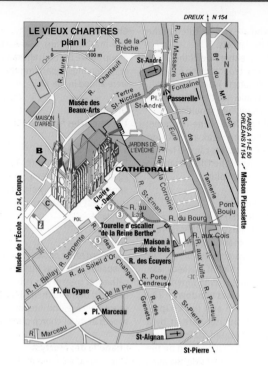

LE VIEUX CHARTRES
plan II

Saint Martin's Chapel (7)
Located by the south gallery, this chapel houses the originals of the statues on the Royal Doorway: the sundial Angel, and others.

▶ A staircase, starting from the ambulatory, leads to a lower crypt.

Crypt Saint-Lubin (8)
This crypt served as the foundations of the 9C church. A thick, circular column with a visible base backs on to a Gallo-Roman wall (9), its bond easily recognisable by the alternating bricks and mortar. The crypt was a safe place that protected the cathedral treasures in times of social unrest or natural disaster. Thus, the chemise of the Virgin Mary survived the Great Fire of 1194.

Puits des Saints-Forts (10)
The lower part of this 33m/108ft-deep shaft has a square section characteristic of Gallo-Roman wells. The coping is contemporary.
The name dates back to 858; it is believed that several Christian martyrs

from Chartres were murdered during a Norman attack, and their bodies thrown down the well.

Chapelle Notre-Dame-de-Sous-Terre (11)
This chapel is a sacred retreat where pilgrims indulge in fervent praying. Since the 17C the chapel, together with the north gallery of the crypt, has played the part of a miniature church. It originally consisted of a small alcove where the faithful came to venerate the Virgin Mary.
The interior of the chapel and its decoration were refurbished in 1976.

OLD TOWN★
(Quartier Saint-André and Banks of the Eure)
Follow the route on the map above.
This pleasant walk leads past the picturesque hilly site, the banks of the River Eure, an ancient district recently restored and the cathedral, which is visible from every street corner. A small tourist train tours the old town in summer.

Collégiale Saint-André

🕐*Open during temporary expositions.*
☎*02 37 21 03 69.*
This Romanesque church *(deconse-crated)* was the place of worship of one of the most active and densely popu-lated districts in town. Most of the trades were closely related to the river: millers, dyers, curriers, cobblers, tanners, drap-ers, fullers, tawers, serge makers, etc. The church was enlarged in the 13C, and in the 16C and 17C it received a chancel and an axial chapel resting on arches that straddled the River Eure and rue du Massacre. Unfortunately, both of these structures disappeared in 1827. The church was renovated in 2009 to house temporary arts expositions.

▶ Cross the Eure River by a metal footbridge.

There is a good **view★** of the old hump-back bridges. At the foot of the short-ened nave of St Andrew's lie the remains of the arch that once supported the chancel. As you wander upstream, the wash-houses and races of former mills have been restored. **Rue aux Juifs** leads through an ancient district that has been renovated and features cobbled streets bordered by gable-ended houses and old-fashioned street lamps.
Rue des Écuyers – This street is one of the most successful restorations of the Old Town. At nos 17 and 19 the houses have 17C doorways with rusticated surrounds, surmounted by a bull's-eye window.

▶ Go along the street to rue aux Cois.

The corner building is a half-timbered villa, with an overhang in the shape of a prow. Opposite stands Queen Ber-tha's stair turret, a 16C structure, also half-timbered.

CENTRAL DISTRICT
Place du Cygne
The street has been widened into a small square planted with trees and shrubs; it is an oasis of calm in this lively shopping district in the town centre.

At the end of rue du Cygne, on place Marceau, a monument celebrates the memory of the local general who died at Altenkirchen (1796) at the age of 27. His ashes have been shared among Chartres (funeral urn under the statue on place des Épars), the Panthéon and the Dome Church of the Invalides in Paris.

Église Saint-Pierre★
This 12C and 13C Gothic church used to belong to the Benedictine abbey of St-Père-en-Vallée. The belfry-porch dates from pre-Romanesque times. The **Gothic stained-glass windows★** can be traced back to the late 13C, before the widespread introduction of yellow staining. The oldest stained glass is that in the south bays of the chancel.

Monument de Jean Moulin
Jean Moulin was *préfet* (chief admini-strator) of Chartres during the German invasion; on 8 June 1940, despite having been tortured, he resisted the enemy and refused to sign a document claiming that the French troops had committed atrocities. As he was afraid of being unable to withstand further torture, he attempted to commit suicide. He was dismissed by the Vichy government in November 1940 and from then on, he planned and coordinated underground resistance, working in close collabora-tion with General de Gaulle. Arrested in Lyon in June 1943, he did not survive the harsh treatment he received from the Gestapo.

Grenier de Loëns
From the 12C onwards, this half-timbered barn with treble gables in the courtyard of the old chapter-house was used to store the wine and cereals offered to the clergy as a tithe. Renovated to house the **Centre international du Vitrail** (♿🕐*Mon–Fri 9.30am–12.30pm, 1.30pm –6pm, Sat 10am–12.30pm, 2.30pm–6pm, Sun 2.30pm–6pm;* 🕐*1 Jan, 25 Dec;* 👛*5.50€;* ☎*02 37 21 65 72; www.centre-vitrail.org),* which organises stained-glass exhibits, the building now features a large hall with restored roof timbering and a 12C cellar with three aisles.

Fontainebleau★★★

It was not until the 19C that Fontainebleau started to develop, due to the growing popularity of country residences and the general appreciation of its unspoiled forest. The area's name derives from a spring at the heart of a forest abounding in game, which was known as the "Fontaine de Bliaut" or "Blaut", probably after a former owner. However, Fontainebleau essentially owes its fame to the castle and the park named on UNESCO's World Heritage list. The town itself is the ideal starting point for excursions to Vaux-le-Vicomte, Barbizon or Courances.

> **Info:** Office du Tourisme du pays de Fontainebleau-Avon, 4 rue Royale, 77300 Fontainebleau. ℘01 60 74 99 99. www.fontainebleau-tourisme.com.
>
> **Location:** Fontainebleau is 60km/37.3mi from Paris, via the A6, and then the N37. To access by rail from Paris take the SNCF rail link from Gare de Lyon.
>
> **Don't Miss:** The Renaissance features of the castle, especially its famous horseshoe staircase.
>
> **Timing:** You can easily spend a whole day here.

A BIT OF HISTORY

The Palais de Fontainebleau owes its origins to royalty's passion for hunting; it owes its development and decoration to the kings' delight in amassing works of art and displaying them in their "family home". This palace has an extremely distinguished past; from the last of the Capetians up to Napoléon III, it was designed for, and occupied by, French rulers.

A hunting lodge

A spring – called Bliaut or Blaut fountain in the middle of a forest abounding in game – prompted the kings of France to build a mansion here. The exact date is not known, but it was probably before 1137, as a charter exists issued under Louis VII from Fontainebleau, dating from that year. Philippe August celebrated the return of the Third Crusade here during the Christmas festivities of 1191, and St Louis founded a Trinitarian convent, whose members were called Mathurins; Philip the Fair was born here in 1268: unfortunately, he also died here following a serious riding accident.

The Renaissance

Under François I almost all the medieval buildings were pulled down and replaced by two main edifices, erected under the supervision of Gilles Le Bre-

ton. The oval-shaped east pavilion – built on the former foundations – was linked to the west block by a long gallery. To decorate the palace, François I hired many artists; he dreamed of creating a "New Rome" furnished with replicas of Classical statues.

The actual building consisted of rubble-work, since the sandstone taken from the forest was too difficult to work into regular freestones. The harled façades are enlivened by string-courses of brick or massive sandstone blocks.

Henri II's château

Henri II pursued the efforts undertaken by his father. He gave orders to complete and decorate the ballroom, which remains one of the splendours of Fontainebleau Palace. The monograms – consisting of the royal H and the two intertwined Cs of Catherine de' Medici – were legion. In a form of ambiguity that was generally accepted in its day, the two Cs placed immediately beside the H form a double D, the monogram of the King's mistress Diane de Poitiers.

When Henri II was killed in a tournament, his widow Catherine de' Medici sent her rival to Chaumont-sur-Loire and

The Farewell

On 20 April 1814 **Emperor Napoléon Bonaparte** appeared at the top of the horseshoe staircase; it was 1pm. The foreign army commissioners in charge of escorting him away were waiting in their carriages at the foot of the steps. Napoléon started to walk down the staircase with great dignity, his hand resting on the stone balustrade, his face white with contained emotion. He stopped for a moment while contemplating his guards standing to attention, then moved forward to the group of officers surrounding the Eagle, led by General Petit. His farewell speech, deeply moving, was both an appeal to the spirit of patriotism and a parting tribute to those who had followed him throughout his career. After embracing the general, Bonaparte kissed the flag, threw himself into one of the carriages and was whisked away amid the tearful shouts of his soldiers.

dismissed the architect in charge of the building work, Philibert Delorme, who was Diane's protégé. He was replaced by the Italian Primaticcio; those working under him, including Niccolo dell'Abbate, favoured cheerful colours.

Henri IV's palace – 17C

Henri IV, who adored Fontainebleau, had the palace enlarged quite significantly. The irregular contours of the Oval Court were corrected, and he gave orders to build the Kitchen Court and the Real Tennis Court (Jeu de Paume). These he had decorated by a new group of artists of largely Flemish, and not Italian, inspiration: frescoes were replaced by oil paintings on plaster or canvas. In the same way, the plain wood panelling highlighted with gilding gave way to painted wainscot. This was the Second Fontainebleau School, whose representatives moved in Parisian circles.

House of Eternity

Louis' XIV, XV and XVI undertook numerous renovations aimed at embellishing their apartments. The Revolution spared the château but emptied it of its precious furniture. Napoléon, who became consul, then emperor, thoroughly enjoyed staying at the palace. He preferred Fontainebleau to Versailles, where he felt haunted by a phantom rival. He called the palace "The House of Eternity" and left his mark by commissioning further refurbishments. The last rulers of France also took up residence here palace. It was eventually turned into a museum under the Republic.

THE PALACE★★★

🕐Apr–Sept Wed–Mon 9.30am–6pm; Oct–Mar Wed–Mon 9.30am–5pm (last admission 45min before closing). Grounds open 24 hrs. 🕐1 Jan, 1 May, 25 Dec. ✆11€, ✆16€ with guided tour. 📞01 60 71 50 70. www.musee-chateau-fontainebleau.fr.

Exterior

Cour du Cheval Blanc or des Adieux★★ – This former bailey was used only by domestics, but its generous size soon earmarked it for official parades and tournaments. It was sometimes called the White Horse Court after the day Charles IX set up a plaster cast of the equestrian statue of Marcus Aurelius in Rome; a small slab in the central alley marks its former location.

The golden eagles seemingly hovering above the pillars of the main gate remind visitors that the emperor had this made into his main courtyard. He gave orders to raze the Renaissance buildings that lay to the west of the court, but kept the end pavilions. It is clear, walking between the two long wings, that only the one on the left with its brick courses has retained the elegance that characterized the work of Gilles Le Breton, François I's favourite architect. The right wing – which boasted the Ulysses Gallery decorated under the supervision of Primaticcio – was dismantled by Louis XV and rebuilt by Jacques-Ange Gabriel.

At the far end of the court the main block, fronted by a balustrade marking the site of the former moat, was com-

Military and Equestrian Tradition

Throughout French history, whether under monarchic or republican rule, independent units have been posted to Fontainebleau. Tradition, it seems, favoured the cavalry, present in the 17C with the king's bodyguard. A number of racecourses and riding schools were created under Napoléon III; the Centre National des Sports Équestres perpetuates this tradition, while the forest caters to riding enthusiasts.

The history of the town has been marked by several military organisations, notably the École Spéciale Militaire (1803 to 1808, before St-Cyr), the polygon-shaped École d'Application d'Artillerie et du Génie (1871 to 1914) and the SHAPE (Supreme Headquarters, Allied Powers, Europe) headquarters of NATO, which gave the town a cosmopolitan touch from 1947 to 1967.

pleted in several stages from the reign of François I to that of Louis XV. Nonetheless, the façades show a certain unity of style. The large horizontal planes of the blue slating are broken by the white façades, the trapezoidal roofs and the tall chimneys of the five pavilions. The celebrated **horseshoe staircase** executed by Jean du Cerceau during the reign of Louis XIII is a harmoniously curved, extravagant composition showing royalty's taste for splendour.

Cour de la Fontaine★ – The fountain at the edge of the pond *(Étang des Carpes)* used to yield remarkably clear water. It was kept exclusively for the king's use and to that end the spring was guarded by two sentinels night and day.

The present fountain dates back to 1812 and is crowned by a statue of Ulysses. The surrounding buildings feature stone masonry and the ensemble forms a pleasant courtyard. At the far end, the Galerie François I is fronted by a terrace; it rests on arches which once opened on to the king's bathroom suite.

The **Aile de la Belle Cheminée** on the right was built by Primaticcio around 1565. The name originated from the fireplace that adorned the vast first-floor hall until the 18C. At that point in history Louis XV (who had turned the room into a theatre and rechristened it Aile de l'Ancienne Comédie) dismantled the fireplace, and the low-relief carvings were scattered. The monumental external steps consist of a dog-legged

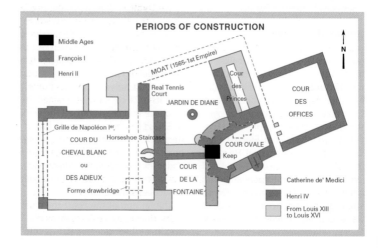

PERIODS OF CONSTRUCTION

Middle Ages
François I
Henri II

MOAT (1565-1st Empire)

Real Tennis Court
JARDIN DE DIANE

Cour des Princes

COUR DES OFFICES

Grille de Napoléon Ier
COUR DU CHEVAL BLANC
ou
DES ADIEUX
Forme drawbridge

Horseshoe Staircase

COUR DE LA FONTAINE

Keep

COUR OVALE

Catherine de' Medici
Henri IV
From Louis XIII to Louis XVI

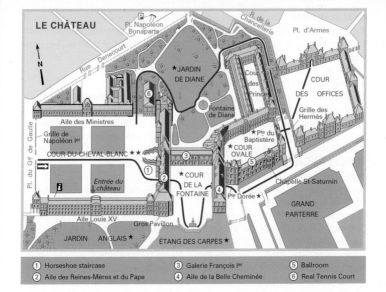

LE CHÂTEAU

N

★ JARDIN
DE DIANE

Rue Denecourt

Pl. Napoléon
Bonaparte

R. de la
Chancellerie

Pl. d'Armes

Cour
des
Princes

COUR
DES OFFICES

Grille des
Hermès

Fontaine
de Diane

Aile des Ministres

Grille de
Napoléon Ier

COUR DU CHEVAL-BLANC ★ ★

Pl. du Gal de Gaulle

Aile Louis XV

JARDIN   ANGLAIS ★

Entrée du
château

Gros Pavillon

★ Pte du
Baptistère

★ COUR
OVALE

★ COUR
DE LA
FONTAINE

Pte Dorée ★

Chapelle St-Saturnin

GRAND
PARTERRE

ÉTANG DES CARPES ★

① Horseshoe staircase
② Aile des Reines-Mères et du Pape
③ Galerie François Ier
④ Aile de la Belle Cheminée
⑤ Ballroom
⑥ Real Tennis Court

staircase with two straight flights in the Italian style. On the left the Queen Mothers' and Pope's wing ends in the Grand Pavilion built by Gabriel.

Étang des Carpes★ (Carp Pond) – In the centre of the pond – alive with carp – stands a small pavilion built under Henri IV, renovated under Louis XIV and restored by Napoléon. It was used for refreshments and light meals.

Porte Dorée★ – Dated 1528, this gatehouse is part of an imposing pavilion. It was the official entrance to the palace until Henri IV built the Porte du Baptistère. The paintings by Primaticcio have all been restored and the tympanum sports a stylized salamander, François I's emblem.

On the two upper levels are Italian-style loggias. The first floor – its loggia sealed off by large bay windows – used to house Mme deMaintenon's suite.

The ballroom is flanked by an avenue of lime trees. The view from the bay windows is splendid, and it is regrettable that the initial plans to build an open-air loggia were changed on account of the climate. The east end of the two-storeyed chapel dedicated to St Saturnin can be seen in the distance.

Porte du Baptistère★ – The gateway opens on to the Oval Court. The base of the gateway is the rustic entrance with decorative sandstone that once held the drawbridge across the old moat. It opened on to the Cour du Cheval-Blanc and was designed by Primaticcio. It is crowned by a wide arch surmounted by a dome. The gateway is named after the christening of Louis XIII and his two sisters, Élisabeth and Chrétienne, celebrated with great pomp on a dais on 14 September 1606.

Cour Ovale★ – This courtyard is by far the most ancient and the most interesting courtyard of Fontainebleau Palace. The site was the bailey of the original stronghold; of the latter there remains only the keep, named after St Louis, although it was probably built prior to his reign. François I incorporated it into the structure he had erected on the foundations of the old castle, shaped like an oval or rather a polygon with rounded corners. Under Henri IV, the courtyard lost its shape, although not its name; the east side was enlarged, and the wings were aligned and squared by two new pavilions framing the new Porte du Baptistère. The general layout of the palace was preserved.

Cour des Offices – The entrance faces the Porte du Baptistère and is guarded by two arresting sandstone heads depicting Hermes, sculpted by Gilles Guérin in 1640. The Cour des Offices was built by Henri IV in 1609; it is a huge oblong, sealed off on three sides by austere buildings alternating with low pavilions. With its imposing porch executed in the style of city gates, it bears a strong resemblance to a square. Walk through the gate and admire its architecture from place d'Armes; the sandstone front presents rusticated work and has a large niche as its centrepiece.

Continue the tour of the palace exterior. The east and north wings of the Cour des Princes are two functional buildings designed or redesigned under Louis XV to provide further accommodation for members of the court.

Jardin de Diane★ – The queen's formal garden created by Catherine de' Medici was designed by Henri IV and bordered by an orangery on its northern side. In the 19C the orangery was torn down and the park turned into a landscape garden. **Diana's fountain**, an elegant display of stonework dated 1603, has survived in the middle of the grounds. It has now resumed its original appearance;

the four bronze dogs formerly exhibited in the Louvre Museum sit obediently at the feet of their mistress, the hunting goddess.

Interior
Grands Appartements★★★

The main apartments are reached by the stucco staircase (a), the Galerie des Fastes (b) and the Galerie des Assiettes (c), which features 128 decorated pieces of Sèvres porcelain.

Chapelle de la Trinité★ – The chapel takes its name from the Trinitarian church set up on the premises by St Louis. Henri IV had the sanctuary reinforced by vaulting and then decorated. Martin Fréminet (1567–1619), one of the lesser-known followers of Michelangelo, painted the arches with strong, vigorous scenes characterized by perspective and a daring use of foreshortening. The scenes represent the mystery of the Redemption and a number of figures from the Old Testament. It was in this chapel that Louis XV was wedded to Marie Leszczynska in 1725 and that Louis Napoléon, later to be Napoléon III, was christened in 1810.

Galerie François I★★★ – This gallery was built from 1528 to 1530 and was originally open on both sides, resembling a covered passageway. When Louis XVI enlarged it in 1786, he filled in the windows looking on to Diana's garden. A set of false French windows was fitted for reasons of symmetry. The greater part of the decoration – closely combining fresco and stucco work – was supervised by Rosso, while the wood panelling was entrusted to an Italian master carpenter. François I's monogram and his emblem the salamander were widely represented.

The scenes are difficult to interpret (there are no explanatory documents), though they seem to split into two groups, one on either side of the central bay, which is adorned with an oval painting depicting two figures: Danaë by Primaticcio and *The Nymph of Fontainebleau* (1860) after Rosso.

Galerie François I

©H. Chajmowicz/Michelin

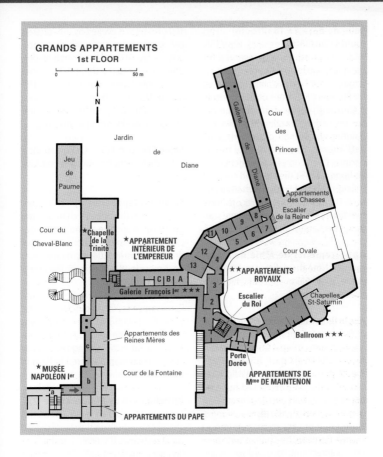

GRANDS APPARTEMENTS
1st FLOOR

The east side, near a bust of François I, features mostly violent scenes, perhaps referring to the recent misfortunes of the French king (the defeat of Pavia, the king's captivity in Madrid), the inescapable nature of war and death (the battle between the Centaurs and the Lapiths, Youth and Old Age, the Destruction of the Greek fleet).

Beneath the vignette depicting Venus and Love at the edge of a pond, note the miniature picture set in a tablet, representing the château around 1540 with both the gallery and the Porte Dorée clearly visible.

On the west side, near the entrance, the décor exemplifies the sacred qualities of the royal function – Sacrifice, the Unity of the State – and the concept of filial piety in the old-fashioned sense of the word (the twins Cleobis and Biton): the

king, his mother Louise of Savoy and his sister Marguerite d'Angoulême were devoted to one another.

The most striking scene is the portrait of an elephant whose caparison bears the royal monogram; the pachyderm no doubt symbolises the perennity of the monarchy.

Escalier du Roi★★ – The staircase was built in 1749, under Louis XV, in what was once the bedchamber of the Duchess of Étampes, François I's favourite. The murals – the history of Alexander the Great – are by Primaticcio (note Alexander taming Bucephalus above the door) and dell'Abbate (Alexander placing Homer's books in a chest, on the far wall). Primaticcio's stucco work is highly original; the upper frieze is punctuated by caryatids with elongated bodies.

Salle de Bal★★★ (Ballroom) – This room (30m/98ft long and 10m/33ft wide) was traditionally reserved for banquets and formal receptions. It was begun under François I and completed by Philibert Delorme under Henri II. A thorough restoration programme has revived the dazzling frescoes and paintings by Primaticcio and his pupil dell'Abbate. The marquetry of the parquet floor, completed under Louis-Philippe, echoes the splendid coffered ceiling, richly highlighted with silver and gold. The monumental fireplace features two telamones, cast after Antique statues in the Capitol Museum in Rome.

Appartements de Mme de Maintenon – Note the delicate wainscoting in the Grand Salon, most of which was executed in the 17C.

Appartements royaux★★ – At the time of François I, Fontainebleau featured a single suite of apartments laid out around the Oval Court. Towards 1565, the Regent Catherine de' Medici gave orders to double the curved building between the Oval Court and Diana's Garden. Subsequently, the royal bedrooms, closets and private salons overlooked Diana's Garden. The original suite now houses antechambers, guard-rooms and reception rooms where the king used to entertain his guests.

Salle des Gardes (1) – Note the late-16C ceiling and frieze.
From the **Salle du Buffet (2)**, a wide arch leads to a chamber in the oldest tower of the castle.

Salle du Donjon (3) – Until the reign of Henri IV, this sombre room was occupied by French kings who used it as a bedroom, hence its other name, the St Louis Bedroom. The equestrian low-relief sculpture (c. 1600) portraying Henri IV on the fireplace came from the "Belle Cheminée". It was carved by Mathieu Jacquet.

Salon Louis XIII (4) – It was here that Louis XIII was born on 27 September 1601. His birth is evoked by the coffered ceiling, which depicts Cupid riding a dolphin (the word dauphin means both dolphin and heir to the throne). The panel with painted wainscoting is crowned by a set of 11 pictures by Ambroise Dubois; the Romance between Theagenes and Chariclea, works dating from c.1610.

Salon François I (5) – Of Primaticcio's work there remains only the fireplace in this room.

Salon des Tapisseries (6) – This room, having been the queen's chamber, the guard-room and the queen's first antechamber, became the empress' principal drawing room in 1804, the guard-room once more in 1814 and finally the Tapestry Salon in 1837.
The fireplace dates from 1731 and the Renaissance ceiling in pinewood is the work of Poncet (1835). The furniture was made during the Second Empire (mid-19C). The tapestries telling the story of Psyche were manufactured in Paris in the first half of the 17C.

Antichambre de l'Impératrice (7) – Formerly the queen's guard-room, this chamber was built on the site of the old royal staircase; the ceiling and panelling are both dated 1835. The Gobelins tapestries, executed after cartoons by Le Brun, illustrate the four seasons. The Second Empire furniture features a console, a carved-oak writing desk (Fourdinois, 1865) and a set of armchairs of English inspiration. Note the two Indian-style enamel vases produced by the Sèvres factory.

Galerie de Diane – This long gilt passageway (80m/263ft) was decorated during the Restoration and turned into a library under the Second Empire.

Salon blanc- Petit salon de la Reine (8) – In 1835 the room was decorated with furnishings from an earlier period: Louis XV wainscoting, Louis XVI fireplace inlaid with bronze, etc. The furniture is Empire: chairs in gilt wood by Jacob Frères, settee, armchairs and chairs from

St-Cloud, mahogany console and heads of fantastic animals in bronzed, gilt wood (Jacob Desmalter).

Grand Salon de l'Impératrice (9) – This drawing room, formerly the queen's gaming room, features a ceiling painted by Berthélemy; the scene is Minerva crowning the Muses.

The furniture dates from the reign of Louis XVI (chests by Stöckel and Beneman, seats upholstered with painted satin, a carpet made by the Savonnerie works) or from the First Empire (seats and chests by Jacob Desmalter, the so-called "Seasons Table" made of Sèvres porcelain and painted by Georget in 1806–7, and a carpet rewoven to an old design). The two sets of furniture are displayed in turn.

Chambre de l'Impératrice (10) – This used to be the queen's bedroom. The greater part of the ceiling was designed for Anne of Austria in 1644; the wood panelling, the fireplace and the top of the alcove were created for Marie Leszczynska in 1747 and the doors with arabesque motifs were installed for Marie-Antoinette in 1787. The brocaded silk was rewoven according to the original pattern in Lyon at the end of Louis XVI's reign.

Among the furniture note Marie-Antoinette's bed, designed in 1787 by Hauré, Sené and Laurent, a set of armchairs attributed to Jacob Frères and several commodes by Stöckel and Beneman (1786). The vases are Sèvres porcelain.

Boudoir de la Reine (11) – This delightful room was designed by Marie-Antoinette. The wainscoting was painted by Bourgois and Touzé after sketches by the architect Rousseau. The ceiling – representing sunrise – is the work of Berthélemy. The roll-top writing desk and the work table were made by Riesener in 1786.

Salle du Trône (12) – This was the king's bedroom from Henri IV to Louis XVI; Napoléon converted it into the throne room. The ornate mural paintings, dating from several periods, were harmonized in the 18C. Above the fireplace is a full-length portrait of Louis XIII, painted in Philippe de Champaigne's studio.

Salle du Conseil (13) – This room was given a semicircular extension in 1773. The ceiling and panelling are splendid examples of Louis XV decoration.

Five pictures by Boucher adorn the ceiling, representing the four seasons and Apollo, conqueror of Night. The wainscoting presents an alternation of allegorical figures painted in blue or pink monochrome by Van Loo and Jean-Baptiste Pierre.

Galerie de Diane

©H. Chajmowicz/Michelin

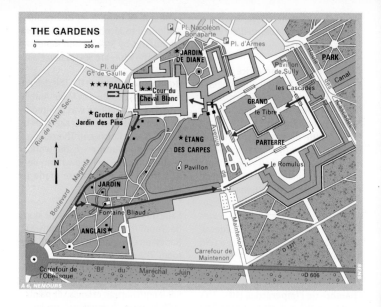

THE GARDENS

0   200 m

Pl. Napoléon
Bonaparte
Pl. d'Armes
★JARDIN
DE DIANE
Pl. du
Gal de Gaulle
★★★ PALACE
★★Cour du
Cheval Blanc
★Grotte du
Jardin des Pins
★ÉTANG
DES CARPES
♦ Pavillon
JARDIN
Fontaine Bliaud
ANGLAIS★
Carrefour de
l'Obélisque
Bd   du   Maréchal   Juin
Carrefour de
Maintenon
PARK
Pavillon
de Sully
les Cascades
Canal
GRAND
le Tibre
PARTERRE
le Romulus
A 6, NEMOURS
D 606
SENS

Appartement Intérieur de l'Empereur★ – *Visit included in the tour of the Grands Appartements.*
Napoléon had his suite installed in the wing built by Louis XVI, on the garden side running parallel with the François I Gallery.

Chambre de Napoléon (A) – Most of the decoration – dating from the Louis XVI period – has survived. The furniture is typically Empire.

Petite chambre à coucher (B) – A little private study which Bonaparte furnished with a day bed in gilded iron.

Salon de l'Abdication (C) – According to tradition, this is the room in which the famous abdication document was signed on 6 April 1814. The Empire furniture in this red drawing room dates back to that momentous time.
The François I Gallery leads to the Vestibule du Fer-à-cheval, at the top of the curved steps of the same name. This was the official entrance to the palace from the late 17C onwards. Both the gallery of the chapel and the Appartements des Reines Mères give on to this hall.

Musée chinois★ – This small museum, commissioned by Empress Eugénie on the ground floor of the Gros Pavillon, comes as a surprise because of the contrast between the comfortable, heavy furniture and the slender elegance of the objects on show. The collection was originally the booty captured during the Franco-British conflict with China in 1860, especially as a result of the ransacking of the imperial palace. The following year, a delegation of Siamese ambassadors completed the collection with a number of opulent presents, an event that was faithfully recorded in a painting by Gérôme.
The tour begins in the **antechamber** decorated with two luxurious Siamese palanquins. The **nouveaux salons** beyond are decorated with crimson wall hangings, padded armchairs, ebony furniture and objects from China and Siam. Most of the collection, however, is to be seen in the **cabinet de laque** decorated with 15 panels from an 18C Chinese fan. Note the four large tapestries on the ceiling and the huge glass-fronted cabinet filled to the brim with objects, including a copy of the Siamese royal crown.

Musée Napoléon I★

Same hrs as the Palace. Admission included in the ticket for the visit to the Grands Appartements. 01 60 71 50 70. The museum is dedicated to the emperor and his family; it occupies 15 rooms on the ground level and first floor of the Louis XV wing. Exhibits include portraits (paintings and sculptures), silverware, arms, medals, ceramics (imperial service), clothing (coronation robes, uniforms) and personal memorabilia. Thanks to the numerous works of art and furniture adorning their interior, these apartments have kept their princely character.

The rooms on the first floor evoke the Coronation (paintings by François Gérard), the emperor's various military campaigns, his daily life (remarkable folding desk by Jacob Desmalter), the Empress Marie-Louise in formal attire or painting the emperor's portrait (picture by Alexandre Menjaud) and the birth of Napoléon's son, the future King of Rome (cradles).

The ground floor presents the emperor's close relations. Each of the seven rooms is devoted to a member of the family: Napoléon's mother, his brothers Joseph, Louis and Jérôme and his sisters Elisa, Pauline and Caroline.

Petits Appartements et Galerie des Cerfs

Same hrs as the Palace. Guided tours daily at 2.30pm (call first). 7€; combined ticket with the Grands Appartements 16€. 01 60 71 50 70. These rooms are on the ground floor below the François I Gallery and Royal Suite overlooking the Jardin de Diane.

Petits Appartements de Napoléon I

– This suite comprises François I's former bathroom suite (located beneath the gallery and converted into private rooms under Louis XV for the king, Mme de Pompadour and Mme du Barry), and the ground floor of the new Louis XVI wing, situated under the Imperial Suite. The rooms opening to the garden have been decorated with Louis XV wainscoting and Empire furniture.

Appartements de l'Impératrice Joséphine★

– This suite of rooms adorned with Louis XV panelling was designed for Joséphine in 1808. It lies beneath the Grand Royal Suite.

The study, with its large rotunda, stands beneath the Council Chamber *(first floor)*. The Empire furniture here has a feminine touch: Marie-Louise's tambour frame, etc. The Salon Jaune constitutes one of the palace's best examples of Empire decoration. The gold-coloured wall hangings provide an elegant setting for Jacob Desmalter's choice furniture ,set off by a large Aubusson carpet.

Galerie des Cerfs★

– The gallery is decorated with deer heads. The mural paintings show palatial residences at the time of Henri IV, seen in perspective. It was in this gallery that Queen Christina of Sweden had her favourite, Monaldeschi, assassinated in 1657.

THE GARDENS★

Daily May–Sept 9am–7pm; Mar–Apr and Oct 9am–6pm; Nov–Feb 9am–5pm.

Grotte du Jardin des Pins★

This rare ornamental composition carved in sandstone reveals the popular taste, copied from the Italians, for ponds, man-made features and bucolic landscapes in vogue towards the end of François I's reign. The rusticated arches are supported by giant telamones. The frescoes have disappeared.

Jardin anglais★

The garden was created in 1812 on the site of former gardens (featuring a pine grove) redesigned under Louis XIV and abandoned during the Revolution. The Bliaut or Blaut fountain, which gave its name to the palace, plays in a small octagonal basin in the middle of the garden.

THE PARK

Daily 24hrs.

The park was created by Henri IV, who filled the canal (in 1609) and had the grounds planted with elms, pines and fruit trees.

ements, Fontainebleau

Where to Stay

Paris offers a wealth of lodgings within the city and on the outskirts, ranging from moderately priced in-home stays and bed and breakfast accommodation to intimate boutique hotels and large, glitzy palaces. Breakfast is sometimes included in the rate, or optional buffet and continental-style servings are available at an additional fee. *See the opposite page for a list of hotels by neighbourhood. For coin ranges, see the Legend on the cover flap.*

ECONOMY CHAIN HOTELS

These are generally located near main roads. While breakfast is available, there may not be a restaurant.

- **Mister Bed** – www.misterbed.fr.
- **B&B Hôtel** – www.hotel-bb.com.
- **Première Classe** – 02 0 75 19 50 45. www.premiereclasse.com
- **Campanile** – 08 92 23 48 12. www.campanile.fr
- **Ibis** – 0 825 882 222 (0.15€/mn). *www.ibis.com*
- **Kyriad** – 02 0 75 19 50 45 (0.15€/mn). *www.kyriad.com*

Note: Some establishments won't accept pets, while others will put them up for a fee. Enquire when you reserve.

BED AND BREAKFAST

- **Bed & Breakfast France** www.bedbreak.com.
- **Alcôve et Agapes** 8 bis rue Coysevox, 75018 Paris 01 07 64 08 42 77; www.bed-and-breakfast-in-paris.com.
- **Une Chambre en Ville** www.chambre-ville.com.
- **France Lodge** – 2 r. Meissonier. 75017 Paris. 01 56 33 85 80. www.francelodge.fr.
- **Good Morning Paris** – 43 r. Lacépède. 75005 Paris. 01 47 07 28 29. www.goodmorningparis.fr.

OTHER WEBSITES

www.parisattitude.com
www.airbnb.com.

HOSTELS

There are two main youth hostel (*auberge de jeunesse*) associations in France.

- **Ligue Française des Auberges de Jeunesse,** 01 44 16 78 78; www.auberges-de-jeunesse.com.
- **Fédération Unie des Auberges de Jeunesse,** 27 rue Pajol, 75018 Paris, 01 44 89 87 27; www.fuaj.org. Members of Hosteling International should contact their country's office for information (US 240 650 2100, www.hiusa.org; UK 44 845 293 7373, www.hihostels.com).

SELECTED HOTELS BY DISTRICT

For each neighbourhood described in the *Discovering* section, the corresponding *arrondissement* is shown in the listings beginning on the opposite page, so that you can choose establishments based on their **geographical location**. A wide array of lodgings has been presented by **price ranges** (*see the Legend on the cover flap*) to suit every budget; the closest **metro station** M is shown (if relevant), as well as the **map** on which the accommodation appears in this guide (a list of maps in this guide can be found on page 459).

Rooms are rented per night and **breakfast** is included unless a price is noted after the coffee cup symbol. It is highly recommended that you **reserve ahead** – Parisian hotels are often fully booked; most lodgings offer online booking. Keep in mind that you are expected to reconfirm if you plan to arrive after 5 or 6pm. This notification is essential in many hotels, where your room may be given away if you fail to call or fax your **confirmation** and your time of arrival. If you are travelling on a budget, you may wish to experience the posh décor and atmosphere of the mythical palace hotels by dropping in for brunch or a cup of tea.

1ST ARRONDISSEMENT

⊖⊜⊟ **Hôtel du Cygne** – *Map Beaubourg Les Halles. 3 r. du Cygne. 75001.* Ⓜ*Étienne-Marcel.* ℘*01 42 60 14 16. www.hotelducygne.fr. Closed third week of Jul and first 3 weeks of Aug. 20 rooms.* ⊑*8€.* In spite of its rather small dimensions from the stairwell to the halls, this hotel, located in an old building in central Paris, has character. Appointed with pretty fabrics and exposed wooden beams, the tiny bedrooms benefit from recently renovated bathrooms.

⊖⊜⊟⊟ **Hôtel Britannique** – *Map Beaubourg Les Halles. 20 av. Victoria. 75001.* Ⓜ*Châtelet.* ℘*01 42 33 74 59. www.hotel-britannique.fr. 39 rooms.* ⊑*14€.* Originally opened by an English family during the reign of Queen Victoria, this hotel has an unmistakable imperial style with cosy rooms and lobby lounge decorated in refined British exoticism.

⊖⊜⊟⊟⊟ **Hôtel Ducs de Bourgogne** – *Map Beaubourg Les Halles. 19 r. du Pont Neuf. 75001.* Ⓜ*Châtelet.* ℘*01 42 33 95 64. www.bestwestern-bourgogne.com. 50 rooms.* ⊑*17€.* A 19C building with small but well-kept rooms, with those on the top floor under a mansard roof. Renovated bathrooms, functional furniture, and a charming lounge area.

⊖⊜⊟⊟ **Hôtel Place du Louvre** – *Map Les Quais. 21 r. des Prêtres St-Germain -L'Auxerrois. 75001.* Ⓜ*Louvre Rivoli.* ℘*01 42 33 78 68. www.paris-hotel-place-du-louvre.com. 20 rooms.* ⊑*15€.* Facing the St-Germain-l'Auxerrois Church, the hotel has named each room for a painter. Breakfast is served in a 14C stone-vaulted-cellar that once connected to the Louvre by tunnel.

2ND ARRONDISSEMENT

⊖⊜ **Hôtel Tiquetonne** – *Map Beaubourg Les Halles. 6 r. Tiquetonne. 75002.* Ⓜ*Étienne Marcel.* ℘*01 42 36 94 58. http://hoteltiquetonne.fr. 45 rooms.* ⊑*6€.* In this modest family hotel in a semi-pedestrianized street near Les Halles and rue Montorgueil, the rooms are bright and have old-fashioned charm; they are well maintained for the price.

⊖⊜⊟ **Hôtel Vivienne** – *Map Les Grands Boulevards. 40 r. Vivienne. 75002.* Ⓜ *Grands Boulevards.* ℘*01 42 33 13 26. www.hotel-vivienne.com. 45 rooms.* ⊑*11€.* At this family hotel just off the Grands Boulevards, rooms are spacious, each with a different style. Some have a balcony, others a mini-terrace, overlooking the Paris rooftops.

⊖⊜⊟⊟ **Hôtel Favart** – *Map Les Grands Boulevards. 5 r. de Marivaux. 75002.* Ⓜ*Richelieu Drouot.* ℘*01 42 97 59 83. www.hotel-favart.com. 37 rooms.* ⊑. The painter Goya stayed at this charming hotel, where a timeless atmosphere prevails. The rooms of the main façade, overlooking the Opéra-Comique, are the most attractive.

3RD ARRONDISSEMENT

⊖⊜ **Hôtel Bellevue et du Chariot d'Or** – *Map Sentier and Temple. 39 r. Turbigo. 75003.* Ⓜ*Arts et Métiers.* ℘*01 48 87 45 60. www.hotelbellevue75.com. 59 rooms.* ⊑*7€.* Even if this hotel is well past its former glory days, its spacious halls and rooms (some large enough for families) can be appreciated. It has a great location in the centre of Paris and good price-quality ratio.

⊖⊜⊟ **Austin's** – *Map Sentier and Temple. 6 r. Montgolfier. 75003.* Ⓜ*Arts and Métiers.* ℘*01 42 77 17 61. www. hotelaustins.com. 29 rooms.* ⊑*10€.* Austin's sits along a calm street across from the Arts-et-Métiers museum. Rooms, red or yellow, are warm and welcoming. Some have original exposed wooden beams.

⊖⊜⊟⊟ **Hôtel Pavillon de la Reine** – *Map Le Marais. 28 pl. des Vosges. 75003.* Ⓜ*Bastille.* ℘*01 40 29 19 19. www. pavillon-de-la-reine.com. 41 rooms.* ⊑*28€.* Behind one of the 36 brick pavillions of the place des Vosges, two buildings, including one from the 17C, house this hotel with its refined rooms overlooking a private garden.

4TH ARRONDISSEMENT

⊖⊜⊟ **Hôtel Acacias – Hôtel de Ville** – *Map Le Marais. 20 r. du Temple. 75004.* Ⓜ*Hôtel de Ville.* ℘*01 48 87 07 70.*

www.acacias-hotel.com. 33 rooms. ⊑9€. This old building isn't much to look at, but it benefits from an excellent location. Rooms are well equipped, decorated in a simple yet contemporary style. The rustic-style breakfast room is very pleasant.

⊖⊟⑤ **Hôtel Andréa Rivoli** – Map Beaubourg Les Halles. 3 r. St-Bon. 75004. Ⓜ Châtelet or Hôtel de Ville. 📞 01 42 78 43 93. www.hotel-andrea-rivoli.com. 32 rooms. ⊑9€. This hotel is located right in the centre of Paris. It has been completely renovated from reception to the rooms and the breakfast area. It now has modern décor and air conditioning throughout. It's a good address.

⊖⊟⑤ **Hôtel Jeanne d'Arc, le Marais** – Map Le Marais. 3 r. de Jarente. 75004. Ⓜ St-Paul or Bastille. 📞 01 48 87 62 11. www.hoteljeannedarc.com. ♿ ⊑8€. Built in the 17C, this hotel sitting behind the Place du Marché-Ste-Catherine has a striking mosaic framed mirror at reception. The rooms are quite comfortable, but be sure to reserve in advance. The colourfully renovated rooms are best, the other are more classic in style.

⊖⊟⑤⑤ **Hôtel de la Place des Vosges** – Map Le Marais. 12 r. de Birague. 75004. Ⓜ Bastille or St-Paul. 📞 01 42 72 60 46. www.hotelplacedesvosges.com. 16 rooms. ⊑8€. This hotel within the 17C walls has real character. The rooms, of adequate size, either have a sober minimalist style, or have been prettily renovated. The lobby combines ancient stone walls, exposed wooden beams and old tapestries. It's near one of the most beautiful squares in Paris.

⊖⊟⑤⑤ **Hôtel du 7e Art** – Map Le Marais. 20 r. St-Paul. 75004. Ⓜ St-Paul or Sully Morland. 📞 01 44 54 85 00. www.paris-hotel-7art.com. 23 rooms. ⊑8€. The name gives it away: the entire establishment is decorated with a cinema theme, particularly vintage films from 1940 to 1960. Rooms on the third and fourth floors have exposed wooden beams. Air conditioning and laundry are available.

⊖⊟⑤⑤ **Grand Hôtel Malher** – Map Le Marais. 5 r. Malher. 75004. Ⓜ St-Paul. 📞 01 42 72 60 92. www.grand hotelmalher.com. 31 rooms. ⊑9€. Well situated for exploring the Marais on foot, this hotel, with an ancient façade, has modern rooms with painted wooden furnishings and colourful fabrics. Those facing the street are as quiet as those on the courtyard thanks to good soundproofing.

⊖⊟⑤⑤ **Hôtel Bretonnerie** – Map Le Marais. 22 r. Ste-Croix de la Bretonnerie. 75004. Ⓜ Hôtel de Ville. 📞 01 48 87 77 63. www. hotelparisbretonnerie.com. 29 rooms. ⊑9.50€. The rooms of this historic 17C Marais mansion come in all sizes, and have a rather rustic, country style, many with exposed wooden beams.

⊖⊟⑤⑤ **Hôtel Saint-Louis Marais** – Map Le Marais. 1 r. Charles V. 75004. Ⓜ Bastille. 📞 01 48 87 87 04. www.saintlouismarais.com. 19 rooms. ⊑13€. This hotel in a building dating back to 1740 has a charming address. Rooms aren't very large, but feature painted wooden beams and recent renovations. The lobby has a rustic country décor and breakfast is served in the vaulted stone cellar.

5TH ARRONDISSEMENT

⊖⊟ **Hôtel de L'Espérance** – Map Port-Royal. 15 r. Pascal. 75005. Ⓜ Les Gobelins ou Censier-Daubenton. 📞 01 47 07 10 99. www.hoteldelesperance.fr. ♿. 38 rooms. ⊑9€. Two steps from the Rue Mouffetard and its picturesque market, this charming little hotel is filled with flowers, from the façade to the patio. Rooms are comfortable and quiet, with brightly coloured décor.

⊖⊟⑤ **Hôtel du Mont-Blanc** – Map Le Quartier Latin. 28 r. de la Huchette. 75005. Ⓜ St-Michel. 📞 01 43 54 49 44. www.montblancparis.com. ⊑10€. On a street that's lively night and day, lined with Greek restaurants, bars and the famous Théâtre de la Huchette, this hotel is perfect for anyone who likes to be in the centre of the action. Rooms are functional, with basic amenities. Those in the back are quieter. Breakfast is served in a pretty vaulted cellar.

⊖🛏🛏 **Hôtel Familia** – *Map Jardin-des Plantes-Mouffetard. 11 r. des Écoles. 75005.* Ⓜ*Cardinal Lemoine.*📞*01 43 54 55 27. www.familiahotel.com. 30 rooms.* ☕*6.50€.* Located close to Notre-Dame and the Collège des Bernardins, this hotel has rooms done in a country style, with frescoes on the walls of Paris monuments. Nice breakfast room.

⊖🛏🛏 **Hôtel Sunny** – *Map Port-Royal. 48 bd. du Port-Royal. 75005.* Ⓜ*Les Gobelins.*📞*01 43 31 79 86. www. hotel-sunny.com. Closed 2 weeks in Aug. 37 rooms.* ☕*7.20€.* This hotel behind the classic Haussmann façade has many attractive traits: a family-run atmosphere, location near the Pantheon and Luxembourg Gardens, and functional rooms with fabric walls (those on the courtyard are quieter).

⊖🛏🛏🛏 **Grand Hôtel St-Michel** – *Map Le Quartier Latin. 19 r. Cujas. 75005.* Ⓜ*Luxembourg.*📞*01 46 33 33 02. www. hotel-saintmichel-paris.com. 47 rooms.* ☕*20€.* This Haussmannian building has plush rooms with painted furniture in a Napoléon III style. Breakfast is served in the vaulted cellar.

⊖🛏🛏🛏 **Hôtel des Grandes Écoles** – *Map Le Quartier Latin. 75 r. du Cardinal Lemoine. 75005.* Ⓜ*Cardinal Lemoine.*📞*01 43 26 79 23. www.hotel-grandes-ecoles.com.* Ⓟ *51 rooms.* ☕*9€.* Made up of three cottage-style houses around a pretty garden courtyard, this oasis in the city is a bit old-fashioned but adorably so. Two of the buildings have been recently renovated.

⊖🛏🛏🛏 **Hôtel Select** – *Map Le Quartier Latin. 1 pl. de la Sorbonne. 75005.* Ⓜ*Cluny la Sorbonne.*📞*01 46 34 14 80. www.selecthotel.fr. 67 rooms.* ☕*10€.* This resolutely contemporary hotel is located in the heart of the student district. Public areas include a bar, a lounge and a patio with a cactus garden. Some rooms have views over Paris rooftops.

⊖🛏🛏🛏 **Hôtel St-Jacques** – *Map Le Quartier Latin. 35 r. des Écoles. 75005.* Ⓜ *Maubert-Mutualité.*📞*01 44 07 45 45. www.paris-hotel-stjacques.com. 36 rooms.* ☕*14€.* Modern comforts with old-fashioned charm characterize the rooms in this hotel. The library holds books from the 18C and 19C, and the breakfast room is decorated in the Années Folles 1920s cabaret style.

6TH ARRONDISSEMENT

⊖🛏🛏 **Hôtel de Nesle** – *Map Les Quais. 7 r. de Nesle. 75006.* Ⓜ*Odéon or St-Michel.* 📞*01 43 54 62 41. www.hoteldenesleparis. com. 20 rooms. No breakfast.* An almost magical address where rooms are each decorated in their own theme (colonial, Oriental, country, Molière, etc.). The garden is planted with Tunisian palms, a haven in the centre of the Quarter.

⊖🛏🛏 **Grand Hôtel des Balcons** – *Map Le Quartier Latin. 3 r. Casimir Delavigne. 75006.* Ⓜ*Odéon. RER Luxembourg.*📞*01 46 34 78 50. www. balcons.com. 50 rooms.* ☕*12€.* "Paris is planted in my heart" wrote the Hungarian poet André Ady after staying in this hotel. Downstairs the style is Art Deco, while the rooms are more basic, some with little balconies. Large breakfast buffet.

⊖🛏🛏 **Hôtel de Sèvres** – *Map Le Faubourg St-Germain. 22 r. de l'Abbé Grégoire. 75006.* Ⓜ*St-Placide.*📞*01 45 48 84 07. www.hoteldesevres.com. 31 rooms.* ☕*13€.* Situated next to the department store Bon Marché, this peaceful hotel has been renovated in contemporary style. The breakfast room overlooks a tiny flowered courtyard. Temporary art exhibits are presented in the lounge.

⊖🛏🛏🛏 **Millésime Hôtel** – *Map St-Germain-des-Prés. 15 r. Jacob. 75006.* Ⓜ*St-Germain-des-Prés.*📞*01 44 07 97 97. www.millesimehotel.fr. 21 rooms.* ☕*16€.* Sunny colours complement fabrics and furniture chosen to create a warm atmosphere in the gorgeous rooms of this hotel. There's a beautiful 17C staircase, a patio and a pretty vaulted lounge.

7TH ARRONDISSEMENT

⊖🛏🛏 **Hôtel de France** – *Map Eiffel Tower and Le Trocadéro. 102 bd. de la Tour -Maubourg. 75007.* Ⓜ*École Militaire.*📞*01 47 05 40 49. www.hoteldefrance.com. 60 rooms.* ☕*12€.* Two buildings with a family atmosphere, housing modern rooms. Those facing the street have views over Les Invalides; those facing the courtyard are quieter.

◎◎🛢🛢 **Hôtel St-Thomas-d'Aquin** – Map St-Germain-des-Prés. 3 r. du Pré-aux-Clercs. 75007. Ⓜ Rue du Bac or St-Germain-des-Prés. ℰ01 42 61 01 22. www.hotel-st-thomas-aquin.com. 21 rooms. ⬚12€. The chic boutiques, antique shops, art galleries and literary cafés of Paris' celebrated Left Bank are right outside this renovated hotel. Rooms have modern comforts and boat-cabin-style bathrooms.

◎🛢🛢 **Hôtel Verneuil** – Map St-Germain-des-Prés. 8 r. de Verneuil. 75007. Ⓜ Rue du Bac. ℰ01 42 60 82 14. www.hotel-verneuil-saint-germain.com. 26 rooms. ⬚15€. This old building has been arranged like a private mansion, with 18C engravings in the cosy bedrooms. Nearby is the house where legendary French singer Serge Gainsbourg lived.

◎◎🛢🛢 **Hôtel L'Empereur** – Map Les Invalides. 2 r. Chevert. 75007. Ⓜ École Militaire or La Tour Maubourg. ℰ01 45 55 88 02. www.hotelempereur.com. ⬚ 38 rooms. ⬚12.50€. Empire style, of course, for this hotel across from Les Invalides. A nod to the memory of Napoléon, who rests eternally beneath the Dome. Ask for one of the renovated rooms, more comfortable and in the same type of décor.

◎🛢🛢 **Hôtel de la Tulipe** – Map Eiffel Tower and Le Trocadéro. 33 r. Malar. 75007. Ⓜ Invalides or La Tour Maubourg. ℰ01 45 51 67 21. www.paris-hotel-tulipe.com. ⬚🅿. 21 rooms. ⬚11€. This yellow house dating back to the 17C is now a Provençal-style hotel with a pretty paved garden courtyard. The small rooms are nicely furnished, with a mix of wicker, exposed stone and wooden beams.

◎◎🛢🛢 **Hôtel du Palais-Bourbon** – Map Les Invalides. 49 r. de Bourgogne. 75007. Ⓜ Varenne. ℰ01 44 11 30 70. www.bourbon-paris-hotel.com. 29 rooms. ⬚. Built in 1730, this hotel between the Rodin Museum and the Invalides is a pleasant surprise. Well-decorated

rooms with air conditioning and wooden furnishings. Singles are quite small. Breakfast included in the rates.

◎◎🛢🛢 **Hôtel Lindbergh** – Map Faubourg St-Germain. 5 r. Chomel. 75007. Ⓜ Sèvres-Babylone or St-Sulpice. ℰ01 45 48 35 53. www.hotellindbergh.com. 26 rooms. ⬚ 12€. One of the craftsmen who helped build Lindbergh's famous airplane *Spirit of St-Louis* stayed at this hotel near the Bon Marché in the 19C. All of the rooms were redecorated in the 1930s–1940s style.

◎◎🛢🛢 **Hôtel Malar** – Map Eiffel Tower and Le Trocadéro. 29 r. Malar. 75007. Ⓜ École Militaire, La Tour Maubourg or Invalides. ℰ01 45 51 38 46. www.hotelmalar.com. ⬚. 22 rooms. ⬚11€. These two buildings constructed under Louis-Philippe's reign (19C) have been renovated many times. Rooms have period furnishings and pretty two-toned bathrooms. In summer breakfast is served in the tiny private courtyard.

◎◎🛢🛢 **Hôtel Muguet** – Map Les Invalides. 11 r. Chevert. 75007. Ⓜ École Militaire. ℰ01 47 05 05 93. www.hotelparismuguet.com. 43 rooms. ⬚12.50€. This hotel has been freshened in a classic spirit, with a lounge in Louis Philippe style. The rooms are lovingly decorated (seven have Eiffel Tower views) and there's a veranda and mini-garden.

8TH ARRONDISSEMENT

◎🛢🛢 **Hôtel d'Albion** – Map Le Faubourg St-Honoré. 15 r. de Penthièvre. 75008. Ⓜ Miromesnil. ℰ01 42 65 84 15. www.hotelalbion.net. 🅿. 26 rooms. ⬚12€. This hotel is located between the avenue des Champs-Élysées and the Madeleine Church, on a surprisingly calm street. Rooms are comfortable, each one personalized in décor. The best face the inner courtyard. Breakfast is served in a tiny garden patio.

◎🛢🛢 **Astoria Opéra** – 42 r. de Moscou. 75008. Ⓜ Rome. ℰ01 42 93 63 53. www.astotel.com. 86 rooms. ⬚12€. Business travellers are big fans of the charming rooms in this hotel, which is located in the business district of Paris. Many have contemporary paintings. Breakfast is served under a glass skylight.

◒🖴🖴🖴 **Hôtel Champs-Élysées** – *Map La Voie Triomphale. 2 r. d'Artois. 75008.* 🅜*St-Philippe du Roule.* 📞*01 43 59 11 42. www.champselysees-paris-hotel.com. 26 rooms.* 🍽*18€.* This welcoming hotel occupies a modernized building dating back to the 19C. The tasteful rooms have been decorated in gorgeous individual styles, and the breakfast room is in a pretty vaulted stone cellar.

◒🖴🖴🖴 **Élysées Mermoz** – *Map La Voie Triomphale. 30 r. J.Mermoz. 75008.* 🅜*Franklin-Roosevelt.* 📞*01 42 25 75 30. www.hotel-elyseesmermoz.com.* ♿*. 27 rooms.* 🍽*18€.* This cosy hotel has pleasant, modern rooms; the bathrooms have wood panelling and lava stone sinks. The lounge is in winter-garden style beneath a large glass ceiling. Breakfast is buffet-style.

◒🖴🖴🖴 **Hôtel Powers** –*Map Alma. 52 r. François-I. 75008. Franklin-Roosevelt.* 📞*01 47 23 91 05. www. hotel-powers.com. 50 rooms.* 🍽*25€.* This attractive building has several bow windows. Compact rooms are stylish and modern with historic touches such as moulding, fireplaces, etc. English bar and cosy lounge bar.

9TH ARRONDISSEMENT

◒🖴🖴 **Hôtel Chopin** – *Map Les Grands Boulevards. 46 Passage Jouffroy. 75009.* 🅜*Grands Boulevards.* 📞*01 47 70 58 10. www.hotel-chopin.fr.* 🍽*7.50€.* Located in a covered passage dating from 1846 that also houses the Grévin Wax Museum, this little hotel is surprisingly quiet in this animated district. The lobby/reception area is stylishly appointed in turn-of-the-century furnishings. The colourful, but rather basic rooms should be reserved well in advance.

◒🖴🖴🖴 **Hôtel Langlois** – *Map Pigalle and La Nouvelle Athènes. 63 r. St-Lazare. 75009.* 🅜*Trinité.* 📞*01 48 74 78 24. www.hotel-langlois.com. 24 rooms.* 🍽*13€.* Constructed in 1870, this building once housed a bank, then a hotel since 1896. Rooms have varying styles and character from Art Nouveau and Art Deco to 1950s.

◒🖴🖴🖴 **Hôtel Peyris** – *off-map. 10 r. Conservatoire. 75009.* 🅜*Poissonnière.* 📞*01 47 70 50 83. www.hotel-peyris.com. 50 rooms.* 🍽*.* Rooms are equipped with functional amenities and the décor is done up in bold, primary colours. The dark-colour lounge is decorated in Napoléon III style. Friendly service.

10TH ARRONDISSEMENT

◒🖴🖴 **Hôtel Albert 1** – *Map Le Canal St-Martin. 162 r. LaFayette. 75010.* 🅜*Gare du Nord.* 📞*01 40 36 82 40. www.albert1er hotel.com. 55 rooms.* 🍽*16€.* This hotel has modern, well-equipped rooms featuring double-glazed windows. Ongoing renovations keep it up to date. Convivial atmosphere.

◒🖴🖴 **Hôtel Paradis** – *Map Les Grands Boulevards. 41 r. des Petites Écuries. 75010.* 🅜*Bonne Nouvelle or Poissonnière.* 📞*01 45 23 08 22. www.hotelparadisparis.com.* 🍽*12€.* This is a practical address to stay in the capital, in the heart of a lively neighbourhood. Renovated rooms are small but decorated with contemporary style, flat-screen TVs, free WiFi, and queen-sized beds.

◒🖴🖴 **République Hôtel** – *Map Le Canal St-Martin. 31 r. Albert Thomas. 75010.* 🅜*République.* 📞*01 42 39 19 03. www.republiquehotel.com. 40 rooms.* 🍽*8€.* Located on a calm street near the place de la République and the Canal St-Martin, this hotel welcomes tourists to its tiny rooms, which are simple and comfortable at this price range.

◒🖴🖴 **Hôtel Libertel** – *Map Le Canal St-Martin. 13 r. du 8 May 1945. 75010.* 🅜*Gare de l'Est.* 📞*01 40 35 94 14. www.hotelfrancais.com. 72 rooms.* 🍽*12€.* This hotel, located across from the Gare de l'Est train station, is in a lively neighbourhood. Rooms are soundproofed, air conditioned, well equipped and renovated with style. The 1900 reception salon beneath a large glass atrium is open for the breakfast buffet.

11TH ARRONDISSEMENT

◒🖴🖴 **Croix de Malte** – *Map Le Marais. 5 r. de Malte. 75011.* 🅜*Oberkampf.* 📞*01 48 05 09 36. www.croixdemalte-*

paris-hotel.com. 29 rooms. ☕*10€.* This hotel is currently undergoing renovation, but it is well-situated in the Oberkampf district. Its breakfast room is brightened with a skylight.

Grand Hôtel Amelot – *Map Le Marais. 54 r. Amelot. 75011.* Ⓜ*Chemin Vert.* ✆*01 48 06 15 19. www.hotelamelot.com. 44 rooms.* ☕*7€.* This hotel near the Bastille has a nice lobby and functional rooms on six floors (with lift). Families appreciate the quad rooms sleeping four. Those with renovated bathrooms are more comfortable.

Hôtel Campanile – *Map Le Marais. 9 r. du Chemin Vert. 75011.* Ⓜ*Chemin Vert.* ✆*01 43 38 58 08. www.campanile-paris-bastille.fr.* ♿*. 157 rooms.* ☕*9.50€.* This is a modern chain hotel situated on a lively street between Bastille and République. Rooms have air conditioning; those on the top floor have a terrace. The buffet breakfast is served in the garden on summer days.

Hôtel du Nord et de l'Est – *off-map. 49 r. de Malte. 75011.* Ⓜ*Oberkampf.* ✆*01 47 00 71 70. www.hotel-nord-est.com. 45 rooms.* ☕*9€.* Located close to République, this hotel has a loyal following thanks to its family atmosphere and fairly reasonable prices. The renovated rooms have a more up-to-date style.

Le 20 Prieuré Hôtel – *off-map. 20 r. du Grand-Prieuré. 75011.* Ⓜ*Oberkampf.* ✆*01 47 00 74 14. www.hotel20prieure.com.* ♿*. 32 rooms.* ☕*12.50€.* This hotel sports a sleek, contemporary interior awash with cream-coloured tones, blonde wood panelling, modern furnishings, and enlarged photos of Paris over each bed's headboard. Rooms are compact, some with windows; bathrooms are spotless.

Grand Hôtel Français – *off-map 223 bd. Voltaire. 75011.* Ⓜ*Nation.* ✆*01 43 71 27 57. www.grand-hotel-francais.fr. 36 rooms.* ☕*12€.* The rooms, small but modern, have been renovated with care to their current décor, with comfortable bedding, thick carpeting and solid furnishings. Good soundproofing.

12TH ARRONDISSEMENT

Lux Hôtel Picpus – *off-map. 74 bd. Picpus. 75012.* Ⓜ*Picpus.* ✆*01 43 43 08 46.www.parisluxhotel.com.* 🅿 *38 rooms.* ☕*9€.* A carved stone building near the place de la Nation. Rooms are modern, in differing sizes, each one personalized with colourful fabrics. A buffet breakfast is served each morning.

L'Interlude Hôtel – *off-map. 258 av. Daumesnil. 75012.* Ⓜ*Michel Bizot.* ✆*01 43 43 61 36. www.hotelinterlude.com* ♿*. 44 rooms.* ☕*11€.* This classic hotel has been well maintained, with tastefully decorated rooms. Ask for a room overlooking the courtyard, in the quiet, recently renovated section of the building. Comfortable suites as well.

Hôtel Amadeus – *off-map. 39 r. Claude Tillier. 75012.* Ⓜ*Reuilly Diderot or Nation.* ✆*01 43 48 53 48. www.hotelamadeus-paris.com.* ♿*. 22 rooms.* ☕*7€.* Seen from the outside, this little hotel doesn't look like much. But don't hesitate to check it out, because inside are nicely renovated rooms with comfortable, rattan furnishings. Good soundproofing.

Venise Hôtel – *off-map. 4 r. Chaligny. 75012.* Ⓜ*Reuilly Diderot.* ✆*01 43 43 63 45. www.hoteldevenise.fr. 30 rooms.* ☕*8€.* This family establishment is located near the Viaduc des Arts and its promenade plantée. The rooms are functional and decorated in a different colour on each floor. Bathrooms all have a tub. Friendly welcome.

Hôtel Paris Bastille – *Map Bastille and Le Faubourg St-Antoine. 67 r. de Lyon. 75012.* Ⓜ*Bastille.* ✆*01 40 01 07 17. www.hotelparisbastille.com.* ♿ *37 rooms.* ☕*14€.* Modern comforts and contemporary furnishings in exotic woods characterize the rooms of this hotel facing the Opéra Bastille. There's a small bar on the premises.

Hôtel Terminus Lyon – *off-map. 19 bd. Diderot. 75012.* Ⓜ*Gare de Lyon.* ✆*01 56 95 00 00. www.hotelterminuslyon.com. 60 rooms.* ☕*12€.* Located across from the Gare de Lyon, this family-run hotel is well maintained. Rooms are simple and somber; the largest ones overlook the boulevard, but the ones facing the courtyard are quieter. Meals can be ordered.

13TH ARRONDISSEMENT

⊜🍽🛏 **Arian Hôtel** – *off-map. 102 av. de Choisy. 75013.* Ⓜ*Tolbiac or Place d'Italie.* 📞*01 45 70 76 00. http://hotelarian.com. 30 rooms.* 🍽*7€.* This hotel is known for having "one star, but it really shines". Located in the heart of Chinatown, it's modest but comfortable and impeccably clean. The guestrooms are moderately sized.

⊜🍽🛏 **Hôtel Magendie** – *Map La Butte-aux-Cailles. 6 r. Corvisart. 75013.* Ⓜ*Corvisart.* 📞*01 43 36 13 61. www. belambra.fr/hotel-paris-magendie.* ♿. *112 rooms.* 🍽. In a quiet residential area of Paris, this hotel with its small rooms is functional and soundproofed. The current décor is minimalist.

⊜🍽🛏 **Hôtel Résidence Vert Galant** – *Map La Butte-aux-Cailles. 43 r. Croulebarbe. 75013.* Ⓜ*Les Gobelins.* 📞*01 44 08 83 50. www.vertgalant.com. 15 rooms.* 🍽*10€.* This hotel embodies the country-side in Paris: the residence hotel has charming and quiet rooms around a large central garden bordered by grapevines.

⊜🍽🛏 **Hôtel Henriette** – *Map La Butte-aux-Cailles. 9 r. des Gobelins.75013.* Ⓜ*Les Gobelins.* 📞*01 47 07 26 90. www. hotelhenriette.com. 32 rooms.* 🍽*10€.* On a cobblestoned street behind the Manufacture des Gobelins tapestry factory, this non-smoking hotel has a Parisian village atmosphere. The rooms are small and simple; some overlook the flowered courtyard patio, as does the breakfast room.

14TH ARRONDISSEMENT

⊜🍽🛏 **Hôtel Apollon Montparnasse** – *Map Montparnasse. 91 r. de l'Ouest. 75014.* Ⓜ*Pernety.* 📞*01 43 95 62 00. www.paris-hotel-paris.net. 33 rooms.* 🍽*11€.* At this family hotel that has been gently renovated, the rooms are tastefully decorated. It's located on a calm street, a few steps from the train station.

⊜🍽🛏 **Hôtel de la Paix** – *Map Montparnasse. 225 bd. Raspail. 75014.* Ⓜ*Raspail.* 📞*01 43 20 35 82. www.hotel delapaix.com. 39 rooms.* 🍽*10€.* While the lobby of this hotel has a particular 1970s style, rooms are a bit more modern, functional and well maintained.

⊜🍽🛏 **Hôtel Delambre** – *Map Montparnasse. 35 r. Delambre. 75014.* Ⓜ*Edgar Quinet.* 📞*01 43 20 66 31. www.delambre-paris-hotel.com. 30 rooms.* 🍽*13€.* André Breton stayed in this hotel, on a quiet street near the Montparnasse train station. There's a modern flair here in the décor with simple but cheerful rooms, many quite spacious.

⊜🍽🛏 **Hôtel Moulin Vert** – *off-map. 74 r. du Moulin-Vert. 75014.* Ⓜ*Pernéty or Alésia.* 📞*01 45 43 65 38. www. hotel-moulinvert.com. 28 rooms.* 🍽*8€.* For an agreeable stay in this residential district, this small hotel offers guests renovated rooms, some a bit small, but pleasant and well maintained. WiFi is available in every room. A family atmosphere prevails.

⊜🍽🛏 **Hôtel L'Aiglon** – *Map Montparnasse. 232 bd. Raspail. 75014.* Ⓜ*Raspail.* 📞*01 43 20 82 42. www.aiglon. com. 36 rooms.* 🍽*14€.* This hotel where Giacometti and Buñuel once lived has been slowly modernized. Bright colours and attention to detail (mosaics in the bathrooms, framed photos, etc.) define the modern décor.

⊜🍽🛏 **Hôtel Lenox Montparnasse** – *Map Montparnasse. 15 r. Delambre. 75014.* Ⓜ*Vavin.* 📞*01 43 35 34 50. www.paris-hotel-lenox.com. 52 rooms.* 🍽*16€.* This establishment makes the most of its elegant style with a cosy and intimate bar and lounge, rooms with personalized décor, and agreeable suites on the sixth floor.

15TH ARRONDISSEMENT

⊜🍽🛏 **Hôtel Avia Saphir Montparnasse** – *off-map. 181 r. de Vaugirard. 75015.* Ⓜ*Pasteur.* 📞*01 43 06*

43 80. www.saphirhotel.fr. 40 rooms. ⊐8€. Complete restoration has given this hotel a nice facelift with modern comforts. Rooms are spacious, well equipped and decorated with coordinated fabrics and carpeting. The breakfast room has a contemporary style.

Lutèce Hôtel – off-map. 5 r. Langeac. 75015. ⓂConvention or Porte de Versailles. ☎01 48 28 56 95. www.lutecehotel.com. Closed 21 Dec–3 Jan and 23 Jul–1st Sept. 35 rooms. ⊐8.80€. This 1920s building has been given a facelif, and rooms have been renovated; those on the sixth and seventh floors have views over the rooftops of Paris. In summer breakfast is served on the inner courtyard.

Hôtel Printania Porte de Versailles – Map Vaugirard. 55 r. Olivier de Serres. 75015. ⓂConvention. ☎01 45 33 96 77. www.paris-hotel-printania.com. 21 rooms. ⊐8€. Right next to the Parc des Expositions, this small hotel has functional, well-maintained rooms that have been recently renovated. The breakfast room has been painted in bright Mediterranean colours.

Timhotel Tour Eiffel – Map the Eiffel Tower and Le Trocadéro. 11 r. Juge. 75015. ⓂDupleix. ☎01 45 78 29 29. www.timhotel.fr. 39 rooms. ⊐13€. Ideally situated near the Eiffel Tower and Le Trocadéro, this renovated hotel has experienced a renaissance with a new décor and comfortable amenities.

Hôtel de l'Avre – off-map. 21 r. de l'Avre. 75015. ⓂLa Motte-Picquet Grenelle. ☎01 45 75 31 03. www.hoteldelavre.com. 26 rooms. ⊐11€. This elegant hotel features a reception hall in bright yellow for a Provençal atmosphere; the green of the garden offers a calm haven to relax at breakfast. Rooms are done in soft beige and white, or bright yellow.

Saphir Hôtel – Map Eiffel Tower and Le Trocadéro. 10 r. du Commerce. 75015. ⓂLa Motte-Picquet Grenelle. ☎01 45 75 12 23. www.saphirhotel.fr. 32 rooms. ⊐10€. A great little unpretentious address ideally located near the Eiffel Tower. Rooms

are functional, clean and modern. Request one facing the courtyard, where breakfast is served in summer.

16TH ARRONDISSEMENT

Camping Le Bois de Boulogne – Map Le Bois de Boulogne. 2 allée du Bord de l'Eau. 75016. Allée du Bord de l'Eau, between Pont de Suresnes and Pont de Puteaux, banks of the Seine. ☎01 45 24 30 00. www.campingparis.fr. ♿. Reservations recommended. 510 places. This campsite set up in the Bois de Boulogne can be noisy (the spots closer to the river are the quietest), but the price is great. Rates are for two people and a spot for a tent. You can also rent small cabins. In season there's a shuttle back and forth to the Porte Maillot.

Hôtel Ambassade – off-map. 79 r. Lauriston. 75016. Ⓜ Boissière or Kléber. ☎01 45 53 41 15. www.hotelambassade.com. 38 rooms. ⊐15€. This air-conditioned hotel benefits from a tranquil residential location while being just a few minutes from the Champs-Élysées. The rooms have an Art Nouveau look; the least expensive ones can be quite small. Breakfast is buffet.

Hôtel Passy Eiffel – Map Passy. 10 r. de Passy. 75016. ⓂPassy. ☎01 45 25 55 66. www.passyeiffel.com. 49 rooms. ⊐14€. On a lively street, this family-run hotel has practical rooms that are well-maintained, overlooking the street (some have Eiffel Tower views) or the pretty garden patio.

Queen's Hôtel – Map Auteuil. 4 r. Bastien Lepage. 75016. Ⓜ Michel Ange Auteuil. ☎01 42 88 89 85. www.queens-hotel-paris.com. 17 rooms. ⊐13€. Contemporary art as well as period paintings decorate the halls and rooms of this grand, eclectic hotel. Its stately character helps guests forgive the compact rooms, which are nicely decorated. Air conditioning and free WiFi round out the amenities.

Hôtel Gavarni – Map Passy. 5 r. Gavarni. 75016. ⓂPassy. ☎01 45 24 52 82.www.gavarni.com. 25 rooms. ⊐15€. Gavarni is an agreeable non-smoking hotel with small yet cosy rooms, many with their original mouldings and fireplace. Fair-trade products are served for breakfast.

🍶🍽️ **Hôtel Hameau de Passy** – Map Passy. 48 r. de Passy. 75016. Ⓜ*La Muette*. ☎01 42 88 47 55. www.hameaude passy.com. 32 rooms. 🚇. At the end of a small passage, this discreet hamlet and its charming garden courtyard offer serenity. Quiet nights are guaranteed in the small yet modern rooms.

17TH ARRONDISSEMENT

🍶🍽️ **Hôtel de Paris** – off-map. 17 r. Biot. 75017. Ⓜ*Place de Clichy*. ☎01 42 94 02 50. www.hoteldeparis-montmartre.com. 30 rooms. 🚇6€. A few steps from the bustling place de Clichy, this establishment has completely renovated rooms, on the small side, but with well-equipped bathrooms. Breakfast is served on the patio in summer.

🍶🍽️ **Hôtel Prince Albert** – Map Monceau. 28 passage Cardinet. 75017. Ⓜ*Villiers-Malesherbes*. ☎01 47 54 06 00. www.hotelprincealbert.com. 33 rooms. 🚇7€. This hotel hidden on a tiny side street has benefited from a major renovation. Rooms are small but functional and well equipped. The breakfast room is on the lower-level.

🍶🍽️ **Monceau Élysées** – Map Monceau. 108 r. de Courcelles. 75017. Ⓜ*Courcelles*. ☎01 47 63 33 08. www.monceau-elysees.com. ♿. 29 rooms. 🚇11€. Just off the Parc Monceau, this non-smoking hotel has compact, individually decorated rooms in orange-, salmon- or yellow-coloured fabrics. The breakfast room is housed in a vaulted stone cellar.

🍶🍽️ **Magellan** – off-map. 17 r. J.B.-Dumas. 75017. Ⓜ*Porte-de-Champerret*. ☎01 45 72 44 51. www.hotelmagellan.com 72 rooms. 🚇17€. Functional and spacious rooms sit within this beautiful 1900 building. There's an Art Deco-style lounge. Breakfast is served in summer in the small garden pavillion.

🍶🍽️ **Tilsitt Étoile** – off-plan. 23 r. Brey. 75017. Ⓜ*Charles de Gaulle Étoile*. ☎01 43 80 39 71. www.tilsitt.com.

38 rooms. 🚇13€. Charming small rooms (some with balconies), pleasant breakfast room and a stylish lounge bar: all this in the swanky Etoile district close to the Champs Elysées.

18TH ARRONDISSEMENT

🍶🍽️ **Hôtel des Arts** – Map Montmartre. 5 r. Tholozé. 75018. Ⓜ*Abbesses or Blanche*. ☎01 46 06 30 52. www.arts-hotel-paris.com. ♿Ⓟ. 60 rooms. 🚇10€. A great location in Montmartre near the Moulin de la Galette and the place du Tertre. The halls are decorated with paintings from Roland Dubuc, a local artist. All the rooms are brightly coloured. Reserve well in advance.

🍶🍽️ **Hôtel Roma Sacré Cœur** – Map Montmartre. 101 r. Caulaincourt. 75018. Ⓜ*Lamarck-Caulaincourt*. ☎01 42 62 02 02. www.hotel-roma-sacre-coeur.fr. 57 rooms. 🚇8€. Here find all of the charm of Montmartre: a garden out front, stairs on the side, and Sacré-Cœur above. Cheerful colours decorate the pleasant rooms.

🍶🍽️ **Comfort Hôtel Place du Tertre** – Map Montmartre. 16 r. Tholozé. 75018. Ⓜ*Abbesses or Blanche*. ☎01 42 55 05 06. www.comfort-placedutertre.com. 50 rooms. 🚇8€. A nice Montmartre location between the Moulin de la Galette and the rue des Abbesses for this updated hotel. Rooms are functional and cosy with their coordinated fabrics and carpeting. Calm and quiet atmosphere.

🍶🍽️ **Ermitage Hôtel** – Map Montmartre. 24 r. Lamarck. 75018. Ⓜ*Lamarck Caulaincourt*. ☎01 42 64 79 22. www.ermitagesacrecoeur.fr. Ⓟ 🍽️. 11 rooms. 🚇. This private mansion from the Napoléon III era was built by a wealthy notary for his mistress. Rooms are personalized: the best have a terrace opening to the private gardens. Four have a nice view over the rooftops of Paris.

🍶🍽️ **Paris-Oasis B&B** – Map Montmartre. 14 r. André del Sarte. 75018. Ⓜ*Anvers*. ☎01 42 55 95 16. www.paris-oasis.com. Closed Aug and 1 week in Dec. Ⓟ 🍽️. 5 rooms. A handful of guestrooms in this Montmartre B&B

make the best use of the available space and are tastefully decorated. Flea market furnishings, painted murals, a lush garden outside where guests enjoy brunch in summer, and a small covered pool are some of the reasons to stay at this B&B.

19TH ARRONDISSEMENT

⊜⊜ **Laumière** – *Map Les Buttes-Chaumont. 4 r. Petit. 75019.* Ⓜ*Laumière.* ℘*01 42 06 10 77. www.accorhotels.com. 54 rooms.* ⌇*9€.* Need some green space? This hotel, simple and well maintained, has a great little garden where breakfast is served. The vast Buttes-Chaumont park is close by.

⊜⊜⊜ **Hôtel Crimée** – *Map La Villette. 188 r. de Crimée. 75019.* Ⓜ*Crimée.* ℘*01 40 36 75 29. www.hotelcrimee.com. 31 rooms.* ⌇*8.50€.* A short walk from La Villette science park, this friendly, recently renovated hotel offers scrupulously clean rooms overlooking a leafy street that leads directly to the capital's trendy canal quaysides.

20TH ARRONDISSEMENT

⊜⊜⊜ **Hôtel Lilas-Gambetta** – *off-map. 223 av. Gambetta. 75020.* Ⓜ*Porte des Lilas.* ℘*01 40 31 85 60. www.lilas-gambetta.com. 34 rooms.* ⌇*9.50€.* The building's 1925 façade in brick and carved stone hides a modern interior. The rooms are compact and simply but tastefully furnished. The quietest rooms face the charming courtyard where breakfast is served in summer.

⊜⊜⊜ **Hôtel Palma** – *Map Le Père-Lachaise. 77 av. Gambetta. 75020.* Ⓜ*Gambetta.* ℘*01 46 36 13 65. www. hotelpalma.com. 32 rooms.* ⌇*8€.* Located next to the place Gambetta and famous Père-Lachaise cemetery, this hotel has small rooms, a bit on the old-fashioned side, which have maintained their 1970s style.

⊜⊜⊜ **Hôtel Paris-Gambetta** – *Map Le Père-Lachaise. 12 av. du Père-Lachaise. 75020.* Ⓜ*Gambetta.* ℘*01 47 97 76 57. www.hotelparisgambetta.com.* ♿. *31 rooms.* ⌇*10€.* This hotel has soundproofed rooms and sits on a street protected from the urban noise; it's in close proximity to the Père-Lachaise cemetery. Calm and quiet, the rooms are well equipped, and there's free WiFi throughout.

⊜⊜⊜ **Mama Shelter** – *Map Le Père-Lachaise. 109 r. de Bagnolet. 75020.* Ⓜ*Gambetta.* ℘*01 43 48 48 48. www. mamashelter.com.* ♿. *171 rooms.* ⌇*15€.* The imagination of designer Philippe Starck has inspired the décor of this vast, contemporary hotel, from the pure lines in the rooms to the popular bar lounge. There are huge bay windows throughout and a long terrace overlooking the historic Petit Ceinture.

VINCENNES

⊜⊜⊜ **Donjon** – *Map Le Bois and le Château de Vincennes. 22 r. du Donjon.* ℘*01 43 28 19 17. www.hotel-donjon-vincennes.fr. Closed 18 Jul–25 Aug. 25 rooms.* ⌇*11€.* This centrally located hotel in Vincennes has rather smallish rooms, each decorated differently. The lounge and breakfast room are nicely furnished.

⊜⊜⊜⊜ **St-Louis** – *Map Le Bois and le Château de Vincennes. 2 bis r. R. Giraudineau.* ℘*01 43 74 16 78. www.hotel-paris-saintlouis.com. 25 rooms.* ⌇*13€.* This building near the Château de Vincennes houses elegant rooms with stylish furniture. Some open right on to the private garden on the ground floor (with a bathroom located downstairs).

Where to Eat

In the eyes of many gourmands, Paris is the world's capital of gastronomy. The city abounds in top-rated restaurants and great chefs. Even the small establishments, often family-run for generations, turn out excellent food. Classic French cuisine is ubiquitous, of course, but a wide variety of fare, from Mediterranean and Asian to traditional British and European dishes, as well as fusion, are served in the city. A host of ethnic restaurants can also be found throughout the city. *See the opposite page for a list of restaurants by neighbourhood.*

FOOD AND DRINK

France may have a well-deserved reputation for its cuisine, but don't assume that you will be guaranteed a high standard of cooking in all the restaurants of its capital city. Much depends upon the area in which you eat as well as the type of restaurant you select.

The World's Cuisines – Dishes from Greek to Spanish, from Japanese to Vietnamese and from West to North Africa can be found in many areas of the city. Some districts specialise in **international cuisine** – for example in the 13th *arrondissement*, the area to the southeast of the place d'Italie, known as Chinatown has many restaurants serving traditional Asian dishes.

In the capital city, a variety of **regional cuisine** is to be found: Lyonnais, Norman, Basquaise and Breton are just some of the regional varieties served. The French food scene is very inventive, and there are many ways to experience good food in Paris, from dining in a Michelin-starred restaurant to treating yourself to a gourmet snack in one of the capital's great department stores while enjoying a panoramic view of the city. The **bistronomy** craze, which combines budget prices with creative dishes made from fresh products, has been popular for a while, but a new rival is emerging: a special type of street food called **mobile gastronomy**, which makes available gourmet burgers and tacos or delicious Breton crepes cooked from a food truck, such as "Le camion qui fume" or "La caravane dorée".

Hours – The **traditional restaurant** usually opens twice a day, from noon to 2.30pm and again from 7pm or 7.30pm until 10.30pm or 11pm. Often reservations are necessary, and while children and pets are usually welcome, they are expected to behave appropriately.

Prices – Restaurants usually offer a **fixed-price** menu and/or **à la carte** with separately ordered courses. *See Prices in Paris p40.*

Check the blackboard for set meals

© Eric Belisle/iStockphoto.com

Types – Apart from the actual cuisine, there are several types of **eating place** that are common to France, and Paris.

Restaurants – Restaurants prevail in Paris, with limited to high-capacity seating and a kitchen commanded by family cooks to famous chefs.

Brasseries – A brasserie is essentially a cross between a restaurant and a café. They are open every day and normally reservations are not required. However, some are quite popular and it can be difficult to get in at peak times. Originally from Alsace – the name means brewery – they tend to serve less sophisticated fare. Some are open all day without a break, while others continue serving until midnight and beyond.

Cafés and bars – Cafés and bars are numerous throughout the capital. They are normally the place to enjoy a coffee, a glass of wine or *pression* (draught beer), but light snacks are often available as well. Many offer a lunchtime *plat du jour*, or dish of the day, which is typically a good value. Some cafés like Les Deux Magots and the Café de Flore are very famous and sophisticated, but the great majority are inexpensive places to relax and watch the world go by.

Bistrots – Contrary to cafés, which mainly serve hot and cold beverages, croissants, tartines, croque-monsieurs and light meals, and where sitting and sipping is the real activity, bistrots are small, informal restaurants set in a casually chic décor (they could actually be quite shabby in the old days, but times have changed). Hearty classic dishes (Coq au vin, soupe à l'oignon, etc.) using fresh, local ingredients are on offer. The meals, often served with a glass of wine, are fairly reasonably priced (for Paris, that is), with some exceptions though: bistrot cuisine has become quite trendy, and many famous star-rated chefs have opened their own (sometimes very fancy) bistrot as a way of experimenting with new dishes and making their cuisine available to a more diverse clientele.

Thus, the price range for a meal in a bistrot depends on just who is behind the kitchen.

SELECTED RESTAURANTS BY DISTRICT
FOR ALL BUDGETS...

The selected restaurants that follow are listed by neighbourhood and by price range *(for coin ranges, ⚓see the Legend on the cover flap)*, along with the nearest metro station. In addition, each of the neighbourhood descriptions in the *Discovering* section tells you which *arrondissement* to look for in this directory.

The following pages contain listings of establishments where you might be able to find a meal for under 16€ (rare these days) as well as elegant restaurants for budgets up to 50€. Top-rate restaurants are also in the list, offering Epicurean feasts and magnificent décors, but at a high price: correct attire is generally *de rigueur* in these stylish places.

...AND FOR ALL TASTES

In order to provide you with as many choices as possible, we have selected typically Parisian brasseries and bistros, as well as traditional, exotic or otherwise distinctive establishments. You'll also find simple venues where you can stop in for a salad, quiche or a sweet snack.

A few fervent defenders of France's regional cuisines are included to give you the opportunity to sample the diversity of the country's culinary heritage. Or follow the guide to Italian, Spanish, Argentinian, Japanese, Thai and other cuisines of the world. Remember to reserve your table, especially in the evening.

Smoking is no longer allowed inside restaurants in France, but still permitted on the terraces and outdoor spaces, something to keep in mind when booking al fresco meals.

For even more choices

Consult the red-cover **Michelin Guide Paris**. It offers a varied list of Parisian

the Aveyron region: free-range meats from Aubrac, duck confit, home made foie gras, etc. Pavement terrace.

LE SENTIER AND LE TEMPLE

☺ **L'Estaminet des Enfants Rouges** – *39 r. de Bretagne.* Ⓜ*St-Sébastien-Froissard.* ✆*01 42 72 28 12. www.lestaminetdes enfantsrouges.com. Closed Sun eve and Mon.* ♿. Aprovincial bistro atmosphere orevails at this amusing restaurant hidden in the oldest covered market in Paris. Local shopkeepers, regulars and the curious visitors settle into the large communal tables that encourage interaction with the neighbours. The short menu is created daily. A good selection of wines by the glass or the bottle.

☺☺ **Chez Omar** – *47 r. de Bretagne.* Ⓜ*Arts et Métiers.* ✆*01 42 72 36 26. Closed Sun noon and eves of 24 and 31 Dec.* ⌷. In the setting of an old neighbourhood bistro, the house couscous has had a loyal following for over 20 years. Trendy since the 1990s when it was discovered by supermodels, the atmosphere nevertheless remains noisy and relaxed.

☺☺ **Les Petits Carreaux** – *17 r. des Petits-Carreaux.* Ⓜ*Sentier.* ✆*01 42 33 37 32. 7am–midnight. Closed 25 Dec.* The retro charm of this friendly establishment has been maintained despite recent renovations. The clientele are a mix of locals, shopkeepers from the rue Montorgueil and the Sentier, and a few tourists seduced by the convivial atmosphere. When the weather is nice tables are arranged on the pavement along the pedestrian-only street.

☺☺☺ **Da Mimmo** – *39 bd Magenta.* Ⓜ*Jacques Bonsergent/Gare de l'Est.* ✆*01 42 06 44 47. www.damimmo.fr. Valet every evening from 7.30pm.* A little corner of Naples under the Parisian sky. The chef Christoforo Manfredi proposes his house specialities (pasta or risotto with seafood, mushrooms, or white truffles) as well as the freshest fish and seafood dishes: sea bass, calmari, scampi, squid, lobster and even sea urchins. You're literally plunged into the Bay of Naples with a very "VIP" atmosphere, as Da Mimo is a favourite establishment among TV personalities.

☺☺☺☺ **Anahï** – *49 rue Volta.* Ⓜ*Arts et Métiers.* ✆*01 48 87 88 24. www.anahirestaurant.fr. Daily 7.30am–midnight.* This little restaurant is the temple of "Gaucho" cuisine in Paris. The façade has the look of an abandoned urban building, while the inside has kept its authentic Parisian butcher shop décor. The speciality is prime cuts of beef, of course: the *churrasco* or strip steak and the *bife angosto*, or filet mignon.

Chez Omar

© Yoshimi Kanazawa/Michelin

LE MARAIS

⊜ **Chez Marianne** – *2 r. des Hospitalières-St-Gervais.* Ⓜ*St-Paul.* ☎*01 42 72 18 86.* Located in the Jewish quarter of the rue des Rosiers, this restaurant-deli combines Mediterranean and central European flavours. The menu allows you to create your own platter of favourite items. Request a table in the dining room across from the wine racks, or on the terrace in summer.

⊜ **L'As du Fallafel** – *134 r. des Rosiers.* Ⓜ*St-Paul.* ☎*01 48 87 63 60. Closed Fri. dinner and Sat.* The most famous falafel establishment on the Rue des Rosiers, Paris' Jewish quarter is worth a stop. There's usually a queue for the take-out, but it moves quickly and the price is hard to beat. Inside it's always packed; food is served on disposable plates, and you'll be asked to leave as soon as you've finished.

⊜ **Candelaria** – *52 r. de Saintonge.* Ⓜ*Filles du Calvaire.* ☎*01 42 74 41 28. www.candelariaparis.com.* A trendy but low-key Mexican taqueria in the north Marais serving authentic house made tortillas and salsa for their tostadas and tacos. Stand at the counter or grab the one table at the

Galette, Breizh Café

front (they also do take out). The door in the back isn't for the restrooms; it's a hidden cocktail bar open from 6pm.

⊜⊜ **Breizh Café** – *109 r. Vieille du Temple.* Ⓜ*Rambuteau.* ☎*01 42 72 13 77. www.breizhcafe.com. Closed Mon, Tue.* A popular, contemporary café specializing in organic Breton crêpes made with only the finest ingredients. There is also a large selection of ciders and a boutique next door where you can order crêpes to go.

⊜⊜⊜ **Autour du Saumon** – *60 r. François Miron.* Ⓜ*St-Paul.* ☎*01 42 77 23 08. www.autourdusaumon.eu. Mon–Sat noon–2.30pm, 7pm–10.30pm; Sun 9am–4pm.* At one end of this establishment is a boutique selling salmon from Denmark, Scotland, Ireland, Norway and the Shetland Islands, as well as marinated herrings, smoked fish, Iranian caviar and a range of champagnes, vodkas and aquavits. At the other end is a restaurant specializing in salmon dishes.

⊜⊜⊜ **L'Enoteca** – *25 r. Charles V.* Ⓜ*Sully Morland or St-Paul.* ☎*01 42 78 91 44. www.enoteca.fr. Closed 2 weeks in Aug.* This Italian restaurant has a good reputation with its extensive Italian wine list and creative cuisine. Housed in a charming 16C building, the décor successfully mixes ancient wooden beams, ochre walls and Murano glass light fixtures.

LE JARDIN DES PLANTES

⊜⊜ **Café Littéraire** – *1 r. des Fossés-St-Bernard.* Ⓜ*Cardinal Lemoine or Jussieu.* ☎*01 55 42 55 44. www.imarabe.org. Closed Mon and 1 May.* This café in the contemporary Institut du Monde Arabe is decorated with Moorish booths features salads, daily specials and a buffet of Oriental pastries. The cuisine is simple and unfussy. In the afternoon come for pastries and mint tea, of course. For those with a larger budget, take the lift up to the Ziryab for the gourmet menu and amazing views.

⊜⊜ **El Picaflor** – *9 r. Lacépède.* Ⓜ*Place Monge.* ☎*01 43 31 06 01. www.picaflor.fr. Tue–Sat from 7pm, Fri–Sun noon–2.30pm.* This colourful restaurant specializing

© Yoshimi Kanazawa/MICHELIN

in exotic flavours wears its name well: Picaflor means hummingbird in Spanish, and this is the best address in Paris to discover Peruvian cuisine: *chicharrones*, grilled pork tenders, every kind of *pollo* chicken dishes accompanied by quinoa, aromatic shrimp soup, and marinated rabbit with spices. Friday and Saturday night there is live salsa, samba and traditional Peruvian music.

Le Jardin des Pâtes – *4 r. Lacépède.* M*Place Monge or Jussieu.* ☎*01 43 31 50 71.* Just outside the exit of the Jardin des Plantes, this tiny restaurant with old-fashioned tiles and white garden-style chairs serves home-made pasta, freshly made each day from organic flour (such as rice, chestnut, buckwheat) on the premises. It's a good place to take a break from visiting the Jardin des Plantes and nearby museums.

Les Délices d'Aphrodite – *4 r. Candolle.* M*Censier Daubenton.* ☎*01 43 31 40 39. www.mavrommatisenligne.fr.* This convivial tavern just off the Rue Mouffetard is known for its Greek-Cyprian specialities with sun-drenched flavours. The walls are covered in photos of local landscapes and ivy covers the ceiling.Pavement terrace seating in nice weather.

Verse Toujours – *3 ave. des Gobelins.* M*Censier Daubenton.* ☎*01 43 31 06 98. www.versetoujours.fr.* A true neighbourhood brasserie where locals congregate throughout the day, from the first morning espresso, to the hearty lunch, and to enjoy a house cocktail late in the evening. French classics are presented with a modern twist. Spacious terrace overlooking the busy boulevard.

LE QUARTIER LATIN

Au coin des Gourmets – *5 r. Dante.* M*Maubert-Mutualité.* ☎*01 43 26 12 92. Mon 7pm–10.30pm, Tue–Sun noon–2.30pm, 7pm–10.30pm, Reservations recommended.* The colours and tastes of Vietnam, Laos and Cambodia make up the menu at this restaurant close to the Sorbonne. Two small dining rooms simply decorated.

Mirama – *17 r. St-Jacques.* M*Maubert-Mutualité or St-Michel.* ☎*01 43 54 71 77. Open from noon to 10.45pm.* Located in the Latin Quarter, this little Chinese is adored by everyone: Asians, tourists and Parisians crowd into the dining room and grotto-like cellar for the copious dishes and reasonable prices.

Bouillon Racine – *3 r. Racine.* M*Cluny-La Sorbonne.* ☎*01 44 32 15 60. www.bouillonracine.com.* This brasserie is known for its Art Nouveau décor (marble mosaic tiling, painted windows, Belle Époque-style wood panelling and floral motif mirrors). The restaurant was created in 1906 by the Chartier brothers. Now classified a historic monument, it continues the atmosphere of Paris in the 1900s. The cuisine is all home-made: stuffed suckling pig and roasted duck with oranges and chicken blanquette.

El Palenque – *5 r. de la Montagne.Ste-Geneviève.* M*Maubert-Mutualité.* ☎*01 43 54 08 99. http://el-palenque.fr. Mon–Thu 7pm–11pm, Fri–Sat noon–3pm, 7pm–11.pm. Closed 24 Dec–2 Jan.* Visit the faraway lands of Argentina without leaving Paris. Try the delicious meats and South American wines in a ranch-style setting. A relaxing, laid-back establishment.

Le Coupe-Choux – *11 r. de Lanneau.* M*Cardinal Lemoine or Maubert-Mutualité.* ☎*01 46 33 68 69. www.lecoupechou.com.Daily noon–3pm, 7pm–11.30pm.* All the charm of the bourgeois countryside in Paris. After passing through narrow halls you'll find a lovely dining room with wood panelling, a 17C stone fireplace and a courtyard terrace. This is an ideal place for a romantic and gourmet meal: duck terrine with figs, scallops in puff pastry.

Les Papilles – *30 r. Gay Lussac.* M *Luxembourg.* ☎*01 43 25 20 79. www.lespapillesparis.com. Closed 1–8 Jan, Easter holidays, 1–21 Aug, Sun–Mon.* This little wine shop and deli also has a few bistro tables where the freshest market finds are served in one unique menu at each meal.

Colourful dining options in Le Quartier Latin

⊝⊜🍽 **Louis Vins** – *9 r. de la Montagne-Ste-Geneviève.* Ⓜ*Maubert-Mutualité.* ☎*01 43 29 12 12.* A welcoming décor with a 1900s spirit (carved walnut bar, mirrors, frescoes), where bistro cuisine is served in generous portions with a large selection of wines.

⊝⊜🍽 **Terroir Parisien** – *20 r. Saint-Victoir.* Ⓜ*Maubert-Mutualité.* ☎*01 44 31 54 54. www.yannick-alleno.com. Closed 22–28 Dec.* A contemporary dining room with bar seating in a historic Art Deco building, this restaurant specializes in locally-produced and sourced ingredients to create modern versions of Parisian classics. Stylish but relaxed atmosphere.

⊝⊜🍽🍽 **Itinéraires** – *5 r. de Pontoise.* Ⓜ*Maubert-Mutualité.* ☎*01 46 33 60 11. www.restaurant-itineraires.com. Closed 4–25 Aug, last week of Dec, Sat lunch, Sun–Mon (reservations a must).* This much talked about bistro deserves all the attention it gets: French cuisine reinvented with finesse, trendy atmosphere and a stylish and modern setting. In the evenings you can dine on charcuteries and tapas at the bar.

⊝⊜🍽🍽 **Méditerranée** – *2 pl. de l'Odéon.* Ⓜ*Odéon.* ☎*01 43 26 02 30. www.la-mediterranee.com. Closed 22–28 Dec.* Two dining rooms decorated with frescoes evoking the blue sea and a

large veranda facing the Théâtre de L'Europe create a wonderful setting for the Mediterranean cuisine.

SAINT-GERMAIN-DES-PRÉS

⊝ **Bar à Soupes et Quenelles** – *16 r. Mabillon.* Ⓜ*Mabillon.* ☎*01 43 25 53 00. www.giraudet.fr. Closed Mon lunch.* The Maison Giraudet, founded in 1910, is known for its dumplings made with passion and French savoir-faire. Over a century later its trendy new boutique offers clients home-made soups and pastries to take away, while seating is possible at the Place des Vosges location at 6 rue Pas de Mule.

⊝🍽 **L'Heure Gourmande** – *22 passage Dauphine.* Ⓜ*Odéon.* ☎*01 46 34 00 40. Daily 11.30am–7pm (Mon until 3pm). Closed 1 Jan, 1 May, 25 Dec.* It's in this charming cobbled passage, sheltered from noise and passers-by, that you'll find this adorable little tearoom. Home-made pastries, each one more appetizing than the last, are displayed on a table in the centre of the cosy dining room.

⊝🍽 **La Tourelle** – *5 r. Hautefeuille.* Ⓜ*Odéon or St-Michel.* ☎*01 46 33 12 47. Closed Sat noon and Sun, Aug.* This restaurant is like a little conservatory of traditional French bistros. The décor is completely authentic and unaffected by modern trends. You almost expect the bill to be in francs! But even in euros, the prices are quite reasonable, especially at lunch. The hearty cuisine will fill you up.

Maison de la Lozère – *4 r. Hautefeuille.* ⓜ*St-Michel or Odéon.* ✆*01 43 54 26 64. www.lozere-a-paris.com. Tue–Sat noon–2pm, 7.30pm–10pm. Closed Sun–Mon. Reservations recommended.* A country atmosphere fills this Parisian restaurant specialising in cuisine from the Lozère region. Guests sit around massive wooden tables and dine on chunks of bread, pork cold cuts, home-made soups, smoked trout, sweetmeats and their famous chestnut cakes. Come on Thursday for the house aligot (cheese, mashed potatoes and garlic).

Azabu – *3 r. A.Mazet.* ⓜ*Odéon.* ✆*01 46 33 72 05 www.azabu.fr. Closed 2 weeks in Apr, Sun noon and Mon.* Good, modern Japanese cuisine served in a small, contemporary dining room, at the tables or the bar facing the *teppan-yaki* (skillet).

La Table d'Erica – *6 r. Mabillon.* ⓜ*Mabillon.* ✆*01 43 54 87 61. http://tableerica.free.fr. Closed Aug, no lunch Sun–Mon.* Cross the little passage to enter the Table d'Erica. Relaxation guaranteed and a short menu made up of Creole dishes of fish, colombo and spicy chicken.

Le Marco Polo – *8 r. de Condé.* ⓜ*Odéon.* ✆*01 43 26 79 63. www. restaurant-marcopolo.com.* This trattoria features dishes direct from Italy: tuna with olives, pasta with aubergines or clams. The regulars enjoy speaking Italian to the servers, and there are often politicians and TV personalities spotted here. It also has one of the nicest terraces in St-Germain-des-Prés. Don't miss the panna cotta.

Ristorante da Alfredo Positano – *9 r. Guisarde.* ⓜ*Mabillon or St-Sulpice.* ✆*01 43 26 90 52. Daily 12.30–3pm, 7pm–midnight.* Alfredo Positano has held reign over the rue des Canettes for many years. As you enter the restaurant he has you pass by the selection of Italian dishes of the day on display, which varies according to what's in season at the local market.

Rôtisserie d'en Face – *2 r. Christine.* ⓜ*Odéon.* ✆*01 43 26 40 98. www.jacques-cagna.com. Closed Sat noon and Sun.* "The Rotisserie across the Street" from what? From the haute cuisine restaurant of Jacques Cagna, who decided to create this more laid-back chef's bistro. A simple elegance reigns with the ochre walls.

LE FAUBOURG SAINT-GERMAIN

Au Pied de Fouet – *45 r. de Babylone.* ⓜ*St-François-Xavier or Vaneau.* ✆*01 47 05 12 27. www.aupieddefouet.com. Closed Sat, and Sun in Aug.* Just like at grandma's house, the family-style cuisine here is served without pretension. The tiny dining room and mezzanine have a real Parisian bistro atmosphere, and the prices are on the light side for the neighbourhood.

Au Bistrot du Palais – *34 r. de Bourgogne.* ⓜ*Varenne.* ✆*01 45 55 80 75. Mon–Fri noon–2.30pm and 7pm–10pm. Closed Sat–Sun and Aug.* This restaurant in contemporary bistro style next to the National Assembly building welcomes as many tourists as business men and women from the nearby government offices.

Grand Bistrot Breteuil – *3 pl. de Breteuil.* ⓜ*Duroc or St-François-Xavier.* ✆*01 45 67 07 27. www.legrand bistro.fr. Daily noon–2.30pm, 7pm–11pm.* This chic and refined bistro with the Costes-style décor is known for its good price–quality ratio. The cuisine is contemporary French, with a large selection of dishes. The desserts are also worth mentioning. Reservations recommended since the dining room is packed daily with well-heeled locals. Reserve a terrace seat in the summer.

À la petite chaise – *36 r. de Grenelle.* ⓜ*Sèvres-Babylone.* ✆*01 42 22 13 35. www.alapetitechaise.fr. Daily noon–2pm, 7pm–11pm.* This is the oldest restaurant in Paris, founded in 1680, under the reign of Louis XIV! Authentic décor, warm welcome, efficient service, and simple yet traditional cuisine. Expect tourists plenty of other tourists.

LES INVALIDES

🍽 **Café du Musée Rodin** – *77 r. de Varenne.* Ⓜ*Varenne.* 📞*01 44 24 27 96. www.musee-rodin.fr. Tue–Sun 8am–10am and from 7pm, except Wed.* In the pretty gardens hides a little pavilion where visitors and regulars looking for a light snack come to eat under the trees of the adorable terrace. Simple salads, sandwiches, and self-serve ready-to-eat dishes.

🍽 **Chez Françoise** – *Aérogare des Invalides.* Ⓜ*Invalides.* 📞*01 47 05 49 03. www.chezfrançoise. com.* A new look, respecting the original décor, has cheered up this restaurant founded in 1949. Situated under the old air terminal on the esplanade des Invalides, close to the National Assembly building, it has become by default the canteen of the Parliament representatives.

🍽 **Miyako** – *121 r. de l'Université.* Ⓜ*Invalides.* 📞*01 47 05 41 83. www. miyakoparis.fr. Mon–Fri noon–2.30pm, 7pm–10.45pm, Sat no lunch. Closed Aug, and Sun.* Located in the Gros-Caillou district, this little culinary voyage to the Land of the Rising Sun specializes in wood stove cooked kebabs and sushi platters.

🍽 **Le Petit Bordelais** – *22 r. Surcouf.* Ⓜ*Invalides.* 📞*01 45 51 46 93. www.lepetit-bordelais.com. Closed last 2 weeks Feb, Aug, Sun–Mon.* This contemporary restaurant features a good selection of wines by the glass, particularly from Bordeaux. Intimate setting with velour booths in red and mocha tones.

🍽 **Le Vauban** – *7 pl. Vauban.* Ⓜ*St-François-Xavier.* 📞*01 47 05 52 67. Daily 7am–10.30pm.* ♿. To admire the Dôme of the church at the Invalides, make sure to get a terrace seat at this popular brasserie with its décor of trompe-l'œil marble. A varied menu is available.

🍽 **Café de l'Esplanade** – *52 r. Fabert.* Ⓜ*La Tour Maubourg.* 📞*01 47 05 38 80. Valet parking. Daily 8am–2am.* It's a restaurant Costes, without the usual stuffy atmosphere. Choose one of the terrace tables facing Invalides. The décor takes the military theme further with cannons facing the esplanade. Sunday afternoons the atmosphere is more family oriented, but at night it's a trendy place to see and be seen: politicians, media stars and other VIPs.

EIFFEL TOWER AND TROCADÉRO

🍽 **Essaouira** – *16 r. de Magdebourg.* Ⓜ*Trocadéro or Iéna.* 📞*01 47 27 57 28. restaurant-essaouira.fr. noon–2.30pm, 7pm–11pm. Closed Mon noon, 15 Aug.* In an authentic Moroccan setting of sculpted walls and oriental friezes, you'll discover pastillas, couscous and tagines served on giant copper platters. Traditional service and uniforms, and tables are low to the ground. Méchoui is available if you order at least two days in advance.

🍽 **Carette** – *4 pl. du Trocadéro.* Ⓜ*Trocadéro.* 📞*01 47 27 98 85. www. carette-paris.com. Daily 7am–11.30pm. (Sat–Sun from 7.30am).* Founded in 1927, this tearoom is a Parisian institution on the place du Trocadéro. The perfectly conserved old-fashioned décor still attracts a loyal following among the chic locals. Don't miss the sweet macaron pastries or the tasty salads served at lunch.

🍽 **Les Cocottes** – *135 r. St Dominique.* Ⓜ*École-Militaire.* 📞*01 45 50 10 28. www.maisonconstant.com. Daily noon–10.30pm.* This convivial establishment where no reservations can be made is casual, with tall bar-like tables and inventive bistro-style cuisine served in cocottes.

🍽 **Sancerre** – *22 av. Rapp.* Ⓜ*Pont de l'Alma.* 📞*01 45 51 75 91. Closed 3 weeks in Aug, Mon–Fri 8.30am–4pm, 6.30 –10pm, Sat no dinner.* ♿. A veritable embassy of the Sancerre region, this country-style restaurant features hearty little dishes including terrines, omelettes, andouillette sausages cooked in Sancerre wine, goat's cheese on toast and home-made savoury tarts.

🍽 **Brasserie Le Coq** – *2 pl. du Trocadéro.* Ⓜ*Trocadéro.* 📞 *01 47 27 89 52. Daily 9am–noon.* This old brasserie was given a facelift and new life as a Costes restaurant. The location is ideal, and the terrace is heated in winter. The décor inside is quite remarkable, with a large glass column lit from the inside, good lighting, a reflective ceiling, plenty of space between tables and minimalist lines.

Le Père Claude – 51 av. de La Motte-Picquet. **M**La Motte-Piquet Grenelle. *01 47 34 03 05. www. leperreclaude.com. Daily noon–2.30pm, 7pm–11.30pm.* Founded in 1988, this French restaurant specialises in steaks and grilled meat dishes. The cuisine is simple, made with high-quality ingredients and served in generous portions. An excellent address for Sunday brunch with its traditional family atmosphere.

P'tit Troquet – 28 r. de l'Exposition. **M**École Militaire. *01 47 05 80 39. Daily noon–2pm, 6.30–10pm (no Sat lunch). Closed 2 weeks in Jan, 2 weeks in Aug.* This tiny bistro is certainly "p'tit". But it has many things going for it: a nostalgic charm (vintage publicity posters and period zinc bar), friendly atmosphere and delicious market-based cooking.

Restaurant Philippe Excoffier – 14 r. de l'Exposition. **M**École-Militaire. *01 45 51 78 08. www.philippe-excoffier.fr. Closed 2-24 Aug, Sun-Mon.* Twelve years as executive chef in the American Embassy had Philippe Excoffier preparing official dinners for numerous heads of state and also legends like Olivia de Havilland. But here, at his bistro, he prepares these exquisite modern French dishes just for you.

ALMA

Aux Marches du Palais – 5 r. de la Manutention. **M**léna. *01 47 23 52 80. Closed 1 week Christmas to 1 Jan.* On the small and tranquil rue de la Manutention, a restaurant with authentic "bistro-style" furniture and traditional "terroir" cuisine.

6 New-York – 6 av. New-York. **M**Alma-Marceau. *01 40 70 03 30. www.6newyork.fr. Mon–Fri 12.15pm–2pm, 7.30pm–10.20pm, Sat 7.30pm–10.50pm. Closed Aug, Sat noon and Sun.* Even if the name tells you the address, it doesn't tell you how a chic little bistro features cuisine cooked in perfect harmony with the setting: resolutely modern and refined.

Oscar – 6 r. de Chaillot. **M**léna. *01 47 20 26 92. www.restaurantoscar.fr. Daily noon–2.30pm, 7pm–10.30pm (no Sat lunch). Closed 2 weeks in Aug, and Sun.* A discreet façade, tightly packed tables, and a slateboard with the specials of the day: even with zero marketing, the clientele of this bistro come from all over Paris!

Thiou – 49 Quai Musee d'Orsay . *01 40 62 96 50. www;thiou.fr. Mon–Sat noon–2.30pm, 7pm–11pm. Closed Sun. noon.* Thiou and Le Petit Thiou, in the 7th arrondissement, are part of the Thiou restaurant group. You'll find signature Thai gastronomic cuisine here: crunchy vegetable nems, mini nems with lobster, and crab claws to die for! The great speciality is still the Tigre qui Pleure (Crying Tiger, a grilled beef fillet chopped in small morsels and served with sticky rice and salad, presented in an original way).

Gusto Sardo – 17 rue Georges Bizet. **M**Alma-Marceau. *01 47 20 08 90. www.restaurant-ilgustosardo.com. Mon–Fri 12.30pm–2.15pm, 7.30pm–10.30pm, Sat 7.30pm–10.30pm. Closed Sat lunch and Sun.* In this Italian restaurant run by a mother-father-son team, the focus is placed on all the flavours of Sardinia. The pasta, for example, is served along with la boutargue (Mediterranean caviar), and the veal escalope with lemon is a real treat.

Noura – 27 av. Marceau. **M**Alma-Marceau or léna. *01 47 23 02 20. www.noura.com. Daily until midnight.* Since 1989 this address has represented excellence in Lebanese gastronomy: authentic flavours and subtle tastes worthy of 1001 Arabian Nights, all served with a little glass of arak. You'll also find Noura at Montparnasse, the Opéra and on the panoramic terrace atop the Institut du Monde Arabe.

LA VOIE TRIOMPHALE

🍽 **Kaiten** – *63 r. Pierre Charron.* Ⓜ*Franklin-Roosevelt.* ☎*01 43 59 78 78. www.kaiten.fr. Mon–Sat noon–3.15pm, 7pm–12.15am.* In a very zen décor you'll find a conveyor belt sushi bar with sushi, sashimi, maki and other Japanese specialities for your selection.

🍽 **Lô Sushi** – *8 r. de Berri.* Ⓜ *George V.* ☎*01 45 62 01 00. www.losushi.com. Noon–12.30am.* At this Japanese restaurant sushi dishes circulate on the conveyor belt in a minimalist modern décor. The concept is fun and simple: have a seat at the bar and choose your sushi as they pass by. Very popular with the *beautiful people* who keep it packed nightly.

🍽 **Flora Danica** – *142 av. des Champs-Élysées.* Ⓜ*Charles de Gaulle Étoile.* ☎*01 44 13 86 26. www.floradanica-paris.com. Daily noon–2.30pm, 7.15pm–11pm.* This café-snack bar in the Maison du Danemark offers guests the possibility of lunch or dinner on the terrace on the Champs-Élysées for a price that beats the competition: hearty salads, sandwiches and Nordic platters.

🍽 **L'Atelier Renault** – *53 av. des Champs-Élysées.* Ⓜ*Franklin-Roosevelt.* ☎*08 11 88 28 11. www.atelier-renault.com. Sun–Thu noon–10pm, Fri–Sat noon–11pm.* Your kids will love this place: the vast Renault exhibition hall has been completely renovated; the model cars are still there. Tables are placed on the catwalks suspended above the hall, for a great view of the cars. Ideal for lunch or a snack break. Brunch on Sundays.

🍽 **Théâtre du Rond-Point** – *2 bis av. Franklin-Roosevelt.* Ⓜ*Franklin-Roosevelt.* ☎*01 44 95 98 44. www.theatre durondpoint.fr. Noon–3pm, 7pm –12am. Closed Aug, Sat noon, Mon eve and Sun.* Cross the hall of this pretty theatre on the edge of the Champs-Élysées to enjoy this completely renovated, modern restaurant. The terrace under the chestnut trees is packed during the summer months and the menu changes along with the seasons.

🍽 **Le 68 Guy Martin** – *68 Av. des Champs-Elysées.* Ⓜ*George V.* ☎*01 45 62 54 10. www.le68guymartin.com. Closed 1 May, 25 Dec, 1 Jan. No dinner Sun.* Enjoying this lovely brunch, lunch and tearoom in Guerlain's flagship boutique is as wonderful as dining here for dinner. Guerlain's "nose", Thierry Vasseur, collaborated with Chef Martin to create dishes based on signature perfume notes: vanilla, rose, jasmine, bergamot.

🍽 **La Maison de L'Aubrac** – *37 r. Marbeuf.* Ⓜ*Franklin-Roosevelt.* ☎*01 43 59 05 14. www.maison-aubrac.com.* Decorated in the style of a farmhouse in the Aveyron region, La Maison serves hearty rustic dishes with a speciality in beef, and has a wonderful wine cave. Come here to discover the tastes of l'Aubrac and you get to people- watch on the Champs-Élysées.

🍽 **Ladurée - Champs-Élysées** – *75 av. des Champs-Élysées.* Ⓜ*George V or Franklin-Roosevelt.* ☎*01 40 75 08 75. www.laduree.com.* How could any sweet tooth resist this place? In addition to pastries, those who prefer a bit of savoury cuisine will find a nice choice of salads, classic French dishes, and house creations, all served in magnificent Napoléon III décor.

🍽 **Victoria 1836** – *12 r. de Presbourg.* Ⓜ*Étoile.* ☎*01 44 17 97 72. www.victoria-1836.com. Closed 1–15 Aug, Sat–Sun mornings.* Elegant walnut with aqua accent the décor by Sarah Lavoine. This turf-and-surf restaurant offers an excellent breakfast, lunch, tea or dinner choice near the Arc de Triomphe. It doesn't hurt that the new Lenny Kravitz-designed nightclub is just downstairs, too.

MONCEAU

🍽 **Les Domaines qui Montent** – *22 r. Cardinet.* Ⓜ*Courcelles.* ☎*01 42 27 63 96. www.lesdomainesquimontent.com. Mon–Sat 10am–8pm. Closed 2 weeks in mid-Aug and some holidays.* This establishment successfully combines its restaurant and wine boutique (wines ordered for dining are priced the same as in the boutique). The owner's recommendations are always spot on, and his passion really comes through as he teaches his clientele all there is to know about "les domaines qui montent" (up and coming wines).

⊜⊜⊜ **Chez Léon** – *32 r. Legendre.* Ⓜ*Villiers.* ☎*01 42 27 06 82. www. restaurantchezleon.com. Mon–Fri noon–2.30pm, 7pm–10.30pm, Sat 7–11pm. Closed first 2 weeks in Aug.* The décor combines the bistro spirit with modern touches in one of the three dining rooms. The cuisine also mixes the traditional with the modern. Convivial atmosphere.

⊜⊜⊜ **Daru** – *19 r. Daru.* Ⓜ*Courcelles.* ☎*01 42 27 23 60. www.daru.fr. Mon–Sat 10am–11pm. Closed Aug and Sun. Valet parking.* Founded in 1918, Daru was the first Russian deli in Paris. It continues to perpetuate the Slavic tradition, with décor that will transport you to a Russia of yesteryear.

⊜⊜⊜ **Chez Karl & Erick** – *20 r. de Tocqueville.* Ⓜ*Villiers.* ☎*01 42 27 03 71. Mon–Fri noon–2pm, 7.30pm–10pm. Closed Aug, Sat–Sun.* A pair of twins, one in the dining room and another in the kitchen, are the ones behind this bistro with the contemporary loft style. A slateboard presents the daily specials, combining the best of traditional and modern bistro fare.

LE FAUBOURG SAINT-HONORÉ

⊜ **Swoon's** – *10 r. des Saussaies.* Ⓜ*Madeleine.* ☎*01 42 68 00 02. Mon–Fri 8am–3.30pm. Closed end Jul–early Aug.* A successful melange for this establishment. They kept the "bistro" décor with the wooden tables, chairs, benches and parquet flooring while featuring a snack-bar-style menu of sandwiches, salads and specials.

⊜⊜ **Village d'Ung et Li Lam** – *10 r. J.Mermoz.* Ⓜ*Franklin-Roosevelt.* ☎*01 42 25 99 79. Mon–Sat noon–3pm, 6pm–midnight. Closed Sun and 1st 3 weeks in Aug.* A cosy and hushed atmosphere at Ung and Li's, where aquariums are suspended from the ceiling and the flooring is embedded with pâté de verre and sprinkles of sand for an original setting. Chinese-Thai cuisine.

⊜⊜⊜ **Chez Cécile la Ferme des Mathurins** – *17 r. Vignon.* Ⓜ*Madeleine.* ☎*01 42 66 46 39. www.chezcecile.com. Closed the week of 15 Aug.* Traditional dishes, in copious portions while remaining refined in taste. A friendly atmosphere with many regulars in this authentic, old-fashioned bistro.

⊜⊜⊜ **Granterroirs** – *30 r. de Miromesnil.* Ⓜ *Miromesnil.* ☎*01 47 42 18 18. www.granterroirs.com. Mon–Fri 9am–5pm and private parties until 11pm. Closed last 2 weeks in Aug, Sat–Sun.* ♿. Large oak communal tables, shelves stocked with regional specialities, baskets filled with wines from independent growers and gourmet foods from the French "terroir". This upmarket deli and restaurant specializes in bringing French country flavours to Paris.

⊜⊜⊜ **Le Griffonnier** – *8 r. des Saussaies.* Ⓜ*Miromesnil.* ☎*01 42 65 17 17. Mon–Fri 8am–7pm. Closed Aug, Sat–Sun.* Located in a 17C house, this wine bistro serves tasty little bistro dishes. A rustic setting, in a bit of a narrow dining room, but it's pleasant and cosy. A larger dining room is upstairs. They also serve the best new Beaujolais here in November.

⊜⊜⊜⊜ **L'Arôme** – *3 r. St-Philippe du Roule.* Ⓜ*St-Philippe du Roule.* ☎*01 42 25 55 98. www.larome.fr. Mon–Fri noon–1.45pm, 7.30pm–9.45pm. Closed first 3 weeks in Aug, Sat–Sun.* A chic "neo-bistro" expertly run by Éric Martins in the dining room and Thomas Boullault in the kitchen. The décor is simple, in coral and taupe tones, with an open kitchen.

OPÉRA AND PALAIS ROYAL

⊜ **Hokkaido** – *14 r. Chabanais.* Ⓜ*Pyramides or Quatre–Septembre.* ☎*01 42 60 50 95. Thu–Tue 11.30am–10.30pm. Closed Wed.* At this Japanese canteen in the Opéra/Bourse business district, as soon as you enter, the smells will get your appetite going. The open kitchen allows clients to watch the chefs as they work with the enormous skillets, steaming vats of broth, and hot woks of veggies and meats.

Véro-Dodat – *19 Galerie Véro-Dodat.* Ⓜ *Palais Royal Musée du Louvre.* ☎ *01 45 08 92 06. www.verododat.fr. Mon–Sat noon–4pm, 6.30–9.30pm. Closed Aug.* ♿. A humble family-run restaurant in the historic Passage Véro-Dodat. The décor of old lace curtains and red velour booths is authentic. Few tables on the ground floor, but there's another tiny dining room upstairs.

Le Bistrot Mavrommatis – *18 r. Duphot.* Ⓜ *Madeleine.* ☎ *01 42 97 53 04. www.mavrommatis.com. Closed 2 weeks mid-Aug, Sat, Sun.* Greece, Italy Spain, North Africa, Provence: you'll find all the flavours of the Mediterranean at this tapas bar. The restaurant is upstairs, with a deli and wine boutique where Iberian hams can be tasted.

Legrand Filles et Fils – *1 r. de la Banque.* Ⓜ *Bourse.* ☎ *01 42 60 07 12. www.caves-legrand.com. Mon 11am–7pm, Tue–Fri 10am–7.30pm, Sat 10am–7pm. Closed Sun.* ♿. This wine boutique and gourmet dry goods deli is one of the must-visit addresses of the city. Here you'll find the great classics as well as the little-known gems and French "terroir" products. The selection as well as the authentic décor are impressive. A communal Table d'Hôte is available at lunch in the dining room facing the Galerie Vivienne.

Yamamoto – *6 r. Chabanais.* Ⓜ *Pyramides or Quatre Septembre.* ☎ *01 49 27 96 26. Tue–Sat noon–2:30pm, 7pm–10:30pm.* This Japanese restaurant has maintained its authentic Japan atmosphere, with its tiny, minimalist dining room and curtained entry. They don't take reservations and there's often a line of people waiting for a table, so come armed with patience.

You – *11 r. Ste-Anne.* Ⓜ *Pyramides.* ☎ *01 42 60 55 50.* If you like Japanese cuisine, the rue Ste-Anne restaurant is like a little trip to the Land of the Rising Sun. Among the multitude of restaurants try You. The setting is simple, the service efficient, and the traditional dishes prepared before you.

Baan Boran – *43 r. Montpensier.* Ⓜ *Palais Royal.* ☎ *01 40 15 90 45. www.baan-boran.com. Mon–Sat noon–3pm, 7pm–11pm. Closed Sat noon and Sun.* This Asian restaurant across from the Théâtre du Palais Royal specialises in Thai cuisine prepared in a wok and served in a contemporary dining room.

Le Saut du Loup – *107 r. de Rivoli.* Ⓜ *Palais Royal.* ☎ *01 42 25 49 55. www.lesautduloup.fr. Daily 10am–2am.* Elegant black-and-white décor from the floors to the ceilings and views over the Louvre's Carrousel gardens make up the décor for this restaurant of the Musée des Arts Décoratifs. The dishes are refined and inventive.

Nodaiwa – *272 r. St-Honoré.* Ⓜ *Palais Royal.* ☎ *01 42 86 03 42. www.nodaiwa.com. Mon–Sat noon–2.30pm, 7pm–10pm. Closed Sun.* The Parisian branch of the Japanese restaurant Nodaiwa in Tokyo specialises in grilled eel, a popular dish in Japan. Sliced into fillets, grilled over hot coals, steam cooked, then marinated several times in a special Také sauce gives it the signature caramelized taste.

Willi's Wine Bar – *13 r. Petits-Champs.* Ⓜ *Bourse.* ☎ *01 42 61 05 09. www.williswinebar.com. Mon–Sat noon–midnight Closed 9–24 Aug, Sun and bank holidays.* A collection of posters created for this convivial wine bistro by different contemporary artists decorate Willi's. The bistro cuisine is always inventive, and the wines carefully selected.

Le Costes – *Hôtel Costes, 239 r. St-Honoré.* Ⓜ *Tuileries.* ☎ *01 42 44 50 25. www.hotelcostes.com.* A trendy "world food" restaurant in the exclusive Costes hotel, so expect a fat bill! However, it's an agreeable place for those who want to spend an evening with the beautiful in the luxurious bar-lounge-restaurant decorated by Jacques Garcia. The courtyard is popular for lunch.

LES GRANDS BOULEVARDS

🍴 **Big Fernand**– 55 r. de Fbg. Poissonnière. ⓂCadet. ☎01 73 70 51 52. www.bigfernand.com. Closed 25 Dec–1 Jan, Sun. The best hamburgers near The Rex, these are thick and juicy and piled high with all the fixings. The burger-flipping, apron-wearing staff infuses this tiny joint with the sense that they're up for anything: they'll even join you in your selfie photos.

🍴🍴 **Chartier** – 7 r. du Faubourg-Montmartre. ⓂGrands Boulevards. ☎01 47 70 86 29. www.restaurant-chartier.com. ♿. An ideal place to dine on a budget, but also to experience the authentic old-fashioned atmosphere of this typically Parisian workers' canteen from 1896. The décor hasn't changed since opening, with its large atrium ceiling, wood panelling, brass luggage racks and little lockers where the regulars keep their napkin.

🍴🍴 **Pooja** – 91 passage Brady. ⓂChâteau d'Eau or Strasbourg-St-Denis. ☎01 48 24 00 83. www.pooja.restaurant. com. Daily noon–3pm, 7pm–11pm. Here, a variety of Indian specialities are served in a welcoming setting.

🍴🍴🍴 **L'Office** – 3 r. Richer. ⓂPoissonnière. ☎01 47 70 67 31. Tue–Sat noon–2.15pm, 7.30pm–10.45pm. Closed Aug, 21 Dec–5 Jan, Sun–Mon, no lunch Tue–Wed and Sat. An address with a minimalist décor, in keeping with the trend for new restaurants. The passionate, self-taught chef proposes a menu based on the fresh market produce.

🍴🍴🍴 **Le J'Go** – 4 r. Drouot. ⓂRichelieu Drouot. ☎01 40 22 09 09. www.lejgo.com. Closed Sun. ♿. The menu at this bistro pays tribute to the cooking of Huguette, the owner's mother. He came to Paris from the Gers region to bring the city the flavours of his childhood. Hams, terrines, chicken and fries, roasted lamb and cassoulets among a selection of rotisserie meats.

🍴🍴🍴 **Les Diables au Thym** – 35 r. Bergère. ⓂGrands Boulevards. ☎01 47 70 77 09. www.lesdiablesauthym.com. Closed 3 weeks in Aug, Sat–Sun. Located near the Grévin Wax Museum, this simple dining room in the bistro spirit has a few contemporary paintings. Modern cuisine that changes with the market and a slateboard listing wines.

PIGALLE AND NOUVELLE ATHÈNES

🍴🍴🍴 **Domaine de Lintillac** – 54 r. Blanche. ⓂBlanche. ☎01 48 74 84 36. www.lintillac-paris.com. Closed Sat noon and Sun. Foie gras, quality preserved goods and appetizing prices: three ingredients that have made this mini-chain of restaurants founded by an artisan preservist from the Perigord region of France so successful. Be sure to reserve a table if you want to enjoy the southwestern cuisine. Bistro décor.

🍴🍴🍴 **La Petite Sirène de Copenhague** – 47 r. N.-D. de Lorette. ⓂSt Georges. ☎01 45 26 66 66. www. lapetitesireneparis.com. Closed Aug, 23 Dec–2 Jan, Sat noon, Sun–Mon. A plain and simple dining room with whitewashed walls and filtered lighting in the Danish style for cuisine coming from the land of Hans Christian Andersen. Attentive service.

🍴🍴🍴 **Momoka** – 5 r. Jean-Baptiste-Pigalle. ⓂTrinité-d'Estienne-d'Orves. ☎01 40 16 19 09. Closed Aug, Sat noon, Sun–Mon. Be sure to reserve well in advance at this mini-restaurant run by a Franco-Japanese couple. Masayo cooks up tasty Japanese dishes for a menu that changes daily. Authentic, family-oriented atmosphere.

CANAL SAINT-MARTIN

🍴 **Couleurs Canal** – 56 r. Lancry. ⓂBonsergent. ☎01 42 40 60 52. Mon–Fri noon–7pm. Closed mid-Jul–mid-Aug. The slateboard offers a selection of daily specials such as savoury tarts and house pastries made on the premises, often with organic ingredients. The décor is simple yet modern to best show off the sculptures of the owner-artist on display (pretty lamps upstairs).

🍴🍴🍴 **Hôtel du Nord** – 102 quai de Jemmapes. ⓂRépublique. ☎01 40 40 78 78. www.hoteldunord.org. It was in front of this façade on the edge of the Canal St-Martin that the French actress Arletty uttered her famous line, "Atmosphere, atmosphere…" in the Marcel Carné film *Hôtel du Nord*. Today this café-restaurant, with its retro setting, serves a menu of classic and modern fusion dishes.

😊🍷🍺 **Le Valmy** – *145 quai de Valmy.* Ⓜ*Château Landon.* ☎*01 42 09 93 78. Daily 9am–2am, Sun until 10pm. Closed Aug, Sat noon.* Huge bay windows overlook the Canal St-Martin right across the street from this recently renovated old local's bar (bright colours, tables in mosaic tiling and wrought iron, walls covered in framed photographs). Family-style cooking, simple yet served in generous portions.

😊🍷🍺 **Porte 12** – *12 r. des Messageries.* Ⓜ*Poissonnière.* ☎*01 42 44 22 64. www.porte12.com. Tue–Sat noon–2pm, 7pm–10pm. No lunch Sat. Closed Sun, public holidays.* Exuding a living room feel, this trendy new restaurant is very contemporary, even though awash with 1950s styling. The kitchen serves an unpretentious, pared-down menu.

BASTILLE AND FAUBOURG SAINT-ANTOINE

😊🍷 **Le Café Moderne** – *19 r. Keller.* Ⓜ*Ledru Rollin.* ☎*01 47 00 53 62. www.cafemoderne-tbmb.com. Tue–Sat noon–2pm, 7pm–midnight. Closed Mon, Sun brunch only.* A nice dining room with a beautiful veranda in the back where clients enjoy couscous and the carefully prepared dishes by the chef. A simple but welcome establishment, usually lacking in this often overrated neighbourhood.

😊🍷 **Barrio Latino** – *46/48 r. du Fbg-St-Antoine.* Ⓜ*Bastille.* ☎*01 55 78 84 75. www.barrio-latino.com.* ♿. *Daily noon–2pm, 7pm–midnight.* This former furniture store is now a sumptuous Latino bar-restaurant of 3 000 sq m on four floors, connected with a grand staircase that's a classified historic monument. The building's façade and metal beam structure were designed by Gustave Eiffel. The ground floor has a tapas bar, a restaurant is on the first floor and a Cuban bar on the second floor with a cigar room and club chairs.

😊🍷 **Grand Bleu** – *Bd. de la Bastille.* Ⓜ*Bastille.* ☎*01 43 45 19 99. www.legrand bleu-paris.com.* No, you're not dreaming, you're still in the heart of Paris. But when you're sitting on the sunny terrace overlooking the Arsenal pleasure port and its charming gardens, it's easy to forget the place de la Bastille is just 50 metres away. Service on the veranda in good weather.

😊🍷 **Les Sans-Culottes** – *27 r. de Lappe.* Ⓜ*Bastille or Ledru-Rollin.* ☎*01 48 05 42 92. Closed Mon–Fri noon.* Before throwing yourself into the nightlife of the rue de Lappe, get your fill at this bistro with the 1900-style décor: a pretty zinc bar with its coffee machine, carved wood panelling, menu on the slateboard and convivial atmosphere.

😊🍷🍺 **Swann et Vincent** – *7 r. St-Nicolas.* Ⓜ*Ledru Rollin.* ☎*01 43 43 49 40. www.swann-vincent.fr. Daily.* A successful mix of Italian cuisine and Parisian bistro décor. Old tile floors, walls with a vintage patina, red banquettes, tables and chairs in wood, and an immense slateboard with the specials of the day. The service is friendly and laid-back.

😊🍷🍺 **Traversière** – *40 r. Traversière.* Ⓜ*Ledru Rollin.* ☎*01 43 44 02 10. Closed Sun eve and Mon, 3 weeks in Aug, 1 Jan, 25 Dec.* ♿. This neighbourhood restaurant has preserved its provincial country inn atmosphere (historic façade, exposed wooden beams), but it's furnished in a contemporary style. Excellent traditional cuisine prepared with care, and game dishes in season.

😊🍷🍺 **La Biche au Bois** – *45 av. Ledru-Rollin.* Ⓜ*Gare de Lyon.* ☎*01 43 43 34 38. Closed 20 Jul–20 Aug, 23 Dec–2 Jan, Sat–Sun, and Mon noon.* Clients sit elbow-to-elbow in this discreet little restaurant, but the atmosphere is lively and the service is charming and attentive. Generous portions for the traditional French dishes, and game served in season.

😊🍷🍺 **La Gazzetta** – *29 r. de Cotte.* Ⓜ*Ledru Rollin.* ☎*01 43 47 47 05. www. lagazzetta.fr. Closed Aug, Sun–Mon.*

This restaurant is dedicated to the Mediterranean. Their "all in one" concept – restaurant, wine bar, café (with international newspapers available) – has made it a trendy place to hang out for the locals. Excellent southern France cuisine.

🍽🍷🍺 **La Pirada** – *7 r. de Lappe.* Ⓜ*Bastille. www.pirada.com.* 📞 *01 47 00 73 61 or 01 43 57 21 96. Daily 5pm–2am. No lunch.* The atmosphere in this restaurant-bar located in one of the popular nightlife districts is hot, young and festive. The décor has recently been renovated, the tapas are as varied and tasty as ever, and the paella is worth a try. Spanish or salsa music.

🍽🍷🍺🍺 **Blue Elephant** – *43–45 rue de la Roquette.* Ⓜ*Bastille.* 📞 *01 47 00 42 00. www.blueelephant.com. Daily except Sat noon.* A gastronomic voyage to the Kingdom of Siam, in a Thai country-style décor with a waterfall, lush plants and orchids. The Thai cuisine is highly refined.

LE BOIS AND LE CHÂTEAU DE VINCENNES

🍽 **Le Bosquet** – *Parc floral.* Ⓜ*Château de Vincennes.* 📞*01 43 28 87 15. Open depending on the weather.* With its serene green dining room, its terrace and buffet, this little garden grove ("bosquet") is ideal for lunch or a snack break in the afternoon. At lunch there's a self-service formula, a full meal menu, or a speciality of the day. From 4pm it becomes an ice cream parlour much adored by the children.

🍽🍷 **Les Magnolias** – *Parc floral.* Ⓜ*Château de Vincennes.* 📞*01 43 74 78 22. www.restaurant-lesmagnolias-paris.com.* A real restaurant, more for parents than the children. But they can still enjoy playing on the terrace. Reservations highly recommended, especially on weekends when the weather is nice.

🍽🍷🍺 **La Rigadelle** – *23 r. de Montreuil. 94300 Vincennes. RER Vincennes.* 📞*01 43 28 04 23. Closed 28 Jul–17 Aug, 20–28 Dec, Sun–Mon.* In a sunny, contemporary dining room with nautical touches, enjoy the dishes of

the day. The speciality of the house is fish and seafood, which comes direct from Brittany each day.

BERCY

🍽🍷 **Fil 'O' Fromage** – *12 r. Neuve-Tolbiac.* Ⓜ*Bibliothèque F Mitterrand.* 📞*01 53 79 13 35. www.filofromage.com. Mon–Sat 11am–7.30pm (Thu–Sat until 10.30pm). Closed 2 weeks in Aug and bank holidays.* ♿. You've heard of wine bars, soup bars, tapas bars: now here is a cheese bar. On the ground floor the deli sells cheeses, charcuterie meats, and wines with a few tables for tasting. Upstairs is the restaurant, which becomes a tearoom in the afternoon. There are also concert evenings and tasting events throughout the year.

🍽🍷 **Café Bibliothèque** – *128–162 av. de France.* Ⓜ*Bibliothèque F Mitterrand.* 📞*01 56 61 44 00. www.mk2.com. Noon–midnight.* The contemporary architecture by Jean-Michel Wilmotte for the MK2 cinema complex forms the backdrop to this modern brasserie with the red walls. Large salads, burgers and small dishes on the menu from lunch till midnight. Play the movie star in your sunglasses on the sunny terrace.

🍽🍷 **L'Auberge Aveyronnaise** – *40 r. Lamé.* Ⓜ*Cour St-Émilion.* 📞*01 43 40 12 24. Closed 2–18 Aug.* This modern bistro-brasserie is solidly anchored in the cuisine of the Aveyron region of France. The huge, neo-rustic dining room is complemented by a nice terrace.

🍽🍷 **La Zygothèque** – *15 bis r. de Tolbiac.* Ⓜ*Bibliothèque F Mitterrand.* 📞*01 45 83 07 48. www.la-zygotheque.fr. Closed 3 weeks in Aug, Sat noon and Sun.* ♿. La Zygothèque? The name may be strange but the décor is cosy and the chef cooks up tasty French dishes.

LA BUTTE-AUX-CAILLES

🍽🍷 **Bambou** – *70 r. Baudricourt.* Ⓜ*Olympiades.* 📞 *01 45 70 91 75. Closed 1–15 Aug and Mon.* People line up for a table at this tiny Vietnamese restaurant. The cuisine is among the best in Chinatown. Simple décor and convivial atmosphere.

😋🍷 **Sukhothaï** – *12 r. du Père-Guérin.* Ⓜ*Place d'Italie.* 📞*01 45 81 55 88. Closed 3–23 Aug, Mon noon and Sun.* The name of this restaurant invokes the ancient name of the capital of the Thai Kingdom (13C–14C). Chinese and Thai cuisine served under the eyes of the Buddha statues (artisan sculptures).

😋🍷🍽 **Auberge Etchegorry** – *41 r. Croulebarbe.* Ⓜ*Les Gobelins.* 📞*01 44 08 83 51. www.etchegorry.com. Closed Sun –Mon.* A brochure describes the history of the neighbourhood and this charming Basque restaurant. Dried sausages, hams, garlic and hot peppers hang from the ceilings for added ambience.

😋🍷🍽 **L'Avant-Goût** – *26 r. Bobillot.* Ⓜ*Place d'Italie.* 📞*01 53 80 24 00. www.lavantgout.com. Closed 3–25 Aug, Sun–Mon.* An original take on fresh market cooking, a good choice of wines by the glass and a relaxed atmosphere in a contemporary dining room have made this little bistro a popular place to dine. Be sure to reserve.

😋🍷🍽 **Les Cailloux** – *58 r. des Cinq-Diamants.* Ⓜ*Corvisart.* 📞*01 45 80 15 08. Closed 1 week in Aug, 24 Dec–2 Jan, Sun–Mon.* This stylish little trattoria and its popular terrace are located at the heart of this lively yet laid-back neighbourhood. The Italian cuisine (pastas, bruschetta, seafood dishes, etc), well-selected wines and reasonable prices have made it one of the best addresses in the area.

MONTPARNASSE

😋 **À la Duchesse Anne** – *5 pl. du 18 juin 1940.* Ⓜ*Montparnasse.* 📞*01 45 48 97 21. Closed Sun and bank holidays.* ♿. An ideal tearoom for having a break at the foot of the Tour de Montparnasse. Food is available to go or to eat in, including sandwiches, savoury tarts, dishes of the day, pastries and ice cream.

😋🍷 **Les Zazous** – *46 bd du Montparnasse.* Ⓜ*Montparnasse.* 📞*01 45 49 32 88. www.restaurant-leszazous.com. Closed 2 weeks in Aug.* ♿. The original outfits worn by the servers at this restaurant fit in with the 1940s "zazou" spirit: blousy white shirts, suspender braces, black trousers and a hat perched on the side of the head. The food is more discreet, with everything from a fish of the day to duck breast confit and steaks.

😋🍷 **Severo** – *8 r. des Plantes.* Ⓜ*Mouton-Duvernet.* 📞*01 45 40 40 91. Closed 24 Jul–24 Aug, 1 week at Christmas, 1 week in Feb and 1 week in Apr.* Products from the Auvergne region (meats, cold cuts) are prominent on the slateboard at this cosy bistro. The wine list is eclectic.

😋🍷🍽 **Ausgustin Bistrot** – *79 r. Daguerre.* Ⓜ*Gaîté.* 📞*01 43 21 92 29. www.augustin-bistrot.fr. Closed Sun.* This industrial chic dining spot is the setting for intimate meals of classic French dishes amid ceiling-high shelves holding a variety of white tableware. There's a cosy bar as well as street-side service.

😋🍷🍽 **L'Opportun** – *62 bd Edgar Quinet.* Ⓜ*Montparnasse or Edgar Quinet.* 📞*01 43 20 26 89. Daily noon–3pm, 7pm–11pm (reserve).* Simply decorated yet convivial, this Lyonnais bistro has a menu full of succulent regional specialities: thick-cut steak with Ambert cheese, Provençal-style scallops, stewed kidneys, andouillette sausages and the best Beaujolais.

😋🍷🍽 **La Cerisaie** – *70 bd. Edgar Quinet.* Ⓜ*Edgar Quinet.* 📞*01 43 20 98 98. Closed 1–11 May, 11 Jul–17 Aug, 19 Dec–4 Jan, Sat–Sun.* This postage stamp of a restaurant is situated in the heart of the Brittany Quarter of Paris.

How about Take-Out?

Tang Frères Takeout 44 Av. d'Ivry Ⓜ*Olympiades* 📞*01 45 70 80 00. Closed Sun afternoon and Mon.* The courtyard of Paris' Chinese grocery emporium houses this little hut that serves up steamed pork buns, fried chicken claws and other Far Eastern delights that are great to take home – or eat while standing.

Each day the owner writes the specials from the southwest on the slateboard.

🍽🍷🍱 **Le Bistrot du Dôme** – 1 r. Delambre. Ⓜ*Vavin.* ✆*01 43 35 32 00 or 01 43 21 40 64. Daily noon–2.30pm, 7.30pm–11pm.* The menu here changes daily depending on the catch of the day. There are always 7 starters, 7 mains and 7 desserts.

VAUGIRARD

🍽🍷 **L'Infinithé** – 8 r. Desnouettes. Ⓜ*Convention.* ✆*01 40 43 14 23. www.infinithe.com. Closed Sun (except first Sun of the month), Mon and eves. Lunch menu.* This charming tearoom has perfectly captured the 1930s retro spirit. The atmosphere is cosy and the décor refined: wood panelled walls, Cupboards, pedestal tables and vintage sugar bowls all found at the flea markets. Delicious pastries, and for lunch there are home made dishes and savoury tarts.

🍽🍷 **Le Mûrier** – 42 r. Olivier de Serres. Ⓜ*Convention.* ✆*01 45 32 81 88. Closed 9–23 Aug, Sat noon and Sun.* A nice little place to stop for a quick bite while shopping around the rue de la Convention. The dining room is decorated with old posters of traditional recipes.

🍽🍷 **Du Marché** – 59 r. Dantzig. Ⓜ*Porte de Versailles.* ✆*01 48 28 31 55. Closed Aug, Sun–Mon.* Situated not far from the Parc Georges-Brassens, this pleasant bistro decorated in 1950s style has a loyal following for its unfussy French cooking.

🍽🍷🍱 **Afaria** – 15 r. Desnouettes. Ⓜ*Convention.* ✆*01 48 42 95 90. Closed 2–24 Aug, 23–28 Dec, Sun–Mon noon.* Creative and carefully prepared dishes are the hallmark of this restaurant with a pleasant bistro décor (wine list written on the mirrors, Basque-style striped napkins). Aperitifs and tapas at the bar are also available.

JAVEL– ANDRÉ–CITROËN

🍽🍷 **L'Os à Moelle** – 3 r. Vasco de Gama. Ⓜ*Lourmel.* ✆*01 45 57 27 27. Closed Sun–Mon.* A haven for foodies. In a tiny but sunny dining room, clients choose their meal from the slateboard.

🍽🍷 **La Dînée** – 85 r. Leblanc. Ⓜ*Balard.* ✆*01 45 54 20 49. www.restaurant-ladinee.com. Closed Sat–Sun.* This stylish restaurant with the contemporary artworks features modern French cuisine. More casual tapas-style food served in the bistro next door.

🍽🍷🍱🍱 **Maison Kaiseki** – 7 r. André Lefebvre. Ⓜ *Balard.* ✆ *01 45 54 48 60. www.kaiseki.com.* An atypical restaurant-with-laboratory, sometimes puzzling, with a new take on Japanese cuisine by an extremely creative chef. The decoration is minimalist and the large tables are communal. A strange experience for first-timers.

AUTEUIL

🍽🍷 **Le Petit Boileau** – 98 r. Boileau. Ⓜ*Exelmans or Porte de St Cloud.* ✆*01 42 88 59 05. Closed Sun, Mon.* A restaurant specializing in "terroir" cuisine where the regulars come to dine in a convivial atmosphere. A husband-wife team cover both the kitchen and the dining room. Interesting selection of wines.

🍽🍷🍱 **A et M Restaurant** – 136 bd Murat. Ⓜ*Porte de St Cloud.* ✆*01 45 27 39 60. www.am-restaurant.com.* This popular "Chef's Bistro" just a few steps from the Seine River has a contemporary décor, in cream and tobacco tones, designer lighting and cuisine reflecting the latest trends.

🍽🍷🍱 **Chaumette** – 7 r. Gros. Ⓜ*Mirabeau.* ✆*01 42 88 29 27. www.restaurantchaumette.fr. Closed Sat lunch and Sun.* This attractive old bistro is just like one sees in the movies with dark wood panelling, tables in a line, and the long counter. The chic locals appreciate the carefully prepared traditional cooking.

🍽🍷🍱 **Rosimar** – 26 r. Poussin. Ⓜ*Michel Ange Auteuil.* ✆*01 45 27 74 91. www.restaurant-rosimar.com. Closed 1 Jan, Aug, holidays, Mon–Tue eves, Sat lunch, and Sun.* This small restaurant enlarged by a wall of mirrors specializes in all the traditional flavours of Spain. A great little family establishment.

PASSY

◷◷ **Le Bistrot des Vignes** – *1 r. Jean Bologne.* Ⓜ*La Muette.* ℘*01 45 27 76 64. www.bistrotdesvignes.fr.* 🅿. Here is a wonderful little bistro in which to enjoy a leisurely meal. The colourful décor and stained wood furnishings gives it a warm atmosphere and the cuisine from Provence and the Aveyron region is remarkable. The young team are friendly and efficient.

◷◷◷◷ **La Gare** – *19 chaussée de la Muette.* Ⓜ*La Muette.* ℘*01 42 15 15 31. www.restaurantlagare.com. Daily noon–3pm, 7pm–11.30pm.* ♿. The old Passy-La Muette Train Station, built in 1854 along the Petite Ceinture railway, is now home to this atypical restaurant. The tables are arranged around the former platform, and the bar-lounge has been set up in the old waiting room. Traditional French cuisine and décor.

BOIS DE BOULOGNE

◷–◷◷ **Le Jardin d'Acclimatation** – *Bois de Boulogne, carrefour des Sablons.* Ⓜ*Sablons or Porte Maillot. www.jardin dacclimatation.fr.* ♿. The Jardin d'Acclimatation has over seven family friendly restaurants, some open on weekends and some all week: the **La Grande Verriere** features hearty salads, burgers, and daily entrées. **Le Pavillon des Oiseaux** serves family-friendly cuisine and brunch on Sundays. **Le Petit Pavillon** offers daily menus for the whole family, while **La Creperie de la Petite Ferme** offers savoury and sweet crepes as well as salads. **La Salon de Thé Angelina** is a perfect place for a tea break or a light lunch of quiche, sandwiches, and salads. Check the website for opening times.

◷◷◷ **Les Jardins de Bagatelle** – *Parc de Bagatelle, rte. de Sèvres.* ℘*01 40 67 98 29. www.bagatellelerestaurant.com. No dinner Fri–Sun. Daily noon–3pm (lunch), 3pm–6pm (tea), Mon-Thu 7pm–11pm (dinner).* ♿. Right in the heart of the Parc de Bagatelle, this pretty pavilion with a large shaded terrace is open for family meals or afternoon snacks.

MONTMARTRE

◷◷ **L'Été en Pente Douce** – *8r. Paul-Albert.* Ⓜ*Anvers or Château Rouge.* ℘*01 42 64 02 67. www.parisresto.com. Daily.* ♿. From Sacré-Cœur Basilica, go down the steps to this little street where tables on the shaded terrace of this former bakery now offer a great setting across from a leafy park for a restaurant and tearoom.

◷◷ **La Mère Catherine** – *6 pl. du Tertre.* Ⓜ *Abbesses.* ℘*01 46 06 32 69. www.lamerecatherine.com. Daily noon-midnight.* A Montmartre institution. And for good reason. Aside from its legendary location, this 17C house once welcomed Danton and his Revolutionary disciples.

◷◷ **Le Cave Gourmande** – *96 r. des Martyrs.* Ⓜ*Abbesses.* ℘*01 46 06 10 34.* Classic and simple Fernch cuisine that changes daily on a chalkboard menu and the market-driven menu make this a popular bistro near the Parc des Buttes-Chaumontin the heart of Montmartre. Fun atmosphere.

◷◷ **Le Templier de Montmartre** – *9 r. des Abbesses.* Ⓜ*Abbesses.* ℘*01 42 54 88 64. www.letemplierdemontmartre.com. Daily.* A little terrace on the pavement, across from the place des Abbesses, precedes a cosy dining room (brick and wood, low lighting, some paintings on the walls) at this establishment. The daily specials are written on the slateboard. Live jazz music every Thursday.

◷◷◷ **Bistro Poulbot** – *39 r. Lamarck.* Ⓜ*Lamarck Caulaincourt.* ℘*01 46 06 86 00. www.bistropoulbot.fr. Tue–Sat noon– 2pm, 7:30pm–10pm. Closed Aug, Sun, Mon.* The name of this bistro evokes the street kids of Montmartre immortalized by the artist Poulbot in the early 1900s. New owners and a convivial setting, with a traditional menu and more elaborate dishes at dinner.

◷◷◷ **Le Café qui Parle** – *24 r. Caulaincourt.* Ⓜ*Lamarck Caulaincourt.* ℘*01 46 06 06 88. www.lecafequiparle.fr. Mon–Fri noon–3pm, 7.30pm–11pm, Sat 10am–4pm, 7.30pm–11pm, no dinner Sun.* In a convivial atmosphere you'll discover cuisine anchored in the classics brought up to date with a talented touch of modernity. The décor is modern with chocolate tones, and art expositions. Brunch on Sunday.

🍽🍽🍽 **Le Vieux Chalet** – *14 bis r. Norvins.* Ⓜ*Abbesses.* ☎*01 46 06 21 44. 12.30pm–2.30pm, 7.30pm–11.30pm. Closed 25 Dec–Mar, Sun eve and Mon.* ♿🍽. Eating well without going broke just 50 metres from the busy place du Tertre is indeed possible. Enter this 100-year-old inn with the country atmosphere and a wonderful courtyard garden terrace far from the crowds, just like former regulars Apollinaire and Picasso.

🍽🍽🍽 **Le Moulin de la Galette** – *83 r. Lepic.* Ⓜ*Abbesses.* ☎*01 46 06 84 77. www.lemoulindelagalette.fr. Daily noon–11pm.* A windmill from 1622, then the setting of a popular dance hall (bal populaire) immortalized by Renoir and Toulouse-Lautrec, this establishment has been restructured with an inviting bistro menu and green terrace.

🍽🍽🍽 **Miroir** – *94 r. des Martyrs.* Ⓜ*Abbesses.* ☎*01 46 06 50 73. www. restaurantmiroir.com. Daily noon–2pm, 7.30pm–10pm.* At the head of this bistro is a young, professional team. A contemporary setting, with one dining room lit by a skylight, and a slateboard menu inspired by the seasonal market.

LA VILLETTE

🍽🍽🍽 **Au Bœuf Couronné** – *188 av. Jean Jaurès.* Ⓜ*Porte de Pantin.* ☎*01 42 39 44 44. www.boeuf-couronne.com. Daily noon–3pm, 7pm–midnight.* Unflagging success for this institution located across from the former Halles de la Villette. The cuisine is copious (especially the meat dishes), the service friendly, and the décor retro.

🍽🍽🍽 **La Violette** – *11 av. Corentin Cariou.* Ⓜ*Corentin Cariou.* ☎*01 40 35 20 45. www.restaurant-laviolette.fr. Mon–Sat 11.30am–2.45, 7pm–10.45pm. No dinner Mon, no lunch Sat. Closed Sun. Covers limited, reserve.* Friendly welcome, convivial setting and trendy décor (black and white, with violet banquettes and walls covered in wine crates), and tasty, modern cuisine.

LES BUTTES-CHAUMONT

🍽 **Le Fleuve Rouge** – *1 r. Pradier.* Ⓜ*Pyrénées or Belleville.* ☎*01 42 06 25 04. Daily 11.30pm–3pm, 7pm–11pm.* It's no surprise that this simple restaurant is unanimously adored by all of the locals, because it always has a convivial atmosphere. The home-cooked cuisine is served in generous portions, with Vietnamese dishes on order. Service with a smile.

🍽🍽 **L'Hermès** – *23 r. Mélingue.* Ⓜ*Pyrénées.* ☎*01 42 39 94 70. Closed Sun evening and Mon.* Delicious country atmosphere with ochre walls, wood furnishings and floral napkins. Generous bistro cuisine listed on slateboards. A great address with a Guinguette-style setting.

🍽🍽 **L'Heure Bleue** – *57 r. Arthur Rozier.* Ⓜ*Botzaris.* ☎*01 42 45 96 55.* You'll need to go up a few steps to reach the dining room at this restaurant decorated with parquet wood flooring, and lovely bistro-style wooden counter and furnishings. Traditional French cuisine with a few vegetarian dishes, jazzy atmosphere and convivial atmosphere.

🍽🍽 **Nakagawa** – *9 r. Lassus.* Ⓜ*Jourdain.* ☎*01 42 08 43 22. www. restaurant-nakagawa.com. Mon–Sat 11.30am–10pm. Closed Sun.* This excellent Japanese restaurant has several little branches in the 20th arrondissement. The dining room is bright if not particularly charming, but the sushi, sashimi, soba and tempura are tasty and fresh.

BELLEVILLE

🍽 **Le Baratin** – *3 r. Jouye Rouve.* Ⓜ*Pyrénées.* ☎*01 43 49 39 70. Noon–16.30pm, 6pm–1am. Closed Aug.* Just a few steps from the Parc de Belleville and its Chinese restaurants, this popular wine bar with traditional French cuisine is frequented by many of the neighbourhood's artists whose studios are nearby.

⊜ **Le Pacifique** – *35 r. de Belleville.* Ⓜ *Belleville.* ☎ *01 42 49 66 80. Daily 11am–2am.* In the heart of Belleville, this Chinese restaurant is a favourite with both the locals and Asians who come for the dumplings and other typical dishes. The dining room has large bay windows overlooking the busy street. Open until 2am.

⊜ **Le Vieux-Belleville** – *12 r. des Envierges.* Ⓜ *Pyrénées.* ☎ *01 44 62 92 66. www.le-vieux-belleville.com. Mon–Sat 11am–3pm, 8pm–2am. Closed Sun.* This wine bar is known for its convivial atmosphere: every night the guests sing along at their tables in spontaneous choirs and the accordion makes the rounds on Friday and Saturday nights. Open until 2am.

⊜⊜ **Le Zéphyr** – *1 r. du Jourdain.* Ⓜ *Jourdain.* ☎ *01 46 36 65 81. Daily 8am–2am.* Discover Paris of the 1930s in this pretty period bistro with Art Deco dining room (Cubist frescoes, wood panelling and period light fixtures). Often packed with locals who enjoy the friendly atmosphere and inventive cuisine.

LE PÈRE-LACHAISE

⊜⊜ **Café Charbon** – *109 r. Oberkampf.* Ⓜ*Parmentier or St-Maur.* ☎ *01 43 57 55 13. Daily 9am–1am.* A neighbourhood institution appreciated for its superb dining room decorated with booths, retro light fixtures, Art Nouveau mirrors and vintage-tile floors. Come for a drink, a coffee, a brasserie-style meal or Sunday brunch.

⊜⊜ **Café Justine** – *96 r. Oberkampf.* Ⓜ*Parmentier.* ☎ *01 43 57 44 03. Daily 8am–2am.* There's a young, festive atmosphere in this trendy café with the cosy, wood-panelled décor that occupies two floors. There's a brasserie menu with classics and top-quality steaks.

⊜⊜⊜ **Le Bistrot des Soupirs "Chez les On"** – *49 r. de la Chine.* Ⓜ *Gambetta.* ☎ *01 44 62 93 31. Closed Aug, Sun–Mon.* This great litle bistro with the oak counter features an eclectic menu of dishes (there's even game in season), and an interesting selection of wines from independent growers.

⊜⊜⊜ **Les Allobroges** – *71 r. Grands-Champs.* Ⓜ *Maraîchers.* ☎ *01 43 73 40 00. www.lesallobroges.com. Closed Sun eve and Mon.* Get off the beaten path and come in here to discover this great little restaurant near the Porte de Montreuil. Simple yet pretty décor and a new chef preparing modern cuisine in generous portions.

LA DÉFENSE

⊜⊜ – ⊜⊜⊜ **Quai Marine** – *Au Cnit: 2 pl. de la Défense. 92800 Puteaux.* ☎ *01 46 92 13 70. Mon–Fri noon–3pm (lunch only).* This restaurant gives the CNIT tower a breath of fresh nautical air. The elegant décor mixes design elements with light wood panelling. Popular with the office workers and executives at La Défense for the relaxing atmosphere and traditional fish dishes.

⊜⊜⊜ **Globe-Trotter Café** – *16 pl. de la Défense. 92000 La Défense.* ☎ *01 55 91 96 96. www.globetrottercafe.com. Daily 7.30am–11.30am (café), lunch noon–2.30pm (restaurant).* ♿. Located in the heart of the towers of La Défense, facing La Grande Arche, this original restaurant will take you around the globe with its exotic, tasty dishes and international wine menu. A large dining room under the veranda, with a terrace overlooking the monumental Agam fountain.

LE MARCHÉ AUX PUCES DE SAINT-OUEN

☞ **Café Le Paul Bert** – *20 r. Paul Bert (at the Marché aux Puces). 93400 St-Ouen. ☏01 40 11 90 28. Sat–Mon and Thu 7.30am–6pm, Fri 5:30am–6pm. Closed Tue–Wed.* Tucked between two boutiques in the heart of the St-Ouen flea market, this old-fashioned brasserie with the retro décor is a favourite for anyone nostalgic for the 1930s jazz atmosphere. Traditional French dishes include a remarkable onion soup.

☞ **Le P'tit Landais** – *96 r. des Rosiers. 93400 St-Ouen. ☏01 49 45 11 55/☏06 21 02 17 67. Lunch daily except Tue. Open Sat eve.* Offers classic French and Italian specialties.

☞🍽 **Brasserie Biron** – *102 av. Michelet. 93400 St-Ouen. ☏01 40 11 18 72. www. brasseriebiron.com.* Serving up fresh market fare (charcuterie and cheeses, oysters, homemade terrines, classic dishes such as grilled steak with chanterelles, tarte Tatin, and a fine selection of house wines) along with a rich program of live music.

VERSAILLES

☞🍽🍽 **La Flotille** – *Parc du Château. Grand Canal. 78000 Versailles. ☏01 39 51 41 58. www.laflotille.fr. Open for lunch daily. Closed eves except during night festivals.* ♿🅿. Overlooking the Grand Canal, in the park of the château, this 19C pavillion with the *guinguette* atmosphere is brightened by a large skylight and a huge terrace. Three options are available to diners: formal restaurant, brasserie or tearoom. The food is nothing to write home about, but the setting is worth the stop.

CHANTILLY

☞🍽🍽 **Aux Goûters Champêtres** – *Le Hameau, Château de Chantilly. 60500 Chantilly. ☏03 44 57 46 21. www.domainedechantilly.com. Open Mar–Nov Wed–Mon noon–6pm.* Dining in Chantilly's park in the heart of the hamlet of the same name offers classic French cuisine, such as duck confit, and certainly, desserts topped with the famous Chantilly cream at the place of its birth.

☞🍽🍽 **La Capitainerie** – *Château de Chantilly. 60500 Chantilly. ☏03 44 57 15 89. www.domainedechantilly.com. Lunch 12.45am–5.45pm during the Château's opening times (Mar–Nov Wed–Mon Apr–Oct daily 10am–6pm).* 🅿. Set under the arches of 17C chef François Vatel's kitchen, La Capitainerie offers fresh seasonal produce and traditional French fare, including grilled fish, lamb, steaks and quail. Outside seating on the terrace in good weather.

Nightlife

LE GRAND LOUVRE

Café Marly – *93 rue de Rivoli, 1st arr.*
℘01 49 26 06 60. Daily. Located in the
Richelieu wing of the Louvre Museum,
this stylish café is a great place to
enjoy pre-dinner apéritifs or late-night
cocktails. From the terrace under the
arcades, there's a view over the pyramid.

Le Fumoir – *6 rue de l'Amiral de Coligny,
1st arr. ℘01 42 92 00 24. www.lefumoir.
com. Closed late Dec.* The bar at this chic
restaurant has an excellent cocktail
menu. Happy Hour attracts a well-
dressed crowd for the large selection of
martinis. A few Chesterfield sofas and
wide bay windows overlook the Louvre
and the Église St-Germain l'Auxerrois.

BEAUBOURG

Andy Wahloo – *69 rue des Gravilliers,
3rd arr. ℘01 42 71 20 38. http://andy
wahloo-bar.com. Closed Sun-Mon.*
This intimate Moroccan-themed bar
decorated with Middle Eastern pop
art attracts a hip, fashionista crowd,
many of whom drop in for cocktails
and tapas before heading out to the
popular Moroccan restaurant, **404**, right
next door, or the French restaurant
Derrière, through the rear courtyard.
A DJ gets the crowd dancing in the
small space late on weekends.

L'Imprévu – *9 rue Quincampoix, 4th
arr. ℘01 42 78 23 50. Daily. Closed
Sun-Mon.* L'Imprévu is an eclectic, cosy
bar with a warren of rooms décorated
with mismatched flea market finds.
The vibe here is casual and relaxed,
but the place is always packed with
clientèle as colourful as the setting.
There's a large menu of cocktails and
small savory dishes for light appetites.

LES HALLES

Le Ballroom du Beef Club – *58 rue
Jean-Jacques Rousseau, 1st arr. ℘09 52
52 89 34. Daily 7pm-5am.* A well-hidden
cocktail bar opened by the owners of
the Experimental Cocktail Club, the
Ballroom sits in the cellar of the Beef
Club restaurant: look for the unmarked
door to the left of the entrance (there
may be a doorman blocking it).

The décor Is low-lit, Prohibition-era
speakeasy cosy, with a very stylish,
hipster crowd.

Duc des Lombards – *42 rue des
Lombards, 1st arr. ℘01 42 33 22 88.
www.ducdeslombards.com. Open
daily 8/10pm, concert, 9pm.* Modern
jazz has pride of place in this small
club and restaurant on the corner of
boulevard Sébastopol. Some of its
regulars have included the pianist
Martial Solal, bass player Henri Texier,
saxophonist Steve Lacy and drummer
Aldo Romano. Free entry for the Friday
and Saturday late-night jam sessions.

O-Château – *68 rue Jean-Jacques
Rousseau, 1st arr. ℘01 44 73 97 80.
www.o-chateau.com. Daily 4pm–
midnight.* The wine bar of the famous
wine-tasting school serves 40 wines by
the glass and gourmet dishes or nibbles
for big or small appetites. The crowd
Is all ages, laid-back, international.

Sunside/Sunset – *60 rue des Lombards.
1st arr. ℘01 40 26 46 60. www.sunset-
sunside.com. Daily.* One of the hotspots
for Parisian jazz, the intimate Sunside
(upstairs) and Sunset (downstairs) host
nightly concerts by musicians from
around the world. All types of jazz,
from the 1940s up until today.

OBERKAMPF

Café Charbon – *109 rue Oberkampf,
11th arr. ℘01 43 57 55 13. Daily.
DJ from 10pm.* This former early 20C
theatre café (which also used to sell
coal – hence the name) is one of the
district's most popular venues. In a
high-ceilinged room, with tall mirrors
and a long bar, a young, arty crowd
flocks here for a dinner and late-night
drinks. Live electronic and rock music
acts and DJs from 10pm in the
Nouvelle Casino club behind
the café.

L'International – *5-7 rue Moret, 11th
arr. ℘01 42 02 02 05. www.linternational.
fr. Daily 6pm–2am.* Music lovers on a
budget can't get enough of this temple
of music, where every night there
are two or three live acts followed by
a DJ set, no cover, and inexpensive
drinks served in plastic cups. The cellar
setting is industrial garage, with young

bodies packed tightly every night for the international and local pop, rock, electro, and folk musicians.

Le Gibus – *18 rue du Fg-du-Temple, 11th arr. ☎01 47 00 78 88. www.gibus.fr. Closed Sun–Mon.* This former rock temple is now devoted to hip hop and French rock, with a succession of the best DJs around. Trendy but not exclusively "clubby", it is focused first and foremost on dance in a low-ceilinged, concrete setting (for some it is a suffocating garage atmosphere, for others, pure heaven).

LE MARAIS

Le Petit Fer à Cheval – *30 rue Vieille-du-Temple, 4th arr. ☎01 42 72 47 47. www.cafeine.com. Daily.* This delightful little bistro, now a fashionable meeting place, owes its name to its old bar in the shape of a horseshoe. A few tables stand on the pavement. Often packed in the evening with regulars drinking wine and French beers.

Les Étages – *35 rue Vieille-du-Temple, 4th arr. ☎01 42 78 72 00. Daily.* One almost wants to tiptoe into this four-storeyed bar, such is the intimate, almost private atmosphere inside. The succession of amusingly decorated little rooms provides a choice of well-worn sofas where you can enjoy one of the house cocktails or glass of Champagne.

Lizard Lounge – *18 rue Bourg-Tibourg, 4th arr. ☎01 42 72 81 34. www.cheapblonde.com. Daily. Closed 1 week in Aug.* Warm, relaxed and intimate, this establishment clearly favours the American bar style. Food is served upstairs and a DJ mixes tunes for dancers in the cellar bar (no cover charge).

Café Charlot – *38 rue Bretagne, 3rd arr. ☎01 44 54 03 30. www.cafecharlotparis. com. Daily.* This 50s-style neo-bistro opened in a former butcher shop is one of the neighbourhood mainstays in the wildly trendy North Marais district. Locals occupy the zinc bar and large terrace from its opening at 7am until closing at 2am. Classic and contemporary cocktails alongside gourmet burgers and fries.

Mary Celeste– *1 rue Commines, 3rd arr. www.lemaryceleste.com. Daily from 6pm.* At this hipster oyster bar in the North Marais district serving original cocktails, try and secure a spot at the bar later in the evening when the dinner crowd has moved on.

Little Red Door– *60 rue Charlot, 3rd arr. t01 42 71 19 32. http://lrdparis.com. Daily from 6pm.* Inspired by American speakeasy bars of the Prohibition era, this North Marais bar specialises in cocktails. The setting is low-lit and comfortable, with seating at the bar or up in the intimate mezzanine.

MOUFFETARD

Place de la Contrescarpe – *Pl. de la Contrescarpe, 5th arr.* This square is lined with cafés and is always full of rue Mouffetard's colourful, motley crowd, who invade the pretty terraces of the numerous cafés. **Le Café Contrescarpe** and **Café Delmas** have the largest terraces, but the nearby Irlandais, Café des Arts, Le Bateau Ivre and the Mayflower are also lively nightspots for a predominantly student crowd.

LE QUARTIER LATIN

Caveau de la Huchette – *86 rue de la Huchette, 5th arr. ☎01 43 26 65 05. www.caveaudelahuchette.fr. Nightly 9:30pm, no reservations needed.* These historic cellars used by the French revolutionaries have hosted international jazz musicians since 1946. Most people dance in the tiny quarters to jazz, bebop, swing and blues.

Caveau des Oubliettes – *52 rue Galande, 5th arr. ☎01 46 34 23 09. www.caveaudesoubliettes.fr. Daily.* Jazz, funk and blues bands play downstairs *(Tue–Sun nights)* at this low-key Latin Quarter beer pub. Free entry, one-drink minimum. Sports matches on the screens upstairs most nights.

Les Trois Maillets – *56 rue Galande, 5th arr. ☎01 43 54 00 79. www. lestroismailletz.fr. Daily.* A friendly feeling emanates through this former wine cellar where you can stop in for a drink, dinner, piano bar entertainment at 6pm, or even get up on the tables and dance with the cabaret performers from 10.30pm.

SAINT-GERMAIN-DES-PRÉS

Castel – *25 rue de Buci, 6th arr.* 📞*01 43 26 02 93. http://germainparis.com. Daily.* A mythical Parisian club that was past its prime in the 1990s, given a new lease on life from its young, new owners, including one of the Costes brothers. If you can get in (it helps to know one of the members), there's dancing with the well-heeled jetset in the little club downstairs until dawn.

Café Mabillon – *164 blvd St-Germain, 6th arr.* 📞*01 43 26 62 93. Daily.* This stylish St-Germain-des-Prés café attracts a trendy crowd for Happy Hour and is prime people-watching from the pavement terrace seats.

Germain – *15 rue Princesse, 6th arr.* 📞*01 40 51 52 80.* A contemporary brasserie in the heart of St-Germain with black-and-white tile floors, brightly-coloured chairs and a canary yellow oversize sculpture of a woman's lower body (her upper body is on the upper floor) to set the avant-garde mood. Drinks and dining possible all night long, this is a popular "before" spot for a fashionable crowd.

La Rhumerie – *166 blvd St-Germain, 6th arr.* 📞*01 43 54 28 94. www.larhumerie.com. Daily.* Founded in 1932, this establishment specializes in rums from all over the world. Live Caribbean jazz some nights.

ODÉON

La Palette – *43 rue de Seine, 6th arr.* 📞*01 43 26 68 15. www.cafelapaletteparis.com. Daily. Closed 1 week in Feb, 3 weeks in Aug and public holidays.* This is one of St-Germain's best-known bistros: its pleasant provincial Parisian terrace has somewhat invaded the pavement (the regulars always sit in the reserved tables by the entrance). Decorated with paintings and palettes, the influence of the nearby art school is obvious. A great place to enjoy a bottle of wine and a platter of cheese and charcuterie.

Hôtel d'Aubusson (Café Laurent) – *33 rue Dauphine, 6th arr.* 📞*01 43 29 43 43. www.hoteldaubusson.com. Daily.* This

café was very popular among 18C philosophers. Renamed the Café Tabou in 1946, it became one of the favourite haunts of Sartre and Camus. Today a modern room opens on to one of the former period rooms with original beams (1606) and hearthplace. Live jazz Wed-Sat nights from 9pm, Sunday jazz aperitif Sunday from 6.30pm.

Compagnie des Vins Surnaturels – *7 rue Lobineau, 6th arr.* 📞*09 54 90 20 20. www.compagniedesvinssurnaturels.com. Daily from 6pm.* A chic and relaxed wine bar with a young and stylish St-Germain crowd. Wines by the glass or the bottle, along with gourmet bar nibbles like Burrata cheese or Iberian ham with truffle oil. Get there early to secure one of the sofas.

Les Étages Saint-Germain – *5 rue de Buci, 6th arr.* 📞*01 46 34 26 26.* This popular establishment fills out the two floors of an old house, leading visitors through a maze of tiny rooms, all decorated differently. From the second floor, there is a good view of rue de Buci and rue Grégoire-de-Tours. Young clientele, but more conventional than its sister establishment in Le Marais.

Prescription Cocktail Club – *23 rue Mazarine, 6th arr.* 📞*09 50 35 72 87. www.prescriptioncocktailclub.com. Daily from 7pm.* The second bar by the Experimental Cocktail Club group is a cosy and stylish cocktail bar on two levels. Aside from the creative cocktails, they also serve Champagne and whiskys from around the world. DJ from 10pm.

La Mezzanine de l'Alcazar – *62 rue Mazarine, 6th arr.* 📞*01 53 10 19 99. www.alcazar.fr. Tues-Sat.* A chic and festive bar overlooking the contemporary British restaurant Alcazar, where fashionably-dressed men and women come Thursday, Friday and Saturday nights for the live DJ evenings after a quick meal. Surprisingly open and spacious, it's perfect for those who can't stand claustrophobic clubs.

SÈVRES-BABYLONE

La Pagode – *57 bis rue de Babylone, 7th arr.* 📞*01 45 55 48 48.* A unique Parisian cinema built within an authentic 19C

Japanese pagoda imported to France by the rich owner of Le Bon Marché as a gift to his wife. Be sure to see films screened in the Salle Japonaise, which is beautifully preserved.

ALMA

Le Bar du George V – *Four Seasons Hotel 124 rue La-Boétie, 8th arr. Daily. ☎01 42 25 18 06. www.fourseasons.com/ Paris.* Comfortable and luxurious, as you would expect of any bar in a Parisian palace hotel. The cocktails, fine spirits and wines by the glass are priced to savour slowly. Gourmet hors d'oeuvres, club sandwiches and other bar snacks available until midnight.

LE QUAIS

Les Berges – *Port de Solférino to Port de la Bordonnais, 7th arr. www.lesberges. paris.fr.* In 2013 the city transformed an expressway along the Seine's Left Bank into an esplanade for pedestrians, cyclists and joggers open year-round. There are several cafés and bars, particularly around the foot of the Pont Alexandre III, where Parisians of all ages come for sunset drinks, late-night cocktails and clubbing until dawn. Some of the most popular locations are **Faust** (under the bridge), the **Concorde Atlantique** (a boat club), and **Rosa Bonheure sur Seine** (boat bar).

Le Showcase – *Port des Champs-Elysées, 8th arr. www.showcase.fr. Fri-Sat from 11.30pm.* A large techno house and bass club at the foot of the Grand Palais, beneath the Right Bank end of the Pont Alexandre III. Purchase tickets in advance online and get there early to avoid standing in the queue all night.

Wanderlust – *32 quai d'Austerlitz, 13th arr. http://wanderlustparis.com.* Opened in a former concrete warehouse on the eastern end of the Seine River known as Les Docks, Wanderlust is a restaurant, bar, nightclub and open-air cinema with huge wooden terraces overlooking the river. All ages mix here depending on the event, from Happy Hour drinks and food-truck fare to late-night clubbing.

Le Batofar – *Quai François Mauriac, 13th arr. ☎01 53 60 17 30. Mon–Sat 8pm until at least 2am. www.batofar.org.*

This former boat-lighthouse, painted red and moored opposite the François Mitterrand Library, is an invitation to travel around Europe's multiple cultures and forms of musical experimentation (electronic and avant-garde jazz). Visitors walk along the gangplanks, through cosy areas in living room cabins to a dance floor playing house and techno music. Pavement terrace in the summer for drinks and dining.

Dame du Canton – *Quai François Mauriac, 13th arr. ☎01 53 61 08 49. Tue–Sat 7pm–2am, Sat–Sun until 5am. www.damedecanton.com.* Formerly known as the Guinguette du Pirate, this old Chinese junk was retired at the foot of the Bibliothèque François Mitterrand. It's now a popular world music venue, with a cosy "Captain's Quarters" restaurant below deck and a vast terrace on the quay opened in the summer months.

CHAMPS-ÉLYSÉES

Cigare Bar (La Maison Champs Elysées) – *8 rue Jean-Goujon, 8th arr. ☎01 40 74 64 94. www.lamaison champselysees.com. Daily.* Black walls and dark brown leather chairs decorate this elegant cigar bar in the newly opened contemporary hotel, La Maison. Open nightly from 6pm, the bar can be privatized for your own group on request.

L'Arc Club – *12 rue de Presbourg, 16th arr. ☎01 82 28 71 32. www. larc-paris.com. Thu–Sat from 11.30pm.* Completely redone after a fire in 2014, the Arc club attracts a well-heeled, jetsetting international crowd of bankers and models for its nightclub overlooking the Arc de Triomphe. Wear your highest stilettos and a lot of attitude to get past the doorman.

Fouquet's (Barrière) – *99 av. des Champs-Élysées, 8th arr. Ⓜ Georges V. ☎01 47 23 50 00. Daily.* Now a listed monument, Fouquet's has one of the few remaining historical terraces on the Champs-Élysées facing the Louis Vuitton flagship store. It is equally in favour with TV and film celebrities as with the literary world, and the Césars Awards (French film awards) are celebrated here each year. Fouquet's has a brasserie and restaurant menu, but you can also just enjoy drinks on the terrace and watch the world go by.

Mini Palais (Grand Palais) – *5 rue de Presbourg, 16th arr. ☎01 40 67 17 37. Daily.* One of the hottest terraces on the Champs Elysées is actually in the Grand Palais, with its immense Imperial columns and views of the Seine and the majestic Pont Alexandre III. Open until 2am for dining or cocktails.

Sir Winston – *avenue Winston Churchill, 8th arr. ☎01 42 56 42 42. www.sirwinston.fr. Daily.* This large bar-restaurant stands behind a very British-looking façade. The interior decoration has combined a whole host of influences: a Chinese room, a leopard lounge in the basement and small private booths. The place is bathed in soft lights, world music rhythms. Live music and DJs Monday-Saturday evenings.

OPÉRA

Harry's New York Bar – *5 rue Daunou, 2nd arr. ☎01 42 61 71 14. www.harrys-bar.fr. Daily. Closed 24–25 Dec.* Forever popular with Parisian expatriate Americans and all those keen on Bloody Marys and Side Cars (just don't try ordering beer or wine). Piano bar downstairs Tuesday–Saturday nights.

PALAIS ROYAL

Bar 228 at Le Meurice – *228 rue de Rivoli, 1st arr. ☎01 44 58 10 10. www.le meurice.com. Daily.* This Parisian palace hotel bar across from the Tuilleries Gardens is sober and luxurious, with wood panelling, leather armchairs and a fine selection of whiskies, malts, Cognac and Armagnac all served in crystal glasses. Try the Cocktail Starcky, named for the bar's designer Philippe Starck, or the Italian bartender's perfect Bellini.

Bar de l'Hôtel Costes – *239 rue St-Honoré, 1st arr. ☎01 42 44 50 25. www.hotel costes.com. Daily.* In what is one of the capital's smartest addresses, a maze of little rooms provides a variety of styles, ranging from Second Empire to Mediterranean. The Italian-style patio is popular in the fine weather. In favour

with the capital's cosmopolitan jet-set, who flock here to see and be seen. Don't even try to get in during Fashion Week.

Café Ruc – *159 rue St-Honoré, 1st arr. ☎01 42 60 97 54. Daily.* This purple-coloured café/restaurant overlooking the busy place Malraux is a favourite among tourists and members of the Comédie Française's troupe, who meet here for tea, a glass of wine or a late supper. Served in a tasteful, but unpretentious décor. It owes its name to one of its early owners.

The VIP Room – *188 bis rue de Rivoli, 1st arr. ☎01 42 61 64 00. www.viproom.fr. Closed Sun-Mon.* This modern dance complex on two floors moved from its former location on the Champs-Elysées to this spot in 2010. Very fashionable with the bling-bling jet-set. The clientele are in their 20s and 30s, and DJs come from around the world. Italian restaurant on the top floor.

Au Caveau Montpensier – *15 rue de Montpensier, 1st arr. ☎01 42 60 12 89. Closed Sun.* A historic bar given a contemporary makeover, this little hole-in-the-wall behind the Palais Royal gardens is a casual and friendly place to enjoy craft beers, cocktails and tapas, open nightly from 5.30pm.

MADELEINE

Le Baudelaire Bar – *Burgundy Hotel, 6-8 rue Duphot, 1st arr. ☎01 42 60 34 12 . www.leburgundy.com. Daily.* A sexy, elegant hotel bar just around the corner from the Rue St-Honoré's fashion boutiques. Plush violet carpeting, comfortable velour-covered chairs and a ceiling fresco inspired by Beaudelaire's Fleurs du Mal create a relaxing and sensual setting for cocktails or Champagne with your date.

Le Forum – *4 blvd. Malesherebes, 8th arr. ☎01 42 65 37 86. www.bar-le-forum.com. Closed Sun.* First opened in 1918 and run by the same family since 1923, this bar has a New York men's club feel with its wood-panelled walls and leather chairs. Serious whiskys and cocktails are served here in a friendly but serious atmosphere – don't dare pull out your smartphone or show up in shorts! Popular with the neighbourhood's business crowd for apéro hour.

LES GRANDS BOULEVARDS

Max Linder Panorama – *24 blvd. Poissonière, 9th arr.* Ⓜ*Grands Boulevards. www.maxlinder.com.* For more than a century this independent Parisian cinema has been showing the latest films in its vast, panoramic screening room on three levels, able to hold up to 560 spectators. Many avant-premières, so be sure to look for "VO" for foreign films in their original language with French subtitles.

Le Rex Club – *5 blvd Poissonière, 2nd arr.* ☏*01 42 36 10 96.* Ⓜ*Bonne Nouvelle. www.rexclub.com.* Some of the greatest electronic DJs in the world have played at Le Rex over the past 20 years, including Daft Punk, Laurent Garnier and Justice. They still have a solid schedule of electro, tech, house and minimal stars alongside up-and-coming talent, and a refreshingly all-inclusive door policy.

Silencio – *142 rue Montmartre, 2nd arr.* ☏*01 40 13 12 33.* Ⓜ*Grands Boulevards. www.silencio-club.com. Tue–Sat from midnight.* David Lynch's private club for the cultural elite opens to the general public after midnight (assuming the doorman likes your look -- go for "arty"), with two bars, a stage and a dance floor.

SENTIER

La Conserverie – *37 bis rue du Sentier, 2nd arr.* ☏*01 42 26 14 94.* Ⓜ*Bonne Nouvelle. www.laconserveriebar.com. Closed Sun.* In the usually quiet street of textile wholesalers, this bar has an almost theatrical, artfully scruffy atmosphere with ist old wooden floors, mismatched furnishings, jewel-toned walls, and old mason jars transformed into lighting (before it was cool, of course). Cocktails and dinner menu from 8pm, DJ from 10pm on weekends.

Club Rayé – *26 rue Dussoubs, 2nd arr.* ☏*01 40 13 72 93.* Ⓜ*Etienne Marcel or Sentier. www.clubraye.com. Tue–Sat 5.30pm–midnight.* An Art Deco-styled piano bar near the trendy Montorgueil district, with a large white grand piano on the ground level and two more intimate spaces downstairs. Nightly performers, full cocktail bar and gourmet cuisine for dining with your music. No cover.

Experimental Cocktail Club – *37 rue Saint Sauveur, 2nd arr.* ☏*01 45 08 88 09.* Ⓜ*Etienne Marcel or Sentier. www. experimentalcocktailclub.fr. Closed Sun.* This is the spot where the craft cocktail revolution took off in Paris back in 2007, birthing an empire that now reaches New York, London and Ibizia. The space istelf is tiny and unassuming, with exposed brick walls and large black Chesterfield sofas in the back. Be there early to get in before the crowd arrives.

PIGALLE

Dirty Dick – *10 rue Frochot, 9th arr.* Ⓜ*Pigalle.* A Polynesian-themed bar in a former "hostess bar" from Pigalle's seedier bygone days. Tropical cocktails (Zombies and daiquiris, for example) are served in tiki cups or giant conch shells in a fabulously kitsch atmosphere, adored by the local hipsters.

Le Louxor – *170 blvd. de Magenta, 10th arr.* ☏*01 44 63 96 98.* Ⓜ*Barbès-Rochechouart. www.cinemalouxor.fr.* First opened in 1921, this Egyptian-themed cinema in the colourful Barès district has been completely restored and re-opened after being abandoned for many years. There are three screening rooms, one with a mezzanine and one with a starry-sky Intimacy. And instead of a generic snack stand, there's a real bar serving fine wines and gourmet snacks on the top floor with views of Sacré-Coeur

La Machine du Moulin Rouge – *90 blvd. de Clichy, 18th arr.* ☏*01 53 41 88 89.* Ⓜ*Blanche. www.lamachine dumoulinrouge.com. Daily.* Just next door to the Moulin Rouge, the former Loco is now dedicated to live bands and DJs, mostly French and European acts. There are three main areas, the Champagne Bar à Bulles, Le Central main space where the largest events takes place, and La Chaufferie (Boiler Room), a smaller space where live acts perform.

Le Monseigneur – *94 rue d'Amsterdam, 9th arr.* Ⓜ*St-Lazare. www.monseigneurparis.com.* Closer to the Gare St-Lazare, this 1930s Russian cabaret has been resurrected as a popular dance club with disco, techno, and hip-hop tunes, album release parties, and live concerts.

Le Petit Trianon – *80 blvd. Rochechouart, 18th arr.* 📞*01 44 92 78 08.* Ⓜ*Anvers. www.letrianon.fr.* Another Belle Époque establishment, known as the Café des Artistes, that has been re-opened after 20 years, with a theatre and adjoining café-bar on the street level. Come for dinner or late-night drinks with live DJ on the weekends to entertain a young nightlife crowd.

CANAL SAINT-MARTIN

Chez Prune – *36 rue Beaurepaire, 10th arr.* 📞*01 42 41 30 47. Daily. Closed 1 Jan, 25 Dec.* Situated on the edge of the St-Martin Canal, the retro bistro Chez Prune is a popular hangout with the local youth who come here for snacks or a drink. A selection of unusual paintings hangs on the walls, giving the place a trendy feel.

Hôtel du Nord – *102 quai Jemmapes, 10th arr.* Ⓜ*Jacques-Bonsergent. www.hoteldunord.org. Daily. Closed Sun–Tue.* Not actually a hotel, but a stylish neighbourhood haunt with a well-regarded restaurant and an excellent selections of wine and cocktails at the bar. There are a few tables on the pavement in summer.

Point Ephémère – *200 quai Valmy, 10th arr.* 📞*01 40 34 02 48.* Ⓜ*Juarès. www.pointephemere.org. Mon–Sat until 2am, Sun until 9pm.* A former cement depot turned into a neo-industrial club and bar on the Canal St-Martin. The cheap drinks (think beer in a plastic cup, not craft cocktails) and casual, Inclusive atmosphere attract a young, university crowd. Regular concerts and art shows are always on tap.

La Scène du Canal – *116 quai du Jemmapes, 10th arr.* Ⓜ*Jacques-Bonsergent* 📞*01 48 03 33 22. www.lasceneducanal.com.* Situated on the Canal Saint-Martin, La Scene presents a regular programme of French chanson, pop rock and slam artists. Tuesday evenings are dedicated to female performers.

FAUBOURG SAINT-ANTOINE

Barrio Latino – *46/48 rue du Fg St-Antoine, 12th arr.* Ⓜ*Bastille.* 📞*01 55 78 84 75. www.barrio-latino.com. Daily.* A bit of Havana in the heart of Paris well known by salsa fans. Spread over four levels and connected by a magnificent staircase, this listed building was designed during the 19C by Gustav Eiffel. A tapas bar on the ground floor is open all day and in the evening the place is taken over by a DJ with his exciting bossa nova and salsa rhythms. South American dishes such as Brazilian *feijoada* are offered on the mezzanine while a Cuban bar on the second and a nightclub with a VIP bar on the third should cater for everyone's tastes. Salsa dance lessons Sundays at lunch.

Baron Rouge – *1 rue Théophile Roussel, 12th arr.* Ⓜ*Ledru-Rollin.* 📞*01 43 43 14 32. Mon–Sat 5pm–10pm, Sun until 4pm.* One of the city's best-loved wine bars just off the Marché Aligre, this unpretentious establishment with large wooden barrels serving as tables is a great place to try French wines by the glass and charcuterie with a friendly crowd of locals.

BASTILLE

Place de la Bastille, with its countless brasseries such as Bofinger (opened in 1864), has become a focal point for night-lovers on their way to and from the Marais and the restaurants, cafés, beer cellars, wine bars and nightclubs of the rue de Charonne, rue de la Roquette, rue de Lappe, rue St-Sabin and rue Keller.

Café des Phares – *7 pl. de la Bastille, 11th arr.* Ⓜ*Bastille.* 📞*01 42 72 04 700. www.cafe-philo-des-phares.info.* It was here that the philosopher Marc Sautet (now deceased) created the first Parisian *café philo* (philosophy café). Still very popular, it is particularly crowded on Sunday mornings when budding philosophers congregate. Pleasant terrace at all hours.

Le China – *50 rue de Charenton, 12th arr.* Ⓜ*Ledru-Rollin.* 📞*01 43 46 08 09. www. lechina.eu. Daily.* Welcome to Shanghai circa 1930. A neighbourhood classic, Le China is a stylish, Colonial-style Asian restaurant with a sexy cocktail bar and an underground music club with live funk, jazz, soul and folk acts. No cover, one drink minimum.

Check their Facebook page for the updated schedule (zouk, salsa, etc.). All age groups. Smoking room.

Le Balajo – *9 rue de Lappe, 11th arr.* Ⓜ*Ledru-Rollin.* ℰ*01 47 00 07 87. www.balajo.fr. Mon (Tea Dance 3pm–7pm), Tue (Salsa), Wed (Swing), Thurs (Cuban Salsa), Fri– Sat (dancefloor).* Founded in 1936 by Georges France (aka Jo), Balajo's is the oldest musette dance hall in Paris. Its old-fashioned atmosphere and preference for hits from the 1950s, 1960s and 1970s continue to attract crowds of all ages.

Pause Café – *41 rue de Charonne, 11th arr.* Ⓜ*Ledru-Rollin.* ℰ*01 48 06 80 33. Closed 25 Dec.* A traditional café with a fine U-shaped bar in the centre of the room. The soft lighting and subdued atmosphere make it a pleasant place for a quiet read. Evenings it's more lively with a young, locals crowd enjoying the cocktails.

BERCY
Bercy Village – *28 rue François Truffaut,12th arr.* Ⓜ*Cour St-Emilion. www.bercyvillage.com. Daily.* Once the hub of the Paris wine-bottling district, this pedestrian-only village is located in the renovated stone wine warehouses known as chais. Today it's a pleasant place to spend the day, with shops, cafés and cinema, and in the evening there's a lively atmosphere on the terrace cafés and wine bars. In the summer there are regular live open-air music performances.

LES GOBELINS
The Butte-aux-Cailles is a lively, bohemian style district and abounds with little bars, cafés and restaurants.
La Folie en Tête – *33 rue de la Butte-aux-Cailles, 13th arr.* Ⓜ*Corvisart.* ℰ*01 45 80 65 99. http://lafolieentete.wix.com/lesite. Closed Sun.* The musical instruments hung on the walls keep watch over this pleasant spot where visitors can play chess, draw, discuss or listen to music. Young crowd.

PORT-ROYAL
La Closerie des Lilas – *171 blvd du Montparnasse, 6th arr.* Ⓜ*Vavin or Port Royal.* ℰ*01 40 51 34 50. www.closeriedeslilas.fr. Daily 11am–1.30am.*

This historic institution may at first seem intellectual, snobbish or intimidating, but it is in fact quite charming. Its wood panelled piano bar and sheltered terrace exude a warm, intimate atmosphere. Although all that remains of Sartre or Hemingway are their names engraved into their favourite spots at the bar, it continues to be popular with some of Paris' literary names of today.

Café Universel – *267 rue St-Jacques, 5th arr.* Ⓜ*Luxembourg or Port Royal.* ℰ*01 43 25 74 20. www.cafeuniversel.com. Closed Sun.* A popular jazz, swing, soul and blues club with live acts Tue-Sat in a somewhat kitsch setting near the Luxembourg Gardens.

MONTPARNASSE
Charlie Birdy – *84 blvd Montparnasse, 14th arr.* Ⓜ*Montparnasse. Daily until 2am, Sat–Sun until 5am.* ℰ*01 40 64 88 00. www.charliebirdy.com.* This large Anglo-American sports pub with comfy booths attracts a young, cheerful crowd. Live jazz and blues music as well as major sporting events on big screens. Good-quality hamburgers, and a large selection of beers and cocktails. More of a clubbing atmosphere at the Rue du Commerce location near the Eiffel Tower.

Le Rosebud – *11 bis rue Delambre, 14th arr.* Ⓜ*Vavin.* ℰ*01 43 35 38 54. Daily. Closed Aug, Christmas and New Year.* Located in a smart street near Montparnasse, this unassuming bar with the illustrious hustory is a favourite of the locals and longtime expats. White-coated waiters take a bit of time warming up to new faces, but the cocktails and hearty bistro fare are worth it.

Le Select – *99 blvd du Montparnasse, 14th arr.* Ⓜ*Vavin.* ℰ*01 45 48 65 27. www.leselectmontparnasse.fr. Daily. Closed Christmas.* An Art Deco institution, it was *the* place for artists and intellectuals when it first opened in 1924. Next door to other flashier brasseries, the Select has retained a quiet, intimate feel.

Perfoming Arts

THEATRE

Comédie-Française – *Pl. Colette.*
Ⓜ*Palais Royal.* ☎*01 44 58 15 15. www.
comedie-francaise.fr. Tickets: 11am–6pm
Closed end Jul–Sept and 1 May.* Founded
in 1860 by Louis XIV, the repertoire
consists principally of traditional
drama composed by the classical
French playwrights. Theatregoers can
admire the famous seated figure of
Voltaire by Houdon in the public foyer,
as well as the chair in which Molière
himself fell ill while playing *Le Malade
Imaginaire* on 17 February 1673.

Kiosque Théâtre – *Pl. de la Madeleine.*
Ⓜ*Madeleine. Tue–Sat 12.30pm–8pm,
Sun 12.30–4pm.* 🎫. Theatre tickets
can be bought here on the day of the
performance for half the normal price
(for the most expensive shows). You
can choose from over 100 shows and
120 plays (more private than state-run
theatres). Go with alternative choices
in mind, as you may not get what you
want. No credit cards.

La Cartoucherie – *Rte du Champ-de-
Manœuvres, Bois de Vincennes.* Ⓜ*Chateau
de Vincennes.* ☎*01 43 74 88 50 or 43 74
24 08. www.cartoucherie.fr.* This group of
theatres of five independent playhouses
(Théâtre du Soleil, Théâtre du Chaudron,
Épée de Bois, Théâtre de l'Aquarium
and Théâtre de la Tempête) was created
in the 1970s on former army land.
The woody, peaceful setting and the
quality and variety of its shows have
contributed greatly to its success.

Odéon Théâtre de l'Europe – *Pl. de
l'Odéon.* Ⓜ*Odéon.* ☎*01 44 85 40 40.
www.theatre-odeon.fr. Tickets: Mon–Sat
11am–6.30pm.* Jean-Louis Barrault and
Madeleine Renaud made this one of
Paris' premier playhouses up until
1968. Productions of Paul Claudel's
Tête d'Or, Ionesco's *Rhinoceros* and
Samuel Beckett's *Waiting for Godot*
and *Happy Days* were staged here.

Théâtre de la Renaissance –
20 blvd St-Martin. Ⓜ*Strasbourg-St-
Denis.* ☎*01 42 08 18 50 or 42 02 47 35.
www.theatredelarenaissance.com.
Ma sœur est un chic type* and *Un air
de famille* (Family Resemblances)
by Bacri and Jaoui are two of this
theatre's greatest hits to date. Guy

Bedos and Fabrice Lucchini have also
graced the stage of this playhouse
dedicated to quality entertainment.

Théâtre des Variétés – *7 blvd
Montmartre.* Ⓜ*Grands Boulevards.*
☎*01 42 33 09 92 (res) or 01 42 33 11 41
(theatre). www.theatre-des-varietes.fr.
Tickets: Mon–Sat 11am–6pm, Sun 11am–
4pm. Closed Jul–Aug.* Feydeau's *La Puce à
l'oreille* (Meet me at the Pussycat),
Marcel Pagnol's *Topaze*, Jean Poiret's
La Cage aux Folles (Birds of a Feather),
and, more recently, *Le Dîner de cons*
(The Dinner Game) were all created
in this theatre, one of Paris' oldest.

Théâtre du Rond-Point – *2 bis av.
Franklin-Roosevelt.* Ⓜ*Franklin-Roosevelt.*
☎*01 44 95 98 21. www.theatredurond
point.fr. Tickets: Tue–Sat noon–7pm,
Sun noon–4pm. Closed two weeks in
August.* First a panoramic view-point,
then a skating rink, Rond-Point has
been a playhouse since 1981.

Théâtre Marigny – *Av. de Marigny.*
Ⓜ*Champs-Élysées-Clémenceau.* ☎*01
53 96 70 00. www.theatremarigny.fr.
Tickets: Mon–Sat 11am–6.30pm. Closed
Jul–Aug. Amadeus* produced by Roman
Polanski, *Cyrano de Bergerac* by Robert
Hossein, *Les Variations Enigmatiques*
with Alain Delon and *La Dame aux
Camélias* starring Isabelle Adjani have
been among this theatre's finest
moments. Long directed by the
Compagnie Renaud-Barrault, then
Elvire Popesco and Robert Manuel.

Théâtre Mogador – *25 rue Mogador.*
Ⓜ*Trinité.* ☎*01 53 32 32 32. www.moga
dor.net. Tickets: Mon–Sat 10am–7pm, Sun
10am–4pm.* Built in 1914 along the lines
of the Palladium in London, this is Paris'
largest private theatre (1 805 seats). Over
the years, the programme has featured
variety shows, operettas, drama *(Cyrano
de Bergerac, La Femme du Boulanger)* and
films. Currently dedicated to musicals,
Jérôme Savary, Jeanne Moreau and Dee
Dee Bridgewater have worked wonders.

Théâtre National de Chaillot – *1 pl.
du Trocadéro.* Ⓜ*Trocadéro.* ☎*01 53 65
30 00. www.theatre-chaillot.fr. Tickets:
Mon–Sat 11am–7pm.* Inaugurated in
1920, from 1930 to 1972 this stage
was home to the Théâtre National
Populaire (TNP) under the supervision
of some of the world's finest directors,
including Jean Vilar and Georges

Wilson. Here Gérard Philipe gave unforgettable performances as the lead roles in *El Cid* and *Lorenzaccio*.

Théâtre National de la Colline – *15 rue Malte-Brun.* Ⓜ*Gambetta.* ☎*01 44 62 52 52 www.colline.fr. Tickets: Mon–Sat 11am– 6.30pm, Sun 2pm–4.30pm. Closed Jul– Aug.* The staging of modern drama is this national theatre's vocation.

OPERA AND DANCE

Opéra-Bastille – *Pl. de la Bastille.* Ⓜ*Bastille.* ☎*01 40 01 17 89 or 08 92 89 90 90. www.opera-de-paris.fr. Tickets: Mon–Sat 2.30am–6.30pm. Closed mid-Jul–mid-Sept.* Designed by Carlos Ott, this opera house marries technical prowess and public outreach. Inaugurated in 1989 by François Mitterrand, it began its first season in spring 1990, with a revival of Hector Berlioz' *Les Troyens*, under the direction of the conductor Myung-Whun Chung.

Opéra-Comique (Salle Favart) – *5 rue Favart.* Ⓜ*Richelieu Drouot.* ☎*08 25 00 00 58 or 01 42 44 45 46. www.opera-comique. com. Tickets: Mon–Sat 11am–7pm, Sun 11am–5pm. Closed Aug.* The Opéra-Comique is also known as the **Salle Favart**. Operas such as Bizet's *Carmen* (1875), Léo Delibes' *Lakmé* (1883) and *Pelléas and Mélisande*, which dazed the world of opera in 1902, all made their débuts here.

Palais Garnier – *8 rue Scribe.* Ⓜ*Opéra, RER Auber.* ☎*01 40 01 18 11 or 08 36 69 78 68. www.opera-de-paris.fr. Tickets: Mon–Sat 11.30am–6.30pm. Closed mid-Jul–early Sept.* Built from 1862 to 1875 by Garnier, a young architect, this theatre's impressive size and luxurious decoration make it a fine example of Second Empire architecture. It has been the home of the National Academy of Music since 1875. The stairwell, foyer and hall are magnificent.

Théâtre de la Ville – *2 pl. du Châtelet.* Ⓜ*Châtelet.* ☎*01 42 74 22 77. www. theatredelaville-paris.com.* Tickets: Mon 11am–7pm, Tue–Sat 11am–8pm. A multidisciplinary people's theatre, featuring ballet, drama, and popular, traditional and classical music. With an eye to encouraging contemporary creativity, this stage has showcased many fine artists, from Pina Bausch to Nusrat Fateh Ali Khan.

CLASSICAL AND CONTEMPORARY CONCERTS

Châtelet-Théâtre Musical de Paris (TMP) – *Pl. du Châtelet.* Ⓜ*Châtelet.* ☎*01 40 28 28 40. www.chatelet-theatre.com. 10am–7pm by telephone or 11am–7pm at theatre.* In 1909, Serge de Diaghilev's Russian Ballet presented Borodin's *Prince Igor* here; the following year, Gustav Mahler conducted his own *Symphony No 2* and Caruso was acclaimed for his performance of Verdi's *Aïda*.

Philharmonie de Paris – *221 av. Jean Jaurès.* Ⓜ*Porte de Pantin.* ☎*01 44 84 44 84. www.philharmoniedeparis.fr. Tue–Fri noon–6pm, Sat–Sun 10am–6pm.* Inaugurated in 2015, the Philharmonie de Paris is comprised of two buildings at the Parc de la Villette: the former Cité de la Musique designed by the architect Christian de Portzamparc in 1995, which houses the Music Museum and smaller performance rooms, and the new main building by Jean Nouvel whose Grand Salle can hold up to 2400 spectators. There are also documentation centres, musicians' workshops, a Music Museum, a bookshop and a café. The musicians and program of the historic Salle Pleyel have been permanently moved to the Philharmonie.

Maison de Radio-France – *116 av. du Président Kennedy.* Ⓜ*Passy.* ☎*01 56 40 15 16. www.concerts.radiofrance.fr.* The Maison de Radio-France hosts a range of music concerts: jazz, classical, traditional and contemporary; performances are inexpensive or free. Olivier-Messiaen Hall stages concerts by Radio-France's choir and orchestra.

Théâtre des Champs-Élysées – *15 av. Montaigne.* Ⓜ*Alma-Marceau.* ☎*01 49 52 07 41. www.theatrechampselysees.fr. Closed Jul–Aug.* Constructed in 1913 and belonging to the historical register since 1953, the Théâtre des Champs-Élysées offers music-lovers a choice between the traditional evening programme and Sunday morning concerts. The world's greatest conductors, including Karl Bœhm, Herbert Von Karajan and many others, have waved their batons here, while the stage has hosted some of the planet's finest ballet troupes and even Josephine Baker's famous Revue Nègre.

Classical Music in Parisian Churches – Regular classical music concerts and organ recitals take place in the churches of Paris, notably St-Eustache, La Sainte Chapelle, Eglise de la Madeleine and St-Germain-des-Prés. Check posters outside the church or ticketing websites such as www.ampconcerts. com or www.classictic.com.

JAZZ-ROCK

Jazz-Club Etoile – *81 blvd Gouvion-St-Cyr.* Ⓜ*Porte Maillot.* ℘*01 40 68 30 42. www.jazzclub-paris.com. Concerts from 9.30pm.* Since 1976, all the greatest names in jazz have played here, including Count Basie and the Modern Jazz Quartet. Traditional jazz (New Orleans, Swing) concerts alternate with rhythm 'n' blues.

Le New Morning – *7–9 rue des Petites Écuries.* Ⓜ*Château d'Eau.* ℘*01 45 23 51 41. www.newmorning.com. 8pm–1am. Closed Aug.* Jazz, world music, folk salsa, blues: the New Morning is an effervescent, eclectic club that has produced Chet Baker, Dexter Gordon, Art Blakey and James Carter as well as The Cranberries and The Fugees…

Le Petit Journal Montparnasse – *13 rue du Cdt-Mouchotte.* Ⓜ*Montparnasse -Bienvenüe or Gaîté.* ℘*01 43 21 56 70. http://petitjournalmontparnasse.com. Open Mon–Sat 7am–2am, concerts: 9.30pm. Closed mid-Jul–mid-Aug and certain public holidays.* A bastion of classical jazz boasting a lengthy inventory of great names: Baden Powell, Claude Bolling, Didier Lockwood, Eddy Louiss and Richard Galliano, in addition to songsters with a jazz, swing or blues slant, like Claude Nougaro, Manu Di Bango and Bill Deraime.

VARIETY

Casino de Paris – *16 rue de Clichy.* Ⓜ*Trinité.* ℘*01 49 95 22 22. www.casino deparis.fr.* Maurice Chevalier and Josephine Baker made their names in this century-old theatre that now produces contemporary stars like Jacques Higelin, Sylvie Vartan, Eddy Mitchell and the hit musical *Starmania.*

La Cigale – *120 blvd Rochechouart.* Ⓜ*Anvers or Pigalle.* ℘*01 49 25 81 75. www.lacigale.fr.* Born in 1887, La Cigale (The Cicada) has vibrated to the tune of the great Mistinguett, Maurice Chevalier and Arletty. Redecorated in 1987 by Philippe Starck, the stage of its handsome Italian-style theatre now welcomes variety artists, together with international rock and pop musicians.

Le Bataclan – *50 blvd Voltaire.* Ⓜ*Oberkampf.* ℘*01 43 14 00 30. www.le-bataclan.com.* Built in 1864, the Bataclan was named after an Offenbach operetta. Successively a café-concert hall, a revue theatre and a cinema, it has hosted stars as dissimilar as Buffalo Bill and Edith Piaf. Today it is a member of the rock and clubbing circuit.

Olympia – *28 blvd des Capucines.* Ⓜ*Opéra.* ℘*01 47 42 25 49 or 08 92 68 33 68 (reservations by phone). www. olympiahall.com. Shows: 8.30pm, Sun 5pm. Closed Aug.* A popular music-hall formerly managed by Bruno Coquatrix, the famous talent scout. Demolished in 1997, the Olympia was entirely rebuilt a few dozen metres from the original site.

Bercy Arena – *8 blvd de Bercy.* Ⓜ*Bercy.* ℘*08 25 03 00 31. www.bercyarena paris.com.* Bercy Arena underwent massive renovations and is opening its fall 2015 season. As for sports, tournaments include figure skating (the Lalique Trophy), go-karting, rollerblading, indoor cycling (Open des Nations) and equestrian competitions.

Zénith – *211 av. Jean Jaurès. Porte de Pantin.* ℘*01 42 08 60 00. www.le-zenith. com.* The Parc de la Villette's vast grey and red hall (6 335 seats) is appropriately named: many artists at the zenith of their careers play here, including the greatest names in rock and pop.

CABARETS, REVUES

Le Paradis Latin – *28 rue du Cardinal Lemoine.* Ⓜ*Jussieu or Cardinal Lemoine.* ℘*01 43 25 28 28. www.paradis-latin.com.* This fêted Parisian cabaret was designed by Gustave Eiffel and inaugurated in January 1889 to mark the World Fair. The dancers (male and female), lights, sets and music all participate in upholding the magic of this revue where the French cancan still kicks up its heels.

Moulin Rouge – *82 blvd de Clichy.* Ⓜ*Blanche.* ℘*01 53 09 82 82. www.moulin -rouge.com. Tickets: 9am–1am.* Since 1889, the Moulin Rouge has enthralled spectators from all over the world

Cinemas

When consulting a cinema programme, it should be remembered that foreign films shown in France can be divided into two categories: VO or VF. VO *(version originale)* means that the film is shown with its original soundtrack and subtitled in French. VF *(version française)* means that the film has been dubbed. This does not apply to French films, which are in French, unless otherwise stated.

© Kris Ubach/age fotostock

Cinémathèque Française

Cinéma L'Entrepôt – *9 rue Francis-de-Pressensé.* Ⓜ*Pernety.* ℘*01 45 40 07 50. www.lentrepot.fr.* Film buffs appreciate this movie house's particularly thoughtful programme: films in VO, experimental feature-length cinema, after-film debates, weekend concerts, etc. A vast bar and a restaurant with a garden terrace are popular in summer.

Cinéma Le Grand Rex – *1 blvd Poissonnière.* Ⓜ*Bonne Nouvelle.* ℘*08 92 68 05 96. www.legrandrex.com.* 7 theatres, including one with 2 750 seats (on 3 levels), and another with 504 places. Two giant screens, one of which is 21m/69ft across; Dolby stereo sound. VF (dubbed) box-office-type films. This cinema, built in 1932, is famous for its starry night-sky ceiling, which rises 24m/79ft above the Oriental/Art Deco interior.

Cinéma Mac-Mahon – *5 av. Mac-Mahon.* Ⓜ*Charles de Gulle Étoile.* ℘*01 43 80 24 81. www.cinemamacmahon.com. Closed Aug.* This cinema was a giant shrine to the Hollywood film goddess during the 1950s and 1960s. Today the Mac-Mahon continues to present movies in their original format and context (with newsreels of the period). One screen. Dolby stereo sound. Classic films, VO only. Cocktail bar.

Cinéma UGC Ciné Cité Bercy – *2 Cour St-Emilion.* Ⓜ*Cour St-Emillion.* ℘*01 36 68 68 58 or 08 92 70 00 00. www.ugc.fr.* 18 theatres with giant screens, 4 500 seats, Dolby AS/R and DTS numeric sound. Films in VO. Primarily box-office-type films. Café and snacks. This large cinema complex is built on the site of Bercy's former wine warehouses.

La Cinémathèque Française – *51 rue de Bercy.* Ⓜ*Bercy.* ℘*01 71 19 33 33. www.cinematheque.fr. Closed Tue, Aug.* Founded in 1936 by Henri Langlois and Paul-Auguste Harlé, the Cinemathèque has been preserving and cataloguing films from all over the world, including the entire works of Marcel L'Herbier and René Clair, as well as a large number of short films and pre-war works. It moved to the contemporary space designed by Frank Gehry in 2005.

La Pagode – *57 bis rue de Babylone.* Ⓜ*St-François-Xavier.* ℘*09 62 23 05 33.* The excellent programme of the 7th *arrondissement*'s only movie theatre puts the accent on artistic and independent films, while the Oriental atmosphere transports one to a universe made of mystery and splendours of the past. This superb Japanese pagoda was a gift that the then director of the Bon Marché store gave his wife in 1896. The home of Oriental galas for over 20 years, it became a cinema in the 1930s.

Max Linder Panorama – *24 blvd Poissonnière.* Ⓜ*Grands Boulevards.* ℘*01 48 24 00 47 or 08 92 68 00 31. www.maxlinderpanorama.com.* 1 giant screen, 615 seats (on 3 levels). THX Dolby stereo SR, DTS and SRD numeric sound. Excellent acoustics. VO films. Box-office programme featuring films with an accent on culture. Bar. Once owmed by Max Linder, a pioneer of silent French film.

Children's Entertainment

Many Guignol shows are available to attend

The main public gardens have marionette shows, usually on Wednesday afternoon, Saturday and Sunday, and during the school holidays. Adults should sit in the back rows!

Cirque d'hiver Bouglione – *110 rue Amelot.* Ⓜ*Filles-du-Calvaire.* ☏*01 47 00 28 81. www.cirquedhiver.com. Nov–late Jan.* The Bouglione family enchants viewers of all ages at this traditional circus with animals, clowns and acrobats.

Cirque Diana Moreno Bormann – *1 rue de la Haie Coq.* Ⓜ*Porte-de-la-Chapelle.* ☏*01 64 05 36 25. www.cirque-diana-moreno.com. Wed, Sat–Sun, school and public holidays at 3pm.*

Théâtre du Guignol – *Jardin d'acclimatation, Bois de Boulogne.* Ⓜ*Sablons.* ☏*07 60 25 77 33. www.jardindacclimatation.fr. Wed, weekends, public and school holidays at 3pm and 4pm.*

Guignol St Lambert –*Square St-Lambert, 15th.* Ⓜ*Félix Faure.* ☏*07 82 15 98 07. www.guignol.fr. Wed, weekends, public and school holidays at 5.30pm.*

Guignol Anatole – *Parc des Buttes-Chaumont.* Ⓜ*Laumière.* ☏*01 43 98 10 95. www.guignol-paris.com. Outdoors theatre (mid Mar–end Oct): Wed, weekends and holidays at 3pm and 4.30pm.*

Guignol Parc Floral – *Parc Floral de Paris, Bois de Vincennes.* Ⓜ*Château de Vincennes. www.guignolparcfloral.com. Wed, weekends, public and school holidays at 3pm and 4pm. Park admission covers events.* Shows include theatre, mime, clowns and marionettes.

Marionnettes des Champs-Élysées – *Rond-Point des Champs-Élysées.* Ⓜ*Champs-Élysées.* ☏*01 42 45 38 30. www.theatreguignol.fr. Wed, Sat–Sun and school holidays at 3pm, 4pm and 5pm.*

Marionnettes du Champs de Mars – *Av. du Général-Margueritte.* Ⓜ*École Militaire.* ☏*01 48 56 01 44. Wed, Sat–Sun at 3.15pm and 4.15pm.*

Marionnettes du Luxembourg – *Jardin du Luxembourg.* Ⓜ*Vavin.* ☏*01 43 26 46 47. www.marionnettesduluxembourg.fr. Wed, Sat–Sun, school and public holidays at 3.30pm (extra show at 11am Sat–Sun).*

Marionnettes du Parc Georges-Brassens – *Parc Georges-Brassens, rue Brancion.* Ⓜ*Porte-de-Vanves.* ☏*01 48 42 51 80. www.marionnettes-parc-brassens.fr. Summer: Wed, Sat–Sun and school holidays at 3pm, 4pm and 5pm; winter: same days at 3.30pm and 4.30pm. Closed mid-Jul–mid-Aug.*

Théâtre Astral – *Parc Floral de Paris (Bois de Vincennes).* Ⓜ*Château de Vincennes.* ☏*01 43 71 31 10. Reservations required. Shows Wed, Sat–Sun, public and school holidays. 3–8 yrs old.* Theatre for children where an acting troupe creates worlds with princesses, knights, robots and fairies.

with its sumptuous productions: from the French cancan – immortalized by Toulouse-Lautrec – to Maurice Chevalier, from Colette to Mistinguett, and from Ella Fitzgerald to Elton John. "Féerie", the Moulin Rouge's new revue, carries on the tradition with dancers who are as gorgeous as ever…

Crazy Horse – *12 av. George V.* M*George V.* ☎*01 47 23 32 32. www.lecrazyhorseparis.com.* One of the capital's most beautiful revues. Magnificent dancers burn up this stage night after night performing original choreographed works in this intimate setting (no dinner served, just caviar and Champagne).

Folies-Bergère – *32 rue Richer.* M*Cadet or Grands Boulevards.* ☎*01 44 79 98 98. www.foliesbergere.com. Tickets 10am–6pm.* Loïe Fuller and Yvette Guilbert, Maurice Chevalier, Yvonne Printemps and Mistinguett, Josephine Baker and Charles Trenet – the legendary stars of yesteryear whose spirits now haunt this theatre all crossed paths here. Note the Art Deco façade and epic hall.

Le Lido – *116 bis av. des Champs-Élysées.* M*George V.* ☎*01 40 76 56 10. www.lido.fr.* Without a doubt Paris' most international revue. The celebrated Bluebell Girls show off their feathers, glitter and stunning anatomy with panache. Over 600 costumes, dozens of décors, fountains and superb lighting.

CAFÉ-THÉÂTRES

Here is a list of a few of the lively *café-théâtres*, which are a speciality of Paris, mixing humour, song and often a bit of late-night carousing. If you don't speak French, you're likely to feel left out, and would be better off taking in a cabaret.

Café d'Edgar-Théâtre d'Edgar – *58 blvd Edgar Quinet.* M*Edgar Quinet.* ☎*01 42 79 97 97. www.theatre-edgar.com. Mon–Sat 2.30pm–7.30pm.* The Café d'Edgar is one of Paris' most famous *café-théâtres* with a reputation for comedy and original shows.

Café de la Gare – *41 rue du Temple.* M*Hôtel de Ville.* ☎*01 42 78 52 51. www.cdlg.org. Shows 7pm or later.* Set in the heart of the Marais, this hallowed hall of merriment has been open for three decades. Patrick Dewaere and Coluche both started their careers here. Today, comedy is staged under the venerable beams of this old carriage inn.

Le République – *1 blvd St-Martin.* M*République.* ☎*01 47 70 97 96. www.lerepubliqueparis.fr. Shows Mon–Sat 8pm or later, Sun 3.30pm.* Open since 1901, this establishment still operates along the same lines as New York's Times Square Comedy or London's Comedy Store: 6 comedians follow for 2hrs 15 mins of stand-up. Laurent Ruquier, François Morel, Smaïn and Patrick Sébastien are just a few famous French comedians who started here.

Le Lapin Agile – *22 rue des Saules.* M*Lamarck Caulaincourt.* ☎*01 46 06 85 87. www.au-lapin-agile.com. Tue–Sun 9pm–1am.* This cabaret located in a rustic little house looks surprisingly bucolic. It owes its name to the sign painted by André Gill in 1875 of a rabbit leaping out of a stew pot. Le Lapin has remained true to its origins, when Apollinaire, Bruant, Modigliani and Picasso used to spend an evening here: song, satire and *sans* microphone.

Les Blancs-Manteaux – *15 rue des Blancs-Manteaux.* M*Rambuteau.* ☎*01 48 87 15 84. www.blancsmanteaux.fr. 7pm–11pm.* A hotbed of talent for the past 30 years, this *café-théâtre* gave many performers their first taste of fame (Renaud, Jacques Higelin, Bernard Lavilliers, Romain Bouteille, Anne Roumanoff and more). Several different artists share the stage every night.

Les Deux Ânes – *100 blvd de Clichy.* M*Blanche.* ☎*01 46 06 10 26. www.2anes. com. Shows Tue–Sat 9pm, Sat matinée 4.30pm, Sun matinée 3.30pm. Closed Jul–Aug.* Since 1922, the tradition of French songs and Montmartre humour has lived on in the political satire of the Two Donkeys.

Mélo d'Amélie – *4 rue Marie-Stuart.* M*Étienne Marcel.* ☎*01 40 26 11 11. www.lemelodamelie.com.* A musical comedy house combining magic, reality and fantasy.

Shopping

FOOD MARKETS

These take place year-round, whatever the weather, usually from 9am to 1.30pm. In Paris, there are 65 open-air markets (one, two or three times a week) and 13 covered markets (daily). Here is a list of the most interesting:

◆ **Aligre**, place d'Aligre, 75012, Ⓜ Ledru Rollin; Tue–Sat 8am–1pm, 4pm–7.30pm, Sun 8am–1pm
◆ **Bastille**, boulevard Richard Lenoir, 75011, Ⓜ Bastille; Thu 8am–2.30pm, Sun 8am–3pm.
◆ **Belleville**, boulevard de Belleville, 75011, Ⓜ Belleville; Tue, Fri 8am–2.30pm.
◆ **Monge**, place Monge, 75005, Ⓜ Place Monge; Wed, Fri 8am–2.30pm, Sun 8am–3pm.
◆ **Raspail**, boulevard Raspail, 75006, Ⓜ Rennes; Tue, Fri 8am–2.30pm, Sun: organic produce; 9am–2pm.

In addition, a number of picturesque street markets take place all day on a daily basis: **rue Montorgueil** (75002), **rue Mouffetard** (75005), **rue de Buci** and **rue de Seine** (75006), rue Cler (75007), rue des Martyrs (75009), rue Daguerre (75014), rue de Passy (75016), and **rue Poncelet**, **rue de Lévis** and rue de Tocqueville (75017).

SPECIALIZED MARKETS

◆ **Art market**
(Marché parisien de la Création): blvd Edgar Quinet (75014), Ⓜ Montparnasse or Edgar Quinet, Sun 9am–7pm.
◆ **Bird market:** place Louis Lépine (75004), Ⓜ Cité, Sun 8am–7pm.
◆ **Book market:** Parc Georges Brassens (75015, entrance along rue Brancion), Ⓜ Porte de Vanves, Sat–Sun 9am–6pm.
◆ **Flea markets:** Porte de Vanves (75014), Ⓜ Porte de Vanves, Sat–Sun 7am–1.30pm; Porte de Clignancourt (75018), Ⓜ Porte de Clignancourt, Sat–Mon 9.30am–6.30pm and Porte de Montreuil (75020), Ⓜ Porte de Montreuil, Sat–Mon 7am–7.30pm.
◆ **Plant, flower markets:** place Louis Lépine (75004), Ⓜ Cité, Mon–Sat 8am –7.30pm; place de la Madeleine (75008), Ⓜ Madeleine, Tue–Fri 7am–1pm; place des Ternes (75017), Ⓜ Ternes, Mon–Sat 8am–7.30pm.
◆ **Stamp market:** Carré Marigny (75008 on the corner of avenue Marigny and avenue Gabriel), Ⓜ Champs-Élysées Clemenceau, Thu, Sat–Sun and holidays from 9am–7pm.

DEPARTMENT STORES

◆ **Le Bazar de l'Hôtel-de-Ville**, 14 rue du Temple, 75004 Paris, Ⓜ Hôtel de Ville, ✆ 01 42 74 90 00,

Flower market, Place Louis Lépine, Île de la Cité

© S.Sauvignier/MICHELIN

www.bhv.fr; Mon–Sat 9.30am–8pm
(Wed 9pm).

♦ **Le Bon Marché,** 24 rue de Sèvres,
75007 Paris, Ⓜ Sèvres-Babylone,
✆ 01 44 39 80 00, www.lebonmarche.
com; Mon–Sat 10am–8pm (Thu 9pm).

♦ **Printemps,** 64 boulevard
Haussmann, 75008 Paris, Ⓜ Havre-
Caumartin, RER Auber, ✆ 01 42 82
50 00, www.printemps.fr; Mon–Sat
9.35am–8.45pm (Thu 10pm).

♦ **Galeries Lafayette de Paris,**
40 boulevard Haussmann, 75009 Paris,
Ⓜ Chaussée-d'Antin, ✆ 01 42 82 34 56,
www.galerieslafayette.com; Mon–Sat
9.30am–8pm (Thu 9pm).

♦ **Franck & Fils,** 80 rue de Passy, 75016
Paris Ⓜ Passy, ✆ 01 44 14 38 00, www.
francketfils.fr; Mon–Sat 10am–7pm
(Fri 8pm).

SHOPPING CENTRES

Carrousel du Louvre, 75001 Paris,
Ⓜ Palais Royal, ✆ 01 43 16 47 10,
www.carrouseldulouvre.com;
daily 9.30am–10pm (shops open
10am–8pm; more than 30 boutiques
selling high-quality gift items).

Centre commercial Italie Deux,
place d'Italie, 75013 Paris, Ⓜ Place
d'Italie; www.italiedeux.com; Mon–Sat
10am–8pm, Thu until 9pm (multi-
level complex with some 130 fashion
boutiques grouped around Printemps,
Carrefour hypermarket and FNAC).

Centre commercial Beaugrenelle,
12 rue de Linois, 75015 Paris, é Charles
Michel; www.beaugrenelle-paris.com,
Mon–Sat 10am–9pm (restaurants and
cinemas until midnight); multi-level
complex in two sections with fashion
boutiques grouped around Marks &
Spencer, Zara, H&M and Uniqlo, etc.

ART
BEAUBOURG
Rue Quincampoix – *rue Quincampoix,
3rd arr.* Ⓜ *Rambuteau*. Among the
many art galleries which are clustered
along this street are contemporary art
specialists Galerie Polad-Hardouin, and

fashion designer Agnès B's Galerie du
Jour, specializing in street art.

LE MARAIS
Galerie Vidal St-Phalle – *10 rue du
Trésor, 4th arr.* Ⓜ *St-Paul.* ✆ *01 42 76 06 05.
www.vidal-stphalle.com. Closed Sun,
Mon, holidays and Aug.* This modern
art gallery exhibits the work of well-
known artists, little seen in France, such
as Rafols-Casamada, Max Neuman,
Christopher Le Brun, Pierre Tal-Coat or
Martin Assig.

Rue Vieille-du-Temple – *rue Vieille-
du-Temple, 3rd arr.* Ⓜ *Filles-du-Calvaire.*
At the top of rue Vieille-du-Temple
(from rue du Perche) and in the
surrounding streets (rue Charlot, rue de
Poitou), there are a large number of art
galleries. Each gallery has a brochure
with a map of the neighbourhood.

INSTITUT DE FRANCE
Rue de Seine – *rue de Seine, 6th arr.*
Ⓜ *Mabillon.* A large number of art
galleries line rue de Seine and
neighbouring streets (rue des Beaux-
Arts, rue Visconti, rue Jacob, rue
Jacques-Callot, etc.). Maps can be
obtained in each gallery.

MONCEAU
Galerie Lelong – *13 rue Téhéran, 8th arr.*
Ⓜ *Miromesnil.* ✆ *01 45 63 13 19. www.
galerie-lelong.com. Closed Aug.* One of
Paris' most famous galleries. It displays
work by several international artists:
Alechinsky, Appel, James Brown,
Chillida, Dibbets, Judd, Kounellis,
Michaux, Miro, Pignon-Ernest,
Rebeyrolle, Saura, Scully, Tàpies…

BASTILLE
Art galleries – The art galleries along
rue de Charonne, rue de Lappe and
rue Keller all exhibit the work of
contemporary artists.

BELLEVILLE
Les Ateliers d'Artistes de Belleville –
1 rue Francis Picabia, 20th arr. ✆ *01 77 12
63 13. www.ateliers-artistes-belleville.fr.*
This gallery is home to the association

of over 200 artists who live and work in Belleville and the surrounding neighbourhoods. They organize regular exhibits and the annual Portes Ouvertes in May.

SAINT-SULPICE

Christian Lacroix – *2–4 pl. St-Sulpice, 6th arr.* Ⓜ*St-Sulpice.* ☏*01 46 33 48 95. www.christian-lacroix.fr. Closed Sun and public holidays.* A designer, known for his flamboyant, flowery, even precious style who seeks to bridge the gap between haute couture and street fashion. Each garment is a celebration.

Cire Trudon – *78 rue de Seine, 6th arr.* Ⓜ*St-Sulpice.* ☏*01 43 26 46 50. www. trudon.com. Closed Sun and holidays.* The former royal candle maker dating back to 1643 is a Left Bank institution, famous for their wax busts too beautiful to burn, but also a large selection of candles and home scents.

Yves Saint Laurent – *6 pl. St-Sulpice, 6th arr.* Ⓜ*St-Sulpice.* ☏*01 43 29 43 00. Closed Sun and public holidays.* A living legend. 40 years of creativity have forged the style of this artist so loved by women and whose inventions have marked the history of fashion. This shop presents four of the Rive Gauche collections.

CHÂTELET-HÔTEL DE VILLE

Le Bazar de l'Hôtel de Ville – *55 rue de la Verrerie, 4th arr.* Ⓜ*Hôtel de Ville.* ☏*01 42 74 90 00. www.bhv.fr. Closed Sun.* This eternally packed department store is one of the capital's landmarks. If you're looking for something in the realms of decoration or home improvement, you will be hard-pressed not to find it here.

Papier Plus – *9 Rue du Pont Louis-Philippe, 4th arr.* Ⓜ*Hôtel de Ville.* ☏*01 42 77 70 49. www.papierplus.com. Mon–Sat noon–7pm.* On a street lined with many artisan paper shops, this is one of the more charming ones, with a large selection of French stationery, cards, journals, sketch pads, fountain pens and ink, calligraphy books, and other gifts.

Rue de Rivoli – Built during the reigns of Napoléon I and Louis-Philippe, this street is one of the main shopping streets in central Paris with arcaded stores between the place de la Concorde and Rue du Louvre, and high-street shops continuing to the metro St-Paul.

LE GRAND LOUVRE

Carrousel du Louvre – *99 rue de Rivoli, 1st arr.* ☏*01 43 16 47 10.* A combination museum-shopping gallery of some 16 000sq m/19 139sq yd, including a performing arts centre (Studio-Théâtre), many brand name shops and a variety of multi-purpose halls (congresses, exhibitions, etc.), is one of the more original ideas invented by the Grand Louvre.

Boutique des Musées Nationaux – Reproductions, books, games, etc.

LES HALLES

Agnès B. – *6 rue du Jour, 1st arr.* Ⓜ*Les Halles.* ☏*01 45 08 56 56. www.agnesb.com. Closed Sun and public holidays.* Clothes for men, women and children, accessories and jewellery. All of Agnès B's collections can be found behind one of the elegant windows of the five shops which line this little street.

La Droguerie – *9–11 rue du Jour, 1st arr.* Ⓜ*Les Halles.* ☏*01 45 08 93 27. Closed Sun.* This shop stocks absolutely everything necessary for the budding dress or jewellery maker.

Stohrer – *51 rue Montorgueil, 2nd arr.* Ⓜ*Etienne Marcel.* ☏*01 42 33 38 20. www.stohrer.fr. Closed 1–15 Aug.* Nicolas

Stohrer

Stohrer started his career in Louis XV's court at Versailles, and opened this pastry shop and delicatessen at its current location in 1730. The décor is a classified historical monument, and the baba rhum is the house speciality.

OBERKAMPF

La Bague de Kenza – *106 rue St-Maur, 11th arr.* Ⓜ*Parmentier.* ☎*01 43 14 93 15. Daily.* This Algerian pastry shop, rare in Paris, sells high-quality, subtly flavoured cakes and pastries, together with a wide range of breads, some of which are exclusive to the house. Particularly in vogue with the press and fine gourmets, famous and otherwise.

Rougier and Plé – *13 blvd des Filles du Calvaire, 3rd arr.* Ⓜ*Filles du Calvaire.* ☎*01 44 54 81 00. www.crea.tm.fr. Mon–Sat 9.30am–7pm.* Arts and crafts galore! Three floors with everything you could need for bookbinding, printing, drawing, graphics, modelling, etc. If you are looking for a bag of colourful feathers to adorn your hat, or a glass-paste gem to repair your favourite brooch, this is the place.

LE MARAIS

Antik Batik – *18 rue de Turenne, 4th arr.* Ⓜ*Bastille, St-Paul or Chemin-Vert.* ☎*01 44 78 02 00. Daily. Closed ten days in Aug.* This ethnic-style fashion shop sells the creations of designers influenced by Latin America, India and Indonesia. Always colourful, their originality has long found followers among Paris' youth.

COS – *4 rue des Rosiers, 4th arr.* Ⓜ*St-Paul.* ☎*01 44 54 37 70. Mon–Sat 10am–7.30pm. www.cosstores.com.* "Company of Style" is the big sister store of H&M, featuring edgy, contemporary Swedish style for men and women.

Sacha Finkelsztajn – *27 rue des Rosiers, 4th arr.* Ⓜ*St-Paul or Hôtel de Ville.* ☎*01 42 72 78 91. www.finkelsztajn.com. Closed Tue and mid-Jul–mid-Aug.* Following in his father's footsteps, Sacha Finkelsztajn upholds the tradition of Yiddish gastronomy and pastries from Central Europe and Russia in his friendly yellow shop. Strange, foreign spices and flavours, delicious, mouth-watering pastries, cheeses, tarama and olive caviar await visitors.

MOUFFETARD

Rue Mouffetard – These colourful market stands (along the St-Médard end of the street) are open Tue–Sat and Sun morning (closed at lunch).

LUXEMBOURG GARDENS

Christian-Constant – *37 rue d'Assas, 6th arr.* Ⓜ*Notre-Dame-des-Champs.* ☎*01 53 63 15 15. www.christianconstant.com. Daily.* Inventor of the Appellation d'Origine Pur Cru, this chocolate, pastry and ice-cream maker is not only one of Paris' best craftsmen, he is also an adventurer of the palate. He creates the most amazing sweets and desserts which both astound and delight the tastebuds.

SAINT-GERMAIN-DES-PRÉS

Debauve et Gallais – *30 rue des Sts-Pères.* ☎*01 45 48 54 67. www.debauve-et-gallais.com. Closed Sun and public holidays.* This chocolatemaker, established in 1800, counted the Kings of France among his customers. The shop is officially listed as a historic monument.

Emporio Armani – *149 blvd St-Germain, 6th arr. Other shop: 25 pl. Vendôme, 1st arr.* ☎*01 45 48 62 15. Closed Sun and public holidays.* The sober, sophisticated style of this designer appeals to the young and the not so young. The shop, in line with the designs, is a tasteful blend of luxury and modernism. It also boasts an Italian tea shop which is very popular with its well-heeled clientele.

L'Écume des Pages – *174 blvd St-Germain, 6th arr.* ☎*01 45 48 54 48. www.ecumedespages.com. Daily. Closed public holidays.* One of the last of the legendary St-Germain book shops, contributing to the neighbourhood's cultural life (book signings, etc.).

Le Carré Rive Gauche – *7th arr.* Ⓜ*Rue du Bac or St-Germain-des-Prés. www.carrerivegauche.com.* This association houses some 120 art galleries and antique dealers spread out through rue des Saints-Pères, rue de l'Université, rue du Bac and along quai Voltaire. Each one has a brochure in which their various specialities and addresses are indicated.

Debauve et Gallais

© Debauve et Gallais

Marché Saint-Germain – *rue Clément, 6th arr.* ⓜ*Mabillon.* ☎*01 43 29 80 59. Closed Sun.* This pleasant covered market houses a number of fashion shops and a large food hall.

Rue de Furstemberg – *rue de Furstemberg, 6th arr.* ⓜ*Mabillon.* Arty Dandy, Flamant, Pierre Frey, Braquénie, Jim Thompson – this discreet little street is almost entirely devoted to home decoration.

Sonia Rykiel –*194 blvd St-Germain, 6th arr.* ☎*01 49 54 60 60. www.sonia rykiel.com. Closed Sun and public holidays.* The designs of this legendary, extremely talented designer are often inspired by her other passions: literature, cinema or food.

Ralph Lauren Flagship – *173 blvd St-Germain, 6th arr.* ⓜ*St-Germain-des-Prés.* ☎*01 44 77 77 00. www.ralphlauren.fr. Mon–Sat 10.30am–7pm, Sun 1pm–7pm.* Housed in an elegant aristocratic mansion on several floors, the Ralph Lauren flagship store sells the American designer's men's and women's collections, as well as sunglasses, jewellery and accessories. The stylish **Ralph's** restaurant in the courtyard is a pleasant stop for lunch or dinner.

ODÉON

Le Coupe Papier – *19 rue de l'Odéon, 6th arr.* ⓜ*Odéon.* ☎*01 43 54 65 95. Closed Mon in Jul, Aug, public holidays.* A bookshop devoted to theatre, cinema, opera and dance, it publishes a full reference catalogue and specializes in contemporary arts. It also has a selection of English and Italian language works.

Un Dimanche à Paris – *4 Cours du Commerce Saint-André, 6th arr.* ⓜ*Odéon.* ☎*01 56 81 18 18. www.un-dimanche-a-paris.com. Mon noon–8pm, Tue–Sat 11am–8pm, Sun 11am–7pm.* On an 18C cobblestone passage, this contemporary pastry boutique and chocolate shop is known for its hot chocolate and artistic confections (some of them gluten-free). The tearoom next door serves their savoury dishes with chocolate touches.

FAUBOURG SAINT-GERMAIN

Barthélémy – *51 rue de Grenelle, 7th arr.* ⓜ*Rue du Bac.* ☎*01 45 48 56 75. Closed Sun, Aug and public holidays.* Barthélémy is not only one of the best cheese merchants in town, he is also a man who adores sharing his love of cheese. This magnificent shop has retained its original 1900 décor.

Le Cabinet de Porcelaine – *37 rue de Verneuil, 7th arr.* ☎*01 42 60 25 40. Closed Sun–Mon, Aug and public holidays.*

This quaint boutique on a street of antique shops specializes in antique porcelain, from delicate tulips and orchids to amazingly life-like fruits and vegetables.

SÈVRES-BABYLONE

La Grande Épicerie de Paris – *38 rue de Sèvres, 7th arr.* M*Sèvres-Babylone.* 01 44 39 81 00. www.lagrandeepicerie.fr. *Closed Sun.* The handsome Art Deco façade of this branch of the Bon Marché houses one of the capital's largest gourmet food halls. Equally excellent wine cellar.

Le Bon Marché – *24 rue de Sèvres, 7th arr.* M*Sèvres-Babylone.* 01 44 39 80 00. www.lebonmarche.fr. *Closed Sun.* This place was founded in 1852 by a highly inventive shopkeeper. His old French style and policy of selecting only the best products and fashion designers has led to the success of this large yet exclusive department store.

Poilâne – *8 rue du Cherche-Midi, 6th arr.* M*Sèvres-Babylone or St-Sulpice.* 01 45 48 42 59. www.poilane.fr. *Closed Sun.* Not so long ago, penniless artists could be found here exchanging paintings for bread with this remarkable craftsman. The decoration has not changed since 1932, neither has the manufacturing method (6hr of preparation) of the bread which remains the best known in Paris.

Rue du Bac – *rue du Bac. 7th arr.* M*Rue du Bac.* A multitude of home-decorators have grouped themselves in the streets between rue de Grenelle and rue de Sèvres: MD Contemporain, Dîners en ville, the Conran Shop, etc.

MUSÉE D'ORSAY

Richart – *258 blvd St-Germain, 7th arr.* M*Solférino. Other shop: 36 av. de Wagram, 8th arr.* 01 45 55 66 00. www.richart.com. *Closed Sun.* This master craftsman excels in the art of producing chocolates thats delight both the eye and the palate. His assortments, which resemble miniature paintings, are composed of exquisitely decorated *ganache* chocolates.

LES INVALIDES

Pétrossian – *18 blvd de La Tour Maubourg, 7th arr.* M*La Tour Maubourg.* 01 44 11 32 22. www.petrossian.fr.

Closed Mon in Aug and Sun. In this magnificent 1920s shop, Paris' caviar and smoked fish specialists introduce their customers to real Scottish and Norwegian salmon, smoked for five days over a fire of different wood essences, as well as wild white salmon from the Baltic. Their foie gras is also delicious.

TOUR EIFFEL

La Maison de l'escargot – *79 rue Fondary, 15th arr.* M*Émile Zola.* 01 45 75 31 09. www.maison-escargot.com. *Open Tue–Sat 9.30am–7pm. Closed holidays and end Jul–mid-Aug.* Open since 1894, this shop only sells hand-prepared snails from Burgundy and Savoy for the *Bourgogne* and from Provence for the *petits gris.*

ALMA

Avenue Montaigne – *Av. Montaigne, 8th arr.* Undoubtedly the smartest street in Paris. All the major fashion designers and luxury brands have an outlet here: Emanuel Ungaro, Loro Piana, Prada, Dior, Bonpoint, Bottega Veneta, Valentino, Vuitton, Céline, Caron, Nina Ricci, Harry Winston.

Noura – *27 av. Marceau, 16th arr.* M*Alma-Marceau.* 01 47 23 02 20. www.noura.com. *Open 9am–midnight.* Perhaps the best place to shop for Lebanese specialities in town. Taboule with parsley, hummus, mustabal, grilled meat, baklavas and other delicious specialities, all of which are presented superbly.

CHAMPS-ÉLYSÉES

Disney® Store – *44 av. des Champs-Élysées, 8th arr.* M*Franklin-Roosevelt.* 01 45 61 45 25. *Daily. Closed 1 May, 25 Dec.* Toys, clothes, disguises, accessories, music, videos, etc. All of Disney's products are presented here in this vast children's bedroom, equipped with a giant screen which projects clips from all the latest cartoons all day long.

Drugstore Publicis – *133 av. des Champs-Élysées, 8th arr.* M*Charles de Gaulle Étoile.* 01 44 43 79 00. www.publicisdrugstore.com. *Daily until 2am.* Don't let the name fool you; more than a drugstore, Publicis is a Paris institution since the 1950s, with a café, restaurant, international press and

Ladurée

© Murat Koç/iStockphoto

tabac, luxury gift boutique, wine cellar, bookshop and even a cinema house. A stylish place to see and be seen.

Guerlain – *68 av. des Champs-Élysées, 8th arr.* ⓂFranklin-Roosevelt. ℘*01 45 62 11 21. www.guerlain.fr. Mon–Wed 9am–7pm, Thur–Sat 9am–8pm.* The history of this illustrious family so acclaimed in the perfume world began back in 1828. Today the marble floors and walls of this perfumery and beauty institute are listed monuments. It sells all of Jean-Paul Guerlain's creations.

Ladurée – *75 av. des Champs-Élysées, 8th arr.* ⓂFranklin-Roosevelt. ℘*01 40 75 08 75. www.laduree.fr. daily.* This historic pastry shop is known for its macarons, in no fewer than 13 flavours.

Stamp market – *Carré Marigny (on the corner of av. de Marigny and av. Gabriel), 8th arr.* ⓂChamps-Élysées Clemenceau. *Thu, Sat–Sun and public holidays 9am–7pm.*

JARDIN DES TUILERIES

Galignani – *224 r. de Rivoli, 1st arr.* ⓂTuileries. ℘*01 42 60 76 07. Closed Sun and public holidays.* Founded in 1801, the bookshop is still run by the Galignani family. This prestigious firm is proud to have been the first English bookshop established on the Continent. Excellent history, art and cooking sections.

Goyard – *233 rue St-Honoré, 1st arr.* ⓂTuileries. ℘*01 42 60 57 04. www. goyard.fr. Closed Sun and holidays.* This reputable luggage maker has recently changed hands but has retained its former spirit. At the back of the shop, an impressive early 20C mahogany staircase leads up to a room where the establishment's first creations are displayed, including a trunk-desk designed for Conan Doyle.

Collette – *213 rue St-Honoré, 1st arr.* ⓂTuileries. ℘*01 55 35 33 90. www. colette.fr. Closed Sun.* The original fashion concept store is still the first stop for Fashion Week editors and stylists who come to Paris looking for the latest in women's and men's fashions, accessories, shoes and an eclectic selection of gadgets and music. There's a Water Bar downstairs.

PLACE DE LA CONCORDE

Bernardaud – *11 rue Royale, 8th arr.* ⓂConcorde or Madeleine. Other shop: Carrousel du Louvre, 1st arr. ℘*01 47 42 82 66. www.bernardaud.fr. Closed Sun, 1 Jan, Easter, 1 May, 4 Jun, 25 Dec.* From sumptuous re-editions of the Royal Manufacture of Limoges to dozens of original new creations, this shop is almost a living museum of porcelain and chinaware. Unusual gift ideas: engraved lithographs, jewellery, etc.

FAUBOURG SAINT-HONORÉ

Hermès – *24 rue du Fg St-Honoré, 8th arr.* Ⓜ*Concorde.* ☏*01 40 17 47 17. www.hermes.com. Closed Sun and public holidays.* Since it first began as a harness maker when Thierry Hermès opened the first shop in 1837, this family business has never ceased to grow, while retaining its original founding spirit. The equestrian influence remains strong in this establishment dedicated to quality before all else.

Les Caves Taillevent – *199 rue du Fg St-Honoré, 8th arr.* Ⓜ*Charles de Gaule Étoile, Ternes or St-Philippe du Roule.* ☏*01 45 61 14 09. www.taillevent.com. Closed Sun–Mon, public holidays and 3 weeks in Aug.* Whether on the shelves or hung on the walls, all the bottles on display are dummies; the real ones are kept in a ventilated cellar. In addition to the best vintage wines, they also stock a fine selection of regional wines. Friendly and efficient staff.

Rue du Faubourg Saint-Honoré – *rue du Fg St-Honoré, 8th arr.* Ⓜ*Concorde or Madeleine.* From rue Royale to place Beauvau, rue du Faubourg St-Honoré is entirely devoted to fashion and luxury goods. All the leading brand names are there: Lolita Lempika, Lanvin, Hermès, Cartier, Guy Givenchy, Versace, Laroche, Dior, Louis Ferraud, etc.

LA MADELEINE

Betjeman and Barton – *23 blvd Malesherbes, 8th arr.* Ⓜ*Madeleine.* ☏*01 42 65 86 17. www.betjemanandbarton. com. Closed Sun, public holidays and 2 weeks in Aug.* This English-inspired brand of high-quality French teas will delight all tea-enthusiasts by the quality of its products and the elegance of their presentation.

Chanel – *31 rue Cambon, 1st arr.* Ⓜ*Madeleine.* ☏*01 42 86 28 00. www.chanel.com. Closed Sun.* Such is its fame, this legendary house needs no introduction, because it is now synonymous with France's reputation for elegance and luxury throughout the world. Leather sofas and an attentive staff continue to uphold Chanel's tradition of high-quality service and products.

Fauchon – *24–30 pl. de la Madeleine, 8th arr.* Ⓜ*Madeleine.* ☏*01 70 39 38 00. www.fauchon.fr. Closed Sun.* Delicatessen pastry maker, high-class grocery and tearoom all rolled into one. Fauchon sells luxury goods from France and abroad. Very popular with the Parisian bourgeoisie and foreign visitors who come to admire the shop's sumptuous decorations at Christmas time.

Hédiard – *21 pl. de la Madeleine, 8th arr.* Ⓜ*Madeleine.* ☏*01 43 12 88 88. www. hediard.fr. Closed Sun and public holidays.* At the entrance, a delicious array of exotic fruits and spices invites gourmets to venture into this house of mouth-watering delicacies. The wine cellar, managed by a competent, young wine expert, is also worth a look.

Lalique – *11 rue Royale, 8th arr.* Ⓜ*Concorde or Madeleine. Other address: Carrousel du Louvre, 1st arr.* ☏*01 53 05 12 12. Closed Sun and public holidays except 8 May, Ascension, 11 Nov.* Lalique's first creations are now owned by collectors from all over the world. Renowned for its specialized work in transparent-satin finishes, this prestigious house manufactures crystal in all shapes and sizes from the famous Bachantes vase to watches and perfume bottles.

Rue Royale – *rue Royale, 8th arr.* Ⓜ*Concorde or Madeleine.* Fashion (Adolfo Dominguez, Gucci), jewellery (Poiray, Fred), crystal (Christofle, Cristallerie St-Louis) or chinaware (Bernardeau), this wide avenue has the flagship shops of many of Paris' most prestigious and most luxurious brand names.

PALAIS ROYAL

Shops Arcades of the Jardins du Palais Royal – *Place Colette, 1st arr.,* Ⓜ*Palais Royal.* Built in the 18C in what used to be the gardens of the king's palace, the stone shopping arcades are now home to luxury boutiques, cafés and art galleries. Fashion brands include Marc Jacob, Stella McCartney, Rick Owens, and Didier Ludot's famous vintage couture.

Le Louvre des Antiquaires – *2 pl. du Palais Royal, 1st arr.* Ⓜ*Palais Royal.* ☏*01 42 97 27 27. www.louvre-antiquaires.com. Closed Mon all year, Sun–Mon in Jul–Aug.*

250 antique dealers have set up shop in this vast building. Paintings, archaeology, jewellery, furniture, etc. This gallery of beautiful objects displayed in superb showcases is worthy of a museum. Ask for a map at the entrance.

Les Salons du Palais Royal Shiseido – *142 Galerie de Valois, 1st arr.* Ⓜ*Bourse or Palais Royal.* ℘*01 49 27 09 09. www.salons-shiseido.com. Closed Sun and public holidays.* Serge Lutens, the former artistic director of Shiseido, now creates his own fine perfumes. Based on the night and day theme, this fan of Morocco has designed a setting full of mystery to present his fragrances of rare essences.

Verlet – *256 rue St-Honoré, 1st arr.* Ⓜ*Palais Royal.* ℘*01 42 60 67 39. Closed Sun, Sat–Sun May–Oct and 3 weeks in Aug.* The pleasant smell of freshly ground coffee seeps out of the establishment of this coffee-shop-cum-tearoom. Since 1880, the house has stocked a variety of coffees and teas and in the winter, preserved fruits, to the delight of the faithful regulars of this genuine craftsman.

PLACE DES VICTOIRES

Jean-Paul Gaultier – *6 rue Vivienne, 2nd arr.* Ⓜ*Bourse.* ℘*01 42 86 05 05. Closed Sun.* Located in the former stables of the Palais Royal, Jean-Paul Gaultier's shop is well worth a visit. Its extravagant design is a distinctive hallmark of this designer whose reputation is worldwide.

Kenzo – *3 & 6 pl. des Victoires, 1st arr.* Ⓜ*Sentier.* ℘*01 40 39 72 03. Closed Sun.* These spacious, ready-to-wear boutiques for men and women present the collections of this Japanese designer who has combined Eastern and Western influences to create his own sober, elegant style.

Legrand Filles and Fils – *1 rue de la Banque, 2nd arr.* Ⓜ*Bourse.* ℘*01 42 60 07 12. www.caves-legrand.com. Closed Sun.* This authentic wine cellar and fine grocery shop is the home of a reputed family of wine dealers. From the classical to the unusual, let yourself be guided by the master of the house and don't forget to take a look at their selection of regional goodies.

LES GRANDS BOULEVARDS

À la Mère de Famille – *35 rue du Fg Montmartre, 9th arr.* Ⓜ*Le Peletier or Grands Boulevards.* ℘*01 47 70 83 69. Closed Sat–Mon, public holidays and Aug.* This sweet shop is steeped in history. The decoration, which has not changed since 1900, endows the place with a mysterious charm, enhanced by the odour of dried fruits and sugared almonds prepared at the back of the shop.

Pain d'Epices – *29 Passage Jouffroy, 9th arr.* Ⓜ*Grands Boulevards.* ℘*01 47 70 08 68. www.paindepices.fr. Closed Sun.* Located in the historic, 19C shopping passages, this charming boutique features old-fashioned and whimsical children's toys and miniatures, but nothing that requires batteries.

SAINT-LAZARE

Augé – *116 blvd Haussmann, 8th arr.* Ⓜ*St-Augustin.* ℘*01 45 22 16 97. www.cavesauge.com. Closed Sun and public holidays.* Founded in 1850, this family enterprise has the oldest cellar in Paris. Venture into its authentic surroundings and discover the best of what France's vineyards have to offer. Foreign wines also available. Reasonable prices.

Galeries Lafayette – *40 blvd Haussmann, 9th arr.* Ⓜ*Chaussée-d'Antin or Havre-Caumartin.* ℘*01 42 82 34 56. www.galerieslafayette.com. Closed Sun and public holidays.* It would be impossible to go on a shopping spree in Paris without envisaging a trip to this major department store, where all the brand names have an outlet.

Printemps – *64 blvd Haussmann, 9th arr.* Ⓜ*Havre-Caumartin, RER Auber.* ℘*01 42 82 50 00. www.printemps.fr. Closed Sun.* This temple to fashion features the work of all the world's leading design houses. Divided into three buildings which are linked by passageways. A large panorama terrace tops the Printemps de la Maison.

PIGALLE

Arnold Delmontel *39 rue des Martyrs, 9th arr.* ℘*01 48 78 29 33. www.arnaud-delmontel.com. Daily.* This boulangerie-pâtisserie not only produces the best baguettes in Paris (official!), but

Shopping under the cupola of Galeries Lafayette

© PhotoTalk/iStockphoto

also superb Renaissance bread and perfect pastries, biscuits and almond croissants.

FAUBOURG SAINT-ANTOINE

La Maison du Cerf-Volant – *7 rue de Prague, 12th arr.* M*Ledru Rollin.* ✆*01 44 68 00 75. www.lamaisonducerfvolant.com. Closed Sun–Mon.* For beginners or experienced flyers, this whimsical kite shop has something for everyone, with both ready-to-fly and kits to build your own.

Marché d'Aligre – *Pl. d'Aligre, 12th arr.* M*Ledru Rollin. Tue–Sun mornings.* Large, noisy, colourful food and flea market. Specialty foods are sold in the covered market, the Marché Beauvau, which is also open late afternoons 4pm–7.30pm.

LES GOBELINS

Cave des Gobelins – *56 av. des Gobelins, 13th arr.* M*Gobelins or Place d'Italie.* ✆*01 43 31 66 79. Closed Sun and Aug.* Following in the footsteps of his father, the equally friendly Eric Merlet has taken over the management of this exceptional wine cellar, with among others, a few very rare vintage spirits (including a cognac from 1809!) together with a selection of practically every fine wine produced over the last 40 years.

Les Abeilles – *21 rue de la Butte-aux-Cailles, 13th arr.* M*Corvisart or Place d'Italie.* ✆*01 45 81 43 48. www.lesabeilles.*

biz. Tue–Sat 11am–7pm. This apiculture boutique sells not only beekeeping supplies, but every kind of honey product, including candies, royal jelly, soap, beeswax, vinegar, sweet bread, and honey by the jar.

MONTPARNASSE

Jean-Paul Hévin – *3 rue Vavin, 6th arr.* M*Vavin or Notre-Dame-des-Champs.* ✆*01 43 54 09 85. www.jphevin.com. Closed Sun, 3 weeks in Aug and public holidays.* One of the capital's best chocolate makers. For over 10 years, this master craftsman has delighted patrons with his bitter *ganaches* made from a variety of cocoa beans. Don't miss his delicious macaroons or his legendary chocolate *millefeuille.*

Marché parisien de la Création – *blvd Quinet.* ✆*08 72 57 89 91. www.marchecreation.com.* Around 100 artists exhibit their works on Sundays.

LA MUETTE-RANELAGH

Franck & Fils – *80 rue de Passy, 16th arr.* M*Passy.* ✆*01 44 14 38 00. www.francketfils.fr. Closed Sun and public holidays.* One of the most elegant department stores in Paris, without the crowds. Small yet well-appointed with the top Parisian and international brands for women and men.

Pascal Le Glacier – *17 rue Bois-le-Vent, 16th arr.* Ⓜ*La Muette.* ☎*01 45 27 61 84. Tue–Sat 10.30am–7pm. Closed public holidays and Aug.* Pascal and his wife are obsessed – with quality. Each sorbet is prepared in small quantities with fruits of the season, distilled water and a great deal of care. Their success has not altered the attention to quality or high standards of this remarkable duo.

Réciproque – *89–101 rue de la Pompe, 16th arr.* Ⓜ*Rue de la Pompe.* ☎*01 47 04 30 28. www.reciproque.fr. Closed Sun–Mon and public holidays.* The 800 sq m/8 612sq ft of this second-hand fashion, accessories and jewellery shop in five buildings are more than worth a glance. Only luxury goods in excellent condition are sold, displayed by designer. From a Hermès scarf to a Vuitton bag, it's all there.

MONTMARTRE

Marché St-Pierre – *Sq. Willette, 18th arr. Daily.* In addition to a pleasant walk, this colourful, lively market provides an excellent choice of cut-price fabric.

Génération – *4 rue Tholozé, 18th arr.* Ⓜ*Abbesses.* ☎*01 42 54 28 08. www. boutique1962.com. Closed Sun–Mon.* A vintage concept store with a charming mix of retro home décor, clothing and accessories from the 1950s and 1960s.

La Piscine – *29bis rue des Abbesses, 18th arr.* Ⓜ*Abbesses.* ☎*01 42 55 94 45. Daily.* A local outlet shop for top brands of men's and women's clothing and accessories from previous seasons' stock.

Art galleries – In addition to the open-air artists on the **Place du Tertre** (check into the small tourism information office there for maps of the neighbourhood), there are also many art galleries around the Butte, including Rue des Trois Frères, Rue Yvonne Le Tac, and Rue Lepic.

CHARTRES

Galerie de Chartres – *10 rue Claude Bernard ZA du Coudray.* ☎*02 37 88 28. 28. Showings: Wed 9am–noon, 2–6pm.* This establishment organizes auctions for an international clientele every weekend in the 16C Église Ste-Foy (ceramics, weapons, stamps, silverware, cameras, radios, etc.). Specializes in the sale of collectable dolls and toys.

Galerie du Vitrail – *17 Cloître Notre-Dame, 28000 Chartres.* ☎*02 37 36 10 03. www.galerie-du-vitrail.com. May–mid-Oct Tue–Sat 10am–1pm, 2pm–7pm, Sun and holidays 11am–1pm, 2pm–7pm; mid-Oct–Apr Tue–Sat 10.30am–1pm, 2pm–7pm.* This atelier was founded in 1946 by Gabriel Loire, and is continued today by his grandchildren. The art e of making stained glass are carefully explained, beginning with artists' models (as designed by Adami, Miro or Fernand Léger, for example) and ending with the finished product created by master glass crafters. Many unique pieces can be obtained in the boutique and a specialized library can be visited.

Marché aux légumes et volailles – *pl. Billard.* Each Saturday morning, the covered Vegetable and Poultry Market displays colourful stands featuring authentic Beauce produce. This carrousel of sights, tastes and fragrances is one of the most popular markets in the area.

FONTAINEBLEAU

Les Terroirs de France – *41 r. des Sablons.* ☎*01 64 22 50 80. Closed Aug.* A speciality cheese shop with the local favourite le Fontainebleau, a soft white cheese with cream. There is also a selection of local products. A pleasant, pastoral setting.

Sport and Leisure

OUTDOOR ACTIVITIES
Luxembourg Gardens
In the summer, open-air concerts take place in the **Luxembourg Gardens** *(boulevard St-Michel side)*. The **Gardens** also have a shady café-terrace.

Tuileries Gardens
In the summer, a carnival with ferris wheel takes place in **Tuileries Gardens** *(rue de Rivoli side)*. The **Gardens** also have a shady café-terrace open late (access through **place de la Concorde**).

Parc de la Villette
Open-air concerts and open-air cinema takes place in the summer. The vast lawns are always open to the public.

OUTDOOR ACTIVITIES FOR KIDS
👫 Luxembourg Gardens
On the rue de Guynemer side, the **garden** has swings, merry-go-rounds and puppet shows. There is a fenced area where young children can play and sandpits for all ages. They can sail model boats in the basin in front of the Palais de Luxembourg. Paying activities are rather expensive.

👫 **Park Monceau** – Children's play areas are scattered throughout the park, such as roller skating, sandpits and merry-go-rounds.

LEISURE ACTIVITIES
Monceau
Salle Cortot – *78 rue Cardinet, 17th arr.* ℰ*01 47 63 47 48. www.ecolenormale cortot.com.* This handsome room with seating for 400 was designed by Auguste and Gustave Perret in 1929. It is part of the Paris School of Music and hosts **concerts** of classical music, but also holds master classes with artists such as Rostropovitch, François-René Duchâble, Felicity Lott.

Bois de Boulogne
Bike Rental – ℰ*01 47 47 76 50. Late Apr–mid-Oct daily; late Oct–mid-Apr Wed, Sat–Sun and holidays.* 👓*6€/hr.* Bike rental stands are located by the entrance of the Jardin d'Acclimatation and the north end of the Lac Inférieur.

Boat rental – *At the north end of the Lac Inférieur. May–Sept daily 10am–6pm; Oct–Apr daily noon–5.30pm.* 👓*10€/hr.* ℰ*01 42 88 04 69.*

Petit Train du Jardin d'Acclimatation – *Service between the Porte Maillot and the amusement park. May–Sept daily 10am–7pm; Oct–Apr daily 10am–6pm.* 👓*2.90€.* ℰ*01 40 67 90 82.*

FONTAINEBLEAU
Cercle de Jeu de Paume de Fontainebleau – *Château de Fontainebleau. Daily 9.15am–9.45pm.* ℰ*01 64 22 47 67. www.jdpfontainebleau. com.* The jeu de paume, a sport whose descendants include tennis and squash, has been played since 1601 in this indoor court of the Château de Fontainebleau. Visitors can watch a match or try a game themselves.

SPECTATOR SPORTS
Palais Omnisports de Paris-Bercy (POPB) – *8 blvd de Bercy, 12th arr.* ℰ*01 40 02 60 60. www.bercyarena.paris.* This is the largest covered stadium within the City of Paris, used for major sporting events such as basketball, motocross, ice skating, go-carting, cycling, martial arts, horse jumping and gymnastics. It also hosts major music concerts.

Stade de France – *St-Denis La Plaine.* ℰ*0892 700 900. www.stadefrance.com.* The largest stadium in France was built in 1998 to host the World Cup Final (France beat Brazil 3-0). It's home to the French national football (soccer) and rugby teams, and is used for domestic sports matches, motocross, and occasional music concerts.

Other sports stadiums, all within the **Bois de Boulogne**, include the **Parc des Princes** (rugby), **Roland Garros** (tennis) and the **Hippodromes de Longchamp** and **d'Auteuil** (horse racing and jumping).

In the **Bois de Vincennes** the **Hippodrome de Vincennes** is primarily used for trotting horse races. The **Tour de France** finishes every year on the **avenue des Champs-Élysées**.

INDEX

INDEX

INDEX

INDEX

INDEX

INDEX

🛏 STAY

🍷 EAT

MAPS AND PLANS

MAP LEGEND

★★★ **Highly recommended**

★★ **Recommended**

★ **Interesting**

Tourism

Sightseeing route with departure point indicated	Map co-ordinates locating sights
Ecclesiastical building	Tourist information
Synagogue – Mosque	Historic house, castle – Ruins
Building (with main entrance)	Dam – Factory or power station
Statue, small building	Fort – Cave
Wayside cross	Prehistoric site
Fountain	Viewing table – View
Fortified walls – Tower – Gate	Miscellaneous sight

Recreation

Racecourse	Waymarked footpath
Skating rink	Outdoor leisure park/centre
Outdoor, indoor swimming pool	Theme/Amusement park
Marina, moorings	Wildlife/Safari park, zoo
Mountain refuge hut	Gardens, park, arboretum
Overhead cable-car	Aviary, bird sanctuary
Tourist or steam railway	

Additional symbols

Motorway (unclassified)	Post office – Telephone centre
Junction: complete, limited	Covered market
Pedestrian street	Barracks
Unsuitable for traffic, street subject to restrictions	Swing bridge
Steps – Footpath	Quarry – Mine
Railway – Coach station	Ferry (river and lake crossings)
Funicular – Rack-railway	Ferry services: Passengers and cars
Tram – Metro, underground	Foot passengers only
Bert (R.)... Main shopping street	Access route number common to MICHELIN maps and town plans

Abbreviations and special symbols

A	Agricultural office (Chambre d'agriculture)	**P**	Local authority offices (Préfecture, sous-préfecture)
C	Chamber of commerce (Chambre de commerce)	**POL.**	Police station (Police)
H	Town hall (Hôtel de ville)		Police station (Gendarmerie)
J	Law courts (Palais de justice)	**T**	Theatre (Théâtre)
M	Museum (Musée)	**U**	University (Université)
			Hotel
			Park and Ride

Some town plans are extracts from plans used in the Green Guides to the regions of France.

COMPANION PUBLICATIONS

MICHELIN MAPS AND PLANS

Make the most of your trip to Paris by keeping a good map to hand as you discover the city. Each of the places described in this guide is associated with the references which correspond to Michelin map 10, a fold-out street map.

Other formats are also available for your convenience:

♦ No **106**, Paris and environs (scale 1:100 000), which covers the road network as far as Fontainebleau to the south and Senlis to the north, provides tourist information.

♦ No **101**, the **suburbs of Paris** scale (1:53 000).

♦ No **18**, **north-west suburbs**, no **20 south-west suburbs**, no **22 south-east suburbs**, no **24 south-east suburbs** (scale 1:15 000).

For getting around Paris, you have a choice of:

♦ **Paris Tourisme**, no **52**, which shows monuments, museums, shopping, shows and practical information. Tourist and metro plans are also included (scale 1:20 000).

♦ **Paris Transport**, no **51**, with a plan of the bus, metro and RER routes. Also includes information on taxi station locations, rental cars and railway stations.

♦ **Paris** no **54** shows one-way streets and car parks; it is very useful if you are driving a car (scale 1:10 000).

♦ **Paris Atlas** no **56**, with a street index, one-way streets, pedestrian only streets, car parks, and metro – RER – bus routes (scale 1:10 000).

♦ **Paris** no **55**, which is the same as no **54**, but with an index.

♦ **Paris Atlas by arrondissements**, no **57**, with street index, one-way streets, car parks, and metro – RER – bus routes (scale 1:10 000).

♦ **Paris Plan Poche** no **50** gives the major roads.

♦ And of course, the **map of France** no **721** shows a view of all of the Paris region, and how to travel to and from the city by road. The whole country is mapped on a scale of 1:1 000 000.

INTERNET

Michelin is pleased to offer a route-planning service on the Internet: **www.viamichelin.com www.travel.viamichelin.com**. Choose the shortest route, a route without tolls, or the Michelin recommended route to your destination; you can also access information about hotels and restaurants from *The Michelin Guide*, and tourist sites from *The Green Guide*.

Moving
for a world

Moving forward means developing tires with better road grip and shorter braking distances, whatever the state of the road.

CORRECT TIRE PRESSURE

RIGHT PRESSURE

- Safety
- Longevity
- Optimum fuel consumption

-0,5 bar

- Durability reduced by 20% (- 8,000 km)

-1 bar

- Risk of blowouts
- Increased fuel consumption
- Longer braking distances on wet surfaces

The Michelin Adventure

It all started with rubber balls! This was the product made by a small company based in Clermont-Ferrand that André and Edouard Michelin inherited, back in 1880. The brothers quickly saw the potential for a new means of transport and their first success was the invention of detachable pneumatic tires for bicycles. However, the automobile was to provide the greatest scope for their creative talents.

Throughout the 20th century, Michelin never ceased developing and creating ever more reliable and high-performance tires, not only for vehicles ranging from trucks to F1 but also for underground transit systems and airplanes.

From early on, Michelin provided its customers with tools and services to facilitate mobility and make traveling a more pleasurable and more frequent experience. As early as 1900, the Michelin Guide supplied motorists with a host of useful information related to vehicle maintenance, accommodation and restaurants, and was to become a benchmark for good food. At the same time, the Travel Information Bureau offered travelers personalised tips and itineraries.

The publication of the first collection of roadmaps, was an instant hit! In 1926, the first regional guide was published, devoted to the principal sites of and before long each region of France had its o Guide. The collection was later extended to mor destinations, including New York in 1968 and Tai

In the 21st century, with the growth of digita the challenge for Michelin maps and guides to develop alongside the company's Now, as before, Michelin is improving

MICHELIN TODAY

WORLD NUMBER ONE TIRE MANU
- 70 production sites in 18 countries
- 111,000 employees from all cultures
- 6,000 people employed in research

forward together
where mobility is safer

It also involves helping motorists take care of their safety and their tires. To do so, Michelin organises "Fill Up With Air" campaigns all over the world to remind us that correct tire pressure is vital.

WEAR

DETECTING TIRE WEAR

The legal minimum depth of tire tread is 1.6mm.
Tire manufacturers equip their tires with tread wear indicators, which are small blocks of rubber moulded into the base of the main grooves at a depth of 1.6mm.

Tires are the only point of contact between the vehicle and road.

The photo below shows the actual contact zone.

If the tread depth is less than 1.6mm, tires are considered to be worn and dangerous on wet surfaces.

NEW TIRE

WORN TIRE
(1,6 mm tread)

Moving forward
means sustainable mobility

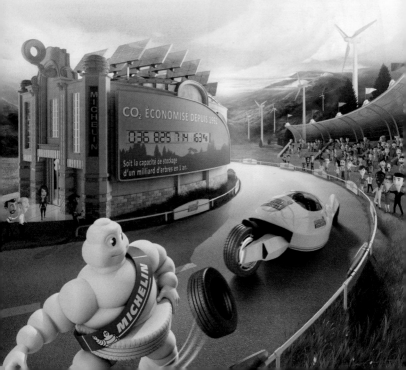

Chat with Bibendum

Go to
www.michelin.com/corporate/en
Find out more about
Michelin's history and the
latest news.

QUIZ

Michelin develops tires for all types of vehicles.
See if you can match the right tire with the right vehicle...

Michelin Travel Partner

Société par actions simplifiées au capital de 11 288 880 EUR
27 cours de l'Ile Seguin - 92100 Boulogne Billancourt (France)
R.C.S. Nanterre 433 677 721

No part of this publication may be reproduced in any form
without the prior permission of the publisher.

© Michelin Travel Partner
ISBN 978-2-067203-54-9
Printed: March 2015
Printed and bound in France : Imprimerie CHIRAT, 42540 Saint-Just-la-Pendue - N° 201503.0461